THIRD EDITION

The Adult Years

AN INTRODUCTION TO AGING

Dorothy Rogers

Distinguished Service Professor, Emeritus

State University of New York at Oswego

Prentice-Hall, Englewood Cliffs, N.J. 07632

Library of Congress Cataloging-in-Publication Data

ROGERS, DOROTHY, (date)
    The adult years.

    Bibliography
    Includes index.
    1.–Adulthood.   2.–Middle age—Psychological
aspects.   3.–Aged—Psychology.   4.–Aging—Psychological
aspects.   I.–Title.
BF724.5.R57–1986   155.6   85-28295
ISBN   0-13-008939-7

Editorial/production supervision
  and interior design by Martha M. Masterson
Cover design: Joe Curcio
Manufacturing buyer: Barbara Kelly Kittle
Cover Photo: T.G. Bell

Printed in the United States of America

10 9 8 7 6 5 4 3 2 1

ISBN 0-13-008939-7 01

PRENTICE-HALL INTERNATIONAL (UK) LIMITED, *London*
PRENTICE-HALL OF AUSTRALIA PTY. LIMITED, *Sydney*
PRENTICE-HALL CANADA INC., *Toronto*
PRENTICE-HALL HISPANOAMERICANA, S.A., *Mexico*
PRENTICE-HALL OF INDIA PRIVATE LIMITED, *New Delhi*
PRENTICE-HALL OF JAPAN, INC., *Tokyo*
PRENTICE-HALL OF SOUTHEAST ASIA PTE. LTD., *Singapore*
EDITORA PRENTICE-HALL DO BRASIL, LTDA, *Rio de Janeiro*
WHITEHALL BOOKS LIMITED, *Wellington, New Zealand*

Contents

Preface

This third edition of *The Adult Years* has been thoroughly updated and revised.

Many topics such as those relating to singles, friendship, and women in the work-world, have been expanded; others have been added, including mentors, the homeless, and commuter marriages. Topics of special current interest—among them positive concepts of health and exercise, organ donation, and life styles of adult baby boomers—are discussed, as well as such current trends as single parenthood and research efforts to prolong life. Still other topics deal with contemporary issues—for example, reproductive choices (sperm banks, test tube babies, and so forth), changing sex roles, and euthanasia.

The Suggested Readings at the end of each chapter are new for this volume, and almost all of them date from the past three years. Also, because of the proliferation of research on adulthood, as well as the rapidly changing environments in which adults live, priority has been given to recent studies in all areas.

The revised volume, like the original one, is designed as a textbook for courses in adult psychology. It deals with adults in general as well as adults at three life stages: early, middle, and later adulthood. The fact that certain topics are dealt with on all three levels produces an illusion of redundancy. Nevertheless, this approach reveals the significance of certain matters at successive age levels. All adults have certain life experiences in common, in addition to those that are unique to particular stages.

The book is organized around a comprehensive, developmental view of adulthood. Part I introduces current theories and research emphases in the study of adulthood. Part II relates to young adults, including their passage into adulthood, their main tasks, and life styles. Part III deals mainly with middle-aged adults—their characteristics, life styles, and activities. Much of the material presented in this section might well apply to adults generally. In Part IV the characteristics and life styles of older adults are described in much the same way. In addition, special emphasis is placed on their problems and crises, including death, and on programs designed to help them. Finally, in Part V an attempt is made to integrate concepts and conclusions about adulthood, and to suggest projections about the future.

Stress has been placed on relevance, special issues, and the uniqueness of personal experience. An effort has been made to sift out purely esoteric material and to retain whatever is of genuine concern to adults today. Human interest has been emphasized, since students—whether adults already or adults-in-the-making—will become involved in, and identify best with, personalized material. Throughout the book the concept of pluralism is recognized; adults have infinitely varied personalities and fall into many differing categories. Attention is also given to "anticipatory" material—that is, issues-in-the-making and what may lie ahead. The status of adulthood is not static but fluid; it has roots in the past and reaches into the future.

I would like to thank my typists, Ann Hoefer and Cherie Blanchard. I would also like to thank my production editor, Martha Masterson, whose expertise and attention to detail greatly eased the task of revision.

Dorothy Rogers
Oswego, NY

CHAPTER ONE

Introduction

In colonial New England, people had fairly clear ideas about old age, childhood, and youth; but "they had scarcely a term, let alone a full-blown concept, of middle age. There seemed to be a kind of gap there."(The age span from 25 or 30 to about age 60 was not considered to be any special phase) or stage in "an ongoing sequence of events, but simply as the full realization of personhood" (Scanlon, 1979, p. 20).

Only recently has adulthood begun to come into its own. Children were studied in the seventeenth century, adolescents in the early twentieth century, and the aged a few decades later. In the wake of the Industrial Revolution, a variety of writers, social reformers, medical personnel, and psychologists focused on the physical and mental limitations of later years. However, not until the 1940s was gerontology, the study of the elderly, recognized as a new field; and only about mid-century did social scientists decide that old age was a significant problem. It was later still, in the 1970s, when the first real interest was shown in the early- and middle-adult years. Even in 1968 there was no article on adulthood in the *International Encyclopedia of the Social Sciences* (Jordan, 1976), and as recently as 1975 Brim and Abeles labeled the middle years as "a largely unexplored phase of the human cycle" (Barnett & Baruch, 1978).

Now, however, social scientists in general have become concerned about adulthood, and more research is being done and more books are being written on the subject. While publications on adulthood are still few in comparison to those about children and adolescents, the interest now being paid adults dwarfs what has been shown them before. It is just possible, surmises Graubard (1976), that we are entering "the century of the adult, at least in America."

T.G. Bell

The study of the elderly has received increased emphasis.

Interest in Old Age. Just in the last decade, the number of professional and scientific journals relating to gerontology has greatly increased, which testifies to the growing concern about later years (Birren, 1980). There are various plausible reasons for the growing interest in adulthood. Concern was first felt about the elderly because of their dramatic increase in numbers and the ever-growing burden on society for their care.

The problem has been complicated by the rapid transition in America from the extended family to the nuclear family; the result is that many older people now need to be helped to make it on their own. In the extended family, which included parents, children, grandparents, and other relatives, older people blended unobtrusively into the society. However, industrialization and technological society made the extended family unwieldy; the streamlined nuclear family, which was capable of moving about the country with relative ease, became the vogue. Hence, the task of caring for the old, cast loose from extended family moorings, raised the question, what are older people like and what are their needs? The answer was a growing interest in gerontology and *geriatrics,* the science of treating and healing the illnesses and disorders of old age. Gerontology is not concerned merely with problems, but also with the possibility of continuing growth in older people. Overall, it is the study of "the whole person" and the aging process as "reflected in all aspects of life functioning" (p. 12).

Interest in Entire Adult Span. Why did a psychology of all the adult years develop? For one thing, television has revealed exciting life-style potentials for average families, and it has increased young adults' desire to achieve such life styles (Scanlon, 1979). Adulthood has also become a focus of attention because researchers have belatedly recognized that this stage was all that was left of the life cycle to study; they needed to study it to achieve closure. Interest in adulthood also derives from the current perception of this stage as a time of development and growth, rather than as a period in which the main dynamic is toward aging and death (Notman, 1980). In addition, certain samplings of children who have been studied over a span of years (in what is called *longitudinal research*) have grown up. Naturally, researchers have become interested in what might happen to these people in decades ahead. For another thing, adults in modern Western society have now become sufficiently affluent and have enough free time to think about their personal development. In former times their energies were largely absorbed by the sheer business of survival and childrearing. Meantime, the possibility of limiting family size has allowed parents to stake out their own claims to "personhood," and to make childrearing fit their own life patterns, instead of the reverse.

Fortunately, the recent and growing interest in life-span development helps provide perspective on adulthood and to relate it to the preceding years. Honzik (1984) notes the tremendous increase in interest in life-span development that began in the 1970s. Especially notable is the large number of excellent books emerging on this topic as well as multidisciplinary, empirical studies and longitudinal research over long periods. Honzik believes the multidisciplinary approach to be especially useful for pursuing comprehensive studies of development over the life span.

WHAT IS AN ADULT?

Just what is an adult? The term "adult" evokes all sorts of associations in our minds. When we were children, adults seemed all-powerful and adulthood itself terribly remote; to be an adult was to pay more to go to the movies, or to drive cars, or to smoke cigars.

Even among adults the term "adult" has no definite meaning. Does anyone know for sure when he or she becomes an adult? The following replies from young adults illustrate the varied ages when people first felt like adults and of their reasons for doing so. (It should be added that a number said they *still* didn't feel like full-fledged adults.)

I still don't feel like an adult, but more like a young adult. When I took off a semester from school to live in Europe, I felt I was on the road to adulthood.

At age 21, when people finally began treating me as an adult.

At age 14, when I held my first job and worked from 20 to 40 hours a week.

At age 17, when family problems placed heavy responsibilities on my shoulders.

The common view is that being an adult means having come to terms with life, coping successfully with crisis, and being in charge of one's world. It is also viewed as a time of stability and maintenance instead of growth (Gill, Coppard & Lowther, 1983).

Postman (1981) contends that television eliminates the division between childhood and adulthood because it requires no special instruction of the viewer and it does not segregate its audience by age. The chief difference between children and adults is that adults understand certain facets of life including its "mysteries, its contradictions, its violence, its tragedies . . ." (Postman, 1981, p. 96). When children move toward adulthood these mysteries are presumed to be conveyed to them in a psychologically comprehensible way. However, television reveals these adult secrets—sexual, social, physical—and "forces the entire culture to come out of the closet" (Postman, p. 97). In attempting to grip its audience, television challenges all taboos. In consequence, "childhood innocence and specialness are impossible to sustain," which is the reason that there are no longer many children on television. Rather, children on television are really portrayed as miniature adults. Nevertheless, though the traditional view of childhood disappears it cannot be concluded that everyone is simply tied up in an adult world. Instead, a new kind of person is projected, one who might be called the "adult child," that is, an adult with attitudes typically associated with childishness: a strong need for immediate gratification, a lack of consideration of consequences, and a strong focus on consumption. It tends to divide the population into three groups: infancy, senility, and between—"a group of indeterminate age where everyone is somewhere between 20 and 30 and remains that way until dotage descends" (Postman, 1981, p. 97).

Even social scientists seldom ask what "adulthood" is. It does not have the kinds of associations for us that the words "childhood" or "adolescence" do. Instead it "seems almost a catch-all category for everything that happens to the individual human being after a specific chronological age—whether 18, 21, or some other" (Graubard, 1976, p. v).

With the exception of English, no European language consciously identifies adulthood as a distinct stage in human development (Rudolph & Rudolph, 1976). The same has been true through the ages and around the world. The term adult itself comes from the Latin *adolescere,* to grow up. It suggests a process rather than the final attainment of a specific status (Bouwsma, 1976). Similarly, in China Confucianism interpreted adult maturity not as a state of attainment, but as a process of becoming (Tu Wei-Ming, 1976).

Images. Typically adults are viewed as being somewhere in the middle of the continuum between youth and old age. Most people hold a far more negative view of older adults than of adults in general. A study of undergraduate attitudes indicated older and middle-aged adults to be equally acceptable as persons, but the older ones were judged more dependent and ineffective (Sherman & Gold, 1979–80).

Beyond such generalities, Americans hold no consistent image of what adults are like. A random selection of views on the subject proves this to be the case. Stegner (1976) suggests that qualities of adults include "sanity, normality, rationality, continuity, sobriety, responsibility, wisdom, conduct as opposed to mere behavior" (p. 39). Adulthood in its highest form is symbolized in the lives of sages, saints, and culture heroes. In our pluralistic society there are so many kinds of ideal figures that they are not always easily reconcilable with one another. Indeed, if the present trend toward increased ethnicity and diversity persists, we may not have an identifiable American adult, but instead diverse and inconsistent life styles and values representing the various subcultures.

The term adult may also suggest less flattering attributes such as "stodgy," "settled," or "practical." Growth is perceived by some as proceeding until adulthood when a certain stagnation sets in, the drama of youth having gone by the wayside. And the older the adult, the truer this image becomes. In old age, some people believe, adults are at the lowest point of their lives; they are inflexibly set in their ways.

THE AGING PROCESS

Factors in Aging

Maturational Factors. Aging includes "processes of change in organisms which occur after maturity, whereas old age refers to the last phase of life . . ." (Birren & Renner, 1980, p. 4). In many people's minds the term "aging" suggests growing old; however, Hayflick (1984) points out the problem in determining just when aging begins. Some date it from conception, which suggests the false conclusion that isolated sperm and egg cells are not alive. It could be argued that aging begins before conception, since sperm and egg cells demonstrate age changes after they mature and before they fuse. The life of living cells has no real beginning since every living thing can trace its origins through linkages of living cells to the origin of life itself.

Anyhow, as a result of aging, the organism proceeds through stages of immaturity, maturity, and deterioration. Even at birth individuals appear to have an inborn potential to live a particular length of life. Thus the life spans of identical (one-egg) twins are more similar in length than those of fraternal (two-egg) twins. Such potential is modified somewhat by personal life patterns and environmental influences (Birren, 1978). Progressively, as people grow older, incoming stimuli are processed more slowly, the rate of biological interaction in the body decreases, and metabolic processes slow down. In fact, "there may even be various pacemakers built in to predetermine some of these changes which, with age, ultimately lead to a type of shut-off or, as Freud suggested, an intrinsic death force or built-in pattern leading to an inorganic state" (Cath, 1975, p. 207). In the biological sense, aging is often viewed fatalistically as the ticking away of an uncontrollable time clock that dooms us to an inexorable process of decline and ultimate demise. Despite its inevitability, it is not altogether beyond our control. (Bernard Strehler believes that the significant factor that initiates the deterioration of aging is loss of capacity for cell division in tissue types such as heart and muscle.) The result is a gradual decrease over time in the functional efficiency of such tissues (Kent, 1980, p. 57).

(Although the average life span is increasing it is also uncertain when it will reach a plateau—do not genetic factors impose a limit?) (Rossi, 1984) (It has been estimated that the average life span at birth for females born a century from now will be 94 and for males 82.)

The sex difference in timing of life's markers exists throughout life. The sexes have different timetables of aging. On the average males arrive at sexual maturing at age 14, women at 12. Muscular strength reaches its peak at age 25. Even before puberty "the level of thymic hormones—which regulate the immune system—begins falling" (Batten, 1984). By age 25 height may already be declining. After age 30, the body's functional capacity declines about 0.8 percent a year; hearing continues to decline—it peaked at age 10; frown and smile lines appear; and skin loses elasticity. The musculature is still intact but the back begins to slump after this decade.

The Morale Factor. The aging process is not solely a matter of genetic destiny, for the stress that the body has experienced during a lifetime is also involved. Every period of stress, expecially those which involve frustration and lack of success, leaves scars that contribute to tissue aging (Selye, 1974). By contrast, success provides exhilaration, leaving one feeling youthful even in advanced old age. Hans Selye tells of entering medical school at age 18 and becoming so fascinated with research about disease and life that he would get up at 4 A.M. and study until 6 in the evening. Even now, in his late 60s, he still gets up at 4 or 5 A.M. and works until late at night with few interruptions and is in

perfectly good health. The trick, declares Selye, is to determine those jobs that one can do, the one that one can do best, and that which oneself and others can best appreciate.

Health Factors. There is (plentiful evidence that healthful living and preventive medicine can retard the effects of aging and increase longevity.) People in the Western world now have a life expectancy of 70 years, a figure that will probably increase to 80 by the end of the century.) By contrast, life expectancy in ancient Rome was 22 years, and in ancient Greece, 18. While much of this difference is due to the decline in infant mortality rates, it is also a fact that far more people are living longer today than ever before.

In recent years growing attention has been paid to the effects diet, exercise, and activity have on retarding aging. Cath (1975) concludes that if there is one significant physiological finding of the last two decades regarding the prevention of aging, it is the advice to remain active, to exercise to whatever degree is tolerable, and to keep busy. When people are no longer active, the prognosis for a long and healthy life is poor, and "atrophy from disuse is almost as certain as night following day" (p. 206). In addition, it appears that those people who average 10 or more hours or less than 6 hours of sleep a night have a shorter life expectancy than those who sleep between 6 and 8 hours (Kent, 1980, p. 97).

Environmental Factors. The unit of analysis in ecological psychology is the behavior setting: "a recurring pattern of human activity that takes place within specific time-and-space boundaries—for example, the colloquium, concert, or baseball game . . ." (Stokols, 1978). The major theme in environmental psychology is the transactional or bidirectional nature of human-environment relations, in that the environment reflects the interplay of environmental and human forces. (The optimization theme stresses efforts of individuals and groups to create environments that are optimally supportive of their activities and goals) (Stokols, 1978). In particular, much attention is being paid to the quality of the physical environment—including pollutants, tobacco, and pesticides, as well as housing and neighborhoods—which may influence health directly or indirectly. (Another factor is diet, since persons who eat improperly almost certainly die earlier.) For example, too much animal fat probably relates to a high mortality rate, although the evidence is not conclusive. The effect of reducing food intake on cancer incidence varies with the type of tumor. Most tumors occur less frequently with low-calorie diets, but some more so (Kent, 1980, p. 94).

History bears testimony to the effect of technological advances and environmental factors on aging. In Old Testament times (1500 B.C.) the average life expectancy was just 18 years; by Shakespeare's time (A.D. 1600), it was 35 years. Of course, throughout history some individuals have lived to age 80 or 90 or longer. In 1900 the average life expectancy in the United States was 49 years; now it is over 20 years longer. In just the past decade 3 years have been added to this average (Cranston, 1980).

Pathogenic Factors. (By contrast, other factors accelerate rather than retard the aging process.) Most individuals do not live to the full human life span of about age 100 because the basic mechanisms of the aging process make people vulnerable to diseases) (Kent, 1980). Such afflictions rob older people of many good years (Cranston, 1980). In addition, certain *pathogenic* (disease-producing) elements—for example, cigarette smoking and excessive exposure to the sun—can cause lung cancer, emphysema, and wrinkled skin; air pollution, to some as yet undetermined extent, may also contribute to aging. It is well known that people who experience long-term malnutrition or who work in coal mines and unsafe factories age earlier than people in more fortunate circumstances. (Evidence is also overwhelming that aging and disease processes are intertwined (Kent, 1980, p. 25). Senility may simply be an accelerated form of aging, and is possibly initiated by some environmental factor. Among factors thus far linked to senility are "slow-acting viruses and elevated brain concentrations of aluminum") (p. 26).

Mortality Versus Morbidity. Butler (1983) notes the need to distinguish between mortality and morbidity rates. Most data indicate diminishing age-specific mortality rates but flat or rising morbidity (sickness), in which case the proportion of the life span with chronic illness will expand and the need for medical care in later years will increase. For example, morbidity—sickness and its attending disabilities—increased between the years 1966 to 1976, mostly in ages 45 to 64. However, it is still unclear whether it is simply that more people are surviving with impairments because of medical and other support) (Butler feels it is important to develop an index of average health expectancy as a parallel to that for average life expectancy. It is possible that changes in life style, including management of stress and diet, and exercise habits, may change the morbidity or sickness picture.)

It should be noted that morbidity and mortality trends do not necessarily go together. (Besides, data about morbidity derive from what people say about their health and can be erroneous;) people report less illness than they actually experience. In any case it seems that morbidity rates are rising, perhaps beause the mortality rate is decreasing, thus throwing a greater burden of serious illness on society. Unfortunately, we lack means for detecting the more subtle changes in functional health, which nevertheless have significant implications for retirement timing and ability to work.

Causes of Aging. There is no shortage of theories about aging, and no one claims to explain all aspects of senescence. (One theory suggests that aging is programmed in the brain, a "hormonal clock"; another that the immune system, which manufactures antibodies against "foreign invaders" eventually becomes ineffective. Still others focus on genetic cellular theory, that "the machinery within each cell wears out, gradually losing its capacity for self-repair)..." (Patrusky, 1982, p. 112).

Most theories fall into two main categories: one that focuses on aging at the cellular level, the other on biological systems, such as the immune system.

Patrusky (1982) sums up the most common theories as follows. The one currently favored centers on "the genetic machinery—the DNA and its associated protein-making apparatus. The idea is that the machinery within each cell wears out, gradually losing its capacity for self-repair and resulting in deterioration" (p. 112). Another theory suggests that there is a mechanism for throwing off faulty components and displacing them with replacement genes. In this theory some species live longer and presumably have greater reserve DNA than others—however, all species finally exhaust such reserves. Another theory hypothesizes an aging gene, suggesting that growing old is part of the "genetic script" from conception onward. Aging genes are preprogrammed and slow down, then halt, the processes critical to the life of the cells.

Still others employ a free radical theory to explain aging as produced by deterioration of a cell's energy-processing center instead of the genetic machinery. Such "free radicals are unstable atoms, transient byproducts of the bucket brigade process by which the cell converts food stuffs to fuel" (Patrusky, 1982, p. 112). If these free radicals are not quickly "mopped up" they can do a great deal of damage to cell structures. Clean-up enzymes perform such mop-ups; however, over time such enzyme levels become lower.

Some specialists on aging point to other factors such as disruptions in the regulatory mechanisms within the whole organism. One theory points to the immune system that manufactures antibodies which protect against "foreign invaders. In time ... the body grows allergic to itself." Still another organismic theory views aging as programmed in the brain. This hormonal-clock hypothesis suggests that at a particular time the pituitary gland "releases a death hormone, which triggers a host of age-associated disruptions, including the creation of excess free radicals and the accumulation of errors in the genetic machinery" (Patrusky, 1982, p. 112).

Patrusky concludes that a number of these theories will prove to be at least partially true, "with some mechanisms acting jointly to produce senescence. If so, the age-old dream of extending the life span will probably remain an impossible one" (p. 112). Nevertheless, if the aging mystery is solved it may "help preserve the health associated with youth to the preprogrammed maximum age, thus making it possible to grow old with more than grace" (p. 112).

Certain generalizations may be said to apply to aging. Aging begins, in a sense, even before conception. A woman is born with all the eggs she will ever have, and the ovum of a woman who gives birth at age 35 is already that many years old (Batten, 1984). In addition, each species has its characteristic age span—45 years for chimpanzees, 60 for elephants, and 100 to 105 in humans—and the oldest are around 110. Throughout recorded history the human life span has remained the same although average longevity or length of life is rapidly increasing. There are three times as many American centenarians now as in 1960. In the mid-nineteenth century half of all people died by age 40, and "half of all the people on earth who ever lived past the age of 65 are alive today." (Batten, 1984, p. 95). Some scientists believe that a commitment to aging research, as great as that given space in the 1960s, "might produce an unprecedented evolutionary breakthrough" (Batten, 1984, p. 95).

Aging: A Complex Individual Process

It becomes apparent that aging is not a simple process, but involves the impact of time on all aspects of an individual's being and behavior (Zarit, 1977). We can be several different ages at the same time—biological, social, psychological, and chronological. Not all humans age in exactly the same way. They differ greatly in the rate and processes of aging. While genetic factors, as well as life style, undoubtedly play a part, just how all these factors mesh together is not well understood. Nevertheless, Cranston (1980) predicts major advances in knowledge about the underlying mechanisms of aging; and control of the aging process may produce major benefits. For example, through learning how to control age changes in the body, physicians will acquire important strategies for preventing disease.

The Chronological Model. Because of the varied factors involved in aging, several frames of reference are employed in approaching the topic. Ordinarily people employ the chronological model—calendar years—with regard to aging. According to Lowy (1975), "gerontologic research has divided aging into three stages: middle age, later maturity, and old age. Middle age would extend chronologically from 45 or 50 to about 65. Later maturity would begin around 65 and would stretch approximately to 75. Old age would begin at 75" (p. 139).

The chronological approach is simple, precise, and easily explained. Yet it also has significant drawbacks. For one thing, chronological age becomes less important as people grow older simply because people are more variable as they age (Dibner, 1975). Indeed, "some 40-year-olds are biologically older than some 80-year-olds, and any individual might 'age' much more or less during one discrete time period in his life than another" (p. 67). Moreover, challenges of midlife, spread out over a decade or so, do not relate to chronological age in any except the most general way (Merriam, 1979).

The significance of calendar age varies somewhat according to sex. Regardless of a man's calendar age, he is viewed as young or middle aged if he is active and vigorous; however a woman's perceived age relates more directly to her calendar age (Shanas, 1980). Actually, men age biologically more rapidly than women in later years.

Chronological age is also an inadequate yardstick for aging because an individual does not age all at once. One can be at quite different ages in physical health, mental capacity, endurance, creativity, or other functions. For example, in the process of writing the centennial history of her college, the author interviewed many of the oldest living faculty members and graduates. One woman was still living by herself at the age of 90. She hobbled about and had arthritis, but she had a sparkling personality and her mind was entirely clear. Another woman, age 88, had had the reputation for being a fireball in her earlier years as a teacher. While remarkably well preserved physically, she was now emotionally bland and mentally senile. The 90-year-old by all odds seemed a decade or so younger.

Bernice Neugarten, an authority on aging, calls the United States an age-irrelevant society because chronological age is becoming an ever-poorer indicator of how people live. Age alone tells nothing about an individual's "economic or marital status, style of life, or health" (Hall, 1980, p. 66). After the first two decades, age diminishes as a basis for prediction.

The Legal Model. The law often employs chronological age as a criterion for legal responsibility (Goldstein, 1976). Being an adult in the eyes of the law is not the same as being adult in one's own eyes or in those of others. The legal age of majority for assuming adult responsibilities varies over time and from one state to another. For example, in Alabama both sexes may marry with parental consent at age 14 and without it at age 18; whereas in California both sexes must be age 18 with or without consent of parents or guardians. In Mississippi males must be age 17 to marry with consent and females 15; without consent both sexes must wait until age 21 (*World Almanac,* 1980, p. 963).

The Biological Model. The concept of biological aging generally considers those physical changes in the organism that have been found in general to be associated with aging. (These changes may be in cell structures, organ systems, or their functioning) (Dibner, 1975). In the biological sense the stages of life might be distinguished by such events as birth, puberty, and menopause. This model also focuses on changes in the body over the years. Bernard Strehler of the University of Southern California conjectures that after ages 25 to 30 the "body relentlessly loses functional capacity at the rate of about 1 percent annually" (Patrusky, 1982, p. 112).

(The concept of biological age has not been stressed, partly because it is uncertain what physical changes best measure the rate of aging (Borkan & Norris, 1980). (The concept is easier to apply in childhood than in adulthood because dental, skeletal, and sexual maturation proceed according to sequences and well-defined stages, whereas aging itself is continuous, without a clear-cut beginning or end.) Hence, the biological age index is employed merely to predict the likelihood of mortality. Studies that have investigated whether biological age distinguishes between groups categorized on the basis of health show that unhealthy persons have greater biological age.

The Sociocultural Approach. In another sense, adulthood is a social concept, for in some ways aging is socially and culturally determined. In other words, people do not determine for themselves whether they are adults; rather they are perceived to be adults by others (Stegner, 1976). A 70-year-old may declare that he's a 50-year-old at heart and that he feels not a day older than he did then. But if he looks like a 70-year-old, his self-concept is socially meaningless (Rosow,

1974). Society perceives him to be 70 years of age and treats him accordingly. How adults are perceived also varies from one era or society to another (Hareven, 1976). The 80-year-old who is revered in China might be considered an old fogy in the United States.

("Social age" also refers to socially assigned roles that a person fills, roles that then determine what his or her social behavior should be.) The role of grandmother, retired person, or old man are examples of socially ascribed roles for the aged (Dibner, 1975, p. 69). These roles, too, vary greatly from one era or culture to another.

The Developmental Frame of Reference. (Most psychologists favor the life-span developmental approach) in which each phase of adulthood is viewed in terms of what has gone before and what is yet to come. In this "life-span framework, human development is perceived as a life-long process and life stages in terms of their antecedents and consequences" (Elder, 1975, p. 1). This approach is concerned with both psychological and biological changes.

The developmental approach also involves studying individuals as they relate to, or interact with, their interpersonal and nonpersonal environments. Hareven (1976) prefers to use the term "life course" instead of "life cycle" because life course considers people not merely as individuals but in terms of the basic institutions such as the family, of which they are a part. That is, people are not treated as though they dwell in a vacuum but in complex ever-changing environments to which they must continuously adapt. Thus there is gradually developing a convergence between developmental and environmental psychology, which is concerned with relationships between all aspects of the physical environment and behavior. Such matters as the effects of crowding, noise, and types of housing are being related to human development (Wohlwill, 1980).

Rossi (1984) complains that life-span psychologists typically "vaccilate between the view that men and women are free, purposive actors charting their own lives . . . and the view that they are chameleons responsive to changing currents of opinion in historical events" (p. 1). She also believes the life-course sciences have ignored the effects of sex in general.

Functional Age. A related concept is that of *functional age.* According to this concept, individuals are viewed as aging at different rates in different functions, and functional age can be estimated in very much the same way as mental age. Thus the functional age concept might be applied to variable retirement programs in which people may retire at varying ages. While chronological age refers to years lived, functional age refers to the changing effectiveness of behavior across the years. Functional age considers what a person is capable of doing and not simply the number of years that he or she has lived.

Personal Age. The concept of personal age refers to the way an individual relates his or her own experience to the aging process. In the decade after age 35, people ask themselves four main questions: why they live and age; how much longer they have to live and to change their ways; how they will age with what human supports; and how they will die (Cath, 1980). Often people rationalize that what they have done has been correct and that the goals they have worked toward are valid.

Perceptions of self with regard to age derive from both personal experience and social stereotypes. No matter how vigorous and robust individuals may feel, if they live in a society that attaches strongly negative stereotypes to aging, they will have difficulty escaping a deteroriating self-image as they age. In such cases much depends upon attitudes toward the self that an individual carries across the years, for these attitudes tend to resist changing external situations.

In *As You Like It,* Shakespeare portays life as involving seven stages:

serves that the adult life cycle is often defined in terms of presumably inevitable life events. For women these would include high school graduation, marriage and parenthood, the empty nest, the husband's retirement, and ultimate widowhood. This framework, however, fails to take into account the significance of alternate life styles and unanticipated and off-time events. For middle-aged women, divorce, early widowhood, and women's entry into the labor force suggest that unanticipated events have a tremendous effect on their experience.

STAGE THEORY

The Concept of Stage Theory

In various contexts we have already referred to stages of life, each with its own characteristics. While these stages follow no fixed chronological schedule, they are presumed to occur in all persons at roughly the same period in development. They are also hierarchical—that is, each new stage is dependent on those that have gone before.

Stage theory is no recent arrival on the psychological scene but is rooted deep in the past. In classical antiquity theories of life stages existed, as evidenced in the writings of Aristotle and Plato. In the eighteenth century, views of human development related to then-current concepts of aging; in the nineteenth century, individual biographies became significant in analysis and therapy (Rosenmayr, 1980). Current views of life stages derive in considerable measure from the Freudian stress on the continuities of psychosexual development and the idea that life unfolds in an orderly sequence.

Bischof (1976) cites some vivid observations regarding stages of life. Disraeli is presumed to have said that "youth is a blunder, manhood a struggle, old age a regret." Gracian observed that "at 20 the will reigns, at 30 the intellect, and at 40 the judgment."

According to a certain Greek proverb "childhood ends at 12, youth at 18, love at 20, faith at 30, hope at 40, and desire at 50."

In *As You Like It,* Shakespeare portays life as involving seven stages:

The infant mewling and puking . . .
The whining school boy . . .
The lover, sighing like furnace . . .
A soldier, full of strange oaths . . .
The justice, in fair round belly . . .
The sixth age shifts . . . with spectacles on nose . . .
his shrunk shank . . . voice turning again
towards childish treble . . .
Second childishness . . . sans teeth, sans eyes, sans
taste, sans everything . . . (Act II, Sc. 7)

A Sampling of Stage Theories

Hall's Recapitulation Theory. G. Stanley Hall played an important part in the history of developmental psychology and popularized the concept that life involves relatively discrete or separate stages. He stressed that ontogeny recapitulates phylogeny—that the individual human growth pattern parallels evolution, and succeeding phases in life demonstrate characteristics relevant to the chief evolutionary (phylogenetic) advances.) During the period of youth, which Hall designated as the years 8 to 12, children pass through the early history of man: cruel and savage, yet moving toward higher human aspirations. The adolescent period becomes the stage that lifts children above the anthropoids; nevertheless it can involve backsliding (Grinder, 1969).

Hall portrayed growing old as "walking over a bridge" that "slowly tapers to a log, then a tightrope, and finally to a thread. But we must go on till it breaks or we lose balance. Some keep a level head and go farther than others but all will go down sooner or later" (p. 437). Thus Hall's conception of aging was pessimistic, contrary to the upbeat version in vogue today. While Hall's theory currently has few if any adherents, it did lay a foundation for understanding human development in terms of progressively higher levels of developmental function.

Havighurst's Developmental Tasks. Robert Havighurst proposed a series of developmental "tasks" appropriate to the various life stages. A *developmental task* "is [one] which arises at or about a certain period of the life of the individual, successful achievement of which leads to his happiness and to success with later tasks, while failure leads to unhappiness in the individual, disapproval by the society, and difficulty with later tasks" (Havighurst, 1972, p. 2). The tasks proposed by Havighurst for earlier adulthood (ages 18 to 30) include selecting a mate, learning to live with the marriage partner, beginning a family, rearing children, managing the home, embarking on an occupation, assuming civic responsibility, and finding congenial social groups. The tasks of middle age (ages 30 to 55) include achieving adult social and civic responsibility, establishing and maintaining an appropriate standard of living, helping

Mate selection is an important developmental task.

T.G. Bell

teenage children become happy and responsible adults, developing worthwhile adult leisure activities, accepting and adapting to the physiological changes of middle age, and adjusting to aging parents. In later maturity (ages 55 and over), the tasks include adjusting to declining physical health and strength, adapting to the death of a spouse, adjusting to reduced income and retirement, establishing relationships with one's age group, and fulfilling civic and social obligations.

Havighurst's theory has both strong and weak points. It helps place adulthood in perspective and underscores the importance of the teachable moment. That is, it is wise to define purposes of education at different age levels so that people may achieve the developmental tasks appropriate for each stage. On the other hand, people can omit some of the steps proposed by Havighurst. For example, many persons never marry and yet live satisfactory lives. Finally, the developmental tasks as defined by Havighurst relate only to life in this culture.

Levinson's Theory. Levinson (1978) terms the basic design, or pattern, of an individual's life its *life structure*, and to understand it, one must consider the interrelationships between self and environment. He identified four overlapping eras in the life cycle, each lasting about 25 years, and each having its own typical life style and as well as psychological, physical, and social aspects: youth, adulthood, midlife, and late life. The three overlapping or transitional periods are viewed as the most critical points in the life cycle. They include the transition from youth into adulthood, the midlife transition, and the late adult transition into later years. Each transitional period becomes a source of "renewal or stagnation" that shapes the character of the period just ahead. It is during this time, as in the late youth stage, that the existing life structure and future alternatives are examined, and a base is built for a new structure.

Erikson's Stage-Task Theory. One widely known concept of the life cycle is that of Erik Erikson (1959), who divides it into eight phases or ages. Each stage involves a specific task, and the stages follow a general chronology, although they do not involve arbitrary, rigid age limits. The first four stages occur in childhood, the fifth in adolescence, and the last three in adulthood. Life tasks belong to particular stages only in that they arrive at critical points of resolution during those stages. Otherwise, they are prepared for in previous stages and elaborated in those that follow. Thus at successive stages, components of all the eight major tasks are present, either as "precursors" or "crises." In this sense adolescence does not mark the end of childhood or the beginning of adulthood. Instead, adulthood is anticipated in childhood, and the child exists in the adult.

To be ready for adulthood, the adolescent, in stage five, must achieve a sense of ego identity. Only after having defined his or her sense of self is an individual ready to establish intimacy with another. This is the first phase-specific task of adulthood (stage six in the total life span). This intimacy involves relationships with oneself, with the opposite sex, and with others of both sexes. Meantime isolation, which is the converse of intimacy, is demonstrated by one's tendency to withdraw from or destroy these forces in people that one perceives as unfriendly to oneself. Thus Erikson defines each phase-specific task in terms of opposites that may or may not be successfully resolved.

The next phase of adulthood, stage seven, is concerned with the conflict between "generativity" and stagnation, the phase-specific task here being the establishment of the next generation through producing and caring for children. Those who do not become parents may achieve generativity through creative and unselfish behavior. The biological status of parenthood, therefore, does not necessarily constitute genuine generativity. The failure of generativity results in stagnation, which may assume the guise of obsessive pseudo-intimacy or narcissistic self-indulgence whereby an individual may treat himself as though he were his one and only child.

The last phase of adult life involves the issue of integrity versus despair and disgust. Integrity (a sense of wholeness) represents the "fruit of the seven stages," and is the result of having successfully accomplished the tasks of all the former stages, including taking care of others, adjusting to oneself, and generating ideas. It suggests having adapted to one's own life cycle, an essential task of life. If one does not accept the reality of one's own life cycle, the outcome is despair because there is no opportunity for a new beginning. This despair in turn produces a disgust with the world and the self.

In recent years Erikson's interpretation of this last stage has changed, perhaps because of the gradually improving status of the elderly and their circumstances. Instead of viewing the old person's task as confronting despair and preserving a sense of self, though diminished, in facing death as he once did, he now sees a long, still-productive period, when people are elderly, before the last stage when they are old. He used to see sex as inappropriate in old age; now he characterizes the last sexual stage as one of "generalized sensuality" (Nissenson, 1984).

Note that Erikson assigned the task of identity formation primarily to late adolescence and early adulthood; however, especially for mothers, issues of personal identity may not become critical until the "empty nest" period of the late 30s and 40s. Erikson suggests that women's identity crises occur only after choice of a mate, a suggestion that Barnett and Baruch (1978) call "onerous." "Women, but not men, require a spouse before they can complete as crucial a task as identity formation; not marrying implies never establishing one's identity" (p. 189).

Erikson's theory was based on intensive interviews with a small sampling of men. He portrays the 20s as the time for launching a marriage and entering the work world; the 30s as the stage for establishing oneself in work and marriage; and the late 30s as the critical period for reexamining one's commitments and often freeing onself from a previously important mentor, the "famous boom phenomenon—becoming one's own man" (Barnett & Baruch, 1978, p. 189). Many women do not fit this theory because many of them do not enter the work world until their 30s. Besides, few women have mentors, and even those with long-term careers are rarely able to reassess their commitment pattern by age 40. In short, Levinson's and Erikson's models apply only to male experience. They focus on chronological age and presume an uninterrupted series of events such as commitment to marriage and occupation; their models ignore the less connected and more variable experience of women.

While most stage theorists acknowledge at least a rough division of adulthood into young adulthood, middle age, and later years, a minority go further and carve out additional stages of life, including the "young-old" and the "old-old." We do not yet know whether these further subdivisions will be useful (Hareven, 1976). Nor do we know what new categories may emerge in the future.

The Significance of Stages. Society's organization of life tasks and roles by stages has certain implications. Matters of age stratification, or generation, relate to the distribution of society's responsibilities, prestige, and resources on the basis of age and define the meaning of belonging to any particular age group in any given society at a particular time. The middle-age generation commands greater resources and influence than do children or the elderly, who command little (Ragan & Wales, 1980, p. 377). Society also assigns people *age* and *role identities:* "People accept the social sanctions related to age norms" (Neugarten, 1968, p. 144). For example, it is easier for the person with a middle-age identity to be viewed as sufficiently responsible and vigorous to be considered for the presidency of the United States than for younger or older adults. Age-role identity also produces *age segregation* in American society. For example, certain clubs and housing developments that cater to young adults would subtly discourage the presence of middle-aged persons.

Critiques of Stage Theory. Stage theory has had many critics. Goodman and Feldman (1975) observe that passages from one stage to another vary "in their desirability, their inevitability, their reversibility, and their repeatability" (p. 166). Stages also vary in terms of their clarity and emphasis. Much emphasis is placed on old age and little on young adulthood. The boundary between middle and older adulthood is clearer than between younger and middle adulthood. Old age, unlike other adult stages, has a formal beginning—age 65—at least as far as work life is concerned. Moving into it is institutionalized by retirement and the beginning of Social Security benefits (Hareven, 1976). Hence, adulthood as a stage should always be related to adulthood as a process. Similarly, Erikson and Martin (1984) agreed that "normative milestones" may be identified, but this global approach ignores differences in the way individuals move through these phases. Not only does it help to identify developmental issues but to determine differential modes of task resolution.

Some authorities question stage theories that portray adulthood as involving life stages unfolding according to some inner logic and necessity. Stage theorists have not often questioned the relationships between adulthood and environment nor analyzed ways in which alternative economic systems lead to different paths to adulthood (Lacy & Hendricks, 1980). Research with over 9,100 respondents failed to produce any consistent empirical support for developmental stage models; stage models of the life course were not congruent with practical problems of living in particular cultures.

Surveys have indicated that such demarcations do exist—at about 7-year intervals—but only within a particular culture. It would appear that such transitions depend upon events experienced by particular cohorts and are not inherent in the developmental process itself (Braun & Sweet, 1983–84). In other words, changes associated with the passing of time are not limited to individuals; aspects of the environment are also changing, including nations, societies, cultures, and institutions. Concepts of development and decline may be applied to the institutions of society just as they are to the life histories of individuals. Thus we have changing individuals relating to a changing society, and the effect of such events will vary with the life cycle) (Bengtson & Starr, 1975).

Society itself is becoming far less rigid and life styles more fluid; no longer do particular years mark optimum times for getting married, getting a job, going to school, or having children (Hall, 1980). Formerly individuals incorporated something of an internal clock, based on society's clock, that told them when to get married, go to school, or retire, but the importance of this clock has greatly diminished. It isn't uncommon today to hear of "a 22-year-old mayor or a 29-year-old university president—or a 35-year-old grandmother or a retiree of 50" (p. 66). It isn't even too uncommon for younger men to marry older women, although the age difference is usually not as great as that between older men and younger women.

(Stage theory derives mostly from research about males; it can be applied to some aspects of females' lives but not to all.) Since females are the childbearers they probably approach the stage of generativity earlier than males. For example, more young women than men adoptees seek to find their birth parents, perhaps partly because of concern about what they may transmit genetically to their own children. However, parallels in stage transitions may also be drawn. After comparing young and middle-aged women, Ryff and Migdal (1984) concluded that Erikson's designation of intimacy as significant for young adult men and generativity for the middle-aged is also valid for women. Certainly the young woman seeks to establish close relationships with the husband and others; and later she shows the breadth of interest, innovation, concern for others, and generosity associated with generativity. Erikson's concept is also global—it does not take into account other highly important aspects of each stage. For example, young adults are interested in career, political involvement as citizens, and conflict resolution, as well as intimacy.

The Concept of Generations

People in the same age group who experience the same problems at any particular time belong to the same *generation.* The time during which generations live limits their range of experience, which in turn modifies their values, thoughts, and behavior. Utilizing data from studies in the Detroit area, Dowd (1979–80) concluded that for the most part, changing values relate to cohort differences and the effects of historical periods rather than aging itself.

Those *cohorts,* or groups within the same generation, who utilize their common experiences in distinct ways are said to constitute *generation units.* Such units share a common destiny in history and time. Hence, it is important to consider historical events experienced by certain generations and cohorts such as economic depressions, political crises, and wars. The cohort concept interprets a generation as an age-homogeneous group; and the developmental stage perspective approaches it in terms of "task-homogeneous" cohorts (Aycock, 1984, p. 152). The "discrete time-span perspective" takes into account the time required—about 30 years—for a new cohort to replace its parents—but displacement is a continuous pro-

cess. A generation as "zeitgeist" subsumes those who share a historically distinct cultural content of values, arts, and style (Aycock, 1984).

Consider this illustration: In the late 1960s college students and their parents constituted different generations. Many of these college students, by their common involvement in antiwar protests and the civil rights movement, attained a certain distinctiveness or identity—that is, they became a generation unit.

In other words, the cultural and historical experiences that we live through leave their mark upon us, and they have a different effect on people of different ages. People who were young adults at the outbreak of World War I were affected more by that war than were the young children of those years. Thus we have the so-called *generations effect,* in which successive age cohorts are different not merely because of age differences but because they have experienced particular historical events differently. The resultant differences between generations are said to constitute a generation gap. It becomes apparent that developmental progression through the life cycle relates to points in historical time. For example, persons aged 65 in 1981 who were young adults during the great Depression may even yet feel undue anxieties over money. It would be easy to ascribe their economic conservatism to their older years, when in fact it arose from their own young adult experiences with financial stress.

The matter of generations becomes more important as ever-greater numbers of people live until late old age. Among a sampling of undergraduate women, many had significant relationships with one or more grandparents, and with grandmothers more often than with grandfathers (Hoffman, 1979–80). Meantime, the middle generation learns through experience with their parents to avoid the same behaviors with their offspring (Rosenmayr, 1980).

Erikson (1982) believes that old people

have a valuable generative or "grand-generative" function. Children, especially, benefit from encounters with them, being helped to realize that after work careers are over life may combine wisdom and enrichment. Consequently, Erikson deplores the discontinuity of family life, often imposed by the distance between younger people and their elders. For their part, the elderly, without this contact, find their sense of well-being and ability to share their life experience reduced. In effect, they then have less reason to remain alive.

THE STUDY OF ADULTHOOD

Historically, developmental psychologists have dealt mainly with the age periods conception through adolescence with the implicit assumption that development concludes with the end of growth or maturity. In contrast, life-span developmental psychologists have focused more on adult years and aging, and currently they are showing greater interest in mature years (Honzik, 1984).

Methods

Cross-Sectional and Longitudinal Research Designs. The most common research method in studying adulthood is a *cross-sectional,* in which comparisons are made of behavior at different ages. For example, early, middle-aged, and older adults can be tested simultaneously to measure their capacities for creativity. The differences that are found might be assumed to be strictly a result of age. However, education is far more common today than it was when present-day older people were young. Hence, the differences are partly a function of educational background as well as changes in health care, nutrition, and density of population. More effective than the cross-sectional method is the *longitudinal method,* in which

the same subjects are studied periodically over a length of time, sometimes even a lifetime. The results are then compared on successive testings, and attempts made to account for observed changes. Because longitudinal studies include such variables as past experience, family history, or medical history, they help determine the causes of particular age changes. They not only identify continuities across the life span but also explain breaks or discontinuities, for one is as significant as the other.

A fascinating book, *Whatever Happened to the Class of '65?* (Medved & Wallechinsky, 1976), suggests just how difficult it is to predict what direction individual lives will take. The thirty students interviewed were by no means a random sampling of Americans, nor were they selected on any other basis than that they were members of the same class. Among the thirty individuals, the all-American quarterback became a minister in a moderately bizarre religious cult while earning a livelihood as a masseur. The most popular boy in the class killed himself, while a gang leader established a million-dollar business empire. The head cheerleader and homecoming queen became a history professor at Princeton, and an idealistic, brilliant loner emerged as an egomaniac and a John Bircher. More predictable individuals who simply embarked upon uneventful, pleasant lives proved to be few and far between. The contrast between what the students had expected would become of each other and the reality of what did happen was extreme.

There are a number of significant longitudinal studies in progress. Among these, the Duke Longitudinal Aging Study, begun in 1955, has included both sexes; its first phase studied volunteers aged 60 to 90. The Boston Normative Aging Society includes over two thousand male veterans who have been examined every 5 years since 1963. Another project, the Baltimore Longitudinal Aging Study, begun in 1958, originally included only men, but since 1978 has included their wives, children, and other relatives as well. The idea is to gain insight into differences in aging between the sexes, especially with regard to the female life-span advantage. The second phase of the Duke study, begun in 1968, includes a random selection of both sexes aged 46 to 70 (Kent, 1980).

The Terman study, begun in 1926, involved 1,470 children with IQs of 135 or higher in California, most of them in grades 3 through 8; 58 younger siblings of the original group were added in 1928 and have been followed ever since (Goleman, 1980a). The data revealed how bright people of a particular generation viewed their lives. However, the sources of problems and happiness differed from one generation to another. Since they were college aged during the great Depression, the majority of the women got less education than they otherwise would. The data are most useful for studying differences among subgroups within the sample—for example, the most versus least successful, or the divorced versus the still married. The Terman study also allows an examination of the sequence of causes in individual development over a span of more than 50 years.

There have been nine followups in the Terman study, including interviews with the subjects and sometimes their spouses. There were also interviews with parents and early teachers. Researchers are still in touch with over 900 of the original 1,528 cases, so that 75 to 80 percent are still being followed. The total number of variables eventually coded for each person will be about 4,000. Four thousand codes for each person and about 1,000 cases will produce 4 million pieces of information.

The Terman study revealed critical turning points in each man's life. The chief turning point was World War II, which all the men perceived as a positive factor in their development. They said it matured them and helped them to understand life better. Most of them very quickly became officers, and their rapid advancement was both traumatic and growth-producing (Goleman, 1980c).

Attempts to predict the ultimate development of excellence in individuals have proved difficult to assess, indeed impossible, by methods currently available (Koch, 1981). For one thing causes may be unique to each individual thus precluding overall valid conclusions. Or the effects of chance may be sufficient to overwhelm those of measurable roots, and the great number of contributory influences may forbid evaluating their individual effects. Besides, effects of genetic factors on individual development are still not understood. Thus, it is not really possible to predict ultimate excellence until acquaintance with heredity mechanisms is vastly expanded. Moreover, being aware that some special constellation of events affected one individual in a particular manner tells us nothing about the effects of some similar occurrence or events on someone else. The effect on H.G. Wells of breaking a leg at age 7 had the effect of encouraging an already bookish child to be bed-bound for a time by his injury, thus allowing him to devote even more attention to written words, and therefore contributing to his becoming unusually intellectual as a child and outstandingly so as an adult.

It is hard to predict future excellence partly because such studies pose certain problems. For one thing, they require long periods of time and a lot of money. Some subjects may outlive the original investigators. Others may die or drop out of the sample. Changes in individuals may be ascribed to age when they are actually due to the historical period. The best way to overcome the deficiencies of both longitudinal and cross-sectional approaches is to combine the two. It is essential to study individuals as they proceed through their individual life spans, but it is also important to compare people at selected points in their lives or at different ages at the same point in historical time (Neugarten & Datan, 1973).

Life Histories. Some of the best, and most continuous, evidence regarding individual variations across the life span can be obtained from biography (Howe, 1982). However, note that such data cannot displace evidence from empirical research. Besides, biographers often do not discriminate between factual evidence and their own inferences. Also, information concerning the very early years, even of very important persons, is often lacking. Even the brief biographical accounts that we have indicate the great diversity of early circumstances of individuals who have attained eminence. Some child prodigies have become outstanding adults and others failures. Successful individuals may have had, in early years, neglecting parents or caring ones, extreme poverty or wealth. The parents of John Maynard Keynes were ambitious for him and carefully arranged plans for instructing him. In contrast, George Bernard Shaw's father was a secret drinker and Shaw was disliked and rejected by his mother.

Another group of questions which biographical evidence may help to shed light upon concerns the specialization of interest and commitment at a very early stage in life (Howe, 1982). Many actors say that from early years they desired to go on the stage; and many novelists say that they had wanted to write from early childhood. Often there was not a straight-line development of such interests—a period of floundering around was common. Charles Darwin's notebooks reveal a succession of self-discoveries, unexpected consequences, and stumblings on the discoveries of others.

Any particular study, regardless of overall approach, may employ several techniques. In Vaillant's study of midlife males, which he originally began during their college careers, a complete record was compiled for each man based on in-depth interviews and psychological tests. A staff member prepared a history of each man's family, and after graduation every individual submitted a questionnaire each year until 1955. Thereafter a questionnaire was completed every two years. A social anthropologist visited each man between 1950 and 1952, and in 1967 Vaillant interviewed 94 survivors of the original 268, whom he randomly selected from the larger sample (Muson, 1977).

Even broad generalizations from such research are dangerous. An individual who had been his mother's darling was predicted to feel triumphant throughout his life and confident of his success (Clark, 1980). Nevertheless, Dylan Thomas declared that "there is only one thing worse than having an unhappy childhood, and that's having a too happy childhood" (Ferris, 1977, p. 49). On the other hand, studies of relatively detailed accounts in the early years of outstanding people may reveal common themes, and patterns, or sequences of events that occurred in their early lives.

Certain types of achievement depend more on early precocity than others. Many outstanding musicians were quite precocious in childhood. Even when such precocity is not apparent an individual may have had the sort of childhood experiences that would lay the proper groundwork for achievement in later life, such as in the childhoods of Charles Darwin and Sir Richard Burton. Burton, whose highly varied achievements as explorer, anthropologist, poet, archeologist, and translator depended on his having proficiency in many foreign languages, spent much of his childhood in countries abroad (Howe, 1980).

In childhood an individual may acquire a reservoir of experiences to draw on in later years. In studying Dickens' childhood one has "the strong feeling that the person whose early years are being described is the one and only person who could conceivably have written the novels that Dickens produced" (Howe, 1980, p. 1076).

Many children known for their intellectual precocity receive special instruction from one or both parents or a sibling or, as in

Francis Galton's case, from the whole family. Often in such cases much of a parent's time was devoted to instructing a child. In the early seventeenth century, Pascale's father went to great lengths to arrange an intellectual environment for his three children.

Biography can provide help in identifying ways that family circumstances may influence an individual over the years. Charles Darwin was certainly influenced by his father, a physician, with special biological interest and by knowing of the career of his grandfather who was a biologist. Vocational choices can be influenced in particular directions for generations. The timing of events is also especially important—the fact that Charles Dickens was ill in his childhood encouraged him to read.

Especially intense childhoods are often characteristic of people who become writers, particularly novelists. The Brontes, Dickens, Kipling, and Balzac had unusually intense childhood experiences that left marks on them for life. Such children also often had highly developed their fantasy world as children. It is also important to pay attention to motivational and intellectual bases of developmental progress, including individual goals. Sometimes it is a matter of knowledge for its own sake, in other cases, a matter of wealth or status. H.G. Wells felt a strong need to avoid poverty, to escape the desolate conditions of his home life, and to achieve something of the comfort he had seen in the house where his mother labored as a housekeeper.

Other Techniques. Another method involves measuring such characteristics as intelligence, dexterity, or memory. Tests may also be of the projective type, the two most common being the Thematic Apperception Test and the Rorschach Inkblot Test. For assessing physiological factors, various biological and organic measuring devices are employed, such as the electrocardiograph for heartbeat and the electroencephalograph for measuring brain waves.

Appraisal of Research

Weaknesses. Research on adulthood, like that on other subjects, is subject to biases that distort conclusions. Erik Erikson and Charlotte Bühler derived their early views from clinical observations and analysis of biographical data. They did not take into account the social context within which human tasks were pursued (Lacy & Hendricks, 1980). Currently, adult development is being studied at Harvard, Berkeley, Chicago, and UCLA, all of which are highly respected institutions. However, most of this research is done by male researchers who are studying other men.

Social scientists also reflect both the biases of people who are influential in their fields and their own values; these biases influence the way they structure their research and the interpretation they place on their findings.

Distortions also arise from limitations on the topics being investigated. Often researchers work on problems that are simple and easily quantifiable because they are short of time and money. Or they may hesitate to investigate certain questions, such as sex relations among the aged, because of ethical problems. In addition, there has developed a "crisis of integrity" created by certain experimental procedures employed in psychological and medical experiments (Goethals, 1975, p. 59). As a result, new standards of ethics have been adopted which some experimenters deplore as hindrances to worthwhile research.

Distortion may arise from the research design and the instruments employed. Shesse, Burstein, and Atkins warn that traditional views of sex roles may be reinforced simply by the content and wording of survey questions (Sexist surveys, 1979). They analyzed over 3,000 national survey questions used from 1936 to 1973 and found that men were the subjects of such questions used from 1936 to 1973 and found that men were the subjects of such questions far more often than women. (None of the questions that described people in professional roles related solely to women.) The result was a picture of women who were mostly married, in dependent roles with husbands who supported them. The preponderance of questions about men results partially from the tendency to use "he" for everyone, but no one knows to what extent questionnaires interpret "he" to mean only males or both sexes.

A problem inherent in all developmental and personality research is determining the various meanings that individuals attach to behavior. Because of the infinite variety and complexity of human behavior, individual differences are easily obscured and distorted whenever subjects are thrown into categories for purposes of measurement. For example, (researchers may categorize an older person as maladjusted because he or she has only a single confidant.) For the individual who is somewhat quiet, just one friend may be enough. More outgoing persons might feel better satisfied with several confidants or would at least expect intense contact with the single confidant. (Antonucci, 1976, p. 138).

Consider another common example from the aging research. People generally remain the same throughout their lives in the degree to which they attach themselves to others, or the reverse. Formerly disengagement or distance from others was associated with aging (Havighurst, Neugarten & Tobin, 1968). Now it is better understood that disengaged people, whether aging or otherwise, exist across the life span.

What Adelson (1979) said of adolescent psychology can also be said of adult psychology: there is no single adult psychology that is timeless and universal. Adults are no one thing; they differ among themselves and at different ages in early, middle, and late adulthood.

The Status of Adult Research. The developmental study of adulthood is in its infancy, except in the field of gerontology. It is much

easier to do research on adolescents and older people because those groups are captive research subjects in schools and rest homes. Meantime, the middle aged are out in the world, working and trying to grasp the complexities of life.

Nevertheless, new trends in research are apparent, one being a concern for all life stages as they relate to each other. Only through studying the total life span, including old age, can one fully understand the complete significance of any earlier period. As Charlotte Bühler observed in a letter to Robert Havighurst: "My interest was in the whole of human life. . . . After some years, I decided that life as a whole could be better understood from its end than from its beginning" (Havighurst, 1974, p. 398). Hence, she and her students studied biographies that were sufficiently well documented to allow following lives to their very end. Interest is also being shown in the more optimistic, healthful aspects of aging as distinct from the almost total concern for its problems that was shown formerly.

Meantime, as behavioral scientists have acquired a growing stake in such research, the individual's privacy has been placed in greater jeopardy. To what extent research may be retarded by regulations designed to safeguard people against possible invasions of privacy is as yet unclear; also unclear are the ethical restraints that scientific disciplines had best impose on themselves (Etzioni, 1978–79).

Perhaps the most important development in research on adulthood, or any age, is the arrival of high-speed computers (Rubinstein, 1980). Researchers have found that they can make calculations in 20 seconds that once would have required 11 months. Even if they have 100 subjects or more in a study they can analyze the impact of dozens of factors simultaneously. When the psychologist Paul Muchinsky published his studies of human subjects at five-year intervals over the past two decades, the average number of individuals included in each study had increased seven-fold between 1957 and 1978 (Rubenstein, 1980).

Special Needs. Looking ahead, it is hoped that certain deficiencies will be remedied. More research needs to be done on the early adult years, from about 21 to 35; and more studies should be made of older people who are not institutionalized and who have aged successfully. To date, research has focused chiefly on the minority of the elderly who are in institutions; the few studies of the healthy elderly who live in the community are providing completely new insights into this age group. Such studies should be greatly expanded, always taking into account the particular life conditions in which successive cohorts have lived.

A second need is to study adults not as a homogeneous group but as subcultures, social classes, and individuals. Race and social class have a special effect on the timing of social events. To date too little attention has been paid to contextual and social factors in the patterns of change through the life cycle. Researchers have also spent little time considering the life styles of people married over a half century (Roberts, 1979–80). In addition, if lifelong education is to be related to life-cycle changes and developmental periods, more should be learned about the corresponding needs of the target population. The focus to date has been on the middle class, with little attention being paid to the poor or the very rich; nor has much attention been paid to the various subgroups within the middle class (Rivera, 1978).

There should be more replication of research so that policies and programs will not be implemented on the basis of studies that lack adequate substantiation or have become out of date. There should also be more anticipatory research–that is, there ought to be attempts to gauge the future in order better to prepare for it. While such research admittedly lacks the solidity of empirical research, it would be better than guesswork about what lies ahead.

Adults should also be studied within the context of interfamilial relationships. Datan (1980) decided that "we have been looking too long at little boys, and too little at their fathers and mothers. I saw the Oedipus complex as only one half of a dynamic interaction between child and parents, in which the second half, the sexual and aggressive passions of the parents, seemed curiously neglected" (p. 6).

THE ORGANIZATION OF THIS BOOK

The following chapters are concerned with three successive age levels of adulthood. Part II deals with young adults, including their transition into adulthood, their main tasks, and their life styles. Part III focuses on middle-aged adults—their characteristics, life styles, and activities; some of the material in this section applies to all adults in general. In Part IV older adults are treated similarly, in terms of characteristics, life styles, problems, and finally death. Certain of the same topics are employed in order to demonstrate more clearly the transitions that occur with age. Topics that relate more specifically to each stage are also covered.

While adulthood conceivably could be subdivided somewhat differently, adult age roles in America are ordinarily defined as young, middle-aged, or old. As treated here, young adulthood will be interpreted as embracing the period from the first assumption of an adult role until the late 30s, when the exploring, getting-ahead-in-the-world phase yields to a more stable, settled stage. Middle age is perceived as beginning about age 35 and lasting until retirement, or age 65, chiefly because old age is commonly presumed to begin then. Because of the vast differences among people in their 60s and 70s, and those in their 80s and 90s, it might be more accurate to think of the young-old and the old-old. It should be clear from the text which of these two levels is concerned.

The last chapter is designed to tie together the preceding chapters and attempt to forecast the future. Because of deficiencies in research thus far, as well as continuously evolving status of adults in modern society, generalizations are necessarily tentative. However, if we are ever to develop a useful psychology of adulthood, it is essential to consider the significance of such data as we have, and to make whatever conjectures appear justified.

SUMMARY

In recent years interest has been shown in the psychology of adulthood for the first time. The growing numbers of old people, the extension of already existing longitudinal studies of children, and the increasing amount of free time in adulthood are among the reasons for this interest. But just what adults are like is still unclear; various images of adults exist.

Aging, or the process that accounts for the successive stages of life, is modified by several factors. In the biological sense, it involves certain pacemakers that establish a general time frame for life stages. However, people are not wholly the victims of genetic destiny, for life satisfaction and healthful living can retard aging. Conversely, lack of activity, cigarette smoking, and a polluted environment can hasten it. Aging itself is a complex process that concerns the impact of time on all aspects of an individual's behavior.

The chronological model of aging treats the life process in terms of calendar years. The legal model involves such matters as the age of majority and the acquisition of certain rights and responsibilities. The biological model relates aging to physical changes in the organism over time; social age refers to socially ascribed roles at successive life stages. The developmental model focuses on life as a changing, growing process from conception until death, whereas functional age suggests that people age at different rates in

different functions. Finally, personal age refers to the way individuals relate their own experience to the aging process.

According to stage theory, the life cycle itself involves stages that occur in all persons at roughly the same period in development. This concept has been variously interpreted by Jung, Havighurst, Erikson, and others. According to one view, people in the same age group who experience the same historical problems at any particular time constitute the same generation. The historical period in which a generation lives limits its experience and influences its values and behaviors. The generational process itself is not constant, but varies according to the speed and nature of change.

The most common methods employed for studying adults are the longitudinal and cross-sectional, while life histories may involve a variety of techniques. All have their strengths and weaknesses, but the longitudinal and life-history approaches are proving especially fruitful. Such research, where adults are concerned, is still in an exploratory stage, but it is rapidly gaining momentum. It appears that exiciting new insights on adulthood will certainly emerge, as was the case in the earlier phases of child and youth research.

SUGGESTED READINGS

ACOCK, A. C. (1984). Parents and their children: The study of inter-generational influence. *Sociology and Social Research, 68*(2), 151–171.

CHINEN, A. B. (1984). Modal logic: A new paradigm of development and late-life potential. *Human Development, 27*(1), 42–56.

DANNEFER, D. (1984). Adult development and social theory: A paradigmatic reappraisal. *American Sociological Review, 49,* 100–116.

ERICKSON, V. L. & MARTIN, J. (1984). The changing adult: An integrated approach. *Social Casework, The Journal of Contemporary Social Work, 65*(3), 162–171.

FREEMAN, M. (1984). History, narrative, and life-span developmental knowledge. *Human Development, 27,* 1–19.

FROLKIS, V. V. (1982). *Aging and life prolonging processes.* Vienna, NY: Springer-Verlag.

HAYFLICK, L. (1984). When does aging begin? *Research on Aging, 6*(1) 99–103.

KASTENBAUM, R. (1984). When aging begins. A lifespan developmental approach. *Research on Aging, 6*(1), 105–117.

LABOUVIE-VIEF, G. (1982). Dynamic development and mature autonomy. A theoretical prologue. *Human Development, 25,* 161–191.

LOGAN, R. D. (1983). A re-conceptualization of Erikson's identity stage. *Adolescence, 18*(72), 943–946.

MONTAGU, A. (1982). *Growing young: Anthropology and Aging.* McGraw-Hill.

NELSON, G. K. (1983). Time in developmental studies: A convergence of the dialectic and phenomenological thought. *Genetic Psychology Monographs, 108*(2), 215–243.

NYDEGGER, C. N., MITTENESS, L. S., & O'NEIL, J. (1983). Experiencing social generations. *Research on Aging, 5*(4), 527–546.

RUNYAN, W. M. (1982). *Life histories and psychobiography.* New York: Oxford University Press.

SIMONS, C. J. R., & THOMAS, J. L. (1983). The life cycle in historical context: The impact of normative history-graded events on the course of life-span human development. *Human Development, 26,* 117–120.

STREEVER, K. L., & WODARSKI, J. S. (1984). Life-span developmental approach: Implications for practice. *Social Casework: The Journal of Contemporary Social Work, 65*(5), 267–278.

SURBER, C. F. (1984). Issues in using quantitative rating scales in developmental research. *Psychological Bulletin, 95*(2), 226–246.

WATKIN, D. M. (1983). *Handbook of nutrition, health and aging.* Park Ridge, NJ: Noyes Publications.

CHAPTER TWO

Induction Into Adulthood

COMING OF AGE

Pubertal Rites

All societies distinguish between the status of child and that of adult. Most simple societies have precise formulas for inducting their youth into adulthood. The youth undergoes certain pubertal rituals, or *rites de passage*, which vary in amount of stress produced, after which the youth is considered an adult. These rites differ for the sexes in varying manner and degree. Rites may be for one sex only, or they may be more elaborate for one sex than for the other. Societies are more likely to have male puberty rites when the society is more integrated sexually—that is, when the sexes are more jointly involved in various occupational activities

(Kitahara, 1982). Perhaps one reason is that men in such a society desire to maintain a distance between the sexes, even though they are integrated in the labor force.

Such rites may be quite different for the sexes or, in a few cases, much the same. Among the Sepiks in New Guinea, for example, boys can become men only by ritualizing birth and taking over as a collective group the function that women perform naturally (Mead, 1950). More attention is given rites for males, because the man's role in most societies is defined as more important. Besides, the boy undergoes no specific physical event which in itself signals the onset of puberty. His pubertal changes occur slowly, and no developmental events give him an immediate right to say "I am now a man." Therefore, simple societies provide the boy an adult identity by contriving rites of passage which make known his status to his tribe or village. His new social status may be proclaimed by visible signs, including body scars, circumcision, pierced ears, teeth filing, and teeth removal, as well as by special gifts. Stressful rites for young males are the rule. The Nandi of East India contrive ingenious tortures during the circumcision of the boy and he is rewarded if he does not show pain. The Apache Indians initiate the boy as though breaking a colt: they compel him to make holes in the ice and bathe, run with water in his mouth, and in general, bully him. Among the Mundugumor of New Guinea, the boy receives blows and curses and is scarred by a crocodile skull.

In contrast, little attention is accorded the girl's puberty. Among the aborigines in Central Australia, elaborate ceremonies are held for the male, but none at all for the female. Since menarche is dramatic and unmistakable, there is no question about the female's new status as a woman. Hence, the girl's rites are usually confined to significant happenings in her development, such as her first menstruation, betrothal, or marriage, and include relatively mundane activities. Only in rare cases—for example, where obesity is considered a sign of feminine beauty—is much attention paid to the girl's growing up. In parts of central Africa, she is separated at puberty from her family and fattened for several years, during which time she performs no physical activities.

Except in rare cases, female rituals are also less stressful, perhaps for similar reasons. During pubertal ceremonies among the Tukuna Indians, a girl's hair is plucked from her head, and the pain may be so great that she faints, but such ordeals for girls are exceptional. In Samoa, which is more typical, there are no taboos surrounding menstruation, and the menstruating girl is even permitted to prepare most foods. Menarche itself is not celebrated at all, although the recognition of defloration, or loss of virginity, is.

Pubertal Rites: Western Style

In modern society, there is no consensus as to what constitutes a rite of passage because growing up by formula is not the rule. Instead of a single ceremony, a sequence of steps leads to adulthood—grade school graduation, high school graduation, and college graduation. Pubertal rites have been displaced by legal definitions of rights and responsibilities. Sometime between the twelfth and the eighteenth birthdays, the protective and restrictive aspects of minor status are progressively removed, and adult privileges and responsibilities instated. The sacrifice of childhood privileges and the acquisition of mature responsibilities do not always go together. For example, 12-year-olds may pay full fare for airplane tickets; but they may not drive cars.

Perhaps the nearest thing we have to pubertal rites in this culture, writes Joseph Kett in *Rites of Passage,* is leaving home, a ritual that has changed greatly over the past two decades (Goleman, 1980). In the eighteenth and nineteenth centuries youth went through many home leavings before finally setting forth in life. It was a commonplace practice for children, even as young as age 7, to be sent to a neighbor's farm as a boy-of-all-work. Or coast merchants might send their sons to sea as cabin boys even before they were 10 years old. Daughters would go out to work as servant girls. Thus there was a pattern of "semi-dependence," alternating between being subject to the parents' authority at home and much freer on the job.

From about the mid-nineteenth century on, cities grew and employment there increased, which meant that young people who went there to work usually stayed instead of making regular trips home, because of expense of transportation. Then, between 1800 and 1900, certain demographic trends importantly modified the quality and character of American adolescence. Small urban families displaced large ones on the farms; fewer teenagers were compelled to contribute to the family income. In consequence, people began to adopt the "romantic view that the innocent young need protection against the pressures and dangers of modern life," so they were no longer sent away to work but to high school instead (Goleman, 1980c, p. 57). The new belief was that parents should carefully look after their teenagers until they were ready for adulthood, which served to prolong adolescence.)

These days there are various patterns for children's leaving home. One is to leave home sooner than parents are ready to let their children go. One girl, age 18, did so after she argued with her parents about staying out late. She left and moved into an apartment in Toronto with some friends. She knew that her parents were upset about her leaving but said that she wanted them to see that she was not a child any more. Others leave home in stages, not leaving for good until they have established a secure base away from home. One girl lived first in her mother's house, then in a small cottage in the backyard, and then in a dormitory on a college campus. By leaving in stages she felt less insecure. Others may feel no pressure to leave at all and may remain at home well into adulthood. In one family five of seven children ages 15, 17, 23, 26, 30 lived at home and the others lived close by. The father said that the family had always been close together and had taken vacations together. Some young people feel ambivalent about leaving home. They may leave but want to be sure there is a home base for them to return to whenever they like.

Psychological counselors in universities indicate that home leaving often brings students, especially freshmen, to clinics, girls more often than boys. Thus, they may have left home physically but not psychologically. Also only and youngest children have more problems leaving home because parents often hold on to them too long and more tightly.

Another problem is that the home-leaving process is not institutionalized, and there are no firm guidelines. In other words, there is no right time or manner in which to leave. Parents themselves are uncertain about how long to hold their children. It is clear that this matter cannot be understood without studying the family as a whole.

Although mounting evidence indicates that adolescence is not extremely stressful, leaving home may represent something of a crisis. A major task of the family, especially the parents, is to permit their grownup children to leave home as a natural consequence of their maturity. Parents must acknowledge to themselves their adolescent children's maturity and renew their own attachment to each other if they are to avoid feeling depressed.

Wechter (1983), a social worker, told of her own experience in leaving her family in Texas to go to New York. The family perceived her leaving as rejection of her own identity as a southerner, a Texan, and small city girl. She had rejected the family's life style, and her accustomed role as mediator in the family, which tried desperately to get her to stay at home. In her first two years in New York the relationship had swung back and forth between "closeness and distance, enmeshment and alienation, acceptance and rejection" (p.99). The family seemed angry at her seeming rejection and caused her to feel guilty. She was trying to find her own vocational life while, at the same time, trying to retain her parents' encouragement, and she zigzagged between attempting to meet their expectations and developing her own.

Obstacles to Establishing Maturity

One obstacle to maturity is the scarcity of association between age groups. Adolescent groups are often set off to the point of encapsulation, and spend their time in teen herds. Since they are denied the exercise of genuine responsibility and direct identification with adults, they are correspondingly denied a true apprenticeship for adulthood. Another obstacle to such apprenticeship is (the parent who refuses to acknowledge that his or her child (usually the girl) is growing up.)Mothers, especially, may not know how to retire from parenthood, and their children cannot cut parental psychic umbilical cords without guilt feelings.

In addition, much that children learn has little relevance for adulthood. The submissiveness of early years must be changed to independence and even aggressiveness later on. Fun and irresponsibility must give way to serious concerns. Even schools, supposed to train students for the business of life, fail adequately to integrate the curriculum with life outside the school. Youth think of graduation as crossing the threshold into real life, as though the years up to that time had been some sort of prolonged prenatal state.

A related problem is difficulty in finding adequate models of adulthood (Porter-Gehrie, 1979).(Often, the adults youth prefer as models are remote from their experience, such as historical figures or athletic heroes.) (Hence, their modeling is indirect, as in images of adults presented in films, books, and television.)

Another problem of maturing is the lack of any standard for determining when adulthood has been achieved since standards for achieving maturity vary with social class, sex, culture, and marital status. Children of the lower class are turned loose earlier and be-come heads of families and wage earners immediately after high school. Despite their later age of puberty, males are accorded recognition as adults earlier than females. College males are often referred to as men, whereas females of the same age are commonly called girls. Marital status also makes a difference. The youth with a wife and family is considered a man, but a single male of the same age is still an adolescent.

(Contributing further to the confusion are society's capricious standards of responsibility.)One teenager is locked up for a crime and held accountable as if he were a man; another of the same age, convicted of an even more serious crime, may be granted reprieve because of his youth. Such ambiguities reinforce young people's uncertainties about themselves. They cannot be sure what privileges they are entitled to or when they will be held accountable.

In the late 1960s and early 1970s young people began to demand their rights and to be treated more maturely, and as a result the voting age was lowered to 18 (Proefrock, 1981). In addition, there was a trend toward trying adolescents indicted for serious crimes in adult, instead of juvenile, courts. Meantime, technical and trade schools requiring brief periods of training had grown more popular. Thus it appeared that the adolescent period was becoming shorter. Never-

T.G. Bell

Many adolescent activities have little to do directly with preparation for adulthood.

theless, there was no real progress toward giving adolescents a greater share in the benefits they wanted from society.

The complex factors involved in establishing recognition as an adult are apparent in students' answers to the question: "At what age do you expect to consider yourself an adult and why?"

I'll be an adult by age 26, because by then I'll have had experiences as a teacher and as a housewife. I'll have a burden of responsibility and a position of respect.

I had so many responsibilities during my teens that I was an adult long before I entered college.

I am young in spirit and will probably not feel like I'm an adult until I am 30.

I already feel like an adult. I began feeling like one about age 18 and certainly by 21. Why? I first lived away from home and learned what sex was (in theory). Above all, college gave me a personal insight into self.

ATTITUDES TOWARD GROWING UP

Adults' Attitudes

Among factors serving either to facilitate or obstruct youth's induction into adulthood are adult attitudes. Some parents, unconsciously or otherwise, resist their children's growing up. It is hard to change perceptions which have become habit. Besides, parents' acknowledgment that their children are growing up is to concede that they themselves are aging. Other adults accept their children's changing status because they assume they are expected to or because they look forward to escaping responsibilities incumbent upon the parental role.

Youth's Attitudes

Individual reactions to growing up vary widely: some adolescents eagerly look ahead; others have mixed feelings; still others cast a wary eye on approaching adulthood as though flying into the eye of a hurricane. Less than enthusiastic adolescents sympathize with the wit who said, "Adulthood is a time when one stops growing at the ends and starts growing in the middle." Adulthood is the time to settle down; fun-seeking as a way of life is over.

Somewhat confused or ambiguous feelings about becoming adult are reflected in these youths' statements:

FEMALE: My perception of the adult world is still ambiguous. Money is very important, too important—the adult world doesn't place much emphasis on self-actualization. It's too deodorized, too antiseptic. It discriminates against women and frustrates their self-actualization.

MALE: My perception of adult society is complex, and my feelings contradictory. I see a world that says one thing and does another. Adult society says be an individual, make your own choices. It also says don't be a rebel, and follow the rules.

Some individuals have a greater stake in prolonging adolescence than others. The girl may dread choosing between marriage and career. The glamourous female and the male athletic star may lose the worship currently given them. For them, adulthood is anticlimax, not climax. As one 20-year-old youth wrote:

I was a three-letter man in high school and accorded all the honors and privileges that went with my exalted status. I had my pick of dates and invitations to parties. It was wonderful while it lasted, but a football injury put an end to my being a Saturday hero. Now I am a has-been, a used-up athlete, trying to get used to the lacklustre role that has been forced upon me.

Many adolescents hold a double orientation to adulthood, like young Bazerov in Turgenev's *Fathers and Sons*. Portrayed as the archetype of adolescence, he is described as trembling on the brink of adulthood while also trembling with anger that he was being restrained. In any case, the majority unconsciously accept the fact that they will soon become adults and must prepare themselves accordingly. Whether they perceive adulthood as climax or anticlimax, they accept its inevitability.

Youth's Goals for Adulthood

The life styles most youth would prefer as adults are somewhat traditional, though in some respects they reflect the times. Among 17,000 high school seniors almost three-quarters thought a happy marriage and family life were highly important (Youth on the move, 1981).

Young men are coming to attach growing importance to their future role in the family and all but a very few college women still rank motherhood and marriage first among their future priorities, although the majority expect to combine marriage and career (Mash, 1978). Nevertheless, young women no longer look on housewifery, motherhood, and conventional feminine behavior as the end-all of women's existence. They want flexibility in career plans, with brief interruptions for motherhood or for reducing career commitments when their children are young.

Young women's fertility expectations have fallen more sharply than the fertility ideal. The decrease in fertility expectation may be linked to a realistic perception of the conflict between having children and holding a job. Decreased fertility expectations are also consistent with their higher educational expectations. Although many young women appear not to regard high level of educational attainment as incompatible with relatively high fertility, expected educational attainment is closely linked to the age when young women begin childbearing. Delay in childbearing is associated with ultimately having fewer children. Moreover, as young women grow older and increase their schooling, they may revise downward their fertility expectations, especially those who obtain attractive positions in the job market. However, this situation may be revised to the extent that child-care programs and flexible policies are provided in the workplace, concepts which are slowly but surely taking hold (Crowley & Shapiro, 1982).

It should be added that, looking ahead, youth not only perceive the roles of making a living, rearing a family, and maintaining the society but also a life of self-expression, creativity, and adventure. They wish to develop their creative potential for developing "expressive styles of living" (Yankelovich, 1983, p.39).

Preferred Life Styles. Undergraduates at the State University of New York at Oswego indicate the type of life styles they would prefer as adults.

After college

MALE: I would prefer to wait about 5 to 10 years after school to get married, or possibly just live with someone; then I would like to have a few children.

FEMALE: My choice would be to get married eventually, but right now I'm not sure that I want to have children. I don't think it is fair to bring a child into a world as problem-oriented as ours. I'd like to adopt a child who needs a home. Society should care for people already living rather than just producing more.

Where to live after college

MALE: Ideally, I would like to live in a small town. I like the easy-going pace, but realize that job opportunities are fewer there. I have to draw a balance between my ideal living conditions and my ideal career aspirations (although I don't even know what they are yet).

FEMALE: I was raised in a rural area and found it very rewarding because I could have pets, and always had a place to get away from it all.

Future vocation

FEMALE: I am looking for a job I can be secure in (both financially and job wise) and a place where I can be creative. I am more of a doer than a sitter and these two parts have to go together for me to function well.

MALE: After college I plan to become a policeman or federal agent. I would like to get married and have at least three children. However, I want to have good financial status when I get married. I want my children to go to school, even to college. My sons, I want to be fair, honest, and athletic; my daughters, fair, honest, healthy. I want to live in the country. I want my family to feel like a family, not like a cardboard structure of a family found in suburbs and cities.

CRITERIA FOR MATURITY

Progress toward adulthood is sometimes measured in terms of developmental tasks. That is, an individual must attain particular attitudes, habits, and skills in order to function effectively as an adult. Adulthood often sneaks up on adolescents, catching them unprepared. Various listings of such tasks exist, generally not conflicting but having different emphases. The following points, derived from various lists, will be summarized here.

1. A basic criterion of maturity is that the normal tasks of adolescence will have been resolved. The young adult must have firm preadult underpinnings; otherwise energies still required for fighting childhood battles and healing old wounds cannot be set free for resolution of adult problems.

2. Youth who are ready for maturity have found healthy channels for expressing emotions and can control them to the extent required. They have learned to inhibit excessive expression of emotion, as well as to ignore many of the stimuli which, in early years, proved to be stress-producing. This is not to say that they remain emotionally insulated from their environments. On the contrary, they make heavy emotional investments, but are resilient, capable of taking in stride the inevitable frustrations of life.

3. Young adults should have a sense of commitment and of belonging to the "human enterprise." On the other hand, they should maintain freedom from undue control by others.

4. Mature individuals can maintain their autonomy more easily if they have established a sense of identity and a way of life consistent with their own potential. They are aware of self—not in a self-conscious way, but in a manner that makes for integration of energies and self-respect. Mature individuals make use of their competencies, capitalizing especially on unusual talents, even if the result is an apparently lopsided manner of life.

5. Another task is to retain the best of the preceding stages, while dispensing with the rest. Adults should preserve the sort of energy, idealism, and *joie de vivre* which is characteristic of youth. However, some aspects of adolescence, if they persist, can become a stumbling block to later adjustment. A case in point is the pressure on American adults to remain pegged at an adolescent stage of sexual development. Marital satisfaction may decline, partly because adults are expected to perform at 40 or 50 as they did at 20 or 25.

6. They have developed an interest in establishing the next generation, implying a faith in life and in their own place in the total scheme of things. This concept subsumes many facets of generation, including all the ways of creating and nurturing new persons, new products, new institutions, and new life styles, through periods of their origin and early existence and early "vulnerability."

7. If not engaged in full-time homemaking, mature individuals have successfully entered a vocation that permits self-actualization, and have become good citizens. They have made satisfactory adjustments to the major social institutions, on both the local and the larger scene.

8. In defining one's relation to the world, the mature individual has developed a rational moral code and a philosophy of life. This philosophy provides the individual with a sat-

isfying concept of the universe and his or her place in it; and the moral code serves as a measuring stick for one's actions. It must also be flexible, designed to effect its basic purpose—to insure the greatest ultimate good of all concerned.

9. Young adults must be sufficiently tough, resourceful, and flexible to cope with giant-sized problems. We can prophesy with some degree of certainty that today's young people will ultimately be required to cope with awesome issues, including problems of population, pollution, the bomb, interracial tension, and perhaps interplanetary relationships.

10. One fundamental task of young adults is the continuation of exploratory activities already developed—a matter of life styles on trial in a wider arena. They do not find themselves all at once; making final decisions at this age stage is neither immediately necessary nor desirable.

HELPING YOUTH TO GROW UP

Although most individuals muddle through to maturity reasonably well, some of them, like those quoted here, might be helped to set their compasses more accurately:

FEMALE: I am only allowed to make unimportant decisions about my life. Most

of our decisions are guided by what other people think.

MALE: I have always concentrated on happiness, but in my childhood I was unhappy and my adolescence is the same. Sometimes I have to stop work and have a good time to sort of regain my childhood. I perceive the adult world with disdain but when I look at our own generation I am not happy. The world of the businessman I don't like, nor the world of competition.

Assistance for such youth might embrace the following points:

1. Youth should not be forced into maturity too soon. If we indulge in overkill where adolescence is concerned, an individual fails to retain aspects of youth, such as hope and enthusiasm, that should be preserved. The adolescent years may be preserved as a psychosocial moratorium, during which individuals remain relatively free from adult pressures. They need time to engage in identity play and other forms of experimentation to determine who they really are.

2. To be appreciated, adulthood should be earned. Adults who excessively indulge young people prevent them from understanding that only through becoming competent do they attain true freedom (Baumrind, 1974). They cannot

Mentors play an important role in helping youth grow up.

Frank M. Gaines, III

feel that they have a future or make a place in the world without appropriate understandings, skills, and attitudes.

3. Conflicting interests between older and younger generations should be resolved insofar as possible; *hence, respective roles of younger and older adults should be clarified.* Parents of young adults should resist the temptation to sacrifice all the fruits of their toil to give their children an effortless start in life. Conversely, young adults must eliminate guilt feelings which tempt them to surrender rights of self-determination to parents who may attempt to run their lives.

4. Youth should be prepared not only to resolve adult problems but to enjoy adulthood actively; yet maturity is rarely pictured as satisfying. In most television programming, the primary emphasis is on romantic love involving young, good-looking subjects in fictional situations. Hence, youth have fuzzy ideas about adulthood in its most productive and satisfying aspects.

5. A more all-embracing goal is that youth should become challenged continuously to develop "new and more inclusive purposes for life" at later ages (Menge, 1982, p. 438). Nor should they perceive "change" as "threatening, as something that happens to one, but rather something that one's own efforts cause to happen, through explicit purposes, new information and skills" (pp. 433–439). Thus, "life continues to hold out the promise for a better tomorrow and when one feels significantly involved in making that future happen, the integrity of one's identity and productivity on earth is enhanced" (p. 439).

6. A national survey (Watts, 1981) indicated that "parents no longer regard their children as wards, whose future lives they must—or even can—orchestrate and plan" (p. 48). However, adults may earn youth's disrespect by too easily abdicating their own convictions. Some impatient youth champ at the bit; they can already taste the power of running a world; hence, adults should not shirk the responsibility of debating issues with the young. All too many adults have become self-doubting and intimidated by the aggressiveness, impatience, and impulsiveness of the young and refuse to engage them in vigorous debate on substantive issues.

7. It is well, too, for people entering their 20s to look at some of the research being done on people of middle age and later years. Many middle-aged people look back, wishing that their values had been different in their 20s. Still later, in old age, both physical and mental health status are rooted in habits, skills, and attitudes established in earlier years. Every youth is an old-person-in-the-making and a significant determiner of what that old person will be.

YOUTH AND THE FUTURE

The foregoing recommendations regarding youth's preparation for adulthood have been couched in terms of the world as we know it. The present discussion is more conjectural, in terms of potential and alternative futures.

Youth must be prepared for uncertain futures and events that seem improbable, even impossible, today (Anderson, 1979). They must be prepared for dramatic technical breakthroughs equivalent in significance to the discovery of electricity, the automobile, the airplane, and the computer. It is thought-provoking to examine predictions made by certain highly respected individuals and publications in the past. The *Literary Digest* for October 14, 1899 declared that "the ordinary horseless carriage is at present a luxury for the wealthy; and although its price will probably fall in the future, it will never, of course, come into as common use as the bicycle." *Science Digest* of August 1948 declared that landing on the moon would involve so many serious problems that at least two more centuries would be required to accomplish it (The worst forecasts, 1978).

The following points are intended mainly to establish a habit of thinking that anticipates the future and involves preparation for the most probable scenarios to come. Also essential is the development of abilities needed to cope with new and complex developments and to learn to live with, even be challenged by, ambiguity.

1. Youth should keep abreast of intelligent prediction, as opposed to unscientific "star gazing." Futurist Paul Dickson calls futurism the "fastest growing educational phenomenon in history, the most important new concept of government in a hundred years, invaluable, too, for industry and a major breakthrough in human thinking" (The worst forecasts, 1978, p. 127). Certainly it would seem that perceptions of any life stage would gain greater validity if related to years that follow. As they go through life, individuals must learn to cope with new and growing threats to health that derive from mankind's assault on the environment. Also, as linkages of computer interactions progress, quantities of data, often very personal, may be made generally available, thus threatening individual privacy (Decades of decision: Micro/macro, 1979, p. 144).

2. Youth need to develop new values if they are to relate properly to a rapidly changing world. Every scientific advance raises new questions of redefining interrelationships in the universe. Brower (1979) advises that adults of tomorrow rethink certain values which have been taken for granted—among them, man's right to dominate the environment. He suggests that "our attitude toward Earth was healthier when we were pagans who believed that spirits resided in everything, that man and beast were on an equal footing—bears becoming men, occasionally men becoming owls—and that a tree had to be placated before you chopped it down"(p. 20).

3. Because of the growing exploitation of earth's resources, youth need a sense of generativity or concern for future generations, more than ever before. Future generations will hardly forgive us "for the erasure of a large fraction of the species of plants and animals—an unnecessary wastage of their heritage, which will undoubtedly be ranked as the worst error committed during the twentieth century." Since children and youth have a notoriously limited time sense, they should be helped *imaginatively* to embrace a sufficiently long time span to consider the long-term effects of behaviors (Decades of decision: Alternating currents, 1979.)

4. Adults of the future must have sound interpersonal relationships for their very survival.

There is a wide gap between humans' genius in natural discoveries and their inability to resolve conflicts between groupings of humans around the globe (Decades of decision: The human family, 1979).

5. Schools must continuously update their offerings, attempting to anticipate what their students need for effective living currently and in the future. A panel of youth and adults, commissioned by the National Education Association, defined certain educational goals if youth were to be prepared properly for the future. In addition to more traditional subjects, they should study human relations and communication skills as well as such related skills as computer languages and information processing. Concepts of work and leisure should be reinterpreted and both become employed as means to greater personal fulfillment. Of special concern was the need to develop ethical character, perceived as requiring up-to-date ethical models and redefinition of values of equity and justice (Shane, 1977).

6. Youth must be prepared to think in terms of all the earth and even beyond the earth. Continued developments in transportation and communication will rapidly increase the tendency, already great, to bring the whole world close together. Author Ray Bradbury concludes that in all the history of the world, nothing is more important than space travel. For him it is "commensurate with the birth of Jesus, Buddha, or Mohammed" (Decades of decision: Micro/macro, 1979, p.100). Presumably, systematic search for radio signals and civilizations that may have far greater expertise than we have (Interview with Philip Morrison, 1979).

7. Tremendous technological advances suggest the potential for greatly enriched lives and increased free time. Merely consider the time saved by the computer. Computers are becoming increasingly simplified and will enable people to simplify coping with problems of managing their daily lives and life styles. To date, society has done too little to help children and youth to develop creative and satisfying ways of spending leisure time for all their years ahead.

Technological breakthroughs will also necessitate making important personal decisions.

For example, through breaking the genetic code, "the master chemical blueprint of life, couples may choose characteristics, including sex, of their children" (Age of miracles, 1983, p. A19). As never before, sophisticated decision-making will be required to maximize benefits and avoid serious errors.

8. Finally, youth should discard the habit of always expecting final, concrete answers. True, psychologists have long associated ambiguity with insecurity and anxiety—people feel more self-assured when their environment is predictable. Nevertheless, it is increasingly clear that the future will require the capacity not only to handle ambiguity but to feel comfortable with uncertainty.

Research Needs

No generation in history has been studied more than present-day youth, yet greater knowledge about youth has not been followed by a comparably increased understanding of how to develop worthy young adults. There is plentiful research concerning the fluid character of adolescent personality, but little about the final resolution of this diffusion, or how adolescence becomes adulthood. Among pertinent questions are these: How might adolescents' experience best be structured to insure that they will consistently continue to achieve in the future? Most famous people produce little of consequence after the beginning of the middle years, although numerous exceptions prove that productivity can continue to extreme old age. Can the achievement motive become so structured that its impact will continue throughout an individual's life?

No solutions to such questions can ever be accepted as final. Researchers must keep their hands constantly on the pulse of young America. Changing times and conditions inevitably outmode currently sound conclusions. The wisest plan is to appraise data critically and, with an open mind, to use the best of what has been learned to date.

SUMMARY

All societies recognize differences between the status of child and that of adult, and all possess ways of inducting youth into adulthood. In modern societies, there is no consensus as to what constitutes an initiation ritual or pubertal rite. Perhaps the requirements of a swiftly changing, complex society have made prescribed formulas for growing up impractical.

There are obstacles to achieving healthy maturity in Western culture, including the discontinuity between training received in childhood and the responsibilities expected of adults. Much that is learned in early years has practically no relevance for adulthood. Adolescents are thereby denied a true apprenticeship for their responsible role in society. Other obstacles are the lack of association between adolescent and adult age groups, the refusal of some parents to acknowledge that their children are growing up, and society's capricious standards for awarding responsibility and for determining when adulthood has been achieved. An individual may be recognized as an adult in terms of military service, while remaining at the subadult level in terms of professional training.

Both adults and youth hold characteristic attitudes about youth's growing up. Adults' attitudes may serve either to facilitate or to obstruct youth's induction into adulthood. Some parents accept their children's changing status because they may desire release from the responsibilities relating to the parental role, or they may resist recognizing their children's increasing maturity because to do so would acknowledge their own aging status. For their part, some youth eagerly anticipate adulthood; others feel anxious about it; still others hold somewhat ambivalent attitudes about it. They may look ahead eagerly, desiring the privileges that customarily accrue to the adult, or they may cling to adolescence because it is more carefree, romantic, and pleasant. Some individuals—among them, college athletes—have a greater stake in prolonging adolescence than others do.

Youth's goals for adulthood are still somewhat traditional, although in certain respects they reflect the times. Almost all expect to marry and have children; a large majority would own their home, living far enough from a city for a measure of privacy and space; and working at a meaningful, reasonably well-paying job. They would like to delay marriage until they are in their late 20s to allow some years for travel and varied experience.

Youth's readiness for maturity may be defined in various ways: for example, in terms of developmental tasks, or the acquisition of those attitudes, habits, and skills required to function effectively as an adult. Youth's progress toward maturity may also be defined in normative terms, or how the individual's progress corresponds with that of others of the same age. For perspective on criteria of maturity, it is well to keep in mind that no one set is adequate and that a composite measure might best be used. We must remember, too, that estimates are subjective in nature, depending upon value judgments of the individuals who devise them, as well as the culture or subculture concerned.

There is considerable difference of opinion concerning how well prepared most youth are for maturity. Some adults have doubts about youth's progress toward maturity; others believe they mature too early and become unduly serious and grim in their attitude toward life. Still others caution that readiness for adulthood is not a once-and-for-all achievement; instead, regressions must be expected from time to time. Individual youth vary greatly in their approaches to and progress toward maturity. Even among the more mature, maturity in all areas is not achieved all at once, and regressions are common.

It is generally conceded that certain measures may help youth in their progress toward maturity. They should not be forced into maturity too soon; they should be permitted a psychosocial moratorium during which to test the ground rules of their society. They also need clear-cut standards of responsibility if their own adult roles are to be adequately defined. Certain customs or rites similar to the aborigines' walkabout, if institutionalized, might facilitate the transition. Certainly, youth must not simply be presented adulthood as a gift; they should earn it if they are to discharge their mature roles adequately. In addition, the adult society should be made more attractive, so that youth are not reluctant to join the ranks of their elders. Adults must present worthy models if youth are to trust their leadership and respect the ranks of those they must ultimately join.

These and other suggestions for helping youth attain a healthy maturity are based on a combination of subjective views and empirical research. Topics heretofore neglected should be investigated, and their scope should be broadened to include youth of all sorts in all countries and subcultures. The research effort should extend backward into the past and forward into the future, anticipating what may lie ahead.

SUGGESTED READINGS

BLOOM, M. V. (1980). *Adolescent parental separation.* New York: Gardner Press.

COOK, A. S., WEST, J. B., & HAMMER, T. J. (1982). Changes in attitudes toward parenting among college women: 1972 and 1979 samples. *Family Relations, 31*(1).

CROWLEY, J. E., & SHAPIRO, D. (1982). Aspirations and expectations of youth in the United States, Part I. Education and fertility. *Youth and Society, 13*(4), 391–422.

GOLEMAN, D. (1980). Leaving home: Is there a right time to go? *Psychology Today, 14*(3), 52–61.

HENDRICKS, L. E., & MONTGOMERY, T. (1980). A limited population of unmarried adolescent fathers: A preliminary report of their views on fatherhood and their relationship with mothers of their children. *Adolescence, 18*(69), 201–210.

LEE, K. (1982). Age at first marriage in Peninsular Malaysia. *Journal of Marriage and the Family, 44*(3), 785–798.

LEIGH, G. K. (1982). Kinship interaction over the family life span. *Journal of Marriage and the Family, 44*(1), 197–208.

LEWIN, B. (1982). Unmarried cohabitation: A marriage form in a changing society, *Journal of Marriage and the Family, 44*(3), 763–773.

MOORE, D., & HOTCH, D. F. (1983). The importance of different home-leaving strategies to late adolescents. *Adolescence, 18*(70), 413–416.

NATIONAL COMMISSION on YOUTH. (1980). *The transition of youth to adulthood: A bridge too long.* Boulder, CO: Westview Press.

RUBIN, Z. (1982). The search for reunion. *Psychology Today, 16*(6), 22–33.

SELTZER, V. C. (1982). *Adolescent social development: Dynamic functional interaction.* Lexington, MA: D.C. Heath Co.

SMITH, M. B. (1982). Hope and despair: Keep to the socio-psychodynamics of youth. *American Journal of Orthopsychiatry, 53*(3), 388–410.

WECHTER, S. L. (1983). Separation difficulties between parents and young adults. Social casework. *The Journal of Contemporary Social Work, 64*(2), 97–104.

WILSON, N. H., & ROTTER, J. C. (1982). School counseling: A look into the future. *Personnel and Guidance Journal, 60*(6), 353–357.

CHAPTER THREE

Tasks of Young Adulthood

OVERALL TASKS

According to developmental task theory, progress through the life span involves constantly learning and mastering new tasks appropriate to each new age stage. At each stage an individual must attain particular attitudes, habits, and skills if the tasks of the next stage are to be performed adequately. However, for various reasons many young people enter young adulthood without adequate preparation for the tasks that confront them. Few parents require their children to perform many household tasks; since children do not learn to work or produce, they become passive consumers of goods and services. Moreover, they learn a passive role toward responsibility for doing things, and they think in terms of following, not leading. Also, since many women are now employed outside the home, children receive little training in running a household (Walters &

Walters, 1980). After they marry young couples often find that neither of them has learned skills in food preparation, home maintenance or resource management.

Young people are also inadequately prepared for adulthood because most adult roles have thus far been invisible to them. Children know little about what their parents do at work or what exactly is involved in full-time adult employment. Ordinarily they see only one model of adult marital or sexual relationships—their parents. (Mortimer & Simmons, 1978).

Definition of Tasks

The tasks of young adulthood have been variously defined. In Chapter 1 we discussed Erik Erikson's portrayal of young adulthood as the time when most individuals must attain intimacy, as opposed to isolation. They must learn to relate unselfishly on a deeply intimate level to another person, as required in a wholesome marriage relationship. And they must achieve generativity by becoming creative in their work or becoming parents. This goal means being ready to commit themselves consciously and willingly to guide the new generation.

Gail Sheehy (1976) based her concepts of young adult tasks on in-depth interviews with young couples from a total of 115 middle-class subjects aged 18 to 55. Early on they had to make hard decisions: Would they take a trip to Europe now or salt the money away for Junior's college education? Should they spend evenings in the office getting a jump on the competition, or join other couples at bowling?

Roger Gould (1975) was able to delineate adult tasks by studying 500 middle-class group-therapy patients at UCLA, ages 16 to 60. He divided their lives into phases. The first phase is that of youth, before the break from the family of origin. In the second phase, ages 18 to 21, changes take place so that by the third phase, ages 22 to 28, independent adult behaviors and attitudes become stable. Among Gould's subjects, the 22- to 28-year olds perceived themselves as being part of the Now Generation. They felt that the time to live was now, but that they should also be preparing for the future.

Also, the 20s involve the question of how to gain a foothold in the adult world. At this time, people spend less time thinking about questions that were vital to them during their late adolescence, such as problems of identity, and become primarily concerned with how to achieve their goals. This preoccupation produces a certain sense of urgency from the mid-30s to the mid-40s.

Tasks of the Thirties

A Period of Reflection. Gould (1975) divides the 30s and early 40s into two phases. The first, from ages 29 to 36, concerns deep personal involvement and self-reflection. The next phase, ages 36 to 43, involves feelings of personal and marital unrest and decreased financial problems. After investing tremendous energies in developing an adult life style and becoming increasingly aware of the all-too-rapid passage of time, a nagging question begins to persistently assert itself: Am I doing what I should be doing, and am I on time in progressing toward my goals?

Appraising One's Progress. Like Gould, Sheehy (1976) perceives the 30s as a time for reflection and evaluation of one's life to date. After spending their 20s considering what they should be doing, young adults pause and look around as they approach age 30. Their choices so far may have seemed appropriate, but now they feel differently about them. They are concerned about satisfying their inner needs, a task that involves making new commitments, or strengthening existing ones. All these tasks involve tremendous personal change and hence may cause crises in people's lives. Some individuals feel simultaneously elated and depressed. One reaction is to tear apart the pattern that the 20s were dedicated to establishing. A married couple may decide to call it quits and resume their single lives or take new partners. A single person may decide that it's time to get married and have a child. The woman who formerly was content to stay at home and rear babies now feels a restless urge to reenter the world.

Settling Down. The 30s are also devoted to putting down roots (Sheehy, 1976). The life style begins to make more sense as these roots sink deeper. Men settle down seriously to making a go of it in their career. Often a couple are less satisfied with their marriage than they were during their 20s. The wife ordinarily focuses on rearing the children, sometimes holding an outside job at the same time. Social life is somewhat neglected. Whether the wife acts on the basis of her life reassessment at this time depends on many factors, and often some "marker event" will determine her future. Her husband may fall ill; or she may obtain a divorce; or she may be offered a job she cannot easily pass up.

Men often react to their wives' crises, and their need to break out of their shells, with considerable alarm. After all, aren't wives supposed to be their husbands' support system? Some husbands are unselfish and perceptive and help their wives jump over the hurdles. Others force their wives back into their shells in order to continue their earlier monotonous existence. Still others, who fail to be supportive, may make their wives that much more determined to "do their own thing," with or without their husbands' approval.

Beyond such broad objectives there has been little effort to identify the tasks of young adulthood more specifically and to explore their significance. Therefore, in this chapter we shall supplement the scanty research on the topic with a sampling of young adults' views. Unless otherwise identified, these people are in their 20s.

TASKS OF PERSONALITY DEVELOPMENT

The Attainment of Autonomy

Basic to the achievement of other adult tasks is the attainment of autonomy—that is, young adults must establish themselves as persons distinct from their families of origin. A minority do not establish independence, but continue to bow to their parents' authority, partly because society tacitly condones it, at least for daughters. Ordinarily young adults need their families' emotional and financial support in order to establish a base for their own lives. However, as they move through their 20s they become less dependent and have fewer contacts with their parents. Typically, the first step is to physically remove themselves to school or college, or to a job in another city, or perhaps to get married and have their own homes (Stein, 1976). Nor do they anticipate having to care

for their parents in the future. Younger people, when asked whether they would prefer to pay higher social security taxes or assume the support of older family members, choose the taxes (Hall, 1980).

It should be added that autonomy is not exclusively a matter of becoming free of excessive parental authority. Sometimes a spouse, usually the wife, merely transfers her dependency on her parents and becomes childishly reliant on her husband. This situation is common when the husband dominates the wife, although the opposite also occurs.

The Search for an Identity

The establishment of autonomy is simply one aspect of the continuing search for, and refinement of, identity. The search for identity continues throughout life in different ways at each age level. For example, it is often in young adulthood that adoptees seek their natural parents because of a critical need to know what sort of biological characteristics they may transmit to their children. Also they may be concerned about generational continuity, both for themselves and their children, especially when the first child arrives. Practically all young adult adoptees who succeed in finding out who their parents are believe the search to have been worthwhile. One young woman was pleased to learn that she was Scotch-Irish, and that both sides of her family were quite healthy (Baran, Sorosky, & Pannor, 1975).

Young adults also try to achieve an identity by patterning themselves after people they admire, who function as role models for their own personal and vocational careers. Such models are plentiful enough for young men, although any particular male may have difficulty finding one appropriate to him. For women the problem is more serious. In one study only 44 percent of the undergraduate women questioned reported that they had found a female faculty member with whom they could identify. Women need such models, not only in schools but later as they establish themselves as adults; they need support in resolving conflicts between traditional femininity and a desire to achieve (Where are the role models? 1977).

Not always, or even usually, does a young adult discover a single adequate role model. There may be different models for different roles. A young male high-school teacher may be especially inspired by some outstanding instructor he once had. In his role as a father he may unconsciously model himself after his own father. Or his models may be composites derived from various people, whom he has strongly admired.

Establishing Emotional Stability

Young adults must somehow settle down; their energies cannot be tied up in emotional problems that should have been resolved by now. Such problems vary by subgroup, individual, and generation. Behavioral scientists Morton Lieberman and Leonard Pearlin report that individuals who are young, female, or of lower economic status experience the most severe life strains (Causes of emotional stress, 1979). After surveying 1,100 Chicagoans, they identified ten major sources of distress in their subjects' roles as workers, spouses, and parents. Half of them related to occupation and eight applied more to women than men. The young more often experienced problems connected with employment such as being laid off or changing jobs. Among the more persistent job problems were depersonalized work environments and work pressures. In time the work life becomes more stable and less eventful, at least until retirement. While women more often find their jobs unrewarding, men more often are exposed to heavy job pressures and depersonalized work experiences.

Developing Guideposts for Behavior

Values. An especially significant task of young adults is to establish values that will help them steer their way through life. Many

middle-aged people believe that they pursued the wrong goals when they were in their 20s and 30s. Men in their 40s may wish that they had not been so consumed by ambition in their 20s, thus depriving themselves of important experiences with their families. In general, young adulthood brings several changes in perspective. Original optimism about the attainment of goals changes to a gradually greater realism, as they begin to accept their fate in life (Scanlon, 1979).

In addition they come to realize the pluralism of values; they no longer think in terms of a single set of values, and "the problem of establishing priorities among values becomes almost insoluble" (Scanlon, 1979, pp. 106–107).

It is often theorized that the world is changing so rapidly that many young people become hopelessly confused and prone to develop shallow value systems that they do not integrate well into their lives. On the other hand, many of them have found it a constructive experience to grow up in times when old value systems were being sloughed off and new ones developed. Many of them are now successful, open, realistic, confident, and more aware sexually and emotionally than earlier generations. Apparently some individuals rise to the challenge when moving over uncharted terrain while others simply fall by the wayside.

Goals. Although goals are less abstract than values, values are vital in determining goals. In fact, peoples' values are often apparent in their statements of goals. Also, as will be seen from the statements below, most young adults' goals are relatively simple and somewhat traditional. Their goals are moderate and involve the need for good, solid, satisfying jobs, a loving family, and contentment. Few are thinking of performing some great mission or service to society.

MALE: Having always been a noncompetitive person, I have tried to make my goals simple and attainable, but worthwhile to me. After having lived for some years completely on my own, I now have confidence in myself and my abilities not to fear the terrible outside world. I have simple goals, mostly trying to surround myself with things that will make me content. The only unusual thing is that I require more freedom than most.

MALE: Travel is of utmost importance, as well as success in the business world. I hope to be able to keep my idealistic views, no matter what job or place in society my life affords me. During my 20s I want to take courses that will enrich my mind, both with regard to my vocation and anything else that interests me. I want to maintain my individuality, but also to interact with people.

FEMALE: My goals for my 20s are ones of exploration and higher education. I want to travel before going to graduate school. I would also like to have some stability by the time I'm 30, location and abilitywise. I'd like to try various jobs, but ones that would enable me to be financially secure.

FEMALE: My goals are to have a job, marry, and work for a while, and have children. I expect to quit work until the children are in school, and then go to work again.

FEMALE: My goals for my 20s and 30s encompass a vast array of things. Travel is one of them. There is so much to see, and new people to meet. In my 30s I see myself as more of a realist, a person who must be responsible for a family, have a steady job, and make money.

INTERPERSONAL RELATIONSHIPS

Establishing Intimacy

As stated earlier, Erik Erikson considered the establishment of intimacy to be a basic task of young adulthood. Intimacy applies to a variety of human relationships, not just sexual feelings. Intimacy "includes the ability to experience an open, supportive, tender relationship with another person, without fear of losing one's own identity in the process of growing close" (Newman & Newman, 1975, p. 270). Each party must be able to give and receive; and while intimacy is ordinarily "established within the context of the marriage relationship, marriage itself does not, by definition, produce intimacy" (p. 270).

Vaillant (1977) reports that the most frequent psychiatric problems of the 20s are problems of intimacy. One problem is that men and women may attach different significance to intimacy and have different ideas about how to establish it. Males have often been taught to deny their dependency needs and to restrain their emotionality, whereas females have been rewarded for nurturant, supportive, and expressive behavior. Men may be threatened by intimacy because it may involve becoming so close to another individual as to threaten their own uniqueness and even if men accept their own right to be vulnerable, women may have difficulty accepting a man's vulnerability (Berger, 1979). Especially important for maintaining satisfactory sexual relationships, as well as quality of marriage in general, is a sense of mutuality, and that both partners contribute to it and benefit (Hatfield, Greenberger, Traupmann & Lambert, 1982).

In one respect young women today have an easier task than their counterparts in other periods in establishing intimacy—and that is with regard to sex. In past times they may have felt at ease with outer expressions of affection and gentle caresses, but unprepared for more intimate sexuality. More recently young women have come to accept their own sexual needs and to relate on a more equal basis with men.

For some individuals the intimate, dependent relationships of marriage weaken the sense of self. They feel a "blurring of the boundaries of their own identity" and unconsciously "erect barriers" in order to maintain an intact sense of identity (Newman & Newman, 1975, p. 173). Such people must somehow learn that achieving a sense of intimacy can actually strengthen their feelings of identity.

A study of young couples married 5 years or less indicated that the quality of the sexual relationship is far more important than its quantity (Greenblat, 1983). After the first year the frequency of intercourse declines sharply; other forms of intimacy become more important, such as closeness and tenderness. Even those who value sex highly, do so mostly for the feelings of bonding and intimacy that it provides. The importance of frequency itself depends largely on the stage of a relationship and the particular individuals involved.

Age of Marriage. These days there is normally about a decade between leaving the parents' home and getting married, a trend with potentially positive and negative effects (Rossi, 1984). On the plus side growing numbers of women are becoming economically and socially self-sufficient, and they are developing expectations of shared family and household responsibilities after marriage. Meantime, more young men are also living on their own, acquiring domestic skills that they can bring into their marriage. It is uncertain, however, to what extent adult independence may impair the couple's inclination to shift from personal gratification to a genuine concern for the welfare of children. Whereas living alone may increase each future spouse's skills in home management, it does not give them greater skill in caring for a child, or in placing others' needs above their own. Moreover, this independent living may increase some individuals' inclination to remain childless, whether or not they marry.

Marriage

Why Young People Marry. In college years youth begin fantasizing about the families they will have and their future roles as parent and spouse. Women place a higher premium on getting married than men do. They often marry the first chance they have, the result being that they marry at a younger age than men. In addition, women are more likely than men to interrupt their education in order to get married (Marini, 1978). Indeed, all but a tiny fraction of young women still rank marriage and motherhood first among future priorities; however, they have a greater desire than women of former times to combine rearing a family with having a career (Mash, 1978).

It is so commonly expected that people will marry, Blake (1973) concluded that "marriage and parenthood . . . are not really chosen, they happen to people" (p. 19). Sheehy (1976) agrees, observing that the idea that people marry for love is largely a myth. Of twenty-seven women interviewed by Spence and Lonner (1978) only nine recalled this period in their references to conflict or turmoil. Economic pressures played a considerable part in their earlier lives. Friends getting married often encouraged them to pursue the same course. Family situations or boyfriend pressures often projected them into marriage. As a result, fifteen of the twenty-seven said that in retrospect their marriages seemed just "to happen." Another factor is society's failure to encourage women to seek a true profession and instead to take marriage for granted. Although these women also had occupational roles, the motherhood role was typically predominant—a situation which produces quite different circumstances from those of career women.

Love as the cause of marriage is secondary. People may marry for security and to have their dependency needs satisfied. Many adults never get over their childhood needs to be taken care of by their parents and yearn for the security and safety of their families. Other reasons for marriage are to compensate for some inadequacy within oneself, or to enhance oneself in some manner. A man to whom career is very important may marry someone who will make a satisfactory show-

Community Relations Office, SUNY Oswego

Premarital cohabitation has become increasingly common.

piece. Still another motive is to get away from home, in some cases to escape responsibilities.

Cohabiting Singles. The increasing delay in marriage has been accompanied by a corresponding increase in "marriage-like behavior" before marriage (Glick, 1984). Over the past decade the number of unmarried cohabiting couples was increasing at a rate of about 15 percent a year, and a doubling of such arrangements is predicted in the 1980s. In the early 1980s about one in twenty-five couples were living together unmarried, and about three in ten had one or more children present (Glick, 1984). The trend is toward an increase in both premarital cohabitation and in number of children in such households (Spanier, 1983). Social scientists may come to perceive it, not as an alternative, but as normative.

Premarital cohabitation is widely practiced in Sweden. A comparison of unmarried with married cohabitants in Sweden indicated them to be alike in their attitudes toward marriage, possibly because the now-marrieds were formerly unmarried cohabitants. Most of the unmarried couples—if their relationship persisted—eventually married. Thus, unmarried cohabitation proved not so much an alternative to marriage as a variety of it. Nor was it in any way a threat to marriage as an institution—the major difference was that one category had a marriage license, the other did not (Lewin, 1982).

In America a comparison of married and unmarried couples, all childless, pointed up the pluses and minuses of marriage. It showed their problems to be mostly similar, with some differences (Cunningham, Braiker & Kelley, 1982). The wives viewed their husbands' careers as a threat, complaining that they received too little attention, and rated this their greatest problem. In general, the cohabiting women possessed a more favorable status in their relationship than did the wives, and the married men seemed better off than the cohabiting men. This finding confirmed other research that has reported married men to profit more from marriage than women. Perhaps married women are more likely to put up with a less-than-satisfying relationship, because of the emotional costs of dissolving a marriage. Besides, marriage typically imposes on wives a greater burden, and wives may be more traditional than cohabitants, who choose not to accept inequity. It may be conjectured, too, that the cohabitants are more in the romance phase of their relationship, during which greater satisfaction and equality are common.

Certainly most young adults today expect to get married, preferably in their late 20s, after they have had their fling. A small but growing minority, however, expect to remain single or to live with a member of the opposite sex without getting married, for an indefinite period or always. Here several young adults consider their own prospects for marriage.

FEMALE: I live with my finance whom I am marrying in 2 months. I hope to have a good marriage, a full social life, and a career. These things take precedence over a family. We are in the process of planning a large home in the country with lots of land and woods. Many young families and couples live there. They still have the fun of kids, but with the responsibility of adults. They are very friendly, casual, warm, and accepting.

FEMALE: I want to get married some day, but I'm not in a hurry. I lived with a man for 2 years and I enjoyed it, but I also enjoy being on my own. I'm very independent and selective, so it may be difficult to find a suitable partner.

MALE: I believe I will remain single, free of responsibilities, at least through young adulthood. If you don't get the adventure out of your system, you'll be frustrated the rest of your life.

MALE: I cannot foresee marriage for a few years. I have to get my own head together and I don't want to put someone else's together also.

Choosing a Mate. In former times, parents played an important part in arranging their children's marriages. Since daughters usually lived at home, parents were in a strategic position for getting rid of undesirable suitors. Parents also played a significant but

lesser role in the son's search for a mate (Cornish, 1979). These days the parents' role is usually more subtle and indirect. Most young people seek someone who conforms to their own ideal image of a mate, an image that is derived from many experiences, including those with their parents. The boy who idolizes his mother may unconsciously seek someone like her (Rogers, 1981a).

Sometimes young adults are confronted with the question, whether or not to marry outside their religion (Glenn, 1982). Increasingly, they are willing to do so, the main exception being Jews. True, many couples of different faiths come to have the same religion, believing it best that their faiths agree. How much, if any, the increase in inter-religious marriages has contributed to the rise in divorce rates is uncertain. However, society's increasing acceptance of such marriages should relieve pressures on the persons involved.

The process of mate selection usually involves one or more breakups before marriage occurs, as demonstrated in a major study of college couples (Hill, Rubin & Peplau, 1981). Over a 2-year period 45 percent of the sample broke up. Among other outcomes the researchers found that women appear in greater control of dating relationships than men, fall both in and out of love more readily, and find it easier to remain friends and to cope after the breakup.

When disengagement occurs, it is not an event, but a process, which may involve cycles of ambivalence and oscillations between deterioration and repair, or a more or less straight-line progression toward dissolution. There is no simplistic series of stages—instead the dissolution process assumes various patterns (Baxter, 1984).

Several factors account for the strength and duration of a relationship. One is matching—similarity in physical, mental, and social characteristics and in attitudes. Men report a greater need to fall in love than women, are somewhat less likely to precipitate its conclusion, and are more disturbed afterward. Rarely is the decision to break up entirely mutual—one party wants it more than the other. Factors external to the relationship—such as one partner's moving or taking a job—combine with internal factors, to limit its duration. Another contributory factor is relative degree of involvement—attachments more often last if the partners are about equal in commitment, and love is more important than liking.

Two factors may account for the woman's tendency to fall in love less readily than men and more often to terminate the relationship. Since the wife's status, life style, and finances depend more on the husband's than vice versa—even in these times—she has more at stake. Hence, the woman may be more sensitive to the quality of a relationship and more disposed to end it if it does not measure up. In addition, the woman's generally greater sensitivity to the quality of interpersonal relations may cause her to monitor their quality more closely.

Having Children

Motivations for Becoming Parents. Overall, just a tenth of young women have no desire ever to have children; nevertheless, families are becoming smaller, partly because parenthood is being delayed (Blake, 1982). On the other hand, there is less disapproval of childlessness than formerly. In 1973 70 percent of a sampling said that remaining childless was selfish compared with 25 percent just 5 years later (Huber & Spitze, 1983). Indeed, young couples do not automatically proceed to have a series of children as their forebearers did; rather the choice of parenthood as one aspect of a life career may result from a combination of personal motives and situational factors. One of the most effective reasons is social pressure, which, though often subtle, is nevertheless real (Blake, 1973). While childbearing is not necessarily perceived as a solution to all marital problems, it is commonly believed to help with adjustment problems, including every-

thing from loneliness to frigidity to marital unhappiness. Parenthood is also encouraged by such social policies as baby bonuses or preferential tax treatment for parents.

Lidz (1980) observes that most women acquire a feeling of fulfillment from creating a child. They are in intimate touch with creation through the menstrual cycle, and "their sexuality encompasses conception, the filled womb, childbirth, and nursing as well as the sexual act" (p. 27). Hence, many women feel incomplete if they do not produce and nurture a child. The father also receives intense gratification from parenting a child. For some men fathering a child is a symbol of masculinity that some ethnic groups deem essential for self-esteem. Fatherhood also allows the men an opportunity to express the nurturant emotions they have acquired from early identification with their mothers, and for which they have few alternative outlets.

Anticipatory socialization—the learning, rehearsal or planning for the role in advance—has a slightly positive effect (Steffensmeier, 1982). For females, the higher their education the greater is the difficulty in assuming parenthood; for males, the higher their education, the lower is their difficulty. For both, the higher their education, the greater is their planning for the pregnancy but the lower is their later gratification for having children. Longitudinal research would clarify the picture further, because the transition to parenthood proceeds over a period of time, perhaps changing for better or worse.

Values of Having Children. After the fact, parents find varying ratios of pluses and minuses in having children. In one sampling of parents, 66 percent of the women and 60 percent of the men claimed that the primary advantage of having children was the expression of love and affection and the feeling of being a family. The second most important was "stimulation and fun." Respondents made such statements as "Children bring liveliness into your life" or "Something is always going on" or "We love playing with them." A third of the respondents named values relating to expansion of the self or having someone to carry on after you are gone. The most common disadvantages were the loss of freedom and financial problems (Advantages, 1979).

The role of mothering, declare Gerson, Alpert, and Richardson (1984), should be interpreted more broadly than in the traditional manner—that is, its impact on children. Instead, it should be viewed within the context of intimate relations in a particular subculture and time in history.

The Right to Become a Parent. In general, people believe they have an inalienable right to become parents. However, the existence of a variety of hereditary disorders suggests that an individual has an obligation to determine whether he or she is capable of transmitting a sound biological heritage. Only recently have we begun to understand the impact of genetic diseases upon society and a couple's responsibility for the health of future children. Yet 15 percent of all Americans are victims of birth defects; and 12 percent of all adult patients in hospitals have a genetically determined disease (Scanlon, 1979). Arthur Robinson, a medical geneticist, notes the growing evidence that adult behaviors are affected by genetic errors that occur at the outset of the life cycle.

Increasingly, as such data accumulate and genetic counseling becomes available, young couples must decide for themselves whether they can give their children a good or even adequate biological heritage, or whether they should have children at all.

One might also ask: Do people who lack proper training for parenthood have a right to become parents? The mere act of having children does not convert young people into knowledgeable parents. Otherwise well-informed young adults often behave toward their children in ways that research has proved is damaging. The answer may be education for parenthood, both for teenagers and adults, in a combination of formal in-

struction and practical experience (Horn, 1975). It would involve learning not only the skills for effective parenting but acquiring a sensitivity to the serious, often burdensome, responsibilities involved.

Many of those who decide to have children simply fail to comprehend parental responsibilities. Nor are they prepared to make the sacrifices or to modify their life style in order to insure their children's healthy development. The idealized image of devotion to a child "bears little resemblance to . . . [the] social reality: that most children are born simply because sex is pleasurable; that the crying, the mess, and the safety surveillances of early childhood are . . . for many parents (especially mothers) a relentless burden; that the condition of a child's sound growth may mean adult sacrifices—confinements, foregone pleasures, and marital tensions that, for many, can be all but unbearable . . ." (Bailey, 1976, p. 36).

Bergman (1978) suggests that parents should be licensed, pointing out that the parenting role—so critical and complex—requires no licensing while a great number of lesser tasks do. Adults take it for granted that they have the right to become parents, but what of children's rights? Courts have begun to acknowledge that children have certain rights, including the right to an education and the right not to be economically, sexually, physically, or psychologically abused.

The almost total neglect of this matter leads to problems both for parents and children. Parents who realize, after the fact, that they are ill-prepared emotionally, financially, or otherwise to take care of children are nevertheless held responsible for them by society. Meantime, parents have almost total power over their children, to the point of beating them and doing anything short of bodily disfiguring them.

Even these days not all adults are acknowledged as having the right to have a child. Individuals or couples who desire to adopt a child must prove their fitness to take care of the child and must go through a rather complex procedure for obtaining one. While society generally approves such screening procedures, it shuts its eyes to the need for screening the first set of parents.

The Parenting Role. There are many reasons that entering upon the parent role is precarious, among them the lack of preparation for that role. Moreover, the transition, once the child arrives, is abrupt—"it is as if the woman shifted from being graduate student to full professor with little intervening apprenticeship experience of slowly increasing responsibility" (Rossi, 1981). A young woman with strong dependency needs may simply adopt a passive role in relation to her husband, but the young mother must be active if she is to maintain a home and bring up children.

A major need is a restructuring of research to consider the impact on the parent and on parent-child interaction, and not just that of parent on the child, as has been prevalent to date. For example, there has been much research regarding the effect of a mother's working on the child—but what if a mother's staying at home to be with the child adversely affects her?

The parental role has certain unique features, one being cultural pressures—mainly on the woman—to assume such a role. Although this pressure has diminished and childless marriages are becoming better accepted—or tolerated—relatives and society at large have caused most women to feel that to be fulfilled they must become mothers (Rossi, 1981). This pressure varies, however, with the times. During the Great Depression there were often pressures not to have children; in the 1950s the tendency was to turn to the private sphere for gratification—hence, the baby boom. More recently women's influx into the work world has caused the birthrate to drop, especially of third and fourth children.

The process of entering upon the parent role has critical components. Unlike getting married, becoming pregnant is not always voluntary. Abortion is still frowned on by a considerable minority, and once a child arrives, unless one places the child for adoption—which is socially frowned upon for the married—one finds oneself, like it or not, in the parent role. As a result the parent who does not physically abandon the child may withdraw from it psychologically.

Stages in Mothering. Gerson, Alpert, and Richardson (1984) translate the various aspects of parenting into stages, focusing on women. Such stages depend somewhat on the age cohort to which a woman belongs and also on subgroups in society. The first stage in mothering is deciding whether or not to have children. Formerly, the decision not to have children was viewed as deviant; however, many young women now choose not to be mothers, perhaps because of career, the cost of childrearing, time desired for leisure activities, and experiences with one's own mother. Some spouses may feel that having children will threaten their relationship with each other—a realistic fear. Having children appears negatively to affect marital satisfaction, producing role conflicts and stress. It should be added that we lack data regarding the satisfaction of persons with or without children in later years. There is also little literature available to help individuals decide on whether or not to parent. On the other hand, some women feel that motherhood facilitates creativity and reduces feelings of alienation and loneliness.

During the next stage, the transition to parenting, a medical model of disease or psychopathology may be employed. Thus, the pregnant woman is viewed as somehow regressed, an image that may be due to her anxiety about the delivery and increased fatigue. A quite different family systems theory takes into account her relationship with her husband and her pregnancy to the whole family. Such research as we have, though inadequate, indicates that pregnancy is a period of developmental crisis or at least transition; however, maternal feelings develop over time, and feelings toward significant others, herself, her mother, and her husband change over the course of pregnancy. She tends to have a more positive attitude toward pregnancy if she has a good relationship with her mother and her husband.

Reproductive Problems. Both retarding and enhancing chances of reproduction may involve problems. Birth control methods, especially, have produced considerable controversy. Salvatore Pizzo, a Duke University pathologist, reports that women who use birth control pills may, through regular exercise, prevent painful and occasionally fatal side effects of blood clots (The latest line, 1981). About 20 in 10,000 women are predisposed to clotting since they possess low levels of a protein called plasminogenactivator. Among women who exercised three times a week, including 10 minutes of stretching and a half hour of jogging or walking, the level of protein rose by at least a half.

Growing numbers of couples either want no children or no more than they already have. The latter, especially, may decide upon sterilization. Sterilization is not uncommon, as shown in a telephone survey in Ohio (Huether, Howe & Kelaghan, 1984). Of the married thus contacted 25.1 percent of those ages 18 to 45 and 33.8 percent of those ages 30 to 45 had been sterilized. A major reason given for not having a vasectomy was lack of enough information. For blacks the ratio of female sterilization to male vasectomy was 8 to 1, for whites 1 to 2, and Protestants had twice the sterilization rate of Catholics.

Views regarding the dangers of male contraception are conflicting. A study of vasectomized males indicated increased relative risks for coronary heart disease to be associated with high blood pressure, smoking, and family history for such disease, but not with vasectomy (Perrin et al., 1984). Experiments with monkeys suggest that vasectomy enhances the risk of *atherosclerosis,* or thickening of arterial walls, that slows blood flow and contributes to at least 800,000 fatal strokes

and heart attacks a year. In contrast, the Association for Voluntary Sterilization has compiled data indicating that vasectomies are safe, and an estimated 6 million American men have had them (The latest line, 1981).

The opposite problem, encouraging fertility, becomes more difficult after the 20s. A small, nevertheless significant, decline in fertility occurs among women, ages 31 to 35, and a strong decline in women older than 35 (West, 1981). Among women who received artificial insemination from anonymous donors because their husbands were sterile, after twelve instances of insemination, once each ovulatory cycle, about 75 percent of women younger than age 30 became pregnant. Among those ages 31 to 35 years old, 62 percent became pregnant, and among those 36 to 40, 50 percent. In contrast, a 25-year-old woman, having regular intercourse with a fertile partner, becomes pregnant within a year 85 percent of the time. In general, the longer the effort to conceive is delayed the more risk that some physical impairment may occur to the reproductive system. It is estimated that one in every six couples has some difficulty either in conceiving or carrying pregnancies to term. The American Fertility Society judges infertility to exist when a couple fails to achieve a successful pregnancy after a year of sexual relations without contraception.

Reproductive ability may also be reduced because of everyday stress, alcoholism, and drug abuse. Neuroses alone may be lowering the reproductive ability of at least 15 to 20 percent of American couples (McFalls, 1980). Stress can prevent ovulation or produce abnormal cervical secretions that immobilize sperm. Among men stress can produce muscle spasms in sperm ducts, thereby interfering with the transmission of semen; and it may even reduce sperm production. Among other causes are nutritional deficiencies, physical disease, and environmental factors, including exposure to sterility-causing chemicals. Overall, problems in having children affect 30 to 40 percent of Americans in their childbearing years.

The failure to conceive proves devastating to most couples. At first they experience a sort of disbelief followed by a feeling of helplessness at being unable to control their lives. They may also distrust their bodies' integrity; women feel "hollow" or "empty," or men feel "like castrates who talk about intercourse as shooting blanks" (McFalls, 1980, p. 104). Feelings of defectiveness extend to an individual's general sense of self-worth and body image and other areas of life. One woman called herself "the sterile cuckoo." Infertile adults are also anxious about their own sexual performance and desirability. They may become angry at themselves, perhaps blaming infertility on some past pregnancy or abortion, or at physicians for failing to come up with an answer. Or they may fear abandonment by the fertile partner. There is also a kind of mourning for the child they cannot have. Even women whose childlessness has been voluntary may undergo depression during their 30s, mourning for a portion of themselves that never came into being.

Coping with knowledge of infertility is difficult, partly because "the loss is so vague . . . and because there are no formal rituals like funerals to assist the bereaved. The loss is 'invisible' to the outside world, and the couple feels isolated in their grief" (McFalls, 1980, p. 108). They must live in a world full of reminders that other people do have babies, although the pain ultimately may fade. Some of them choose to adopt a child, but the adoption does not cure infertility.

Preparation for Parenthood. One usually neglected task of young adults is preparation for parenting. Interviews with women during their first pregnancy disclosed certain themes. One of these concerned the reevaluation of the women's relationships with their own parents, especially the mothers. Another theme among the pregnant women was the ascription of characteristics to the unborn fetuses, which Arbeit (1975) called the "emerging definition of the fetus as child." A related theme was the differentiation of self from the unborn other. The mother who makes no such differentiation and becomes obsessively introspective may create a distance between herself and her husband and fail to recognize the unborn child's personhood. It may also "presage an unhealthily symbiotic and overprotective mother-infant relationship" (Lamb, 1978, p. 140).

Couples should be aware that childbirth has the effect of traditionalizing marital and gender roles. The baby's insistent needs make it essential to designate parental tasks specifically—and society's definition of the nurturing maternal role is very clear. At the same time, young fathers are under pressure to fulfill the provider role. In earliest years, therefore, the young child is exposed to traditional parental role models (Wente & Crockenberg, 1976).

Current approaches to obtaining such information are often haphazard, ineffectual, and of varying quality. Over the past decade the number of men participating in childbirth classes during the pregnancy period, and being present when their children are born, has increased dramatically—and most men react very positively to such experience (Gearing, 1978). On the other hand, such classes do not lessen the difficulty of the initial adaptation to parenthood (Wente & Crockenberg, 1976). Those parents who attend such sessions make their own individual adaptations, in contrast to the more hypothetical situations proposed in the classes.

The popular literature on preparation for parenting is highly variable in quality, and much of it is poor. A sampling of popular books on childrearing obtained at the usual places such as drug stores, supermarkets, and bus depots, showed them to be sexist and traditional; none discussed the matter of sex roles in parenting at all (Parenting by the book, 1978).

Another subject about which couples need information is the use of drugs during the childbirth process. Aleksandrowicz (1974), after studying relationships between various obstetric drugs and behaviors of the newborn, decided that "there is enough evidence to date that obstetric analgesia and anesthesia in any form involve an element of calculated risk to the infant." However, it is difficult to separate the effect of obstetric medication from other sources of potential effect such as a parent's age, socioeconomic level, and prenatal anxiety. Unmedicated childbirth has been reported to have quite beneficial results. At the same time natural childbirth has become associated with high socioeconomic status, which would insure that the birthing environment is generally favorable.

Young couples should also be aware that women typically suffer postpartum blues in the first ten days after delivery. To what extent this reaction is due to hormonal imbalances (which often succeed parturition) or other factors is uncertain.

Family Size. Over the past few decades there has been a sharp decline in the number of children women expect to have. In 1955, 37 percent of women ages 18 to 24, anticipated having four or more children compared with just 8 percent in 1974. In 1980 11 percent of women in this age group expected to have no children and 17 percent of college-educated women expected never to have a child (Gerson, Alpert & Richardson, 1984). Meantime there has been a marked decrease in the number of unwanted births, from 1 in 5 in 1966 to 1 in 12 a decade later. There has also been a change in the span of years for active mothering. In the early 1900s childbearing occupied a period of 10 years, usually between ages 23 and 33, and in the 1970s just 7 years, ages 23 to 30. Another change is that women are having children later in the lifespan, reflecting their higher education. In 1960 76 percent of married women had already had children by age 24 compared with 67 percent in 1977.

Also rapidly increasing has been the incidence of one-parent families, especially among blacks. In one decade, 1970 to 1980, the number of such households doubled— those maintained by men having increased 95 percent and those maintained by women by 97 percent. A parallel development has been the increased employment of women outside the home, especially for mothers with young children, which increased by 57 percent between 1960 and 1975. In 1955 just 18.2 percent of married mothers with children under age 6 were employed, compared with 25.3 percent in 1965 and 49.9 percent in 1982. Still another trend has been the increase in number of adolescent mothers, this rate being five times as great among black as among white teenagers.

The current generation of young adults intends to limit the size of its families. Over the last decade or so, the family size preferred by young people has steadily declined (Juhasz, 1980). Of 287 college students questioned, 59.5 percent expected to have children, 8.5 percent did not, and the remainder were undecided. About half (49 percent) of them wanted two, 26 percent three, and 17 percent four.

This trend is primarily due to better birth-control methods and changing attitudes toward having children. In the past children were valued for what they could contribute to the family welfare, such as performing farm chores. Most families grew much of their own food, which made feeding an extra mouth inexpensive. However, labor-saving devices, urbanization, and changed living patterns have made children an expensive luxury. They no longer pay their way. Nor can parents any longer count on their children to support them in later years.

The number of children desired depends somewhat on a couple's situation. When Jan Harrell and Nancy McCunney had 342 unmarried college men complete a questionnaire on how many children they would want under various circumstances, the men were found to desire fewer children if the wife was a poor mother or homemaker. The number of children desired sharply declined if the marriage was characterized by heavy debt, unrewarding work, and poor communication. Fewer offspring were also desired when the wife-husband relationship was more egalitarian. If their wives should desire no children, the men appeared willing to accept that conclusion. They also wanted few or no children if the wife believed that it was the husband's job to take a major role in child care (The dad decision, 1978).

The Best Age for Having Children. If parents decide to have children, when is the best time? The worst time is when parents are in their teens. Most very young parents have yet to achieve emotional and financial stability and may be still in need of parenting themselves. Besides, before age 20, young women have usually not matured physically and often have trouble delivering a normal child. For such women the incidence of still births, birth defects, and infant mortality is high (Lasswell, 1974).

On the other hand, problems may arise from delaying parenthood too long. A 40-year-old parent may lack sufficient energy and patience to cope with a 2-year-old. It is also conjectured that aging egg cells may increase the possibility of birth defects. In particular, Down's syndrome (mongolism) has been linked to aged eggs, which may contain chromosome defects. In physiological terms, the best age for women to give birth is between 21 and 35. Still, older couples have an advantage financially, and often they are more stable psychologically.

The Childless Marriage. An increasingly popular option, the childless marriage, was formerly frowned upon by society. Veevers (1974) tells of a woman, age 21, who asked to have her tubes tied.

The intern conerned went scurrying out. He came back in with a female gynecologist who had three children of her own and proceeded to tell me all about how it is possible to work and have children and how they fulfill your life. . . . I said, "Yes, but

I don't want two children. I just don't want to have them"; so they went and got the head gynecologist who called me a silly, idiotic female and told me to shut up. I didn't know what I was talking about, and I didn't know what I would want . . . (p. 403)

Of course, taking such measures to prevent pregnancy is an irreversible decision. It is often assumed that young couples do not know whether they might desire children later on. On the other hand, the matter of having a child is irreversible too (LeMasters, 1973, p. 59). In any case, it seems likely that many reluctant parents would reject their children, at least on the unconscious level.

There is still considerable pressure on many young couples to have children. In-depth interviews, which matched samples of women undergraduates who did or did not desire children, indicated that 85 percent of each sample believed that parents or other close relatives would prefer that they have a child. Both samples thought that other people would think they were selfish if they waited for quite a while before having children (Houseknecht, 1977). Those desiring to remain childless expressed less concern about others' opinions and were supported by their own reference groups in their decision. They were also relatively autonomous, capable of resisting the pressures and sanctions of the dominant society. Both groups, it appeared, had reference group support for their different decisions.

A minority of couples expect to remain childless for widely varied reasons. One reason is that the younger generation has come to accept the childless marriage as a viable option. Another is the threat of overpopulation; and while some experts believe that such a "diffuse objective" is hardly relevant, some couples do insist that the population problem is a factor. Certainly it becomes a legitimate reason for accepting a childless marriage. A third reason is the great expense of childrearing. In addition, having children is a considerable gamble, perhaps the biggest of a lifetime. Parents cannot know in advance the characteristics of their child-to-be. Other couples may prefer to remain childless because of the greater freedom that childlessness affords (Veevers, 1974). Childless couples maintain more flexible schedules and have greater latitude with regard to their behavior, language, and hours kept. In any individual couple the motivations for childlessness are complex and, to a certain extent, ill-defined and even unconscious.

In contrast to former times couples who prefer to remain childless can do so. They may engage in contraception to avoid conceiving, or in proceptive behaviors designed to increase the chances of conception (Miller, 1983). Beyond these two opposites there are other choice-related problems. Some parents are caught between the desire not to remain childless and lack of inclination to make the necessary sacrifices. They must also cope with whatever internal pressures may be generated by shifting changes in society's views about reproduction and by technological advances in this area. Already we are seeing development in such areas as "amniocentesis, genetic screening, sex preselection, semen storage, artificial insemination, ovum transfer, and *in vitro* fertilization (the so-called test-tube babies) (Miller, 1983, p. 1202). Almost certainly, in decades ahead, human abilities to influence reproduction will grow dramatically, including how to have children and even what kind to have. The goals of progenesis, deliberately manipulating reproduction, may embrace avoiding undesirable characteristics in offspring, or seeking to achieve desired ones. The former would mean preventing congenital abnormalities or genetic diseases; the latter would include sex selection. As a result young couples will become involved in greater ethical and value-related decisions than ever before.

Sometimes career women hesitate to have children because they fear they will not have enough time to spend with their infants. Many young parents these days, and those who advise them, have bought the popular belief that mothers should have ample physical contact with their newborns and young babies, a practice said to promote bonding (Lamb, 1982). However, follow-up studies indicate that such "skin contact" provides no long-term advantage, although mothers may gain satisfaction from it. Those who, for whatever reason, are unable to provide it, should take comfort from this follow-up research.

In general, childless women are as well-adjusted as those with children. Psychologist Judith Teicholz interviewed over 75 childless married women in their 20s and 30s, half of whom were planning to have a child and the other half to remain childless. The two groups proved to be about equally well adjusted and feminine, as gauged by a femininity scale and a projective technique. The groups portrayed their marriages as happy and both were successful in their careers. Since 1900 the proportion of couples electing to remain childless has remained about the same, about 5 percent (Albin, 1980).

Two common assumptions regarding childless couples are unjustified. First, the fact that a couple has had no children during the first years of marriage is not proof that they never hope to have them. Seventy percent of childless couples involved in a nationwide study desired to have children eventually, the majority wanting two. Seven percent wanted no children and another 8 percent were uncertain. The rest were already expecting a child (Advantages, 1979). A second false assumption may be that husbands and wives share equally in child-bearing decisions. A study that compared the processes of arriving at fertility decisions in marriage (Marciano, 1979) indicated that the husband's preference, either for childlessness or for children, was more often the deciding factor. Perhaps the reason is that most men are socialized to please themselves and most women to please others. Women are more likely than men to be vulnerable both to their husbands' and to society's pressures.

It seems incongruous, therefore, that family-planning agencies commonly treat fertility decisions as purely the woman's sphere.

Abortion. Abortion means quite different things to different people. Feelings of those who elect abortion vary from immediate relief to lifelong guilt feelings to ambivalence. For some individuals, this ambivalence is terminated after the abortion; for others it persists for years, damages their lives, and wrecks marriages. Usually the more meaningful the relationship between a couple, the greater their ambivalence toward abortion (Francke, 1978).

A theologian and moral philosopher, Joseph Fletcher, insists that aborting a defective fetus is morally the right thing, and that not aborting, in cases of genetic disease, is morally wrong. An individual who knowingly causes a defective or diseased child to be born hurts society, the family, and the individual born with defects. Such an individual is "just as blameworthy, ethically speaking, as 'typhoid-Marys' who knowingly carry infectious diseases" (Chedd, 1981, p. 40). Those who oppose abortion for reasons relating to genetic disease cite several reasons, one being that the decision might be made purely on the basis of economic benefits to society. The expense to society of caring for a handicapped child is far greater than for aborting fetuses with genetic defects. Yet the concept of "a bookkeeping God" is an inhuman and cruel way to deal with human beings. In addition, in view of the limited capacity to diagnose defects prenatally, it is uncertain how wide a range of weaknesses or defects might become bases for abortion. Would abortion be in order where a predisposition is shown for alcoholism or heart disease? Would society come to demand perfect babies based on current notions of desirable traits? Does every fetus, regardless of the parent's wishes, have a right to be born? On the other hand, does a fetus have a right not to come into a world with a minimum chance of a meaningful life?

Relevant cases have appeared in the courts—for example, parents have brought suit to gain the costs of rearing children because a physician failed to inform them of the results of a test or to conduct it properly, in the case of a defective child. In one case in California a Court of Appeals judge ruled that children with genetic defects could sue negligent physicians or laboratories, or even parents, claiming that they should not have been born. In contrast, a New Jersey court declared that even life with genetic impairment was better than no life at all. The California verdict disturbs some physicians and lawyers, raising the question whether increasing numbers of defective individuals or persons with anything less than a perfect life could have a right to sue.

Many legal issues remain to be decided regarding abortion, one being the relative priority of maternal and fetal health. Should a physician, for example, be required by law, to inform a woman of the potential hazards involved in relating to abortion decisions (Glantz, 1984)? Even lately, when a majority of the Supreme Court have defended women's rights to make abortion decisions, states have tried to interfere with details of doctor-patient guidelines. Any changes in the courts, in a greater fetal rights' direction, might place greater limitations on a woman's options, and these will be determined by whatever legislation and court decisions currently exist regarding them (Glantz, 1984). Women in some states may be ordered to undergo Caesarean sections because doctors are anxious about the well-being of the fetus. Under its fetal-vulnerability policy a North Carolina plant forbids women of childbearing age employment in certain high-paying blue-collar jobs that are deemed dangerous. These and other decisions are balancing the rights of fetuses against those of women; and right-to-lifers are exerting all the pressure they can to have the fetus treated as a real person. Depending on the outcome, young couples will be influenced in their decisions about parenting and, indirectly, in their adaptation to marriage.

Apparently abortion by single women has no great impact on their relationships with their partners. Robbins (1984) found that single women who did or did not carry their pregnancies to term did not differ in this regard, although the women who aborted had weaker ties to their partners preceding the pregnancy. However, aborting women who had strong relations with their partners felt more stress afterward than did those with weaker relationships.

Immediate reasons for abortion vary greatly. For single women, abortion may result from social and financial pressures and often breaks up a sexual relationship. For married women, it is often a choice of life style; many experience emotional stress prior to the abortion and gradually return to normality later on. Some women report lifelong regret, guilt, and stress. For men the chief emotion is relief, sometimes mixed with varying degress of anger and helplessness. For parents, a daughter's abortion may bring shame, anxiety, and a refusal to accept the daughter's sexuality.

Young Adult Testimony. To sum up, the vast majority of young adults plan eventually to get married; and almost, but not quite, all those who marry expect to have children. The great majority want two or three, although a few want more. Most young adults today perceive parenthood as a unique, challenging experience, and as one way of enriching their own lives.

MALE: I would like to have children, partly because of wanting an extension of myself.

FEMALE: I plan to have two or three children after age 28 to 30, depending upon my spouse, finances, and the care and affection levels that I can handle.

FEMALE: I want children, basically because it would be a tremendous accomplishment to help shape someone's life.

FEMALE: I want children in order to fulfill myself as a woman—and also I enjoy children. I grew up in a family of nine children, and watching them grow up was quite an experience. It would be even more of an experience if they were my own children.

MALE: I want no more than three children but not less than two, because it is important for a child to have a brother or sister. I would not have too many children because of the potential population explosion.

MALE: I don't know if I want to get married or have a family. I hope I find alternatives to this mode of self-fulfillment.

FEMALE: I'm getting married in June, and we do not plan to have children right away. If we do decide to raise a family it won't be for 6 or 7 years, as we both want to pursue our careers. We also want as much time together as possible, and having children right away would interrupt what we want to do.

The next period, after the child arrives, may be viewed as either a transition or a crisis, especially for women who had careers before mothering. One critical factor is the timing of the first birth. Women who have births between the ages of 30 and 39—and their numbers are increasing—in some ways provide a healthier emotional environment for their children. They tend to encourage verbalization, seek involvement of the spouse in childrearing decisions, and encourage independence.

Establishing Friendships

In adulthood friendships vary with each stage of the life cycle. Almost all young adults, married and single, establish a supportive network of friendships within the context of their newly defined lives. Often their paths or new interests have taken them away from friends of earlier years. They must form friendships with people whose personalities and life styles are congenial to their own. Young couples develop friendships on the basis of special interests including decorating, homemaking, the Little League, the P.T.A., and community participation. These friendships may not be deep, but may broaden as the parties involved find common interests (Bensman & Lilienfeld, 1979). At this stage and beyond, it becomes difficult to admit others to the inner core of one's personality. By young adulthood, individuals have become clearer about their identity and commitments, and their possibilities for deep friendships more limited. In earlier years individuals are somewhat open to others and, because of a lack of boundaries and because of anxieties about growing up, form deep commitments to their friends—and these friendships tend to last.

It is especially important that the married woman have supportive relations with other women; however, among a sampling of married women in London, only a third had a "true" relationship with another, which involved a high level of interaction and intimate confiding (O'Connor & Brown, 1984). Such an actively supportive relationship is to be distinguished from those that merely reflect a search for attachment and contribute far less to one's emotional health.

In both youth and adulthood, men have fewer intimate friendships than women, hence do not fare as well in terms of affiliative needs. In childhood, most boys' fathers are somewhat strong, aloof, and silent—and they communicate these values to their sons. Thus many boys learn that to be a real man they must deny their intuitive, fun-loving, and nurturing feelings. Such attitudes transfer to their relationships with other males, who have been similarly socialized. When males meet there is typically a noninteraction, either a glad-handing, back-slapping superficiality or a self-conscious interchange of monosyllables, characterized by Gary Cooper's taciturn cowboy who says little more

than "Yep" (Crites & Fitzgerald, 1978, p. 12).

Nevertheless, adults of both sexes place a high value on friendship. In a survey of *Psychology Today* readers of all adult ages (which was skewed toward young adults), friendship appears to be "a unique form of human bonding" (Parlee, 1979, p. 43). Two-thirds (68 percent) of all the respondents had between one and five close friends; 38 percent had friends from other racial groups; and 47 percent from different religious backgrounds. A small majority (55 percent) said that most of their close friends were of the same sex. All said that opposite-sex friendships differed from same-sex friendships, mainly because sexual tensions can come into the relationship. Other reasons were: having less in common with the other sex, and society's discouragment of opposite-sex friendships. In general many friendships were long lasting, often originating in childhood or college. They depended more on quality of interaction than physical nearness. The reasons for cutting off friendships, in descending order, were: "One of us moved"; "I felt that my friend betrayed me"; "We discovered that we had very different views on issues that are important to me"; and "One of us got married."

The main activities of friendship included relying on each other for help and trading confidences about intimate matters such as failure and success at work, sexual activities, and illness. When faced with a crisis, about half (51 percent) sought out friends ahead of family, younger more often than older ones.

Canadian sociologist R. N. Whitehurst identifies a new type of relationship that is similar to the strong bonds formed by people in armed forces in situations of stress. Buddies in the armed forces help each other and can be relied on for aid and comfort under any circumstances; "buddyships" are built on sharing problems. If there's any sexual activity at all, it is on a friendly, therapeutic basis, with no real commitment. A similar relationship is emerging among many young men and women. While women have always been able to sustain nonsexual relationships with men, only in the past few years has the reverse been true. The freeing of men's sex roles and the downgrading of machismo have made men more comfortable with women and able to relate to them as equals. A heterosexual buddyship may begin in typical boy-girl fashion, then develop into a special relationship; ordinarily such a pair does not wish to damage their relationship with sexual playing around (Buddyships, 1979).

In a survey of individuals, ages 25 to 30, the matters of social isolation, rejection, and happiness were of great concern for both sexes (Abrams, 1982). As consumers they showed a great need for human contact—and the financial community has reacted in kind. Various companies are engaged in providing goods and services that facilitate social communication. These include vacations, health clubs, and telecommunications. "Social surrogates," such as video games and computers, that make people who are alone feel less so are also available.

The trend is toward enjoying life now and worrying less about the future. Among the age group 25 to 50, mostly early middle-agers, 67 percent described leisure and recreation as necessities, not luxuries. Six in 10 agreed that vacation time is not when one should cut corners to save money (Abrams, 1982).

For young adults, the task of making friends relates to articulating their family life with their life outside the family. Philippe Ariès, France's great historian of the family, feels that today's young adults have become too demanding of each other, and that the parent-child relationship has become unbearably confining. He sanctions a more open family instead of the contemporary family, which is too often a "prison of love." The woman's movement is inducing many young women to rebel against their erstwhile imprisonment within the confines of the family (Mousseau, 1975).

Marriage impacts differently on men's and women's friendships. Young married women who are childless work in the same proportions as do men but women's jobs provide fewer opportunities for developing work-related friendships (Fischer & Oliker, 1983). The higher social status, pay, and friendship incentive attached to men's work encourages wives to look on their husband's friends as more important to their own social status, and these inequalities allow the husband greater privilege in selecting the couple's mutual friends.

The impact of marriage on friendship is limited somewhat by the couple's division of labor at home. Often marriage diminishes the amount of housework that men do but increases it for women—for example, women's home duties include social entertainment, whether the friends are his or hers. This division of home duties is little affected by the wife's working and reduces the time that young married women, most of whom work, have for socializing, while increasing the time that men have for companionship. Also, the woman is frequently responsible for chores relating to both spouses' kin.

Another factor, the effect of parenthood, causes many young women temporarily to quit working, thus forfeiting a significant opportunity for making friends. Those who continue to work are handicapped by parenting responsibilities in matters of social involvement with their colleagues and other friends. In contrast, most fathers give up neither colleague friendships nor advancement opportunities after children arrive.

It might be argued that parenthood reduces wives' friendships because they are, by disposition, more concerned with family attachments than friends. However, those young mothers with smaller numbers of friends are not as happy as those with more friends; married women at home without any children are less satisfied than practically all categories of men. In other words, children do not compensate psychologically for women's loneliness (Fischer & Oliker, 1983).

THE ORGANIZATION OF LIFE TASKS

Type and Place of Residence

Housing. Life also has its more mundane practical aspects, such as choosing a place to live. In the late 1970s, two-thirds of the American people were living either in small towns or in the suburbs, and about two-thirds owned their own homes. Since home ownership is a middle-income norm and a symbol of middle-class status and success, most renters would like to become homeowners (Scanlon, 1979). The current back-to-the-city movement shows that young adult renters are purchasing their homes in city neighborhoods. Looking for a house becomes a matter of finding surroundings that will support one's life style. For example, two young college professors who got married shopped for a three-bedroom house, not because they expected to fill it with children but because each spouse wanted a private study (Donnelly, 1976). Most couples, certainly those with children, can hardly be so specific in their requirements. Many of them must at first settle for small units such as apartments, townhouses, mobile homes, and no-frills houses. However, in a mobile society such as ours, decisions about housing must often be made several times.

The vast majority of young adults today share a common dream, with minor variations. They expect to delay marriage for several years while they establish their career, travel, and have varied experiences. While they are single, they are content to live in apartments; once they have a family they want their own home, a good-sized one, in a small town or rural area, not too far from a city. They seek such ideals as freedom, simplicity, privacy and quiet—yet want to be close enough to a city to avail themselves of its advantages. Most young adults express variations on these basic themes:

FEMALE: During my 20s I want to remain single to pursue my career, a goal very important to me; then I want to marry and have two children. While I'm single I'd like to live in an apartment complex with other young people. Later, with my own family, I want to live in an apartment complex or a medium-sized town. I'll continue my career, too, taking classes from time to time to keep up to date.

FEMALE: After I get married in my late 20s and have two children, I want to live in a one-family dwelling in a large-enough community so that everyone does not know everyone else's business.

MALE: During my 20s I'll stay single and live in diverse community settings. I want to spend some time in a major city like New York, but my heart belongs in the country. In my 30s, I plan to marry, or live with someone on that level, and settle there. I want one child, and to adopt another two or three.

The Trend Toward Simplicity. A recent theme in choosing a habitat and life style has been a search for simplicity. Duane Elgin and Arnold Mitchell say that about 10 million people live according to voluntary simplicity today; and by 1987 the number could be greater than 40 million and by 2000 over 90 million. Such simplicity may be vital to human fulfillment or even survival (Peter, 1978).

Health

An important aspect of life style is maintaining good health. At age 30 the male is a little plumper than earlier, a little slower and balder, and his body has just passed its peak. His body has begun dying a very little bit every day, losing about 1 percent of its functional capacity each year. His tissues are becoming less flexible; his chemical reactions are slowing (Tierney, 1982). Similar changes are occurring in the female. Hence, it becomes imperative that young adults preserve and improve upon their physical characteristics.

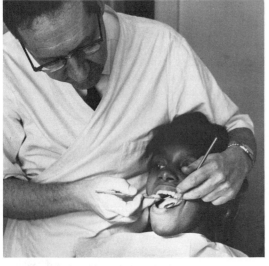

Mike Sullivan, Columbia University

Appropriate health and dental care is an important foundation for later years.

A major task of both sexes is the preservation and improvement of health. An individual's overall health status in earlier years tends to persist. Among the bright individuals in the Terman study, there was a distinct continuity of health from the teens over the next five decades (Goleman, 1980a). Habits established in adolescence and young adulthood lay the foundation for health in old age.

It is imperative, therefore, that physical problems be identified and treated in young adulthood, especially in individuals with a family history of diabetes, heart disease, emphysema, arthritis, and other diseases of genetic origin. Such treatment helps increase the effectiveness of medical care in later years when these diseases have their greatest impact.

Perhaps more young people would respond to warnings about the wrong or excessive use of drugs if they realized that the effects of these drugs may appear as early as the next stage of life. One such effect—abnormalities of the red blood cells—is evident even in young adulthood. Almost every drug produces toxic reactions, which are fairly common among young adults; however, the long-term effects of marijuana are still controversial. It is difficult to make generalizations because the amount of smoking or drug use that produces addiction in one individual may not in another, for whatever combination of genetic or environmental factors may be involved. (Scanlon, 1979).

Edmund Pellegrino, clinical professor of medicine, recommends that doctors make a life-style review of young adults on a one-to-one basis. The idea is to "detect potentially damaging personal habits and attitudes and to write an individualized prescription for prevention for *this* patient. This prescription takes cognizance of life-style aspirations, as well as physical risk assessment in *this* person—those factors we know affect the probability of illness . . ." (Scanlon, 1979, p. 51). The goal is to lessen health risks and stress prevention by recommending needed changes in life style.

Of special significance is society's growing emphasis on positive concepts of health. When asked what young adults might do to lengthen their lives, Donald King, chairman of the College of Physicians and Surgeons at Columbia University, suggested that sustained moderate exercise may be extremely helpful if it is not too strenuous (Scanlon, 1979). The problem is that some individuals rush to embrace diet and health fads without fully understanding them.

Money Management

A task of special importance for young people is money management. In other times almost all family income was spent for items of survival. Now that incomes are greater and the range of choices wider, the problems of determining how money will be spent are correspondingly more difficult. One by-product of economic, technological, and cultural change has been the proliferation of new consumer products. Besides, products are constantly being improved, making each year's model obsolete by the next year.

Another important factor is that many families now have two incomes. Where both husband and wife have blue-collar jobs, their combined income might place them in the top 25 percentile in terms of total earnings. This higher income enables them to live better in the blue-collar style. They may buy season football tickets or build a game room in the basement rather than move into a new house in an upper-middle income neighborhood (Scanlon, 1979).

LAUNCHING A CAREER

Attitudes Toward Work

The Significance of Work. All people, young adults included, have come to attach more value to the meaningfulness of their jobs rather than to monetary rewards alone. In a random sampling of 1,992 men, aged 18 to 49, there was little difference in work attitudes among the younger and older men. In general they attached a high value to rewards inherent in the work itself (Miller & Simon, 1979). They considered it very important that their work provide challenge, automony, growth, and a sense of making some meaningful contribution. Fewer than a third of them emphasized comfortable routines or not having to work hard; about half emphasized a need to have enough free time to enjoy other things. Despite a slight antiwork attitude among some younger men, values between the age groups were impressively continuous. However, more of the younger men reported a gap between their ideals and the realities of the work experience (Miller & Simon, 1979). They may be impatient to attain their goals and have an intense need for self-realization.

Perhaps the most dramatic change in the workworld has been the rapid influx of women, which is due to several factors (Fer-

ber, 1982). Women are paid less than are men, hence they are more affordable to employers. Attitudes have changed because of the civil rights movement and women's job performance during war time, when they had to replace men. It is taken for granted that young women these days will work, and that they will prepare for it. Formerly, the husband's attitude had a strong influence; now the woman's own attitude is more important. Even now wives view their working more favorably than husbands do, although they are the ones who work longer hours and forfeit more leisure time. Working women, compared to those who remain at home, more often have charge accounts and more to say about how they spend their money; and a higher status is attached to paid work than to the domestic role. There is the economic factor, too: the dual-worker family can maintain a higher quality of life. Most men have come to view their wives' working more favorably, in large measure because it is the prevalent practice. In consequence, it reflects less than formerly on their competence as providers. However, a severe prolonged recession might well cause men to do whatever they could to see that they received precedence in employment.

Younger upper-middle-income women, who are career oriented and well educated, enjoy what they do and attain a sense of self-realization and satisfaction from their work. Their salary is important, too, because it increases their feelings of self-worth. Some work mainly for the extra income, others for a higher status than that of housewife. Some simply dislike housework and want to get out of the house. Many want to have a greater say in how the family spends its money (Scanlon, 1979). Among *Psychology Today* readers, mostly young and well-educated, about 80 percent of the married women worked outside the home and had higher self-respect than those women who did not. Wives who worked had fewer psychological problems and were generally happier than housewives. Work gave them feelings of worth as human beings (Rubenstein, 1981).

The impact on children of mothers' employment outside the home is a matter of special importance since about 43 percent of all children, ages 3 to 13, have mothers thus employed. At least among school-age children there appears to be little cause for worry as it produces neither emotional nor cognitive deprivation. Nor is there any interference in the development of bonding between mother and child (Gersen, Alpert & Richardson, 1984). In general, it seems that mothers who work prefer child-care arrangements within the family and a small minority by nonfamily members. Least often reported are daycare centers. However, conclusions depend partly on the social class or individual life styles of individuals concerned.

Let it be added that most research focuses on effects on the child, but effects on the mother should also be considered. The child might want the mother to stay at home, but the mother may feel a deep need to have a career. The impact of working is different for career mothers and for middle-class professionals who can pay for round-the-clock childcare.

Increasing numbers of women, especially college-educated ones, are choosing traditionally male careers. Data from women enrolled in a vocational training program disclosed three categories: those preparing for male-dominated career programs, those who preferred traditional programs, and those who settled for traditional careers despite an inclination for the typically masculine ones (Houser & Garvey, 1983). The nontraditionals had received more support than had the others, and the main difference between the first-choice traditionals and those who considered but rejected nontraditional choices was in amount of support from the males in their lives. To expand women's options, males must become educated to assume less sexist attitudes, or women must be helped to ac-

quire sufficient self-confidence to resist manipulation by them.

The Timing of Vocational Choice

It is generally assumed that by the early 20s everyone should have made a firm vocational choice and established a toehold in some field. This erroneous assumption derives from the common view that maturity has been reached by the end of adolescence (Levinson, 1978). However, it is more realistic "to speak of forming an occupation—a complex, sociopsychological process that extends over the novice phase [the 20s]" (p. 101). Between the ages of 17 and 29, most people make their first serious vocational choice; however, this decision is often preliminary to a more mature choice later on. A particular individual may need several years "to sort out his multiple interests, discover what occupations, if any, might serve as a vehicle for living out his interests, and to commit himself to a particular line of work" (p. 101).

Certainly, career choice, which involves a logical matching of person and career, is not the rational process it is often portrayed to be (Miller, 1983). Some logical planning may be possible, even desirable, but all sorts of peripheral factors including friends, social networks, and sheer change are often critical. Vocational theorists focus more on an individual's internal characteristics, when much hinges on external factors. It would seem desirable, therefore, that those anticipating careers keep their options open and be prepared to adapt to, and take advantage of, unforeseen opportunities. Those who are inflexible or who will take no chances are often precluded from taking advantage of rare opportunities.

On-The-Job Adjustment. Newly employed persons must not only learn the specific requirements for a new job but unlearn certain unrealistic higher expectations (Mortimer &

Simmons, 1978). Often graduates of professional schools idealize their profession, and their later reaction on the job has been described as reality shock. They may come to realize that their occupation has less prestige than they had believed, or that opportunities to enter the profession are scarce. Often, too, the young worker is assigned the most undesirable task, hence experiences disillusionment.

Nevertheless, most young workers make a reasonably good adjustment, partly because, to a certain extent, occupations select people who have certain traits. That is, people choose occupations on the basis of their particular attitudes and values. Subsequently, these initial characteristics are further intensified by experience in the chosen occupation. Over the years occupational experiences produce significant changes in personality, particularly in life involvement, internal control, self-esteem, and attitudes toward work (Mortimer & Lorence, 1978).

Continuous on-the-job readaptations also occur throughout the work history due to technological advances, changes in occupational roles, and obsolescence of workers' skills. Most people move to other occupations that are highly similar, especially after their mid-30s (Gottfredson, 1977). Those individuals who adapt best to these role passages have higher self-esteem, are more flexible, and more open to new ideas (Morrison, 1977).

Especially significant for many young careerists is having a mentor, a relationship which helps both individuals (Bridgwater, 1984). The younger person receives guidance and support; the mentor gains personal satisfaction and sometimes peer approval for helping to develop young talent. This relationship, reported Kathy Kram after interviewing young managers and their mentors, often has three phases. During the initiation phase, of about 6 months to a year, each party begins to notice and become interested in the other. During the second, the mentor

guides his or her protege. In the third, the younger person forges ahead and becomes autonomous. As the former relationship wanes, the two sometimes develop negative feelings toward each other. For others the mentorship evolves into a friendship, with the roles of both altered.

Men Versus Women. Vocation has different implications for young men and women even today. Traditional life-cycle theorists, such as Erikson and Levinson, portray men's work careers as following a somewhat predictable pattern (Berger & Wright, 1978). After choosing a career and preparing for it, the young man learns to play the game by both written and unwritten rules for success. Many young men become workaholics and spend little time at home. They expect to be mobile and are willing to move about in order to get ahead; and their families, including their wives, are supposed to subordinate their own goals to those of the husband's career.

Meantime, the working wife can hardly give as much to her career as a man can (Sheehy, 1976). She can hardly establish a firm commitment to a job, given the problem of coping with "competing priorities." Hence a career that would bolster her husband's confidence and stability might create havoc in her own life. Her husband may doubt her fidelity if she dines with a business client after work, or she must cope with her husband's fears if she earns more money than he. Psychologists Madeline Heilman and Lois Saruwatari determined that physical attractiveness is an advantage for men seeking both managerial and clerical positions. However, attractive women are top ranked for clerical but not managerial positions. Most Americans perceive executive positions as requiring masculine skills, and attractive women are believed to perform less well in these jobs (Carin Rubenstein, 1979, p. 102).

Another problem is that most men cannot tolerate their wives making more money or achieving higher status than they. Blue-collar men, especially, who have little status outside the home, are jealous of their prerogative as breadwinner within the home. Women encounter additional obstacles if they delay by some years returning to the workplace. New developments with which they are unfamiliar have occurred in their field of specialty, and they must often settle for work below their potential.

There are signs that sex roles are being modified in a positive direction. Developmental tasks, traditionally assigned to each sex, are less differentiated than formerly. For both sexes vocational preparation is moving away from technical production skills to working with people and ideas, skills traditionally related to women's supportive roles. This change underscores the trend among college men toward becoming more open and affiliative. The better educated at least are displaying a trend toward sex-role depolarization (Super & Hall, 1978).

Life Style

The achievement of all the foregoing tasks must somehow be integrated into a way of living that reflects an individual's skills, habits, goals, values, and philosophy of life. It is in early adulthood that a relatively permanent life style is established (Newman & Newman, 1975). During this period an individual experiments and evolves a style of life. Those who marry, and the majority of young adults do, "develop a pace that reflects the activity levels of both [partners]. Within that framework, most couples find that the presence of children requires somewhat more planning and less freedom for spontaneous activities. Finally, the work setting largely determines the structure of time, including when one goes to work and returns, how tired one feels after work, how much time is allotted for vocations, and what kinds of preparation must be made during nonwork hours for one's daily occupation" (Newman & Newman, 1975, pp. 267–268).

One aspect of developing a life style is determining how to apportion one's time effectively—for example, between work and leisure (Newman & Newman, 1975). For some individuals time spent with the family has higher priority than that spent in occupational advancement. The life styles of wife and husband may develop somewhat separately, depending partly on the degree to which they split or share their roles. If both wife and husband work, there may be little time except on weekends for any activities other than those involving care of the household and family. This limitation makes it all the more important that they devote weekends and vacations to personal growth.

Several young adults describe below certain aspects of their preferred life styles:

MALE: I expect to travel as much as possible, see Europe and the U.S.A. I like to spend a lot of time camping and fishing, as I love the out-of-doors. I'd love to remain fairly active sportswise, pursuing my bowling. I like a life style in which I'm not afraid to spend some money. I really don't want to live high on the hog, but at least comfortably. I want to own a boat and a really nice sports car. Most of all, I want good health so that I can pursue the above life.

MALE: I prefer the life style which allows me to do the things I enjoy, such as fishing, and camping, as opposed to working 24 hours a day to reach high social status.

FEMALE: I'm pretty much of a homebody. I like to spend the evening by the fire, reading or baking bread. On the other hand, I want to take advantage of cultural activities—plays, movies, and so on. I'm very adaptable, so any environment suits me fine.

FEMALE: I want to live in a community where there is a lot of land, and I would like to have neighbors but not too close. I come from a family-oriented home and therefore would like to spend a lot of time with my family—camping, traveling, cultural activities—and any kind of activity that would include the whole family.

Life styles, as will become obvious in the next chapter, vary according to many factors including sex, age, and social class; and they reflect the extent to which developmental tasks have been mastered. These life styles may be either relatively ineffective or rewarding; and in any case, are important harbingers of the years that follow.

SUMMARY

The tasks of young adulthood have been variously defined. They include living now while building for the future, exploring options, and ultimately settling down. In their personality development, young adults achieve autonomy, search for identity, and establish emotional stability. They continue to define their values and goals as guideposts for their behavior. Forming families involves establishing intimacy, getting married, and having children. Young marrieds must deal with such matters as whether or when to have children and how many, problems of conception and, in some cases, abortion. Other tasks include establishing friendships, choosing a residence, forming sound health habits, and managing their money properly.

Launching their careers requires developing and maintaining healthy attitudes toward work, choosing and trying out jobs, and adjusting on the job. These tasks pose somewhat different challenges and problems for men and women, and they vary widely from one individual to another. Finally, there is the task of integrating all these facets of living into an appropriate life style—an accomplishment critical for the years to follow.

Overall, young adulthood is a busy period, and a critical one for the stages that follow. The early 20s are so chock-full of such major tasks as getting established as an adult, starting a family, and embarking on a career that there is little time for reflection. Following this period comes a more uncertain time when doubts regarding one's success arise. Such doubts, though tension-producing, are healthy because only through reassessment and change can growth occur. The danger is in getting bogged down with the many details of life so that progress toward more basic goals suffers. It is the nagging suspicion that one is stagnating—that one's life is not headed in any particular direction—that often provokes unrest in people in their 30s. There has been little recognition of this problem by society, and very little preparation or education for it. Generally, young adults must work out the task of steering their lives on their own.

SUGGESTED READINGS

BAHR, S. J., CHAPPELL, C. B., & LEIGH, G. K. (1983). Age at marriage, role enactment, role consensus, and marital satisfaction. *Journal of Marriage and the Family, 45*(4), 795–803.

BAXTER, L. A. (1984). Trajectories of relationships disengagement. *Journal of Social and Personal Relationships, 1,* 29–48.

DeMARIS, A., & LESLIE, G. R. (1984). Cohabitation with the future spouse: Its influence upon marital satisfaction and communication. *Journal of Marriage and the Family, 46*(1), 77–84.

FOOTE, F. H. & SLAPION-FOOTE, M. J. (1984). Do men and women love differently? *Journal of Social and Personal Relationships, 1,* 177–195.

GALLAGHER, J. (1984). The fetus and the law—Whose life is it anyway? *Ms., 13*(3), 62–66; 134–135.

GERSON, M. J., ALPERT, J. L., & RICHARDSON, M. S. (1984). Mothering: The view from psychological research. *Journal of Women in Culture and Society, 9*(3), 434–453.

GREENBLAT, C. S. (1983). The salience of sexuality in the early years of marriage. *Journal of Marriage and the Family, 45*(2), 289–300.

HATFIELD, E., GREENBERGER, D., TRAUPMANN, J., & LAMBERT, P. (1982). Equity and sexual satisfaction in recently married couples. *Journal of Sex Research, 18*(1), 18–32.

HOUSER, B. B. & GARVEY, C. (1983). The impact of family, peers, and educational personnel upon career decision-making. *Journal of Vocational Behavior, 23,* 35–44.

KAPLAN, H. B., ROBBINS, C., & MARTIN, S. S. (1983).

Antecedents of psychological distress in young adults: Self-rejection, deprivation of social support, and life events. *Journal of Health and Social Behavior, 24,* 230–244.

LEE, L. (1984). Sequences in separation: A framework for investigating endings of the personal (romantic) relationship. *Journal of Social and Personal Relationships, 1,* 49–73.

LOBEL, T. E. (1982). Parental antecedents of need for approval—A longitudinal study. *Journal of Research in Personality, 16,* 502–510.

PORTER, N. L. & CHRISTOPHER, F. S. (1984). Infertility: Towards an awareness of a need among family life practitioners. *Family Relations, 33,* 309–315.

ROBBINS, J. M. (1984). Out-of-wedlock abortion and delivery: The importance of the male partner. *Social Problems, 31*(3), 334–350.

STEVENS, J. H. JR. (1984). Child development knowledge and parenting skills. *Family Relations, 33,* 237–244.

CHAPTER FOUR

Life Styles of Young Adults

THE CONCEPT OF LIFE STYLE

The concept of *life style*—the way in which individuals bring together all aspects of their lives—is considered increasingly important today. Life style is the self in action, the pattern of one's life. It includes such matters as how people structure their days, the relative amount of time they devote to specific activities, and what those activities are. It involves whether people live in a hectic, stressful fashion or a leisurely, composed one; in a closed or open family style; a good deal outdoors or almost wholly indoors, and so on.

Throughout childhood and adolescence, life styles are strongly influenced by schooling; but when youth move into adulthood, life styles must be restructured. Although the new life styles bear a relationship to the earlier ones because basic personality characteristics remain the same, ways of living must be completely restructured to accom-

modate the special tasks of this age. And while young adult life styles have certain overall similarities, they differ according to subgroups, as will be seen in this chapter.

THE YOUNG MARRIEDS

The Prechildren Stage

The most common young adult life style involves marriage, and marriage involves three levels of commitment; minimum, limited, and maximum. The degree of couple involvement is at a maximum during the initial, childless stage and again at the "empty-nest" stage, when husband and wife associate constantly with each other. Involvement is minimal or limited during the period in between, depending on how many children there are, whether both wife and husband work, compatibility, and other factors. Once the children arrive, some individuals—mothers in particular—concentrate on the children. (Lowenthal et al., 1975).

Young Adults at the Preparent Stage. The launching of a marriage has its hazards, one being the different backgrounds that partners bring to their new enterprise. Often many aspects of life style in the two families of origin are quite incompatible, making it difficult to effect a congenial fusion.

Despite this situation, the prechild stage of marriage is typically happier than the years just following. In one study the happiest of any group studied—including both singles and marrieds, young and middle aged—were married couples in their 20s who had not yet had children. To a certain degree this prechild period is a time in which both partners share the delusion that they are more alike then they actually are; it is "a happy but fragile stage" (Stern, 1976, p. 18). Later on, reality destroys this delusion; but at least while it lasts, most couples are happy. Each spouse becomes lost in the other and robbed of his or her own individuality. Young wives, particularly, are "positively euphoric," apparently enjoy housework, and are relieved to have arrived at what may still be judged "a woman's greatest achievement . . ." (Campbell, 1975a, p. 38). Young husbands

The preparental stage of marriage is often happier than the years that follow.

Community Relations Office, SUNY Oswego

are also happier after they marry, although they feel more stress about money.

After the first child arrives, the original euphoria becomes tainted by brushes with reality; and the young couples' submerged egos reassert themselves; they no longer believe in the fantasy that their identities are the same.

A couples' life style before children arrive is often distinguished by considerable joint activity to the exclusion of others, at least on an intimate level. Anthropologist Ray Birdwhistell believes that the closed dyad constitutes a "diseased social form" (Sheehy, 1976, p. 147). The wife especially, after beginning a family, often lets friendships with other women deteriorate. She also gives up her nonsexual friendships with men because she feels her husband would not like them.

Certainly most marriages are not all harmony and bliss. Among *Psychology Today* respondents to a survey, mostly well-educated young adults, half had had an extramarital affair by their 40s. One in three of the married couples thought their marriage might end in divorce. Half felt that one partner in their marriage loved more than the other. A third had sex only once or twice a month; and about 40 percent of the women and 28 percent of the men admitted that lack of desire prevented them from expressing sexual feelings.

On the other hand, most of these respondents still believed in romance, and the younger adults were more conservative than were their counterparts of just a few years ago. In 1969 17 percent of the men and 29 percent of the women thought sex without love was either unacceptable or unenjoyable, compared with 29 percent of men and 44 percent of women in 1983 (Rubenstein, 1983). A majority of the current respondents thought that romance was important and that a single love could last for life. They perceived romance as the first stage of love and placed love above companionship or sex. Romance was portrayed as some heightened state of consciousness; love's most important components were devotion, friendship, and intellectual compatibility.

Marital Problems of Young Adults

Problems of Personal Development. Problems inevitably arise for young couples in the process of sorting out priorities and managing their lives. Some problems at this time relate to inadequate income, disillusionment with "the American myth of love and the amount of effort that a successful marriage requires" (Streever & Wodarski, 1984).

To adapt, a couple must develop mutual trust and commitment to complementary life styles (Streever & Wodarski, 1984). The young wife often experiences greater stress than her husband because she has the task of balancing maternal and career roles. If she decides, even for a time, to become a full-time homemaker she may feel somewhat isolated and displeased with the lower status that housework provides in this society. Because of this factor her self-esteem more often relates to her husband's accomplishments.

Another problem is that people's self-concepts and needs change. Young people are becoming more aware of the importance of growth and development in adulthood and that they have alternatives if marriage does not work. In time, observes Sheehy (1976), the male, having attained a certain competence on his job, and feeling increasingly sure of himself, may become bored with his wife's role as substitute mother. He now expects his wife to extend herself as he has, and be more of a companion to him rather than remain in a dependent position. He perceives that his wife has not grown much and is discontent with her less worthy status. If he could admit it, he would say that he cannot bear his wife's relatively dull and non-productive way of life. He is willing to tolerate, even encourage, his wife to do something more on her own, as long as it is not at any cost to himself. That is, he could

not bear to think of her becoming as tied to a job as he is because she would not be able to pay as much attention to him as before. Yet he has no guilt feelings on this score because he has learned from early childhood that it is women's nature to nurture their men and tend their children. He believes that what might be boring to him just comes naturally to her. For her part, the wife's satisfaction decreases sharply from the early stages of parenting through the period of "launching" the children (Scanlon, 1979, p. 82). Although wives are more satisfied with marriage at first, they become less so at subsequent stages until old age. Thus marriage appears to meet the needs of husbands better than wives. In particular, the wife may feel that her husband has gotten ahead of her in the world—that he has become more sophisticated and has developed more as a person. At other times a wife may also feel somewhat impatient, though she may not yet be prepared to do anything about it. Her readiness to undertake something new will depend upon what she has accomplished in the past, for most people are afraid of change.

Aside from matters of personal development, couples disagree at first mostly about in-laws. Later on, especially if the wife gives up her job to have a baby, they argue over money and not having time for joint recreation. They do not fight over specific modes of child care until the children are old enough to get into trouble (Troll, 1975).

Financial Matters. Financial resources are also critical factors in the marriage relationship. In surveys of *Psychology Today* readers, who are mostly middle-class youth and young adults, the majority are now more relaxed than formerly about discussing their sex lives but somewhat secretive about their money (Rubenstein, 1981). Among two-income families (87 percent of this group), money is a frequent cause of friction, especially when the wife earns more than her husband. Young adults are more conscious of money than their elders are and worry more about it;

nevertheless, they have greater hope of making more money in the future.

Problems relating to parenting begin to arise during the pregnancy period. Often the young wife is concerned about inadequate financial resources, especially if she has now retired, at least temporarily, from the workforce. Meantime, the expectant father may have trouble coping with his wife's preoccupation with her pregnancy (Streever & Wodarski, 1984). And he, too, may worry over money, now that he is the sole breadwinner, at least for a time.

How they felt about money depended somewhat on how they felt about themselves and their general adjustment. Youths who are most satisfied with their finances were not always those who made the most money; satisfaction depended more on their degree of content with job, self-respect, social relationships, and personal growth.

Among the *Psychology Today* readers the free-spending individuals appeared healthier and happier than the tightwads. The latter group had lower self-esteem, fewer friends, and less personal growth. Among those earning over $50,000 a year almost a third were tightwads. They often felt their mates spent too much money, feared losing their money, and could hardly enjoy it because of their own feelings of insecurity. About a third of the married respondents had mates with the same spending habits.

Money has come to play an important part in relationships between the sexes. One young woman said that "the bottom line in every relationship is economic" (Rubenstein, 1981, p. 38). Many young wives today feel that they are expected to contribute not simply sexually and emotionally to a relationship, but also financially.

Twice as many of the wives as husbands felt that the money they made was their own. One of them said, "Intellectually I realize it's our money. But to be really honest, his money is ours, and mine is a little extra I spend the way I want" (Rubenstein, 1981, p. 38). Problems often arose when wives earned more

than their husbands, as was true among 23 percent of the wives surveyed. Of these, 57 percent often argued with their husbands about money.

Contrary to what was expected the sexes in this study attached equal importance to love, parenthood, work, and finances. However, the men felt more confident regarding money than the women, felt more control over their financial situation, and set a higher standard for what it takes to feel financially adequate.

Some women feel uncomfortable about earning a great deal. One 33-year-old woman quit her job because she was concerned about threatening men with her earning power, maintaining friends who had less money and were jealous of her, feeling guilty about have-nots, and changes in her personal values. Very few men have such problems and those who do rarely admit them frankly.

Infidelity and Divorce. For financial and other reasons the age period from 28 to 32 involves increasing strains in marriage; and couples feel less strongly that marriage was a good idea (Sheehy, 1976). It is generally during their 30s that husbands are unfaithful for the first time, usually with someone they meet on the job. This new woman is often young and interesting, although her job is subordinate to his, and she poses no real challenge to his status. Sometimes the man who becomes bored with his wife and seeks a divorce finds out after the divorce, that his ex-wife has broken out of her shell and become more interesting.

In other cases it is the wife who initiates the separation. The growing acceptance of divorce has created an alternative to enduring marriage problems for a lifetime. Formerly, married women were admitted to mental hospitals 128 percent as much as men, but now married women have lower rates than married men for mental hospital residency. Perhaps greater availability of divorce has lessened some of women's stress because it gives them an alternative to remaining married (Scanlon, 1979). In fact, for many young women, divorce becomes not just a mode of escape from an unhappy situation but a rite of passage. While the man may have divorced his wife because she was dependent and uninteresting, after the shock wears off she may become a far more dynamic person than before.

Couples who obtain divorces differ from those who remain married in certain critical respects. Often they married quickly, without knowing each other well. The husband and wife may differ regarding perceptions of marriage and their expectations of it. The husband may have used marriage as an excuse to make demands not made in advance—for example, the demand that his wife do housework. Most importantly, these couples often hold differing role expectations of each spouse (Rank, 1981).

A major problem of divorcing parents is dealing with matters of child custody. Albert Solnit, child psychiatrist and psychoanalyst, disapproves of joint custody; he believes that children should rely on only one adult for stability (Dullea, 1980). In contrast Melvin Roman, professor of psychiatry, thinks that children should have continuing contact with both parents, and that at least half of all divorced couples could, with proper counseling, work out satisfactory joint custody arrangements. Often visiting arrangements are so poor that noncustodial parents rarely see their children, and the visit may be so painful that they eventually stop coming at all. In joint custody arrangements children may alternate frequently, for a few days, or perhaps every year. Or parents may take turns living in the children's home. It may turn out that each form of custody works better in certain situations.

A relatively new category in society is that of the noncustody mother, where the divorcing father has received custody of the children (Fischer & Gardes, 1981). Their numbers are still small, but steadily increasing—over 40 states now recognize equal claims by the parents over the children.

However, such arrangements remain somewhat fluid even after the decree, for problems can arise that cause the children to be transferred to the noncustodial parent, a grandparent, or even an institution. Such women have special problems, beginning with the battle for custody. They may lose custody after putting up a fight, which often costs more than they can afford; and they have less money than their spouses for legal fees. Even if they had deeply desired custody, they may be viewed as derelict in their parental duties, because of society's ascribing to women the child-care role. They may experience rejection from former friends, pro-family churches, or even their families, though many remain supportive.

The Gradual Diminution of Problems. During their 30s most young marrieds are somewhat less involved in activities and social relationships, and focus instead on their families. This age period involves many psychological changes, including preparation for the 40s. Life begins to appear harder and more complex (Gould, 1975). Couples still have their dreams, but these are now closer to reality. Most of them have either found their niche or made some compromises.

Young Marrieds and Their Children

Rewards and Problems. Some young couples, observe Jurich and Jurich (1975), overidealize "the single, carefree life," especially if they married early or had limited dating experience. As adolescents, some individuals may have had inadequate opportunities to experiment with different roles, or to choose those that were most suitable for them. That is, their adolescence was "short-circuited" before they could firmly establish a satisfactory identity. After the children are born, either one or both spouses may feel trapped, burdened by responsibilities, and bored by marriage routines.

At least some young women are beginning to question the institution of motherhood in our society. Depression among women is increasing, especially at young adult ages and in the case of women with young children. Those women who are single parents and have low-paying jobs are especially at risk for depression (Barnett & Baruch, 1978).

However, most couples welcome the arrival of the first child, especially if it has been planned. They feel a certain wonder at this small creation of their own flesh and blood who establishes a link between themselves and future generations. Most young fathers also feel an immediate bond with the child. After a time the bubble bursts. So dramatic is the effect of the first child on the parents that it disrupts friendships between couples who are close friends when one couple precedes another couple into parenthood (Bram, 1974). Satisfaction with life in general drops to an average level, and does not rise much again until the children are grown up. (A. Campbell, 1975).

Childrearing. Immediately after the first child arrives, fathers and mothers are eager to hold and play with it (Parke & Sawin, 1977). Nevertheless, the traditional parental roles emerge very early, with the mother's role dominant. The father may also play a strong role but he does it differently. In studies of feeding infants during the neonatal period (the first two weeks after birth), fathers proved as active or more so than mothers in socially stimulating infants during the feeding process, although they spent less time in routine care-giving activities.

Women may feel threatened when men demonstrate effectiveness in childrearing. Traditionally, homemaking has been the woman's special way of showing her own worth; to acknowledge a man's competence in this role may threaten a woman at a time when alternative roots to proving her competence are limited (Berger, 1979).

The mother is the main child caretaker, even in less formal families. A longitudinal study of four family forms in the Los An-

geles area, including communal living groups, unmarried social contract couples, unmarried solo mothers, and traditional two-parent families, indicated a shift to more social conventionality after children arrive and a reversion to more traditional gender roles (Rossi, 1984). In all four types it was the mother who provided the main care for children until the age of 18 months. The unmarried mothers in this study were of two types: those who had unintended pregnancies but kept their babies and those who became pregnant intentionally, ordinarily well-educated ones holding jobs. These solo mothers experienced a problem common to divorced mothers, that their sons manifest more behavior problems than did those in the other three family patterns. In none of these types did men play an important part in childrearing. Thus, it seems that marriage styles are more subject to change than are parenting styles.

In none of these families did the father assume main control until the children were 18 months of age. It appears that men distance themselves from the role of parent during their children's early infancy and deliberately show less skill than they actually possess. They reify the babies, acting toward them as though they were things, instead of little persons. By contrast, women usually embrace the mother role, perhaps acting more skillfully than they feel inside. For later babies the fathers persist in acting the same way, placing a distance between themselves and their young infants. Moreover, fathers differ in manner of interaction with children under 1 year of age. They play with the babies while the mothers take care of them and quiet them. In general, women manifest "greater empathy, affiliation, sensitivity to nonverbal cues and social skills," and men place "greater emphasis on skill mastery, autonomy and cognitive achievement" (Rossi, 1984, p. 8).

It is estimated that 45 percent of mothers with children under age 6 will be employed by 1990; hence, the matter of shared child-rearing becomes critical (Verzaro-Lawrence, 1981). In the past such assistance has come mainly from fathers, relatives, and neighbors in homelike informal settings. However, the trend is toward more formal groups, as in nurseries and preschools. Such caregiving, if of high quality, may constitute a plus for a child, especially for those from disadvantaged backgrounds. Typically, children thus cared for have fared as well as those reared in home settings. The key is quality, and that can be produced on a broader scale, given increased monies and improved training of the caretakers.

An interesting alternative to common modes of caregiving is proving successful in Seattle. In a Hands-Across-the-Years Program daycare centers have been established in certain nursing homes. Both children and the homes' residents appear to profit from the interaction thus provided.

In dual-career marriages, the father's role relative to the children is affected. Raden

In dual-worker marriages fathers are assuming more responsibility than formerly.

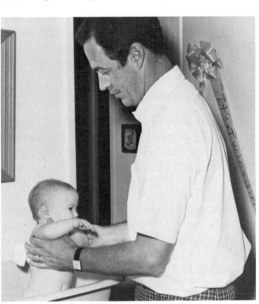

Frank Gaines, III

(1982) studied middle-class couples' children, ages 3 to 6 years, comparing families where the man assumed primary child care while the wives worked with traditional couples where the women were the main caregivers. Fathers who were the main caregivers reported personal costs in terms of their careers, while their wives experienced some loss of close involvement with their children. Both parents felt certain pressures to carry out the tasks for which they had been mainly socialized.

Where the fathers were the main caregivers their children scored higher on internal locus of control and on verbal intelligence than did those in traditional families, and children of solo mothers did more poorly on mathematical attitudes and tasks.

One problem that married women face is how much time to take from work for childbearing. Education has much to do with how early a woman stops work before giving birth, or how soon afterward she returns to her job (McLaughlin, 1983). By 3 months before the birth 63 percent of the college-educated are still working, perhaps because they value their work more, or their type of work may more easily allow it, compared with 41 percent of high school graduates, and just 5 percent of those with less than high school education. Almost no women still work during the month of birth. More of the best educated return early, but the differential is less, probably because of the less well educateds' economic need.

One pattern, which a miniscule number of couples have tried, is shared parenting and part-time work for each. This life style, writes one who tried it (Daloz, 1981), has its problems. While there are a growing number of models for women who work outside the home, there are few for male nurturers. They have a problem yielding part of the job which gives one status and more of themselves to chores to which little status is attached. Nevertheless, concluded Daloz, caring for a child "can be enormously fulfilling."

Because of changing child-care needs, relevant public policies require revision (Gerson, Alpert & Richardson, 1984). Parenting responsibilities have been interpreted as the mother's—rather, such functions should not be gender specific. Also, not just the child's, but both parents' needs, should be viewed simultaneously, and each balanced against the other. As for policies, more child-care facilities should exist, in community daycare centers and at work sites. Innovative programs should encourage all sorts of nonparents to assist with child care. Other alternatives should include more flexible work schedules, child care leaves for both parents, 4-day work weeks, and part-time jobs. Preparing-for-parenthood programs should help with all related issues: when to parent, sources of support, and gender roles.

An increasingly popular alternative is the placement of young children in daycare centers. Daycare at worst is usually harmless and at best can be tremendously effective in a child's development. Quality daycare suggests the following characteristics, among others. There is a low child-to-adult ratio; the staff is well trained; each child is assigned to primary caretakers who play with him or her individually for an hour or two a day. The curriculum provides opportunities for every child to have many mastery experiences. Such schools do not interfere with the bonding of child and mother; when young children are placed in situations where they may choose betweeen the mother and adults closest to them at the daycare center, they choose the mother (Norman, 1978).

Child care may prove an especially problematic area as couples who assume new sex roles decide how best to rear their children. Knox (1980) predicts that each parent will be more aware of what the role involves, and will share more in parenting the children. Also parents will be more informed about what the parent role signifies before their children are born.

In addition, parents-to-be need better training about child care and development. Few of them know much about it or how to design a quality home-learning environment (Stevens, 1984). It seems incredible that society, with its rapidly increasing sophistication, has done so little to educate future parents in such matters.

The Demography of Parenthood. Rossi (1984) points out the impact of demographic trends on parenthood and childrearing. For one thing, the trend toward families becoming smaller with more closely spaced births, added to greatly expanded life spans, means that childrearing will constitute a much smaller fraction of life than it did formerly. Already just one in four American households includes even one dependent-aged child. In time, since fewer people will be rearing children, children's needs may occupy a lesser priority on the social agenda. Already a smaller fraction of each sex is bearing family responsibilities. Although there is a slight increase in both shared and primary father custody of children, women in general carry a far greater childrearing responsibility after divorce. Moreover, since growing numbers of women are having children outside marriage, more women than men are involved in communal activities; and a population with unattached males tends to have a greater amount of alcohol, drug abuse, crime, and violence.

Sex Roles Among Young Marrieds

Adjustments in young adulthood differ in certain significant ways for men and women. The greatest handicap for most men is inherent in the cultural concept of masculinity itself. Because they have been taught to be self-sufficient, many males are awkward in human relationships. They are less comfortable about expressing support and warmth than females are. They focus on the outer world and ignore the inner world (Crites & Fitzgerald 1978).

As for women, it was formerly thought that their personal development ended with marriage, and was interpreted chiefly in terms of family relationships with transitions from wifehood to parenthood to grandparenthood (Scanlon, 1979). For the average young woman who marries at about age 20, the "traditional roles include housewife and mother, companion, and partner. In the beginning of marriage, the companion role is usually at its peak, partly as a carry-over from the courtship relationship. But as time passes—and particularly if children intervene—intimacy wanes, and wives turn to God, other people and housework" (Troll, 1975, p. 80). Of course the situation is somewhat different for those women who work outside the home.

Mothers of young children, in particular, lead a sharply restricted life; and since most of them stop working at least for a time, their situation now stands in stark contrast to their former, broader, adult-oriented lives. Now the young wife relies chiefly on her husband and the TV set for a "pipeline" to the outside world. When the children grow older her world broadens, mostly through returning to work or participating in community activities. Nevertheless, since childrearing is still considered to be more the mother's obligation than the father's, her own development as a distinctive personality slows down. Her satisfactions come mainly from the happiness and success of her husband and children.

Tongue in cheek, Gail Sheehy (1976) hazards a guess that if women had people to keep house for them and take over all their chores—including childrearing, shopping, cooking, and caring for their husbands—they would be as productive and as politically powerful as men. She notes that many high-achieving women maintain expensive housekeepers in order to perform these services for their husbands.

Sex Roles Reflected in Male-Female Interaction. Subtle differences in the roles and status of the sexes in mixed-group situations are of special significance, because of the large numbers of women who have entered the work world. Sociologist Pamela Fishman analyzed sex differences in conversations between men and women and determined that women expend more effort in keeping the conversation going, although they have less control over its subject (Parlee, 1979). She placed tape recorders in the homes of three couples (with their permission) and recorded over 50 hours of conversations. The three couples described themselves as being liberated from the usual sexual stereotypes. Fishman analyzed the conversations to determine how often each sex introduced topics that succeeded, or were developed into a conversation, or failed, in that the listener did not pursue the subject. Topics introduced by the man succeeded 96 percent of the time, compared with 36 percent for those introduced by women, although the women initiated 62 percent of the topics. Women went to more trouble to initiate conversation, saying something like, "I have something interesting to tell you."

Linguist Robin Lakoff suggests that the speech of men and women might be regarded as different dialects or "genderlects." Women use more polite speech, intensify their descriptions with words like "so many people," and use weak modifiers such as "sort of" or "I guess," and empty adjectives such as "lovely" or "divine." Duke University anthropologist William O'Barr believes that people of either sex who employ the tentative style of the woman's dialect have less credibility.

Selected Studies of Young Marrieds

Young Adult Men. Many young adult men in the 1980s are not the corporation-defying, emancipated-from-money-making freelancers that the alienated youth of the late 1960s and early 1970s might have become. Instead many, like their fathers before them, are preoccupied with making it in the world and establishing a career. In Sheehy's (1976) interviews, most young male adults talked

~~actions that they had under-~~
~~is, what progress they had made~~
~~reers; and they measured their~~
~~rms of how close they were to~~
~~their career dreams.~~ Their wives
were secondary in importance to what they
wanted—success through work. When they
spoke of their wives and children, it was chiefly
in terms of how they had contributed to their
own progress in fulfilling their dream.

Not all the young men had followed the
same pattern. Some had settled down quickly;
others, the seekers, had experimented and
explored and made tentative, reversible decisions. Such individuals had breezed through
one job after another during their 20s. Other
men had tried combinations of these two
patterns.

Nevertheless, young men are changing.
While career is still most important, their
lives have taken on a subtly different orientation. They are more expressive than men
of earlier generations, and they take more
interest in their children. They are on a more
equal plane with their wives; and middle-
class males, at least, help more around the
house. They spend more time pursuing interests unrelated to their careers and feel
unembarrassed about having aesthetic concerns. To some degree, at least, they are
throwing off the baggage of having continuously to prove their masculinity.

Young Adult Women. The middle-class
young adult women interviewed by Sheehy
(1976) fell into several categories. One group,
the transients, had kept their options open,
at least during their 20s. They had avoided
permanent commitments either to work or
marriage. Single, healthy young women, especially, had piled up a wealth of life experience by postponing firm commitments.
Ultimately many of these women had settled
down and married, thus assuming a more
traditional way of life.

Another group, the "either/or" women involved two types. First was the nurturer who
delayed her career until she married and

had started a family. However, she expected
from the beginning to go to work at a later
date. At the opposite pole was the achiever
who deferred nurturing, and who spent a
half dozen years or so completing her
professional preparation and postponing
motherhood and marriage.

The nurturer who put off achievement
often had a difficult time realizing her dream.
Many such women had been led to expect
that they would find work they cared about,
once they had put in a number of years as
a homemaker. Yet, by the time they had had
their children and were ready to return to
their careers, so many advances had been
made in their fields that they were no longer
qualified. Such women are becoming increasingly common, for today's mother ordinarily bears her last child by the age of 30
(Norton, 1974).

The most traditional category of women,
the caregivers, had married early and had
nothing else in mind but to pursue the domestic role. In the past, this option was the
most popular; women simply lived for others and took vicarious satisfaction in the
achievements of their husbands and children. Many such women hold part-time jobs,
or work occasionally, simply to supplement
their husband's salary or to provide some
extra money for things around the house;
but such work has nothing to do with their
own self-realization.

There has been considerable speculation
concerning how well women will manage to
combine marriage and career. In general,
professional women with preschool children
express satisfaction with their lives, dependent largely on their personal and situational resources (Elman & Gilbert, 1984). Such
women are normally highly committed to
both their career and parenting roles, but
few make major efforts to defy social attitudes, which continue to stress the woman's
primary mothering role. Perhaps they realize the futility of fighting such deeply en-
trenched attitudes, no matter how unfair they
may be. They do fare much better, however,

when their husbands voluntarily assume greater domestic and parenting responsibilities than men normally have. The emotional support is probably just as important when significant persons, including the husband, endorse the mother's career commitment. Career mothers may anticipate easing of their strains as their numbers grow and as society comes, however slowly, to adapt to and facilitate such a life style.

LIFE STYLE VARIATIONS BY SOCIAL CLASS

Most of what is written about life styles of young adults (or of any age) derives from research about the middle class. The picture of the upper and working classes is fuzzy, for so little research on them has been conducted. The following thumbnail sketches of young adults in these neglected classes are based on two of the rare articles that deal with them specifically.

Upper-Middle-Class Vacationers

Young adults of the upper middle class are described here only in terms of an increasingly important aspect of their life style—their vacations. In a questionnaire survey of *Psychology Today* readers, who are, on the average, a bit younger and more affluent than the general population, it appeared that men enjoy vacations less than women do and spend less money (Rubenstein, 1980). Men are more ready to return to work after vacations, probably because they enjoy them less. About 16 percent took six weeks of vacation or more during the year, and these supervacationers were less often disturbed than others by irritability, anxiety, and fatigue at home.

The majority of these respondents were well-educated young adults; 60 percent of them were women. The average age was 34; 90 percent had had some college education; and almost half had children. Of these respondents, 32 percent took a month or more

off in a year, compared with 21 percent of Americans in general. The readers were asked what goals they desired more time for pursuing. Personal growth was more important than work; 27 percent desired more time for developing special skills; and 20 percent more time for improving intellectual abilities. Nearly 9 percent desired more time for advancing their careers.

With regard to vacation preferences, two thirds of the respondents said they wanted mainly to rest and relax. A mere 11 percent were content to remain at home, and 5 percent would use the time for catching up on work. A large majority felt a need to get renewed and to escape routines. Of all the respondents 89 percent took a vacation trip of at least 100 miles last year, compared with only 48 percent of adult Americans in general. The most popular vacation spots were local beaches, parks, and forests. Men more often than women preferred revisiting familiar places to discovering new ones (22 percent compared with 14 percent). Despite their Protestant work ethic heritage, most of them were "eager vacationers." (Rubenstein, 1980, p. 65).

A small minority (13 percent) of the readers were "workaholics"—people who worked more than 65 hours a week and considered vacations a waste of time. They described themselves as "more energetic" than the others. Women were workaholics as often as men; and many workaholics of both sexes used their vacations to catch up on their work. The workaholics were as energetic in play as in work. They also had more broken marriages (30 percent).

The question regarding main reasons for taking vacations disclosed several distinct profiles. The most popular reason for vacationing was relaxation—a third (37 percent) said they needed time to "recharge their batteries and get renewed" (Rubenstein, 1980, p. 73). Most of these people were in their 30s and had responsible, stressful jobs. Since they spent much of their lives living and working for others, they needed vacations their energy supply" (p. 74). They end some time simply loafing or taking a luxury cruise. For 18 per- the readers, the chief reason was to learn —to enrich their lives intellectually or spiritually, to investigate places they had never known; and they especially desired to live abroad a year. While 13 percent of the sample usually vacationed with their families, most of them were happier at home and placed family life ahead of work. About 12 percent of the sample sought adventure, danger, and sexual episodes on vacations and appeared to find what they sought. This group included more male, young, single individuals than their opposites. About the same number (11 percent) wanted to be alone to solve their personal problems rather than merely enjoy themselves. They believed that they could find themselves on their vacation. Often they were the least happy; they enjoyed their work least, and believed it to be relatively unimportant. Finally, for 8 percent escaping routine and getting a tan were the most important reasons for vacations. This category included more women (54 percent) than men (26 percent) and over half were under 25 years old. They carried psychological burdens and were somewhat unhappy in general.

The Upper-Upper Class

Many people have foretold the end of the upper class (Blumberg & Paul, 1975). Factors accounting for this forecast include: the continuing thrust for equality within society, efforts to include students from all classes in private schools and Ivy League colleges, and the increasing affluence of the general population. However, a study of upper-class young adults revealed the upper-class way of life to be alive and well. In this study, which was based on the society pages of the Sunday *New York Times,* young people listed in the social register were classified as upper class, while the merely rich were classified as

upper middle class. The survey shows that upper-class education distinguishes the social-register rich from the merely rich and those below. Private school attendance at the secondary, if not the primary, stage is practically a must for upper-class youth—and that means not just at any private school but at a particular set of highly select nonchurch-related schools in the Northeast. Indeed, 90 percent of the social-register men, compared to 57 percent of the merely rich, attended private schools. From among the over 2,000 accredited institutions of higher education in the United States, over half the upper-class men chose the eight Ivy League schools.

These select private schools, in turn, serve as "an antichamber to the upper-class marriage market"; their students are invited to fashionable dances and debutante parties. The trend toward coeducation in such schools has strengthened their matchmaking function. This factor, in turn, has increased the already strong tendency of members of the upper class to marry each other.

For upper-class youth of both sexes, higher education is taken for granted, and 19 out of 20 attend college. Most of the females go to the elite Eastern private schools. Three in ten attend the female counterpart to the Ivy League, the Seven Sisters Schools (Smith, Wellesley, Radcliffe, Vassar, Barnard, Bryn Mawr, and Mount Holyoke). Most of those who do not attend the Seven Sisters attend quality private schools elsewhere. Overall, 95 percent of the social-register women, compared to 74 percent of lower upper-class or merely rich, attended private schools. Nor do most of the young women stop there. Over the past decade, the number of upper-class women in graduate or professional schools has doubled from 7 to 14 percent. Yet only 12 percent of the young women, compared to 49 percent of the young men, had a postgraduate education.

The young women, like the young men, are maintaining upper-class traditions. True, the great debutante affairs of past generations have become less frequent, and coming out is less popular.

Despite leveling forces that have erupted in American society in the last generation, the "upper class has maintained itself remarkably intact, and having done so, is perhaps the most untouched group in American life. Moreover, it is the upper-class territory of school, neighborhood, club, and bluebook that remains the most racially segregated turf in America" (Blumberg & Paul, 1975, p. 75).

The Working Class

Youth and young adults of the blue-collar class differ sharply from those of the upper and middle classes (Simon, Gagnon, & Buff, 1972). Working-class youths move into the work force early, sometimes before finishing high school. Such boys may hold several part-time jobs, and then a full-time dead-end one. Their major motive for beginning to work at such a young age is to gain economic independence. They buy a car immediately and make the first of never-ending series of car payments. While their jobs are appropriate enough for ages 22 or 23, they represent an uncertain future in years ahead. The majority, who finish high school, may obtain a job in a post office, on the police force, or in the fire department. Especially after they marry and have a child, their main aim is job security.

The values of the working class have remained pretty stable; "patriotism, personal responsibility, self-help, hard work, and resignation all still coexist with values of political cynicism, distrust of strangers, male dominance, demands for obedience from children, and relative moral and personal inflexibility" (Simon, Gagnon, & Buff, 1972, pp. 32–33). Their unchanging values widen the gap between them and the dominant urban middle-class society.

The working-class girl who does not go to college is committed mainly to becoming a wife and mother. Before then she obtains some low-paying jobs, perhaps as a salesperson. Only if marriage fails or becomes indefinitely delayed does she become more committed to her job. Even then, because of her sex and educational limitations she finds it hard to get ahead. Hence she is committed to maintaining a job rather than working toward a career.

Aside from work, the initial task of working-class young people is to get married and establish their own households. Their ideas are somewhat vague about what their lives should be like, partly because they often fail to find adequate role models in their own parents. Both sexes are relieved once they have decided to marry—after all, they want to be adult; and being married and having a job is considered the proper route to adulthood.

Unlike middle-class couples, they do not ordinarily indulge in recreational pursuits together. The young wives associate mostly with other married women while husbands hang out with "the boys" during nonworking hours, often at a bar. The husband finds married life less supportive than does his wife because it eats up his extra money and to a degree limits his freedom.

Sex roles are more strictly traditional than among middle-class couples. In the home, sex roles are strictly divided: the woman does the traditionally feminine chores and the man the masculine ones. If the wife works, she continues to do most of the domestic chores. The man may help out a bit, but even less than his middle-class counterpart.

SPECIAL CATEGORIES OF YOUNG ADULTS

During the last 15 years there has been a great increase in alternative families, including households headed by never-married women, lesbian and gay couples, communal living arrangements, post-divorce nuclear families (including step families and joint custody arrangements), and cohabitation among unmarried heterosexual and gay couples (Gerson, Alpert & Richardson, 1984).

Gay Couples

A not uncommon life style is that of gay couples. Such individuals, as adults, almost never wish they were heterosexual. Nor do they, by this age, have guilt feelings, despite the still negative way they are viewed by most Americans. True, they are better accepted than formerly, but much hostility remains. Personal interviews with Japanese-American gay men indicated that half had experienced homosexual feelings in the early teens, and the others by the early 20s. All had worked through original feelings of guilt and apprehension, and all with varying frequency socialized in gay establishments (Wooden, Kawasaki & Mayeda, 1983).

Growing numbers of gay couples have children, usually through a previous marriage, adoption, or artificial insemination in the case of lesbians. The evidence is that children of such couples are as well adjusted as those of heterosexual couples; nor do they become gay in greater than usual numbers. Perhaps female couples have the easier time, for they are trained and perceived to be nurturers. However, most gay fathers also manage to integrate their homosexual and parenting roles in positive ways, depending somewhat upon their own commitment to parenting and the support they receive from significant others (Bozett, 1981). Some do not try to integrate the roles, but keep them separate—and these men, too, may achieve a satisfactory life style. Still others simply relinquish the father role and seldom see their children.

In various ways male and female homosexual couples differ. In a comparison of gay and lesbian couples both sexes indicated the same level of commitment; however, the lesbians more often confided in their partners and talked things over together, were more certain of the worth of living together, and thought less often about the possibility of breaking up their relationship (Lewis, Kozac, Milardo & Grosnick, 1981).

Young Servicemen

For a considerable fraction of young adults, a stint in the service produces a distinctive life style, yet little research has been done in this area. This writer's own informal research on the topic has been limited to males, so the following discussion will apply only to them.

Almost all young ex-servicemen report that their period in the service left an indelible and significant imprint on their lives. They also report many rewarding outcomes of the experience such as the following:

Traveling around Europe, meeting people my own age who were nationals of that particular country and learning about them first hand. I still write back and forth with a few. Confidence in myself that I could do "the impossible" at times. Learning to operate heavy equipment. I drove a tractor-trailer for 2 years after being discharged and made $250 a week.

The young men also felt that being in the service had altered their habits and life styles. Here several of them tell how it affected their habits, including drinking, smoking, and drug use.

I did not drink before I was in. By the time I got out I was almost an alcoholic and still do drink to excess occasionally. I smoked before I was in, but by the time I got out I smoked four packs a day. I am now down to one pack a day. It has been said that anyone who was in the service who says they did not experiment with drugs is a liar. I'm not a liar.

I really started to smoke cigarettes in the service—nerves I guess. Not too much drinking. Started smoking grass in Nam though.

I became a heavy drinker in an effort to socialize with the boys.

Most of the young men had problems such as these in adapting to life in the service.

While in boot camp, I realized that I resented taking orders from fellow recruits who were in a higher position yet were younger than I was.

It was my first time away from home. Taking orders from persons I had no respect for and had no respect for me.

Lack of personal freedom and having to take orders from people who you didn't feel were fit for their rank.

Almost all the men, with a few exceptions, said that the experience affected them as people, usually for the better.

I felt that being in the service made me a better person. I was encountering many problems with my family at the time of my entry into the service. By being in a neutral environment, and away from my problems, I was able to develop and mature. I was better able to accept responsibility and perform under pressure.

Made me lose any values I had and corrupted me totally.

For the most part it changed me for the better. I became stronger (mentally). The military madness caused me to become stronger.

I am more confident of myself and I now question many of the values the government has tried to socialize me to. The worst part is that I am much more racist.

The change from service life back to civilian life was not always easy. One problem was relating to persons not familiar with the problems of vets. Another was the resocialization process, or readapting to life outside the service.

Finances were the biggest problem I encountered when I got out of the service, as there were no jobs available to me.

I had to learn to hide what I really felt, you had to be "insane" to keep your sanity and do what you were told even if it was against your better nature. This presented many problems when I first got out, because after being in for so long it was difficult for me to realize I was no longer in. I also found myself resenting people who had

not gone in and experienced what I had. I had been trained to be violent and "on my toes" at all times. I scare myself sometimes (even now) when somebody comes up behind me or wakes me unexpectedly, because at times I will still lash out before I can stop myself. Hopefully I will break myself of this some day.

There is no question but that life in the service is a maturing experience. It causes young people to assess their own values, their former life style, and their goals for the future. It is strange indeed that researchers have almost totally ignored the effect of this period on young peoples' personality development.

Young Adult Students

Young adults in college, from their early to late 20s, include those whose education has been delayed or who are pursuing graduate study. They may have taken time out for travel, to earn money for further study, to begin a family, or for other reasons. They include both marrieds and singles, undergraduate and graduate students. Often such students have worked to save up money to return to school. Their funds may be supplemented by some form of scholarship. Young men may also receive help from their wives, especially if they remain in school a long time.

Until 1940 married undergraduates were unwelcome on college campuses and were few in number. Today, however, such students comprise approximately a fifth of the American undergraduate college population. While such students have characteristic problems, they seem somewhat better adjusted overall than do the single ones (Busselen & Busselen, 1975). They get higher grades, are more satisfied with their living quarters, have better places to study, and are better off economically. The married students' good adjustment may derive from several factors. Those who marry in college may simply be more mature than other students. Besides, since they have already chosen their mates, they need not concern themselves with dating. On the other hand, these students have their special problems, one being that domestic activities leave them little time for cultural experiences. Also, since they are more vocationally oriented than single students, they lead a narrower life. Much of the foregoing also applies to adult, single undergraduates. The latter usually combine work with schooling, and otherwise associate with persons their own age. They, like the married undergraduates, take little part in campus life.

By means of a series of interviews, Taylor (1976) concluded that graduate students are alike in many ways. They are observers, which causes them to separate themselves from objects and people. They have few outside involvements because they must spend long hours in libraries and laboratories. So, to a certain extent, they are in exile. They often have less money than is required for truly adequate living. They develop a strong emotional attachment to their field of inquiry, which they believe is truly significant for life itself even though their studies may be quite esoteric.

Graduate work does have its positive features. Graduate students insist on intellectual freedom; and they believe that they can be different so long as they are decent human beings. They do not seek the same kind of power and wealth as people in nonacademic surroundings. They take a tremendous satisfaction in exploring the depths of their culture. Ideally they transcend their overly deferential attitudes toward scholarly authority and attain a sense of their own scholarly worth.

Young Adult Singles

Characteristics. Young adult singles— older ones will be discussed later—include those who never intend to marry and those who for one reason or another are putting off marriage. Both sexes are remaining single longer than formerly (Rossi, 1984). In just 13 years, from 1967 to 1980, the proportion of unmarried to married women in the population increased from 9 percent to 30 percent, which Rossi attributes to "voluntary postponement of marriage, an increase in preference for remaining unmarried, an increase in homosexuality, and the toll of divorce which leads to fewer remarriages among women than men" (p. 3). Men, too, are postponing marriages to an older age partly because of the social acceptability of their having sex outside marriage, current economic uncertainty, and the knowledge that they will have little trouble getting married at older ages. Women experience an average of a half to two-thirds of their adult lives without a husband.

The number of singles is increasing for a variety of reasons. One reason is that there are now three times as many young women enrolled in college as there were in 1960. Other reasons include: expanding economic opportunities for women, the woman's movement, the availability of birth-control methods (which limits the number of marriages precipitated by pregnancy), and the increasing number of those who declare that they will never marry. Society's reduced pressures on the young to marry constitutes a subtle but real factor in prolonging singlehood.

Single women include a disproportionate number of superior individuals, partly because men feel threatened by them and avoid marrying them (Glick, 1975). Or such women may deliberately postpone marriage until they are well established in their careers or find husbands of their own caliber. Tidbal (1975) studied 1,500 achievers randomly selected from several editions of *Who's Who of American Women*. Slightly over half of these women had married; but once they had received their bachelor's degrees, they had first devoted an average of 7 years exclusively to their careers. Since no such factors operate among men, male singles are more representative of the general population.

For women, age 30 is an important marker. Most under 30 have married, while those who are still single after age 30 are far less likely to do so. Older single women are more positive about life and feel less stress than do younger ones, because they are better adjusted to being single and also may possess better paying, more satisfying jobs. Another reason is that most women who were especially concerned about getting married eventually did so.

Single men experience both advantages and disadvantages because of their unwed status. They may be viewed as swingers who are somewhat carefree. Hence, they evoke a less responsible image than married men. For this reason they are discriminated against in terms of salary and promotion, especially after they reach the age when most of their contemporaries are married. On the other hand, they have had broader experiences with women that they could not have had if they were married. For this reason they are more liberal and sympathetic to movements for social change than married men. They also have more money to spend exclusively on themselves, which allows them to exploit their greater freedom.

Life Styles. Young adult singles have their own life styles. They can and do live a more varied, less rooted life than young marrieds. They socialize chiefly with other young singles, especially those with similar interests and outlook. Those who intend to marry one day will spend more time dating and looking ahead to marriage. They may have the feeling that they must crowd into the here-and-now whatever extensive traveling and fooling around they want to do. They deliberately cultivate the sort of social life that permits them to meet eligible members of the other sex and to test their relationships with different kinds of personalities. The women

who anticipate marriage spend relatively more money on their clothes and social life than do those who expect to remain single.

Those who believe they will remain single early on establish a commitment to career. They too travel and have varied experiences, but with less sense of urgency. They are fully aware that their chosen life style is sufficiently flexible to accommodate such experiences at any stage in life. Many of them associate mainly with their own sex, others with both sexes. They may have both casual and more serious sexual encounters, but they avoid legally binding commitments. While they may lack the security and satisfactions that young couples achieve in establishing a family, they can lead an equally satisfying life.

Single people may be involved in both serious and casual homosexual or heterosexual affairs. However, most women, even sexually liberated ones, find sex acceptable only within the framework of a warm relationship (Hunt, 1973). These relationships may, or may not, signify future intent to marry. In one study, 30 percent of the college men and women questioned felt that traditional types of marriage are growing obsolete, and 25 percent agreed that the traditional nuclear family no longer works (Stein, 1976). Some young people move from campus to city and form friendships with persons quite different from their families and former friends. While they may find the city somewhat threatening, they do have a chance to meet varied people, to gain valuable life experience, and to have fun.

Studies of Women Singles. Such women include the divorced, in rare cases at this age the widowed, and, increasingly, those having out-of-wedlock births. The proportion, ages 25 to 29, who have never married rose 70 percent between 1960 and 1978. Most of them wanted to pursue broad interests that would be denied them after marriage or to establish a career before having children. As one of them said: "I always wanted to be an actress or a movie star or *something*. I never thought about just growing up, getting married, and having babies" (Berman, 1979, p. 188).

These young women differed about whether, when, and why to marry. One mainly wanted the security of family life; two would not marry unless the right man came along; a divorcee was disillusioned by an unhappy marriage and was now ready for a career. ". . . It's not so much the idea of getting married as of having a family; a unit to go through life with that seems important." "For myself the panic is . . . that I may never meet someone that I would really love" (p. 189). "I left [my marriage] with incredible anger. . . . Now I can get on with my life" (p. 190).

In general they expressed special gratitude for their women friends; many believed that single career women feel somewhat condescending toward other women who have forfeited a career for a family. Many also found considerable fault with most men. One suggested that while men might not have changed so much from before, feminist consciousness-raising has made women more clearly perceive men's failings in their relationships with women.

A study of never-married women, aged 24 to 34, who lived alone indicated the majority to be androgynous, combining whatever they found compatible of both male and female roles. They were ingenious in devising ways of avoiding loneliness—for example, by making their home environments comfortable and supportive (Kanter, 1978).

A study of women working in traditionally male professions, disclosed them to be relatively isolated and not involved in the women's movement. With a few exceptions, they had achieved an important professional goal. The late 20s and early 30s was a critical period for them. They greatly valued their independence, but some at least were often lonely and expected ultimately to marry (Kangas, 1978).

Over the years there has been a marked increase in single adult-headed households—from 25 percent in 1960 to 35 percent in 1975, and a projected 45 percent in 1990 (Rossi, 1984). In 1950 just 17 percent of unmarried women in their late 20s headed households; by 1980 this number had increased to 60 percent (Masnick, 1983). Meantime, the number of out-of-wedlock births has been increasing. The overall rate for unmarried women, ages 15 to 44, is higher than ever recorded, representing about 18 percent of all births, partly because there is a trend toward destigmatizing such births (Rossi, 1984).

It is unclear how many of these births to unmarried women are due to the desire for a child without any wish for a spouse. Most women who become artificially inseminated do so because their partners are infertile. Some of these women, mostly in their late 20s or early 30s, with a strong desire for a child but without any "Mister Right" at hand, seek this solution. The Feminist Women's Health Center in Oakland, California added insemination to its services in late 1982, and within the next year almost a hundred women were being inseminated each month, a third of them single (Bagne, 1984). Some of these women are lesbians, many with stable sexual relationships. There seems to be some trend, therefore, toward separating parenting from marriage. Reflective of this trend is the parallel development of unmarried couples' becoming increasingly drawn into, and being accepted by, mainstream society. That is, society is coming to attach less significance to marital status in its treatment and evaluation of individuals.

Studies of young single mothers who had not planned to have babies but did, and decided to keep them, showed that they were less likely to have career plans, had less education, were more often brought up in single-parent families, and more often had single unmarried-mother friends. Also, they more often had remained in touch with the father, suggesting that they may have hoped he would marry them, or help support the children. They were also more likely to have had psychiatric treatment. Overall those less well-qualified for childrearing were those most likely to keep the child (Single mothers, 1980).

Three categories of men carry important primary child-care responsibilities (Rossi, 1984). The first includes solo fathers whose wives have died or who have custody of their children after divorce. A second type embraces men in nontraditional families, perhaps communal groups; and a third includes those in intact marriages who are committed to parenthood as a full partnership.

There is considerable impact on a man of having sole control of his children. Some leave their jobs to meet their parental responsibility; others lose overtime pay because of their children's schedules. Such men also have fewer social ties with their business associates.

The problems relating to solo parenting for the sexes are somewhat different. Solo fathers ordinarily receive more voluntary help from kinspeople and friends, and they make fewer new social contacts. They feel anxious about handling children after the age of puberty, especially the daughters. Solo mothers are mainly concerned about maintaining past living standards and problems of discipline control.

Cohabiting Singles. Despite their growing numbers, young cohabiting adults are becoming more cautious about the legal implications of their relationships (Knox, 1980). The country is absorbing this practice into the family system and converting it more and more into the first stage of marriage (Cherlin, 1980). It is difficult to get correct figures on this subject because the U. S. Census lumps together people of the opposite sex living in the same household, calling them roomers, partners, boarders, and so on. Hence, those sharing an intimate relationship cannot be identified.

As cohabitation is becoming more popular, it is also becoming more regulated. The courts seem to be saying that rights of cohabitants and societal interests are too important to leave solely up to the couples themselves. Much publicity was given to the case of actor Lee Marvin and Michelle Marvin who had lived together for 7 years without benefit of marriage. In this case, Michelle Marvin had served as a companion and homemaker with no pooling of earnings or property. Lee asked Michelle to leave his household, supported her for 2 years after the separation, and then refused further support. She brought suit to acquire half of the property gained during the period of their relationship.

Michelle Marvin was awarded $104,000 for rehabilitation purposes in order to learn new employable skills and reeducate herself. *Palimony,* a term created by the media to decribe such awards, can be awarded even though there has been no contract, either implied or expressed between two parties, while alimony presumes a marital contract. Hence palimony seems to be more of a moral than a legal phenomenon and is justified on principles of fairness. This conclusion and subsequent ones arrived at in similar cases have tended to strengthen institutional support for individuals who have embarked on family relationships without benefit of marriage. At the same time they represent a hazard for individuals who have chosen such arrangements mainly to avoid any such possible outcomes (Myricks, 1980).

Considerble controversy has surrounded the question: Does premarital cohabitation enhance or reduce chances for a successful marriage? In a study of remarried couples, who had or had not cohabited prior to remarriage, the cohabitants judged their remarriage to be more successful and perceived their support from children, friends, relatives, and community as significantly higher (Hanna & Knaub, 1981).

A comparison of young adults who did or did not cohabit prior to marriage revealed both similarities and differences (Rank, 1981). For both categories getting married introduced conventional expectations into the relationship. However, the ex-cohabitants were more likely to retain their surnames, to have small ceremonies, and in some cases to dispense with wedding bands and other traditional customs.

Most young adults themselves—80 percent in Macklin's 1972 study—reported cohabitation to be pleasant, maturing, and helpful for understanding themselves and the other sex. Even those individuals who experienced problems in the relationship reported that personal growth had occurred. Such individuals differed in some ways from young adults generally. In a comparison of unmarried couples who simply "went together" with those who lived together, the going-together couples held more traditional views of each other and were more committed to marriage. Among the living-together couples, more of the young women than men wanted ultimately to marry their cohabiting partners. When young women pressured them to marry, the young men often broke off the relationship and eventually chose new living mates (Lyness, Lipetz & Davis, 1972).

Despite the persistence of the traditional division of labor, there is no significant power struggle between spouses regarding the performance of household tasks, either among married or cohabiting couples. Those young people who are most strongly committed to traditional sex roles tend to come from families in which there is a traditional division of labor, to be from a lower rather than a higher social class, and to be Catholic rather than Protestant. A minority of couples simply structure household tasks along traditional lines while they attempt to implement more equalitarian relationships. It appears that cohabitation and the partial erosion of traditional male authority will not automatically end traditional sex roles. Most young women are still too conservative and concerned about their femininity to alter the current situation.

INDIVIDUAL TESTIMONY

The foregoing discussion has dealt with subgroups of young adults. Within each subgroup there are individual differences. For a better perspective on young adult life styles, here are several young adults' replies to three questions about their lives.

1. What do you find most satisfying about your present life?

MALE, AGE 23:   Good family, challenging job, and recreational opportunities.

MALE, AGE 33:   That my past education and experience, coupled with my capabilities, make it possible for me to do just about anything I want.

FEMALE, AGE 33:   My family and career— also that I am able to choose to stay at home for a year or two and not feel guilty about it.

FEMALE, AGE 35:   The free, open feelings I have about my life style.

FEMALE, AGE 29:   I'm assertive, love myself for the first time, and feel completely turned on and in tune with God and the rest of the world. My work with Spanish-speaking migrants makes me feel very needed and worthwhile.

2. Is there anything unusual or different about your life style?

FEMALE, AGE 27:   I am so traditional in my work, marriage, and so on, that I am "unusual." I have a happy home and marriage—that's unusual.

FEMALE, AGE 33:   I guess being gay is different in that we're a minority, but I feel better about myself, having found my true self. I don't feel that I am different.

FEMALE, AGE 29:   I've lived on several socioeconomic levels, sunk to the lowest levels of life (drugs, prostitution, alcohol), have risen above my past, and now live a respectable, satisfying Christian life.

MALE, AGE 29:   Ninety-five percent of my

time is regulated by me. I eat when I'm hungry, sleep when I'm tired, work when I want to.

3. What are your chief interests and most pleasant forms of recreation?

MALE, AGE 33: I obtain a great deal of joy from traveling and several hobbies, such as woodburning and making things from wood.

FEMALE, AGE 33: I enjoy creating things. I watch TV, sometimes for diversion, sometimes for escape. Crocheting, sewing, reading.

PERSPECTIVE ON YOUNG ADULT LIFE STYLES

Adults have more flexibility in their lives than do children and adolescents because adults can choose their own places of residence, change careers, obtain divorces, and choose friends on the basis of congenial interests from a broader area (Mortimer & Simmons, 1978). On the other hand, young adult life styles are rooted, to some degree, in the adolescent experience. In a study in which high-school students were followed for a 2- to 5-year period, Newman (1979) found that life-style orientations begun by the tenth grade established a pattern for certain global aspects of adjustment in young adulthood.

Changes in young adult life styles in the United States have been less dramatic than is commonly believed; yet they are significant in certain ways. Most young adults focus their main energies and commitments on family and vocation, but in ways that differ from those of their parents. Since most young women work, sex roles are changing; but the changes have not been worked through well enough to satisfy adequately the needs of many husbands and working wives. Ordinarily parents find real satisfaction in their children, the more so because childbearing

has become a matter of choice rather than an obligation or as the price of sex.

No homogeneous picture of young adult life styles can suffice because life in the United States is becoming more and more complex, and there are many subgroups within society. True, certain generalizations apply to most young adults: they are searching for a style of life that suits their needs, and they desire a more satisfying life rather than a largely life-sustaining existence. Beyond such broad goals, considerable differences exist according to such variables as sex, social class, marital status, and vocation. No longer is membership in a nuclear family viewed as the only valid life style, although it is still the most popular. It is increasingly accepted that nontraditional ways of life are the most satisfying for some people for part or all of their lives.

There is nothing in the picture to suggest that today's young adults are any less emotionally healthy than their counterparts of earlier generations. In fact, the reverse is true. As birth-control methods have improved; as the great majority are becoming better educated; and as economic and technological advances reduce the need for drudgery, young adults are expecting more and gaining more from their lives. Even such transactions as obtaining a divorce, joining a commune, or participating in consciousness-raising groups of various kinds may be less symptoms of failure or discontent than a positive reaching-out for greater personal fulfillment.

SUMMARY

Life style varies according to marital status, absence or presence of children, social class, and current involvement, as in graduate work or military service. The most common young-adult life style involves marriage and children. Before the children arrive, couples engage in much activity with each other; afterward, the huband focuses on his job and the wife on the children. Young adults experience problems relating to personal development, marital relationships, childrearing, and differential sex roles. Neither sex attains optimum satisfaction from following traditional sex roles.

Life styles vary even more greatly according to social class. Upper-class individuals manage to maintain their own distinctive life style remarkably intact. Working-class individuals differ sharply from both upper and middle classes. They move into the work force early, sometimes before completing high school, and typically resort to dead-end jobs. Their values and sex-role orientations are traditional, and couples ordinarily indulge in few recreational pursuits together.

Special categories of young adults have their own characteristic life styles. Young adults who spend some time in the service generally find the experience rewarding and maturing. Young adult students take their studies very seriously and gain great satisfaction from exploring areas of knowledge in depth.

Young adult singles often spend time in travelling or in a wide range of activities before settling down. Those who believe they will remain single establish a commitment to a career, taking satisfaction from the fact that their single status allows a flexible life style. Some singles cohabit for varying lengths of time, often with no intent of marrying.

On the whole, young adults' life styles today reflect the changing times, but despite the differences, they are probably as healthy as those of former generations.

SUGGESTED READINGS

ATKINSON, J. & HUSTON, T. L. (1984). Sex-role orientation and division of labor early in marriage. *Journal of Personality and Social Psychology, 46*(2), 330–345.

BOZETT, F. (1981). Gay fathers. Identity conflict resolution through integrative sanctioning. *Alternative Lifestyles, 4*(1), 90–107.

CALLAN, V. J. (1983). Childlessness and partner selection. *Journal of Marriage and the Family, 45*(1), 181–186.

COLE, C. L. & GOETTSCH, S. L. (1981). Self-disclosure and relationship quality. A study among nonmarital cohabiting couples. *Alternative Lifestyles, 4*(4), 428–466.

ELMAN, M. R. & GILBERT, L. A. (1984). Coping strategies for role conflict in married professional women with children. *Family Relations, 33,* 317–327.

FISCHER, J. & CARDEA, J. M. (1981). Mothers living apart from their children. A study in stress and coping. *Alternative Lifestyles, 4*(2), 218–227.

HANNA, S. L. & KNAUB, P. K. (1981). Cohabitation before remarriage. Its relationship to family strengths. *Alternative Lifestyles, 4*(4), 507–522.

HENNON, C. B. (1981). Conflict management within cohabitation relationships. *Alternative Lifestyles, 4*(4), 467–486.

KREPPNER, K., PAULSON, S., & SCHUETZE, Y. (1982). Infant and family development: From triads to tetrads. *Human Development, 25,* 373–391.

LEWIS, R., KOZAC, E. B., MILARDO, R. M., & GROSNICK, W. A. (1981). Commitment in same-sex love relationships. *Alternative Lifestyles, 4*(1), 22–42.

MITCHELL, J. V. Jr. (1984). Personality correlates of life values. *Journal of Research in Personality, 18,* 1–14.

RANK, M. R. (1981). The transition to marriage. A comparison of cohabiting and dating relationships ending in marriage or divorce. *Alternative Lifestyles, 4*(4), 487–506.

RATCLIFFE, W. D. & WITTMAN, W. P. (1983). Parenting education: Test-market evaluation of a media campaign. *Prevention in Human Services, 2*(3), 97–109.

SCHRAG, K. G. (1984). Relationship therapy with same-gender couples. *Family Relations, 33,* 283–291.

SPANIER, G. B. (1983). Married and unmarried cohabitation in the United States: 1980. *Journal of Marriage and the Family, 45*(2), 277–288.

THOMPSON, A. P. (1983). Extramarital sex: A review of the research literature. *Journal of Sex Research, 19*(1), 1–22.

TOKUNO, K. A (1983). Friendship and transition in early childhood. *Journal of Genetic Psychology, 143*(2), 207–216.

VERZARO-LAWRENCE, M. (1981). Shared childrearing. A challenging alternative lifestyle. *Alternative Lifestyles, 4*(2), 205–217.

WOODEN, W. S., KAWASAKI, H., & MAYEDA, R. (1983). Lifestyles and identity maintenance among gay Japanese-American males. *Alternative Lifestyles, 5*(4), 236–243.

CHAPTER FIVE

Characteristics of Middle Age

THE SIGNIFICANCE OF MIDDLE AGE

What is Middle Age?

Definition. When does middle age begin? Middle age has no generally accepted boundaries: some United States Census reports define it as covering ages 45 to 64; other sources date it from 30 to 70. In terms of human biology, the *climacteric*—the end of the human reproductive potential—might be considered the end of the middle years and the beginning of old age (Troll, 1975). Socially, however, the climacteric is considered as occurring in middle age. Psychologically, middle age is a stage of growing awareness of time, a period of introspection and self-analysis that is critical for future development. It is the most significant stage of life in terms of the individual's influence on others, earning power, and impact on society. In the area of family development, mid-

dle age is ordinarily judged synonymous with the *empty-nest period,* (the period between when the children leave home and the husband retires)(Targ, 1979).

It is apparent from reactions to the question "How old do you feel?" that there is usually a gap of variable size between the way people see themselves and their actual chronological age.

FEMALE, AGE 58, MARRIED: Forty mostly, although there are days! I feel younger because I think young always and so does my husband.

FEMALE, AGE 54, WIDOWED: I think I feel my age! If I don't and I get too overactive, I know soon enough.

MALE, AGE 51, MARRIED: I feel about age 34 or 35, partly because I'm in good health and remain physically and mentally active. I feel that unpleasant things will pass. I'm very conscious of always having challenging things to do. When I stop creating things, life gets dull. I'm conscious of keeping things dynamic, alive, and growing.

MALE, AGE 42, MARRIED: I don't feel any different from the way I did when I was 18, although I think differently. I'm not temporally oriented and don't think of things like this from day to day.

FEMALE, AGE 64, MARRIED: Some days pretty old but usually young at heart. I don't have the stamina I used to.

The Middle-Aged Portrait. The Census Bureau identifies midlife as the years 45 to 64, characterized by such major events as retirement, widowhood, chronic illness, the children's leaving home, and care of parents (Challenges, 1984). Nationwide, about 90 percent of the middle-aged live with their families, most often with their spouses. A relatively high fraction (16 percent) of the currently older middle-aged, 55 to 64, for economic reasons have had childless marriages compared with 9 percent of the younger middle-aged.

The understanding of midlife years is still limited. They are sometimes characterized as a period of conflict and transition. In terms of career, midlife has its special issues and problems, including balancing work with other activities, conflicts over career goals and reality, and decisions whether to generalize or specialize. On a broader level, the middle-aged are becoming aware of their mortality, experiencing changing relations within their families, and realizing that aging will further limit opportunities (Gill, Coppard & Lowther, 1983).

The Middle-Aged Male. The magazine *Esquire* describes physical changes in the middle-aged male—and those in the female are similar. At age 40 he is about one-eighth of an inch shorter than a decade ago, and his hair is thinning. His waist and chest are rounding; his stamina has diminished. By age 50 his eyes have begun to fail, especially at close range. His speaking voice is not as low, and his erections are not completely horizontal. The 60-year-old is three-quarters of an inch shorter than at maximum height, and his lungs draw about half what they did at age 30. He has become less sensitive to differences in color, taste, and smell. At age 70 his vision is still worsening; his heart is pumping less blood; and, on average, he has 11 more years to live (Tierney, 1982).

Self-Perceptions of Middle Age. The process of seeing oneself growing older is gradual and often begins in the 30s. Most working people do not view themselves as middle-aged until they become anxious about the retirement period to follow soon. The question arises: If the forced retirement age were eliminated, would concepts of becoming old be delayed? Or is the idea of life stages simply not relevant to most adults today? (Fiske, 1980, p. 345)

In the late 20s and early 30s, people's lives seem to be at their peak—their health is good, their sex lives satisfying, their incomes rising. But they begin to feel older; and as people move from one stage to another, or from one decade to another, as at ages 30, 40, and 50, they suffer "birthday depressions" (Scanlon, 1979). They notice that their peers look older, and realize that they do too.

Nevertheless, healthy individuals continue to feel younger than they are. A comparison of working-oriented returning women students with unemployed, domestically oriented women, disclosed both similarities and differences (Hooper & Traupman, 1983). Both groups, whose mean age was 55, thought of themselves on average as younger than middle age. Nor did they differ much on when one might be considered old. Over two-thirds (65 percent) named 80 years, the others about 70; but 63 percent said their own age was relatively unimportant or not at all important in their lives, and just 23 percent somewhat important (Perosa & Perosa, 1983).

Self-perceptions of age vary greatly according to health, social class, how well life crises have been resolved, and personal outlook in general. People who have led a hard life, have experienced much sickness, and have prematurely aged physically, may feel old. Working men may feel themselves to be middle-aged at 40 and old by 60, whereas professionals and business executives may not perceive themselves as middle-aged until 50, or old until after 70 (Neugarten, 1972). In a study of middle-class men, about half those over 80 considered themselves old, while the other half saw themselves as middle-aged (Eisdorfer & Lawton, 1973). Another factor in determining how one sees middle age is personality. Some people wrap up their lives at a relatively early age. They dwell in the past and the present, not the future. Others look eagerly ahead and live too full a life to be aware of the passing years. In other words, middle age may be meaningful for one individual but not for another.

Symptoms of Middle Age. There are several signs of middle age, one being that people begin counting "backward from death instead of forward from birth" (Butler, 1976, p. 30). There is an awareness of the limits of the life span and an "existential anxiety concerning the insignificance of the individual life in an infinity of time and space" (Lidz, 1980, p. 29). Yet at the beginning of middle age, "there is still time to revise, time to start afresh or at least to salvage the years that are left, but there can be no further delay" (Lidz, 1980, p. 29). Another symptom is that people begin sizing themselves up and evaluating what they have done, deciding whether they have achieved what they had hoped. This trend of thought can be very painful. Other symptoms are the personalization of death, or its referral to oneself, and an increasing sense of self and solitude (Datan, 1980). Researchers have also observed "a sense of bodily decline and a recognition of one's mortalities; a sense of aging—the feeling of being old rather than young" (Targ,

1979, p. 377). There is a growing preoccupation with the body, or "body monitoring." Middle age is sometimes characterized by drug addiction, excessive drinking, or obesity.

The middle-aged must also articulate their life styles with their changing needs. Some developers see among the 55- to 64-year-old "empty nesters," who possess about one-fifth of the nation's discretionary income, a lucrative market for preretirement homes. By now the children have left home and they no longer need those extra bedrooms (Preretirement home, 1981). Like retirement homes, these ban children—after all, prospective residents have reared their families—have single-level construction with quality interior finishes and security systems, and nearby golf courses. Unlike retirement homes, such homes are found in preretirement communities within commuting distance of jobs in large cities, but not so far as to involve unusual commuting time.

The Tasks of the Middle Years

The Tasks Defined. Various authorities provide a picture of what the middle aged are expected to accomplish in modern Western society. They must answer the important questions, "Who am I? Where am I going? What is life all about?" That is, the middle aged, like adolescents, face an identity crisis (Kerckhoff, 1978). They must also cope with managing their households, childrearing, and careers, which means problems in managing time, dealing with work, family conflicts and in-laws, and developing a concern for something outside themselves—that is, for making a contribution to society (Streever & Wodarski, 1984).

Another task is taking care of aging parents, a difficult one in view of the relatively recent phenomenon of small mobile nuclear families. Adults are often torn between responsibilities to their own families and responsibilities for parents. Persons over age 50 confront several other tasks as well. These include coming to accept one's own life, re-directing roles and activities after retire-ment, developing a point of view regarding death, and adjusting to the grandparent role and sometimes to the lack of a spouse.

LeShan (1973) believes that the middle years provide a chance to become truly one-self, to discover one's own truths, especially one's own identity. She compares the process that the middle aged experience in exam-ining their identities with the lobster's pe-riodic shedding of its shell; it leaves the lob-ster vulnerable, but it also permits it to grow.

Middle age is also a time when many fa-milial, community, and societal obligations converge, which explains why the middle aged have been called the "caught" generation, and why they experience "role strain" and "midlife crisis" (Levinson, 1977, p. 249).(Men are at the peak of their careers; women's long-range plans are contingent upon the expectations of others. They depend on the husband's retirement or the children's grow-ing up and getting married.(As their chil-dren grow up and develop their own re-quirements, a married woman's role becomes less well defined)(Spence & Lonner, 1978). Sometimes the children return home, cre-ating the *refilled-nest* problem—the problem of mature children returning home after college because they cannot find immediate work.(A couple whose children return home may experience considerable stress in rea-dapting to them) (The American family, 1980).

The tasks of middle age depend some-what on the relationship of people at this age to older or younger generations. As members of the older generation die, their adult children become the oldest generation and assume certain of the characteristics pe-culiar to it, while the older generation's grandchildren then become the second gen-eration (Duvall, 1971). To a degree they be-come watchdogs of society, evaluating cur-rent trends against earlier ones. And while members of the oldest generation have too little power and are too out of step with the

times to block change, they nevertheless af-fect what happens.(The in-between middle-aged generation to some extent serves as a moderator between the older and the younger generations.)The younger generation is often impatient and wants to make radical changes in society, while the older generation re-mains somewhat cautious, unwilling to turn its back on solutions to societal problems that have proven themselves over the years.

A Study of the Middle Aged. On the basis of interviews with relatively successful mid-dle-aged persons, Neugarten and Datan (1981) reached certain conclusions, one being that middle age is indeed a distinctive pe-riod, and that one may feel different in different phases of one's life or at different times. On the job, the executive may feel he has arrived—hence, is further advanced in his life span than as a father, a role in which his abilities may not yet have fully matured. Both men and women felt farther from the young than from their parents, perhaps be-cause of their feelings of "acute responsibil-ity" for the younger generation (Neugarten & Datan, 1981, p. 275). This writer suggests, too, that their failure to perceive their par-ents as old may have constituted a defense mechanism against recognizing that they, too, would be viewed as old before long. Both sexes, men more than women, perceived time differently, thinking of time left to live in-stead of time since birth, and displaying a growing awareness of the finiteness of life. Another prevalent theme was the percep-tion of middle adulthood as "the period of maximum capacity and ability to handle a highly complex environment and a highly differentiated self" (p. 381). They felt that they had greater judgment and control of their environment than earlier in life.

In certain ways there were important sex differences. Women defined themselves in relation to the family life cycle, men in terms of their work. As the children grew older and left home women saw middle age as a period of increased freedom, with more energy and time for oneself. Their husbands, meantime, often felt increased work pressures or job boredom. For them, the most significant middle-aged markers were biological. Their bodies seemed less efficient and, especially after age 50, feelings of sexual adequacy diminished. In contrast, women less often referred to biological changes or health concerns. By late middle age, many of their friends were becoming widowed, so they monitored their spouses' health more than their own (Neugarten & Datan, 1981). However, the increasing number of women in the work force, and women's still growing numbers in the work force may already have somewhat modified these attitudes.

For men, middle age is a time of taking stock concerning their careers (Neugarten & Datan, 1981). Some of the better educated had continued up the status ladder in their 40s, even in their 50s. Most of the others had simply held their own after about age 35, although for some slippage in status or income occurred between ages 35 and 55. However, the working-class family's income may increase as wives reenter the work force after the children are older.

A Critique of Erikson's Theory. As discussed in Chapter 1, Erik Erikson (1959) perceives middle age as the (phase of generativity, which refers to caring for others in the broader sense, through being productive and creative and thereby making a contribution to others) Many men in their 40s move away from dedicating all their energies to their own personal career advancement and undertake community service. But for every individual who becomes philanthropic or assumes the role of guide to younger individuals, there are several who hang on to their career fantasies as zealously as ever (Sheehy, 1976). Some men at this period, realizing they will never attain their goals or finding that those goals no longer mean anything to them, will drink too much or overeat in or-

der to cope with feelings of disillusion or failure.

Sheehy calls attention to a major limitation in Erikson's theory, which is that he, like most life-cycle theorists, is concerned only with the male life cycle. Most women have always been concerned with generativity or serving others. It is not simply through more generativity that many women manage to recreate themselves during the second half of their lives. Rather, if the crisis for men at midlife is a matter of overcoming stagnation through generativity, the midlife task for women demands that they overcome their dependency and realize their wholeness.

Other writers perceive a certain "biological determinism" in middle-aged women's behavior. Certain common stereotypes of women are reflected, though not always specifically stated, in research: that mind-body relationships are more relevant to women than men. Women are viewed largely in terms of such biological variables as reproductive role, menopause, and the empty nest; the roles of wife and mother are assumed to be critical to any woman's happiness. Any evidence to the contrary is usually explained away in some fashion. When Lowenthal (1975) found that women were looking forward to the empty-nest period, the researchers suggested that women's despair might have been too deep to be discovered even in long interviews. Yet most women do not perceive these events as especially central or distressing at the time (Barnett & Baruch, 1978).

Crisis as a Spur to Growth. This survey of theories about the tasks of middle age suggests that middle-age crisis is normal, and if properly resolved can produce growth. For example, for some individuals the realization of having little time left and limited energies for accomplishing their goals produces a shift in their values. They may either abandon as unrealistic or pursue even more vigorously their former activities. Also the confrontation with their parents' mortality and aging may spur them to greater creativity. The new stage, thus achieved, may be on a higher, not lower, level than that of young adulthood. It is important for researchers to identify the factors that distinguish people who experience renewal after midlife crises from those who get stuck in the same old rut.

Not all authorities view midlife as a major transition. Paul McHugh, chief psychiatrist at Johns Hopkins University, brands this view "fiction." Midlife tasks may be distinctive, but no worse than those at other ages. Writes McHugh: "The message that in midlife we can expect to come apart—that we are entitled to come apart—is a myth. . . . Life is a series of difficulties and challenges" (Midlife, 1983, p. 5E).

MENTAL AND PERSONALITY CHARACTERISTICS

Mental Characteristics

The Pattern of Mental Development. Piaget believed that mental development proceeds through several relatively discrete stages. After going through the first three stages in childhood, normal individuals presumably reach the highest—the *formal operations stage*—in adolescence and become capable of systematic, deductive reasoning. That is, they can now use abstract rules or generalizations to attack a whole class of problems, and think abstractly without the use of concrete proofs. Abilities stabilize at this point and remain reasonably constant until later adulthood, when they begin to decline.

This theory has been subject to certain important criticisms and changes. In the first place the pattern of adult intelligence may sometimes emerge prior to early adolescence (Fitzgerald, Nesselroade, & Baltes, 1973). Second, only half the adult population ever reaches the stage of formal operational thinking, or the problem-solving stage.

In the third place, formal operational thinking is not necessarily the final stage. Instead, thought structures, or patterns of intellectual function, may continue to change progressively beyond this level throughout adulthood (Gruber, 1973).

What happens to intelligence after adulthood appears to depend on an individual's personality and experience (Goleman, 1980c). In the Terman longitudinal study of superior individuals, the most successful appeared to become brighter as they grew older; the less successful remained above the general population in IQ, as they had always been, but their IQs increased less. Life styles in particular related to maintaining or improving intellectual performance—and men's were more favorable than women's. Both sexes showed an IQ gain between the years 17 and 18 and 36 to 48, with the men gaining more in performance IQs, and the women more in verbal IQs. Those whose IQs decreased the most had demonstrated a disproportionate incidence of heavy alcohol use and of debilitative illness. Among those with the greatest increase there were no heavy drinkers; many had traveled outside the United States, and had had stimulating intellectual experiences in early adulthood. In summary three in four of "the decreasers had drinking problems; others were depressed and case history evidence indicated very little mental stimulation" (Honzik, 1984, p. 325).

Conclusions about adult intelligence may be flawed because of the commonly narrow interpretation of cognitive processes (Block & Block, 1983). As ordinarily researched, psychologists have dealt with only a small fraction of cognitive experience; and individuals' mental lives rarely involve the solely cognitive matters with which researchers have been concerned. Practical day-to-day cognition does not involve tasks such as evaluating factors that might influence swings of a pendulum. Moreover, conclusions about intellect have derived mainly from evaluating peoples' interactions with the physical world, which is more orderly and subject to identifiable rules than cognitive processes of the personal world.

The Complex Nature of Adult Achievement. The extent to which individuals capitalize on their mental potential depends on the complex interaction of intelligence, special abilities, personality characteristics, and circumstance. In the Terman study, very bright individuals, followed over six decades from childhood until their 60s, did not prove entirely prisoners of their past. To the extent that they had a capacity for continuing growth, it is significant that they approached the future constructively. As we mentioned, the most successful individuals seemed to grow brighter as they grew older; the least successful were still superior in intelligence to the general population, but their IQs did not increase as much (Goleman, 1980c).

Special abilities in early years appear to have important outcomes in later ones. In the Terman group, those women who had special mathematical ability as children and youths proved more career oriented than did average women and showed more ambition and concern for excellence on the job during their adult years (Goleman, 1980a). On the other hand, Christopher Jencks (1979) reported only a slight correlation between IQ scores in school and successful performance in later years.

Mental Content. More ordinary individuals spend most of their time thinking of somewhat mundane matters. Hurlburt (1979) had subjects jot down in notebooks every time a device beeped what their thought was just prior to the beep, and to turn off the device while they slept. Fewer than 1 percent of them reported a blank mind. The subjects had thought mainly about "mundane matters (work, tests, being late), personal concerns (relationships, anxieties), and having fun (TV, food, sex, sports)" (Gibbs, 1979, p. 137). People may behave somewhat mindlessly in purely routine situations, not because they are thoughtless, but because they

are thinking about other matters. On the other hand, they do little that is mentally challenging in their daily lives.

Differences According to Age and Sex. Younger people react more speedily behaviorally, and by inference, mentally, than older ones, but to what degree is uncertain. Older people are often more deliberate, having grown accustomed to weighing alternatives before accepting answers as conclusive.

Sex differences in adult intelligence may also exist. Women perform well in verbal meaning, reasoning, and word fluency, which reflects their more verbal type of life, whereas males are superior in numbers, spatial relationships, and general intellectual ability (Schaie, Labouvie, & Buech, 1973). Nevertheless, intellectual abilities vary greatly within each sex and can be explained in terms of differential sex roles. For example, men's superiority in spatial relationships and numbers may be due partly to the nature of the games they played and the toys they had in childhood. From infancy boys' toys, games, and activities in general are more mentally challenging than those provided females. To some extent, education can become a compensatory factor. In middle age, after the children have left home, better educated women find it easier to find new interests and activities, whereas the less well educated have more trouble finding substitutes for their erstwhile caretaker role. In contrast, more poorly educated men have had greater opportunities over the years to interact with stimulating work and social environments—hence, they perform better (Shanan & Sagiv, 1982).

The significance of education and culture in intellectual function is especially apparent in cross-cultural comparisons. Sex differences in intellectual performance are significant in the United States and certain Western European countries but stronger in Middle-Eastern countries, notably Iran. Overall, the evidence is clear that sociocultural factors account for men's superior intellectual performance, and that the sex differential varies along with ways that sociocultural factors impinge on the sexes differently.

Personality Characteristics

The Process of Personality Development. Many studies suggest that, once established, basic personality characteristics, as distinct from more peripheral ones, are relatively persistent. Although personality development throughout life is a complex and often obscure process, its basic design persists. Overall, personality "development is a cyclic process with competencies developing and then disappearing to reappear anew at a later age; development is not a continuous process but rather a series of waves, with whole segments of development reoccuring repetitively" (Bower, 1974, p. 322). On the other hand Kagan, Kearsley, and Zelazo (1978) emphasize the potential for personality change, noting that longitudinal studies do not prove that early behaviors are highly predictive of adult behaviors. On the basis of cross-cultural studies, especially in Guatemala, they have concluded that large changes in environment can produce considerable change in personality.

As individuals move through adult life to later years, there are both consistencies and change, varying considerably by sex (Zube, 1982). In general, current adaptations reflect earlier experience. Changes are gradual, and involve moving in the direction of greater reflection and constriction of personal and social space. Both sexes tend to commit themselves to activities and roles different from earlier ones—men away from work to more interpersonal commitments and women away from mostly serving others toward greater self-expression.

Gradually as men move toward and through middle age they show less aggressiveness and less concern for mastery and power, and they have more of a present than future time orientation. They turn toward the family, manifesting more nurturance than in earlier years. Philosophically, they become more realistic, closing the gap between their goals and achievements. They may have become bored and frustrated with their jobs and look forward to retirement.

In contrast, women become more assertive and dominant. They may no longer be satisfied with their current life and are desirous of personal growth. Now free of the childrearing role, their focus on the family may diminish just when that of their husbands increases. More resourceful women find this stage a challenge; those with few resources and who are more inhibited may experience frustration. Meantime, some wives dislike their husbands' greater intrusions into their sphere and demands on their time.

Tendencies toward stability or change are not necessarily built in, but relate to people's social environment. On the one hand, personality development is at least partially a

Women often become more assertive in middle age.

T.G. Bell

response to changing internal and external demands. On the other, personality cannot simply be changed on demand (Nydegger, 1976).

In a second adult follow-up, subjects studied from birth to age 42 (Berkeley Growth and Guidance Studies) and those followed from ages 10 or 11 to 50 (Oakland Growth Study) revealed important relationships between different aspects of development. The study participants showed strong gains in the factor "cognitively invested" between ages 14 and 47, as well as marked gains in self-confidence; and the women became significantly more nurturant during adulthood. The pervasive influence of personality was shown in its significant relationship to IQ, occupational attainment, and physical health (Haan, 1981).

General Characteristics: Miscellaneous Findings. Certain studies have concerned the personality characteristics of adults in general. As indicated earlier, some authorities suggest it is important that individuals redefine their goals in middle age. For example, the realization that time is running out leads to a period of self-examination and assessment of life to date and of life's goals. If these dreams are not fulfilled, does one succumb to a sense of failure and disillusionment? Or is there still a chance to achieve them? There is a deep need to acquire a feeling of fulfillment and completion (Lidz, 1980). However, a survey of adults and university students in Los Angeles, Australia, and Britain indicated that few adults, even the most highly educated (with the exception of university students), had thought at all about the question, "Who am I really?" (Turner, 1975).

Apparently, most people's self-appraisals are not too unsettling; a great many American adults are reasonably content. In 1977 a Gallup Poll revealed that 42 percent of Americans were very happy and another 48 percent fairly happy, whereas only 10 percent were not too happy. Americans are among the happiest people on earth, five times as happy as the people of the Far East and twice as happy as West Germans (Etzioni, 1978). However, in terms of their public life, as members of the broader national community, they are pessimistic and perceive themselves as dissatisfied and unable to cope with the future.

The middle aged are active mentally and physically, and are accustomed to getting things done. At this age most people are at the peak of their potential. Even though they have passed their physical prime, they have learned how to conserve their energies. They are aware of their areas of competence and have moved to "center stage" and assumed responsibilities (Lidz, 1980, p. 30). On the other hand, observes Fiske (1980), there are fewer "self-generating and evolving people now than two decades ago, representing a shift from inner to other directedness" (Fiske, 1980, p. 369). Increasingly, both the young and the middle aged want to be told what to do.

We have also suggested that adults undergo a certain mellowing in middle years. They acquire greater tolerance regarding both self and others, as well as greater insight into the complexities of their world. Nevertheless, aging gracefully cannot be taken for granted. It requires foresight and preparation. The great majority settle down and look upon themselves as relatively stable; for whatever is done, "the die is cast" (Gould, 1975). Such understanding in healthy persons does not represent resignation, but the resolution of conflicting alternatives and the definition of a life style based on their experiences.

All the foregoing data obscure two important truths: people vary greatly among themselves and many possess resources of which even they are only vaguely aware until tested. For example, situations arise in which older middle-aged individuals show remarkable courage, ingenuity, and strength. In more than one instance, an older woman who has never flown a plane has managed to pilot it to a safe landing after the pilot collapsed. In one such case a 60-year-old woman kept a plane in the air until it ran out of fuel, after her pilot husband became unconscious, and then managed a crash landing. Despite having been injured, she managed to crawl to a home for help (Woman survives, 1982).

Results of Selected Studies of Adult Personality

The Grant Study Certain studies—for example, the Grant study—suggest how early personality characteristics and life styles relate to later adjustment. A number of Harvard students, initially selected for study because of their psychological health and high level of independence, had been followed from their freshman year to age 48. The results indicate how people with relatively similar backgrounds and apparently similar personality characteristics eventually follow different paths, and either grow or stagnate. Between the ages of 25 and 35, these young men worked hard at their careers and dedicated themselves to their nuclear families. They were poor at self-reflection, followed the rules, were good at peforming tasks, anxious to become promoted, and dedicated to the system. By age 30 they had given over to conformity. Meantime, most of these young men were masterful at deceiving themselves. Their early 30s were especially empty, and there had been little personality expansion during the previous years. By the time they were 35, they couldn't wait to take charge. However, at 40 most of them found themselves in a state of turmoil greater than anything they had been through in adolescence. The years 40 to 50 proved a difficult decade for all aspects of their lives. Yet they proceeded with self-appraisal in midlife and came out with their lives restructured. They looked back on the years 35 to 49 as the happiest of their lives. But some of them, who had been adventuresome in their 20s (especially the lawyers), seemed to settle down in a very

mundane fashion in their 40s. In midlife they simply failed to grow and, compared with their classmates, appeared to be prematurely aging.

Those individuals who came out best became less concerned in midlife about their personal advancement, and shifted their emphasis from making money and career rewards to caring for others. This reorientation included a concern for children, consulting, teaching, and serving as models and guides to younger men. In Vaillant's (1977) interviews of ninety-five men from the original 268 in the Grant study, individuals who had been organized, integrated, and practical in adolescence were best adapted at age 50, while those who were asocial in adolescence were least likely to achieve the so-called best outcomes.

The Berkeley Study. The Berkeley study began when many of the subjects, now in their middle and late middle age, were small children. In follow-up studies at successive stages of adulthood, some of those who had the "most unfortunate childhoods and least promising personalities" turned out to be among the most creative, healthiest, and happiest (Fiske, 1980). These greater-than-anticipated changes suggest the importance of sociosituational factors.

The Oakland Growth Study. Let us look at one more study, which shows how characteristics that may interfere with adjustment at one age may prove functional at another (Freeing up after forty, 1976). The Oakland Growth study began in 1932 and involved 200 11-year-old boys and girls. They were observed in depth in their junior and senior years in high school and were interviewed again at ages 40 and 50. At 40 the more traditional subjects had moved smoothly into middle age with little change in life style; they appeared emotionally healthy. Those individuals who had been "sex-role rebels" in adolescence experienced some conflict and depression at 40, perhaps because they had "suppressed their freer instincts and emotionality." The male sex-role rebels were more expressive than most males and the females' interests lay outside the home (Freeing up after forty, 1976, p. 50). However, apparently something had happened between the ages of 40 and 50, because by age 50, these individuals had come to appreciate and respect their inner natures. (These nonconformist men were outgoing, giving, sensual, and freely expressed their feelings. They also needed much less power) (The women sex-role rebels had become more perceptive, nonconformist, and strongly intellectual) Researcher Livson concluded that both sexes had become more androgynous by age 50, perhaps because the women no longer devoted themselves to mothering, and the men no longer needed to prove their prowess. Or it may simply be that sex norms are more flexible by this age.

Limited Generalizations. Such studies suggest the complexity of personality research and the difficulty in drawing conclusions. Rough patterns of personality development can be defined within various segments of the population according to social class, ethnic group, and such other factors. Considering the large number of cultures around the world and the many kinds of life styles within a single culture, such patterns could be endlessly noted. To what extent they can be categorized according to overall patterns of human personality development, and pinned down according to the forces that produce them, is uncertain. The task is to integrate findings from the various longitudinal studies on a continuing basis, and to derive sound principles from them.

MORALS AND RELIGION

Adult Morals and Values

Stages of Moral Development. Moral, like mental, development is often portrayed as developing by stages. Kohlberg's well-known

theory (1975) depicts the development of moral reasoning in three stages. The first, or *preconventional stage,* involves egocentric, self-centered concepts of right and wrong. In the second, or *conventional stage,* characteristic of late childhood, the individual simply accepts and follows social standards of law and order.

In the third stage, the *postconventional stage,* an individual follows personal principles and abstract reasons. Originally Kohlberg believed that the final stage of *conscience,* or *principled orientation,* was reached by the end of adolescence. He later found support for the idea that moral development continues in adulthood (Bielby & Papalia, 1975). At a later time, Kohlberg added still further stages.

This theory, like cognitive stage theory, has undergone some revision. For one thing, it has been assumed that once people reach the advanced stages of moral development, they stay there forever. (For another, Kohlberg's concept of moral stages is based on having children of different ages react to certain moral dilemmas portrayed in stories representing values important to this society.) Authorities holding other values might interpret these moral dilemmas in such a way that a different picture of development emerges. (Besides, there is a gap between individuals' behaviors and their reactions to stories.) Nor can people be placed definitely in one stage or another, because responses often embrace several stages at the same time. (Note too, that moral development may not always proceed upward—sometimes people seem to regress to earlier levels) (Muson, 1975).

The most significant challenge to Kohlberg's theory, writes Damon (1983), is relating his conclusions to "real life morality" (p. 283). That is, do an individual's expressed moral views convert into behaviors? In addition, stage 5, representing orientation toward social welfare and stage 6, toward individual concerns, may represent individual differences rather than stages. A new stage 7 tries to answer the question: Why be moral? Does some transcendent morality of love govern which would cause one to recognize some natural universal law?

The Stability of Values. In general, concludes Troll (1975), most adults remain rather stable in their interests, values, attitudes, and feelings about themselves and others. True, "there are fluctuations in values, goals, attitudes, and interests over the adult years, [but] they seem more like waves on the surface of a slow-moving tide of historical shifts than like impressive individual changes" (p. 48).

Some values and interests are more variable among certain individuals and in certain areas of behavior than others. In a longitudinal study (Kelly, 1955) in which several hundred engaged couples were tested in their mid-20s and again 20 years later, the most stable measures were values; but even in this area about half the subjects indicated some change. The least stable measures regarded such matters as church, marriage, child-rearing, entertaining, housekeeping, and gardening. Few individuals felt the same way about these matters as they had two decades before; and the men had changed more than the women.

Adult Morality. Research regarding the status of moral development in adulthood is conflicting (Pratt, Golding & Hunter, 1983). Moral development in the elderly has been viewed sometimes as involving decline, with regression to more primitive modes of thought; at others it has been portrayed as a stage of more sophisticated use of cognitive structures. A study of three age groups—18 to 24, 30 to 50, and 60 to 75—supported the latter view, that people grow increasingly philosophical, mature, and consistent in moral judgment over the years. (A more reflective pattern of moral orientation was apparent with increasing age, especially among the 60- to 65-year-olds.) Otherwise, no important differences in moral development were found at different periods of adulthood.

Yankelovich (1984) describes how ethics and values have changed over recent decades. In the late 1950s people were quite conformist—women were wives, men providers, and success was defined in terms of status and wealth. In the 1960s and 1970s, after people voyaged to the moon, people felt a limitless power—they could do anything, and self-fulfillment and expressiveness became watchwords. In the 1980s Americans are sorting themselves out—they are pragmatic and reality oriented but there remains the residue of the 1960s. People now want both inner and outer success, but the criteria for success are more flexible. Americans want comfort, but not great wealth; they want material well-being and self-expressiveness, too. They are more accepting than formerly of diversity.

In the 1960s self-satisfaction was sought in terms of lack of restraint and doing things naturally, from seeking natural foods to sexual expression. Today, the "nose-to-the-grindstone" ethic is passé; there is still a self-orientation—but the search for pleasure is mixed with self-restraint, as in exercising and dieting. Success does not simply mean acquiring status, but suggests freedom and adventure. In general, it appears that needs must continuously be rediscovered and redefined by each generation in terms of current times and circumstance.

Today's middle-aged—at least the younger among them—moved into adulthood at a time when America's values were in a high state of flux, and in considerable measure, have remained so (Yankelovich, 1983). (Hence, it is more difficult than in years past to choose among competing, shifting values.) Even those chosen are fluid, not absolute—more appropriate for fast-changing times. Among the newer values are tolerance of broader options, sexual freedom, and less emphasis on self-denial for its own sake. Even individuals who have relatively firm values constantly mingle with those who do not and with types whose values are highly varied.

In addition, the middle-aged, the chief architects of society and its government, must be prepared to assess the values involved in current issues)(Pratt, Golding & Hunter, 1983). As citizens they must consider ever more complex ethical questions involved in public policy decisions. Is it ethical to place animal hearts in humans? Should marriage contracts have full legal support? However, despite some increase after youth in "philosophical reflectiveness," there appears to be little advance in level of moral and ethical judgment.

A Study of Moral and Religious Behaviors. (Among *Psychology Today* readers, who are mostly younger and better educated than the general population, more respondents admitted having cheated on their spouses than on expense accounts or tax returns) (Bassett, 1981). Eighty-four percent felt guilty about cheating on marriage partners, and 59% about their tax statements. Over half said that if their tax returns were audited they would very likely owe the government money. About 1 in 3 had deceived a best friend about something significant during the last year and 96 percent felt guilty about it. Amost half said that if they were driving a car and scratched another car in a parking lot they would simply drive away and leave no note. Although 89 percent said it was immoral, 26 percent would simply pocket the difference if a clerk gave them extra change. About a third, when asked their most difficult moral dilemma, described a situation involving sex, most often an extramarital sex affair. About 29 percent of the sampling said they would violate their own standards in 1 in 8 scenarios, 18 percent in two scenarios, and 16 percent in 3 or more. Few of the respondents appeared to lie or cheat frequently—54 percent who had padded their expense accounts and 73 percent who had deceived their friends said they had only done it once or twice. Yet 43 percent said they speeded almost every day, or even more often.

Among predictors of moral behaviors religious commitments and age seemed most important. Individuals judging themselves

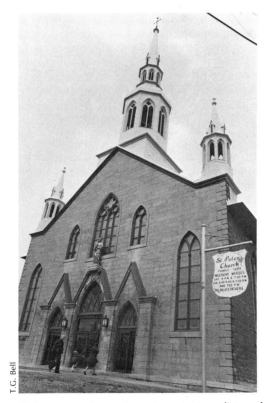

T.G. Bell

Religious commitment is an important predictor of moral development.

very religious were less likely to deceive their friends, have extramarital affairs, cheat on expense accounts, or even park where it was forbidden. Older people expressed stronger moral judgments than younger ones, reported fewer departures from their beliefs, and confessed fewer questionable behaviors. Even more important than age was religious commitment, which was the best predictor of institutional morality, including not cheating on taxes or expense accounts, using office supplies for personal reasons, using business phones for personal calls, or cheating on customs declarations. It had much less influence on personal issues such as not deceiving friends about things that were important, telling white lies, and cutting ahead in line. The impact of religion was especially strong regarding tax paying; nevertheless, it accounted for only about 10 percent in variance of replies. There were many antireligious people who scored as high on any of the scales as did the most religious. One may legitimately wonder to what extent the respondents either consciously or unconsciously departed from the truth.

Individual Testimony. In the process of life evaluation, people arrive at conclusions that together make up their philosophy of life. In the following, several middle-aged adults talk about the most important conclusions that they have reached about life.

FEMALE, AGE 58, MARRIED: Not to be afraid to take a chance, to explore every avenue. Nothing is impossible if you really want it.

FEMALE, AGE 61, WIDOWED: Don't cry—pray. Don't worry. Leave it up to God. All things are possible with Him. Accept people the way they are and don't be shocked if you are deserted by husband, children, or friends. We see it happen to others.

FEMALE, AGE 41, MARRIED: One's attitude toward life reflects an individual's state of mind. We have the capacity to control our minds and in turn, our lives. People need an honest identity. They must feel life has worth, or mental destruction is inevitable.

FEMALE, AGE 53, MARRIED: Your energy slows down after middle age. Make the most of every day. Thank God for the blessings we possess.

FEMALE, AGE 62, SINGLE: If you make mistakes, don't constantly wish you hadn't made them. Have a healthy self-respect, and also respect others to the extent that they deserve to be respected. Life has a lot to offer if you know how to avail yourself of opportunities.

Factors That Modify Values. Various factors cause people to accept certain values. One of these factors is historical. A recent trend in the middle years has been toward seeking greater self-realization, especially among more affluent people, who can afford the leisure time required for it. Earlier in life, and among those who are not well off financially, one's energies are consumed by the struggle to make a living. Later, as people's obligations decrease, they become more preoccupied with their inner selves and concerned with philosophical issues and personal insight (Lionells & Mann, 1974).

Values are also modified by the so-called *generations effect.* This means that cohorts of people who experience radically different life circumstances will have quite different values. (In other words, differences in values between generations are not the result of aging, but of the circumstances they experienced during unusually impressionable periods of their lives, especially adolescence and youth.) Psychologist Gerald Greenberg had commuters at a suburban train station in the Midwest fill out a brief questionnaire and found that older commuters more often supported traditional values. Those scoring highest on a Protestant ethic scale more often carried work with them on the train (Jack Horn, 1978).

An especially significant factor in shaping values is social class. About five years after ideas regarding sex, family, and life style are put forth by the middle class, working-class people take them over (Yankelovich, 1972). The working class differs in turn from the lower-lower class. Blue collar workers accept the dominant value system and have a great respect for such qualities as self-direction, obedience to parents, and the worth of work. Since they do essential work, they are genuinely integrated into the industrial society. Among the lower-lower class the situation is quite different. They have no real status in society and are alienated from it. They are often unemployed or on welfare. One spouse may simply desert the other rather than go through a socially approved divorce (Segre, 1975).

Values also differ across cultures even in Western countries (Western world's silent revolution, 1978). A study embracing the United States and ten Western European nations over the past decade disclosed a shift in focus away from values of materialism and physical security and toward a concern for self-expression and overall quality of life. This value change has been gradual but fundamental, and has created important changes throughout the Western world.

Values always reflect a country's overall culture. Today's technological society is often portrayed as unfriendly to the establishment and maintenance of stable values. LaMott (1978) declares that the United States is on the road to becoming a "modern Babylon" whose citizens' main aim is to make money and to enjoy the fruits of their earnings. Money occupies "the vacuum created by the wasting away of old commitments" (p.23).

Others are more optimistic about the times. According to Dubos (1976), "history shows that crises usually [result in] . . . new phases of creativeness . . ." (p. 172). A change in values is often wrongly identified with a dissolution of values. Crises pave the way for new values that will be more effective for guiding current behavior.

Relevant Research. Comparatively little research exists regarding the place of religion in the lives of adults. We do know that people of various religions give different weight to different kinds of behavior. We also know that family experience, age, and sex importantly modify religious behavior. Very religious parents are likely to have religious children, and if the parents are not religious their children are not likely to be either.

People over age 30 are somewhat more religious than those under that age. Of a national sampling in the 1970s, 45 percent of people under age 30 believed religion to be very important, 35 percent fairly important, and 5 percent not at all important. Of those 30 to 49 years old, 58 percent judged it very important, 30 percent fairly important, and 5 percent not at all important (Gallup, 1977). In the under-30 group, more interest in religion is shown in adolescence than in young adulthood. Young adulthood, in fact, has been called "the least religious period in life. Down-to-earth problems are too pressing at that time to permit much thought of such things" (Rogers, 1981b, p. 178).

Theologian James Fowler (1983) points out that religious experiences differ widely, and are quite personal. For example, conversion and born-again experiences vary. Some individuals experience a series of events that gradually lead them to a deepened sense of the significance of their religion; others make a radical shift over a short span of time. The latter type was Charles Colson, a President Nixon advisor who was convicted for his role in the Watergate affair. His values shifted from a focus on power to one of a quality of love that meant serving others.

Religions differ significantly in the values they attach to God, to society, and to the self, which are reflected in subtle differences in value orientations of their adherents (Christenson, Hougland, Gage & Hoa, 1984). The distinctive values of the various churches are reinforced "by the social dynamics" of individuals brought together because of their common religious heritage, social class background and desire to share their common beliefs" (p. 205). That is, the frequent interaction of persons of the same faith reinforces the importance of certain values. Hence, the relatively distinctive value systems of persons of different religions are products of both indoctrination and socialization.

In recent years, some people have shown an interest in alternative religions, a sign of the fluid state of society. Such religions symbolize a revolt against "dogmatism and cold morality; a strong disapprobation of the exploitive mentality, pollution of the biosphere, and the wasting of natural resources, whether by industry or through the country's endemic gluttony" (Ahlstrom, 1978, p. 28).

It is uncertain what part religion plays in adults' lives today, or even how people define religion. The vast majority say that religion is meaningful for them, but different people interpret both religious concepts and meaning in highly varied ways. While the vast majority express a belief in life after death there is a marked increase in the number of those who no longer hold such beliefs (Hertel & Nelson, 1974).

Individual Testimony. Here several middle-aged people indicate what religion means to them.

A great deal. It always has been and always will be of utmost importance in my life.

A small part—less than in the past. I feel at present that I am on trial. I feel better when I look around me and see some of my friends enjoying life with their husbands.

Religion is a big part. To live content and to find happiness, one must have faith, more now than ever before.

It has never meant anything at all, except negatively. I was compelled to go to Sunday School as a child and I hated it. I gave up any idea of God at about the time I found there was no Santa Claus—they were both just fantasies. However, religion contributes a great deal to many people—and I fully respect other people's religious beliefs.

SUMMARY

Middle age is a somewhat fluid concept. It changes over time as society revises its image of what people in these years are supposed to be like. What are now the middle years in the United States were once the later years for most of the population. This observation is still true in certain countries. The middle-agers' self-image reflects both society's notion of what people at this stage are like and personal experiences with aging.

The middle years have their own special significance. Life's goals are often redefined after the strains of childrearing and vocational competition are nearing an end and preparation for retirement is being made. They are years of accomplishment and of transition between the earlier and later phases. The younger middle-ager is a doer who controls society and serves as an advocate for children, youth, and the very old.

In later middle age, adults reevaluate their goals and life styles. They may not have achieved all their vocational objectives; but they are resigned, even relieved, that the struggle is over, and these years are often their best. They often settle back and enjoy a less hectic, fuller life.

In terms of both mental and personality characteristics, middle-agers fare well. They are no longer considered to be victims of an inevitable but slow decline in mental powers. While they may not learn or respond as speedily as younger people, their experience often more than compensates for whatever decline may occur. To what degree their mental prowess declines or improves depends largely on the quality of their experience over the years.

Middle-agers' personalities depend on the interaction of their genetic makeup with all their experience to date. Hence, personality is more an individual matter than a reflection of how long someone has lived. Nevertheless, since people at any stage in life do share the rewards and strains of that stage, they may display certain similar behaviors. For example, the mellowing of the middle years may result from no longer having to be concerned with childrearing and status seeking. Since life experiences vary according to sex, race, and social class, personalities at middle age will likewise vary.

Middle-aged peoples' morals and values, too, are based on foundations built up over the years. Since they have by now tested themselves in many situations, their values have stabilized somewhat. Nevertheless, regressions or progressions can still occur, depending upon the stability of one's life and one's continued capacity to grow.

Whatever religious views people have when they emerge into adulthood, they usually retain, in broad outline, in middle age. While the middle aged today are not as overtly religious as were their forebears, most of them profess that religion is important in their lives. While research on this topic is inadequate, it is clear that people vary greatly in their religious views and practices.

SUGGESTED READINGS

Baby boomers push for power. (1984, July 2). *Business Week*, pp. 52–59.

BRABECK, M. (1983). Moral judgment: Theory and research on differences between males and females. *Developmental Review, 3*(3), 274–291.

CHRISTENSON, J. A., HOUGLAND, J. G. Jr., GAGE, B. A., & HOA, L. V. (1984). Value orientations of organized religious groups. *Sociology and Social Research, 68*(2), 194–207.

EBAUGH, H. R. F., RICHMAN, K., & CHAFETZ, J. S. (1984). Life crises among the religiously committed: Do sectarian differences matter? *Journal for the Scientific Study of Religion, 23*(1), 19–31.

EDELSTEIN, W. & NOAM, G. (1982). Regulatory structures of self and "postformal" stages in adulthood. *Human development, 25,* 407–422.

FOWLER, J. (1983). PT Conversation. Stages of faith. *Psychology Today, 17*(11), 56–62.

HANDEL, A., KIMHI, S., & LEVIATAN, Y. (1983). Perceived retrospective change of self among the middle-aged in the kibbutz. *International Journal of Behavioral Development, 6*(2), 241–260.

HEDLUND, B. & EBERSOLE, P. (1983). A test of Levinson's mid-life re-evaluation. *Journal of Genetic Psychology, 143*(2), 189–192.

HOLAHAN, C. K. (1984). Marital attitudes over 40 years: A longitudinal and cohort analysis. *Journal of Gerontology, 39*(1), 49–57.

KAUSLER, D. H. & HAKAMI, M. K. (1983). Memory for activities: Adult age differences and intentionality. *Developmental Psychology, 19*(6), 889–894.

PRATT, M. W., GOLDING, G., & HUNTER, W. J. (1983). Aging as ripening: Character and consistency of moral judgment in young, mature, and older adults. *Human Development, 26*(5), 277–288.

SHAPIRO, D. H. & SHAPIRO, J. (1983). "Self-control" concerns for men and women: Refinement and extension of a construct. *Journal of Clinical Psychology, 39*(6), 878–892.

YANKELOVICH, D. (1984, December-January). Talking with Daniel Yankelovich. American values. *Public Opinion,* pp. 2–8.

CHAPTER SIX

Physical and Mental Health

PHYSICAL CONDITIONS AT MIDDLE AGE

Aspects of Physical Aging

Physical aging is basic to all aspects of the aging process (Palmore, 1974). It involves a progressive "decline in physiologic competence that inevitably increases and intensifies the effects of accidents, disease, and other forms of environmental stress" (Timiras, 1972, p. 465). Such changes are most commonly associated with old age, but are already apparent in the middle years. The changes described below are typical; however, the physical condition of middle-aged adults, like that of people of all ages, varies greatly.

Height and Strength. Changes in height and strength are easily recognized. Most people arrive at their full height by adult-

hood, although some reach it in their early teens and others in their 20s. Maximum strength is usually attained sometime between the ages of 25 and 30, after which there is a slow but steady decline, perhaps 10 percent, between the ages of 30 and 60. Much loss of strength occurs in the leg and back muscles, and less in the arm muscles. Exercise can help to retain, even to restore, strength to muscles that have not been used for a while; and individuals can help keep their strength in later years by exercising regularly. For some people, muscle tone declines in their 20s and for others not until their 70s (Timiras, 1972).

The Senses. All body systems, including the senses, become less efficient over the years. Lens changes in the eye occur over the years, and by age 50 almost everyone has at least a pair of reading glasses (Timiras, 1972). With regard to taste, there is little change up to age 60. The number of taste buds decreases from about 250 in young adults to fewer than 100 in 70-year-olds.

Nevertheless, food complaints of older persons, especially those in institutions, do not relate to taste receptors so much as to particular food preferences and emotional attitudes (Bischof, 1976).

Both speech and hearing decline somewhat with age. As the voice-producing apparatus ages, the vocal cords lose their elasticity, and the ability to speak clearly diminishes (Botwinick, 1973). All adults hear more poorly as they age, and high-frequency tones are not heard as well as lower ones (Marsh & Thompson, 1973).

Factors Relating to Health. A wide variety of factors relate to physical health, one being general quality of life. Not surprisingly, therefore, among the generally well-off participants in the Berkeley Longitudinal Studies, when between ages 42 to 50, over 80 percent believed themselves in good health although medical protocols accorded them

Many middle-aged individuals remain quite vigorous.

T.G. Bell

many and increasing numbers of illnesses and complaints. For women the chief source of health concern was their reproductive system and for men the digestive system. For both sexes acute complaints diminished and chronic complaints increased. The men reported more degenerative disease and the women more physical malfunctions. The women seemed more aware of any physical problems and were more resilient. An interesting finding was that responsible self-control and calm personality, even as early as 11 to 15 years of age, related to health in middle age (Bayer, Whissel-Buechy & Honzik, 1981).

Personality factors are also important to maintaining good health. In one year-long study, an individual's sense of low control over life events was associated with less self-initiated preventive health care, poorer self-rated health, more illness episodes, and more physician dependency (Seeman & Seeman, 1983). However, this effect may have been bi-directional. The sense of low control may have tended to produce ineffective health-related behaviors; or a history of illness may have led to a feeling of lower control.

Other researchers, too, have reported that personality characteristics modify the effects of life events on health (Rhodewalt & Agustadottir, 1984). Those with stress-resistant personalities, or hardiness, have high feelings of commitment, are responsive to challenge, and possess an internal locus of control—that is, they control events instead of being controlled by them. Others, the Type As, are similarly hardworking and committed, but prone to stress and coronary heart disease. Like hardy individuals, they have an internal locus of control, but experience greater anxiety in the resolution of problems.

Marriage, parenthood, and employment roles all relate to good health, and the married are healthier than any group of the unmarried. Among the unmarried the never married are healthiest, the widowed next, and the divorced or separated least (Verbrugge, 1983). The reasons for this finding are several: socially active people are healthier; those with jobs are less sensitive to symptoms; and healthy people are more likely to assume multiple roles.

Nevertheless, certain exceptions should be noted. Accumulated life roles relate to good health up to a point. Women with few or numerous life roles have poorer health than those with a moderate number. Also, women with young children have more physical symptoms than those with older children. Nor is the impact of particular roles equal. Employment relates more strongly to good health than do marriage or parenthood. Unemployed men, especially, tend to experience poor health. Parenthood has just a slight effect, much less than marriage. Finally, while these roles separately relate to good health, multiple roles appear not to relate to health, either positively or negatively.

Physical Disorders

Illness. Respiratory illnesses are the most acute ones for people of all ages. After about age 45, heart disease, high blood pressure, and arthritis begin to increase. Other conditions such as diabetes, chronic bronchitis, asthma, and hay fever do not increase consistently after 45 or 50 (Kimmel, 1974). The leading chronic conditions, and the sex most prone to them are as follows: "Diseases of heart, male; arthritis and rheumatism, female; lower-extremity impairments, male; back and spine impairments, male; mental and nervous conditions, female; hypertension without heart involvement, female; visual impairments, male; asthma, male" (Verbrugge, 1975, p. 401).

Of course, the status of illness in adulthood will change as medical and biochemical breakthroughs occur. For example, testosterone, the "male" hormone, increases the chance of high blood pressure, while the "female" hormone, estrogen, suppresses it. However, ways may be found of protecting

men from the effects of testosterone without simultaneously interfering with their sexual function (Kolbenschlag, 1976).

Heart Ailments. Heart conditions are especially common in middle age. High blood pressure, or *hypertension,* plays a direct role in the deaths of at least 60,000 Americans each year, most of them in their 50s. Heart disease is the leading cause of death for males over age 40 and the chief cause of permanent disability.

Heart disease strikes a million people each year, and 20 percent of these first attacks are fatal (Pardini, 1984). The chief factors contributing to heart disease are smoking, hypertension, a high cholesterol diet, and diabetes (The quality, 1980, p. 1). Hypertension, or high blood pressure, begins early and progresses over the years. About 1 in 6 persons has hypertension, which is a risk factor in coronary heart disease. About 1 in 3 persons over age 65 has high blood pressure. Overweight and obesity affect between 40 and 80 million people, who have a greater than average risk of hypertension, diabetes, and heart disease and other disorders.

In a study of men ages 39 to 59, those who were aggressive, competitive, ambitious, and restless were especially prone to coronary collapse. Those who were relaxed, patient, and unconcerned with high achievement were apparently immune to coronary disease, despite such high-risk factors as family problems, smoking, and lack of exercise (McQuade, 1972).

Arthritis and Osteoporosis. Another major crippler is arthritis, which assumes over a hundred types, and affects 31 million people, 4.4 million severely (Pardini, 1984). Osteoporosis, the gradual weakening and thinning of bones, is experienced by most adults. It contributes to hip fractures, which total 200,000 annually, mostly in older women. Shortened height and pain, accompanied by the so-called "dowager's hump" or hunchback, are the chief symptoms of advanced osteoporosis.

Among women bone loss proceeds at an annual rate of 0.75 percent to 1 percent beginning at ages 30 to 35, and increases to 2 to 3 percent in the half decade after menopause. Thus, women may lose 30 percent of their bone mass by age 70. Men also experience such decrease but at a slower rate, and for them it does not usually become serious before age 80. The causes of bone loss are not fully known, but factors associated with it are inadequate activity, inadequate absorption of calcium, loss of estrogen at menopause, and smoking. Possible factors may include high protein and caffein intake. Calcium loss increases with physical inactivity, including prolonged bed rest.

Menstruation and Menopause. Among the most grossly exaggerated views are those related to menstruation. A small minority of women do experience such problems, but for the others they are minimal. One such disorder that has attained considerable publicity because of its presumed relationship to committing crime is premenstrual syndrome—emotional and physical disturbance related to hormonal fluctuations and the menstrual cycle (Angier, 1982). Often progesterone is prescribed—and victims of PMS as it is called, often claim very positive results—but some experts question the effects of its long-term use; and others note that its effects are uneven.

Historically, views of menopause have been quite negative. During the nineteenth century physicians saw it as a sign of decay and sin; the Freudians labeled it a neurosis; and when synthetic estrogens became easily available in the 1960s, physicians portrayed it as a deficiency disease. More specifically, argues McCrea (1983), most male physicians interpreted women's main funtions as biologically destined, determined women's value by their fecundity and physical attractiveness, saw aging women as "useless and repulsive," and portrayed rejection of the traditionally feminine role as bringing about "physical and emotional havoc" (p. 111).

Therefore, despite much research linking estrogen therapy to cancer, vast numbers of physicians continued to prescribe estrogens and tranquilizers for women reporting menopausal complaints. They promised women that estrogen would help preserve their "cosmetic youth" and "unflagging libido."

Others call this disease model of menopause nonsense, pointing out that just 10 to 20 percent of women experience severe symptoms, which are generally temporary. Older women need less estrogen; and hormones from the adrenal glands at least partially compensate for the diminished ovarian production. Besides, such physical problems as may arise can be treated effectively, or perhaps prevented, by proper nutrition, exercise, and vitamins. The overwhelming majority of women proceed normally with their activities throughout the menopausal years. Hence, critics call the disease model, supported by physicians, sexist—a form of social control. If women are perceived as physically and emotionally handicapped during this period, they are deemed unable to compete on a par with men.

Overall Physical Status

General Vigor and Mortality Rate. Many middle-agers enjoy excellent health, chiefly because they have maintained sound health habits over the years. Indeed, overall physical condition declines so gradually that one may hardly be aware of it until many years have passed. After ages 50 to 55, for example, the eyes and teeth may deteriorate more rapidly than muscular strength. These differential aging processes have been neither adequately measured nor researched.

The health of both young and middle-aged adults has been steadily improving over the years, as we can see from the steadily declining death rates. The reduction for the elderly has been even more dramatic. Since deaths from accidents, especially automobile accidents, have sharply increased during this same period, the decline in nonaccidental deaths is even more dramatic (Golenpaul, 1977).

Current Trends in Health Care

Many people are assuming a more active and positive approach toward their physical and mental health. They are showing increased interest in health and health care and attaching greater values to physical well-being and personal fulfillment (Family health, 1979). Over a third of adults engage in planned exercise either daily or several times each week. One in four families report that they count calories more carefully and eat more nutritiously than they did in the past. Four in five realize the dangers of overmedication and favor greater openness about conditions such as alcoholism and mental illness.

Sex Differences in Longevity, Illness, and Disease. Females have higher illness rates, but die later than males; and the greater female longevity (life span) is increasing. In the past people conjectured that men have a shorter life expectancy than women because they smoke more, drink more, and experience greater life pressures (Greenberg, 1980). However, women may live longer because their bodies offer better protection against diseases and poor health habits because females' hormones help immunize them against certain diseases. Among people under age 70, men are eight times as likely to have heart attacks as women (Moriyamo, 1968). Certainly the higher rate of prenatal deaths and birth defects among males suggests that they are inherently less resistant to disease than females. In short, it may be that males "are physically sicker from both acute and chronic conditions, but . . . social and psychological factors enhance females' reports to such an extent that" they appear to be sick more often then men (Verbrugge, 1975, p. 399).

Women report more minor illnesses than do men. After reviewing the research, Gove and Hughes (1979) conclude that women's greater susceptibility to such conditions is real and derives from greater role demands and poorer mental health. Women's nurturant role requires that they be on duty around the clock. In general, their greater role demands and inadequate time for relaxation impact upon mental health.

Sex as a Factor in Mortality. Excluding dangers associated with reproduction, young women have biological advantages over young men and their longevity increases due to a lower incidence of cancer and heart disease (Gee & Veevers, 1983). Among younger adults the chief cause of death is motor vehicle accidents, and the rates are much higher for men. However, the gap has narrowed in recent years because women drive more than formerly. Controlling for distance driven, they have no more accidents than men and fewer fatal ones, presumably relating to males' greater risk-taking. However, women's own accident rate has increased. The incidence of suicide and homicide has increased among the young, with the rates for males increasing faster. Thus the widening gap in sex mortality ratios among young adults relates to social factors.

Among the old, medical advances have helped women significantly more. For all causes of death, except malignant neoplasms, death rates for both sexes have declined, but more for women, which suggests a healthier constitution. The greater reduction in women's cancer deaths is due partly to dramatic gains in treating uterine cancer. On the other hand, as the number of men who smoke has sharply declined, and more women smoke than they did years ago, the sex gap in mortality may decrease.

Gee and Veevers (1983) conclude that the male role has potentially hazardous effects on health. Males take more chances and, unwilling to acknowledge any weakness, they seek medical help less often than women. However, the male's image is less aggressive and risk-taking than formerly, and his death rate has declined. As women come to act more like men, their biological advantage may be modified.

Individual Reaction to Personal Health

In middle age most adults feel that their health is reasonably good, and they have their own ways of maintaining it. Here several individuals answer the question, "How good is your health, and what do you do to preserve it?"

FEMALE, AGE 51: I'd say my health was pretty good except for the usual aches and pains that come with old age.

FEMALE, AGE 54: It's good, except for arthritis. I watch my diet, keep active.

FEMALE, AGE 41: I am in good health. I take vitamins daily and am fairly active. My health currently is not of major concern.

FEMALE, AGE 53: My health is fair. I care for myself by rest and doctoring. I am concerned, as I have always been real active and ambitious. Now arthritis in my feet has slowed me considerably, as well as other minor ailments. It's hard to slow down as I have always hurried. I never want to be a burden to anyone.

MALE, AGE 53: I try to eat right—that is, a lot of roughage with bran. I take sitting-up exercises every morning. I drink only an occasional glass of wine and do not smoke. Consequently I feel good most of the time. My careful diet and daily exercise probably take me out of the average life-style category.

Awareness of Aging. One of the first ways that the middle aged become aware of physical aging is by witnessing heart attacks and episodes of cancer in their contemporaries. As a result, death and illness become less impersonal. Another reminder of passing years is gradual physical deterioration. Middle-aged individuals also experience a jolt when they recognize the gap between themselves and youth, often as a result of quite casual incidents, sometimes merely from

gazing at themselves in the bathroom mirror (McMorrow, 1974).

Hypochondria

Sometimes middle-aged individuals' preoccupation with their bodies assumes the form of *hypochondria*—an excessive preoccupation with the body and physical symptoms; the suffering and anguish, however, are genuine. Some individuals are "closet" hypochondriacs, who try to hide their condition, while others are overt ones, who may constantly seek help.

It is estimated that over half of all patients seen by physicians in the United States suffer from various degrees of hypochondria (Meister, 1980). Despite this estimate, there is "no evidence of ongoing research in hypochondria; and in the existing literature no agreement is to be found on any aspect of the condition. Much worse, the majority of physicians and therapists feel that seeing hypochondriacal patients is a waste of time and they do so very reluctantly" (p. 30). Most hypochondriacs are men, not women, contrary to what most doctors think. It relates to being exposed in early life to numerous complaints and evidence of illness, and to life-threatening experiences of various sorts.

HEALTH PROBLEMS OF SPECIAL INTEREST TODAY

Cancer

Few health topics have been publicized more in recent years than cancer, partly because of increasing numbers of malignancies and partly because we are just beginning to suffer the consequences of past exposure to cancer-causing agents. Two decades or more may be required after exposure to cancer causing agents before a malignancy appears (Schwartz, 1979). Nevertheless, much of the cancer phobia, compared to concern for other diseases, may be unnecessary. In 1978 about half of the 1,924,000 Americans who died were victims of cardiovascular disease, while heart disease claimed 728,190 lives and cerebrovascular diseases 172,520. About 20 percent of these deaths were from cancer. The two most common forms of cancer were tumors of the digestive system, and lung and other respiratory-system cancers, which accounted for 99,000. Another cause of similar magnitude was accidents, half of them involving motor vehicles.

Several factors help keep the incidence of cancer death in perspective. The most important reason for the increase over the past decade has been the aging of the American population. An American is less likely than a decade ago to die from a heart attack, stroke, or other related disorder; but in the end everyone dies from something. In consideration of that fact, the 2.5 percent increase in age-adjusted cancer death seems modest. Only lung cancer and related respiratory malignancies have risen sharply, and these forms of cancer could be sharply reduced by eliminating smoking.

Infertility

Several factors account for a woman's diminished fertility rate over the years. During the interim she may be exposed to diseases or conditions that are harmful to her reproductive system. Sometimes repeated abortions, venereal disease, or viral infections may scar and close off the tubes or impair reproductive organs—or aging alone may be the culprit. The ovarian chamber that releases the egg may be less sensitive to hormones, and the egg less easily fertilized; or the egg may not become fertilized at all or not implant in the uterus.

Some types of age-related infertility are treatable, depending partly on their severity, but half the women treated by drugs or surgery for endometriosis (a condition in which uterine lining cells grow outside the uterus and bleed every time the woman men-

struates) can become pregnant. Tubes that have been scarred and closed, have been opened 15 to 50 percent of the time.

Older women bear more children with birth defects related to genetic damage, since age affects the quality of the egg and the conditions under which it grows. On the other hand, American women are reducing the changes of such negative outcomes through their high protein diets, general fitness, and viral vaccines.

The Climacteric

In recent years much attention has been focused on certain physical phenomena of middle age, among them the *climacteric*. While the climacteric is a normal physical process, it can be a cause of stress. Since most people associate the climacteric with menopause, they believe it applies only to women. But many professionals feel it also happens to men. While *menopause* refers to the permanent cessation of menstruation due to aging, climacteric is a broader term that includes a complex of physical and emotional changes. Technically speaking, the term climacteric, but not menopause, is applicable to men, although the two terms are often used synonymously (Katchadourian, 1976).

The Female Climacteric. Females follow a general pattern of sexual maturing and decline. They are born with several hundred thousand ova, which begin maturing at puberty. About 300 to 400 cycles later, ovulation becomes quite erratic and finally stops. The period of menopause, which marks the end of ovulation, generally occurs around the age of 47, although it can occur before 45 and after 50 years of age. The cessation of ovulation results in infertility and decreased levels of estrogen. As estrogen levels go down, they no longer counter or offset the masculinizing effects of androgen, which continues to be produced by the adrenal cortex. In consequence a woman's voice becomes lower and her face hairier. The reproductive system atrophies. Other symptoms that may accompany menopause include headaches, dizziness, joint pains, palpitations, and hot flashes. While practically all women experience some of these symptoms in menopause, only about one in ten is significantly disturbed by them. Nor does menopause produce sexual dysfunction or apathy. Some women become more erotically responsive, because of the effects of androgen as well as because they are no longer concerned about the possibility of pregnancy.

In the mid-1960s, the so-called *menopausal syndrome* became highly publicized. A book called *Feminine Forever,* which sold 100,000 copies in its first 7 months, encouraged women to take ovarian hormones as long as they lived, which would help them keep the skin smooth and the breasts firm. Between 1967 and 1975 the use of estrogen therapy almost tripled in the United States, and over half of all menopausal and postmenopausal women were taking estrogen.

However, mounting research evidence cast doubt on the wisdom of estrogen therapy and on the existence of a menopausal syndrome. Most women in all cultures welcome menopause, and the only common symptom is flushing. Nor is there any particular association between menopause and severe depressive illness, or evidence that lower estrogen levels produce emotional disturbance. Estrogen may help to control loss of bone mass; however a combination of exercise, calcium, and vitamins is equally effective without the negative side effects. The use of estrogen therapy is associated with risk for "cancer, heart attack, high blood pressure, stroke, gall bladder disease, and probably a host of other metabolic disorders . . ." (Bruck, 1979, p. 46). However, physicians continue to prescribe it, for "the medical mind . . . fixes not on normalcy but pathology and its treatment . . ." (Bruck, 1979, p. 49). As a result, women have become dependent on physicians for a dangerous drug to which they may become psychologically addicted.

It is easy to exaggerate the effects of the menopausal period. After comparing the behavior of middle-class women with that of their husbands through two menstrual cycles, Alice Dan found no more variability in women's than in men's behavior. That is, the men too had their peaks and depressions. While the women's ups and downs related somewhat to the time between the end of one period and ovulation for the next, neither sex proved any more erratic or unpredictable then the other. Nor did Dan find any support for the common belief that there are behavioral deficiencies in women at any special time of the month ("Menstrual myths," 1977).

The Male Climacteric. The male climacteric is a somewhat vague concept, for the male reproductive function does not ordinarily diminish as abruptly as the female does. Beginning in middle age, there is more often a gradual decline in testicular function along with diminished fertility and potency. Some men produce viable sperm into their 70s; however, gonadal hormones begin to decline in the late 40s, after which time there is "a decrease in the viability of the sperm and firmness of the penis" (Bruck, 1979). The sperm ducts get narrower; and the prostate gland does not contract with the same speed or provide the same volume of spermatic fluid. As a result, the frequency of erection and ejaculation tapers off. On the other hand, males can remain sexually active, and sometimes even fertile, into old age. For both sexes, more direct tactile stimulation in sex is required; and putting the penis into the vagina is physiologically more difficult because the penis is less rigid, the vaginal opening smaller, and vaginal lubrication has decreased. Achieving orgasm also takes longer, and it may be less intense than before. Thus sexual activity changes but does not cease.

Alcohol, Smoking, and Drugs

Alcohol. Little attention has been paid to the problems of drinking, smoking, and pill-taking in adults, except for extreme cases. Although most people aged 50 to 70 drink less than younger people, it is unclear whether this difference relates to age. It could simply be a generational effect. That is, today's youth may drink more heavily in later years than older people do now, because of changed drinking patterns.

In order to dilate the arterial-venous system, some physicians prescribe a certain amount of alcohol (often wine) for older patients. Others caution against this practice, believing that it is addictive (Zimberg, 1974). In any case, as many as nine million Americans may be alcoholics, and alcoholism is among the nation's most serious health problems (Butler, 1975b).

Smoking. Most authorities stress the relationship of cigarette smoking to poor health and reduced longevity, especially when combined with such factors as obesity and inactivity. Since smoking satisfies certain needs, people who stop may instead become victims of hypertension or obesity (Botwinick, 1973).

While there is no doubt that cigarette smoking is harmful, the reasons are still not entirely clear. Forty percent of tobacco smoke consists of tar and nicotine, and about 60 percent of it is presumably harmless gases. Carcinogenic agents are presumed to be in tar, while nicotine causes harm to the cardiovascular system (Katchadourian, 1977).

More specific data about the effects of smoking can be summarized as follows: (1) Male smokers, as compared with nonsmokers, have a 70 percent higher death rate; and the risk for women smokers is significantly higher than for nonsmokers. (2) Risk of death from emphysema or chronic bronchitis is anywhere from 3 to 20 times greater, depending on amount smoked and age. (3) Coronary heart disease, the chief killer of both smokers and nonsmokers, occurs 70

percent more often among smokers. (4) The more cigarettes smoked daily, the higher the death rate—men who smoke fewer than 10 cigarettes a day have a 40 percent higher death rate than nonsmokers; those smoking 10 to 19 cigarettes a 70 percent higher rate; and those smoking 40 or more a day a 120 percent higher rate. (5) Young men's life expectancy is reduced on average by 8 years among heavy (over 2 packs a day) smokers and four years among light (less than half pack a day) smokers; and the risk is greater for those who smoke in earlier years. The risk is also greater for smokers who inhale. (6) Death rates for pipe and cigar smokers who normally do not inhale are not much higher than those of nonsmokers. (7) Individuals who have smoked heavily over long periods of time may reduce future risks by giving up the habit—unless disease has already taken hold.

Caffeine. A considerable amount of research relates to the possible effects of drinking excessive caffeine. A large intake has been related to various birth defects, cancers, and cardiovascular diseases, but the evidence is inconclusive. It is clearer that large intake may affect blood pressure and various physiologic and psychotropic variables. However, there seems to be no significant association between tea or coffee consumption and self-reported anxieties (Eaton & McLeod, 1984).

Drugs. Addictive drugs are dangerous because they require increasing dosages if they are to have any real effect, and withdrawal from them produces physiological and psychological stress. These effects do not ordinarily accompany the use of nonaddictive drugs such as aspirin. Drug addiction is more prevalent among young adults, especially those in large urban and suburban centers, because drugs are more available there. There is some decrease in drug use after young adults marry, especially after they have children (Henley & Adams, 1973). The long-term use of addictive drugs reduces longevity for several reasons, including general bodily deterioration, overdoses, or suicide. Hence there are few heavy drug users in the older age group (Capel et al., 1972).

The worst form of drug addiction among adults is excessive or unwise pill-taking, and this trend is increasing. Since little is known about its long-term effects, this habit might prove hazardous. Among the most popular pills are tranquilizers, which are widely prescribed, most often to women. Women are far more likely to go to a physician for any disorder than are men, and are often given tranquilizers or antidepressants to help them deal with current difficulties (Scarf, 1979a). In fact 70 percent of persons using mood-altering drugs are women. Between the ages of 30 and 40, men's use of such drugs increases to 12 percent, females' from 23 to 32 percent. About a third of all women in this age group used prescription drugs to treat their moods. These drugs are commonly prescribed by family physicians or internists—85 percent of persons using such drugs have never consulted a psychiatrist.

Nutrition, Obesity, and Exericise

Nutrition. Some authorities view Americans' dietary habits as alarming; others perceive some recent improvements. Keen observes that in the 1970s "the average American was consuming 125 pounds of fat, 250 pounds of meat and poultry, 130 pounds of refined and processed sugar and 295 12-ounce cans of soda per year," a diet increasingly characterized by fast foods and highly refined carbohydrates (The pure, 1978).

However, in comparison with a decade ago, Americans now consume less refined sugar, and have reduced their cholesterol consumption by eating fewer eggs, less butter, and greater quantities of chicken, fish, and oleomargarine. These changes in eating habits may have helped reduce the number of deaths from heart attacks and strokes. Much of this improvement is due to gen-

erally better eating and living habits, including reduced incidence of smoking, more regular exercise, a 50 percent decrease in consumption of animal fat, and more attention to hazards of high blood pressure.

The growing concern over proper nutrition has encouraged the growth of varied diet cults as well as government-sponsored research. Keen (1978) observes that "America is in the middle of a nutritional revolution" (p. 62), and he warns that zealous nutritionists may turn the search for health foods into "a neurotic life style" (p. 66). [The most "explosive event in recent nutritional politics" has arisen from certain dietary goals set by the Senate Select Committee on Nutrition and Human Needs (p. 65).] This controversial advice, which recommends semi-vegetarian diets, brings the government close to assuming a "nutritional activist position" (p. 65). Its goals include increased consumption of fruits, vegetables, and whole grains and decreased consumption of refined and processed sugars and foods high in total fat and cholesterol.

Biochemist Roger Williams stresses the idea of *biochemical individuality*. While people share certain nutritional needs, they differ with respect to optimum amounts of separate nutrients. Some persons require two to ten times more of a particular nutrient than others. The determination of each individual's optimum dietary needs is "clearly the wave of the future for nutritional research" (Keen, 1978 p. 77). Meantime Williams suggests that people diversify their diets, avoid refined foods, limit the use of alcohol and sugar, supplement their diet with an effective mineral and vitamin formula, and experiment in order to determine what foods are best for themselves individually.

Obesity. The problem of obesity involves not only diet, but genetics, biochemical individuality, and emotional factors, in varying proportions. Dr. Theodore Van Itallie, head of the nation's first large-scale obesity research center at St. Luke's Hospital in New York City, cites certain facts known so far about extreme overweight: (1) Obese people's main problems are to get their weight down to desirable levels and to maintain that weight once it has been achieved. The recidivism rate is about 70 percent—obese persons are less apt to be "cured" than cancer victims. (2) Obesity derives from various combinations of emotional, genetic, environmental, metabolic, and other factors as well as patterns of eating behavior. Some people have a more difficult time keeping their weight down than others. (3) Treatments involve various combinations of diet and behavior therapy. It is best first to go on a low-calorie or even liquid diet in order to lose fat rapidly before growing completely discouraged. (4) Group therapy is especially helpful in such problems because people can provide support to one another. (5) People differ greatly in the nature of their food problems. Some may be especially sensitive to certain foods; others may have learned to eat as a means of relieving anxiety. It is unclear just how or to what extent differences in basic physiological mechanisms account for differences in weight.

The research suggests that truly obese persons and heavy smokers have little chance of breaking the habit, even after psychiatric treatment (Schachter, 1982). However, the prospects for improvement or success may be greater than that suggests. For one thing, most inferences regarding the effects of therapy are drawn from single attempts to cure the habit—multiple efforts might produce better results. Another factor is that some studies have focused on persons with severe problems—those with lesser ones have greater success. Also, there is little research concerning people who attempt to break these habits without professional help; yet these persons have a better record of success. This writer conjectures that persons inclined to take the bull by the horns are more likely to possess the will power and self-assurance to stick to a program.

Margules (1979) believes that "a previously unknown branch of the autonomic nervous system—the endophinergic division—helps trigger the urge to overeat typical of obesity. The effects of this division are counterbalanced by another hitherto unrecognized division of the autonomic nervous system, the endolozonergic division. Normally these two divisions balance each other; however, when the balance slips, for reasons not yet understood, the endorphinergic dominance may tend to produce obesity and various other 'addictionlike attachments'; and the same dominance may also stimulate hyperactivity, anorexia, and hypersensitivity" (p. 136).

Among all age groups in America, the numbers of those exercising is increasing. The surge began in the 1960s; and in 1971 47% of all Americans were exercising, double the number of a decade before. However, such exercise declines with age, with almost 60 percent of those over age 45 reporting no regular exercise.

The U.S. Surgeon General summarizes the values of exercise, saying that it makes people feel better, possess more energy, and need less sleep. More specifically, dynamic aerobic exercises—or large-muscle activities performed rhythmically, at sufficient intensity—help to reduce the risk of cardiovascular disease. Such activities also improve muscular endurance, strength, flexibility of joints, balance, coordination, and agility. To take care of such factors a balanced program is best, geared to individual needs and physical status.

Exercise is especially helpful in relation to certain major disorders, including coronary heart disease, hypertension, arthritis, and osteoporosis, or bone loss. Exercise also plays a role in reducing mild depression. Regular exercise has a certain tranquilizing effect for persons of all ages.

There is no one complete consensus on the proper amount of exercise. Some experts recommend an hour of brisk walking every other day, or a minimum of 20 to 30 minutes. Exercisers are advised to be realistic, to start slowly, to begin the day's exercise with warm-ups, and to cool down afterward (Pardini, 1984).

One negative aspect of the current obsession with exercise is that many people do not know the basic health rules relating to it. For example, problems may arise when an individual exercises strenuously and stops abruptly, with no cool-down period (Exercise peril, 1984).

A Brief Comment

In concluding this discussion of physical health in middle adulthood, a few general observations are in order: (1) It is essential not only to maintain one's health, but to assure that it is good enough to support a rewarding life style. (2) Because of constant medical and biochemical advances, the public should be more effectively educated in order to make better use of newly emerging knowledge. (3) People should integrate their knowledge about health with other kinds of information so that they can adjust their lives accordingly. For example, what are the hazards to family nutrition when both partners work? In many cases childless couples develop unhealthy eating habits. (4) Exercise is an especially important factor because it improves strength and the circulation to cardiac muscles. Yet what may be good for one individual or group in terms of climate, exercise, and diet may be poor for others. (5) As longitudinal data clarify the long-term effects of various health habits and remedies, such information should become a part of health instruction at all levels. Since present-day adults will be living longer than ever it is important that they maintain a life-span view of their health, instead of the all too

common present orientation (If you live, 1983).

Note that many physical conditions that threaten adults today may succumb to new treatments (Ten forces, 1984). Already pacemakers, new drugs, open heart surgery, and emphasis on exercise and diet, have reduced deaths from stroke and heart disease by 40 and 25 percent respectively, just since 1970. Nor is every cancer patient looked upon as doomed to die. Almost half (48 percent) of such persons now live at least 5 years after treatment, and two-thirds of those with certain major types are now cured. Transplants of new hearts, kidneys, and corneas have rapidly increased, and where human organs are unavailable, artificial devices such as artificial hip joints may be used.

Looking ahead, more miracles are possible, some certain. By the year 2000 it is predicted that the cause of hardening of the arteries which produces heart attacks, will be found. Lasers that vaporize the plaque produced by hardening arteries will decrease the need for coronary bypass surgery. Artificial kidneys, electrically powered limbs, even artificial ears and eyes, are being researched and developed.

The gloomy side of this picture is cost—expenses of health care and research are soaring. Ethical issues arise: Will not this expense create a two-tiered society of those who can afford these modern miracles and those who cannot? If resources are insufficient to go around, who should be the beneficiaries?

Four elements contribute to causes of death, notes Michael (1982). About half of all mortality may be due to unhealthy behaviors or life styles, 20 percent to environmental factors, 20 percent to human biological factors, and about 10 percent to inadequate health care. Since unhealthy behaviors are not "disease-specific," the main focus should be on behaviors such as overeating or smoking, that lead to disease. Individuals with a specific disease, such as diabetes, will require specific modifications in life- and work-styles. Another factor in mortality, environmental hazards, accrues mostly from urbanization and industrialization. For example, certain pesticides can damage the functioning of the central nervous system. Middle-aged people must, as citizens, decide how the value of jobs and business should be balanced against the conservation of health.

EMOTIONAL HEALTH

Emotionally Healthy Behavior

Criteria. There is no general definition of emotionally healthy behavior. Smithson (1974) gives these criteria: being independent and being able to accept reality, adapt to change, respond sensitively to others and handle feelings of hostility. Emotionally healthy persons are usually distinguished by those characteristics.

They accept their right to be human and enjoy life. They express normal anger or fear without feeling guilty about it. They control their emotions, rather than being controlled by them. They experience inner freedom derived from confidence in their ability to utilize emotions properly. Emotionally healthy individuals can express feeling in whatever gradation is appropriate. If doors are stuck, they do not smash them down. Such individuals keep things in perspective and do not constantly seek molehills to make into mountains (Rogers, 1977, p. 108).

Common Problems of Middle Age

Impending Old Age and Changing Physical Image. There are increasing physical disabilities and anxiety over whether enough money has been saved for the years ahead. There is also the problem of adjusting to one's own aging physical image, and to others' perceptions of that image. Some individuals almost panic; others who have long

since learned to accept rather than deny the inevitable, accept it, often with a sense of humor. One 62-year-old man, upon being shown a picture that his son had taken of him on vacation, jokingly asked, "Who is that old man?"

In general those individuals who take special pride in their strength or looks begin aging psychologically as soon as they perceive their bodies aging; while those whose self-concept depends on nonphysical characteristics such as intelligence or vocational competence, may feel young until relatively late in life. In many cases, the former try desperately to remain young-looking (Troll, 1975).

The middle aged are keenly aware of the importance of their physical image; and they may resort to various devices—wearing wigs, paying unusual attention to attire and grooming, and dieting to achieve a more youthful figure. Facial surgery may be undertaken for reasons of personal vanity in order to avoid self-consciousness or unwelcome attention, to gain social acceptance, or to increase opportunities for vocational advancement (Belfer, Mulliken, & Cochran, 1979).

Vocational Problems. The middle aged also experience vocational problems, which will be discussed in greater detail in a later chapter. Note here that a major source of stress is making a living in a competitive society. (Most adults endlessly struggle to improve their financial position, even after they are already well off.) The resultant stress becomes a cause of physical problems, depression, and excessive drinking (Kiev, 1974). During the height of the space program at Cape Kennedy, young men experienced a higher rate of divorce and alcohol consumption than their age and numbers would justify, apparently because the project required an almost frenzied pace of production and participants were "rewarded" with dismissal once the project was completed. Three young men who had worked especially hard to obtain a space agency contract for their company died when they learned that competitors had won out (Fisher, 1979). Autopsies of space workers' heart muscles disclosed a type of damage different from that ordinarily associated with heart attacks. It seemed that the heart had been precipitated into "overdrive" by "a deluge of chemicals that transmit nerve impulses" (Bishop, 1979a, p. 28). People at middle age may also go through a period of indecision as to whether they should retire. They may feel pressure from impatient young workers who are trying to push them out.

Sex-Related Problems. Other problems in middle age relate to sex, pregnancy, and menopause (Kisker, 1977). Extramarital sex may cause stress, though less than it did formerly because of changing attitudes and the pill. Pregnancy and childbirth may also produce stress among women in their late 30s or early 40s, and the incidence of mental illness following this period is relatively high (Cohler et al., 1974). Stress may also be connected with abortion, particularly among women with ambivalent feelings about it.

Health-Related Problems. Another threat to happiness is ill health, especially from late middle age on. The potential for more chronic disorders increases with age. Any part of the body affected by surgery is a potent cause for stress. Anxiety is unusually great when it involves the eyes or vital organs, especially the heart. Reactions to open-heart surgery include hallucinations, delirium, and mood disorders (Braceland, 1974). Gynecological operations may also prove emotionally traumatic; for example, removal of the uterus is associated with a loss of femininity. Those women who deliberately choose hysterectomy as a means to avoid pregnancy show few, if any, negative symptoms; but women who have experienced

therapeutic hysterectomies may feel an impaired sense of femininity.

Matters of Situation and Timing. The impact of any particular event or circumstance depends on when and in what total context it occurs. Divorce impinges more heavily on the housewife with six children than on the one with no children and a job. An event that might be handled with comparative ease becomes the straw-that-breaks-the-camel's-back in an already tense situation. Stress-related illnesses and deaths are especially common when death-producing events pile up during the same period. Many soldiers in World War II experienced "combat exhaustion," which was seen to be due to a combination of physical exhaustion and the loss of social support when about two-thirds of their companions had been wounded or killed. The cumulative effect of many small stresses may also produce severe stress (Bishop, 1979a).

Individual Testimony. Individual middle-agers report quite varied problems, as indicated by these answers to the question: *"What are the most serious problems that you face at the current stage of your life?"*

FEMALE, AGE 54: Trying to save enough so that when I retire I won't have to depend on my children.

FEMALE, AGE 61: I don't feel that I have any serious problems. Or maybe at this age I have learned that things work out.

FEMALE, AGE 53: Health problems. Since I reached 50 years of age, I have many ailments.

FEMALE, AGE 62: Trying to sort out from my many life goals those most worth doing; I've roughly a couple of thousand years' worth of projects in mind and somewhat less time than that for doing them.

MALE, AGE 55: Lack of energy. I do not experience financial problems. We live within our means. No foolish spending.

Stress

There is plentiful evidence of stress in America today, stress being the "body's non-specific response to any demand placed on it, whether that demand is pleasant or not" (Cherry, 1978). Four out of five adults indicate a need for less stress in their daily lives. More adults now experience difficulty in coping with everyday problems than just a few years ago (Family health, 1979). Besides problems relating to their specific situations, they absorb the major tensions of the times. Every age has its own anxieties. While there is the threat of nuclear holocaust today, there was the threat of plague some centuries ago.

For many adults these days a major cause of stress is constantly feeling under time pressure. According to the Survey Research Center at the University of Maryland the number of people who feel rushed all the time increases steadily until middle age, from 27 percent among those ages 18 to 29 to 39 percent for those ages 40 to 49. After that age the figures drop to 21 percent for those ages 50 to 59, and to 13 percent for those ages 60 and older. The number of those always feeling rushed rises with income until the middle income range is reached and then declines (Harris, 1981).

It is still unknown just how mental stress produces physical damage in the body (Bishop, 1979a). It is known that when an individual perceives a threat, portions of the nervous system become very active, producing an accelerated heart beat, such as in stage fright. There are also changes in body chemistry such as rising cholesterol levels. Certain drugs that block nerve impulses to the heart from the "emotional" layers of the brain may reduce stress, as indeed may meditation.

Hans Selye, the world's most famous stress researcher, suggests various ways for adults to deal with stress. People should determine their own stress level in order to decide whether they should lead relatively more active or restrained lives. They should choose goals that are genuinely their own and not imposed on them by someone else. They should build themselves up by becoming essential to others and by earning their good will (Cherry, 1978, p. 71).

The most commonly used stress inventories have a major flaw, in that they fail to take into account wide individual differences. Some individuals are race horses who thrive on stress and a fast-paced, vigorous life style; others are happier in a quiet and tranquil environment.

Depression

Over 250,000 persons are diagnosed as clinically depressed and are hospitalized each year; another 200,000 are treated for depression as outpatients (The depression epidemic, 1979).

Most people from time to time feel depressed, about 1 to 2 percent chronically so. While a measure of relief can be obtained from life-style engineering, particular genes may predispose some people to feel depressed (Researchers find, 1981).

Fifteen percent of the chronically depressed commit suicide, and far greater numbers attempt it. Depressions are milder today because people less often feel that they have no way of escaping it. While divorce, for example, produces unhappiness, many who go through it experience only mild depression because they see a way out. Formerly, when divorce was socially disapproved, an unhappy spouse who felt trapped in an unbearable situation might feel severely depressed. The individual who sees no light at the end of the tunnel and lacks any viable alternatives may simply commit suicide.

Psychiatrist Frederic Ilfeld found that most depression is caused by "everyday hassles"

(Connubial depression, 1977, p. 52). The most important factors relating to strain, from highest to lowest, were: marital problems, parenting, child-care burdens, and work and financial problems. Single men found social strains to be more depressing than did single women. Neighborhood problems had little to do with depression.

Also more women over age 65 are in mental institutions simply because women live longer. Moreover, to be diagnosed as depressive one must go to a psychiatrist, and women are more likely to admit that they have problems and to seek professional help. Males, because they are taught not to acknowledge any inability to deal with problems, might consult a physician about a digestive complaint but fail to admit to emotional problems that might have contributed to the disorder. That is, the male, having been taught to suppress feelings of unhappiness and weakness is more reluctant to assume "the sick role" (Scarf, 1979b).

Various factors distinguish between those who react to loss and separation or other trauma through deep depression and those who make normal progress toward recovery. The majority of people cope pretty well with such disturbing family experiences as the death of a parent or a child; and 85 percent of those who are widowed and bereaved are back to normal within a year. The differences in adaptability may be due to genetic characteristics, circumstances that lower self-esteem, self-perceived ability to cope with difficulties, and the presence of family members and friends. Attachments to others are important for an individual's sense of self-worth. Certain drugs or biochemicals may temporarily reduce feelings of depression, as indeed may two or three martinis, through alterations in the nervous system (Roots of depression, 1979). However, the only lasting remedy is by altering the negative aspects of one's situation or somehow achieving a more positive perception of them.

The Midlife Crisis

Conflicting Evidence. Life is often portrayed as involving a series of crises that are presumably experienced by most people at certain periods. Midlife is often portrayed as a critical turning point, a time of transition. In his mid-40s Charles Dickens left his wife and took a 19-year-old mistress. Freud, Jung, Goya, Gandhi, and Eugene O'Neill all experienced crises around age 40, from which they emerged as creative geniuses. For others, crises merged into decline. William Shakespeare is said to have ceased marital sex before age 45 and to have retired from work at 45 (Midlife, 1983).

For every man who suffers from depression, two to six times as many women do, for reasons as yet unclear. It may be argued that male psychotherapists and physicians are more likely to label women as depressives; also women are more likely to acknowledge feelings of depression. Others feel that women are more depressed, not because of anything inherent in being female, but because they must accept and adapt to the rules of a male-dominated society. After studying 553 middle-aged women hospitalized for depression Pauline Bart, psychiatrist, nominated as a prime candidate for such a condition the "super-devoted" mother who gives her whole adult life to her children, reserving no role for herself to fulfill her own special potential (Experts, 1981).

Most observers agree that a midlife change—sometimes called a "crisis"—occurs, although they differ about when it occurs. Some observers portray the crisis as involving a reevaluation of one's life pattern; others describe it as a decrease in life satisfaction and the ability to cope. Some of them believe its effects to be temporary, others see them as irreversible.

Men, especially, are presumed prone to such crises. Farrell and Rosenberg (1981) estimate that about half of all males, ages 39 to 43, undergo a midlife crisis or slump. The specific ways they demonstrate this decline vary according to their earlier life patterns. This depressive experience is "filled with images of death, illness, disability and decay," and feelings of "diminution of self." A man's relationship to his family changes, too. He has been so work-involved he has failed to develop supportive affective bonds, even within his own family. The children and wife he once dominated have begun to assert themselves—he is no longer undisputed head of the house.

Reactions to such crises vary somewhat with social class. Middle-class men deny their distress, despite manifesting symptoms obvious to those around them. They even refuse to acknowledge they are middle-aged, claiming instead that they are in their prime. Working-class men freely express their anxieties and resentments, placing the blame not on themselves, but on their families, neighbors, and work organizations. Men of both classes avoid deep personal explorations because they were socialized into the male pattern of self-sufficiency.

Various factors can precipitate midlife crises. Upper- and middle-class professionals, especially, may not have met their high expectations. Blue-collar men may worry about how long they will be able to continue in their jobs, which often require considerable stamina. Circumstances that may trigger crisis are deaths of parents and friends, signs of personal aging that enhance feelings of vulnerability, or even achieving goals only to find them disappointing. Or a couple may have grown apart and find each other boring and unattractive (Midlife, 1983).

The idea of the age period 40 to 50 as being a crisis has derived mainly from clinical studies and nonrandom populations of subjects (Mortimer & Simmons, 1978). Systematic studies are raising questions about the generality or severity of such crises (Harry, 1976). Unusual stress or redirection of goals

at this stage of life are more common among the higher-level managerial and professional persons (Kanter, 1978). At this level personal involvement is high and individuals have their own timetables for progress toward goals. However, most people's aspirations gradually contract to match their achievements without undue turmoil or distress.

The vast majority of commentary and research regarding midlife crisis relates to men. A significant feature of men's midlife transition, observers Levinson (1977), is that those who have worked very hard at their jobs and supported the values of their culture come to question both the meaning of their work and their values.

Contrary to earlier views, most women are relatively content during the empty nest stage, after the children leave home. Questionnaire data obtained from 232 married women, ages 46 to 61, all graduates of a large mideastern university, disclosed them to be generally quite happy (Black & Hill, 1984). Nine in ten judged their work, marital satisfaction, and overall contentment favorably. After having fulfilled their childrearing obligations they could now "explore new self-satisfying alternatives of careers and life styles" (p. 289). The small number of exceptions, who were quite unhappy, represented all levels of employment and empty nest status.

One cannot generalize from this study that most women at this age stage are well adjusted. For one thing, adjustment related not so much to level of employment or empty nest status as to other factors. These included varied meanings of the empty nest status and career advancement to individual mothers and their ability to cope. In addition, these women were all from intact homes, well-educated, and had at least one child.

Psychologist Wallace Denton theorizes: The middle aged undergo a grief process similar to that experienced when a loved one dies. He has noticed this phenomenon in individuals aged 30 up through age 55, or whenever they decide they are becoming middle aged. The first stage is one of denial; individuals are preoccupied with their appearance (and try to prove that they can do whatever they did when they were age 21.) They develop an obsession over losing weight, adopting new hair styles, and displaying the latest clothing. They may express their need to remain young through extramarital affairs or a revived sexual interest in their spouse. (Women more often engage in extramarital affairs between ages 36 and 40 than any other period, out of a preoccupation with remaining youthful and a need to prove their continued desirability.) The second stage is anger; they regret what they have not done, and take their anger out on the world in general, especially on young people. In the third stage, depression, they experience a letdown and just "run out of steam" (p. 355). Finally comes acceptance, when the middle aged come to terms with themselves; some even conclude that this stage is exciting and rewarding. Now they are old enough to "appreciate the various dimensions of life, but are still young and healthy enough to enjoy life thoroughly" (Middle-age grief process, 1978, p. 355).

During the late 30s, many men feel that they have failed merely because they have not accomplished all that they set out to do. In this sense, every man fails in his career, observe Berger and Wright (1978), and his midlife crisis becomes a family crisis. Having failed to achieve the successes in the world of work that he had dreamed of, the man now turns to his family for consolation. During this sample period, the wife may begin looking outside the home for satisfactions, and the children may be preparing to leave home. Hence, the man may not receive the support that he needs.

Rosenberg and Farrell (1976) feel that the middle-aged male's crises are intensified by demands made on him by the outside world. At the same time he has to be a role model for his maturing children, who are having identity conflicts like his. While his own physical strength is declining, he is reaching the height of his personal and social power. On the job, in the community, and in his family, he is expected to demonstrate a commitment and strength appropriate to his status. He cannot give expression to his conflicting feelings about arriving at middle age, because that would undermine his image of stability. At the same time his own father is getting older, losing his status, and giving up his dominant roles in family and society. The middle-aged son now assumes the status of a patriarch. He is the family head in the eyes of the larger culture, and "the rock" that supports the family network. This new role symbolizes the standard against which his adequacy is measured by both himself and others. At one time he may have wanted to outdo his father; but now that he is on top, his "victory" holds no meaning for him. By now his father arouses his sympathy, so that any enjoyment the son might feel at his own success is tinged with guilt. Now that he is in a position of control, he cannot admit feeling vulnerable or wanting to lean on others. Thus, "like an adolescent, a middle-aged man is confronted by biological, status, and role changes" that make him try to redefine who he is. Unlike an adolescent, he is not allowed to take time off to explore these questions.

By contrast, in their study of middle-aged San Francisco couples, Lowenthal and Chiriboga (1972) found no evidence of a midlife crisis. Many couples had critical problems, but these were a continuation of past ones rather than new developments. Most of these couples felt considerable relief after the youngest child left home; and when asked to name the most significant turning points of their lives, they often mentioned such events as completing their education, obtaining their first job or a better job, getting married, and having children.

The Meaning of the Midlife Crisis. In addition to conflicting evidence regarding the midlife crisis, it is also unclear what significance such a crisis has. At best, it can be liberating, for it allows a person "to take a fresh look at himself and his environment and emerge with a kind of wisdom, maturity, and insight which is beyond the grasp of youthful capacity. At worst, the crisis is kept from becoming fully conscious and results in destructiveness toward both the self and others." Attitudes may become more rigid, and people may feel a "dominating need for others to confirm the very mode of being that is experienced as painful" (Rosenberg & Farrell, 1976, p. 157).

Factors That Relate to Mental Health

Gender Differences. Analyses of mental health data indicate that if all forms of mental illness are included, such as alcoholism, a commonly overlooked category, women are no more disturbed than men. However, women do suffer from more particular disabilities such as neurotic disorders, functional psychoses, and depression (Barnett & Baruch, 1978). Whether women's quality of life is lower than men's is unclear (Barnett & Baruch, 1978). Campbell, Converse, and Rodgers (1976) found no proof that women's lives are any less satisfying or rewarding than men's. However, other studies indicate considerably more distress among women. Among groups of men and women facing life transitions—high-school seniors, newlyweds, empty-nest couples, and preretirement couples—Lowenthal, Thurnher, and Chiriboga (1975) found that middle-aged women were the unhappiest. They were lowest in life satisfaction, highest in despair, most pessimistic, and held the most negative feelings toward their spouses.

Occupation is a common source of stress among men, especially among some personality types. When a certain public utility undertook a job evaluation program that resulted in a large number of either promotions or demotions among its upper-level executives, certain of the threatened men took their situation in stride and others did not. The most highly stressed executives appeared to have some aversion to change and lacked the sense of control over their lives that their healthier counterparts had. When faced with stress, they tended to become depressed, to withdraw, and to reduce their other activities. The hardier executives had a greater feeling of control over their lives, and they saw change as a challenge. They could perceive being overlooked for promotions in terms of their entire lives, and had an overall sense of "vigorousness toward all aspects of life" (Bishop, 1979, p. 28).

Marital Status and Employment. Different kinds of adults vary in terms of life satisfaction and mental health. Some individuals who report satisfaction nevertheless lead very dull, unself-fulfilling lives. They may have developed defense mechanisms that make them blind to their own deficiencies or the emptiness of their lives. For example, married women express greater satisfaction than single women, but single women are emotionally healthier (Campbell, 1975).

The emotional health of housewives depends chiefly on the women's own personalities, goals, and individual situations. In a comparison of domestically oriented women and career-oriented women, both groups indicated a high degree of self-esteem and self-love; however, significant differences were found in measures of autonomy and self-control (Hooper & Traupmann, 1983). The domestics reported much poorer health for the preceding years as well as certain more depressive symptoms including trembling, heart pounding, sleep difficulties, and lack of energy. Such women, after the children left home, may have wanted to spread their wings and engage in more self-fulfilling activities, yet did not because of guilt feelings about evading family responsibilities. They then felt depressed because they could not bring themselves to break out of their world.

The career-oriented women (who had returned to school) were also higher on the spontaneous self, or autonomy factor. The domestics let things happen to them; the students were take-charge people. However, the students did more often feel pushed, because of role strain—being homemakers, students, and sometimes workers, all at once. On the other hand, not all American housewives are unhappy. An important determinant is whether or not the woman wants to work. In a study by Fidell and Prather, many housewives proved healthy, comfortable, and happy in their roles because they did not want to work. They had happy marriages, felt in control of their lives, and had better physical and mental health than working wives. The working wives were less happily married, but felt more competent and had greater self-esteem (Tavris, 1976).

Social Class. Another factor in mental health is social class. Sheehy (1976) concluded that members of the well-educated middle class have the greatest number of options and the fewest obstacles to choosing their life styles. They are not hampered by upper-class traditions that tend to predetermine life styles and result in a certain inertia. Nor are they frustrated by the lack of higher education and economic disadvantages of lower- or working-class people. As they move from one life period to another, they experience a greater feeling of flux but have a greater chance for variety in their development.

It is easy to underestimate the mental health of the lower socioeconomic classes. Among the more affluent strata of society there is comparatively little of the alienation and apathy that working-class people ex-

perience (Sheehy, 1976). However, white-collar professionals often lack the family network that poorer people often rely on for companionship and assistance. Besides, poverty is a relative concept. People who have always lived frugally may not feel as poor as they are perceived to be.

Even within the same social class, mental health will vary according to the type of personality involved. A study of 300 managers (Coping with stress, 1976) revealed both high- and low-stress types. Among the high-stress groups, many had a specific behavior pattern: "excessively competitive, aggressive, hostile, and often neglectful of all but job-related aspects of their lives—that is, significantly related to heart disease" (p. 38). The high-stress people dealt with their tensions by working harder. The low-stress men typically used five coping mechanisms: "Building resistance by regular sleep and good health habits; keeping work and nonwork life separate; getting exercise; talking things through with on-the-job peers; and withdrawing physically from a situation when necessary" (p. 38). The difference between the two groups was "the difference between working smarter and working harder—of changing gears or keeping the foot on the accelerator" (p. 38). The same distinction could be made in other occupations as well.

Personality Characteristics. In another study, Chiriboga and Lowenthal (Horn, 1975) defined the positive and negative personality characteristics that interact to produce a feeling of well- or ill-being. Positive factors, which they call ("resources,") include such characteristics as self-satisfaction, hope, insight, and competence; while the negative elements, called "deficits," include self-criticism, anxiety, hostility, and emotional problems. They tested four groups, including high school seniors, newlyweds, middle-aged parents whose first child was about ready to leave home, and persons within two or three years of retiring. The percentage of those who reported high or low deficits remained pretty constant across the years. The high school seniors were high with regard to both deficits and resources—a "psychologically complex" combination) (p. 34). (The happiest newlyweds were characterized by many resources and few deficits.) The happiest middle-aged persons had few deficits but only moderate resources, while the happiest retirees were low in both deficits and resources) Perhaps, concluded the researchers, when various avenues of self-expression are closed to older people, having a complex personality may become maladaptive, at least from the individual's own perspective. It is possible that complex persons can grow old gracefully in this society only if they belong to privileged classes, where a variety of options remain open to them.

Margaret Hester

Most middle-aged persons are reasonably content.

Overall Assessment. Despite the problems and crises we have discussed here, most middle-aged people are reasonably content. The large majority have begun to withdraw from activities which they never really cared for anyhow. They are modifying their style of life in order to be able to do what they consider truly important. Meantime, they profit from their past experience, take stock, and develop a healthy perspective (Kerckhoff, 1976).

A national cross-section of persons, ages 25 to 50, indicated certain emotional concerns (Abrams, 1982). Losing close friends was named as often as heart problems, which 4 in 10 named as their first fears. Other common fears included loneliness and becoming less happy, each named by 34 percent, and marital problems by 29 percent. Their chief concern with regard to changes with age in personal appearance was that of developing varicose veins.

However, in general, the middle-aged are emotionally healthy. One authority, Richard Kerckhoff of Purdue University, believes middle age can be the happiest time of one's

life, since one is less likely then to be pressured, exhausted, or exploited. It is not a time of doubt but of recognition of values. Few such people, when questioned, said they wanted to be 20 again (Experts, 1981). In a Health, Education and Welfare study, 75 percent of those who married in later years rated themselves as very satisfied or satisfied, with a serenity greater than in earlier marriages (Cawthon, 1981).

It is difficult to reconcile the crises and problems of middle age with evidence of general satisfaction at that age. Often such crises occur on the brink of middle age, and once resolved, a period of calm follows. Besides, the resolution of a crisis is growth-producing and personally satisfying. In the developmental sense, a crisis is not equivalent to stress, but is rather a critical or significant point in life.

Individual Testimony. Middle-aged adults, with some exceptions, feel reasonably well satisfied with their lives to date, although the majority do have certain regrets.

FEMALE, AGE 58: It's been a very exciting life, socially, and materially better than average.
FEMALE, AGE 51: I'm not particularly satisfied with it. I'm sorry I married.
FEMALE AGE 54: I am happy. I'm married and had four beautiful children and eight lovely grandchildren. But I wish I had stopped to smell the roses more often. I also wish I were a more outgoing person.
FEMALE AGE 62: I feel that I could have accomplished a lot more in my early adulthood. Young people have far more opportunities today. I spent my first few adult years teaching public school—and that work is so taxing that there's little time or energy left for a really stimulating life. Nor did I feel any satisfaction with teaching. I felt I was marking time.

Here are some responses to the question, "Is your feeling about the future one of hope, fear, dread, resignation—or what?"

FEMALE, AGE 51: At times I feel all of these—fear, hope, dread, and resignation.
FEMALE AGE 61: The older we get we certainly can't expect things in any area to get better—not health, wealth, or love of life. I don't feel dread or fear and I hope to accept whatever comes with a smile.
FEMALE, AGE 41: I think very little about the distant future; when I do, it is vague but optimistic.
FEMALE, AGE 53: I fear suffering in sickness.

In summary, life satisfaction at middle age is relatively good, although it varies by category and individual. However, such a situation should not obscure the challenge to make life more fulfilling. Becoming satisfied without being mentally healthy can be coun-terproductive and make one pull away from potentially enriching activities.

PREVENTION AND THERAPY

Commonly Used Techniques

Everyday Self-Help Devices. Certain informal approaches, as distinct from more formally organized ones directly guided by professionals, may help upgrade the level of mental health and the quality of life. One of these is facing up to, rather than running away from, reality. Another important ingredient for good mental health is irregular change, even a crisis, if an individual is to grow (Sheehy, 1976). The alternative is to settle back in a rut and dredge up rationalizations for having done so. The individual who has weathered life's crises up to this point and developed a life style that is truly satisfying has achieved what Erikson calls integrity. However, getting there may require breaking out of life patterns that have kept a hammerlock on the development of one's best self. Such a step requires awareness that counterproductive behaviors exist and the courage and persistence to change them.

Ways of coping with the inevitable, but continuing, daily tensions may be healthy, unhealthy, or somewhat neutral in effect. For example, couples may avoid strife in their daily interaction by such apparently trivial activities as shopping, going to a bar, escaping to home workshops, watching television, reading newspapers, or simply sleeping. Parents may also take out on their children the tensions they feel toward each other (Rosenblatt, 1974).

While they may not recognize it as such, people are increasingly engaging in *environmental engineering*. This concept means that they seek to create environments that support personal growth. A favorable environment contains factors that not only preserve sound physical health but also promote aesthetic and emotional satisfaction (Dubos, 1976). Environments must always be evaluated in terms of the age, personalities, and life styles of persons concerned.

Effectiveness of Therapy: An In-Depth Study. It is beyond the scope of this book to deal with major mental problems that deserve professional attention. However, people should have some idea of the effectiveness of such treatment for themselves or others for whom they are responsible. Improvement among untreated persons is often called *spontaneous remission,* but this term overlooks their efforts to help themselves, or help that they may receive from others. But what about those who do seek professional help? Basing his conclusions on 15 years of research clinical psychologist, Bernie Zilbergelt (1983) explodes certain myths surrounding psychiatry. Contrary to what many therapists proclaim there is no one best therapeutic technique—for example, equivalent results may be reported in individual, group, or couples therapy. Nor is counseling equally effective for all problems. It works best for less persistent, less serious problems. It may help with phobias, sex problems, and building self-esteem, but is not most effective for treating depression, addictions, and schizophrenia. Even when patients report a therapy experience to have been positive, changed behaviors may not follow; nor are great changes the norm. It would seem that therapists who have undergone therapy themselves and know much about its processes, should be the healthiest of all people, but they are no healthier mentally than others.

Nor do other findings add much to therapy's image. The results of brief treatment—twenty-five sessions or less—are as good as therapies lasting even twenty times as long. Even when positive results emerge they often do not persist. They do for some individuals; but "relapse rates of over 50 percent are not uncommon, and for treatment of addictions can go over 50 percent" (Zilbergeld, 1983, p. 74).

At least counseling is harmless, most people think—but such is not always the case. A review of family therapy studies indicates that 5 to 10 percent of such patients become worse than before; and another study showed that 16 percent of persons who had participated in encounter groups became worse off than before. It is not unusual for someone to seek a therapist to undo damage done by a previous one. The truth is that "there is absolutely no evidence that professional therapists have any special knowledge of how to change behavior, or that they obtain better results—with any type of client or problem—than those with little or no formal training" (p. 74). That is, most people receive about as good help from relatives or friends. Anyhow, people's behaviors are not easy to change, and what therapy can accomplish may best be described in the old French maxim: "To cure sometimes, to help often, to comfort and console always" (Zilbergeld, 1983, p. 74).

The relationship between religion and adaptation to stress is unclear, with some research reporting it to be a positive, others, a negative, force in people's lives; however, the answer may lie in differentiating the categories of persons involved (Ebaugh, Richman & Chafetz, 1984). Those who are most vulnerable to crisis—for example, the severely deprived or disadvantaged—may find a religion especially palatable that endows its members with feelings of being special. Sects vary in what they promise they can do, the aura of security they cast, and modes of coping that they recommend. Hence, members of different sects would handle their stress differently, depending on how their religious leaders told them to cope. Some who find solace in achieving what is to them a superior religious status are those who attended, but did not complete, college. They had hoped that their college education would give them some advantage, but found the lack of a degree a continuing stumbling block. The role of religion in stress would also vary according to individual differences in personality, amount of anxiety, coping abilities, and degree of religious commitment.

With regard to the effect of physical fitness programs on mental health, much of the relevant research has been poor and its conclusions dubious. However, such programs do appear to contribute to self-concept and improved mood (Folkins & Sime, 1981). Richard Suinn recommends a combination of *relaxation* and *environmental control* (Jordan, 1976). More specifically, he suggests learning to relax—perhaps through deep muscle relaxation—meditation, using imagery to break up emotional reactions that are aroused by pressures, managing the environment properly by such means as scheduling appointments realistically, and walking, talking, and eating more slowly.

Certain therapies are clearly designed to meet newly emerging needs. For example, "encounter groups and therapeutic communities and growth centers serve people's social needs by offering instant intimacy" in a culture in which people move around a great deal and the nuclear family is very unstable, making it difficult for people to rely on one another (London, 1974, p. 68). As a result people are seeking deep relationships wherever they can find them; they even attempt to transform brief encounters into intimate ones.

Meditation. Some people have rejected traditional therapies in favor of "biogenics," sex therapy, food, dance, art, music therapies, . . . massage and breathing-relaxation therapies. These techniques serve people's sensory needs in a culture where there is so much leisure time available that it must be given some deeper meaning in order for

people to truly enjoy it" (London, 1974, p. 68). Still other therapeutic forms, including yoga and nude therapy, combine social and spiritual activities.

Many researchers, as well as laymen, are turning to nonchemical ways to cope with stress. Coleman (1976) speaks of his sojourn in India while on a Harvard fellowship, where he met Indian yogis, Tibetan lamas, and Buddhist monks, who impressed him with their general warmth, openness, and intellectual alertness. All were from highly different backgrounds, possessed highly varied beliefs, and shared just one thing in common—meditation.

Meditation itself is a relatively simple process. If you want to try it, simply choose a quiet place and sit in a straight-back chair in a comfortable position, with your eyes closed. Focus on your breath as it enters and leaves your body, observing the full passage of in-and-out breathing. Whenever your mind tends to wander, simply draw your attention back to the rhythm of your breathing. Don't try to control your breath; just be aware of it. Whether it is fast and shallow, or slow and deep, does not matter. If you have difficulty concentrating on your breathing, count inhalations and exhalations up to ten, and then begin again. Another version is to say some simple word such as "one," in rhythm with your breathing. You should meditate for 20 minutes, and do it regularly, twice a day at the same time and place.

Medical research shows that meditation does indeed prove helpful. While being shown stress films in laboratories, meditators are more relaxed the entire time than are nonmeditators. All meditation techniques seem to be equally effective in reducing anxiety and coping with stress.

Mutual Aid Organizations Another type of self-help therapy includes the large network of voluntary organizations that offer mutual aid and share information. Such organizations include Alcoholics Anonymous, Narcotics Anonymous, Parents Without Partners, and the Gay Liberation Front (Self-help movement, 1978). Thomas J. Powell, professor of social work, deplores either dismissing such movements as harmful or idealizing them and overlooking their limitations. He recommends that professionals become sponsors and consultants to such groups and help them become more effective (Self-help movement, 1978).

A Warning. There are so many therapies and therapists that people have difficulty deciding among them. There is nothing to prevent licensed practitioners from devising new therapeutic techniques about which they may make large claims and use as they like on their patients. In addition, many unlicensed individuals, who are under no professional control, practice their own particular brands of psychological counseling and psychotherapy, and call themselves marital therapists, counselors, and psychotherapists (Bergin, 1975).

Another weakness that exists in all psychotherapy is the lack of any firm criteria for what constitutes a healthy life. Since humans are infinitely variable, so may optimum life styles and characteristics vary endlessly. For example, it is commonly assumed that change is important for continued growth, and a basic ingredient in a good life. But what constitutes a good life is endlessly debatable, even among the so-called experts.

middle-aged persons are in excellent health, and their appearance shows few effects of the passing years. The extent of physical change varies widely according to social class, sex, individual health habits, and emotional status over the years. Furthermore, the physical health of those in middle age and older is progressively improving because of the widespread and growing interest in nutrition and exercise.

While there are no clear-cut criteria for determining what constitutes emotional health, it is certain that middle-agers have characteristic problems. These include concern over their changing physical condition and body image, responsibilities for both the older and younger generations, and midlife crises relating to vocation, sex, and personal goals. Such crises have a positive effect when they result in a realistic assessment and rearrangement of goals and life styles. Most individuals somehow muddle through their problems alone, although growing numbers make use of such preventive and therapeutic measures as meditation, encounter groups, and sometimes psychiatry.

Overall, the outlook appears promising. People today are not merely concerned with resolving problems that cause difficulties in their lives, but are striving for genuinely rewarding lives. While they may find this goal somewhat elusive and continuously in need of redefinition, a large majority achieve relative contentment after they emerge from their midlife crises.

SUMMARY

Aging inevitably changes all the parts and systems of the body. People first become consciously aware of aging in middle adulthood. Certain disorders, such as heart disease, high blood pressure, and arthritis, become more common. Also people become aware that their physical image is changing, as grey hair and a paunch begin to appear. However, many

SUGGESTED READINGS

FREUDIGER, P. (1983). Life satisfaction among three categories of married women. *Journal of Marriage and the Family, 45*(1), 213–219.

GOLEMAN, D. (1982). Staying up: The rebellion against sleep's gentle tyranny. *Psychology Today, 16*(3), 24–35.

HOOPER, J. O. & TRAUPMANN, J. A. (1983). Older women, the student role and mental health. *Educational Gerontology, 9*, 233–242.

KEITH, P. M. & SCHAFER, R. B. (1984). Role behavior and psychological well-being: A comparison of men in one-job and two-job families. *American Journal of Orthopsychiatry, 54*(1), 137–145.

McCREA, F. B. (1983). The politics of menopause: The "discovery" of a deficiency disease. *Social Problems, 31*(1), 111–123.

McCRAE, R. R. (1984). Situational determinants of coping responses: Loss, threat, and challenge. *Journal of Personality and Social Psychology, 46*(4), 919–928.

MARANTO, G. (1984). Exercise: How much is too much? *Discover, 5*(10), 18–22.

McLANAHAN, S. S. (1983). Family structure and stress: A longitudinal comparison of two-parent and female-headed families. *Journal of Marriage and the Family, 45*(2), 347–358.

PARDINI, A. (1984, April-May). Exercise, vitality and aging. *Aging*, pp. 19–29.

PEROSA, S. L. & PEROSA, L. M. (1983). The midcareer crisis: A description of the psychological dynamics of transition and adaptation. *Vocational Guidelines Quarterly, 32*(2), 69–79.

RHODEWALT, F. & AGUSTSDOTTIR, S. (1984). On the relationship of hardiness to the type A behavior pattern: Perception of life events versus coping with life events. *Journal of Research in Personality, 18*, 212–223.

SEEMAN, M. & SEEMAN, T. E. (1983). Health behavior and personal autonomy: A longitudinal study of the sense of control in illness. *Journal of Health and Social Behavior, 24*, 144–160.

TAYLOR, S. E. (1983). Adjustment to threatening events. *American Psychologist, 38*(11), 1161–1173.

VERBRUGGE, L. M. (1983). Multiple roles and physical health of women and men. *Journal of Health and Social Behavior, 24*, 16–30.

WITZLEBEN, J. (1982). Dr. Jekyll and Ms. Hyde. *Discover, 3*(11), 28–34.

CHAPTER SEVEN

Adult Sex Roles

The first part of this chapter concerns adult psychobiological sex roles—that is, the psychobiological consequences of the sex drive, sex awareness, and sex interest. The second part discusses social sex roles, or the broader roles of men and women in society.

PSYCHOBIOLOGICAL SEX ROLES AND BEHAVIORS

Female Sexuality

Psychoanalytic Theory Questioned. Major research fails to support much past psychoanalytic and related theory regarding female sexuality (Chilman, 1974). Women who have physical problems with infertility, pregnancy, menstruation, and childbirth are not, as the Freudians assert, more likely than other women to be mentally ill or neurotic, or to deny their sexual role and functioning. Nor

do problems in one area of sexual functioning necessarily relate to difficulties in others. Women who have problems with menstruation are no more likely than others to have difficult pregnancies; nor does a difficult pregnancy necessarily portend a difficult childbirth. Women are more accepting of their bodies and less anxious about "their body safety" than most males are. Nor is there any scientific support for the penis-envy concept (Fisher, 1973).

On the other hand, middle-class women, at least, may indeed be more dependent than males on their mate relationships, partly because they equate sex with love. Many males enjoy sexual relationships for their own sake, without becoming emotionally involved with their sex partners. It is even uncertain how many "liberated" women can engage in random sex without developing psychological problems.

On the other hand, the old notion that

women passively submit to their husbands without enjoying sex themselves is no longer valid.

Other Research. There have been other reports regarding female sexuality. Chilman (1974) found that physiologically the female's sexual response was much like the male's, and that women probably have as strong a sex drive as men. Within a specific time period, females are more capable of multiple orgasms than males. Yet females have more difficulty than males in attaining orgasm, at least in heterosexual relationships (Fisher, 1973). About a third of them fail to achieve orgasm at least some of the time, and at least 8 percent all of the time. Nevertheless, all females are readily orgasmic if and when they engage in masturbation or lesbian relationships. The female clitoris is analogous to the male penis; and it, rather than the vagina, is the female's chief erogenous zone. In most cases, females achieve more satisfaction through clitoral than vaginal stimulation.

Male Sexuality

In their approach to sex males have traditionally been more physical and less emotionally involved than women. Most males place a high value on their "reproductive equipment" and are quite concerned about their potency (Chilman, 1974, p. 126). This attitude probably relates "to the actual physical vulnerability of the penis and testicles, the need for males to have an erection, to have intercourse and impregnate, their inability to hide erectile or orgasmic failure from their mates, and the fact that, unlike females, they can never be sure that they are actually biological parents" (p. 126). A man's penis is so important to him that he believes it should also be important to the woman, and that she must feel deprived in lacking one.

An overview of sex surveys indicates that men are far more interested in extramarital sex (EMS) than women are, more often seek several partners, and are less selective about partners when having casual sex. Women's election of EMS more often stems from unhappiness in marriage and desire for a better, lasting relationship.

Women are also more selective about whom they marry, perhaps because they have more at stake. In questionnaires filled out for a dating service, women showed greater concern about a potential partner's intelligence, status, race, and religious affiliation. The men were more selective only with regard to their dates' physical attractiveness.

At least partly because some men must endlessly prove to themselves their masculinity, male violence against women is apparently on the increase, especially rape and wife abuse. Rape has been the fastest growing crime reported over recent years, and perhaps three to ten rapes occur for each one reported. Rape, declares Doyle (1983), is not an expression of lust but of need to dominate another, deriving partly from men's traditional authority over women. As for marital violence, society in general has honored the "unspoken rule" that what transpires within families is no one else's affair. Indeed in a national survey almost 25 percent of the women questioned believed violence was a normal, perhaps essential part, of marriage, and about 30 percent of the men thought it a good feature of marriage (Straus, 1977). It is not surprising, therefore, that about 70 percent of assault victims in Boston's City Hospital are women attacked in their homes by husbands or lovers.

Doyle (1983) debunks several myths about male sexuality which men themselves believe. They often think other males' sexual experiences are better, and that only they find them cause of concern. Other myths are that sex performance is easy, that men "can't get enough sex," that men should run the whole "sex show," and that "sex is all that matters in a relationship."

The truth is that many men suffer from

sexual dysfunctions, one being impotence, or erective deficiency, which may assume several forms (Doyle, 1983). Organic deficiency derives from some "defect, injury or disease which affects the general structures, the reproductive system, or the central nervous system" as in spinal cord injuries (Doyle, 1983, p. 205). Functional impotence, as from excessive drug intake, is often temporary; psychological impotence inhibits proper function because of emotional stress such as caused by fear or grief. Other dysfunctions include premature ejaculation, retarded ejaculation, and lack of desire. Overall, perhaps no more than 10 percent of dysfunctions have a biological base—the rest are mainly psychological. Often men fail because of their expectation to "perform at the drop of a hat," or from too great a need to satisfy a sexual partner.

Vasectomy. In recent years some men have been undergoing *vasectomies*, which permit intercourse without conception; a vasectomy involves surgical removal of a portion of the duct (*vas deferens*) that conveys sperm from the testicle to the ejaculatory duct of the penis. In general, postoperative attitudes of persons who have had a vasectomy have been positive, although there are exceptions (Cole & Bryon, 1973). Research into a new kind of birth control has recently begun. It involves the male production of antibodies that sometimes cause infertility. In any case, "rejoining the vas is an expensive, tedious procedure that requires full hospitalization and offers absolutely no guarantee of success, even if the vas deferens are reunited" (p. 216). The chances at present are probably no more than fifty-fifty.

Research on Both Sexes

It is difficult to achieve high validity in sex surveys, although conclusions about overall trends seem justified. Questions may be poorly phrased, sampling techniques flawed, and respondents often inclined to hedge their answers.

During this century two periods could be justified as embracing sexual revolutions. The changes in the 1920s were fueled by good times and by reactions against Victorian repression and the period of austerity embracing World War I. Other factors were increased urbanization and the growing economic and intellectual freedom of women. This trend extended, not just to campuses, but across America. The divorce rate soared and so did that of illegal abortions.

The sexual revolution of the 1960s, broadly embracing the years 1965 to 1975, stemmed from women's increasing liberation, dramatic developments in birth control, and growing economic and social freedom. Self-fulfillment was the order of the day. Then, in the late 1970s, the liberal movement plateaued for life styles in general, including sex, as the economy faltered. Students became more serious—and they wanted a career, not just a job. A mood of cautiousness prevailed and extended to attitudes about family and sex. An additional sobering influence was the spread of genital herpes, a sexually transmitted disease for which no cure is known. Already it infects 10 to 20 million Americans, and extends to another 200,000 to half a million a year.

In the 1980s the trend toward conservatism continued. The year 1982 saw the seventh straight annual increase in marriages, the first decline in the divorce rate in two decades, and the highest number of births in 12 years. Births to women over age 30 were rising, suggesting that family was taking precedence over career. Moreover, 60 to 70 percent of young divorcees remarry within 5 years.

However, it is generally believed that changes in men's attitudes toward sex have been relatively small. Women are still "the gatekeepers" of sex, says anthropologist Lionel Tiger (Men in Groups, 1984). After casual sex experiences, it is the woman who is

left with the unwanted pregnancy and the decision about abortion.

On campus, one-night stands are less common, and going out in groups more so. Many college students still engage in sex, but they are more cautious and sophisticated. The women, at least, are more likely than their counterparts of the late 1960s to couple sex with commitment.

The current conservatism is not equivalent to a revival of Puritanism. The sexual mood of the 1960s subsided, but left its mark. Americans are more relaxed and open about sex than before the 1960s; and practices long questioned, if not tabooed, are widely accepted. Premarital sex and sexual cohabitation, oral sex, and masturbation are widely approved. Only a modest minority question an adult's legal right of access to sexually explicit movies or novels. A large majority do clearly reject certain other practices including open marriage and child sex, while homosexuality remains a "gray area, increasingly tolerated but not approved" (p. 83).

In addition, premarital sex has become widely accepted, especially among the younger generation. At the same time, the search for sexual partners has become more noticeable and widespread. Most cities have public places where sexual pickups are the norm. Growing numbers of underground newspapers and magazines carry advertisements by people seeking sexual partners. Homosexuals have formed over 600 gay organizations; they have their own meeting rooms on campuses, and their publications are circulated nationwide. Some of them are attempting to make homosexual marriage legal. Most dramatically, by 1974 about 1,500 transsexuals had switched from one sex to another through radical surgery. Of more fundamental significance are the increasing numbers who have begun to advocate and practice alternatives to monogamous marriage, such as open marriage, swinging, and homosexual unions. Finally, the courts in certain states have made fundamental revi-

sions in sex laws. For instance, all p acts between consenting adults are decriminalized in several states.

Of course, the final chapter in of sexual behaviors has not been sexual scenario will continue to the times. Sexologist Wardell author of the Kinsey studies, p to sexual conservatism within years. Others, however, see no sion of sexual needs now.

AMERICAN SEXUAL STYLES

In the only study of American se haviors conducted by means of a probability sample, eight main style identified (Ubell, 1984). Sexual style of an individual's thoughts about, and ities relating to, sex. Those responding ra from ages 18 to 60 and included both ried and singles.

Each style, in turn, has varying degr of three components, one being Life Sat faction. Typically, persons high in Life Sa isfaction are also satisfied with their sex lives marital status, and how their bodies looked. They are relatively at ease with sex talk and have intercourse frequently. A second component, Sensuality, concerns satisfaction with such behaviors as kissing, hugging, genital touching, and breast fondling—the so-called foreplay behaviors. Those high in a third component, Eroticism, respond to such stimuli as pornography, oral or anal sex, and genital contact. Those high on this trait have a strong sex drive, find sex important, and often masturbate.

Certain overall conclusions emerged from the research, some of them unexpected. Contrary to what most sex researchers have reported, the sexes were more alike than different. Nor was age a factor—once a sexual pattern is adopted it persists. Religiosity and marital status may have exerted some influence, but not demonstrably so. Homosexuals

generally erotic; and 11 percent of all
respondents had had such experience.
With regard to the sexes, here are the
that they differ most. Sex is important
percent of the men and 66 percent of
women, whereas orgasm is important to
ercent of the men and 60 percent of the
men. More of the men (73 percent) than
women (57 percent) say their sex drive
strong; more men (55 percent) than women
percent) are happy with their bodies;
d more men than women (9 to 7) achieve
gasm in the sex act. Women find it harder
an men (86 percent compared to 59 per-
nt) to have sex without love.

In other respects the sexes were quite sim-
ar. Happiness with sex life was reported by
57 percent of the men, 64 percent of the
women; happiness with married life by 87
percent of the men and 83 percent of the
women; enjoyment of sex in the nude, by 87
percent of the men and 92 percent of the
women; and excellence as a lover by 76 percent of the men and 71 percent of the women.
About half (56 percent of the men and 52
percent of the women) reported high Life
Satisfaction and half of each a high Sensuality score. Each sex averaged having intercourse 6 times a month; and men's long-
est relationships averaged 3.7 years compared
to women's 4.1 years.

With regard to sexual styles, almost equal
numbers of respondents had settled for each.
Of the Pansexuals (198 persons per 1,000)—
those who are happy with all aspects of their
lives, including sex—45 percent were women
and 55 percent men. Sex is important to them;
they often masturbate and have erotic fantasies. The Satisfied Erotics (117 persons per
1,000; 30 percent women, 70 percent men)
have sex often, experiment sexually, and are
happy with themselves and their lives. The
Unsatisfied Erotics (127 persons per 1,000;
51 percent women, 49 percent men), are unhappy with their lives, including sex, although sex is important to them. They often

masturbate because they have trouble finding satisfactory sex partners. The Lonely
Erotics (121 persons per 1,000; 27 percent
women, 73 percent men) engage more in
imagery than in actual sex. They are unhappy with their lives, including sex, and
their main sexual outlet is masturbation.

The Sensualists embrace two main categories, one being the Satisfied Sensualists (109
persons per 1,000; 54 percent women, 46
percent men). They are high in life satisfaction and sensuality, but low in eroticism. They
enjoy foreplay and intercourse but dislike
the erotic, such as oral sex and pornography.
In contrast, the Unsatisfied Sensualists (85
persons per 1,000; 85 percent women, 33
percent men) are generally unhappy and
would like sex, but often lack partners. They
are roused somewhat by sensual acts, but sex
is an unimportant part of their lives. Many
of them are unmarried and lonely, especially
the women.

Two other styles are also comparatively
less sexual. The Conservatives (111 persons
per 1,000; 67 percent women, 33 percent
men) are generally happy, like themselves,
and are satisfied with their sex experience,
but engage in little foreplay. Finally, the
Nonsexuals (132 persons per 1,000; 68 percent women, 32 percent men) are unhappy
with their lives and their bodies. They report
no real interest in sex and no arousal by
sexual stimuli.

In conclusion, it seems that there is no
one normal pattern of sex, that a sexual pattern is part of an overall life style, and that
about 1 person in 7 has a sex problem, men
as often as women. Women most often complain about sexual incompatibility with their
partners (18 percent), trouble achieving orgasm (17 percent), and low sex drive (17
percent). The men more often experience
impotence (18 percent), low sex drive (11
percent), and feeling sexually inadequate (13
percent). Undoubtedly successful therapy for
such problems must take into account indi-

vidual approaches to sex within the context of the total personality and life style.

Issues Relating to Both Sexes

The Double Standard. A long-standing subject of controversy is the sexual *double standard*. This concept means that the sexes are judged differently by society for engaging in the same behavior. (The double standard is based on the mistaken assumption that males have stronger sex drives than females and therefore cannot be expected to control their sexual behavior (Chilman, 1974). "Good" women are perceived as being relatively asexual; they have intercourse primarily to satisfy their husbands' sexual needs.) Their "sexual purity" supposedly makes them superior mothers and guardians of the family morals.

In earlier times the double standard may have had a certain value. Before contraceptives were available, the woman was vulnerable to pregnancy and needed a husband to support her if she had a baby. Since property was the chief form of wealth and was passed down from father to son, a man wanted to be sure that the children born to his mate were really his own. Besides, in days when a male's physical strength was vital for livelihood and security, a female wanted a male to support and protect her. In order to insure that her husband would stay with her and fulfill these needs, she gave him special sexual consideration. (Chilman, 1974).

Another reason for the double standard is that for males, siring a child is merely a matter of copulation, whereas for women, the minimum effect consists of "copulation plus pregnancy plus (throughout most of human history) several years of nursing—a vast commitment of time and energy" (Diamond, 1985).

For such reasons, historically, adultery laws have been highly sexist, partly to insure that husbands only be obligated to provide for children they felt confident were their own. (Even these days, in at least twenty-three countries, from Africa through Arabia to Indonesia, female circumcision and infibulation are practiced.) Through infibulation the woman's labia majora are sewed almost completely shut, to make intercourse impossible, and are opened only for intercourse with the husband, or to allow childbirth. Or she may be circumcised, which involves removing the clitoris or most of the female external genitalia to reduce female interest in sex, so she will never actively seek it. Also, these days, men's adultery is far less condemned than women's and the man who kills his wife or her lover caught in an adulterous act often has the charges reduced to manslaughter or is entirely acquitted.

To date the most significant developments have been women's entry in large numbers into the workworld and the development of the birth control pill. When women can support themselves and control their own reproduction, they are far more independent of male decision-making, in all matters, including sex.

Nevertheless, even in the United States, large remnants of the double standard still prevail. While Americans self-righteously raise horrified objections to various forms of cruel treatment in other countries—as in South Africa and Afghanistan—they ignore this barbaric treatment of women. Even in the United States, women who have entered the workworld continue to be held responsible for most of the child care, meal preparation, and other domestic chores—which, in effect, amounts to a modified form of slavery. Future changes will not necessarily be rehearsals of practices in time past. Although waves of liberalism and conservatism will continue to rise and fall in harmony with social trends, there is also the effect of unforeseen developments. For example, consider the revolutionary impact of the Pill. What now-unpredictable development may have equally as great an impact in the future can only be conjectured.

An Assessment. Are sexual morals "declining," or are they simply adapting to new conditions? Some critics see recent changes in sexual behavior as symptomatic of decay, both within the family and the larger society. By contrast, many authorities believe that today's freer, more egalitarian sex practices are healthier than the traditional, often distorted, views and practices of former years (Cowing, 1975).

SOCIAL SEX ROLES

Earlier we briefly discussed young adult social sex roles. Here we are concerned about sex roles for adults in general, especially those in their middle years. A *social sex role* is a way of prescribing behavior patterns that are considered proper for each sex. It carries with it a whole array of attitudes, feelings, and activities. In short, it may involve anything and everything associated with being a male or a female within a particular culture" (Rogers, 1977, p. 335).

Certain other terms place the concept in sharper perspective. The term *sex-role identity* suggests an awareness of one's biological identity and of what attitudes are associated with being male or female (Dreyer, 1975). Most American children develop this sex-role identity by the time they are 6 or 7, and they maintain it for the rest of their lives. The term *sex-role preference,* on the other hand, suggests an individual's conscious preference for particular sex-typed attitudes and behaviors. An individual's sex-role identity is stable, but one's sex-role preference may change over time. The way most individuals perform their sex roles represents a compromise between their own sex-role preference and social stereotypes of what each sex role should be.

Factors Affecting Sex Roles

Historical Origins. The traditional sex roles of man, the doer, and woman, the nurturer, have deep roots. Western religion and philosophy are based upon patriarchal principles. In the Bible it is stated that "man . . . is the image and glory of God; but the woman is the glory of the man. . . . Neither was the man created for the woman, but the woman for the man" (1 Cor. 11:14). In another place it says "Let the woman learn silence with all subjection. But I suffer not a woman to teach, nor to usurp authority over the man" (1 Tim. 11:15). As a result of this tradition, reinforced through the years, the vast majority of adults were socialized as children to accept these sex-role stereotypes.

Biological Factors. The question of the extent to which sex roles are rooted in biology or simply shaped by environment, has caused considerable controversy. There has been a tendency to think of sex differences as being firmly rooted in biological fact, and that those sex roles that harmonize with biological potential will function best. Rossi (1977) believes that sex differences are permanently rooted in biology; that family systems depend upon the woman's role in childrearing; and that current views of sexual equality and variant family forms do not take into account biosocial fundamentals. In contrast, John Money (1977) believes that any such distinctions are relatively insignificant and that the focus should be on encouraging both sexes to realize their best potential and to dispense with artificial sex-role barriers.

Early Socialization. Even in infancy the sexes are treated differently, and during the second year, sex-role stereotyping is apparent; once established, sex roles are extremely resistant to change (Flerz, Fidler & Rogers, 1976). From their earliest years, boys are exposed to models of males who value "material success, physical and psychological strength, leadership, and invulnerability; who suppress their fear, control their emotions; who are pragmatic, know all the answers, never seek help, are tough and independent")(Farrell, 1978, p. 22). They are also encouraged to be tough and aggressive. For thousands of years, young men have been trained to be warriors, and thus society has capitalized on their aggression and toughness. "If universal conscription should be at 50 instead of 17," observes Skovholt (1978), "negotiations instead of combat would solve territorial disputes" (p. 6).

(Athletics have become the counterpart of combat for most young American boys.) By the age of 5 or 6, boys have introjected the idea that they should not show fear or cry or behave in any way like girls. They come to despise in themselves any so-called feminine feelings of self-doubt or needs for tenderness and love. Thus, even these days males are reared to defend their rights aggressively to be men. Some males still believe that women like them more if they are a "little rough" (Doyle, 1983, p. 185). In situations of violence, most men favor strong action in dealing with persons who are socially disruptive.

Recent Influences. The revision of sex roles is rooted in and supported by basic changes in society (Bell, 1981). In our postindustrial society, with its emphasis on professional and technical occupations, services and knowledge, the sexes are equally competent, and education is valued. And as women attain college degrees as often as men, they reject sex roles at odds with the level of their training and ambitions. Meantime, both sexes' growing access to higher education has led to in-depth examination of values and a concern for personal development and fulfillment (Bell, 1981).

Other factors have also had an unsettling effect on sex roles. Since machines now perform most of the work that once required masculine brawn, the vast majority of jobs can now be performed equally well by both sexes. Women's entry into the workaday world has also freed many men from the exhausting burden of being the sole family provider. Meantime, higher education has increased both sexes' interest in humanistic values and desires for self-realization. Such interests and desires naturally transcend traditional sex roles. The woman's liberation movement, as an outgrowth of these factors, has had an impact on liberating men from their even more confining traditional roles.

Adult sex roles and children's sex-role socialization experiences will become more similar as women spend less time in child-rearing and more in other occupations. As the socialization experiences become more similar, male-female personality differences—including cognitive styles and social orientation—will diminish. Impetus for change in sex roles will also stem from women's rapidly growing participation in the work world, and as the sexes view each other more as individuals and less as sex objects (Kopkind, 1977). As a result "gone would be the classic Rubenesque female, two thirds breasts and hips; gone the stallionoid male, the walking phallic symbol" (p. 47). Kopkind concludes that "androgyny doesn't mean a race of sexless androids, but a wider variety of sexual possibilities than exist now" (p. 47). *Androgyny* refers to the integration of characteristics of both sexes within one individual.

In the mid-1980s certain factors are tending to threaten progress toward healthier sex roles—mainly the reversal toward traditionalism. In particular, the extreme religious right's growing, though still small, minority of the total population has made solid gains of significance to women. The extreme right champions the cause of the traditional nuclear family with the father as head of household, the wife as homemaker, and at least two children. Men are encouraged to be individuals, but women are above all nurturers who place others' goals ahead of their own. The extreme right views alternative family life styles as inferior and calls the nuclear family the pillar of society. Children are fully subject to their parents' authority, especially the father's (Libby, 1983).

The Female Sex Role

Disadvantages. Certain aspects of women's roles are damaging to their personalities. Even some of the presumed advantages of those roles, when they are carefully examined, are of questionable worth. Women often feel protected by men, but is it healthy to feel a need for protection? Many women feel it is a divine blessing that they can become mothers, but males become parents with far less pain and trouble. Besides, women who spend most of their time at home, often tending young children, often do not remain intellectually active and involved. Many married woman who go to work may find that their status depends on how important their husbands are. They are not treated as being persons in their own right (Felson & Knoke, 1974).

In addition, women in general are taken less seriously and given less respect than men. Consider the difference in status accorded men's and women's sports; a woman's airplane competition is frivolously labeled the Petticoat Derby. Female household heads have less prestige in the community and less status than men with the same education and income; and they may have less status than married women who derive their status from their husbands.

The woman's role also subtly interferes with her potential for professional success. Women fail to take themselves seriously enough, for they have not been brought up to have confidence in their abilities (Movius, 1976). In addition, because they are responsible for child care, working women do not have enough time for reading in their field,

for overtime work, and for the sort of personal involvement with a job that helps win promotions. If the children are ill, it is simply assumed that the mother, not the father, will take time off from work to care for them.

When they seek help with their problems, women often have to confront a typical male psychiatrist, which is another disadvantage. A sampling of 184 therapists revealed that the women therapists were considerably better informed, less stereotyped in attitudes, and more liberal than the men (Sherman, Koufacos & Kenworthy, 1978). Although the men's attitudes were in general more liberal than stereotyped, many of them held stereotyped attitudes toward women patients or were inadequately informed to deal with them.

The women therapists knew considerably more than the men about women and their functioning. They knew more about a woman's body functions including pregnancy, childbirth, and menopause. About one in five of the male therapists expressed uncertainty that rape victims had been deliberately seduced; and 26 percent were unaware that most women electing abortions do not suffer serious psychological consequences afterward.

While the therapists' overall scores were fairly liberal, they were less so on certain items. Over half (57 percent) of them believed that acceptance of one's sex role is essential for mental health. Over half (70 percent), more males than females, were either neutral or believed that marriage or its continuation was a significant goal for all women in therapy. A small majority (55 percent), again more males than females, either did not know or agreed that women with young children should remain at home.

Psychotherapy seems to be an institution for easing societal conflicts, simply helping people to adapt to society as it is, not as it ideally should be. Psychotherapy is often no more than a mechanism for helping women accept their traditional sex role rather than changing society so that they can play a more optimally satisfying and fulfilling role (Sherman, Koufacos & Kenworthy, 1978).

Women's sexist upbringing gives rise to certain personality characteristics—for example, in locus of control. *Locus of control* concerns whether one believes that what happens to oneself depends on one's own behavior (internal locus) or is outside one's own control (external locus). The sense of being in charge of one's life develops self-esteem, while the sense of being swept along by circumstances produces feelings of depression and helplessness. Women more often than men attribute their successes and failures to factors over which they had no

In dual-career households women still perform most of the traditionally feminine tasks.

T.G. Bell

control, an attitude that is easy to understand since in their childbearing years they were commonly dependent on others.

Advantages. Nevertheless, the female sex role has its good points. It is more flexible than the male's, and women are penalized less for stepping out of it. Many people believe women are warmer than men, since traditionally they have been freer to express emotion. It could also be argued that certain of the presumed disadvantages of traditional women's roles result from using masculine criteria of satisfaction to evaluate women's status. For example, evaluations based on masculine standards would tend to derogate the housewife's role. Most housewives, however, would rank themselves somewhat higher. A comparison of housewives returning to college with full-time housewives staying home indicated that both groups were equally content with their life styles. Both groups agreed that women's individual growth was compatible with the wife-mother role; and the majority did not believe being married had hampered their creativity or intellectual development (BA or MRS?, 1978).

The Impact of the Women's Movement. The impact of the women's movement on women's sex roles is as yet unclear. First, the movement is not a single entity; there are actually several women's movements. There are radical feminists who desire drastic change; there are moderates; and there are those who are primarily concerned with obtaining better salaries and day care for children, both of which are supportive of family roles. Harmonizing such contrasting role demands—that is, the occupational, marital, and familial—is a difficult task. Lauducina (1973) suggests broadening the scope and meaning of the "women's movement" in order to make it congruent with the needs of more women and men.

A major obstacle to sex-role change is many women's internalized feelings that are rooted in their past. Although women are gaining more freedom, the individual woman will profit little from these gains if she is not psychologically prepared to do so. The woman's movement has made it more acceptable for a woman to go to a singles' bar and initiate relationships on her own, but few women do such things (Knox, 1980).

On the other hand, women have made much more progress in updating sex roles than men. There is somewhat more confusion today than formerly because the sexes may be at different points in their trend toward changing sex roles.

The Male Sex Role

Historical Perspective. The male ideal has changed over the centuries, with successive ages redefining the male role according to then-current concepts of men's proper duties (Crites & Fitzgerald, 1978). Among these models in Western thought was "the Renaissance man," which itself constituted a revival of the classical Greek model. This Renaissance ideal encompassed not simply rational aspects but affective characteristics that are now labeled as feminine. Thus, the Renaissance man was liberated from the rigid confines of medieval times. One result was the production of some of the world's greatest works of art, architecture, and literature.

In time, this Renaissance ideal became fractured as Reformation theologians attributed rational characteristics exclusively to men and assigned affective responses exclusively to women. This duality was apparent some centuries later in the Industrial Revolution, which assigned men to the instrumental world of work and women to the home.

Historically, men have always played the dominant role, in earlier centuries because survival depended so much on brute strength and brawn (Doyle, 1983). Later, after the Industrial Revolution, men became the sole providers—so-called good providers—and because of the great worth attached to material goods, they held greater power and

higher status than females. In the stock market crash of 1929 men lost their jobs, and with them their self-respect because masculinity was identified with competence in the workplace.

After World War II, and a return to better economic times, men's status-giving "good-provider" role was restored, but it subtly began eroding in the following years (Doyle, 1983). Several factors accounted for the change, one being women's influx into the workplace. About 25 percent of married women were employed in 1950 compared with 55 percent in 1978, and a projected 2 in 3 will be employed by 1990. For one thing, inflation makes that second pay check almost essential; for another, it symbolically affords the earner a greater sense of worth and dignity.

Overall, in the twentieth century, the ideal male has been "rational, physically impressive, sexually potent, and more than occasionally violent in the attainment of his goals" (Crites & Fitzgerald, 1978, p. 11). He lacks tender feelings, revels in sexual activity for its own sake, and is inept at intimate love. He is intelligent but hardly intellectual, cares little for pure culture, and is devoted to satisfying his material needs.

In terms of the traditional macho male image, writes Vittitow (1981), men drive themselves unmercifully, always seeking "more money, more power, and more recognition. . . . They are in a double-bind," dissatisfied with their successes and "acutely aware of their failures." In "his pursuit of manhood," the man rarely experiences his real self. In striving to meet the demands of the male role, "he gives up his connection with his unique self . . . and neglects the . . . nourishment of the person he really is." (Vittitow, 1981, p. 291). That is, he is dominated by an unhealthy image and unable to be himself.

From childhood he has been socialized to acquire the characteristics of detective and adventure-story heroes. He must possess solely instrumental characteristics and lacks capacity for nurturance, gentleness, or self-disclosure. He unconsciously longs for this part of himself that he has been taught to hate, and is unable to develop nurturing, cooperative, intimate relationships with either sex. To be a "competent male," he must be "half a human being" (Crites & Fitzgerald, 1978, p. 11).

Another element in the masculine image is aggression, a characteristic Americans both condemn and praise. They claim to abhor violent behaviors yet "scream for blood" at hockey games, and they praise presidents who get tough when dealing with other countries, which may be quite small and relatively defenseless (Doyle, 1983, p. 184).

It is generally agreed that males hold more of every kind of power, as commonly defined (Kahn, 1984). Men receive greater rewards, in terms of money and resources. Men also hold more power to coerce; and though women may withhold love as a means of coercion, men may then seek love elsewhere. Men are more often chosen as models, as being deserving objects of emulation. In a small Iowa town subjects listed both sexes as role models, but females named male role models ten times more often than males listed females (Gaeddert, Kahn, Frevert & Shirley, 1981). Men are rated as being more expert, too, even in traditionally female-dominated areas. A mother may know what medicine her child needs but must get the prescription for it from her doctor, usually a male. In terms of power derived from information, males again hold the edge, as they have higher education on average, and their sphere of activities outside the home is broader. Finally, males are brought up to believe it is their right to dominate, a belief amply supported in society's laws and institutions.

Men may demonstrate their greater power in subtle ways. They adopt a superior or protective manner toward females, touch them, and occupy greater space. They devalue women's accomplishments and deny them positions of unusual responsibility.

The respective stereotypes of the sexes clearly reflect this power differential. Men are perceived as "more aggressive, not easily influenced, very dominant, very skilled and worldly, acting as leaders, and rough" (Kahn, 1984, p. 238). They avoid appearing feminine, thus strengthening the dichotomy suggested by the phrase, "the opposite sex" (p. 238). Male's feelings of superiority over women is vital to their definition of self; "without it they are not better than women."

Since women are denied more direct access to power they may seek it in devious ways. They may rely on such resources as flattering the male or pretending helplessness so he will share his resources with her. Note that the personality traits thus encouraged in women can hardly be called desirable.

A psychiatrist, Leonard Glass (1984) declares that the percentage of men who attain mature masculinity is small and describes two model forms of hypermasculinity: the Man's Man and the Ladies' Man. The image of the Man's Man is that of "the trail-riding, rough and ready cowboy.... This category includes the blunt, direct, purposely unprettied 'jock' whose insignia is his muscular strength and apparently unequivocal masculine presence," (Glass, 1984, p. 261). He feels at ease with machines; his "passion is function (performance, speed)" and his "style" is an "implicit denial of the importance of style (grimy hands, rumpled clothes)." Such men may also be "men of ideas . . . with single-minded intellectual drive whose brains are incisive weapons. . . ." The Man's Man hesitates to marry, and if he does, prefers being out with "the boys." He sees women as "fickle, undependable and alien" in contrast to the "no-nonsense world" of men (p. 262).

The Ladies' Man is the "familiar Don Juan, the smooth, suave 'lady-killer' of fact and fiction" (p. 263). His role is that of a "a consummate, wily hunter collecting female trophies . . . often with the implicit cooperation of his prey. He has a compulsion at once to seduce and control women while shoving them away, to avoid becoming entangled in any authentic or sustained" way (p. 263).

Not often does one encounter a pure type—these are "polar positions." The same individual may have components of both, with a blend of "triumphant contempt and distance-seeking revulsion" in dealing with women, or he may display one or the other mode to a less-than-extreme degree.'

Disadvantages. The male is typically thought of as an efficient doer and achiever. Most men are brought up with the attitude that they must work, take on difficult jobs, and overcome obstacles. They are taught to be competitive and to want to win.

The typical ideal male focuses on dealing with the outer world and ignores his inner world. Even when he has reached the pinnacle of success in middle age, he may face a severe crisis when he realizes that he has missed many of the most significant experiences in life (Crites & Fitzgerald, 1978).

This thumbnail sketch of the ideal male fits no male exactly, but people believe it. Males may be no more competitive than females (Maccoby & Jacklin, 1974). Many of them are warm and loving and place human values ahead of material achievement. Nevertheless, each male must somehow cope with society's stereotype of men. Males are taught to be self-sufficient, which is often interpreted by men to mean that they should not be intimate with others. In unstructured groups males are more competitive and less comfortable about expressing warmth and support than females (Ariès, 1975). In addition, the excessive stress placed on masculine achievement prevents males from relaxing.

Many persons question whether the traditional cultural concept of masculinity is mentally healthy. The ideal is often destructively aggressive and competitive. Furthermore, the concept of masculinity is over-idealized. The "complete male" is the embodiment of courage, independence, effectiveness, success, and a host of other virtues. The individual male's reach is almost sure to exceed his grasp. He applies the cultural measuring rod to himself and often feels like a failure.

One problem that males face is always having to act completely self-reliant, while fearing that others will find out that they are not really all that tough. Actually, men fear many things, from aging, baldness, and excess weight to loss of virility (Doyle, 1983, p. 216).

Advantages. The male role, however, has some advantages. For one thing, men ordinarily are assumed to be the heads of households.

In addition it is ego-strengthening for males to live in a world of work, and a world of big affairs in general, that is ordered by males. Men usually are trained for the higher positions that carry the most power and prestige.

Also ego-strengthening is the male's sex advantage. . . . From adolescence onward, females outnumber males. In social situations, an extra male is an asset, an extra female is a liability. Besides, the unmarried male has a freedom of movement and action denied the unmarried woman (Rogers, 1977, p. 348).

Why the Male Sex Role is Changing. The male sex role is subtly changing, for several basic reasons. Advances in technology have weakened the influence of sex roles in the division of labor. In our earlier agrarian and poineer economies men were called upon to perform tasks requiring physical strength, while women's roles required interpersonal skills and dexterity, including childrearing and homemaking. With the coming of the industrial and postindustrial economies, men performed their tasks away from the home, while women typically remained at home. Nowadays, however, such factors as shorter working hours, increased leisure time, more service occupations which involve interpersonal skills, and the increased availability of mechanical devices to take care of household chores, have weakened the need for sex-typed roles (Dreyer, 1975).

Contributing especially to men's increasingly expressive role is the growing emphasis on leisure time. These days most men report more satisfaction from their leisure activities than their work (Doyle, 1983). In the last decade or so, there has arisen "a whole new subculture of ball-playing men who live only for the macho camaraderie that they find on the field or in the local tavern" (p. 171). However, the greatest threat to the male's provider role is technology, which has robbed many workers of any real sense of identity on the job.

A major factor affecting men's sex roles has been women's progress in the workworld. As women gain power, men will lose it in both concrete and symbolic terms (Kahn, 1984). When women enter jobs formerly held almost exclusively by men, men will no longer automatically receive such employment. As women become better educated and more widely experienced men feel less like the great authorities.

Men are also coming to reject the success ideal as integral to the masculine sex role. Males were expected to work very hard, to compete unmercifully, and to be a success in everything—and their successes have often proved their failures. In achieving success they assumed overpowering obligations, were required constantly to maintain unrealistic standards and found themselves living, not their own lives, but society's image of the successful life style (Doyle, 1983).

Future Prospects. Changes in male sex roles may require more radical adjustments than changes in women's roles. For one thing, men have become used to their higher status, and what dominant group wants to give up its power? For another, men may be called upon to develop values that they have been taught to suppress throughout their early years. Consider, for example, the man who is asked to take care of the baby while his wife is at work. He must diaper the baby, tend it when it cries, feed it, and perform various tasks that he learned as a boy to associate with femininity (Douvan, 1975). The concept of being a sissy has been so strongly associated in the male mind with being repulsive, weak, or even mentally sick, that it is extremely difficult for men to rid themselves of these feelings.

Nevertheless, Gerzon (1982) is optimistic, speaking of the "emerging masculinities—Healer, Companion, Mediator, Colleague, Nurturer—" which all share one common feature. They symbolize "human qualities" which "transcend sexual identity. They reflect awareness of the earth, of work and family, and of the human body, mind, soul. . . . These traits are based on values; they are not sexual, but ethical. . . ." The old stereotypes of the ideal male were "for men only; the emerging masculinities are, in fact, emerging humanities" (Gerzon, 1982, p. 262).

As these humanities gain strength, men will no longer deem it necessary to make a strong distinction between sex roles; instead, they will be shared, and boundaries between the responsibilities of wives and husbands will become blurred. Responsibilities for breadwinning and homemaking will be shared, "and as they are shared they will be transformed. Some couples may wish to reverse roles completely; others may retain clearly divided roles. But if the freedom to choose is increased, the outcome, whatever its form, will be liberating for both men and women" (Gerzon, 1982, p. 238). Thus, "couples will write their own scripts, and construct their own plots, with unprecedented freedom" (p. 237). The author, who agrees with this scenario, would add that the result need not be a complete homogenization of the sexes. Under these circumstances whatever genuine sex differences exist will inevitably, and naturally, produce distinctions; just as individuals within each sex differ, so will the scripts for their behaviors.

Bell (1981) agrees that the male's role is inevitably changing, in response to new "social and economic structures, but the transition will not be smooth" (p. 321). There is the matter of "ideational and institutional

lag, for attitudes typically change more slowly than the socioeconomic circumstances in which they are embedded" (p. 322). Thus, notions of male superiority and patriarchy continue to play a significant role despite changes in the sexual division of labor that supported such ideas. Men increasingly express a belief in equality while clinging to "the earlier stereotype of the self-sufficient and unemotional male" (p. 322).

Inevitably, males will experience stress for changing "from a perspective which rewarded instrumental male behavior to one which promotes expressive activity, and creates a degree of conflict and confusion and a sense of difficulty in fulfilling role expectations" (p. 323). Historically, men have held the greater power, and the newer models of men require giving up some of it—yet "the potential benefits are great." That progress is being made, concludes Bell, becomes clearly apparent through examining contemporary life.

Sex-Role Relationships in Marriage

Changing Relationships. In several ways the relationships between husbands and wives are changing. Because the average family now has fewer children, married couples frequently have no children at home for most

of their lives. Hence, for a significant portion of their lives, sex is leisurely and private (Long, 1976). In addition, sex-role responsibilities are shifting in the home. Sixty percent of married women with jobs outside the home are sharing the responsibility for family support, while some married men are assuming greater domestic responsibilities.

Often working women intend, after marriage, to insist upon shared parenting when children arrive; but most of them retreat to more traditional patterns (Wessel, 1984). One woman who had a child on condition that her husband share the parenting role equally, worked only part-time after her son arrived.

Less traditional, better educated fathers feel conflicting emotions these days. They may feel guilty about neglecting their careers in favor of home duties—or the reverse. Many do, however, perform tasks—such as taking children to a day care center—that wives ordinarily have done. A rare man even stays at home, sometimes pursuing his career there. In most cases, however, it is the wife who remains in charge of scheduling children's activities. It is usually she who gets up to take care of children when they require help in the night.

There is a tendency to look upon men as very liberal if they share such duties, though far from equally, because doing even that

In rural America men still perform most of the outdoor work.

much is a shift from long-ingrained masculine patterns that eschewed doing anything viewed as feminine.

Certain large corporations have developed policies designed to allow men in dual-worker families to do more of their share; however, few men avail themselves of such options. One survey showed that 119 large companies offered paternity leaves to fathers, but just eight said that even one man had requested them. Merck, Incorporated, which offers either parent 6 months of unpaid child care leave, with a job guarantee and paid benefits, reported that 500 women but just ten men had taken such leaves (Wessel, 1984). Reasons given are that the family cannot afford the father's leave, and that men feel they must hang in there, on the job, to remain competitive for success. In one study, 80 percent of two-career couples said it was the mother who stayed at home when a child was ill.

Sex role, coupled with other variables, is an important factor in a wife's depression. Because society still assigns to women a lopsided disproportion of responsibilities for parenting, and since the role carries little status, the majority experience "a depressed sense of self worth, if not actual personality deterioration" (Rossi, 1981). Such feelings are greater among women with more than one child, and they increase with the years, while no such relationships between parenting and age exists for men.

In families where the wife is full-time homemaker, she suffers more stress than her husband. The working wife experiences less stress than the wife-homemaker, but more than her working husband, probably because she performs most of the homemaker role, too. Whether, and to what degree, men whose wives also work feel greater stress than those of full-time homemakers is controversial (Gore & Mangione, 1983). Certainly much would depend on how much the family needed the wife's money, whether the wife's job held higher status, and how traditional the husband might be.

Even though the new sex-role ideology is helping both sexes find out what they are like and what they can really do, they may experience problems in working out their new roles. Often in processes of growth there are so-called growing pains—pain is often the price of true progress. Many couples may blame themselves for their problems in establishing new sex roles when the fault actually lies in institutional and socialization patterns (Berger, 1979).

Meantime, the whole concept of marital roles is changing, partly because greater numbers of adults are now college educated. Traditionally, marriage was viewed as providing for sex, procreation, and the rearing of children, while the marital partners filled rigidly defined complementary roles. One reason for the change in this concept is that increased geographic mobility has removed married couples from their kin and thrown them increasingly on their own resources. The result is that wife and husband look more to each other for friendship and support. At the same time, increasingly better-educated wives have become more satisfactory companions and social assets for their husbands.

Another factor that has fundamentally altered marital relationships is birth control. Until recently there was no way for a woman positively to avoid pregnancy unless she gave up sex with men (Douvan, 1975). In consequence, girls were taught both to expect and look forward to maternity, and they thought it essential to their fulfillment as women. If, for some reason, a woman did not have children, her maternal feelings might be directed into nurturant activities such as nursing or teaching. These were considered legitimate alternative expressions of femininity. However, birth control has divorced maternity from feminine identity. It permits women to think of themselves as fully developed without being mothers.

Nevertheless, there is no evidence that tendencies toward more androgynous sex roles threaten a couple's adjustment in marriage. Individuals who assume a somewhat less polarized sex role may be better prepared than more traditional persons for adult life. As women move into the work world and as men take on more of the jobs at home, both sexes need to develop their fullest human potentials. Moreover, as the sexes modify the traditional sex-role norms, concepts of what is typically masculine or feminine will change. Eventually, new interpretations of sex roles will be perceived as natural, and not as violating what is appropriate for each sex.

Life Stage. The relations between the sexes change over the life span. In general, there seem to be some changes in sex-role behaviors in adulthood (Holahan, 1984). Men adhere more closely to traditional sex roles in young adulthood than they do later, whereas women change more in the direction of masculine role behaviors as they grow older. Perhaps one reason is that in young adult years the husband's provider role in a competitive society encourages his more aggressive tendencies whereas motherhood encourages the woman's affiliative disposition. After the husband retires and the children leave home, the male feels less need to compete and to dominate, while the wife now has less need to forfeit her own special needs in favor of those of others.

New Types of Sex Roles

The Modern Role. New concepts of sex roles have two main features. One is the idea of *sex-role equality,* or putting females in the work force on an equal basis with males (Osmond & Martin, 1975). The second concept is more fundamental and involves a complete reorientation of sex-role concepts. Traditional sex roles clearly differentiate the roles of men and women. Modern sex roles, by contrast, are characterized by "flexible and dynamic transcendence of sex-role constraints. That is, modern definitions of social

roles are not specified by sex" (p. 745). Instead, they focus on "individual human potentiality" (Naffziger & Naffziger, 1974, p. 257). The ideal is that both sexes learn to "define themselves in terms of humanness and not what men do that women should not do." (p. 257).

This new sex-role orientation has several advantages. First, it acknowledges repressed needs in both sexes. Males, who have been taught to repress their emotions, need to get back in touch with them. It also permits women to experience a hitherto repressed need to escape domination. A mutual need for love equalizes the power of both sexes in the couple relationship. The new roles also "facilitate individual growth so that females and males are primarily human beings, sure in ego strength, and capable of making actualized, caring relationships" (Hirsch, 1974, p. 170).

The Androgynous and Bicultural Concepts. There are several alternative interpretations of these new sex roles, although they are basically alike in rejecting the rigid dichotomy of traditional ones. One conception, the *androgynous gender role,* suggests that individuals of either sex should freely incorporate characteristics traditionally associated with either males or females. Both sexes may develop attributes characterized as extremely masculine or extremely feminine without violating their own gender identity. O'Leary and Depner (1976) warn that the androgynous role may produce a "superwoman syndrome," in which a woman enacts both male and female gender roles. This dual role may prove exhausting both physically and psychologically. It is better to encourage either sex to function without limitations imposed by biological gender; but neither sex should feel compelled to enact all the roles traditionally associated with both sexes.

For his part the androgynous male would simply be concerned about developing his own unique potential, without regard to proving his masculinity or having a fear of appearing feminine. The male artist or teacher might devote considerably more of his time and thought to expressive activities than the forester or construction worker, yet neither would feel less masculine than the other. According to the androgynous concept, the most effectively masculine male is the one who comes to appreciate and develop those characteristics that are uniquely his own.

Spence and Helmreich (1978) perceive androgynous individuals as high in both feminine and masculine attributes rather than lacking any particular masculine and feminine characteristics. Thus, androgynous individuals possess both the high achievement motivation and high self-esteem ordinarily associated with males and the superior parenting attitude and warmth traditionally associated with females (Berger & Wright, 1978).

The Concept of Equity. The Rapoports' (1975) concept of *equity* between the sexes agrees, in the main, with the foregoing view, but it has a different twist. This concept does not necessarily mean an equal division of tasks, or performing the same tasks. Instead, it means providing for equal and fair opportunities when conditions are not strictly equal. This concept suggests possibilities for variation instead of a rigid adherence to a new stereotype. It embraces the principle of equality of choice and a fair distribution of responsibilities and privileges. It may involve inequality in the sense of not being exactly the same, provided that the situation is freely entered into and approved by the individuals concerned. The danger in the equity concept is that traditional arrangements may simply be accepted as equitable because the parties concerned lack any real awareness of the inequities actually involved. Nevertheless, argue the Rapoports (1975), over the life cycle the balance will change and shift, and at various times partners to the arrangement will be doing and receiving more or less.

Current Status and Prospects of Change

Current Status. Considerable research suggests that most of the changes resulting from women's liberation have been superficial. In a study of middle- and lower middle-class adults, Lowenthal, Thurnher, and Chiriboga (1975) perceived few signs of sex-role change, even in adolescents and young adults, and less in the older groups. The life styles anticipated by both sexes were "family-centered and male dominant" (p. 244). Only college and university students were making substantial changes in traditional sex roles.

Middle-aged women are often more strongly feminist than younger ones. As Bernard (1975) points out, the life style of middle-aged women (ages 35 to 55) has changed. Often they do not have elaborate hairdos. They use less make-up, and some use none. Their clothes are more casual, and they often wear slacks instead of skirts. Instead of encouraging their daughters to be coquettish, many mothers are often disappointed if their daughters do not take the initiative in asking boys to dance with them at high-school parties.

Gardner (1974) believes that women's lib has had its most dramatic effect on the working-class woman. "Traditionally her role in life was to be the wife, mother, and homemaker—and . . . her primary goal and duty was to fulfill that role as best she could" (p. 17). As the result of her restricted role, the blue-collar woman was isolated from the outer world. She felt that she had little worth outside her home and felt ill at ease in it. She accepted without question that women must serve their husbands, and that women workers must receive lower pay than men for the same work and have fewer opportunities for advancement. Moreover, she reared her sons and daughters to look on the woman's role the same way. She did not feel that her *ers* needed much education because *s* not necessary for homemaking.

The truth is that the traditional divisions *in* sex roles remain basically the same, despite many small changes. To what degree these changes will work their way through to the core is uncertain. One problem has been that many conclusions about sex roles have, to date, been rooted in inadequate research. Kaufman and Richardson (1982) pinpoint flaws they perceive to exist regarding women's achievement motivation. Theories derived from achievement research are based mostly on male subjects and are not equally relevant to women. It is also assumed that establishment of achievement motivation is mainly determined early in life; instead, motivation to achieve is an ever-changing, continuous process, influenced by both personal and historical variables. Recently women have begun to assert their worth in both the public and private areas of their lives. However, they are still handicapped by social sanctions that make it difficult to transcend barriers that confine the large majority to positions of lower status.

Reasons for Modifying Sex Roles. Some people have questioned whether sex roles should be—or even can be—modified. To what extent are they biologically decreed? Should the liberated woman or the happy housewife be the ideal? Those who urge conformity with the old standard say that individuals who find it easy to go along with the prescribed roles are happier. In the area of sex roles, as in any other, those who can accept the status quo are naturally more comfortable (although not necessarily happier) than those who attempt reform (Rogers, 1977, p. 352).

However, there are even more reasons for altering sex roles than those given in the preceding discussion. For one thing, strict adherence to traditional sex roles is emotionally unhealthy. Freeing people from such roles would make them more flexible and would place fewer restrictions on what they

can do. That is, "men need to be humanized; women to be energized. Men need to become more secure, compassionate, and less violent, women to achieve their full status as human beings . . ." (Rogers, 1977, p. 481).

Some progress has been made, but it cannot be assumed that a trend will continue in the same direction. Already a subtle change has occurred in the women's liberation movement. The new feminism is not

an organized movement; nor does it hold meetings or press conferences. It is an all-pervasive rise in female awareness that has permeated virtually every level of womanhood in America, at all ages. Today women believe they have more options, that they can do things that will change their lives, that they have the wherewithal to improve their economic status (Adler, 1975, p. 114).

In short, the transition to sex-role equity will not be easy. Since power is a significant aspect of male-female relationships, any progress women make in their efforts to achieve equity will be at the expense of males' hitherto largely unchallenged dominance (Kahn, 1984). Males' response to their loss of power, in turn, will importantly influence how hard they will fight to maintain their superior status.

An Evaluation

While research reports regarding middle-age sexuality do not agree in detail—primarily because different kinds of sampling were used—it seems clear that practices have become more liberal and attitudes healthier. While sexual problems still exist, there is a more open attitude toward acknowledging and dealing with them.

The same can be said of sex roles; they have evolved in a healthier direction. Each sex role still has its disadvantages, but these are being more widely recognized and are diminishing. It is unclear at present whether sex roles will continue to become depolarized in years to come. The author believes that a rigid dichotomization of sex roles limits the development of personal potential, and that artificial restrictions on behavior, in the name of sex-role appropriateness, should not be tolerated. In a free environment, sex-role differences would reflect individuals' natural predispositions. Both sexes would interpret sex roles in a wide variety of ways, depending on which was the most comfortable and self-enhancing for each individual.

Nevertheless, just how males will respond to women's struggle for equality, is hard to predict (Kahn, 1984). Even those men who protest that they believe in equality often fail to act upon their stated beliefs. Men who rely strongly on their male superiority as an ego support will certainly fight harder to maintain dominance than men who have other sources of power, or more self-confidence in general. Relatively powerless men may go to extremes of wife abuse, rape and battering. A telephone survey confirmed that wife abuse increased when the women involved held higher status or better paying jobs than those of their husbands.

Effecting basic change in such matters will be difficult, as already indicated (Kahn, 1984). Gender is "the prime identifying characteristic of human beings," and results in "we-they groupings" (Kahn, 1984, p. 244). Kahn calls such a dichotomy "arbitrary." If men and women could be taught that to be a man or woman is of no particular importance, no more so than to be tall or short, left-handed or right-handed, it would be more difficult for men to retain power. Equality would be easier to achieve because the sexes would not be seen as opposite. On the other hand, there are those who believe sex differences to be firmly rooted in biology, and that a "natural" distinction is both inevitable and desirable.

SUMMARY

The issues regarding psychobiological sex roles involve defining the distinctions between male and female sexuality and evaluating the status of sex behaviors. In gen-

eral, sexual attitudes and practices have become more permissive than a generation ago, and the double standard by which males and females are judged differently for the same behaviors is weakening.

Social-sex roles, or patterns of behaviors deemed appropriate for each sex, derive from both biological and sociocultural factors, and they change with the times. Each sex role has its advantages and disadvantages; each is currently in a state of flux, partly as a result of the women's movement. Certain changes are occurring, notably in spouse relationships, but how fundamental these changes are and how far they will, or should go, is in dispute. Various alternatives for current roles, all basically alike in rejecting the rigid dichotomy of traditional ones, have been proposed.

SUGGESTED READINGS

ACOCK, A. C. & EDWARDS, J. N. (1982). Egalitarian sex-role attitudes and female income. *Journal of Marriage and the Family, 44*(3), 581–589.

BABLADELIS, G., DEAUX, K., HELMREICH, R. L. & SPENCE, J. T. (1983). Sex-related attitudes and personal characteristics in the United States. *International Journal of Psychology, 18*(1-2), 111–123.

BELL, D. H. (1982). *Being a man; The paradox of masculinity.* Lexington, MA.: Lewis Publishing Company.

BLACK, S. M. & HILL, C. E. (1984). The psychological well-being of women in their middle years. *Psychology of Women Quarterly, 8*(3), 282–292.

BOWEN, G. L. & ORTHNER, D. K. (1983). Sex-role congruency and marital quality. *Journal of Marriage and the Family. 45*(1), 223–230.

D'AMICO, R. (1983). Status maintenance or status competition? Wife's relative wages as a determinant of labor supply and marital instability. *Social Forces, 61*(4), 1186–1205.

DOYLE, J. A. (1983). *The male experience.* Dubuque, IA: William C. Brown.

EAGLY, A. H. (1983). Gender and social influence: A social psychological analysis. *American Psychologist. 38*(9), 971–981.

FISCHER, C. S. & OLIKER, S. J. (1983). A research note on friendship, gender, and the life cycle. *Social Forces, 62*(1), 124–131.

GOLD, D. & BERGER, C. (1983). The influence of psychological and situational factors on the contraceptive behavior of single men: A review of the literature. *Population and Environment: Behavioral and Social Issues, 6*(2), 113–129.

GORE, S. & MANGIONE, T. W. (1983). Social roles, sex roles, and psychological distress: Additive and interactive models of sex differences. *Journal of Health and Social Behavior, 24* 300–312.

KAHN, A. (1984). The power war: Male response to power loss under equality *Psychology of Women Quarterly, 8*(3), 234–247.

LEE, A. G. & SCHEURER, V. L. (1983). Psychological androgyny and aspects of self-image in women and men. *Sex Roles, 9*(3), 289–306.

LERNER, H. E. (1983). Female dependency in context: Some theoretical and technical considerations. *American Journal of Orthopsychiatry, 53*(4), 697–705.

LEWIS, R. A. (ED). (1981). *Men in difficult times: Masculinity today and tomorrow.* Englewood Cliffs, NJ: Prentice-Hall.

PLECK, J. H. (1982). *The myth of masculinity.* Cambridge, MA: MIT Press

CHAPTER EIGHT

Middle Age in the Nuclear Family

In a national sampling of adults, a large majority placed family roles higher than job roles. The only exceptions were older women whose jobs provided more self-actualization than marriage; however, even for them parenting has provided more self-actualization than their jobs (Changing attitudes, 1979). In the family, the spouse role proved more important by a 3 to 2 margin than the parent role for men and just less so for women.

For this reason, almost all Americans marry at some time or other—in the early 1980s about 95 percent of those over age 45 had married, but the situation for younger persons is quite different (Glick, 1984). In 1970 64 percent of women and 45 percent of men had married in their early 20s; a decade later these figures had diminished to 50 and 31 percent. To what extent young people are merely postponing marriage or electing singlehood is as yet unclear (Glick, 1984).

Looking ahead, it appears that about 96 percent of today's adults will marry by age 75 (Glick, 1984). However, three times as many of those still unmarried at age 25 to 29 will not marry. By age 75 3 in 4 women and 5 in 6 men who divorced have remarried; however, the remarriage rate is falling.

MIDDLE-AGED PARENTS

Parental Roles

Within the family, parents still play a large role, but the emphasis has changed. Even motherhood is not static; it contains at least three stages: (1) early motherhood, when the children are preschoolers and the mother is about 25 to 34; (2) middle motherhood, when the children are school aged and the mother is in the 35-to-54 age range; and (3) late motherhood, when the children are 18 or over and the mother is past 55. When women live to old age, the mother-child roles sometimes become reversed (Bernard, 1975). In middle age, the mother—and of course, the father—have children of high-school age or older. The mother often becomes an important confidante of her daughter, and sometimes of her son.

The father's role changes somewhat, too. The very young father takes an interest in his children for a while and then, because of work pressures, becomes much less involved. Later on in middle age, middle-class men, at least, often seek to establish a closer bond with their children (Sheehy, 1976). To some extent they may succeed—adolescents typically admire their fathers (but at this age

In late middle age men spend more time than formerly with young grandchildren.

Joe Franco

teen-agers are seeking autonomy and spend little time with either parent).

The father's role depends partly on his social class, for lower-class fathers are generally less involved and more authoritarian than middle-class ones. Fathers with less education may feel somewhat inadequate as their children's education equals or surpasses their own. Middle-class parents reason with their children more, whereas lower-class parents use physical punishment (Troll, 1975).

As children move into and through adolescence, the parents' roles subtly change. In the family, middle age is associated with children growing up and leaving home. The man may be threatened by the increasing power of his almost-grown sons at a time when his feelings of "physical potency" are declining (Fried, 1967). There may also be a shift in the locus of power within the family in middle age. As time goes on, the woman becomes increasingly important, to the point that "she pushes the father from the stage and seems to draw strength from his decline" (Rosenberg & Farrell, 1976, p. 163).

In recent years greater attention than before has been paid to the reciprocal nature of parent-child relationships. Elkind (1979) speaks of three basic contracts between parents and their children, one being responsibility and freedom. Parents allow their children freedom to the extent that children prove themselves responsible. Adolescent children may have friends over for the night if they make no disturbance in the house. A second contract concerns loyalty and commitment. Parents will spend time with their children, being loyal and committed to them, if their children show respect for the parents' beliefs and values and care more for them than for other adults. A third contract concerns support and achievement. Parents will be supportive of their children in various endeavors if the children achieve goals that the parents perceive as worthwhile. They will pay for their children's college education if the children receive acceptable grades.

The Pluses and Minuses of Middle-Aged Parenthood

Problems. Certain problems are involved in being a middle-aged parent. Young people often experiment with activities that their parents disapprove of, including cohabitation, smoking pot, and having premarital sex. Parents also worry about their almost-grown children's dates, driving habits, and vocational choices. Nevertheless, they must avoid appearing to dictate to their children for fear of alienating them and severing lines of communication.

Parents must also help their children become independent and resist the urge to bind them to themselves. While considerable attention has been paid to parents' attachment to their children, far less has been paid to their separation from them (Bardwick, 1974). Nevertheless, the bonds must be loosened if children are to mature. Healthy children are created not only through attachment but also through separation.

In a national sampling of married couples, the most often named anxieties concerned children's illness or general worries about childrearing. Over half the mothers of preschool children mentioned worries about their children's sickness, whereas parents of teen-agers were concerned about what their children did away from home. Some parents worried about drugs, alcohol, sex, and getting into trouble. They worried more about girls than boys because of concern over the girl's reputation or possibilities of sexual attack or premarital pregnancy (Hoffman & Manis, 1978).

The most commonly mentioned disadvantage of having children was the loss of freedom—they "tie you down"—especially in the early parenting stage. The second most often cited disadvantage was the expense and the interference with the mother's employment. Parents viewed world conditions in terms of the problems they might present to their children, while childless couples questioned whether they should bring children into such a mess. Parents also worried about children's health and safety. Overall, less-educated women reported less dissatisfaction with parenting, perhaps because educated women had more alternative activities (Hoffman & Manis, 1978).

Rewards. There are compensations in childrearing, but they are somewhat different from what they used to be. In the past many parents relied on their children to perform chores in the home or supplement the family income by working. Parents also expected their children to support them when they grew old. Nowadays children's own occupational achievements may provide prestige to their parents, particularly at a time when they are leaving the working world themselves.

There is less child-parent conflict today, too, partly because the gap between the generations in basic values has narrowed, and the hierarchical power relations in the family has diminished. The matter of power within the family, predicts Yorburg (1973), will ultimately disappear, for parents will "defer to and learn from children, if the occasion suggests, as they will defer to and learn from each other" (p. 258). Indeed, there has been something of a reversal in the traditional socialization patterns. Considering the current rate of social change, parents may imitate their children's behavior rather than the reverse. Thus parents may seek to keep up with the changing world through their almost-grown-up children. Examples include "language accumulation, even four-letter words, music patterns, and the new dance steps, and in some cases, hair styles and drug experimentation" (Gunter & Moore, 1975, pp. 203–204). Some authorities believe that the erosion of adult authority can go too far (Baumrind, 1974). They believe that "the roles of guide and guided are essentially hierarchical . . . and that youth will hardly seek advice from those whose status is exactly on a par with their own" (Rogers, 1977, p. 430).

In the national sampling cited above, when

Pit Piucci

Some couples postpone parenting until middle age.

Individual Testimony. Here several middle-aged men and women indicate to what degree and in what way they have found their children satisfying.

FEMALE, AGE 59, HOUSEWIFE: My children have enriched my life enormously. I'd probably be a rigid old female without them.

FEMALE, AGE 41, TEACHER: I am enjoying them more now as a parent-friend since they are older and we can mutually share our enjoyment of the things we do together.

MALE, AGE 50, STOCKBROKER: I have always been so busy with my work that I haven't had much to do with my children. However, I do love them and am proud of them.

So far our discussion has concerned children who are almost or completely grown, but sometimes couples have their first child when they are middle aged. They do so despite certain risks. The chance of having a Mongoloid child after age 40 is much greater than in earlier years—about one in a hundred. However, the process of *amniocentesis*, by which a small amount of amniotic fluid is drawn by a needle from the uterus, has become 100 percent accurate in detecting Down's syndrome (Mongolism) and various other chromosomal abnormalities. If it is discovered that a woman is bearing a seriously handicapped child, the fetus may be aborted. Besides, a growing body of data suggests that the physical dangers of having a baby after age 35 have been exaggerated.

The wisdom of having children at this age depends partly on the parents' motives. In some cases a woman may become pregnant in order to avoid making certain decisions, perhaps about reentering the work world. Sometimes the wife becomes pregnant because she finally decides that she does not want to miss the experience of bearing and raising a child. When older couples genuinely desire a child, they are usually very

couples were asked how much satisfaction they gained from particular areas of life—their job, their spare-time activities, being married, work in and around the house, and being a parent—96 percent of the mothers and 98 percent of the fathers indicated great satisfaction from being parents. For mothers at every stage no other area provided as much satisfaction as the parent role; but no such consensus existed among fathers. The educated working women reported satisfaction with their jobs more often than did either the men or the other women. Nevertheless, they enjoyed parenting even more. Very often parents reported that their children were "fun." Most young adults viewed parenthood with mixed emotions, but older ones viewed it very positively. (Hoffman & Manis, 1978).

successful, level-headed parents, and better prepared financially than younger couples to provide care.

The Empty-Nest Stage

The increasingly long *empty-nest stage*, the time after the children have grown up and left home, may be the most dramatic period in the family life cycle. This time has increased on average from 2 to 13 years, chiefly because people are living longer. This has many implications, the most significant being that not only does the empty-nest period occupy a notably longer fraction of the parents' total life span, but also husband-wife relations subtly alter—for better or for worse—after the children leave home.

In the empty-nest period, parents are often portrayed as feeling desolate and alone. With certain exceptions, especially among women, the opposite is more often true. Many middle-aged couples feel considerable relief when their children no longer consume so much of their money and time. Thus, "raising a family seems to be one of those tasks, like losing weight or waxing the car, that is less fun to be doing than to have done" (Campbell, 1975, p. 39).

Of course, there are individual differences; and a mother who has devoted full time to the task may experience a feeling of emptiness. However, after a brief period of depression, most women begin to feel liberated. In general, women with professional commitments experience less depression as their mother role changes. Mothers sometimes experience depression when children fail to leave home at an age normally expected (Gerson, Alpert & Richardson, 1984).

Women's adjustment at this stage varies somewhat according to social class. In a longitudinal study of transitions, newly married working class women, more often than older women, reported that their husbands were the boss; in these not highly educated, somewhat conservative segments of society, women experience many sociocultural barriers. Af-

ter their chilren leave home, they have ambivalent feelings and often rather negative concepts of themselves; many wonder whether they have any other potential that can be developed. Some find new activities and consequently attain higher self-regard. Those who continue self-sacrificing tasks persist in not liking themselves very much and being dissatisfied with their lives (Fiske, 1980, p. 368).

For some women, the initial empty-nest stage is brief. Many more young girls today are keeping their babies born out of wedlock and calling on their mothers to help with the rearing. The result, suggests Bernice Neugarten, is to place on younger middle-age women tasks they would prefer not to have. These women are mostly in the job market and do not wish again to become full-time mothers and homemakers (Hall, 1980).

In general, the children's departure from home does not affect fathers as much as mothers because children have typically played a lesser role in their lives. Only a minority of fathers feel very disturbed by the children's leaving home. A study of 118 postparental fathers, whose children had recently left home, indicated that most of the fathers felt either neutral (35 percent), somewhat happy (26 percent), or very happy (16 percent) about the last child's leaving, while 22 percent felt unhappy (Lewis, Freneau, & Roberts, 1979).

Aging Parents. A major problem for many middle-aged individuals is caring for aging parents, who often possess some chronic complaint or physical disability (Montgomery, 1982). Indeed, over twice as many severely disabled older persons live at home, usually being cared for by family members, as in institutions. Often, when older people have no children, care is provided by siblings, nieces, or nephews. Hence, the chief family form for the elderly is the modified extended family, including members of their own family, siblings, or other relatives. Thus, the kinship network continues to be the chief support of older Americans, cushioning "later-life crises, and constituting a last resource to retaining a measure of independence."

The host families or individuals, in such cases, receive far more financial support for such care-giving than years ago, but not nearly enough; and available resources such as government help are distributed unevenly. Although the government does little to fund home care for older people, contributions are made for it indirectly through Social Security, Medicare, Medicaid, and various subsidized programs. An experimental program in Athens, Georgia, designed to delay entry into a nursing home, provides home delivered services—therapy, homemaker, meals, and the like; foster care, or placement in some family in the manner of foster child care; and adult day rehabilitation which includes socialization, activities, and meals for persons who otherwise would be isolated.

Certain factors make family care for the elderly difficult. Families are smaller, hence fewer persons are available; and many families are headed by single parents. Houses are often too small to accommodate an older relative adequately. Adult children themselves may be disabled, or at least not very robust. In dual-worker families, caring for an elderly person can cause unusual strain. And almost always, even when a number of relatives or children are available, the bulk of the responsibility falls on one individual, usually female.

MARITAL RELATIONSHIPS

Marital Problems

Shortcomings of the Spouse. Not all problems relate directly to the sex-role dichotomy. Sometimes the marriage relationship is strained because one partner has outgrown the other (Tsoi-Hoshmand, 1976). A lag by one partner may develop for a variety of reasons; for example, a working wife may

have supported her husband through college. In other cases mothers may spend all their time looking after their husbands and children and neglect to develop their own potential.

A second and related problem is the new focus on escaping traditional sex-role stereotypes; many men simply do not know how to behave in the tender, warm, and sharing fashion that women are coming to demand. For their part, women often have ambivalent or guilty feelings about placing their own needs on the same plane with those of their husbands and children; although they are no longer willing to settle for the selfless, passive role bequeathed them by earlier generations (Koch & Koch, 1976).

Traditional Problems. In addition, marital partners still experience traditional problems—lack of communication, unfulfilled emotional needs, undisciplined children, sexual difficulties, infidelity, lack of money, interfering in-laws, alcoholism, and physical abuse (Koch & Koch, 1976). The very fact that such problems are common may tend to perpetuate them. We may come to look on them as inevitable instead of developing new and creative ways to solve them. Yet their very persistence alerts us to the fact that they are extremely difficult to solve.

Here several men and women evaluate their married life and its chief problems:

MALE, AGE 45, TEACHER: My wife has not grown over the years. She's a bore and I've only endured it by having affairs over the years.

MALE, AGE 41:   My hardest problem has been trying to understand my wife and having her understand me. It's not a serious problem but one of constant concern.

MALE, AGE 63, REAL ESTATE BROKER: My chief problem in married life has been the struggle to make ends meet. Finances were strained during the 1940s and 1950s.

FEMALE, AGE 51, OFFICE CLERK: I have found my married life unsatisfactory due to mother-in-law problems, plus a husband who wouldn't face reality and grow up.

Haley (Pines, 1982) believes that economic factors are at the bottom of many marriage problems. Long ago, families stuck together because they had to for survival. These days those who want to move out do; although in hard times or after marriage breakups, grown children who have moved out may return, causing disruption. Families which had reorganized without them must now embrace them again. Sometimes the children may have left home because they did not get along well with one or both parents, so this reconstituted family may not be a happy one.

Special problems also exist in blended families, which bring together children from several marriages. Often there are problems of discipline and of hierarchy. Age difference settles the hierarchy in most families but in others there may be little such distinction.

Another relatively common problem is that of extramarital relationships. Among a sampling of 378 married and cohabiting couples 43 percent admitted to at least one of three dyadic relationships: love without sexual intercourse, intercourse without love, or both (Thompson, 1984).

Spouse Abuse. Sometimes marital problems end in *wife abuse*, a topic which is finally receiving the attention it deserves. A quarter of all American couples have had violent episodes during their marriage, and wife beating may account for as many as 18 percent of the injuries treated in emergency rooms (Miller & Miller, 1980). In one study there were 490 battered wives compared to 2 battered husbands. In another study, of 600 female divorce clients, 60 percent had been beaten by their husbands two or more times. And of 360 beaten wives at least 30 percent were beaten while pregnant. Moreover, many husbands who abuse their wives also abuse and neglect their children. In time, sons who

are beaten by their fathers grow up to be husbands who in turn beat their wives and children. In such homes boys acquire patterns of violence toward girls and women, whereas girls acquire an expectation of being attacked and exploited by males.

Both tradition and legal policy conspire to encourage wife abuse. Social services, police, courts, and hospitals often refuse protection to battered wives. Often the battered wife is assumed to be the guilty party and deserves a beating; and women are sometimes portrayed as encouraging, provoking, and even enjoying being beaten.

In-depth interviews with members of forty-nine families in which women had been beaten, disclosed that certain important factors influence the actions taken by abused wives (Gelles, 1976). One determinant is how much violence the woman experienced as a child. The more she was hit by her parents, the more likely she is to stay with an abusing husband. (Wives are more likely to seek help who have completed high school and are employed.) In general, the fewer resources the wife has, and the less power, the more abuse she will take from her husband before seeking outside help. Another deterrent to seeking help is the lack of support on the part of the police, the courts, and social agencies, which often treat marital violence as a private matter. One woman who called both an agency and the police without receiving any help, was eventually strangled by her estranged husband.

Battered husbands, though relatively small in number, also constitute a problem. Often such husbands are old, ill, and physically smaller than their wives. Over 3 percent of 600 husbands in mandatory conciliation interviews mentioned physical abuse by the wife as a main reason for seeking divorce.

Factors Relating to Family Adjustment. Conger (1981) identifies several factors that are changing family life. Among these are the relative isolation of the family from other institutions, and the woman's movement, perhaps the most significant occurrence of the 1970s, which has changed the way the sexes view each other and themselves. The 1970s were also a "me decade" when people began to put their personal welfare above that of others, even in the family. Even earlier, with the rise of the nuclear family, its members came to perceive themselves as individuals and not as part of a "collective effort." Meantime, a legacy of the 1960s was the right to do one's own thing and greater respect for different ways of life, which paved the way for family life alternatives.

To improve the family, advises Conger, a sense of community should be reestablished. Parents should communicate more with each other and with other parents. Old stereotypes need reexamination, and appropriate institutional accommodations should be devised to meet current needs.

Saving and Improving Marriages

Marriage Contracts. Couples typically make decisions regarding the wife's work and childbearing before they marry, as well as decisions regarding each spouse's obligations for child care that may include an agreement that the husband will not do any such work at all. Sometimes these "negotiations" are merely implicit with little or no actual discussion but simply understood because they coincide with traditional patterns. At other times, especially if the couples are more "modern," the negotiations are made quite definite and sometimes involve considerable conflict. Most of these bargains are struck before or around the time of marriage, and have lasting consequences that later efforts to renegotiate may be unable to change. After the children are born, especially if they are close together, the young wife's bargaining status regarding employment is weakened.

Women are able to negotiate more effectively with their husbands if they are sex-role egalitarian and better educated. Before

marriage they are more likely to negotiate very specifically for the fertility control patterns they desire and for more innovative work while the less well educated are more often willing to go along with traditional sex-role patterns (Mueller, Parcel, & Pampel, 1979).

Contracts have certain drawbacks, one being their questionable legality. Massachusetts has passed legislation for upholding the validity of such contracts, but the vast majority of states have no laws pertaining to them. If the contract violates any exisitng laws, or if its provisions are clearly contrary to tradition, most judges would probably not uphold it. There are other very real problems, one being that young people who have never been married before do not know what the marriage relationship involves. Another problem is that marriage relationships change over the years and so do the marital partners themselves. In addition, such contracts may be so tightly drawn that they do not allow for alternatives.

On the other hand, such contracts may serve useful purposes. In drawing up a contract, a couple will make a serious effort to anticipate their married life realistically. Negotiating a contract may even persuade them that they should not marry at all. In addition, the contract may be a flexible one, with a built-in provision for periodic renegotiation on the basis of what the situation is at a given point in time. The contract may also help clarify and facilitate communication between the couple and determine whether, in fact, they can arrive at harmonious outcomes. There has been little empirical evidence regarding how such contracts fare in the long run.

Marriage Counseling. Traditionally, people learned from their parents how to run their families; now such training is inadequate. The traditional nuclear family, though still the most common, is just one of many types. Neither the larger society nor its segments are prepared to adapt effectively to the various alternatives—single-parent, dual-career, or reconstituted families (after divorce or death of parents) (Rogers, 1985). In consequence, much attention is being paid to marriages in trouble, and couples are increasingly resorting to marital therapy. In the process they seek to learn how to communicate with each other and to gain new insight into their problems. Whether they do or not depends upon the type of therapy employed, the therapist, the couple themselves—and the special "chemistry" of all of these combined. (Marital therapy often involves two stages. In the first, couples simply try to make their lives tolerable. In the second, they seek not simply to make their relationship tolerable, but good.)

Middle-age adults may need to be counseled about various problems including those of parenting their adolescent children, launching their young adult children, divorce, widowhood, and aging (Knox, 1979). Counseling may be provided through home ecomonic extension services, family life education programs, special school and college courses, or self-help groups such as Parents Without Partners or Widow-to-Widow. In other research, a sampling of 25 percent of the membership of the National Council of Family Relations indicated the following topics, in descending order, to be of greatest concern for marriage counselors in the next decade: "(a) divorce, separation, and desertion; (b) variant life styles; (c) child abuse and family violence; (d) marital communications/marital enrichment; (e) age and aging families; (f) single parenting; and (g) both changing sex roles and public policy and the family" (Axelson & Glick, 1979, p. 155).

If counseling is to be effective, it must also take into account changing concepts of marriage. This change would involve more flexible concepts of motherhood, sex roles, and privacy. Neither parent would live exclusively for the children and would more openly weigh the anticipated benefits of rearing them. In other times parents received some compensation for their sacrifice through

various material and symbolic benefits. Nowadays couples are more likely to go their own way, without inviting their aging parents to reside with them.

Finally the concept of marital adjustment suggests a process, not a static condition (Medley, 1977). Marriage is a dynamic relationship that involves continuous change and "not a fixed mechanical sequence. Therefore, no mere list of suggestions for enhancing marital adjustment will do justice to the complexity of the process" (p. 10).

Marital Satisfaction. Considerable research testifies to the importance of a good marriage. Among a nationwide sampling of married couples factors that negatively affected spousal interaction were the presence of children, a traditional division of household tasks and amount of workforce participation by either spouse (White, 1983). However, none of these was as important a determinant of such interaction as was the quality of the marriage.

Though marital satisfaction is important to all wives, its significance differs for presently employed women, those formerly employed, and the never employed, but in different ways or degrees (Freudiger, 1983). Working wives and formerly employed ones value marital happiness above anything else. The traditional, never-employed housewife gains more satisfaction from finances than from marital satisfaction; suggesting that she places her husband's breadwinner role above those of lover and companion. Another reason may be that having to make do with a single income automatically raises the importance of that role. Working wives gain satisfaction from their own career status and become less satisfied as their husbands' occupational prestige outstrips their own. In contrast, the formerly employed or never-employed wives gain some satisfaction from their husbands' achievements, which may place greater strain on them to succeed.

In a study of middle-aged residents in the Syracuse, New York area, 4 in 5 of both sexes said their marriages were going well all or most of the time; however, this evaluation varied by life stages (Rollins & Feldman, 1981). Happiness and companionship are greatest in the first years, followed by a plateau, then a low period as the children are "launched," followed by a rise in satisfaction punctuated temporarily by the husband's retirement.

Marital satisfaction for wives relates more to the family cycle, for men more to their work lives. Men's satisfaction shows little relationship to the child-bearing and -rearing phases of family life; whereas, women's satisfaction with marriage sharply deteriorates through these years, until the children leave home (Rollins & Feldman, 1981).

In other research, in a midwestern community, the degree of stress experienced by individuals depended on the complex interaction of certain variables. In general, marital satisfaction had less effect on depression of working women than of working men or housewives, and job satisfaction was more important for men. Working women with children—especially small ones—were more stressed than those without, especially because of the disproportionate time that working women, relative to their husbands, spend in parenting-housekeeping roles. Employed women are affected more than men or housewives by the presence of small children in the home, but less so by other events. They experience less stress than housewives unless there are children, especially small ones, in the home.

The division of labor in the home appears more resistant to change than that in the labor market, and whether or not the woman works has little effect on how household chores are divided (Clear & Mechanic, 1983). Even more egalitarian couples, who shared in quite nontraditional behaviors during the pregnancy-birth period, assume traditional roles after children arrive. While they believe in equal pay for equal work on the job, they still buy the notion that it is the women who should take care of preschool children.

Defining the Good Marriage

The characteristics of a good marriage, as defined by Tsoi-Hoshmand (1976), reflect the underlying philosophy of many marriage counselors. A good marriage has an unusual degree of mutuality, which suggests the sharing of values and personal feelings as well as the rewards and strains involved in living together. A good marriage will survive even demanding changes within the relationship. Over a period of time, the partners will change in the process of seeking increased psychological maturity; and the relationship should have the capacity to stretch and adapt to the stresses of change.

Such values connote each partner's capacity to respect the other's direction of self-fulfillment, and to see marriage as a context for personal growth (Levinger & Snoek, 1972). Middle-aged men, especially, have often been characterized in literature as "feeling drowned in the dullness of life."

Often problems of middle-aged couples have to do more with boredom than with real stress. The middle-aged marriage, therefore, can often be described as "suffering from success"; and this very security may contain within it "the seeds of destruction" (Tsoi-Hoshmand, 1976, p. 9). In time, however, the so-called middle-aged crises may become a stimulus to growth that challenges a couple to take stock of themselves and live a better life (LeShan, 1973).

To a certain degree, success in marriage is relative—no one should expect perfection. Based on a study of marriages judged to be happy and successful, Ammons and Stinnett (1980) determined that successful marital partners possess personality characteristics that encourage sexual expressiveness, otherness rather than selfness, determination, and high ego strength. Such couples have similar sexual needs, yet make adjustments for additional compatability. They have a mutually gratifying relationship based on the cooperation of both partners, and they honor the commitments of their marriage. Both partners have strong egos that allow them to behave autonomously and preserve their individuality. There is much give and take, including a continuing mutuality while preserving individual autonomy.

Appraisals of Marital Success

The Positive View. Most authorities on the family give it high marks. Eleanor Luckey (1974) believes that the "great quest of life is seeking how to be a loving person. And ... living in a family provides most of us our greatest opportunity for loving one another" (p. 312). While the divorce rate is high, 25 percent of divorcees marry again within 4 to 5 months of the final decree; 50 percent within a year and 75 percent within 3 years. What these people are rejecting is not marriage, but a partner with whom the relationship did not work (Marriage—still a popular institution, 1978).

In a national sampling, when couples were asked to check among the following those items most important to them: "being close to your husband (wife)," "having a happy family," "being financially secure," "having a sense of accomplishment," "having fun and enjoying life," and other such items "happy family" was most often chosen by parents to whom "family" meant both children and spouse (Hoffman & Manis, 1978, p. 177).

The question arises: Why does marriage increase happiness, especially for older women? A main reason is that it provides a love relationship. Three in four married people say they are very or moderately happy in their love relationship, as compared to 40 percent of singles. A second major advantage of marriage is that it provides a stable relationship in which someone is there when needed. While many singles may have such a relationship, marriage in effect insures it.

While some marriages fail in this regard, more succeed—partly because marriage is validated through ceremony, laws, and custom. The married couples' homes provide them security; they do not have to seek out singles bars or people to meet to avoid being lonely. "They have a guaranteed, steady Saturday night date. It may not be a great date; it may not be as romantic and wonderful as they would like, but they can usually count on it" (Freedman, 1978, p. 51). In addition, marriage generally takes care of the major problem of most single people—loneliness. Almost half of all single people often feel lonely, as compared with a fifth of married people.

The Negative View. Although evaluations of family life are mostly positive, some are negative. Choosing a spouse is a source of great stress, but an even greater disturbance is caused by persistent problems within marriage, such as lack of reciprocity and feelings of unfulfillment of marital expectations. One detractor of marriage, France's great family historian, Philippe Ariès, contends that the family that has evolved over the past few centuries has become "both an all purpose refuge and a prison" (Mousseau, 1975, p. 52). On the one hand, the pressures of modern life tend to drive people to seek refuge among their intimates in the home; on the other, this tendency, plus the assumption by the family of many significant life tasks, produces invisible boundaries between its members and the rest of the world. Thus the refuge confines its members by emotional bonds and sometimes limits their growth.

Some individuals idealize traditional marriage and deplore recent trends. Levine (1984) reviews the roots of the patriarchal family, calling it the most functional one for its time, and deplores recent familial forms and trends. Before industrialization family forms, structures, and roles were dictated by survival needs. Since the mid-1960s, however, variations in family forms have increased such as open marriages, single parenthood (by choice), homosexual "marriages," divorce, marriage contracts, and joint custody. Such variations, observes Levine, are viewed by many sociologists as flexible, imaginative ways to cope with complex technological and social changes. However, he adds, they have "undermined the moral consensus and normative standards that have upheld the nuclear family as the one legitimate form of family life whose well-being and prosperity were the primary responsibility of both spouses" (p. 157). What we have now is confusion and uncertainty about what the family is or should be. Complicating the matter further is the current tendency for parents to put their own welfare ahead of the children's and that of self ahead of the spouse's.

Social scientists themselves, notes Levine, simply report such matters—they take no judgmental view lest they contaminate their objectivity. Besides, the value-free approach is more compatible with tolerance of cultural, ethnic, and personal differences, which are hallmarks of a pluralistic society and a many-faceted world population.

Other Factors. Comparisons of marriage satisfaction at different life stages reveal no great variation, despite the common belief that satisfaction decreases after the early glow wears off (Rollins & Cannon, 1974). It is true that marriage satisfaction dips slightly in the middle years and rises again in later years, but the dip is slight.

Medley (1977) describes three ideal types of conjugal relationships, which may or may not last throughout the marriage. All three may provide each partner with feelings of self-fulfillment and well-being. The "husband-wife" type emphasizes the couple's shared, more intimate relationships. While the focus is on husband-and-wife roles, other roles are not excluded. In the "parent-child" type, one partner assumes the role of parent, and the other, the child. The parent-spouse acts in a dominant, nurturant, protective manner, while the other behaves depen-

dently and submissively. Such a relationship may develop when one party becomes incapacitated or assumes a sick role. In the "associate" relationship, couples are more or less friends who appreciate each other's company and find their most rewarding moments outside the more intimate marital relationships.

In general, marital status is more important to men than women, but the quality of the marriage—marital happiness—is more so for women (Gove, Hughes & Style, 1983). Men gain more simply from the status of being married—having the house cleaned, meals prepared, and their personal services rendered, whereas women are more emotionally invested in marriage. For neither sex does sexual gratification or companionship explain the better mental health of marrieds than singles. Certain of the constraints involved in living with others may outweigh the positive effects of social support and companionship. What the marrieds have is participation in an institution strongly supported by society with its own values and meanings.

New Directions

Suggestions for Improving Marriage. Despite its apparent success, most authorities believe that the institution of marriage could be improved. Mace and Mace (1975) are of the opinion that society should provide married couples the support, training, and guidance that they need. Philippe Ariès believes it is essential to reopen the family structure, an idea promoted by the women's movement. The important thing is not so much granting a housewife equality with a working woman, as allowing her to get away from the home "where the nineteenth century had imprisoned her, and where the baby boom had chained her even more tightly" (Mousseau, 1975, p. 57).

Future Prospects. Others predict that specific changes will take place in the future. The parental role itself may be supplemented by experts trained in effective techniques for childrearing. Ariès's (1975) predictions are even more radical. If the life span is extended much further, an individual can hardly be expected to stay with the same spouse for the entire duration. For instance, a woman might choose to remain attached only during her childbearing years.

Most authorities believe that the family will persist in the foreseeable future, but with some changes. Mace (1974) perceives the family "as a very tough institution" that is nevertheless undergoing a significant transition from institution to companionship (p. 291). This new form is based on "depth relationships combined with individual autonomy."

Bernard (1972) agrees with Mace, predicting that the future of marriage is "as assured as any human social form can be," although it may change in form or name (p. 301). People may even refer to themselves as pair-bonded instead of married. The chief characteristic of the marriage of the future will be "the array of options available to different people who want different things from their relationships with one another. . . . In brief, marriages in the future will be as different from conventional marriages of today, as those of the present are from those of our forebears in the nineteenth century . . ." (p. 303).

Overall, predicts Emory University Professor Levinson (When "family," 1983), the next century's families will be as different from current ones as were the patriarchies of old testament days—and the concept of mother as homemaker and husband as breadwinner will be "an historic curiosity." The family will remain strong, though "sprouting some odd branches" (p. A3). As people live longer, serial marriages will grow more common, and children will consist of assorted half- and step-siblings. However, as such developments occur, society will develop more adequate ways of dealing with them. Technologies will have their effects, too. They will allow families to spend more time together as computers make possible more careers at home, shopping from home and even being educated there.

A Caveat. Jay Haley (Pines, 1982) warns against over-generalizing about families, for their diversity is immense. There are Italian families, Asian families, rich ones and poor ones, those with adopted children or those from three marriages. Each type of family has its special functions apart from the basic purpose of child production and rearing.

SUMMARY

Most middle-aged persons are parents within their own families. During their earlier middle age, their children are often teen-agers, and by later middle age their children have left the "nest." Parents find both rewards and frustrations in dealing with their nearly grown children, but the rewards have become greater as families have grown more democratic and the generation gap has narrowed. Despite pride and satisfaction in their children, parents often lead a more relaxed, satisfying life after the children leave home.

The family roles of men and women are distinctively different. Most women—even those who work outside the home—still find their greatest satisfaction in the wife-mother role; nevertheless they have their problems. Their dual role in family and on the job is exhausting, for husbands do not assume an equal work role at home. However, men are gradually assuming more responsibilities in the home; and middle-class men, at least, are taking their father roles seriously.

So far it is unclear what is the healthiest form of relationship between a man and a woman, or how best to achieve it. A complementary relationship, where the ideal is equity, not simply equality, has been proposed as one solution. In order to prevent problems or cope with them when they arise, such techniques as marriage contracts and marriage counseling are employed.

Overall, it seems that most middle-agers find family life reasonably satisfying, with the inevitable problems found in all close human relationships. While family roles and married life are changing as the result of changing times, the family remains the cornerstone of society.

SUGGESTED READINGS

ANDERSON, S. A., RUSSELL, C. L., & SCHUMM, W. R., (1983). Perceived marital quality and family life-cycle categories: A further analysis. *Journal of Marriage and the Family, 45*(1), 127–139.

ARGYLE, M. & FURNHAM, A. (1983). Sources of satisfaction and conflict in long-term relationships. *Journal of Marriage and the Family, 45*(3), 481–493.

BEER, W. R. (1982). *Househusbands: Men and housework in American families.* New York: Praeger.

BORLAND, D. C. (1982). A cohort analysis approach to the empty-nest syndrome among three ethnic groups of women: A theoretical position. *Journal of Marriage and the Family, 44*(1), 117–129.

BOWEN, G. L. & ORTHNER, D. K. (1983). Sex-role congruency and marital quality. *Journal of Marriage and the Family, 45*(1), 223–242.

CLEARY, P. D. & MECHANIC, D. (1983). Sex differences in psychological distress among married people. *Journal of Health and Social Behavior, 24,* 111–121.

COLEMAN, M. & GANONG, L. H. (1984). Effect of family structure on family attitudes and expectations. *Family Relations, 33,* 425–432.

DAVIDSON, B., BALSWICK, J. , & HALVERSON, C. (1983). Affective self-disclosure and marital adjustment: A test of equity theory. *Journal of Marriage and the Family, 45*(1), 93–102.

FRIEDMAN, H. J. (1982). The challenge of divorce to adequate fathering: the peripheral father in marriage and divorce. *Psychiatric Clinics of North America, 5*(3), 565–580.

GLENN, N. D. & MCLANAHAN, S. (1982). Children and marital happiness: A further specification of the relationship. *Journal of Marriage and the Family, 44*(1), 63–72.

GOLDSCHMIDT-CLERMONT, L. (1983). Does housework pay? A product-related microeconomic approach. *Journal of Women in Culture and Society, 9*(11), 108–109.

GOVE, W. R., HUGHES, M., & STYLE, C. B. (1983). Does marriage have positive effects on the psychological well-being of the individual? *Journal of Health and Social Behavior, 24,* 122–131.

HILLER, D. V. & PHILLIBER, W. W. (1982). Predicting marital and career success among dual-worker couples. *Journal of Marriage and the Family, 44*(1), 53–62.

LANG, A. M. & BRODY, E. M. (1983). Characteristics of middle-aged daughters and help to their elderly mothers. *Journal of Marriage and the Family, 45*(1), 193–202.

LEIGH, G. K. (1982). Kinship interaction over the family life span. *Journal of Marriage and the Family, 44*(1), 197–208.

NORTON, A. J. (1983). Family life cycle: 1980. *Journal of Marriage and the Family, 45*(2), 267–275.

POULSHOCK, W. S. & DEIMLING, G. T. (1984). Families caring for elders in residence: Issues in the measurement of burden. *Journal of Gerontology, 39*(2), 230–239.

CHAPTER NINE

Alternative Life Styles

ALTERNATIVES TO THE NUCLEAR FAMILY

Family Groupings

The Extended Family. The most common type of family in America is the *nuclear family*. It is composed of the mother, father, and children. The traditional ideal of the family has been: "father works at an outside job; mother stays home and works at raising their two children" (Monogamous laws, 1978, p. 26). However, by 1975 only seven families in a hundred conformed to this description, and probably fewer than that do now. The "evidence is overwhelming," concludes Butler (1980), that the nuclear family will probably remain the dominant family form, but growing numbers of people will have some experience with the alternative family patterns described in this chapter.

One current alternative, the *extended family*—in which grandparents or other relatives are included in the home—was once the norm; and is still the dominant family form in many parts of the world. Even in this country there are a considerable number of extended families. Extended families fulfill certain important needs, both instrumental and psychological. Relationships within such families provide their members with feelings of self-esteem and well-being. Parents are not the only source of care and affection for the children, or the only adult objects of identification and social learning. The presence of grandparents helps children develop an empathy with older persons, including their own parents, as they grow older. Since such families include several generations, they permit *anticipatory socialization*—that is, they prepare children for the age roles they will occupy in the future (Kempler, 1976). The presence of several generations also gives children a feeling of historical continuity.

On the other hand, the extended family may hurt individuals who have less independence, initiative, and sensitivity to the need for change. The achievement of adulthood involves detaching and differentiating oneself from the parental models, and attaining a distinct sense of self. Hence the extended family functions best when at least some of its members are capable of responding to environmental and historical change (Rudolph & Rudolph, 1976).

The Commune. In the commune, a number of families join together in a sort of miniature socialistic society. Communes vary greatly in purpose, composition, and durability. Leach describes one that has lasted for over 20 years. It is made up of middle-class professionals who have continued in their jobs. The children are all in a play group, and those wives who want to care for the children do so, while the others work (Hall, 1974). In other communes, babysitting cooperatives are used. In still others children are excluded altogether (Kinkade, 1973).

It is debatable to what degree communes constitute a viable alternative to the family. Anthropologist Edmund Leach describes kibbutzim, communes, and group marriages as "artificial," and doubts that such groups can hold together. Yet such arrangements do sometimes work out. The growing need for communes—for example, among single parents, never-marrieds, and the elderly—may result in sounder, more creative approaches to communal living. Sufficient testimony already exists, from those in more successful communes, to prove their potential worth.

It is important to remember that communes vary greatly among themselves. A study of sixty urban communes in six major cities (Ferrar, 1982) indicated much variation, and some provided far more satisfactory settings for family life than others. Communal households designed specifically to accommodate family needs prove more satisfying to parents than those in which

family life is incidental to the communal idea. In multiple-family households parents tend to come into conflict over childrearing, whereas in households maintained separately commitment to parental and communal needs may conflict. In the latter type turnover is high, which proves upsetting to children.

The Family Network. Other useful variations—the *family network* and *family cluster*—are possible substitutes for the extended family (Stoller, 1970). The family network may consist of three or four nuclear families who decide to live in the same neighborhood; they meet regularly to exchange services and to share problems and leisure pursuits. Such an arrangement reduces isolation often experienced in nuclear families today.

The Family Cluster. The deficiencies of these living arrangements are, to a considerable extent, compensated for in the family cluster, in which persons of different age and marital status and their children meet regularly. They participate in leisure-time activities and afford mutual help and personal growth in solving problems—all without living together, pooling incomes, or swapping mates. For several reasons this living arrangement may help reduce the social isolation of a complex, impersonal urban society. For one thing, household units rarely embrace more than two parents and two children, and sometimes include only one of each. Also an increasing number of adults are single, divorced, or widowed (Pringle, 1974). Nor do many people have the advantage of living in three- or four-generation households.

Cluster members need not necessarily live in the same neighborhood: the composition of the group is the important factor. One study was made after several family clusters had been in operation for over 4 months (Wolfarth, 1973). About three-quarters of the participants mentioned having gained interesting companions; and over half said that they now spent more time doing things for fun, profiting from others' experiences, and having friends with whom to share their ideas and feelings.

Several factors may contribute to a cluster's falling apart, including lack of effective leadership, the departure of key members, disagreement as to activities and procedures, and personality clashes. Nevertheless, some of them have operated successfully for a considerable period of time (Pringle, 1974).

Cooperative Enterprises. Some support systems between individuals and families also take the form of various cooperative arrangements—"for example, car pooling, the common ownership of machines like snow-blowers and tractors, and co-ops, especially in urban communities" (Kempler, 1976, p. 148).

The Dual-Worker Family

One alternative to the traditional family, the dual-worker couple, has become the norm. Thus, only from historical perspective can it be judged a truly alternative life style. In 1980 almost 60 percent of American families had two or more wage earners (Job and family, 1980). Yet, many husbands and even more wives are only marginally committed to their jobs. Dual-worker and dual-commitment families may be differentiated, depending mainly on types of occupation pursued. In dual-commitment families, husbands and wives actively pursue occupations that require a high degree of commitment and that have a developmental character over time. In contrast, dual-worker couples take any type of gainful employment. Over 40 percent of all married couples in the United States conform to the dual-worker pattern (Rapoport, Rapoport, & Bumstead, 1978).

There are two major types of dual-worker couples: in one the woman simply works to supplement her husband's pay; in the other, her work is a career. In the former, the woman is usually less well educated and from a working-class traditional background. She

spends as many hours on the job as her h band does, but she does most of the cooking and household chores. Both spouses seem to accept this arrangement as decreed by society, even nature.

In contrast, career couples often possess an ideal of equality, but usually practice something different. In one national study (Barrett, 1984) over half the respondents agreed that working couples should share meal preparation, but in three out of four cases the woman did it all. Another study showed that even the unemployed husband does less housework than his full-time employed wife.

Most women workers, as distinct from careerists, place a higher value on their wife-mother role. A longitudinal study that involved married couples in two Illinois communities indicated that early employment had a minimal effect on either early or later patterns of childbearing. There was no indication that early work experience "set into motion a chain of events" that would lead to greater ultimate fertility or higher levels of future occupation. It may be, conjectured the researchers, that these wives work mainly because of financial need rather than to achieve future success goals. Even on their jobs they reflect more the wife-mother role than the self-fulfilling career model (Ewer, Crimmins & Oliver, 1979, p. 737).

Sometimes two mothers of young children will share a single job, but more commonly such mothers work half time for half pay. However, thus far, part-time individuals do not qualify for benefits such as pensions that are available to full-time workers.

Certain problems are common in such unions (Barrett, 1984). Both spouses want emotional support and both need "wives" to provide it. Sex activities may suffer—they are exhausted, or the modern wife more often asserts her sexual needs. The couple may not fully understand each other's career needs; or the husband may not have been aware that his wife had such needs at the time of marriage.

hand, two-career marriages
...vantages. It allows a higher
...g, and both parties are proud
...and the other's accomplish-
...ough men may like to be taken
...ome, they respect the work-
ing wi... ...e. For their part career women report greater marital satisfaction than housewives.

Sometimes situational factors simplify the dual-worker couple's problem. Retired parents may live nearby who can help out and take care of the children. Or due to the nature of the work, one spouse might operate from the home. Well-off couples may hire housekeepers and persons who specialize in expert child care. Another approach is simplification of one's life—a couple may use paper plates, or decide not to have children; and they may lead an informal social life with just a few friends. Whatever solution is hit upon is easier if both spouses support it.

Discussions with experts and with couples themselves suggest this advice. Couples should clarify joint expectations and priorities, and they should be realistic about what their career obligations involve. They should carefully arrange for times to be together or alone or to relax. They should also support efforts to promote institutional adjustments to make such marriages work.

Only recently have corporations begun revising their personnel manuals to suit the requirements of the two wage-earner family. The major fringe benefit that two wage-earner families desire is better childcare facilities. Only a minority are provided them today. Daycare brings certain benefits to the employers, too. The employees are happier and less likely to quit their jobs. Parents are also happier on their jobs when their children are in the vicinity.

One marriage alternative, the commuter marriage, is an increasingly frequent outcome of the dual-career relationship, chosen mainly to enhance wives' career mobility. (Rhodes & Rhodes, 1984). Most of these couples are well-educated professionals and half have children. Patterns vary greatly—couples may see each other every weekend or once a month. Some are just a few hours apart, others must fly across the country. Some commute for months, others for years.

Such couples are usually alike in certain respects. They arrive at the decision alone, without expert advice. They do not like commuting, and most of them expect it to end. Much of the time commuting wives spend at home is devoted to a disproportionate part of the household chores. Short-term commuters rarely make role adaptations; medium-term ones (1 to 3 years) more often cross sex-role boundaries and often maintain the new roles when the commuting ends. Long-term commuters adjust roles but often grow apart. Men get no real satisfaction assuming the woman's role; however, women often enjoy performing traditionally male roles.

Both hardships and benefits are involved in commuting marriages. Loss of intimacy, less time to spend together, and sexual infidelity are some of the typical problems. The degree of difficulty hinges on such factors as financial resources, distance of commuting, time spent separated, and presence or absence of children (Grossman & Sussman, 1982).

On the plus side, when separated, there may be more personal, concentrated time to work and more independence. If commuting is the only way to allow both spouses to advance in their careers it may be worth the price.

Prospective commuters may do well to heed certain advice. They should review all options; decide which spouse can best commute; decide whether they can adapt to revised sex roles; and consider realistically the toll that separation will take, in terms of emotions, child-, and household care. Since no specific body of law applies to commuter marriages, it also seems best to settle property ownership between the spouses and determine the primary legal residence. They should consider all costs, and talk to couples who have commuted, comparing their situation with those of others. Support networks are especially important. Relatives may help take care of the children and friends may fill the time normally spent with the spouse.

The Childless Couple

Most childless households consist of adults living alone, and their rate of increase for the 1980s will be twice that of all households (Glick, 1984). A fourth of these are persons over age 65; but the most rapid increase in such households is among the never-married and divorced under age 65.

As distinct from couples who have simply delayed having children, childless couples fall into two categories; those who would like to have children and cannot, and those who prefer to remain childless. In a study of 555 married women, aged 30 to 49, those who chose to be childless numbered about 4 percent, while another 4 percent would have preferred to have children but could not (Rao, 1974).

The number of childless couples is increasing.

Joe Franco

Those couples choosing not to have children are similar to those with children in terms of maturity, self-esteem, and life satisfaction, but whether their numbers will continue to increase can only be conjectured. Much will depend on women's future career opportunities; for so long as women are largely confined to low-status, low-paying careers, motherhood will be considered a more favorable life (Knox, 1980).

Despite its growth in incidence, society continues to regard the childless marriage as deviant, and social support for this status is still missing (Houseknecht, 1982). However, this type of marriage has its advantages. There is a positive relationship between egalitarianism and childlessness, suggesting that the maternal role, as ordinarily transacted, deprives women of equal opportunities.

Childless couples are better satisified than those with children. In fact, childless husbands feel unusually satisfied with their lives and experience less pressure than other men their age. The quality of their lives is higher than that of any other group of males, except possibly those whose children are past the age of 17. Part of the reason is that childless couples are freer of financial worries. Childless wives past 30 are just as satisifed as women with children. They usually describe their lives quite positively, though less so than their husbands do. Their status is relatively good, for childless marriages are typically far more egalitarian than those with children (Veevers, 1974).

The following testimony indicates the advantages that several couples have found in being childless:

FEMALE, AGE 40: The chief advantages my husband and I have found are these: (1) We have enough money to do the things we like. (2) We don't really enjoy children, so why have them when they might somehow detect that we would prefer not having them? (3) We don't have to worry about how they will turn out. (4) As a female, I haven't been encumbered with the sort of domestic responsibilities that children impose on a mother.

MALE, AGE 44:   My wife and I put off having children until a time when children would have proved an intrusion upon the life style we had developed. We simply felt complete as a marriage and family unit and had no feeling of anything missing. Originally we had intended having children simply because it was expected of us. Now the population explosion makes us feel we've done our bit toward helping society cope with the problem.

Reasons for Having Children Later. Of course, some long-term childless couples ultimately have children. As women progress through their 30s, they may panic at the realization that they must have a child now or never. In some cases, children become a couple's compensation because of failures or deficiencies in other areas of life. In other cases, a wife may unintentionally become pregnant, and for religious or other reasons, the couple may decide against abortion. Parenthetically, since the voluntarily childless are usually among the better educated, such older parents usually do a good job of parenting.

Bill and Susan Hobby were both well educated, reasonably well off financially, and committed to having no children. Bill taught in a university and Susan did part-time teaching. Otherwise, they stayed at home, engaged in many joint interests, including raising flowers, boating and reading. To their chagrin Susan became pregnant at age 40; however, after the baby, a son, arrived, Bill and Susan became transformed into proud parents. The son, who was attractive and precocious, simply begame programmed into their former way of life.

Essentials for Happiness. For voluntary childlessness to be a viable family form, it should meet certain criteria (Veevers, 1975). Both wife and husband should fully agree that they do not want children. The one condition necessary for the satisfaction of the voluntarily childless wife is that she partici-

pate in meaningful activities outside the home such as holding a job (almost all childless women do so). In addition, a childless wife may gain satisfaction from avocational pursuits such as dancing, painting, writing, or other expressive activities. It is important that both husband and wife take advantage of the free choices made possible by this life style. Through the centuries, having children has been viewed as natural and normal. It has been considered a reflection of sexual competence, as well as a religious, civic, and moral responsibility. Having children is still perceived by most people as making marriage complete and giving it a deeper significance. It is often portrayed as necessary for attaining true social and personal maturity, and for maintaining a healthy personality. Therefore, those married who voluntarily decide to have no children are viewed, especially by older generations, as somehow deviant—ethically, socially, and psychologically (Veevers, 1975).

In general, most childless couples are undisturbed by criticisms relating to "the dominant fertility norms" (Veevers, 1975, p. 485). In effect, they succeed in "discrediting [their] discreditors" (p. 485). They are typically unconventional in other ways as well. They associate mostly with those who are childless or who would prefer to be, which reinforces their own commitment to childlessness. They realize—either from first-hand observation or experience—that following conventional norms is no guarantee of good adjustment. In general, they are quite committed to their careers and they seek varied experiences. They highly idealize the husband-wife relationship; and they also view themselves as advantaged compared to couples with children. They may perceive most mothers as having had little choice about, and having been dragged reluctantly into, parenthood.

Over the past decade, adults in general are becoming more accepting of childless marriages. No longer do they perceive "childlessness as either neurotic or morally reprehensible" (Changing attitudes, 1979, p.

7). Relevant data support the view that many parents do indeed envy childless couples, or would enjoy participating in a child-free life style.

Unconventional Family Life Styles

Group Marriage. In group marriages ordinarily three to six persons consider themselves to be "pair-bonded" or married to others in the group (Peabody, 1982). They may exist within communes or within a single unit. One study showed that participants in more successful groups were over age 30. Compared to the general population they were "more inner-directed, held more internally derived values but used them flexibly, were more aware of feelings and needs, were more spontaneous, and more willing to have intimate contact with others" (p. 430). They appeared to be as well-adjusted in their marriage as did monogamously married persons.

These arrangements dissolve on the same basis as conventional unions do; for example one person may dominate in both monogamous and group marriages. In addition, group marriage partners may indulge in too much mutual soul-searching, when they might come to know each other better by doing things together and interacting in everyday matters. Neither swinging nor group marriage is a genuine alternative to conventional marriage. Such arrangements are too few, fragile, and hazardous to attract the more traditional majority.

An egalitarian, nonmonogamous "utopia" in San Francisco consists of a "polyfidelitous family" which, in 1981, involved nine women, six men and two young children. All the men claimed to love each other and so did all the women, and whatever jealousy arose was dealt with speedily and openly. The Keristans, as they are called, reduce to a minimum anything that may trigger jealousy. To do so, they discarded romantic love in favor of "nonpreferential" or "universal" love; and they maintain absolute fidelity

within the family itself, sharing lifelong commitment to each other. A comparison of these adults with other Americans and Israelis on a sexual jealousy inventory showed that they did indeed feel significantly less sexual jealousy (Pines & Aronson, 1981).

The Open Marriage. The *open marriage* has several distinctive characteristics (Wachowiak & Braga, 1980). It combines here-and-now living with realistic expectations. There is greater role flexibility, personal privacy, and open communication than in traditional marriages. Such couples also believe in "open companionship," which may mean developing deep personal, sometimes sexual, relationships with others. Such marriages are also characterized by equality of power and responsibility, and placing a high evaluation on personal identity or individual uniqueness. Finally there is the assumption of trust—that neither spouse has anything to hide.

Spouses in an open marriage reject the idea that each partner can fill all the other's emotional needs and believe this alternative allows for more personal and emotional growth (Peabody, 1982). An open marriage is based on mutual trust and free communication. It may be open mainly in the sense of encouraging outside relationships; or it may also include agreement not to be sexually exclusive. Generally, partners in open marriages, like swingers, have reported no threat to—or even an improvement of—their marriage bond. Nor were there any significant differences, on psychological measures, between such people and the general population, except that the group marriage partners were "less neurotic, anxious and defensive, and more self-assured" (Peabody, 1982, p. 429).

Although open family systems have sometimes been judged healthy some are characterized by "excessive and chaotic interaction, prolonged conflict and ambiguity, tending to overtax individual resources, eventually leading to collapse and separation" (Constantine, 1983, p. 725). Children may develop somatic problems because of less involved parenting and excessive independence. Hence, it is ill advised categorically to call a particular family system healthy. The health of any family system depends upon its specific practices and organization.

Swinging. A less socially acceptable form of marriage is called *swinging,* or the agreed-upon exchange of marriage partners, at least on occasion. Certain "respectable" national publications accept advertisements for swingers and swing clubs, and a communications network helps swingers locate each other (Fox, 1980, p. 44). Most of those seeking partners make clear that they are not "screw-and-run types" but prefer "long-term loving relationships with interesting couples" (p. 44).

To gain some insight into such arrangements, Gilmartin (1975) compared middle-class married suburban swinging couples with 100 socioeconomically matched nonswinging couples. The swinging couples attended swinging parties about once every 2 weeks. That is, swinging was no more important than other leisure activities. At swinging parties, wives typically engage in erotic activities with perhaps three or four different persons, while husbands may average two or three for each party. Ordinarily they indulge in petting, massaging, mutual masturbation, and oral-genital sex; and the majority have intercourse at least once at each party. Over half of the women sometimes engage in sex with other women, often with the husbands watching, but none of the husbands reported any homosexual activity.

By comparison with the nonswingers, the swingers had looser ties to family, community, and church. As might be expected, the swingers were considerably freer in their attitudes on such matters as sex education for children, abortion, premarital sex, nudity, and contraceptives for teen-agers. Not a single one of them believed that their marriages had become worse as a result of swinging; instead the great majority felt that their mar-

riages had improved. Nor had swinging negatively affected their sex lives, for they normally had sexual intercourse with each other more frequently than the control couples. Among the controls, thirty-one of the husbands and eight of the wives had engaged in adultery. The swingers were even slightly happier than were the nonadulterous controls.

Swinging is not adultery because both partners accept it and a single sex standard of morality prevails (Peabody, 1982). Dedicated swingers view it as recreational and avoid emotional involvement with swinging partners. The majority report that it strengthens their relationship and sex activities with their spouses; however, few swingers persist long in the practice.

The Homosexual Union. In the United States there is a minority of uncertain size composed of homosexual couples who live together in quasimarital unions. In San Francisco as many as a quarter of its 750,000 residents are homosexual, and there are over thirty gay activist groups. Its large gay population is reflected in "relatively high incomes (both gay partners working and no children), and superior restaurants, recreational facilities, book stores, music, and theatres" (Sheff, 1980, p. 108). The vast majority of gays never proclaim their status and are generally indistinguishable from any other roommates or housemates of the same sex. They experience the disadvantages of belonging to two minority groups—singles and gays.

Many people still look upon gays as deviant, socially undesirable, and psychoneurotic, and they consider homosexual unions to be illegitimate, sick, and undeserving of legalization. For example, a male homosexual couple was denied a marriage license in Minneapolis (Weitzman, 1975). Such couples lack the economic advantages of heterosexual couples in filing joint income tax returns, as well as in obtaining certain disability, unemployment, social security, and pension benefits. They also lack certain prerogatives of heterosexual couples in obtaining mortgages, apartments, homes, and insurance.

Freedman (1975) reports that most homosexuals do not adhere to standard sex roles, an observation that most gays themselves would endorse. When two men or two women live together, they quickly perceive the limitations of stereotyped sex roles. The dichotomies of breadwinner-versus-homemaker or dominant-versus-submissive are not important to most of them. Lesbians appear to be better adjusted sexually and play more active sexual roles than do heterosexual women. They focus on sex as an expression of tenderness and warmth. While some of them "come out," or make their homosexuality known, the majority live quite inconspicuously. They have both gay and "straight" (heterosexual) friends and possess a remarkable adaptability. For example:

Kim was a college teacher, a pilot, and a very personable, athletic young woman. When she was visiting her parents at their cottage on a lake, she met Gladys, an attractive divorcee with a small son. Before long, Kim and Gladys established a homosexual relationship and lived together, along with the son. Formerly the boy had been a young terror, but Kim, the butch in the combination, took firm but kindly control of him. Kim's parents sharply disapproved of the arrangement; therefore Kim broke off with them. These events happened twenty years ago. Kim and Gladys, with the boy in tow, went to the West Coast and prospered. They were both creative, active, and congenial. Ultimately the boy grew into a fine young man and left home. Kim and Gladys are a happy middle-aged couple with many friends and fond memories of the past; they are both optimistic about the future.

Data obtained from questionnaires administered to 241 gay men in the Detroit area indicated that there is no single type of gay relationship or gay marital career. The nature of the relationship depends on the characteristics of the men involved. While certain heterosexual marital types and careers are reasonably predictable and derived from institutional definitions in society, variations in gay relationships depend on individual and situational factors (Harry, 1979). Gay relationships range from brief, stressful encounters to long-term intimate and faithful relationships. The couples were typically egalitarian, and the role of houseperson was rare. Nor did problems of dominance occur, as they do in heterosexual marriages.

The commonly held belief that gays are more psychoneurotic than straights has been disproved, and homosexuality is no longer classified as an illness by the American Psychiatric Association. In fact, when homosexuals and heterosexuals not in therapy are compared on personality tests, researchers cannot tell one group from another (Freedman, 1975). In some ways gay people seem better adjusted. They often show a wider range of emotional expression because they are not limited by standard sex roles.

While it is commonly believed that gay men have an undesirable effect on their children, such is not the case. In general, gay fathers do not sexually abuse their children nor expose them to a homosexual atmosphere; nor do they have a disproportionate number of gay children. Their relationships with their children are satisfying, and those men who relinquish their unpleasant marriages and adopt gay life styles often report improved relationships with their children (Miller, 1979).

Since they are more invisible and experience less prejudice, lesbians are often better adjusted than male homosexuals. In a survey of 140 lesbians. Marilyn Fleener of California State University found that they were not the products of any special kind of family situation. Most of them had acquired their present sexual orientation by their early teens, despite pressures to be heterosexual. About four in five had been tomboys as children, but few wanted to be men and those few only because of men's social privileges. Most of them were faithful to their partners, and 98 percent denied playing butch-fem roles. In sexual relations, just 7 percent did not experience orgasm every time or most of the time, which is small compared with the far greater percentage of heterosexual women who rarely or never experienced orgasm. Although society focuses on the sexual activities of their lives lesbians perceive sexual activity as only one aspect of a generally rewarding life style (Lesbian life styles, 1977).

It is commonly assumed that children reared by homosexuals are at risk, but such is not the case. Studies show that children of homosexuals, usually lesbians, are as well adjusted as children in general; nor do they differ in gender preference (Maddox, 1982). The same is even true of children reared by transsexual parents who have had a surgical change of sex.

Nevertheless, judges, who usually do not know the research, are prone to deny acknowledged homosexuals custody of children. In court cases in Seattle lesbians were awarded custody just 1 percent of the time in 1970 and 15 percent in 1982. It is even more difficult for male homosexuals, who may even be denied visiting rights to their children after a divorce.

Lesbians sometimes settle for artificial insemination; and homosexuals of either sex may adopt children, especially if they remain quiet about their sexual preference. In such cases, however, the child may be legally awarded to only one partner, not both.

SINGLES

Single adults in the United States include the never-married, the widowed, and the divorced. They include people before marriage and between marriages. Among single adults in this country, 58 percent have never married, 27 percent are widowed, and 15 percent are divorced (Economics of being single, 1976). About 35 percent of all Americans over 18 are single; and adult singles now head one household in five. By 1990 it may be one in four, mainly because people

are divorcing more often, getting married later, and waiting longer to remarry. Older singles consist mostly of the widowed, separated, or divorced because by this time, many of the formerly single have married. If a person is single and entering middle age, that individual is likely to remain so, for only 1 percent of all first marriages involve the middle aged (U.S. Bureau of the Census, 1976).

For several reasons it is important to study the never-married (Anderson & Braito, 1981). Hitherto, much of the rather limited research about singles has lumped together all the currently unmarried—the never-married, widowed, divorced, and separated. Such research as exists about them is often limited to atypical samples, mostly middle- and upper-income persons, or just one sex. Also, rightly or wrongly, singlehood has been viewed as a deficit status. Finally, singles' numbers are growing as the age of marriage has been increasingly postponed.

Relevant research questions the long-held belief that singles are less healthy mentally than marrieds, although they vary in this regard just as marrieds do (Anderson & Braito, 1981). Low socioeconomic status and isolation are key variables, although some say that their autonomy is worth the occasional loneliness involved. Married people can be lonely, too, especially if they are not congenial. Anyhow, the quality, not the quantity, of contacts may be what is important.

Single Women. Never-married women, especially, are growing in numbers; and those ages 25 to 34 have doubled over the past decade (Levine, 1984). The majority had intended to marry when they were 18, but circumstances prevented. One reason for the growth in numbers of female singles is that they wanted a meaningful life and felt that woman's traditional role would sustain them neither emotionally nor economically (Spake, 1984). Men, and often women, still expect the wife to "embody primarily 'feminine' values—cooperation, nurturance, and impulse to yield" (p. 48). Though the more creative, ambitious woman's values have changed, the man's ideal has changed little. Perhaps for this reason women, ages 35 to 44, with post-graduate degrees and incomes over $20,000, have four times the divorce rate of lesser achievers. In other words, conflicts arise from "the schism between women's new realities and men's (and women's) old expectations" (p. 48). Some women turn to other women, and find deeply rewarding relationships there. However, says Levine, these women still feel a need for men, whether because of biology or upbringing. Nevertheless, single heterosexual women do rely heavily on intimate same-sex friendships.

Increasingly, some singles, mostly female, seek parenthood—both sexes through adoption and women through artificial insemination, or perhaps a man friend who is not interested in marriage or filling a father role. One such individual who induced a friend to be the father, found the experience difficult but gratifying (Mack, 1982). Her family emotionally distanced themselves from her; the child proved very expensive to rear; and she felt somehow different—but she found great delight in her small daughter.

One should also note that many singles, especially the women, live with someone, sometimes on a permanent basis. In this case one might ask whether they may, in fact, be regarded as single. It would also be interesting to compare the mental health of never-marrieds who live alone with that of those who live with others, and of those who would prefer to marry with those for whom singlehood is the choice.

The Divorced

A group of singles who share many of the advantages and problems of singles in general, is the divorced. In growing numbers, individuals married over two decades are ending their marriages (Knox, 1980). In the meantime, states are increasingly adopting no-fault divorce laws, granting alimony to either sex, granting child custody to both parents, and including visitation rights of grandparents in divorce settlements.

Causes of Divorce. There are several reasons for the growth in the divorce rate. Today couples feel less restricted by societal sanctions against divorce than in the past. Wives also feel sure of being able to make a living on their own (What future, 1976). As women enter the labor force, thereby gaining power and money, many couples simply grow apart. Although the vast majority believe in a lifetime marriage commitment, they think that a couple should divorce if they cannot get along, even when children are involved.

A related reason for divorce, suggests Ariès, is that couples may simply become fed up with each other after so many years. In earlier times couples were often separated by death, but because of increased longevity, today's couples spend a half century or more together. Hence, adults simply have replaced death with divorce. The current wide acceptance of divorce assures a couple who cannot tolerate each other for too long that they can separate (Mousseau, 1975).

Certain factors tend to increase divorce rates, others to limit them. Enhancing rates are relaxation of social and religious sanctions against divorce, and women's entry in large numbers into the work force. Hard times, on the other hand, militate against it, since it is more expensive to support two households (Leahey, 1982). Other factors associated with maintaining marriage include marital interaction—doing things together, staying home in the evening, and favorable home environment—especially lack of household crowding—while the presence of children may have a mixed effect. Parents may feel obligated to stay together on account of them or driven apart if they are a source of conflict and tension (Palisi, 1984).

Over recent years the incidence of divorce has risen sharply. Only 15 percent of persons aged 65 to 74 have ever divorced (Glick, 1984). But given current divorce rates, about half (49 percent) of today's young adults, ages 25 to 34, will divorce by age 75, over three times the rate for their grandparents. In general those with a college education have a better chance of achieving a permanent marriage, although over half of all women who take postgraduate degrees divorce.

It appears that the number of divorces and remarriages in years just ahead will rise only moderately (Glick, 1984). The decline in the birth rate has made it easier to maintain two households, but it is unlikely to decline much further. Women's improved education made it easier for them to support themselves after divorce and less willing to endure marital unhappiness, but the increase in educational levels may have about peaked.

Nevertheless, the numbers of persons divorcing at older ages is continuing to increase. Two-thirds of American women who divorce do so by age 30, when their children are generally under age 7; and it is estimated that 1 in 9 children will be living with a divorced parent in 1990. One in 3 (32 percent) will have lived with a divorced parent during some stage of childhood (Leahey, 1982).

A study of divorced individuals (Thompson & Spanier, 1983) reported having received varying degrees of disapproval from others. Fewer than a third of the women and somewhat more than a third of the men received disapproval from their parents, but their friends were mostly neutral. Fifty-eight percent of the women's friends approved, compared to just 36 percent of the men's. Acceptance of dissolution of marriage depended on several factors: the degree of approval of others, attitudes toward marriage, and loss of companionship—but not the length of marriage.

The divorced woman dwells in "social limbo" (Brandwein, Brown & Fox, 1974, p. 506). No longer does she enjoy the pair re-

lationships that she and her husband once shared. In addition, she suffers a certain stigma; for example, consider "the societal myth of the gay divorcee, out to seduce other women's husbands, which leads to social ostracism of the divorced woman and her family" (Brandwein, Brown & Fox, 1974, p. 499).

Divorce is less an event than a process, notes Leahey (1982), with ripple effects over time. Not only affected is the marital relationship but relations between parent and child and between siblings. For example, after the divorce children with older brothers, in comparison with those without, are more aggressive and independent. Also affected are persons and institutions outside the family, especially the kinship system. Extended family members often take sides, thus enhancing the general stress and anxiety of all parties involved. Impacted, too, are the housing market, schools, health care facilities, and community agencies, partly because mother-led single families, the prevalent type, are usually downwardly mobile.

A study of stages of progression through divorce disclosed three stages: those of separation and/or filing, separation and/or filing to final decree, and final decree to penultimate closure. Within these stages is much variation, although generally one party tends to be the active, the other the passive agent, who moves through the process more slowly (Crosby, Gage & Raymond, 1983).

In the following, a 38-year-old woman who has been separated for three years and was now finishing the divorce procedure answers several questions:

I imagine that you did a good many things as a couple when you were with your husband. Since you have not been with your husband, have you found much difference in your social life? I like to be alone a lot and I'm not lonely. I experienced loneliness for the first time going through the process of divorce. I didn't know what was happening to me.

Why would you feel more lonely during this process? For the first 12 years there was a certain intimacy in being married—a feeling I had that someone was always there and that I could talk to—and after he left, I was depressed. But the kind of socializing that we did as a married couple I don't miss at all. I found it phony and superficial. My real friends, people I have shared the most with, have not changed. They are my same friends, whether I am married or not. I have not been to any occasion where there have been couples for the last 3 years.

That particular feature hasn't bothered you? No, I feel relieved at missing these couples' affairs—you never ever get a match. I mean that either the husband part of the team was okay and the wife was a dog; or the husband was a dog and the wife was wonderful. I never found both interesting at the same time.

I gather that your feelings have changed from the time that you first separated until now. In other words, there has been a process of adjustment. How long has that been? It has been about 3 years. I had been aware for maybe 5 years prior to the separation that I had defined myself in terms of my husband. Alot of people said I was lucky to get this person, and a part of me still reacts to this. It's become much diminished but I do feel a tinge of failure. That I failed something, especially because of the terms on which he wanted to end the marriage—that I physically failed him. That I was physically repulsive to him. After all, I'd married at 19, and married with all of the norms that were prevalent in the 50s and early 60s—that you stay married to one man, that you had children, and settled in the suburbs, while he got a good job and became successful. Then came living through those years of finding out that that was really so much crap, and that I didn't want to live in someone else's shadow, that I want to have a career, that I didn't want to just be a mother.

Do you think that you might ultimately get married again? Right now I can't envision myself ever again living with someone in a possessive relationship. I would like to meet someone at a convention and say, "Hey, I'll meet you again next year" or "I'll meet you next month" or "Let's fly here for a vacation, no strings attached." It would be strictly a relationship that has some caring and involvement but in which there are no demands on either party to conform to the expectations of the other.

Divorced men have certain advantages, but their handicaps are greater than is commonly believed. On the one hand, they feel less pressure than do married men, and have less worry about paying bills. Only 25 percent of divorced men describe their lives as difficult. Some of them have to make alimony payments that keep them financially strapped; also, it is usually they who must change their residence. As noncustodial parents they see their children at times not of their own choosing, and many risk losing any real involvement with them (Kressel, 1980). In many cases they are not used to housekeeping for themselves and lead somewhat haphazard, dreary lives. Certainly the image of the "free-swinging ex-husband" is a distortion (Rising divorce rates, 1975).

Nevertheless, divorced people do adjust, and some of their lives become better than before. The vast majority eventually remarry; meantime they carry on, often quite well, after the shock of the divorce wears off. Some of them learn to live alone and like it, especially if they were overshadowed by their former mate's personality. They also enjoy their new freedom and develop a new self-reliance.

Although the divorce process—including the loss of the noncustodial parent, separation and decision to divorce, and adapting to a single-parent household—are stressful, few individuals report that they have been hurt, long-term, by the experience (Leahey, 1982). The impact hinges significantly on the situation of the persons involved, including their socioeconomic status and whether children remain in mother- or father-led families.

Remarriage

Most individuals who divorce ultimately remarry—about three-fourths of divorced women and five-sixths of the divorced men. Men are more likely to remarry than women and more often remarry someone not previously married. Most divorced men with child custody remarry soon to obtain childrearing help. Divorced women without a college education tend to remarry sooner (Glick, 1984).

In a questionnaire study of 500 once-divorced persons, of 490 giving reasons that their first marriage had failed, 68 listed infidelity as the chief reason. Another 103 said their marriages dissolved because they no longer loved each other, and these factors accounted for 55 percent of first-listed reasons. Other frequently listed reasons, in order of importance, were: emotional problems (53 percent), financial problems (30 percent), physical abuse (29 percent), alcohol (25 percent), sexual problems (22 percent) problems with in-laws (16 percent), neglect of children (11 percent), communication problems (10 percent), married too young (9 percent), job conflict (7 percent) and others (7 percent).

Overwhelmingly these remarried persons found their second marriages satisfactory, 88 percent saying their present marriage was much better than the first one, and another 7 percent a little better. In a sampling of 1,800 adults in Nebraska, White (1979) found that remarried men reported greater happiness than did men in first marriages; whereas remarried women reported less happiness than women in first marriages.

Both sexes report role changes in their new marriages. Men share parenting and household tasks more and women expect more of them than they did of their former husbands. Women and men feel they must be primarily in charge of "their own" children.

Usually the shift to this relationship takes place with little or no help. Generally such couples are not closely associated with other such pairs, from whom they might gain support. A few do have such linkages and their children often do. Often such parents send their children to private or parochial schools, where they presumably obtain greater support. Also this practice connects their children with more than one neighborhood.

The main problem is in reconstituted, or blended, families where children from former marriages are involved (Kompara, 1980). The term "stepfamily" itself carries a somewhat unpleasant connotation. Parents have

to deal with children who have been socialized by another set of values. Also disturbing are constant reminders of former spouses—comments by the children, family traditions, and inadvertent remarks by the parents themselves. In addition, the parent who did not receive custody of the child may turn the children against the stepparent. The role of stepmother is judged to be more difficult than that of stepfather. She must cope with the traditionally unfavorable view of stepmothers. She must spend more time with the stepchildren than does the stepfather; and society gives more assistance to stepfathers. There is also the matter of establishing relationships with the stepchildren. Stepmothers under 40 years of age have better relationships with them than those over 40.

Authorities' views on the topic are sometimes conflicting. They disagree about whether the stepparent should encourage stepchildren to maintain close relationships with the natural parent. They differ, too, on whether stepfamilies have a generally difficult time; some studies report greater problems, others do not. In any case, empirically tested programs for helping such families are needed; and ambiguities of cultural norms should be resolved.

Child Custody. Under early common law, the father received priority in child custody decisions. Then over the centuries custody decisions began to favor the mother, as she was deemed better able to care for a child (Woody, 1978). More recently, the emphasis has been on the best interest of the child; and as a result, growing numbers of fathers are receiving custody of their children.

Often the noncustodial parent feels distraught and sometimes desperate at losing contact with his or her children. Parents are kidnapping their own children after divorce at the rate of 100,000 a year and few have been legally punished. However, a recently enacted uniform child custody jurisdiction act, passed in forty states, makes custody decisions in one state binding in others. Efforts to impose greater penalties on the abducting parent are being made in Congress. Some men's groups protest these developments, because they feel that custody decisions discriminate against men (Ramos, 1979).

Contrary to many—probably most—psychologists, the writer favors some form of joint custody in most cases, unless one parent is unfit or disinclined to care for the children. Kristine Rosenthal and Harry Keshet studied 127 divorced fathers in the Boston area with children aged 3 to 7 to determine which form of fathering was most satisfying; full-time custody of the children, half-time, quarter-time, or just once in a while (Happy daddies, 1978). Clearly, the half-time fathers were the happiest; and they had worked out a "kind of equity" with the other parent. Both parents acknowledged their dependence on each other and that each would profit by the other's being a good parent. The half-timers paid less money for child support, had more say in the childrearing process, and greater access to their children. Unlike the full-time fathers, they had time for social lives; and their arrangements for custody were voluntary, in contrast to the full-time fathers who usually had the children because the mother, for one reason or another, could not cope with them. All these half-time fathers worked full time, and the children interfered with their work to a certain extent; but the parenting opportunity made up for it. Most of the fathers were middle-class, college-educated professionals in their 30s.

In general, noncustody mothers, those who live apart from their children, have fewer and less satisfactory relations with them than do custody mothers. They have less contact with their sons than their daughters and less contact with children of either sex than do noncustody fathers (Fischer & Cardea, 1982). It may be conjectured that society is less supportive of noncustody mothers and tends to create in their children the feeling that the mother somehow failed them.

For several reasons the status of children in stepparent families is of increasing concern (Giles & Sims, 1984). For one thing their numbers are growing and should reach 15 percent by 1990. Besides, there are no clear norms for judging reconstituted families. Stepparents simply do not know what their role should be regarding stepchildren, which tends to create inconsistent behavior patterns. Many people attempt to transfer to their step families ideologies more applicable to a nuclear family. Stress diminishes, however, when they adapt their behaviors to the new family structure. For example, women more often than men, expect to be as close as birth mothers to their stepchildren, and their failure to achieve this ideal leaves them frustrated.

The Single Parent

Given current trends, married couple households are expected to decline over the 1980s from 60 to 55 percent, while one-parent households increase by a third. About 2 or 3 percent of children under 18 may be living with fathers only, another 1 in 10 with the mother and a stepfather. About 59 percent of all children born in the early 1980s will spend part of their childhood in a one-parent home. Contributing to this phenomenon is a tripling of children born out of wedlock over the past decade. In 1980 11 percent of white, and 55 percent of black, births were to unmarried mothers, a trend which is predicted to persist but at a lesser rate (Glick, 1984).

Various terms are used to describe single-parent families including "broken," "disorganized," and "disintegrated," all of which carry unfavorable undeserved connotations (Leahey, 1982). Families without two parents are viewed as deviant and abnormal, a perception shaped by and shaping social attitudes. It may even be wrong to assume that divorce creates a single-parent family, for the noncustodial parent may become even more involved in parenting after the separation (Leahey, 1982). Gongla (1982) argues that society should cease viewing the single-parent family as deviant and regard it as a legitimate alternative.

Single parents have certain special needs, including children's daycare and part-time jobs which carry full benefits. They also have limited resources, less assistance with household tasks and child care, and less emotional support from another adult. Such parents also have less time for social activities and community participation. They do gain some help from other adults in the home, social support from neighbors or friends and relatives, and sometimes from community organizations. However, since they are ordinarily busier, they are more isolated from their neighbors than are two-parent families. One result is a feeling of powerlessness or lack of control over their lives (Smith, 1980). Another problem is feeling isolated and lonely, because of dual obligations of work and child care (Smith, 1980). However, the single-parent status is usually transitional, as remarriage is the rule for most within a few years.

Despite their problems, single-parent families can take heart from the available data. A study of third-, sixth-, and eighth-grade children indicated no significant differences in self-concept scores between children from intact, single-parent, reconstituted, and other types of families. (Raschke & Raschke, 1979).

The Single Mother. Over 85 percent of single parents are women, most of them legally separated or divorced. Unfortunately, society portrays the one-adult family as a deviant rather than a workable and increasingly common alternative family form. In addition, such women are tainted with the stigma of being divorced, separated, or single, and the notion that they have been unable to win or to keep their husbands. It is also assumed by many that if these women would either marry or remarry, the situation would then be all right.

An increasingly common type of single parent is the woman who does not desire to marry or is not ready to marry, but chooses to have a child, perhaps by adoption or artificial insemination (Havim, 1983). In such cases certain questions may arise: What will be the effect on the child? Is a child entitled to two parents? Does the child have a right to know who the father is in cases where a sperm donor is employed?

The Single Father. For at least three reasons the number of single-parent families headed by fathers—now about 14 percent—can be expected to increase. Society is placing greater stress on fathering than ever before. In consequence, boys will, in time, begin to receive family-life training along with girls—some already do. Second, men are coming to enjoy and insist upon their rights as parents. And finally, the equal rights movement suggests that fathers' claims to children are as valid as mothers'; women who care little for mothering should not have children foisted on them.

The man who is a single parent has his own special problems. Society tends to question his ability to be a parent, an attitude reflected by the prevailing practice of awarding custody of children in divorce cases to mothers. The father may in fact be somewhat inept because he has not been socialized for the parent role.

On the other hand, no research exists to prove that single fathers do a poorer job than single mothers. They are usually quite conscientious and resourceful about their tasks (Sheehy, 1976). In one study of single fathers (Mendes, 1976), a large majority (28 out of 32) did the cleaning, cooking, and home management, and none of them felt they lost any masculinity in performing these functions. All the fathers loved their children, and all but two believed that their children loved them. The fathers typically showed preadolescent children considerable physical affection, but gave less of it to adolescents. Instead, they reassured the older children by the way they took care of them.

Among the 32 fathers, 20 were rearing

daughters aged $2^1/_2$ to 15. They felt no special concern about taking care of their daughters except in matters of sex. In particular, they expressed concern about how the daughters would accept their sexuality as adolescents. They also expressed some anxiety that their daughters lacked appropriate female role models for learning to be feminine. Sometimes the daughter still had a good relationship with the mother; in other cases the fathers had women friends with whom the daughter interacted.

The Adjustments Involved. Other problems involved in divorce are both immediate and long term. For one thing, the decision to seek divorce is usually made only after a considerable period of time and much emotional strain. Also stressful are the legal proceedings. Due to the traditionally adversarial nature of legal proceedings clients' needs are unmet, even under presumably nonadversarial no-fault laws (Glass, 1984).

Society and Singles

It would be foolish to overgeneralize about singles because they are of such varied types: the never-married, the divorced, and the widowed. Some of the never-married have no intent to marry; some plan definitely to do so. In consequence the latter may identify more with the married than the single. Some singles are in effect married, including gay couples and cohabitants. Singles also vary greatly according to sex, age, occupation, and the presence of children or other persons in their homes (Hayim, 1983).

The reasons that people remain permanently single are somewhat different for either sex. Women who remain single are more likely to be better educated than their married peers. Female scientists and engineers are six times as likely to be single as their male counterparts, often because such women choose not to marry (Havens, 1973). Very successful women, especially, may avoid or terminate intimate commitments (Kan-

gas, 1978). Males may remain single for somewhat different reasons. They may dislike feeling tied down, and they may have easy access to sex.

Singles of both sexes value close relationships but also have a strong need for independence. However, many seek close attachments and find them the most meaningful aspect of their lives. They also have a strong need to achieve and be successful. Factors that dispose either sex to remain single change over the years.

Social Attitudes. Traditionally, singles have been considered somewhat deviant, even a bit pathetic. In the nineteenth century, the superintendent of a mental hospital declared that single and widowed persons were more likely to become insane than married people. As he expressed it:

We remember that the unmarried so often give unbridled indulgence to the feelings, propensities, and passions of depraved human nature, and that uninfluenced by the wholesome and purifying restraints of matrimony, they plunge recklessly into dissipation and vice, reaping as their reward, a broken constitution, ruined fortune, and blasted reputation. We must cease to feel surprised, that in so many instances, they present the pitiable spectacle of a "mind in ruins" and become the tenants of our asylums for this afflicted class of citizens (Stribling, 1842, pp. 15–16).

Unhealthy stereotypes of singles persist in society today, one being that they are lonely and neurotic and that they run away from deep commitments. Yet interviews with thirty-two never-married adults, ages 25 to 37 (average 29)—half employed in the mental health profession, the remainder in other professions—supported neither of these stereotypes (Lynne & Howe, 1979).

Since people do not know how singles satisfy their sexual needs, their imaginations have a field day, suspecting that any single person "sleeps around, is gay, or hamstrung with sexual hangups" (Weaver, 1979, p. 589). Society correctly assumes that singles need intimates, but views them as loose and unanchored.

Older single women especially are viewed as lonely—and it is true their status may present problems. Singlehood also becomes problematic for them after age 30 because their reproductive ability is limited by age (Weaver, 1979). In addition, women, in contrast to single men, lose their marketability for marriage and jobs from age 30 on.

Married people may be somewhat uncomfortable with singles socially. They may feel compelled to invite a single person of the opposite sex to a dinner party to complement this lone person. They may not know how to talk with people who are not interested in children's or spouses' problems. On social occasions, single professional women often enjoy talking with husbands more than wives and thereby raise suspicions about their motives (Weaver, 1979). For their part, many single people simply avoid married couples.

Reactions of Single People to Social Stigmatism. Single people's reactions to societal criticism are highly varied and depend on the personalities of the individuals involved and the reasons they are single. Because of their socialization, they often feel ambivalent about life issues. They are torn between the traditional values of marriage and parenthood, and the just recently acknowledged values of remaining single. Part of the problem arises from pressures to marry from parents, relatives, colleagues, and friends.

Those who are single by choice often feel no defensiveness at all about their status. They may feel that their way of life is superior, at least for them. Their only real concern is that they are the subject of various kinds of discrimination that cast them into the role of a minority group.

Because of society's gradually diminishing, though still powerful, double standard, the older single man is viewed as socially eligible, while the older single woman is viewed as a social liability (Freedman, 1978). In addition, in romantic relationships men

are supposed to be older than women. Men in their 40s or 50s who go out with much younger women are accepted by society, while women the same age who date much younger men are considered to be somewhat strange. This situation means that men of 40 have available as potential partners practically all adult single women, whereas women the same age are greatly restricted.

Discrimination Against the Single Person. Society discriminates against single people in many ways. In many countries unaccompanied women cannot be served at certain bars. Even in this country there are public places where women cannot go without an escort. While hardier women have always defied tradition, less defiant ones have succumbed to such discrimination.

Singles are also victims of legal discrimination. For example, they pay up to 20 percent more in income taxes than a married couple filing a joint return (Economics of being single, 1976). Joint-return taxpayers normally do not pay 50 percent of their income in federal taxes until their gross income reaches about $53,000, while single persons reach that bracket when they earn $40,000 a year.

Singles must also cope with job discrimination. A man's marital status makes little difference in his job until he reaches his early 30s; after that age the unmarried man may be suspected of homosexuality or of not being responsible (Economics of being single, 1976). Married, or even divorced, adults often receive job preferences over singles with the same qualifications. In a survey of major corporations, only 2 percent of the executives, including junior ones, were single. Over 60 percent of corporations responding said that single executives tend to "make snap judgements"; and 25 percent portrayed singlehood as "less stable than marriage" (Jacoby, 1974).

Among women, it is hard to distinguish discrimination based on sex from that based on being single (Stein, 1976). In any case, young single women have to convince employers that they are serious about their careers. In addition, the married have fringe benefits that singles do not. For instance, companies often provide married employees with free group life insurance. Employees can often take their spouses on company trips, but single employees cannot bring along the people they live with. Childless singles will have no one to depend on when they are old, hence have a special need to plan carefully for retirement. Yet even in Social Security laws, single people suffer discrimination. Currently a single man who retires at the age of 65 receives much less than a married man whose wife has never worked at all. Nevertheless, both men may have contributed the same amount in Social Security taxes (Economics of being single, 1976).

Being single carries a variety of potential satisfactions, however. One is having the time and opportunities to make friends. Singles can also lead more varied lives in terms of "taking classes, dating widely, learning music or a sport, travelling, trying new roles they have been afraid to try before" (Stein, 1976, p. 98). For many singles, living with others provides a strong source of emotional support as well as certain economic advantages. Singles also have a degree of choice about work that the married do not because they do not have to look out for the well-being of their families. They can make vocational choices on the basis of motivation, and they can afford to take chances. Both sexes feel a certain satisfaction in not having to spend their money on the basis of joint decision.

Life Styles

Housing. Singles have a variety of living situations. Some live alone; others with roommates; still others live in urban communal groups where they find support and friendship (Stein, 1976). In one urban project, almost 700 adults, most of them single, live in various communes including the "re-

ligious, political, craft, music, art, and apeutically oriented . . ." (p. 94). In s[communes people share a particular ide ogy; in others they gather together mainly for economic advantages.

Singles find this kind of living quite supportive because they meet new people there, and they receive help with emotional problems. They can be the kind of people they want, can relate to others freely, and are cared for when they need it (Zablocki, 1975). Most of the singles who live in communes are quite "normal," and are not at all "freaks" or "way out people" (p. 96).

Weaver (1979) recommends that singles participate in "communities of intimacy, not just work or play groups." The author believes it is healthy for congenial singles to live in pairs, or in small groups that are sometimes within larger groups. Far more of them do so than is commonly recognized. These intimates constitute their "families"; they are more than just friends—yet society totally ignores this status. Normally both members of a married couple are invited to dinner, but not always members of a single couple.

Social Relations. The greatest need of single people is to develop networks of human relationships that provide the basic satisfactions of "intimacy, sharing, and continuity" (Stein, 1976, p. 109). While single people value varied relationships, they place a high value on close enduring friendships.

Singles find considerable support from various groups and group activities. One of these is an organization called Zero Population Growth, which is for those who wish to have few or no children. Another, the National Organization of Nonparents, includes both married and unmarried people, and is concerned with developing workable options outside marriage. There are also networks of human relationships that provide for sharing and intimacy, such as rap sessions and consciousness-raising groups.

Other areas of involvement for singles are

Florence Elizabeth Moody

This middle-aged single woman gets emotional satisfaction from her nephew's child.

therapy and encounter groups, as well as associations that focus on specialized interests. Though often not restricted to singles, they are usually adapted to the needs of singles and are more frequently patronized by them. Carolyn Bird (1972) observes that the degree of caring, interpersonal involvement, and personal support permitted by such groups is often stronger than in traditional marriages.

Mental Health

Since singles are heterogeneous, their mental status must be discussed in terms of subtypes. Older single men are more likely than married men to have mental problems, including neurosis, passivity, and depression; and they are more likely to commit suicide. Never-married men are also twice as likely as never-married women to have mental health problems (Srole et al., 1962). Apparently, observes Campbell (1975b), "women can get along better without men than men can without women, [for] single women of all ages are happier and more satisfied with their lives than single men. So much for the stereotype of the carefree bachelor and the anxious spinster . . ." (p. 38). Single women are also more likely to become parts of warm, supportive networks. Nevertheless, single men are now participating more in friendship organizations and networks.

Given such a situation, it is strange that society persists in depicting single women as lonely, maladjusted spinsters. Many of the outstanding women in history have been single. After reconstructing the lives of women poets over a period of four centuries, Louise Bernikow observed that "women who do not love men, and women who do not have sex with men, in the eyes of men, have loveless and sexless lives . . . [but] most of these women poets have loved women, sometimes along with loving men. Women have found in other women exactly that companionship, encouragement, and understanding that they did not find in men" (cited in Sheehy, 1976).

Another factor in singles' mental health is age. Older singles are more concerned about their careers, and have more money for leisure-time activities and for advanced educational experiences (Glick, 1975). Yet, despite their more stimulating lives, they may feel more discouraged than younger singles. They may feel anxious about the prospects of future loneliness; and if they have not established supportive relationships, they may find the middle years depressing (Stein, 1976).

The Future of Singlehood

We might ask: What is the future of singlehood? Certainly, as greater numbers of people choose to remain single, singlehood will become a more attractive status. At present there is growing social support for the option to remain single. If still more support becomes available, even fewer people will model their life styles around marriage and the family (Stein, 1976).

Singlehood is emerging as a viable alternative life style, but whether it will attain the status of a movement is debatable. Such a movement, and the development of singles' political power, hold the only real hope for reducing discrimination against the unwed. Yet major obstacles stand in the way. One is that singles are so heterogeneous that agreement upon objectives for singles programs would be difficult. Another is that most singles eventually marry, so that enduring, hardcore support for singles programs would be relatively small.

The greatest help may come, in future years, from the population threat. In order to encourage more people not to have children, society may decide to reward singles rather than risk worldwide starvation and poverty.

The Future of the Family

In view of all the foregoing alternatives, the question naturally arises whether traditional marriage is doomed. On this score authorities seem to differ. Although the phrase "do your own thing," has become widely adopted, a growing minority express concern over departures from traditional family life. The rapid increase in alternative life styles which began in the 1960s, because of counterculture movements and the rising incidence of divorce, gave impetus to the so-called pro-family movement. Concern has been greatest among certain religious groups, especially Roman Catholics, Mormons, and fundamentalist evangelical Protestants. One source of concern is traditional support of the patriarchal household, which has predominated throughout the Christian era. For such reasons the pro-family movement has a strong religious element.

The pro-family movement has several avowed goals, and some implicit. Their dislike of "singlehood, cohabitation, dual earner/dual-career marriages, voluntary childlessness, single parenthood, open marriages and same-sex relationships" is apparent in their support of policies that are "anti-ERA, anti-

abortion, anticontraceptive/sex education and anti-welfare. . . ." (Houseknecht & Pankhurst, 1983). They oppose free sexual expression, especially in women, as encouraging collapse of authoritarian ideologies. They believe in their own moral superiority and dismiss individualism as defying legitimate controls. Abetted by a sympathetic Reagan administration and a trend toward traditionalism, they have made some progress in realizing their goals.

Others view alternative family styles as legitimate and deserving of support. Bernard (1975) suggests that within the lifetime of today's youth, the stable lifelong marriage may become "deviant"; and the views of youth today lend some support to that theory. If family forms do change, observes Ariès, it is unclear at this time what new forms they will take, and whether these will be very different from those known before. Ariès perceives attacks against the family as simply one part of the current revolt against technological society, for people are rebelling against an increasingly confined and restricted world (Mousseau, 1975).

Traditional, monogamous marriage has its weaknesses, concludes Peabody (1982). Couples these days have less external support than formerly in the way of closeknit, stable kinship groups and friends. Because of the mobile society of today, an undue strain may be placed on the marriage to make up for the deficit. Other factors tending to weaken such marriages are ability to control conception, undue possessiveness in such a limited relationship, the feminist woman's entry into the workworld, and the lengthening life span. Moreover, as increasing stress is placed on adults' individual personal development, rather than on their sacrifice for the children, the chances increase that they may drift apart.

Nor does marriage operating as a closed system engender richly varied interpersonal relationships. In the past such relations have been defined mostly in terms of "a formally recognized entity—that is, marriage, family, church, etc." However, an individual's reference group may cut across such boundaries (Peabody, 1982, p. 422). Emotional intimacy then becomes a unique structure for each individual.

In addition, the very rigidity of the marriage bond, as traditionally defined, may contribute to its decline. These days individuals often want more flexibility and richness of relationships than that provided in so strictly structured a relationship. Marks of traditional marriage's failure to adapt to modern times are the increasing divorce rate, sex relations outside marriage, especially by the wife, and alternatives to marriage such as swinging, open marriage, and group marriage.

Kempler (1976) recommends that society experiment with alternative marriage arrangements, and provide them with support and encouragement. In the process, different families and individuals may find the mode of life most suitable for their own and their dependents' welfare. Ultimately society itself must provide the environment and technological support, including human service systems, which will help all kinds of families and group living arrangements to function successfully.

SUMMARY

While the nuclear model remains the family form that comes to most people's minds, alternatives do exist, although their levels of popular acceptability vary widely. The childless couple, the single-parent family, and communal living are becoming increasingly, though not universally, approved. Other life styles such as homosexual marriage, swinging, and group marriage are still widely condemned. The divorced and the single no longer provoke the pity and criticism they formerly did. Single-parent families, formerly believed to penalize children, fare pretty well if there are no major financial problems. In short, though the nuclear family remains the preferred life style of the vast majority of adults, certain alternative family forms appear to work quite well.

SUGGESTED READINGS

BEER, W. R. (1982). *Househusbands: Men and Housework in American Families*. New York: Praeger.

CORNFIELD, N. (1983). The success of urban communes. *Journal of Marriage and the Family, 47*(1), 115–122.

FRIEDMAN, H. J. (1982). The challenge of divorce to adequate fathering: The peripheral father in marriage and divorce. *Psychiatric Clinics of North America, 5*(3), 565–580.

GOLD, D. & BERGER, C. (1983). The influence of psychological and situational factors on the contraceptive behavior of single men: A review of the literature. *Population and Environment: Behavioral and Social Issues, 6*(2), 113–129.

HANSSON, R. O., KNOPF, M. F., SOWNS, E. A., MONROE, P. R., STEGMAN, S. E., & WADLEY, D. S. (1984). Femininity, masculinity, and adjustment to divorce among women. *Psychology of Women Quarterly, 8*(3), 248–260.

HORWITZ, J. & TOGNOLI, J. (1982). Role of home in adult development: Women and men living alone describe their residential histories. *Family Relations, 31*(3), 335–341.

KITSON, G. C. & SUSSMAN, M. B. (1982). Marital complaints, demographic characteristics, and symptoms of mental distress in divorce. *Journal of Marriage and the Family, 44*(1), 87–101.

LEWIN, B. (1982). Unmarried cohabitation: A marriage form in a changing society. *Journal of Marriage and the Family, 44*(3), 763–773.

McLANAHAN, S. S. (1983). Family structure and stress: A longitudinal comparison of two-parent and female-headed families. *Journal of Marriage and the Family, 45*(2), 347–358.

MOSKOFF, W. (1983). Divorce in the USSR. *Journal of Marriage and the Family, 45*(2), 419–425.

MOTT, F. L. & MOORE, S. F. (1983). The tempo of remarriage among young American women. *Journal of Marriage and the Family, 45*(2), 427–436.

PAPERNOW, P. L. (1984), The stepfamily cycle: An experiential model of stepfamily development. *Family Relations, 33*, 355–363.

SPANIER, G. B. & FURSTENBERG, F. F., Jr. (1982). Remarriage after divorce: A longitudinal analysis of well-being. *Journal of Marriage and the Family, 44*(3), 709–720.

WATSON, M. A. (1984). Sexually open marriage. Three perspectives. *Alternative Lifestyles, 4*(1), 3–21.

CHAPTER TEN

Work and Leisure

WORK

The Significance of Work

In America family and work are the focus of most adults' lives (Berger, 1979). The work role stabilizes an adult's identity and influences an individual's self-concept throughout life (Mortimer & Simmons, 1978). The work role also determines an individual's status, income, and prestige; it regulates daily schedules, social contacts, and chances for self-development. An individual's satisfaction with work changes with time and situation.

The burden of work is heaviest for the middle aged because it is during this time that they normally reach the peak of their influence in all areas of business and government. Although Americans in the 40-to-65 age category comprise only a quarter of the population, they earn over half the na-

tion's income; and the average age of top business executives is 54 (Generation in the middle, 1970).

The New Work Ethic. Attitudes toward work have changed greatly through history. When it was performed mostly by slaves, work was regarded with contempt. With the rise of Christianity it became a duty (deBoer, 1978). In contrast, these days certain trends are transforming the American work ethic and reducing the work burden (Yankelovich, 1974b). One of these is a new way of defining success. From World War II until recently, most Americans defined achievement in terms of material things. Today, new concepts of success involve quality rather than quantity, self-fulfillment rather than high earnings. The stress is on the self and its unactualized potential, a self that demands full consideration. Paralleling this change has been a shift in feelings about obligations

187

to others, including family, society, and vocational associates. In the past, the "key motif . . . was 'keeping up with the Joneses'; today it is 'I have my own life to live, let Jones shift for himself'" (Yankelovich, 1974b, p. 81). While concern for the material things still exists, these things are now considered no more important, and perhaps less, than such self-fulfilling activities as "being closer to nature, finding ways to be creative, spending more time with friends, and more time on self-understanding" (p. 81). As a result, employer-employee relationships have changed, and employers can no longer count on the total loyalty of their employees.

A third development, equally important for the work ethic, is decreased anxiety over economic matters at least in comparison with the years of the Great Depression and those before the arrival of Social Security. While 3 out of 5 adults still name economic security as their primary goal, 40 percent would take economic risks in order to improve the quality of their lives (Yankelovich, 1974b).

A fourth development has been a "spreading psychology of entitlement." Rather than saying that they would like to have a satisfying job, many believe they are entitled to such a job.

Middle-Aged Women at Work

Economist Eli Ginzburg has called the increase in working women the "single most outstanding phenomenon of our century. Its long-term implications are absolutely unchartable. . . . It will affect women, men, and children; and the cumulative consequences will only be revealed in the twenty-first and twenty-second centuries (*New York Times*, Sept. 12, 1976, pp. 1, 49; cited in Parker, 1978).

A longitudinal study of women who entered adulthood in the early 1960s indicated that work commitment is stable over time and distinct from sex-role attitudes (Bielby & Bielby, 1984). Those who participated less in the mainstream of college life were more committed to the work role, as were those who completed their families early so they could return to their jobs. Although women

Community Relations Office, SUNY Oswego

Self-fulfillment of the job is of prime importance.

interrupted their careers to have children, the mothers' subjective feelings about their work role remained constant. It appears that for many women the work role has become an important component of their adult roles.

Reasons for Working. Women give various reasons for returning to work, including the desire to be recognized for their efforts (society puts small value on housekeeping skills); the desire to do something meaningful; and the need to fill their time after their children leave home (When middle-aged women, 1979). But the main reason that women work is because they need the money. Aside from this, however, many of them want to work outside the home anyway. In the home women often work without getting much appreciation from their families or feeling of accomplishment; on the job they are paid for their labor, they can interact with their peers, and they enjoy a stronger feeling of individual identity.

Special Problems. Although sex roles are changing in American society, modifications in stereotypes of women and men workers have not kept pace. Women are still viewed as having personality characteristics—such as lack of firmness and instability—that ill-equip them for higher level positions (Ruble, Cohen & Ruble, 1984). For advancement, women workers depend on evaluations by their superiors, who are usually men. Females may be judged without bias when objective evaluation of their work is available, at least in terms of immediate performance. However, men distinguish between short-term performance and estimates of long-term potential, in which men are given a large edge. Moreover, this inequity is significant because it profoundly affects the relative advancement of the sexes. In addition, women's successes are typically attributed to effort or luck, men's to stable personality traits.

A majority of women still enter traditionally female occupations despite depressed wage levels (Mott, 1978). Over half seek employment in teaching, health services, and clerical work. Even in occupations that women enter in large numbers, sexual stereotyping still persists, with men often holding the higher-status positions. For example, in the public schools, women constitute 83.5 percent of elementary teachers and men 53.6 percent of high-school teachers. Men hold the better jobs: only 13.5 percent of principals and 0.1 percent of major city school superintendents in the United States are women (Parker, 1978).

Women also experience the special biases and assumptions associated with women at work. While over 90 percent of all women are employed for pay at some time in their lives, such employment has not been viewed as of any great importance in their lives; nor is work expected to affect their identities or self-esteem to any real degree (Barnett & Baruch, 1978).

Women experience special problems when they resume their careers after rearing a family. They often find that today's technology has passed them by, so they must return to school for retraining. Or they may take whatever is available, often making do with dead-end jobs. Many times temporary or part-time jobs are their only alternatives.

Despite the fact that the job market is still sex-segregated, and women make less than 60 percent of what men do, women tend to deny their being victims of discrimination (Crosby, 1984). Indeed, the sexes are equally likely to say they currently receive the benefits they deserve and to deny that they are presently victims of sex discrimination. Women may simply be unwilling to confront the fact of discrimination, or be unaware how it operates in their case. Also they may be unconsciously unwilling to seem too agressively feminist or too traditionalist in attitude to acknowlege women's right to equality.

Of course women's experiences are highly individual. One woman who had been a homemaker for 25 years and became separated from her husband had to apply for low-level jobs (When middle-aged women, 1979). She was first a library clerk, then a part-time secretary. Another woman, who had been a stockbroker before having her first child, became an executive director of a day-care council. Still another, whose husband walked out on her after 31 years, found that little help is given middle-aged divorced women who have few work skills.

The significance of solo status—that is, being the only member, or just one of a few, of one's sex or ethnic membership in a group varies by sex (Crocker & McGraw, 1984). One study revealed that solo females were unlikely to become group leaders; overall group satisfaction diminished when solo females were present; and gender-related issues were most often raised in groups with a solo female. In contrast solo males often became integrated into the group as leaders, which promoted smooth group function. This result was not surprising, when we consider the long-standing traditions of all-male work groups and leadership. To date, given the still gross inequities in this area, women leadership emerges most easily, and often brilliantly, within all-female groups.

Career women who have an attractive physical appearance, personality, and manner, and who enjoy high status and are successful in their chosen fields often experience unique advantages and disadvantages on the job (Kaslow & Schwartz, 1978). They are aware of others' jealousy of them; some do (and others do not) utilize their feminine wiles and have special problems with unattractive women colleagues and wives of some of their male colleagues. They also face certain problems that all women do, including the lack of recognition of their true capabilities and the tendency to downgrade women who are especially ambitious and achievement oriented. The final handicap is the "folklore that attractiveness and competence cannot go hand in hand" (Kaslow & Schwartz, 1978, p. 315).

Women who place their work role secondary to their family role pay a price. They give up work while their children are young, and they limit their own career-striving in deference to their husbands' vocational needs. They choose flexible occupations, such as teaching, or work that will allow time for childrearing. They may select women's specialties, such as dentists who treat only children or doctors and lawyers who work for the government and are directed by others. The result is that they make less money than men and have lower status (Stryker & Macke, 1978).

Better educated women have a higher than normal rate of separation and divorce, perhaps because their husbands cannot adapt to their revised marital relationship (Houseknecht, Vaughan & Macke, 1984). Entering graduate school after marriage results in more cases of marital disruption than when school is completed before marriage. Perhaps after the spousal roles have already been established, husbands object to the renegotiation of responsibilities that the woman's student-career requires. Then, if the husband is unwilling to support his wife's career, she may find it difficult to advance and decide to divorce.

Even career women often encounter the assumption that they will inevitably put family welfare ahead of their jobs. A survey of 1,500 male executives indicated that they had more confidence in men's than in women's abilities to meet the needs of both family and employer (Gaylin, 1976a). A man who is devoted to his family is judged to be a well-rounded, emotionally healthy individual, while a woman with exactly the same feelings is seen as lacking commitment to the firm.

The truth is that married career women often do put their families first, because they have been taught from early childhood to do so. They are also brought up to hold certain false notions about a career. They assume they can take time out for childbearing and then continue their career without penalty. However, only in very exceptional cases can such women compete on an equal basis with men.

Typically the question is still asked of women: If you work how will you take care of the children? The question should become: Should the total society provide for its children? (Berger, 1979).

Dual-Career Couples

There are growing numbers of dual-career couples in the country. Ninety percent of today's college males anticipate that their wives will earn as much money as they do. This raises the question: How will such husbands and wives decide about where to live? (Maynard & Zawacki, 1979). The usual solution to this problem has been to encourage women to think of homemaking as their first priority. If the husband's career is perceived as being more significant, the wife makes the necessary adjustment, either by giving up her job or taking whatever work she can. Women without careers in the true sense follow their husbands as they move about. Then, regardless of how able or well-prepared a woman may be, she may find few opportunities for self-realization in many communities.

This situation is slowly changing, because dual-career couples are becoming common, and women are becoming more career oriented. Moreover, many couples have become committed to having two careers in order to maintain a certain quality of life. This new ethic is reflected partly in the growing number of individuals who refuse to transfer at their employer's request. Employees at 42 percent of the companies surveyed by Dun & Bradstreet refused to relocate, an increase of 10 percent in just 1 year. They named family considerations, personal preferences, or conflicts with their spouse's career as their reasons. Over a third of male executives would not transfer unless the move also satisfied the wife's requirements.

A major obstacle in the lives of dual-career couples is managerial attitudes, especially toward women. Upwardly mobile people are expected to make transfers and to acknowledge that their refusal to do so may damage their careers. A related obstacle is management's view regarding women's duty to follow their husbands.

What solutions are available to dual-career couples? Many do not find any solution, as divorce statistics indicate. Some husbands cannot accommodate their wives' greater pay or success, and divorce becomes the solution. Or the wife may give up her career and stay at home "where she belongs." Some women find that maintaining a house and pursuing a career—the so-called supermom syndrome—is too strenuous.

More imaginative couples may integrate their job seeking and work out which spouse's welfare should take precedence in each case. Other solutions include these: (1) A couple may use a balance sheet approach, deciding what is best for each and compromise. (2) They may alternate giving precedence to each career. (3) Career goals of at least one partner may be altered, a difficult compromise if both are "high achievers." (4) They may both negotiate at the same time for two positions—so-called spouse bargaining. If a company wants to employ one of them, that individual will agree if the company provides something for the other. (5) The couple may give precedence to the spouse who has more specific skills, assuming that the one with more generalized skills will find it easier to become employed elsewhere. (6) They may obtain help from the employer in obtaining a job for the spouse in the new location. (7) A couple may have a joint career or work in closely related fields so that they can remain together. (8) They may live half way between two cities and commute from the same home base. (9) In some commuter marriages, a couple may be separated for several days each week, or they may live across the country from each other and see each other rarely. This situation may be precipitated by their inability to find two good jobs in the same area. One of them may be offered a job in a new city, and the other decides to stay where he or she is. In some cases, both partners may already have two jobs in different cities when they marry and simply delay getting together. (10) Sometimes a husband and wife become a "company couple," who are employed by the same company and are also transferred at the same time.

On the corporate level, companies are increasingly having to adapt to the needs of dual-career families (Maynard & Zawacki, 1979). A majority would rather not get involved with their employees' personal affairs. However, if they block individuals who cannot or will not move, they may lose valued employees and must recruit and retrain replacements. Instead, they may arrange staggered schedules for employees to allow more time for commuting. They may also employ "relocation" experts to expedite a couple's move to a new city and provide subsidies until a spouse obtains new employment. In addition, corporations may have several industrial complexes within the same area so that an individual can move about within this structure without leaving the community. Overall, what is required from both couples and corporations is "a great deal of flexibility, creativity, and a willingness to try innovative ideas" (p. 472).

Middle-Aged Men at Work

The Good Provider Role. Historically, the husband's role as "good provider" had both its costs and rewards (Bernard, 1981). The male's masculinity was identified not only with the work place but with success there. He derived feelings of strength and power from the provider role. (All the purchases around the home were symbols of the family's dependence upon him.) He was considered the "ultimate decision maker" and the head of the family. If his wife worked, the size of her salary related to his status as head of household.

Then, women's entry in numbers into the work force diminished the prerogatives and advantages accruing to that role. In less than three decades, 1950 to 1978, the proportion of married women workers over doubled (from 25.2 percent to 55.4 percent) and was expected to reach 66.7 percent by 1990. Men now felt compelled to seek appreciation for their provider role, a feeling they had taken for granted before. And since their work role now afforded less sense of power than before, many men came to question the large fraction of their lives that they gave to toil.

For some men the escape from being sole providers brought a sense of relief; but many found that the wife provider could now make demands on them, two in particular. First, the husband was expected to become more expressive and nurturant, and second to assume greater responsibility for household chores and child care. In years past he was obliged only to support the family—they gave him emotional support; he was not obligated to give it in return.

As a matter of fact, men have as yet assumed little of the house and child care role. To do so would threaten their masculinity—those tasks are within the female domain. The husband can skillfully mend a fishing net, but not his shirt. The insecure male, especially, feels threatened. Even more sophisticated ones, who profess they believe in equality, have difficulty putting their professed beliefs into practice.

On-the-Job-Advantages. Most middle-aged men also enjoy certain advantages at work. Ordinarily they have found their niche and have at least worked out a reasonably agreeable style of work life. Often their wives work too, so that money pressures are not as great. A man may help out at home if the wife works, but society still assigns the major homemaking responsibility to her, even after the husband retires, however unfair that may be. In recent decades women's work lives have lengthened, while men's have shortened. More women are working than ever before, and they are remaining in the work force until a later age. In the meantime, men are retiring at a younger age.

Men also make more money than women who do the same work, and fare better at the hands of hiring committees, yet not all men receive equal treatment. In one study, married men were often aided in their search for jobs by wives they described as "gems" or "marvelous cooks" (Only married men, 1976). Their wives, along with a "charming family" or "two fine sons," gave them a certain "aura of responsibility, maturity, and stability . . ." (p. 63). The single men, by contrast, were considered somewhat immature. The single women fared more poorly than the men but somewhat better than the married women, especially those with children.

A Study of Family Structure and Job Satisfaction. Interviews with men having three different life structures disclosed significant relations between such structures and career satisfaction (Osherson & Dill, 1984). Both traditional and dual-career families may produce equal satisfaction, depending on the man involved. The traditional structure was supportive of the man who possessed traditional family standards: that a man undertakes work and family obligations early, is upward mobile, and provides for his family successfully. In contrast, the man who shared marital roles in dual-career families had more options in his career. Having two pay checks to rely upon, he could utilize his career for self-development and not feel at the mercy of the work place. In consequence, he felt more self-actualized than did the traditional man. Another reason may be that the sort of man who pursues this path is also more capable of seeking and achieving self-actualization. On the other hand, childless men within two-career marriages were more dissatisfied than either of the types above. Being childless, such men lacked a marker of adulthood, as well as the satisfaction of protecting and providing for children. Often, too, they had entered the work-

world later than the others—hence, were behind them on the career ladder.

Problems. Even married men with charming wives have their vocational problems, one being that men must earn their status on the job while women can attain status simply through marriage. Consider the high status of presidents' wives who, with notable exceptions such as Eleanor Roosevelt, have achieved little on their own. Women have greater social mobility (both upward and downward) through marriage than men do through their occupations, and more readily cross the boundaries of major status groupings.

Men have their own special problems who assume traditionally female careers, one being viewed as somehow deviant (Lemkau, 1984). Such a choice is perceived as reflecting atypical sex-role socialization. Boys are reared to prefer high-status, high-paying jobs—that is, those associated with males. Such men's neglect by researchers has allowed the stereotype to persist.

These men do have distinctive characteristics, one being that they, like women who choose masculine careers, are more androgynous. They have more of certain traditionally feminine, desirable characteristics, including warmth, gentleness, subjectivity, and kindliness. More often than other men, they name women as having influenced their career choices, have greater emotional distance from their fathers, and have experienced some major family stress, which may have sensitized them to others' feelings. Also they are often of lower status—hence, even these jobs represented upward mobility from their families of origin. Given the difficulties their origins imposed, they may have found attractive the easier permeability of so-called female careers.

For men in general, unemployment is devastating, especially at middle age. Unemployment brings not merely loss of income but loss of self-respect and well-being. It also disrupts feelings of stability and continuity. Being without a job often results in new psychosomatic disorders and the revival of old ailments, such as peptic ulcers. Even the wives of laid-off workers experience an unusually high incidence of ulcers. As economic turndowns and consequent unemployment increase, mental hospitalization rates increase; and so do rates of alcoholism and crime (Hesson, 1978).

An especially poignant problem, most often experienced by white-collar workers sometime during middle age, is the growing apprehension and ultimately the stark realization that they will never reach some long-cherished goal. They have identified the accomplishment of this goal with their fulfillment as individuals, and to abandon it is to lose a significant part of themselves. Such a loss may precipitate a serious middle-age crisis and a desperate effort to fill the vacuum thus created with alternative goals and values. An individual's devastation is greater when a colleague, often younger and less capable but with the right connections, is awarded a coveted position.

Even if some men have been successful, they may still have vocational problems. They may feel ambivalent about their increased power and the concomitant strains that arise. When goals are reached, they may not prove very satisfying; and reaching the ceiling in a career may produce a certain apathy unless new goals are established. While some successful persons take an interest in the careers of younger workers, others simply stagnate.

Men who decide to invest more of themselves in their families meet resistance in the workplace. Employers may resist promoting them, and colleagues may reject them for placing family responsibilities ahead of work demands.

Worker Satisfaction

Extent of Worker Satisfaction. Despite such problems, over the past decade most workers have been pretty well satisfied. Those

who are dissatisfied are mostly in lower-status jobs, including nonfarm labor, factory work, clerical work, and so on. However, Sussman declares that 15 to 20 percent of the current work force is unhappy, and that job dissatisfaction is on the rise (Why millions, 1976).

What factors contribute most to peoples' satisfaction with their work? Certainly most workers can name features of their jobs that they dislike. The truth is that achieving vocational satisfaction is an extremely complex matter, and few ever really attain it. As Thoreau said: "Most men live lives of quiet desperation"; the only difference, in modern terms, is the fact that "young people are not so quiet in resigning themselves to a life of despair" (Story, 1974, p. 372).

In the following, two middle-aged adults indicate whether they find their work satisfying.

FEMALE, AGE 63:   No. I find it a bore. I get very tired of all the petty jealousies and selfishness of my co-workers and the pettiness of the bosses. I believe I do a good job, while receiving a minimum of appreciation.

MALE, AGE 51: I enjoy my profession very much, particularly since I seem to have developed an aptitude for it. I am also able to help people in distress, which gives me a great deal of satisfaction.

Factors Relating to Satisfaction. For many people, the critical test of satisfaction is whether the job makes maximum use of their abilities; if they feel "underutilized," they are generally not satisfied (Why millions, 1976). Having a large salary is less important than other factors, and obtaining a raise may not bring about the desired satisfaction. If workers are dissatisfied with their pay, it is usually because they are making less than others with similar skills, abilities, and seniority.

Another factor that is important to job satisfaction is whether workers continue to progress steadily up the promotional ladder.

Individuals accustomed to a succession of promotions and salary increases may ultimately find themselves on a plateau in which their salaries do not keep rising, and promotions may be awarded to persons younger than they. Hence middle-aged workers' salaries may not keep pace with rising consumer prices.

Higher education at times can lead to dissatisfaction with jobs. Because of the rapid increase in number of persons receiving higher education, correspondingly more individuals are finding themselves either unemployed or over-qualified for their jobs (Burris, 1983). A study of clerical workers showed most of them to feel over-qualified for their work and discontented. Thus, given limitations on higher status jobs, higher education comes to create job dissatisfaction, weak feelings of job involvement, high turnover rates, poor co-worker relations, and a focus on future opportunities rather than on the job at hand. One reason is that college education has been viewed more as the route to economic success than the acquisition of habits and attitudes that will permit a higher quality of life.

Worker satisfaction cannot be determined with accuracy at specific points in the career cycle. Often there are years of adjustment and readjustment before an individual decides to settle in a particular niche. As Story (1974) points out, it would be very hard to find even one "successful individual . . . whose early career was not a notorious series of false starts, often in totally unrelated fields" (p. 372). However by the time they reach their 40s, most people have settled down and have a fairly clear idea of how contented they are.

After extensive interviews with working-class men and women, Rubin (1981) found that for the men achieving jobs with "meaning, purpose and dignity" is still important, but the road to achieving that goal is difficult. By age 25 they have worked almost 8 years and have held as many as six, eight, or ten jobs. Most begin as laborers, where there is much worker dissatisfaction, and some move into better jobs that still require hard work. Since more and more jobs require additional skills, the majority move on, not up.

The majority of these men feel a sense of "bitterness, alienation, resignation and boredom"; however, some have a feeling of greater autonomy on the job (Rubin, 1981, p. 259). Their work has little intrinsic reward and little status. Construction workers, truck drivers, and skilled mechanics who control the pace of their work, make independent judgments, and order the tasks to be done, feel more gratification.

Under the pressure of financial strain a majority of working-class women work outside the home, mostly in part-time jobs. Of those who stay at home two-thirds say they are glad to do so and that the homemaker-mother role is important. Also, in this social class, not having to work may prove gratifying. However, even in the poor-paying, lower-status jobs in which they are usually employed, working women often feel better satisfied than homemakers. True, they carry a full burden at home as well, but they like to get outside the home and make some money on their own. Only their lifetime orientation toward homemaking makes it possible for them to like jobs that "require the same qualities of service, submission, and suppression of intellectual development"—jobs shunned by men with even less education than theirs (p. 261). They must also endure negative reactions from husbands who want their financial help, but miss the greater power men have when the wife does not work. The women feel more independent, engaged more in a joint enterprise—but in a third of the families the husbands feel their wives have become too independent.

Inadequacies of Research. Research about careers at this stage is, to date, inadequate and unrepresentative (Gill, Coppard &

Lowther, 1983). It has focused mainly on male managers and administrators, who constitute a tenth of the workforce. It is also largely limited to the upper middle class and college educated. Such research as we have indicates that crises are not tied to life stages, or to particular ages through the midlife years. The causes of crises at this time, and the effects of change, relate more to individual responses to environment than to age. Values that influence life decisions at any one stage of career vary greatly within any single age cohort.

A major problem has been one-dimensional theories employed to explain highly complex behaviors. All too often career is treated as somewhat static when, in actuality, it is continuously evolving. Career status changes in terms of changing personalities within a steadily changing environment. Change within a particular work role, or from one occupation to another, is also a complex process, not an event, and the factors causing them are also complex. Career change does not always involve crisis. Often it represents progress toward greater stability, rather than a dramatic change in the life course. An important factor is education, and educators should become more flexible, taking into account these persons' special needs.

Looking ahead, certain trends in vocational adaptation can be anticipated. For one thing, more stress will be placed on finding work congenial to individual tastes and needs. The idea of a one-time job choice will be displaced by that of matching a changing self to changing jobs. Such a concept will require that seniority and other benefits be easily transferred from one job or place to another. Continuing job reeducation will also be needed, but it will concentrate more on basic concepts than specifics, because specialties quickly become obsolete. For example, "the modern aerospace engineer is in the same plight as that of a hypothetical veterinarian who, after years of intensive

preparation, finds that he has specialized in the unique diseases of extinct animals" (Story, 1974, p. 169).

In future years, increasing numbers of people will have a second career. After all, people are in better health and live longer than ever before. Futurologist Fred Emery of Australia believes the concept of a lifetime career is doomed and that people will have several careers during their working lives (Future work, 1977). Distinctions between leisure and work will become increasingly vague in people's behaviors and minds. People in knowledge-oriented industries will often take their tasks home at night and use their free time to increase their knowledge and upgrade their skills. Meantime, "a myriad of leisure-oriented markets . . . will beggar the imagination" (p. 47).

Especially significant for future careers will be technological developments. Best (1984) perceives the computer to be at the core of profound changes affecting personal and occupational lives in all industrialized nations. Over 3 million Americans bought home and personal computers in 1982 and that figure doubled the next year. The impact of this technology on the total society will be phenomenal. Up to 45 percent of American jobs will be importantly affected by technological changes over the next two decades and will require upgrading of skills. By 1990 it is estimated that 35,000 robots will be installed in America and their "applications will skyrocket" during the 1990s (Best, 1984, p. 61).

The result is that workers will be given tasks requiring knowledge of new, more complex technologies—hence, must upgrade or develop new skills. General Motors Corporation anticipates that by the year 2000 half its work force must be skilled tradespersons (technicians, inspectors, monitors, and so forth) compared to 16 percent in 1980 (p. 61). While some workers will be displaced because of technological innovations, a company's failure to provide such innovations will cause it to lose out in international competition, thus producing even more loss in employment and growth.

LEISURE

The Significance of Leisure

Work generally involves obligation and efficiency, while leisure implies doing what one wishes at one's own pace. We participate in leisure activities when we do not have to work to maintain our household or ourselves. That is, "leisure is doing what we don't have to do" (Neulinger, 1974, p. 186). Free time is not equivalent to leisure, but it does make leisure possible. Leisure "is a state of mind, it is a way of being, of being at peace with oneself and what one is doing" (p. 120). The way in which we determine how to use free time can be called the *leisure style*.

Leisure activities may be classified as individual, joint, or parallel (Orthner, 1975). *Individual activities* demand no communication with others; in fact they may discourage any interaction. *Joint activities* involve a considerable degree of interaction and encourage communication. *Parallel activities* are essentially individual activities within group settings which require little interaction between participants. In a study of upper-middle-class husbands and wives in a medium-sized urban area, it was found that the husbands spent 31 percent of their discretionary (free) time on weekends in individual activities, 34 percent in joint activities with their wives, and 27 percent in parallel activities with their wives.

Recent changes are producing an "inversion of the concepts of work and leisure" (Best, 1984). Classical philosophers restricted leisure to "reflection and the fine arts"; they were deemed "freely chosen leisurely pursuits of the elites" (p. 64). Now, as growing numbers of persons are employed in white-collar jobs and "knowledge work, activities become more like the leisure activities of the past" (p. 64). That is, jobs which now require more autonomy and freedom of expression were viewed as "non-manual" in pre-industrial and early industrial times. The nature of work in the future will become still more removed from what it is today.

Technological advances are changing the relationship between work and personal activities. Just as the arrival of heavy machinery and the industrial revolution took workers away from homes into factories and offices, "new technologies may cause households and neighborhood groups to become more self-sustaining and to abandon institutional settings for many productive activities" (Best, 1984, p. 64).

The Growing Significance of Leisure. The topic of leisure is becoming increasingly significant. Ripley and O'Brien (1976) suggest that "how to live with leisure may become as important for tomorrow's generations as learning to live with work has been for yesterday's" (p. 56). Colleges and universities are already offering courses in leisure, and adult education courses in leisure-time activities are proliferating. Corporations that make leisure equipment such as boats, fishing tackle, and camping gear are thriving, and clothing manufacturers are expanding their range of leisure attire.

Leisure activities are significant for several reasons. Perhaps the most important is the need to compensate for the strains of high-pressure living. In addition, many people must perform jobs that provide less than they might desire in terms of fulfillment; so satisfaction must be achieved for the most part through leisure activities. Also, leisure activities are often the glue that binds families together. The National Recreation Association has a slogan: "The family that plays together, stays together." While this slogan may be an exaggeration, certain trends have made family recreation important. One is the family's transition to being a more companionable institution (Orthner, 1975). On the other hand, recreation in itself is no guarantee of better family relationships. In a family of highly divergent personalities, joint activities may satisfy no one.

Also enhancing the importance of leisure activities is their legitimization by society. Formerly they were perceived as wasteful; now they are regarded as a means of personal growth and fulfillment. Authorities believe they can become far more so when we learn to utilize them more effectively. The task will be to achieve this goal without overstructuring it or making "work" of it.

In a study of residents' perceptions of the importance of, and their satisfaction with, various dimensions of community life, the leisure dimension was most predictive of overall community satisfaction (Allen & Beattle, 1984).

One presumed reason for the growing emphasis on leisure—the increase in free time—may be more illusory than real. It is a myth, observes Butler (1975b), that almost all middle-aged persons have a great deal of leisure, many of them moonlight at other jobs. In addition, housewives have increasingly assumed jobs outside the home, but they still have domestic responsibilities.

Each sex has special reasons for developing leisure activities. For the middle-aged woman there is the empty nest, which either strips her of her childrearing functions or blesses her with their absence, depending upon her outlook. Also, the chances are high that she will spend her later life alone due to the death of her spouse (Sheehy, 1976). For the man, leisure pursuits help defuse tensions that build up from the job. These pursuits also become the focus of his life after he has retired. For both sexes, leisure activities become important avenues of self-

realization that were closed until now because of more pressing obligations.

Leisure Pursuits

Favorite Activities. Certain activities are widely favored by adults in America. One popular form of reading is romance, and estimates of such readers in the country are about 20 million, "which rivals the numbers who view most popular television shows" (Thurston, 1983). Romance readers mirror the total population by education, age, socioeconomic, and marital status. About 40 percent are middle class, and nearly half have had some college education. They watch television, but less than the national average. In these romances they find relief from stress; this is especially true for wives and mothers who need some time alone. Contrary to earlier romances, the heroines are often assertive and independent and the heroes are "sensitive and fallible" (p. 14). Also the new heroines engage more openly and assertively in sex, and the readers see nothing pornographic about it so long as sex is combined with love.

A rapidly growing activity among the middle-aged is continuing education. The interest in lifelong learning has been precipitated by various factors. Adults have become greatly interested in self-development; rapid shifts in the job market have made retraining necessary; certification requirements exist in certain professions; and greater amounts of discretionary income and leisure time are available (Sawhill, 1978–79).

Sawhill (1978–79) believes that adult education is too often of mediocre quality. Professors may scorn students' "dipping back briefly into formal education" (p. 80); or adult students may be considered as less able and less worthy of professors' attention. Sawhill suggests that since newspapers and magazines print reviews of concerts and exhibits, educational programs available to adults should be similarly described and advertised.

Individual Preferences. In the final analysis, each individual organizes free time activities in his or her own way. In the following, several middle-aged persons answer the question: *What are your chief, and most pleasant, forms of recreation or special interests?*

FEMALE, 58, MARRIED, LICENSED REAL ESTATE BROKER: Reading, travel, sewing, creating things, keeping in step with changes and applying them to my home and self.

FEMALE, 51, SEPARATED, OFFICE CLERK: At this age athletics and sports don't turn me on. I'm more interested in meeting and visiting with people, eating out, working for the church, knitting, and doing projects.

FEMALE, 54, WIDOWED, LPN: I like to travel. I like to dance—slow. I do a lot of different kinds of craft work. I like working outside, especially with my flowers.

In other words, participation in any one leisure category varies according to specific activities within that classification and characteristics of the participants. For example, a study of participation in physical recreation activities of college-educated adults indicated significant differences according to sex, marital status, age, and type of activity (Unkel, 1981). Women participated less than males in outdoor activities and team sports, but not in individual or dual (two-person) sports. Neither marital status not children affected the differential participation of the sexes. Participation decreased faster with age for single persons, perhaps because it is easier to initiate such activity when others are readily available.

The findings suggest that certain matters need further research; for example, since participation in team sports declines rapidly in adulthood, should schools' large emphasis on such sports, especially for boys, be reduced? Also, the relationship between age and activity may be, in some measure, spurious. Available research is based mainly on cross-sectional studies—today's exercise-oriented young people may carry their activity orientation with them into later years. Also deserving study is how best to encourage singles to continue physical recreation.

Personality traits also relate to choice of leisure activities. Wilderness users, compared to a random sampling of other adults, were more self-actualized, and potential wilderness users more than potential nonusers. In addition, such actualization also related to attitudes toward the wilderness experience—those scoring highest being more committed to, and concerned about, nature and the habitat. However, frequent wilderness users were not more self-actualized than less frequent users (Young & Crandall, 1984).

Simply listing leisure pursuits provides no great insight into their significance, for a single activity has many facets and may be employed by different people in varied ways. One adult may watch soap operas endlessly, looking for vicarious pleasures. Another may watch television selectively, ignoring all but the more sophisticated programs. A man may go camping in order to get away from the telephone and be outdoors, while his wife may go in order to strengthen the family.

Factors in Choosing Leisure Activities. The factors that determine the choice of leisure activities are many and complex; they include genetic influences, personal characteristics, family background, and age. Some inherited characteristics make a difference in people's interests and skills—some individuals will never have the acute vision necessary to be jet pilots, while others will never have the coordination to become ballet dancers (Grotevant, Scarr, & Weinberg, 1978). In addition, cultural influences, including

Joe Franco

Men spend some of their leisure time doing odd jobs around the house.

often so prominent as to be a distinguishing feature. Realistic persons are ordinarily aggressive, rugged, and practical, and enjoy working outdoors and using their hands (Grotevant, Scarr & Wineberg, 1978). Investigative ones are more scientifically oriented and spend their time thinking over problems. Artistic individuals like to express themselves creatively and appreciate works of art, while social persons are humanistic, concentrating their efforts on helping others. Enterprising types like to sell, lead, and dominate; conventional ones prefer structured competitive activities, either numerical or verbal. Each individual possesses these interests but in widely differing proportions.

The choice of leisure activities varies considerably by nationality. Among all tour groups at the Grand Canyon, the percent of time devoted to particular activities was: shopping, 8.8 percent; viewing scenery, 6.4 percent; photography, 2.9 percent. These were the popular pastimes. The Japanese were more interested than the other tourists in shopping and in photography, perhaps because they have more money to spend, and photo mementos are very important to them (Machlis & Wenderoth, 1984).

Leisure activities also vary according to age, sex, and other factors (Kelly, 1983). Over the life span they change according to developmental needs, interests, opportunities, education, occupational level, marital status, and race. Nevertheless, there is a core of leisure activities common to most adults: watching television, reading, informal interaction with other members of the household, and taking outings with family and friends. Sports interests are more characteristic of males and persons at earlier ages. For those who have completed high school differences are not great, except perhaps in activities such as skiing that require more money. Young men also more often participate in team sport contests, and men of all ages visit bars more than women. Education is a factor

family and sex roles, influence types and levels of interest. Women are coming to feel freer than before to participate in scientific, outdoor, and mechanically oriented activities. In general, adults' interests often resemble those of their parents. Aesthetic parents have aesthetic children, and intellectual parents have intellectual children, although the specific aesthetic or intellectual areas that parents and their children follow may be quite different. Thus certain life styles and values become hallmarks of particular families.

Even within the same family, individual differences in personality may produce a variety of interest patterns. John Holland, a psychologist, portrays each individual's personality as including six interest styles, one in cultural interests, but which concerts or drinking locales are chosen vary with life style. Leisure styles also vary according to marital, parental, and retirement status. In any case, the core of such activities is close to home, and leisure style is one aspect of total life style.

The factors that tend to discourage or enhance particular activities are complex—for example, in wilderness use. One study disclosed that it made more resources and vacation time available; having few or no small children; and being male rather than female, although female users were as committed as were the men. Those with a high leisure ethic, who believed in the constructive value of leisure, were also high users, as was love of, and concern for, wilderness itself.

The privacy that spending time in the wilderness provides fulfills several functions—among them, personal autonomy, emotional release, a congenial environment for self-evaluation, and protected communication—when one can do what one likes with impunity. Of these, emotional release seemed the most important function while within this broad area, resting the mind from anxiety and mental fatigue was the most important individual item (Hammitt & Brown, 1984).

Leisure Styles. Among adults differences in choice of activity by both sex and age are more a matter of degree than kind. In a study of leisure activities among middle- and lower-middle-class adults, the large majority mentioned such pursuits as "radio listening, reading, household chores, shopping, visiting, being visited, and helping others. Those [activities] seldom reported included playing a musical instrument, dancing, solitary games, picnics, and physical exercise" (Lowenthal, Thurner & Chiriboga, 1975, p. 6). The older groups were more selective about their activities than the younger ones. Middle-aged men had the least varied activities, and those

anticipating retirement in the near future were doing what they could to improve their income before they retired. This factor, coupled with their decreased energy, resulted in fewer leisure activities such as club and church affiliations. They might still belong to certain groups, but their participation was erratic. Middle-aged women also engaged in fewer activities than younger women, but not for the same reasons as the men. True, half of them worked, chiefly to supplement the family income, but they were not preoccupied with their jobs, and focused their interests on the family.

Patterns of leisure vary according to the stage of marriage. Before the children come, people engage in recreational activities similar to those they shared before marriage. But the most significant change in leisure patterns comes after the children are born (Kelly, 1975). There is a slight decrease in what are primarily companionship activities, and a slight increase in worklike activities. The change is from activities that are selected chiefly for their intrinsic satisfaction to those that relate to role expectations. That is, family roles tend to structure the parents' leisure styles, and having children significantly limits their choice of activities.

The postparental period, after the last child has left home and retirement begins, does not represent a complete return to the unconditional activities of the preparental stage. Professionals shift slightly back toward work-related activities; and many activities associated with role expectations are exchanged for those related to personal satisfaction (Kelly, 1975).

The choice of leisure activities can be further modified by all sorts of situational and circumstantial factors, including the length of vacations, the amount of disposable income available, the climate, the local culture, or the type of housing people occupy. Leisure styles become modified according to new roles, opportunities, associations, and changes in geographical environment such as moving from an apartment to a single-family house with a yard.

A Perspective on Leisure

Various suggestions have been offered for improving leisure programs. William Glasser, educator and psychiatrist, believes that much, but not all, recreation should be active and energetic (Recreation for all, 1977). Going to a concert is a desirable activity because music affects an individual personally. In reading, the individual translates the written message into personal meanings. Some recreation should involve doing nothing at all except simply "lying on the grass and opening yourself to feelings and thoughts . . ." (p. 74). Human beings are "doing" creatures, though at times they should learn to relax completely.

It is also important to find ways to diminish barriers to participation in leisure activities. Among the most common barriers are inadequate time, money, opportunity, and partners; overcrowding, as in a national park; personal characteristics, including shyness; lack of transportation and lack of knowledge about available opportunities. Barriers, of course, vary with type of recreation, area of the country, and the situations of persons involved. Often a combination of barriers, more than any one specifically, accounts for nonparticipation (Jackson, 1983).

Glasser advocates a "Department of Recreation and Appropriations" that would supplement state and local governments' efforts to provide tennis courts, places to hike, play golf, swim, or engage in other recreation. Local incentive is simply not sufficient. Glasser would not stress activities such as softball leagues, that are dependent upon getting groups together. He advocates instead such activities as tennis, golf, bike riding, skiing, fishing, or jogging. Overall, what is needed is ready access to nonteamed, sim-

ple, relatively uncompetitive recreation—and not merely in physical activities. Music, chess, art, and bridge should be available, as well as yoga, which encourages self-discipline and meditation. These recreations should not have "much of a goal" because the activity should "literally allow your mind to be free" (p. 76). People should have available those kinds of recreation that free the mind and help them to escape strenuous daily tasks "in a deeply felt way, whether through playing golf, painting a picture, or camping in the woods. The secret of happiness is to get involved doing something you believe in enough to accept yourself completely in the process; and doing it is a thousand times more satisfying than watching it" (p. 76).

Interpersonal Relationships

Primary Networks. Three types of social networks typically labeled as primary are family kin, friends, and neighbors (Hoyt & Babchuk, 1983). None of these is invariant—for instance, simple proximity of residence does not make neighbors primary. Nor may it be assumed that kin are always intimate or primary. Children may dislike their parents, and siblings may dislike each other. Friendships, unlike kinship relations that are more or less permanent, are voluntary and change over time. Thus, all such relationships vary among themselves.

Confidences and intimacies within the family vary according to category, sex, age, and frequency of action. Confidences between spouses differ from those shared with siblings. Females, more often than males, confide in kin, and are more often confidants themselves. Kinship ties grow stronger with age, and older kin more often confide in each other than with younger kin—perhaps because there is growing dependency on types of assistance ordinarily provided by kin. In short, common assumptions about kinship networks are often overly simplistic, not taking into account the many variables involved.

Friendship. Tesch (1983) calls friendship "the most ubiquitous" of human relationships, and its study as having the greatest potential for understanding life-span social development. Friendships in early childhood involve mutual liking and shared activities, and in late childhood they include loyalty and mutual aid. In adolescence intimate self-disclosure becomes a part of friendship, for females more than for males. In later years people are increasingly sensitive to, and concerned about, such relationships. Throughout adulthood reciprocity in forms of dependability and intimacy increase. Indeed, among older persons, friends often afford greater satisfaction than do relatives.

Aside from friendships between married couples, close friends are usually of the same sex. Cross-sex friendships among adults are potentially sexual, and are therefore discouraged. Such friendships are rare even in childhood, when they are sanctioned, though hardly encouraged, and also in old age, partly because there are more women than men. They are only fully approved in marital and love relationships. Though numerically rare, they do exist, especially where the situation makes them unthreatening. For example, cross-sex friendship ties may exist between opposite-sex homosexuals or between men and women on the job who share the same interests but are not sexually attracted to each other.

Studies of both younger and older middle-aged married couples indicated certain patterns of friendship (Babchuk, 1981). For one thing couples listed other married couples as their primary, or closest friends, although they were not equally close to both individuals. Typically each spouse had a closer relationship with the same-sex member of the other couple. Three in four couples cited no more than two other couples in their community as primary friends; however, they found that number sufficient. Married couples reacted to other couples as units—indeed, about half reported not a single primary friend independent of the spouse. Children appeared to be no real obstacle, and couples looked on whatever problems they presented as transient. Nor did the number of primary friends increase or decrease from early adulthood to middle age. If a primary-friend couple should move another might be substituted. Primary friendships apart from the couple relationship involve less frequent contact and are less stable. In general, relationships to kinsfolk are independent of those of friends, and are more constant and "inevitable."

In terms of establishing primary friendships the husband's role is dominant throughout the marriage. However, over the years the wife exercises growing influence. The researchers observe that it is unclear how many primary friendships one needs for a healthy life, and how many less-primary associations.

Social Networks. Recently considerable emphasis has been placed on the importance of social networks, which may consist of relatives, neighbors, co-workers, or others (Ell, 1984). Often their membership is based on reciprocal role interaction—hence, they change along with one's roles. Network ties may be closeknit, loose, intimate, or casual. Such networks are not equivalent to social support. Only a few are truly supportive, and these are characterized by frequent interaction, proximity, trust, and reciprocity. Social support includes both practical and psychological encouragement, making a person feel cared for and loved.

Close social networks, if supportive, are usually quite beneficial to health. They may transmit information, provide resources and care, and help one maintain self-esteem. In general, persons with high rates of mental or physical illness and high mortality rates have weak social ties or live in conditions of social disintegration. Nevertheless, the effect of close-knit networks can be negative—for example, when their group values inhibit proper use of medical care, or the network itself may have a poor over-all health status.

Marital Status. Marital status interacts with age in determining social relationships. In general, when people arrive at the stage in life when their children and spouses are the focus of their existence, they relate chiefly to kin and neighbors, in addition to some friends. At this stage the nuclear family provides much of their needed companionship, and fewer new friendships are established outside the family. Close relationships require time and emotional energy and married persons have less time for intimate associations outside the family (Shulman, 1975).

Of course, there is much variation in the way individual adults interact socially. There are the loners and the extroverts, those with many superficial friends, and those with a few close ones. But the most common pattern among adults is to have a few close friends who share certain things in common, whether children, leisure activities, or personal traits.

SUMMARY

Work is still very important to middle-aged adults, although a bit less to men and much more to some women than formerly; nevertheless, its meaning is changing. Today both sexes want something more than a job—they want a vocation that gives them a measure of fulfillment. They also expect to earn a high enough income to be able to afford the good things in life, including satisfying leisure activities. Both sexes still have their vocational problems, though working wives find

such pursuits rewarding, and both sexes are reaping the benefits of improved working conditions. Nevertheless men may feel devastated by unemployment, even when the wife's paycheck plus his unemployment benefits can sustain the family.

While leisure is still less important in most middle-agers' life style than work, it is gaining rapidly in significance. These people engage in widely varied pursuits that are somewhat dependent on social class, education, sex, age, marital status, and individual tastes. People have their characteristic leisure styles that evolve over time; leisure activities change, to some extent, as the total life situation changes—for example, when the children leave home or retirement approaches.

SUGGESTED READINGS

BERNARD, J. (1981). The good-provider role. *American Psychologist, 36*(1), 1–12.

BURRIS, B. H. (1983). The human effects of unemployment. *Social Problems, 31*(1), 96–110.

COSTA, P. T. & McCRAE, R. R. (1984). Personality and vocational interests in an adult sample. *Journal of Applied Psychology, 69*(3), 390–400.

ELL, K. (1984). Social networks, social support, and health status: A review. *Social Service Review, 58*(1), 133–149.

FELD, S. L. (1984). The unstructured use of personal associates. *Social Forces, 62*(3), 640–652.

GILL, S. J., COPPARD, L. C., & LOWTHER, M.A. (1983). Mid-life career development theory and research: Implications for Education and work. *Aging and Work, 6*(1), 15–30.

HOUSEKNECHT, S. K., VAUGHN, S. & MACKE, A. S. (1984). Marital disruption among professional women: The timing of career and family events. *Social Problems, 31*(3), 273–284.

KEMP, A. A. (1983). The excluded ones: Males and females in small or very segregated occupations. *Sociological Spectrum, 3*, 181–202.

MUCHINSKY, P. M. (1983). Vocational behavior and career development, 1982: A review. *Journal of Vocational Behavior, 23*, 123–178.

OSHERSON, S. & DILL, D. (1983). Varying work and family choices: Their impact on men's work satisfaction. *Journal of Marriage and the Family, 45*(2), 339–357.

PHILLIBER, W. W. & HILLER, D. V. (1983). Relative occupational attainments of spouses and later changes in marriage and wife's work experience. *Journal of Marriage and the Family, 45*(1), 161–170.

RIDDICK, C. C. & DANIEL, S. N. (1984). The relative contribution of leisure activities and other factors to the mental health of older women. *Journal of Leisure Research, 16*(2), 136–148.

RUBLE, T. L., COHEN, R. & RUBLE, D. N. (1984). Sex stereotypes. *American Behavioral Scientist, 27*(3), 339–356.

TESCH, S. A. (1983). Review of friendship development across the life span. *Human Development, 26*(5), 266–276.

UNKEL, M. B. (1981). Physical recreation participation of females and males during the adult life cycles. *Leisure Sciences, 4*(1), 1–27.

YOUNG, R. A. (1983). Toward an understanding of wilderness participation. *Leisure Sciences, 5*(4), 339–357.

CHAPTER ELEVEN

Characteristics of Older People

ESTABLISHING A FRAME OF REFERENCE

What Should Older People Be Called?

There is no single accepted designation for the last stage of life. Many terms used for the aged evoke negative images, including "the elderly," "the retired," and even "senior citizens" and "golden-agers." Some terms are contemptuous and degrading. Older people may be described as " 'fading fast,' 'over the hill,' 'out to pasture,' 'down the drain,' 'finished,' 'out of date,' and old 'crock,' 'fogy,' 'geezer,' 'biddy' " (Butler, 1975c, p. 2).

In the following, several persons over age 60 tell how they feel about the term "senior citizen," and what they think older people should be called. (Significantly, younger persons had no objection to the term "senior citizen.")

MALE, AGE 72: Silly euphemisms usually amuse me. This one is no worse than "interment director," for "undertaker," which I saw in a newspaper advertisement.

MALE, AGE 69: I can't think of a better term.

FEMALE, AGE 73: Yes, I object to it. Why use any special name?

FEMALE, AGE 84: Any term is agreeable to me. I just don't like for people to be always trying to "honor" us.

FEMALE, AGE 62: I dislike very much the terms "the aged" and "the elderly," and feel lukewarm about "senior citizen." I prefer "older persons" or "the long-living" better, but haven't encountered the ideal term as yet.

Butler advises that either the least objectionable of the common names—perhaps "the older" or "the elderly"—should be given a respectable status, or we should have a new name altogether. The Abkhasians in the Soviet Union simply describe older persons as "the long-living," which emphasizes life rather than death (Butler 1975c).

Neugarten (1980) favors dropping the term "old" because of its "complex connotations. The average person who says 'old' generally has in mind a set of physical attributes and behavior that make the bearer different from the rest of society" (p. 78). She prefers the terms "young-old" and "old-old," to differentiate the more from the less vigorous.

Whatever names older people may be called will inevitably become colored in the popular mind by their status in society. Hence, the best way to insure that names will be ego-building rather than ego-eroding is to upgrade the status of older people.

Instead of calling the last stage of life maturity, Erik Erikson (1982) terms it "old age." He believes it is time we acknowledged that one becomes old, not just mature; and we shouldn't simply lump all adults together as "the mature." Erikson, age 80 himself, feels all right about the word old, but complains that "elderly" transforms "elder" from a token of respect to something deprecating.

Demographic Data

Meantime, the composition of the older population has changed. For one thing, the older population itself has grown older. Since 1900 the over-age-75 population has increased eleven-fold, and the 85-plus population by about eighteen times. During the same period the life expectancy of white women grew by 27 years, compared to 22 years for white men. Based on 1980 mortality rates, white females can expect to live 78 years on average, and white males 70 years; and the older the age the greater becomes the sex imbalance. In the age 60-to-64 group women outnumber men 116 for every 100, and among those age 85 and older by 229 to 100 (Fowles, 1983).

Older people are growing in number much faster than the general population. The over-age-60 population grew in size from 4.9 million in 1900 to over seven times that number (35.6 million) in 1980 (Fowles, 1983). In 1900 just 1 in 16 persons was over age 60; now they are 1 in 6 and will be over 1 in 4 (27 percent) by 2030.

The gain in life expectancy has been chiefly at older ages. The average age of the pop-

The young-old are still relatively active and vigorous.

ulation is older simply because factors contributing to death in infancy, childhood, and middle age have been reduced. The decline in the death rate among the elderly themselves has been dramatic. This decline has resulted mainly from improved treatment of heart disease, but also from reduced smoking and new medical technologies. The death rate for heart disease held at 24 percent in the last decade for persons over 85; for stroke 33 percent; for influenza and pneumonia, 37 percent (Hyatt, 1979). Overall, it is simply a matter of more people reaching old age, for basic longevity has remained pretty stable.

A concomitant of the rapid increase in the average life span has been a parallel growth in number of multigenerational families. Among persons age 65 and over, four in five have living children and almost half are members of four-generation families. Among individuals 80 years and older, almost three-fourths are great-grandparents; and even a fourth of those ages 65 and 66 are great-grandparents (Shanas, 1980).

When Is One Old? Frames of Reference

Chronological Age. Kalish (1975) raises the question, "When is one old?" (p. 2). The answer depends on one's frame of reference, as discussed in Chapter 1. From the chronological point of view, old age is most often considered to begin at age 65, but only because retirement commonly dates from that time. The same chronological years represent a condition today different from the one in the past, just as people at present may be quite different from those of the same chronological age in the future. Yet we continue to confine our operational concept of aging largely to calendar years, although it has both pluses and minuses. It simplifies compiling statistics because age is universally used in data sources. However, notes Fowles (1983), people of the same calendar age vary greatly in biological age. Besides, no specific chronological age applies—older persons are

variously defined as those over "age 55, age 60, or age 65, or some other age." Fowles himself arbitrarily defines all those over 60 as older people.

Old age is sometimes divided into categories. Neugarten (1974) divides the older population into three categories:((1) The young-old, between 55 and 65, are still working and at the peak of their social and vocational status. On the other hand, one might as easily call them the older middle-aged. For one thing, these people identify themselves as middle-aged; and for another, their health, life style, and activity, aside from vocation, more nearly resemble those of the middle-aged than of the elderly. (2) The middle-old, aged 65 to 75, constitute much of the retired population. The majority are in good health and have plenty of time for enriching their lives. (3) The old-old, over age 75, are the frailest, loneliest, poorest, and sickest. Ordinarily we refer to this group when we speak of the "problem elderly" and the deplorable status of the aged (Streib, 1976).

The chronological definition of old age has changed over time. In societies where life expectancy is only 35 to 40 years, an older person is much younger chronologically than in those places where the life expectancy is over 70 (Hauser, 1976). In modern countries—including the United States, Japan, and Western Europe—retirement laws and health and pension plans have established the beginning of old age between ages 55 to 65.

Psychological Age. Another approach to old age is psychological. It considers older persons' feelings, perceptions, and attitudes. Bailey (1976) says that the signs of approaching old age are "easily identifiable: the death or degenerative illness of a relative or close friend of approximately the same age; an increase in aches and pains; the tendency of others to mumble their words and of publishers of phone books to reduce the type size" (p. 39).

There are also psychological stereotypes—for example, that the older person is senile, a "catch-all label . . . to explain any behavior about an older person that violates . . . expectations of normal behavior" (Branco & Williamson, 1982, p. 385). Senility may result from hardening of the brain's arteries or cerebral arteriosclerosis or other brain disease, but it is not a normal part of aging. This stereotype also connotes intellectual decline, which derives partly from cross-sectional data. Currently old persons had less education than younger adults have, which tends to distort conclusions. Moreover, scores vary according to the component of intelligence being measured. Although still controversial, it appears that intelligence does not necessarily decline sharply with age.

Phenomenological Age. The concept of phenomenological age refers to an individual's self-perception of aging, which is highly variable. Traditionally, older persons' sense of feeling younger than their chronological age has been interpreted as defensive, a denial of a socially stigmatized status (Baum, 1983–84). That is, they have been viewed as simply deceiving themselves. From this point of view, such persons should be less psychologically healthy than those who admit that they feel their age. However, research consistently shows that the majority of older persons feel younger than their age, and are psychologically healthier than those who feel their age. That is, they describe their status much more favorably than the public assumes.

For Mary Tompkins, social leader, it happened during her daughter's freshman year in college. Trim Mary—tennis playing, party giving, club going—looked into the lighted makeup mirror one morning and saw deepening lines from nose to mouth, shadows of other creases around her eyes, and three new grey hairs. . . . When is a person old? For Harrison Caldwell old age was still a future shadow on his eightieth birthday. Although he had retired (and had the gold watch to prove it) when he was 65, the lumber company which he had served still used him as a consultant several days a month. Besides, he kept up his golf game and volunteered to help several young parolees (Bailey, 1976, pp. 13–14).

Various factors contribute to feeling young, including psychological and physical health, higher socioeconomic status, gender identity, being married, greater social involvement, delayed retirement, advantaged ethnic status and younger age. Over the life span such factors contribute to making one feel more or less active, useful, or in control of his or her life—in effect, younger or older. That is, feelings of being old—ineffective, used up—are at one pole of the continuum, those of vitality and purpose—being young— at the other.

Commonly, self-perceptions of aging are not a matter of a single crisis but a series of events, often cumulatively critical. It is easier to "make sense of being old if we recognize that we begin to age almost as soon as we are fully adult—that aging and dying are part of everyday life and that . . . nothing is immutable, and whatever we want to continue must be constantly retrieved from loss and reincorporated (Marris, 1978–79, pp. 134–35).

Social Age. Older persons' psychological age differs from their social age. Some individuals are psychologically ancient in their 20s; others are psychologically youthful in their 80s (Smith, 1973). That is, psychological age "is measured in terms of what a man is, how he experiences life" (p. 12). By contrast, "social age becomes that age which is gauged by social roles and habits. Forced retirement at 65 makes a social-role definition of old age" (p. 12). Hence older persons' social roles are defined by the way people at large perceive them. Thus the way individuals respond to people who have retired, defines their role in society.

Physical Age. Aging may also be defined in physical terms with regard to body posture, hair color, voice, and the ability to see and hear. Physically, an individual's body does not age in homogeneous fashion, for some parts of it may decline sooner than others. A man aged 70 may "retain a perfectly smooth, unwrinkled face, a full head of black hair, and a heart performing like that of a man in his 50s—while his renal functioning may be like that of an 80-year-old" (Kalish, 1975, p. 5).

Tierney (1982) provides a picture of the average 70-year-old man, and how he has changed since young adulthood. Consider first how the 70-year-old man looks. His skin wrinkles as it becomes less moist and elastic, and particular lines derive from his customary facial expressions. His skin thins and spreads out, like a wrinkled case a bit too big for its contents. By age 60 he has excess skin and bags under his eyes, and by age 70 there are many wrinkles, and the skin is less uniform in color. Meantime, he has gained weight from an average 165 pounds at age 20 to 178 at age 70. Since he has become more sedentary and his basal metabolic rate is slowing he has twice as much fat, 30 percent of body weight compared to 15 percent. He has shrunk, too, from an average height of 5 feet, 10 inches at age 30 to five feet, 8 7/8 inches at age 70 as muscles weaken and the back slumps, as disks between the spine bones deteriorate, causing the bones to move closer together. His features become bigger and more distinctive; the ear lobes flatten, and grow longer. The head has increased about an inch in circumference, because the skull has thickened. He has lost a third of his teeth, not because of age; however, future 70-year-olds should fare better because of fluoridated water and better dental care. He gets hairier in his ears and nostrils, and sometimes on his back; and his eyebrows grow longer. Men grow bald or turn grey at different rates, and some never experience balding. Hairs are thickest at age 20 and thin as a baby's at age 70.

His senses are not as sharp or discriminating either. He can discriminate colors, sounds, and tastes less well. The lens of the eyes continue to harden through life, and cause problems to most men by the 40s. Less light reaches the retina, making it harder to see in the dark.

The taste sense also declines—he has about 245 taste buds at age 30 but just 88 by age 70. His mouth is drier, and his voice begins to quaver as he has less control over his vocal cords. He speaks more slowly and at a higher pitch. He cannot hear sounds as high-pitched as earlier, but his hearing diminishes little in the range of ordinary human speech.

Other changes occur in general stamina, muscles, and reflexes. As heart, lungs, and muscles weaken, less oxygen enters, and the heart dispenses it more slowly through the bloodstream through the muscles. His bones and joints have deteriorated, too. His bones have lost calcium, becoming more brittle and slower to heal. Few men develop rheumatoid arthritis, but most of them acquire degenerative arthritis which creates slower, stiffer movements. The muscles that control the lungs weaken and tissues in the chest become less resilient, so deep breaths are shallower than formerly. At age 70 he can still run a marathon if he has trained, but it will take him longer than at age 30. His reflexes have slowed, because his brain processes information and dispatches signals more slowly.

His brain shrinks as it loses billions of neurons, the loss varying in different parts of the brain. The part controlling posture holds up, but that guiding sleep patterns deteriorates—he sleeps 2 hours less a night at age 70 than at age 30.

By age 70 most men are much less active sexually, for a number of reasons. Psychological changes, decreased vitality, and a lower hormonal level all play a part. With increasing years, the testes sag, more time is required for penile erection, orgasm, and recovery. At age 30 he averages 121 orgasms a year, 10 alone; at age 70, 22 a year, 8 alone. At age 30 the angle of erection is 20 percent above horizonal, at 70, 25 percent below.

Here are some brighter comments about young-old men's physical aging. People become less sensitive to pain, probably because of nerve fiber deterioration and slower processing of sensory information (Tierney, 1982). Perhaps one should worry less about gaining a bit of weight—the mildly overweight live longer. Smokers who manage to make it past age 65 are no more likely than nonsmokers to have heart attacks. The effects of disease are worse than those of aging. Physically, a healthy 70-year-old is more like a 30-year-old than a contemporary who has certain chronic disorders.

In general the same picture applies for women, with some variations and exceptions. Men's skin ages more slowly, because it has more oil and they shave, scraping away dry skin. However, as the years pass women prove generally hardier and live longer.

Developmental Age. The alternative—as suggested in Chapter 1—might be a developmental concept, but even this approach poses problems. Developmentally, aging would be viewed holistically—that is, in terms of all the processes and areas of behavior. Such an approach becomes increasingly complex because the older people become, the greater the asynchrony of the aging process within their bodies. A more limited view might be more practical. The physical criterion alone would be more appropriate in determining whether a man should retire from a construction job. It may be best simply to make clear the current frame of reference while keeping in mind all the options that exist.

Aging as Pathology. It is often assumed that older people always have poor health (Branco & Williamson, 1982). Not even a majority of older people have health problems, although a considerable minority do experience some limitations in major activities due to ill health. Also certain chronic conditions such as rheumatism, arthritis, and high blood pressure are more common in the elderly. Nevertheless, the Shakespearean idea of old age as a period of "sans teeth, sans eyes, sans taste, sans everything" is er-

roneous. The assumption that older people will have serious health problems has led to such practices as age segregation and mandatory retirement.

Most older persons rate their own health better than it actually is. About two-thirds rate their health as good or excellent compared to that of others their age. True, 4 in 5 older persons report some one or more chronic, long-term health conditions but a large majority function adequately. However, age exacerbates such conditions and significantly impact the lives of about half the over-age-85 population (Fowles, 1983). The percentage rises from 5 percent of persons ages 65 to 74, to 12 percent for those 75 to 84, and to 31 percent of those age 85 and older.

Here are certain health rules which minimize the ravages of aging. People who exercise live longer, but is it that healthier people exercise? Anyhow, monkeys reduce risk of heart disease if they work out regularly on a treadmill. Exposure to ultraviolet rays of the sun makes skin dry and stiffen, and produces age spots. Perhaps it is a good idea to avoid eating too much fat, but what constitutes the best diet is still at issue. Cigarette smokers' lung capacity is that of nonsmokers 10 or 15 years older. Perhaps drinking a little alcohol is better than drinking none. Very moderate drinkers outlive both heavy drinkers and abstainers.

The best-known pathological theory of aging, which treats aging as a diseaselike process, was put forward by a Russian zoologist, Elie Metchnikoff. According to this concept, aging results from "cumulative self-poisoning—auto-intoxication—by the toxins of bacteria normally resident in the gut" (Medawar & Medawar, 1977, p. 57). Although this theory has not proved popular, Metchnikoff deserves recognition for first treating aging as "an epiphenomenon of life—something superimposed upon the normal processes of living—rather than as a phenomenon somehow entailed by the life processes themselves" (p. 57). Another theorist,

Leslie Orgel, views aging as resulting from "accumulated errors of information-processing in the body. Among dividing cells such errors may of course arise in the nucleic acid information source itself, but in addition mistakes are bound to occur in the transcription and translation of genetic information into bodily constituents; and if these happen to be enzymes, then the products whose manufacture they make possible will be awry as well" (p. 57).

Thus far neither of these views regarding the cause of aging nor any others have gained firm support. On the other hand, there has been some concern expressed about the possible negative consequences if scientists find ways to greatly prolong life. Overpopulation, and other problems arising from tampering with the natural order, might result. After all, death is nature's way of removing successive generations to make room for those to come. Almost all medical advances in the field of aging serve to prolong life, and it is difficult to discriminate between socially constructive research and that which may disturb the natural order. With regard to "all life-saving and life-prolonging measures, the real mischief arises from their being adopted piecemeal and haphazardly, instead of being part of a well thought out program" (p. 57).

Aging as Positive. A review of the research indicates that the elderly are viewed in largely negative terms (Branco & Williamson, 1982). Particular individuals may be viewed as exceptional and as persons to whom the stereotypes do not apply. Also, some people, most of them individuals who find their own later years satisfying, paint a brighter picture of older people in general. Ashley Montagu (1982) perceives growing older as an art which he calls growing up. Characteristics needed for growing up include a continuation of learning, the need to organize, to develop curiosity, and to sustain a sense of wonder. Other elements in continuing to grow are imagination, explorativeness, a sense of humor, flexibility, honesty, optimism, and trust. He places special stress on continuing education and continuous exercise of the mind.

Perspective on Aging. Whatever one's frame of reference with regard to age, certain observations should be kept in mind. It is difficult to determine the effects of aging because older persons differ so much from each other. Some individuals change far more than others, and aging proceeds at different rates in different parts of the same body. Apparently aging does not function as an independent variable, but as a function of other variables. Individual differences in changes that occur over the years involve the interaction of diverse factors, including life experiences, psychological well-being, and alterations in physical status, including those caused by smoking, illness, and disease.

It is especially important to distinguish between the effects of biological aging and those of diseases, especially those which are common in later years. It is true that there is a general decline in resistance to disease and infection (Branco & Williamson, 1983). [However, losing one's teeth is not necessarily age-related. It is related more to diet and dental hygiene than to age.] The decrease in pulse rate is a biological matter, whereas heart disease may be more a reaction to smoking or environmental stress.

Attitudes Toward Aging

Cultural Variations. Attitudes regarding later life are highly variable, ranging from positive to neutral to negative, but heavily skewed in the unfavorable direction. The Japanese have a strong awareness of aging and are preoccupied with changes, especially of seasons and years. But their attitude toward the elderly as such is neither strongly positive nor negative. The majority of people in the United States believe aging is somewhat sad and that it is accompanied by inevitable decline. Those who view aging positively, at least in this country, are the exception.

The Times as a Factor. At any one time, attitudes toward the aging are related to an economy's ability to support its population (Berman, 1975). Whenever a population outgrows an economy's capacity to support it, the weaker elements of humankind, including the aged, the infirm, and the handicapped, become vulnerable. Life becomes relatively cheap, and the basic need for self-preservation—as demonstrated in the law of the survival of the fittest—produces attitudes and practices that operate subtly to deplete the older population. Certainly when there are excessive numbers of old people in a society while many younger ones are struggling for survival, it becomes easier to rationalize turning off life-giving machines or cutting Social Security payments. Older people may lose their value simply because they have become so numerous. We feel a certain veneration for the rare person who lives beyond age 100. But such veneration does not extend to the growing numbers of old people in their 70s and 80s (Shanas, 1980). Sometimes they are seen as "funny" old people who behave inappropriately in the eyes of younger persons. "At others, they are 'cute' old, bright, productive, and active persons, and thus, assumed to be like clever children" (p. 14).

Variations in Views by Age. Older and younger generations vary somewhat in the way they perceive the elderly. In a study of young, middle-aged, and older persons, all three age groups indicated that the death of a 75-year-old was less tragic than that of a younger person of any age (Kalish & Reynolds, 1976). In another study, Cameron and Cromer (1974) determined generational preferences by sampling three groups: young adults, the middle aged, and the elderly. The two oldest generations expressed a next-younger generational preference, thus demonstrating an antiold, proyoung preference. The young adult generation was the most,

and the older generation the least, preferred.

How Older People View Themselves. The fact that older people do not devalue themselves as much as do younger people, does not mean that they view themselves positively. Many elderly Americans have negative attitudes toward aging and toward themselves. When older people speak of others their own age, they hold the same kinds of stereotypes about aging as the general public; they consider themselves to be all right, but see others of about the same age as "old fogies" (Moore, 1975).

The elderly have developed various defense mechanisms to offset the negative stereotypes assigned them. They may try especially hard to behave in more acceptable ways; or they may refuse to accept themselves as elderly at all, concealing their age both from themselves and others. In a study of persons aged 20 to 80, those under 30 thought of themselves as young, and those between 30 and 60 as middle-aged (Tuckman & Lorge, 1954). At age 60 only a few thought of themselves as old, and at 80 slightly over half called themselves old. A small percent of the 80-year-olds insisted on describing themselves as young. In general the older people are, the later they think old age begins. Hence there is a gap between their self-image and the image others hold of them (Rosow, 1974). Some older individuals even think that aging should not exist and that they should defy it and remain vigorously youthful to the last. Thus, a man may undertake very strenuous work such as building a house, which overtaxes him and produces a fatal heart attack (Marris, 1978–79).

In the following, several older adults react to the questions: *How old do you feel? Why do you feel older or younger than your age?*

FEMALE, AGE 73: Age as such does not bother me. I am still able to garden, travel, and entertain whenever I wish. I guess I feel younger than my age.

FEMALE, AGE 71: At times I feel much younger, at times the reverse.

FEMALE, AGE 74: I do not feel old. I try to think young and be around young people as much as possible. I feel much younger than my years. I am usually taken for being younger than I am.

MALE, AGE 72: I am aware that I can't do some things that I did at age 50 but it is silly to spend time thinking of such things, and I don't.

FEMALE, AGE 92: I guess I feel about age 75—oh well, sometimes age 80.

MALE, AGE 65: I still feel young at heart except when my physical problems become untenable.

These people's apparently distorted views of their own aging may be quite realistic, at least in the psychological or physical sense. It is apparent that aging is highly variable in all but the chronological sense—and while it has been tacitly assumed that it is healthy to confront one's aging, which age are we talking about?

Current Status of The Image. Neugarten observes that many Americans think of all older people as being needy. This stereotype, however, is not an accurate picture of what most older people are like; older people are not a homogeneous group. The general view is that people become more alike as they age; instead, they become less and less alike (Hall, 1980). There are signs that the popular image of the elderly may be improving (Seltzer & Atchley, 1971). In a national survey, Louis Harris and Associates (1975) found little evidence of *ageism* (negative feelings about old people) in public attitudes generally, and that the elderly portrayed their own life situations—including social interaction, economic status, and self-perceptions—as far more positive than they are commonly assumed to be.

A study of how television commercials portray aging also revealed considerable discrepancies from reality (Hiemstra, Good-man, Middlemiss & Vosco, 1983). Of 136 commercials analyzed, just 12 percent included persons who appeared to be over age 50 and 3.1 percent over age 60, compared with 15.7 percent of those over age 60 in the population. Of those portrayed two-thirds were males, although females considerably outnumber them at this age-stage. The focus was also on the young-old—few bald persons or those with wrinkled skins were shown. In general they were "nondescript," with "no observable family ties." Old people were shown mostly in relation to consumer services and to health, food, and household products, and were less likely to be shown in connection with automobile or household appliances or recreation items, despite their large amount of leisure time.

Overall, Hiemstra et al. concluded that these commercials hardly acknowledged the existence of older people. They ignored the fact that millions of older Americans are healthy and buy a wide range of items. Nor did they take into account the large purchasing power of this age group. Meantime, it must be acknowledged that advertisements of products to remove age spots, to color gray hair, or to help arthritis sufferers, will tend to reinforce the commonly negative view of older persons.

In another study, of Saturday morning cartoons on television, older people were mostly absent or inconsequential. Even incidental remarks about aging were rare, and nearly always negative or stereotypical. In a sense, older people were symbolically annihilated or trivialized. Being old, on Saturday morning television as in the public eye, is "not healthy, not attractive, and not good" (Bishop & Krause, 1984).

Upgrading the Stereotype. Certain trends may succeed in modifying negative stereotypes of the elderly. The growing popularity of the life-span developmental approach, and of courses on adulthood and aging, may help young people perceive themselves from the life-span point of view. From this perspective, all of us are all ages, which in effect minimizes age-stage barriers. We all have in us aspects of the child and youth we once were, and the forces that will inevitably project us into later stages. Perhaps we will shift from the "I-we" and "others perspective," to the "us-all perspective," the collective point of view (Christoffersen, 1974).

CHARACTERISTICS OF OLDER PEOPLE

Personality Characteristics

The Validity of Popular Concepts. Commonly held views of personality in later years are often erroneous, while a few rest on more solid ground. One myth is that the elderly inevitably grow inflexible and conservative. Life is typically viewed as progressing from "innovation to conservatism." The truth is that some people continue to change until the very end of their lives.

Another myth is that older people are unproductive. Although decreases in productivity may occur, they may be more a result of diseases and other circumstances than of the process of aging itself. Besides, some older individuals are as productive as they ever were. Women whose energies may have been tied up for many years in nurturant activities may even become more productive. Congressman Claud Pepper (1980) writes: "Don't talk to me about doddering old people—I know some people who dodder at 25 or 30. George Bernard Shaw was fond of saying, 'Some people are younger at 70 than 17.' Colonel Sanders didn't start his fried chicken business until he was past 65. Margaret Mead—at 75—was perhaps the nation's foremost anthropologist. Arthur Fiedler, at 83, and Leopold Stokowsky, at 94, were among our leading conductors . . ." (p. 16).

In the past the elderly were relatively uneducated. However, the gap between generations is being rapidly closed. In 1960 the median number of school years completed

by older persons was 8.3; by 1990, it will be 12. Already the number of college graduates has doubled since 1960 (Cohen, 1980, p. 991). Distortion arises from the tendency to think of the present and future old in terms of the past old. Older people of the future will be better educated, healthier, more secure economically, and better able to take care of themselves than the currently old are (Hyatt, 1979).

Nor is the social isolation stereotype valid, for more younger than older adults mention loneliness as a problem (Fowles, 1983). The institutionalized elderly may feel somewhat isolated from society, but few live in institutions. Besides, 4 in 5 of the elderly have living children and, on average, see their children at least once a week.

Older people are also often viewed as rejected by younger generations. It is true that there is a social barrier between the generations, and close friendships do not often develop between the very old and the very young. However, age segregation may be as much the preference of older as of younger people. The old enjoy talking with others their own age because they have lived through the same periods and they can share recollections and talk over common problems (Kalish & Reynolds, 1976).

Some older people do perceive themselves as losers, as is commonly believed. A study of gambling and aging suggests that old people expect to lose while the young anticipate winning, the difference perhaps being locus of control (Stone & Kalish, 1973). However, this attitude may derive from realistic appraisals of obstacles that society puts in the way of older persons rather than from any pessimism that arises in the process of aging.

As often presumed, people do indeed become wiser with age as a result of their experiences (Butler, 1975a). Old age is the only time when one can attain an individual sense of the entire life cycle. This perspective involves a subjective awareness of death, a sense of the unfolding process of change, and an understanding of human time as distinct from objective time. At this time people also understand what life is about; they have accumulated factual knowledge of what to expect during different phases of the life cycle, and they have certain concepts of those stages and phases.

A theme of later life is reviewing what one has done to decide what one has accomplished or what one thought one should. Ideally, people are able somehow to harmonize their past with their present and to feel reasonably content with what they have accomplished to this date (Streever & Wodarski, 1984).

The aged also have a nostalgic attachment to familiar objects, including their home, pets, and keepsakes. They have a sense of legacy, too, a need to leave something behind when they die, whether it is money, jewelry, or furniture. Another important task of later life is knowing when to give up power to the younger generation; it is often given up too late or too early.

A sense of satisfaction with one's life is more common than most people realize, but not as common as it might be. Feelings of wisdom and serenity may derive from a sense that one has done one's best or perhaps survived against great odds. The capacity for surprise, change, creativity, and curiosity does not necessarily decline over the years. Some older persons first develop their creativity in later years after other burdens have lessened.

It is also believed that the elderly are somewhat neutral sexually. Young and middle-aged adults are judged to have strongly marked characteristics of masculinity or femininity, while older ones are not. Masculinity and femininity are commonly believed to peak during the middle years and become somewhat more diffuse in old age. It would seem that masculinity plummets, but femininity increases more slowly and then decreases more gradually. However, Cameron (1976) found no evidence that adult females had any weaker gender identification than did males. For either sex, gender identity, once established in early childhood, is maintained at a somewhat constant level throughout life.

This writer believes that the discrepancy between older persons' self-perceptions of gender identity and the cultural stereotype can easily be explained. In early life, people establish a concept of themselves as masculine or feminine, in varying ways and degrees, and this self-perception persists. However, the way people appear to others in later years suggests weaker gender identity. Older women appear less feminine in that their voices are a bit deeper, their faces hairier, and their busts flabbier. They may lack the kind of physical attractiveness that is considered to be the feminine ideal. They have gone through menopause, and their life tasks are no longer dedicated to such traditionally feminine preoccupations as caring for children. Older men appear less masculine since their voices are not as deep as they were before, and they no longer possess the strength or the capacity for vigorous activity that is associated with maleness. Furthermore, many of their activities are less "masculine" than before. For one thing, after they retire, they help more often with household tasks, including cooking. They also become more sedentary and passive, which are characteristics associated with females.

Often the poor image of the elderly is reflected in subtle ways. Low status and power within a society, as reflected in both deferential speech patterns and body language, are apparent both in women and in the elderly (McGee & Wells, 1982). For example, in mixed-sex discussion groups at senior centers men exercise conversational control over women, and the middle-aged assume a more forceful stance than do their elders. Speech and behavior patterns are also affected by transitory factors such as audience and setting. In situations of dependency—for example, nursing homes—males may display powerless speech and a certain deference. However, such behaviors are less obvious when their wives, women in general, or persons inferior in status are present.

The above scenario is modified somewhat by historical forces, such as the feminist movement. Beliefs and identities acquired in early and middle adulthood, deriving from such forces, tend to carry over into later years. Present-day elderly women grew up in times when a women's place was in the home, and have maintained their deferential attitude toward men. Future cohorts of the aged may be expected to reflect the impact of women's entry in large numbers into the workworld and of the feminist movement.

Common Characteristics of the Elderly. There is no such thing as an aged personality type or even several distinct ones. Instead, older people may have typical adjustment reactions because of problems attached to the current status of old age. However, personality is far more continuous than discontinuous through life, and "at any point in time, a person is more like he has always been than he is like peers of his age group" (Dibner, 1975, p. 80).

Nevertheless, there are some characteristics that are found more commonly among older people than younger ones, one being preoccupation with the self. This inner orientation, which Neugarten (1968) calls *interiority*, begins to develop in middle age. As time goes on, "older people move toward more egocentric, self-preoccupied positions and attend increasingly to the control and satisfaction of personal needs" (p. 140). This orientation is more a response to the growing bodily needs that focus attention on the self than to any basic change in personality.

Older people are presumed to be more conservative—that is, they are characterized by an attitude of maintaining the status quo rather than favoring change. This tendency takes the form of "behavioral rigidity, unyieldingness, and greater consistency in social and political attitudes" (Dibner, 1975, p. 82). A related characteristic, cautiousness, undoubtedly stems from a decreased ability

to cope. On the other hand, older people often manifest a certain disregard for what is socially proper. They may be outspoken to the point of bluntness, or show utter disregard for style or custom. This not-as-yet researched characteristic may derive from older persons' growing isolation from their surroundings and an accompanying insensitivity to them. Such isolation may produce a reliance on internal rather than external standards of behavior.

Explanations of Personality Changes. Most psychological changes associated with age derive from nonuniversal biological causes such as illness, or from life events such as retirement or widowhood. Genetically programmed changes appear to be subtle and are rarely universal. Instead, changes that occur in adults derive chiefly from their own interaction with the environment, and the slowing down that characterizes older persons is simply evidence of basic alterations in the organism. As a result, older people come to prefer simplicity to complexity. Younger persons, with their high energy and abundant resources, "adapt to the environment through seeking complexity, stimulation, and novelty. . . . However, in states of illness or fatigue, even the young organism will evidence preference for simplicity. Preference for simplicity [serves a definite purpose] in the case of waning energy and lessened resources" (Dibner, 1975, p. 86). Simplicity, in turn, permits conservation of energy and easier adaptation at a stage when motor skills are deteriorating and senses growing less acute.

Disengagement Theory. Older people are often described as increasingly disengaged or detached from others. Social disengagement involves the mutual withdrawal by aging persons and those in their social environment from each other. This process arises not from some mysterious function of aging, but from conditions that often relate to it. As individuals age, significant persons in their lives drop off one by one; and even their familiar surroundings, including the childhood home, the neighborhood, and the community, die in the sense that they disappear or change beyond recognition.

In consequence, older people may turn away from their social environment to their inner resources. However, this statement is only relative. Older people are more diverse than any other group; some simply give up and others remain very active. A 91-year-old New York judge still hears some of the appellate court's most important cases. He studies Spanish and Latin, and he drinks martinis. A garment district worker, age 86, opens his shop for 4 hours every day. George Burns, the actor-comedian, resumed his film career at age 87 and worked on a film just 3 months after having open-heart surgery (Bronson, 1979).

Intellect

Cross-Sectional Data. Mental abilities have been presumed to decline so slowly as to be imperceptible in middle age, and then more rapidly, depending somewhat on the specific ability or individual concerned. Intellectual factors that depend directly on speed of response tend to decline relatively early (Cunningham & Clayton, 1973). Decrements in verbal ability, spatial relationships, reasoning, and mathematical ability may not occur until people reach their late 60s (Schaie & Labouvie-Vief, 1974). More extreme declines may derive from senility or *terminal drop,* a phenomenon recognized only recently. Individuals who show an accelerated decline in any of the various cognitive performance areas are more likely to die within a few years than those who manifest no special change (Riegel & Riegel, 1972).

In one such study, Baltes and Willis (1982) found among subjects, ages 62 to 80 (with an average age of 70), considerable plasticity in fluid intellectual performance. Schaie (1982), after 24 years of studying adult intelligence, concluded that reliable age changes

in psychometric abilities are not demonstrated before age 60, but reliable decrements may be shown for all abilities by age 74. Nevertheless, he emphasizes that there are great individual differences in intellectual change across the adult years, which produce early decrement in some individuals and maintain mental function into quite advanced age for others. Especially important for maintaining intellectual capacities are "favorable environment, varied opportunities for environmental stimulation . . . and a flexible life style" (Honzik, 1984, p. 325).

Intellectual declines in problem solving that occur before the late 50s are not normal but pathological (Schaie, 1980, p. 279). From the early 60s to the mid-70s, some—but not all—abilities normally decline. However, decrement is the rule for people over age 80. Beginning in the 50s most people experience some decrement in abilities that depend on speed of response and in those that are sensitive to modest impairments of the peripheral nervous system. Decrements occur in most abilities in persons with severe cardiovascular disease at any age; people who live in socially deprived, relatively undifferentiated environments also undergo a decline, beginning in their late 50s or early 60s.

As for complex problem solving, the answers are still unclear because the available data are based chiefly on cross-sectional studies.

Research regarding cognitive processes in later years indicates an overall stability in most people until a few years before death, the main exception being speed. Fewer than 5 percent of the over-age-65 population is institutionalized for physical or mental capacity at any one time, and only 15 percent will ever be in an institution. Moreover, many of these will be there for physical rather than mental incapacity (Woodruff, 1983). In general, age is a lesser factor in cognitive functioning than ordinarily believed. A comparison of the cognitive performance of twenty college students and twenty college-educated elderly persons, showed no difference according to age; however, both curriculum and gender proved to be significant predictors (Blackburn, 1984).

Only about 10 percent of people over age 65 manifest obvious deterioration, such as partial memory loss. Conditions of *senility* or *dementia*, a group of illnesses causing a decline in intellectual function, affect only 8 percent of the over-65 population. Alzheimer's disease, or *senile dementia*, formerly believed to be separate but now thought to be the same illness, accounts for 50 to 75 percent of dementia cases (Bronson, 1979). The progressive deterioration of brain tissue produces a gradual breakdown of mental capacities, such as in abstract thinking or short-term memory. Other effects are apathy and personality change. Symptoms are treated with psychotherapy and drugs, and life expectancy is about eight to ten years after diagnosis. Often what seems to be a cognitive impairment in later years is reversible; and modification of stress conditions may improve the situation of individuals with irreversible brain disease (Gaitz & Varner, 1980).

Perhaps the most significant aspect of aging involves those changes in the brain that account for numbers of elderly persons in nursing homes and mental institutions. It is clear that there is some brain-cell loss from birth to age 20 and then little from adulthood to old age. Brain weight remains practically unchanged through maturity and declines in later years (Kent, 1980, p. 27). The decrease is about 10 percent from the maximum weight in early adult life until the ninth decade (Drachman, 1980, p. 506). "There is an atrophy and functional weakening with age of many systems of neurons at all levels of the nervous system. . . . These are more or less universal and the deficits are gradual all through the adult years and increase in later life" (Adams, 1980, p. 506).

While hardening of the arteries, or *arteriosclerosis*, may be a contributing factor to senility for 1 case in 6, additional causes account for the others. The dementia of most older people relates to an organic disease of the nerve cells, synapses, and neurites. It is possible that biological research may, at some not too distant date, produce ways of preventing the lesions that produce senile dementia. The dementia in aging may be either chronic, deriving from cardiovascular disease—the natural concomitant of aging—or it may be acute, involving treatable conditions such as benign tumors, intoxication, infection, or nutritional defects (Sinex, 1975). There are certainly some elderly people in mental institutions whose dementia derives from treatable conditions.

It should always be kept in mind that older people vary greatly in mental characteristics. Some subjects, regardless of how old they may be, never show any measurable memory impairment (Botwinick, 1973). It is more accurate to think of decline in memory and other mental functions as descriptive of increasing numbers of individuals as they grow older, rather than as an invariable characteristic of all aging persons.

Demographic factors make it important to determine the mental capacities of older people and which are maximized with age (Woodruff, 1983). Persons now in their 20s and 30s will have to work until age 70 to receive Social Security benefits; by 2020 there will be too few of the young and too many of the elderly to maintain the traditional social structure. In other words, older people must then contribute more actively to society and not simply be beneficiaries of it. Therefore, it must be determined at what ages people are "the most efficient decision makers, information processors and integrative thinkers" and when they are wisest and "most effective in planning and achieving goals" (Woodruff, 1983, p. 140).

More people than generally recognized perform on a high intellectual level in later years. An insurance magazine which researched the histories of 400 famous people found that 35 percent of their greatest achievements were between the ages 60 and 70, 23 percent between 70 and 80, and 8 percent when they were over 80 (Cawthon, 1981).

Longitudinal Data. Except in instances of terminal drop and senility, recent longitudinal data present a far more encouraging picture of intellect in later years than has emerged before. While Piaget (Flavell, 1963) hypothesized that the final stage of intellectual growth (formal operations) is reached by about age 12, researchers are reporting consistent gains in conceptual development of young adults and older subjects (Papalia, 1972; Storck, Looft & Hopper, 1972). Some studies reveal little or no age decrement except in very old people or during the period shortly before death (Jarvik, Eisdorfer & Blum, 1973). Baltes and Schaie (1974) found "no strong age-related change in cognitive flexibility. For the most important dimension, crystallized intelligence, and for visualization as well, we see a systematic increase in scores for the various age groups, right into old age. Even people over 70 improved from the first testing to the second" (p. 36). *Crystallized intelligence* refers to cognitive performance (perceiving relationships, reasoning, and so on) in which culturally acquired skills are used. By contrast, *fluid intelligence,* which connotes cognitive performance relatively independent of those skills, may decline in later years.

Reconciling Discrepancies. Several factors account for the overly pessimistic reports of earlier researchers. For one thing, the differential results of cross-sectional and longitudinal studies can only be appreciated if cohort differences are analyzed with reference to changing social conditions as well as changing biological conditions within the subjects involved (Riegel & Riegel, 1972). Changes in cognitive functioning may not result from aging per se but from the declines in physical health that often accompany aging (Kalish, 1975). Besides, the poor performance of the elderly in some studies may be due to a lack of formal education,

and the fact that in the past, schooling relied more on memorization than on problem solving (Baltes & Schaie, 1974). It is significant that the specific age of decline is with successive generations (Schaie & Labouvie-Vief, 1974). Also, despite an apparent regression of cognitive functioning during advanced years, no longitudinal study has proved conclusively that specific abilities, once present, deteriorate in old age (Papalia & Bielby, 1974). Deficits observed by researchers may reflect differences in performance rather than a decreased ability to learn (Schaie & Gribbin, 1975).

Sociocultural factors may also distort the results of mental and sensory tests in later years. In short-term longitudinal studies, sociocultural differences have proved more important than age in accounting for differences in test results (Rudinger, 1972). Besides, older people may hesitate to make a response for fear of making the wrong one; thus cautiousness may contribute to what are thought to be performance deficiencies (Schaie & Gribbin, 1975).

The performance of the elderly also varies according to test content and the way tests are conducted (Furry & Baltes, 1973). Much of the data about cognitive performance comes from intelligence tests whose contents are aimed primarily at the young (Baltes & Schaie, 1974). Besides, most of the tests are timed, and again, older people have learned through experience to be cautious.

Recommendations. The Task Force on Aging of the American Psychological Association, among others, recommends that greater attention be given to understanding and eliminating unnecessary causes of decline in intellectual functioning in old age. Gerontologists have begun to consider the extent to which intellectual performance in older people can be enhanced; and the results so far, although still somewhat meager, are promising (Baltes & Schaie, 1974). The response of elderly subjects has improved dramatically, as much as 20 to 35 percent, among women 65 to 80 years of age, after as little as 2 hours of training. In addition,

The breathing of concentrated oxygen for extended periods, to increase oxygen supply to the brain, seems to improve memory for recent events. . . . Treatment of hypertension . . . also seems to be promising. . . . In view of the positive results already obtained, it seems plausible that breakthroughs in research may ultimately produce far more dramatic retardations or regressions in the decrements of aging than we can even imagine today. What is necessary is persistent, dedicated effort on a broad scale, involving researchers from a number of disciplines (Baltes & Schaie, 1974, p. 38).

Economic Status. There is also the stereotype that older people are poor. They do have a higher poverty rate than younger people, but it is not large. Three in four of the aged are certainly not poor; however, more females than males are in the poverty category.

Actually, the income of older persons has improved somewhat over recent years (Fowles, 1983). They are better educated and have larger public and private pensions, Social Security, and Medicare. They also sometimes have the savings and benefits deriving from having been dual-income couples. Nevertheless, subgroups among the elderly—mainly women, minorities, those who live alone, and the very old—are still below the poverty level. Those who fall into two or more of these categories are especially likely to be poor.

Physical Status

Appearance. Troll (1975) summarizes the changes that take place in physical appearance during adulthood. In the early years there is little change, followed by gross transformations in middle age. The body grows shorter as cartilage degeneration produces calcification and discs between vertebrae become smaller, causing the body to shrink and

sometimes to curve. There is some tendency to put on weight, and fat is redistributed. While body fat is a mere 10 percent of one's total weight in adolescence, it becomes at least 20 percent by middle age, with much of it concentrated around the waist. The chest or bust diminishes, while the hips and abdomen enlarge. The portion of the face that changes most is the bottom third. The distance between the bottom of the nose and the chin decreases because of changes in muscle, bone, teeth, and connective tissue. Because of a certain stiffening of the joints and decreased muscular resilience, posture becomes less erect and movements less fluid (Wiswell, 1980). Meantime, the skin becomes less elastic, and wrinkles appear. The pouches and dark circles that often appear under the eyes become more apparent because the remainder of the skin lightens.

The most visible change is in the hair; during the 40s, the hair thins, the hairline recedes, and baldness increases, especially in men. Also in the 40s, grayness appears and increases so that by their 50s, the majority of Americans are gray haired and a few white haired. Less obvious hair changes include diminished facial hair in men and increased facial hair in women; stiff hair in the eyebrows, ears, nose, and eyelashes of men, and on the chin and upper lip of women.

Next to impairment of mental function, deterioration of motility and gait are the most frequent neurologic accompaniments of aging. The strong stride of young adults changes to a "hesitant broad-based, small-step gait that has many of the characteristics of incipient parkinsonism" (Drachman, 1980, p. 508). Dizziness is a common complaint of the elderly as well as normal dementia, or normal cognitive changes with aging.

Differences in physical aging vary according to social class, sex, and the individual. On the individual level, differences among people of the same age are obvious. Middle-class people show the effects of aging far less than lower-class people because they are often engaged in less physically strenuous activity and have more time and money to spend on their appearance. On the individual level, too, losses in physical function vary greatly with aging. The rate of decline reflects several factors, one being history of exercise (Wiswell, 1980).

Any reduction in sexual activity up to age 60 can be attributed more to psychological and social than biological factors. Most individuals experience decline in sexual behavior in later years; however, older men appear to be more active and interested in such activities than older women. The main reason is that more women than men over age 65 are not remarried, because the pool of available men is much smaller (Branco & Williamson, 1982).

Sexual Functioning. The physical basis of male sexuality changes considerably. After the age of about 50, purely psychic erection—that is, without direct stimulation—occurs with gradually decreasing frequency. The tactile sensitivity of the penis may also decrease with age, and the intensity of the ejaculatory process is reduced. The time required to reach full erection is doubled or tripled for males over age 50 in comparison with younger men; however, the older male maintains an erection more easily for longer periods of time before feeling a need to ejaculate. Whether this effect may be attributed to the aging process or to coital experiences is unclear. Excessive use of alcohol may produce episodes of impotency in males of any age, although older males are more susceptible to its effects. There is no hard evidence that androgen therapy has any long-term effect on libido or sexual responsiveness (Corby & Skolnick, 1980).

In females the vagina becomes shorter and narrower and loses some of its flexibility; vaginal lubrication is reduced in rate and amount. But the woman's clitoral response remains essentially unchanged. Overall, there are gradual declines in response for both sexes with age. The critical point "is that there is much physiological potential for sexual pleasure remaining for both male and female" (Corby & Solnick, 1980, p. 896).

Sensory and Perceptual Abilities. Wide variations exist from one individual to another in levels of sensory, perceptual, and motor abilities in later years. In vision, more time is required to recover from exposure to glare or to adapt to the dark, so that night driving becomes harder after middle age. Color vision is maintained very well throughout middle age, although more light may be required to fully distinguish colors. Vision itself does not decline significantly during adult years because retinal changes rarely occur before age 60. In general, visual acuity peaks at around age 20 and remains constant until the 40s, after which a very gradual decline begins (Timiras, 1972).

Hearing deficiencies are very common among older persons. Hearing changes during adulthood are so subtle and so constant, albeit slow, that many individuals possess a hearing loss of which they are not aware. Losses in hearing appear mostly in the upper frequencies, and the decline begins at about age 10. The older the adult, the poorer the perception of high-frequency sounds (Dibner, 1975).

In general, body sensations become strongly diminished over time. Older people may report no pain after contracting such diseases as peritonitis or pneumonia; they are more sensitive to touch, and have a lower tolerance for hot and cold. Finally the tactile senses become generally less sensitive, especially in the hands and feet (Dibner, 1975).

Adults generally sleep the same number of hours each night (Thompson & Marsh, 1973); but after they reach their 40s, they awaken more often during the night, and their sleep is progressively less deep. Sleeping patterns change with age, but the total time spent asleep does not decrease. Sleeping time is broken into smaller segments; and individuals who sleep little at night often compensate through afternoon naps (Bronson, 1979). In all, they may spend more time in bed as they grow older, but not feel as rested.

Changes in psychomotor performance also occur with age. There is a gradual loss in muscular strength after the 20s, and there are noticeable effects after unusual or continuous exertion. Since older people inhale less oxygen and exhale less carbon dioxide, their bodies are less prepared for strenuous work (Dibner, 1975).

Sometimes problems do arise from vigorous exercise. In an exercise class of 50 people meeting three times each week, a cardiac fatality might normally occur every $6^1/_2$ years (Wiswell, 1980). However, preexercise medical examinations aren't always necessary or practical in low-intensity exercise programs. Medical clearance is necessary for aerobic programs that involve comparatively high-intensity exercises such as jogging, swimming, and other activities. Wiswell argues that "low-intensity exercise can have as dramatic an effect on mental health status in older adults as does aerobic conditioning" (p. 954).

The Nervous System. With regard to the nervous system, Timiras (1972) cites data that indicate a reduction of conductivity across synapses and in peripheral nerves. Those changes in the nervous system that accompany the aging process reflect a generous slowing down of practically all bodily processes and functions. Although this process is gradual, it occurs throughout the body.

Emotional Health

Conflicting Stereotypes. Two opposite views exist about emotional adjustment in old age. Each is partly false and partly true. One view is that the elderly become serene, living in a sort of "adult fairy land," as suggested by pictures of carefree grandmothers and "rocking-chair" grandfathers. The other is that older people are inevitably sad, dejected, and rejected, and are just waiting to die. Each stereotype is partly true. Older people do experience greater stresses than any other age group, stresses that can prove devastating (Butler, 1975c). The highest rate of suicide is among white males in their 80s; and the elderly, who constitute 10 percent of the total population in the United States, account for a quarter of all reported suicides—a rate typical of all Western countries (Lowy, 1980).

The number of alcoholics among older age groups is also large. About 10 percent of all people age 60 and older are heavy drinkers (Simon, 1980, p. 661). The habit may have been present in early adulthood or may have begun in middle or even old age. In cases of later onset, individuals are reacting to age-related stresses, often depression and physical illness. As these problems diminish so does their drinking (Simon, 1980, p. 662). Effects of alcoholism in later life include social isolation, malnutrition, falls, general physical deterioration, and dementia; many effects of alcoholism are sometimes mistaken for those of chronic illness and age, and attributed to senility.

Chronic brain syndrome and *functional psychosis* account about equally for over 93 percent of the mental disorders of old people in mental hospitals. Chronic brain syndromes of cerebral arteriosclerosis and senile brain disease are characterized by relatively permanent deficits in intellectual functioning; and symptoms are impairment of memory, knowledge, judgment, and confusion. However, there are many exceptions to this dismal picture. In a study of healthy, socially autonomous community residents, researchers found some surprising results. In general, "psychological flexibility, resourcefulness, and optimism characterized the group . . . rather than the stereotype of rigidity" (Butler, 1975c, p. 370). Maddox (1979) concludes that social integration and not social isolation for older persons is the rule. Older persons interact with kin, participate in politics, and live in separate households by choice.

Mental Health. Overall, the status of older persons' mental health is somewhat uncertain. However, a 1981 Harris poll indicated that most older persons are satisfied with their lives, and a third called these the best years of their lives (Fowles, 1983). At the other extreme 27 percent called this "the dreariest stage of my life," and 13 percent called loneliness a serious problem. About 4 percent, or twice the national average, reported emotional conditions that hampered their activities. As a result, suicide rates rise with age. In 1981 17.4 percent of all suicides were committed by persons ages 65 and older, who numbered 14.7 percent of the population.

Various factors are associated with older persons' feelings of well-being, health status being the strongest. Among women, next to their own health status, the strongest factors were the spouse's health, the quality of the marital relationship, and, in varying degree and complex ways, pet ownership (Ory & Goldberg, 1983). Among a community sampling, pet ownership was not predictive of greater happiness. Women who had pets, but with little attachment, were unhappier than those attached to their pets or without them; and women of higher socioeconomic status with pets were happier than lower-status women without them, the exact mechanism of such differences being unclear.

In other research Mussen, Honzik, and Eichorn (1982) reported that the satisfaction at age 70 of mothers who participated in the Berkeley Guidance Study was predictable from two characteristics measured at age 30: marital compatibility and satisfaction with the husband's job. In contrast, the father's traits at age 30 predictive of life satisfaction at age 70 were his health, stamina, energy level, an emotionally stable wife, job satisfaction, and marital compatibility.

A study of young, middle-aged, and older adults indicated more age similarities than differences in emotional experience (Malatesta & Kalnok, 1984). The older people did not feel that their emotions had changed over the years, and they inhibited their emotional expression less than did younger adults. Nor did they experience more negative emotion, or shame and embarrassment—indeed, the literature in general indicates no decrease with age in sense of well-being, when demographic factors are controlled. Perhaps older people are perceived as having more negative feelings because they express them more openly. Neither was age a factor in causes of emotion—for example, for all adults anxiety and sadness were most often caused by personal losses and physical problems, although the latter figured more prominently with age. For young and middle-aged adults anger related most to demands and responsibilities, for older ones to personal loss.

Certain sex differences were apparent— for example, at all ages, women found emotion more central to their lives, and more men than women agreed that their sex should conceal their feelings. However, in actuality, women inhibit and mask their emotions more than men do. Possibly 15 to 25 percent of older adults have significant symptoms of mental illness; and the incidence of psychosis, or serious disorder, rises sharply after age 75 (Fowles, 1983).

Characteristics of Successful Aging. A number of authorities have identified some characteristics that apparently relate to successful aging. DeCarlo (1974) found that successful aging correlated with physical and mental health, and intellectual performance. The active pursuit of leisure activities was critical to satisfactory adjustment, both in retirement and aging. Age and marital status were also significant. Among their subjects, Eisdorfer and Lawton (1973) discovered that the unmarried, most of them widows, were in by far the worst situation. The younger aged, those 65 to 70, were considerably better off than those 75 or older; and the distance between the two groups was widening.

Those subjects in the Longitudinal Study of Transitions (which involved mostly lower middle-class subjects) who had both strengths and weaknesses proved most adaptive. The more complex of the late middle aged "grow older gracefully and comfortably only if they have the kind of open options, alternatives, and choices, usually more readily available only in more privileged sectors of our society" (Fiske, 1980, p. 342). As such people reach late middle and old age, they often lack situations in which they can achieve self-fulfillment. In studies of transitions of adult life, from youth to later years, most differences between sexes within any one stage are greater than those between the young and old of each sex (Fiske, 1980, p. 343).

On the basis of his far-ranging experience with the elderly, Robert Butler (1975b) has concluded that there is no "secret of life." However, certain things may help. For instance, "having a partner is very crucial to survival" (p. 32). It is also important to have continuing tasks and goals, with certain things to do each day. Another factor is maintaining physical fitness, although it is unclear just how such activity relates to adjustment. Other aids to survival are resourcefulness, flexibility, and the capacity to continue learning. Heredity is important, too; however, people can do much to compensate for genetic weaknesses by taking good care of themselves.

On the basis of studying sixty-five older people in San Francisco, Hochschild (1973) identified six general themes that constitute a basis for successful aging: (1) sufficient independence to allow continued feelings of integrity; (2) pleasant, satisfying relationships with other people, some of whom are willing to provide assistance when needed, without in the process showing a disrespect for older persons; (3) a reasonable degree of emotional and physical satisfaction and a comfortable physical environment; (4) stimulation of the mind in ways that are not too strenuous; (5) sufficient mobility to be able to experience varied environments; and (6) some type of intense life interest or involvement, at least partly to avoid preoccupation with thoughts of death.

Another characteristic of people who age successfully is being able to endow their experience with meaning, through continuous evaluation. The sense that people make of their own lives depends on the interpretations that they bring to bear on their past acts and that give meaning to their life as a whole. Such conclusions may provide a certain generational connectedness and help to find meaning in one's life, so that life review produces a sense of satisfaction (Freeman, 1984). Meantime, the profound impact of significant others in one's early experience is underscored by elderly individuals' references to them while reminiscing. Hence, reminiscing should not be interpreted as clinging to the past but as reexperiencing vital activities of former years that help to preserve one's identity and self-esteem (Carlson, 1984).

Some aging persons avoid life review, since such rehearsal would force them to confront unresolved tasks. Some are discouraged in such review by others who will not listen to them. In the process, older persons sense a lack of support from significant persons around them (Freeman, 1984).

A Comprehensive Portrait

Some authorities have attempted more general characterizations of older people. On the basis of his comprehensive study of older people, Butler (1975c, p. 408) constructs the following image of aging:

Older people are as diverse as people in other periods of life, and their patterns of aging vary according to the range they show from health to sickness, from maturity to immaturity, activity to apathy, useful constructive participation to disinterest, from the prevailing stereotype of aging to rich forms of creativity.

Caroline Bird (1983) distinguishes between the old, in need of welfare services, and the ageless, who are exemplars of the good life. On the basis of interviews with many outstanding persons throughout the country, she concluded that the ageless share certain characteristics in common. They appear to "have outwitted Mother Nature. They are not slow, timid or disengaged. . . ." (p. 36). They do not mumble their words; they speak clearly and distinctly. They do not dwell on the past but look to the future. A 94-year-old and his wife were cross-pollenating orchids, not expected to bloom for another 5 years. The ageless have great curiosity and are as excited as children about trying out new things. They describe their lives in terms of continuous growth. A former woman college president defined her life as a "spiral," always returning to the same problems but resolved each time on a higher plane. Most of those interviewed thought of their lives as a journey, not in terms of arrival. They had not followed a specific life plan, but creatively reacted to chance situations and encounters. A woman editor saw her life as a voyage of discovery through stormy seas.

After finally giving up the long career climb the ageless feel free. They are free from self-interest and ready to work for the common welfare. They are free from concern about what others think. They feel free to be individuals and to develop still undeveloped parts of themselves. They may face something of an identity crisis but, having worked it out, have a surer sense of self. Finally, they do things they always wanted to do but did not have time to do.

THEORY AND RESEARCH ON THE ELDERLY

Theoretical Framework

Covey (1983) examines certain popular theories relative to older people. The subculture theory of aging suggests that older people as a category have many characteristics required of a subculture. They are

group-conscious, share common interests, and, to some degree, are excluded from participation in society, and are often responded to negatively by others. Nevertheless, this theory may be criticized on several points. Many older people do not identify themselves as such; older people are even more heterogeneous in their behavior than younger ones; and they are not discriminated against by society in all respects.

Closely related to subculture theory is minority theory, which portrays older people as sharing characteristics with other minority groups in that they are subject to discrimination on the basis of certain biological characteristics.

Implicit in disengagement theory is the notion that individuals who try to maintain all their earlier activities are aging unsuccessfully. The disengagement process is portrayed as a way of effecting an "orderly transmission of power from one generation to the next, which incidentally leads to increased efficiency of the total society. It is functional for society to disengage older people from their roles and statuses to make room for younger, more efficient people" (Covey, 1983, p. 96). Therefore, older people should not continue to perform social roles that ideally would be reserved for young people. However, research shows that individuals may disengage in some areas and not in others; and engagement, not disengagement, relates more closely to psychological well-being. Besides, age is not the critical, but rather an incidental, factor in determining disengagement.

Perhaps the most popular theory these days is activity theory which emphasizes that degree of disengagement is more a function of individuals and their background than any "inevitable process" (Covey, 1983, p. 98). Moreover, amount of activity remains relatively stable through old age and relates directly to degree of satisfaction.

There are criticisms of this theory, too, one being that the emphasis is on people maintaining their middle-age role, thus denying that old-age roles are valid and worthwhile. One might also counter by arguing that there is no need to differentiate middle age from later life roles because life is continuous and activities in one age flow into the next. Note, too, that decreasing activity is perceived as somehow undesirable—but one might ask why an individual should persist in maintaining the middle-age rat race?

The life-span approach portrays life as embracing alternative paths that individuals follow, punctuated by points of transition or markers, which produce stages. Particular roles and their corresponding behaviors are presumed to be sequential and involving a relatively smooth process. Life-span theory is not without its critics, one common disagreement being that within stages there are great variations, as well as between different groups within the same stage. The basic idea that all kinds of people are governed by the same underlying sequences and developmental periods is also questioned.

Another promising theory is that of continuity, which maintains that in the process of becoming adult, individuals develop differences, habits, and dispositions that become a fundamental part of the personality. Then, as people grow older they become disposed to maintaining continuity in preferences, associations, and so on. It does not presume that any lost roles should be replaced (Covey, 1983).

Inadequacies of Personality Research

With regard to aging research, it is still at the immature level. Much of the older literature regarding both personality and intelligence is shot through with methodological flaws. While significant improvements are being made, much research is still weak, or relatively thin, and cannot be replicated.

An especially common flaw in aging research is the employment of inadequate—or no—controls, partly because of the difficulty of obtaining them. In studying the effects of institutionalization, finding and obtaining the cooperation of a matched noninstitutionalized population is difficult. Just as serious a flaw is using research instruments and methods that were developed for dealing with nongerontological populations (Schonfield, 1980).

Another common deficiency of aging studies is the presentation of data without meaningful interpretation. Mortality tables provide no information about functional losses preceding the events leading to death; nor do averages reflect individual experience. Besides, death removes progressively more subjects from samples of the aging after the period in which an acutely declining function may occur. Reliable data can only be derived from longitudinal research that follows the aging processes of individuals.

If we return to our original question of who are the old, we can answer: all of us and none of us—all of us in the sense that we are older persons-in-the-becoming, and none of us in the sense that no overall categorization fits. The task is to find models among older people who are sufficiently flexible to reflect the major and minor categories of persons in an increasingly pluralistic society, yet who are not so fluid and fragmented that they have no functional value.

A related task is to uncover processes by which successfully aging individuals maximize their personal potential through longitudinal studies or the analysis of autobiographies. Such persons have been overlooked because researchers have often focused on the less able fraction of the elderly, those in nursing homes (Carlson, 1984). The reason is obvious—they are the most available, singly or in groups, for questioning. As a result we may be misled by the fact that many persons past 90 are hypotensive, or manifest lower than average tension. Yet one cannot conclude that merely through the aging process do people's reactions become less intense. On the other hand, most hypertensive individuals, whose blood pressure has increased along with their age, do not make it to age 90.

SUMMARY

The concept of age is confusing, and varies with one's frame of reference. While the chronological frame of reference is common, others—such as social, physiological, temporal, and cultural—are often full of implicit attitudes toward older persons. Aging itself is an almost meaningless concept, because people vary so much in any age grouping.

Older people undoubtedly do have to cope with exceptional problems of a different kind and degree from those encountered at other ages. They are assigned negative stereotypes, which are fortunately diminishing. Many experience progressively greater physical and mental declines and disorders as the years go on; and many undergo little physical or mental change until very old age. To what extent the degenerative or pathological conditions of aging might be prevented, mitigated, or reversed, given more favorable conditions and scientific breakthroughs, is uncertain.

A similarly confused picture exists regarding the personality characteristics of the elderly. Older people are often stereotyped as inherently unproductive, asexual, and cautious; however, such traits often reflect their changing circumstances. The more negative features of the stereotype are grossly exaggerated. Most older people have quite positive traits, such as mellowness and kindliness. Even their present status is far less gloomy than is frequently presumed. Granted a more favorable environment, their adjustment will be correspondingly improved.

SUGGESTED READINGS

BAUM, S. K. (1983–84). Age identification in the elderly: Some theoretical considerations. *International Journal of Aging and Human Development, 18*, 25–30.

BISHOP, J. M. & KRAUSE, D. R. (1984). Depictions of aging and old age on Saturday morning television. *Gerontologist, 24*(1), 91–94.

BODEN, D. & BIELBY, D. D. (1983). The past as resource: A conversational analysis of elderly talk. *Human Development, 26*(6), 308–319.

BLACKBURN, J. E. (1984). The influence of personality, curriculum, and memory correlates on formal reasoning in young adults and elderly persons. *Journal of Gerontology, 39*(2), 207–209.

BRANCO, K. J. & WILLIAMSON, J. B. (1982). *Stereotyping and the life cycle: Views of aging and the aged. In the Eye of the Beholder.* New York: Praeger.

BUTLER, R. N. (1983). Current data inconclusive about aged's health and work. *Aging and Work, 6*(3), 187–196.

CARLSON, C. M. (1984). Reminiscing: Toward achieving ego integrity in old age. *Social Casework: The Journal of Contemporary Social Work, 65*(2), 81–89.

COVEY, H. C. (1983). Some theoretical considerations, Part II. *Educational Gerontology, 9*, 95–109.

DOWD, J. J. (1984). Beneficence and the Aged. *Journal of Gerontology, 39*(1), 102–108.

ERIKSON, E. H. (1982). *The life cycle completed.* New York: W.W. Norton & Company.

FENGLER, A. P. (1984). Life satisfaction of subpopulations of elderly. *Research on Aging, 6*(2), 189–212.

FOWLES, D. (1983, May–June). The changing older population. *Aging,* pp. 6–11.

HAZAN, H. (1983). Discontinuity and identity: A case study of social reintegration among the aged. *Research on Aging, 5*(4), 473–489.

HIEMSTRA, R., GOODMAN, M., MIDDLEMISS, M. A., & VOSCO, R. (1983). How older persons are portrayed in television advertising: Implications for educators. *Educational Gerontology, 9*, 111–122.

LAWTON, M. P., KLEBAN, M. H., & deCARLO, E. (1984). Psychological well-being in the aged. *Research on Aging, 6*(1), 67–97.

MALATESTA, C. Z. & KALNOK, M. (1984). Emotional experience in younger and older adults. *Journal of Gerontology, 39*(3), 301–308.

McGEE, J. & WELLS, K. (1982) Gender typing and androgyny in later life: New directions for theory and research. *Human Development, 25*, 116–139.

NESSELROADE, J. R., MITTENESS, L. S., & THOMPSON, L. K. (1984). Older adulthood: Short-term changes in anxiety, fatigue, and other psychological states. *Research on Aging, 6*(1), 3–23.

OKUN, M. A., STOCK, W. A., HARING, M. J. & WITTER, R. A. (1984). The social activity/subjective well-being relation. *Research on Aging, 6*(1), 45–65.

ORY, M. G. & GOLDBERG, E. L. (1983). Pet possession and well-being in elderly women. *Research on Aging, 5*(3), 389–409.

ROTHSTEIN, M. (1983). *Review of biological research in aging* (vol. 1). New York: Alan R. Liss, Inc.

SCHEIDT, R. J. (1984). A taxonomy of well-being for small-town elderly: A case for rural diversity. *Gerontologist, 24*(1), 84–90.

SWENSON, C. H. (1983). A respectable old age. *American Psychologist, 38*(3), 327–334.

WOODRUFF, D. S. (1983). A review of aging and cognitive processes. *Research on Aging, 5*(2), 139–153.

CHAPTER TWELVE

Life Styles in Later Years

TYPES OF HOUSEHOLDS

The Married

Satisfaction with marriage usually becomes greater during later years. Skolnick (1981) concluded that marriages change over time, more often in a positive direction, and life circumstances importantly influence marital satisfaction. In data obtained from 1,056 married members of three-generation families, no differences were disclosed by sex or by first versus second marriages; nevertheless, marital satisfaction did vary by generation (Gilford & Bengston 1979).

The youngest generation demonstrated the greatest frequency of both positive and negative feelings. Although they found much of their interaction fulfilling, the period was characterized by instability and extremes of behavior and feeling. The middle generation couples had not only the fewest good times but also most bad times together. They were possibly too involved with parenting the younger generation and taking care of the older generation, besides earning a living, to place a high priority on the marital companionship—or they might have come to take it for granted.

The grandparent generation reported a medium level of positive interaction and the fewest negative feelings as they approached old age. Younger ones among them had begun to look at their lives in terms of time left to live. They argued less and enjoyed the stability and freedom of their postparental lives. Older couples were happy to be together, in contrast to the alternatives of dependency and widowhood. In these somewhat companionate marriages, negative sentiment was reduced to its lowest level while positive interaction remained moderate. The lack of sex differences in reports of satisfaction indicated that they evaluated their relationships similarly (Gilford & Bengtson, 1979).

Among older couples, the performance of tasks around the house typically remains sex-related, though less so than formerly. A study of retired couples disclosed that husbands increased their participation in household activities after retirement, whereas wives reduced theirs somewhat (Keith & Brubaker, 1979). Men might wipe the dishes or help clear the table, and some of them helped do the laundry, the grocery shopping, or even cooking—at least occasionally. Yet they were far more likely to become involved in the more stereotypically masculine household activities such as home repairs, yard work, or disposing of the trash and garbage.

Living Alone

Reasons for Being Alone. Each major grouping of older persons has its characteristic problems, tasks, and life styles. One such category, those who live alone, totals about 81 percent of all persons over 65. Over the past two decades, the number of single-person households of persons aged 75 and over has doubled that of those aged 65 to 74 and tripled that of those aged 60 to 64. In 1950, 10.3 percent of men and 18.1 percent of women in all age groups lived alone; in 1975 the figures increased to 15.4 and 39.4 (Bengtson & Treas, 1980).

There are certain main reasons that so many older people live alone. One is that women live longer than men; the other is that most older people want to remain in their own homes even when it means financial deprivation. Also the current trend toward self-actualization, which involves more concern with oneself than in the past, contrasts with the more old-fashioned ideal of helping others.

Housing. Often younger people fail to comprehend older singles' feelings about housing. They may doubt older persons' ability to maintain their own households, but most older people are quite capable of it until their late years. Besides, most older people see their friends or relatives often. A third of all older Americans live within 10 minutes of a child, and only 23 percent over 30 minutes' distance (Bengtson & Treas, 1980). Often housing that seems less than appealing to the observer may be the older single's choice. Some move into age-segregated communities such as trailer camps because they find their age mates satisfying company. Others—self-reliant loners who place a higher value on their autonomy—may prefer single-room occupancy hotels (SRO's) (Gerber, 1980). They have no desire for public housing, or much broader social involvement, although there is a considerable amount of social interaction and mutual aid among themselves.

A large majority (7 in 10) of heads of household 65 years or older own their own homes, 85 percent of them with no mortgage (Fowles, 1983). Nevertheless, they devote a larger fraction of their own income than younger persons to housing expenses, a fourth compared to just 9 percent of younger persons who own their homes outright. This difference derives from older persons' smaller incomes and older houses, although just 12 percent have serious deficiencies.

Several factors may operate to affect older persons' place of residence (Fillenbaum & Wallman, 1984). If economically feasible, they prefer to live alone; however, financial stress may compel them to move in with offspring. Or they may be more willing to live with their children if their own income allows them to help. Another factor is self-care capacity; if functionally impaired, they may find it necessary to forfeit independent living. However, if both wife and husband are impaired, they may retain their own separate residence longer because they compensate for each others' infirmities. Also, persons with close-at-hand families are more likely to be helped to live at home or invited to live with them. Certainly, the childless and unmarried are disproportionately represented in nursing homes.

To facilitate their adjustment, the National Policy center on Housing and Living Arrangements for Older Americans makes certain suggestions. The manufactured housing industry should be given the same legal and financial status as builders of conventional houses, which would allow production of appropriate, low-cost units. The government should provide subsidies for rehabilitating homes of the elderly, and local communities should change zoning laws that discriminate against shared housing. Such housing allows two or more older persons to live together, sharing expenses, sometimes with those better off physically but poorer financially making part of their payment in services (News notes, 1984).

Loneliness. Older people living alone are viewed as lonely and are thus subject to the unhealthy by-products that this status entails. Stress from loneliness harms an individual in certain major ways: first, long-term emotional stress changes the neurochemical processes in the body. The immune system may break down and heighten susceptibility to disease (Warning: Living alone, 1980). Second, loneliness may lead to self-destructive behaviors such as excess drinking, smoking, or reckless driving. In addition, observes psychiatrist James Lynch, people who live alone have an unusually high death rate. Simply giving lonely patients antidepressants complicates their problem and increases their sense of loneliness. What they are greatly in need of is the human touch. Even people who are in deep comas have improved heart rates when their hands are held. (Petting even has an effect on the cardiovascular systems of dogs.) Bachelors under age 65 have twice the death rate from

cancer and heart disease as married men (Lonely die young, 1978, p. 61).

Such figures, as always, should be kept in perspective. As we have seen, many older singles who maintain separate households have supportive people close by. Some of them, especially the never-marrieds, are used to being alone and prefer it. Nor is there any hard evidence that older people are more lonely than younger ones. Besides, people can be lonely when living with others if little compatibility exists.

The Older Never-Marrieds. About 8 percent of the over-65 population, the never-marrieds, often live alone and are generally better adjusted than widows of that age. For one thing, never-marrieds do not experience the disruption of having a spouse die. People who have typically been isolated report less loneliness than those only recently isolated. Older never-married singles are no lonelier than the married, while the widowed are twice as lonely.

Significant data regarding the adjustment of older singles comes from a study (Gubrium, 1975) of twenty-two such persons in Detroit. When asked how they thought of themselves in terms of age, they avoided locating themselves in any particular period of life; they indicated that life was pretty much what it always had been. Some of their answers are included here.

In general these single people denied ever being lonely.

I need 8 days in the week. I'm so busy now. I'm not unhappy.

I don't think of it at all. I'm pretty good. I have never compared it. In our Scottish way, we don't like to analyze ourselves. I don't give it much thought.

Never lonely! You can put that down twice! I've been the same right through. At 45 I was still the same. I'm satisfied. I was always satisfied and I'm still satisfied! I didn't change at all (Gubrium, 1975, p. 33).

In general, they believed their future would simply be an extension of the past. They did not worry about it, which suggests that they thought things would not change very much. They looked on death as simply one more event in a chain of ongoing experiences.

Older singles looked upon their status as just another way of life. They did not perceive themselves as deviant or abnormal. Their lives were just as acceptable to them, as they imagined having a spouse was to married persons:

Half the married people have children to keep—even when they are old. I have nobody to keep but me. I have no complaints.

A married man—he is going through the same maneuvers everyday. A single man can meet many people. He has a free hand. He can go and come as he pleases.

Clearly these people value their independence. They do not have the burden of dependents, especially children, although some of them said that they had never married because they had been responsible for ailing parents. With regard to social relationships, they had often associated more with friends than with relatives, when they were younger. They visit with others occasionally; however, compared to older married persons they engaged in more solitary activities, and said that they are satisfied with them.

I do knitting and watch TV. Visit with my neighbors. I watch TV in the morning and in the evening.

Sometimes I knit; sometimes I play solitaire. In the morning I straighten out my clothes. After lunch, I sometimes read or take a nap. Evenings I watch TV and read the paper.

The Widowed. By far the largest category of older persons living alone is the widowed. By age 65, 3 in 5 women no longer have their spouses; and by age 75 the number is 4 out of 5; and about 1 in 3 men over age 75 is a widower (Bengtson & Traes, 1980, p. 418). Their large numbers derive from the differential longevity of the sexes—a woman's life expectancy is 7 years greater than a man's—and the practice of women marrying men older than themselves.

The prelude to becoming widowed, as well as the adjustment period that follows, is especially difficult for all concerned. Often one spouse tends the other through a terminal illness, sometimes for years (Bowling & Cartwright, 1982). Despite stresses and strains, this task is discharged willingly, although about 1 in 5 must eventually obtain additional help. Most often daughters play this supportive role, and the widowed may move in with the daughter after the spouse's death. Some of the children involved are themselves over age 60, and concerned with their own problems of aging. However, those experiencing greatest strain are somewhat younger, with full-time jobs and children to tend, a situation which often causes serious role conflict.

Both widows and widowers share certain stresses, and both rate themselves lower in life satisfaction than married people. The original, and immediate, problem is to cope with grief after losing their mates. The bereaved "may mummify themselves in the past, retreating into a way of life, still absorbed in the lost relationship. Or they may plunge busily into a new life, whose hollowness betrays its failure to retrieve a real sense of purpose: the crisis is driven out of mind, but not resolved" (Marris, 1978–79, p. 132). Nor does time solve their problems. As the years roll on, their close friends die off one by one; and after their spouse dies, the problem is doubled. However despite such problems, many of the widowed make a relatively good adjustment.

Widowed women have their own distinctive problems. One is money, for most did not work outside the home until after their children were grown, and then only in low-paying jobs.

For several reasons a widow's sense of well-being seems to derive more from intimate peers than from family members (Bankoff, 1983). Immediately after her loss, her children may fail to give her sufficient support because they are too involved in their own grief. Besides, they have their own lives and special concerns. Sometimes, her children may attempt to help out by assuming a protective role, thus reversing the parent-child relationship. In contrast to this dependent role, friends who share her new life style are equals, with common interests. What she needs is a renewed sense of self and a revised but healthy sense of identity. Later, in the transition stage from the married to single role, as she picks up the pieces and sets about reorganizing her life; family relationships may interfere with making new friends or developing a new life style.

Indeed, what helps her most is forming ties with networks more supportive of her new needs as a single person. Since friendships are based on common interests and life styles, her erstwhile married friends are no longer compatible and contribute little to her sense of well-being.

At least two programs have proved of some value to the widowed. In the Widow-to-Widow program, women who have adjusted to their own situations help those who are recently bereaved to work out a new life style and destiny in a positive fashion (Silverman, 1972.) Another approach, Group Therapy for Widows, involves relatively homogeneous groups in terms of age and socioeconomic level, and has also been quite successful. Group members learn to give up old identities and establish new ones. However, not all the participants achieve these results. Some find the experience depressing or of no special value. Others complain that they want the group to serve a social rather than a therapeutic purpose. On the whole, however, group discussion can be effective for those who are able and willing to relate to other members (Hiltz, 1975).

Problems of Being Widowed. The statements below are typical of views expressed by widowed women when asked: "Do you experience special problems?"

FEMALE, AGE 74: Many, many, many! When you have had a good husband it is terrible to try to live without him. Loneliness, decisions, lack of escorts, lack of companionship, small tasks he used to do, and many others.

FEMALE, AGE 73: When one lives near a large city, there's the fear of being alone at night. It limits attendance at symphony, opera, theatre, and so on.

Living Alone in the Very Late Years. As time goes on, problems for all those who live alone become accentuated. Some give up and move to retirement or nursing homes; others hang on as long as they can. Some older persons are maintained for years in their own homes by their friends and neighbors (Butler, 1975a).

Mr. Billings is 92 years old and totally blind, yet he lives alone in his own home in Minneapolis. He prepares some of his meals and takes care of the house himself. Since he is familiar with the house and with household routines, he manages very well—with the considerable assistance of relatives and neighbors.

This man's stubborn determination and courage are not unusual. A great many people prefer the risk of falls and broken bones to being placed in nursing homes. In terms of the financial costs to society and the morale of the persons concerned, community homecare services are the best solution for old people who live alone.

The Divorced

Divorce in later years is infrequent, but becoming more common. Older divorced men find partners for remarriage much more easily than do older divorced women, and more so as times goes on. In early adulthood, the probability of a single woman's remarrying is 3 in 5; by age 65 it is 1 in 32 (Cleveland, 1979). Older single women must also confront society's attitude that older men become interesting and distinguished, but older women simply become old.

Women who remain single have several alternatives regarding sex experience. They can deny their sexual outlets altogether and simply validate their female roles as mothers or grandmothers. They can masturbate, fantasize, and otherwise engage in autoerotic sex activities. They can maintain social relationships with younger men, or they can have affairs with them. Finally, they can develop lesbian relationships, an alternative that may become more acceptable as a result of the women's movement and the gay movement (Cleveland, 1979).

Divorce has a considerable effect on grandparenthood, partly because relations with grandchildren are mediated by the parents (Matthews & Sprey, 1984). After their child's divorce, the grandparent relationship usually changes somewhat, especially if the former in-law child is awarded custody of the grandchildren. The relationship is most vulnerable for paternal grandparents, since mothers are usually awarded custody. It should be added that grandparent visitation rights are currently being sought in certain state courts.

Relations with Others. Simons (1983–84) observes that older people's interpersonal relations serve three main psychological needs: for security, intimacy, and self-esteem. Normally, adult children and spouse become the primary source for security, the spouse for intimacy, and participation in organizations for self-esteem. However, when one such source is missing another may compensate or substitute reasonably well in satisfying the same need. In the absence of a spouse or adult children siblings or friends may provide security; and when a spouse is

lacking a close friend may provide intimacy. When participation in groups and organizations is missing, confidants or adult children may provide self-esteem. However, adds Simons, participation in groups and organizations may enhance feelings of loneliness among the unmarried. This writer would add that this result is a function of the type of group involved. Singles find loneliness significantly diminished by association with groups involving mostly unmarried persons, especially of their own sex; whereas groups of mostly married people plan activities that enhance the spousal relationship, and in effect, discriminate against singles.

Living with Others in Primary Relationships

Those older persons who live with others fall into two main categories—those who live with a spouse, children, or a friend; and those living in some kind of group such as a nursing home or commune. Older women, especially, may live with a close friend, sharing expenses, household tasks, and companionship. Others live with a spouse and often enjoy a richer, fuller life than they did in middle age because they are free of the responsibilities of work and childrearing. Those with a reasonable income may travel, often in motor homes.

Living with One's Children. Fewer older people than ever before live with their children, partly because society no longer demands that younger adults share quarters with their parents. In certain societies today, and in our own in the past, younger family members provided for older ones as a matter of course. However, today the cost of such care has grown, and greater numbers of people are living a longer time.

Traditionally, women were the "mainstay of family support systems" for the elderly (Bengtson & Treas, 1980). They would run errands for widowed mothers, provide custodial care, and take them into their households. However, women's entry into the work world occupies their time and energy, and too little is left to take care of elderly parents. Another factor that diminishes family feelings of responsibility for day-to-day care of older relatives is the growing movement for midlife options. Increasing numbers of the middle aged are launching second careers, returning to college, vacationing abroad, or in general upgrading the quality of their own lives.

Nevertheless, families still provide an important support system, both potential and real. They may help older members during illness, provide financial assistance, and sometimes give them a place to live. They also importantly reinforce the older person's self-concept by providing identification with the family.

Support patterns within the kinship group take various forms, including gifts, advice, financial assistance, emotional support, or joint living arrangements. Surprisingly, the proportion of older parents who help their children is greater than those who receive help from them (Kivett, 1976). Older parents have low expectations in terms of receiving assistance, especially money, from their children.

A study of persons ages 60 and over indicated that the majority had access to family, friends, and neighbors, as well as both instrumental (helper) and expressive (emotional) support (Ward, Sherman & LaGory, 1984). Whether they appeared to have sufficient social support was much less important than whether they felt they had enough. Low network involvement may not produce poor morale, especially in persons who are less gregarious. Nor does having children, in itself, produce feelings of well-being—the quality of the relationship is important. Older persons' reactions may be ambivalent because they dislike feeling dependent or being perceived that way. On the other hand, for older persons who doubt their abilities to cope, instrumental support is essential.

The Grandparent Role. The great majority of older people, including both those who do and do not live with their children, become grandparents. A full 70 percent of people over 65 now have living grandchildren (Atchley, 1972; American family, 1980). Fully 9 out of 10 older people have weekly contacts with their children's families. This fact takes on increasing importance as life roles—for example, that of worker—disappear or diminish. In addition, since many mothers work, grandparents often take care of the children. Meantime, since their relationships with grandchildren require fewer responsibilities than did those with their own children, grandparents can afford to be more objective and relaxed. Hence, the relationship is often quite satisfying, both to grandparents and grandchildren.

Not all grandparents feel the same about their role, as a study by Neugarten and Weinstein (1964) proved. They interviewed grandmothers, most of them in their early 50s to middle 60s, and grandfathers a few years older. While the majority were satisfied with being grandparents, about a third of the grandmothers and almost as many grandfathers had reservations about it. Some of them felt too young to be comfortable in the grandparent role, because it suggests being old. The remainder who rejected the role simply had little interest in their grandchildren or were too involved in their own concerns. Among those who enjoyed the role, a third said it provided a kind of biological renewal ("I feel young again") or biological continuity ("I see my life going on into the future through these children"). About 30 percent said that being grandparents had little influence on their lives one way or the other.

A study of middle-class, white, suburban grandmothers showed that they shared the

same stereotype of the ideal grandmother—
"a traditional woman who is old, domestic,
and nurturing" (Johnson, 1983, p. 564).
However, this conception was quite different from their own self-images. They were
more inclined to pattern their behavior after
a "young, playful image, who is intermit-
tently helpful, but not obliged to be so" (p.
565). The older ones in the group were less
active with their grandchildren, probably because the latter were older. Few of the women
found acceptable role models of grandmothers within their own families; hence,
they had "to invent" roles more appropriate
to the times. This conception usually resulted in a warm relationship with children,
grandchildren, and sometimes children-in-
law. The fact that few were moralistic about
their children's permissive life styles undoubtedly contributed to the harmonious
relationship.

Nursing Homes

Often there comes a time when people
cannot take care of themselves and in some
instances have no one to take care of them.
Hence they must go to nursing homes. Persons are entering nursing homes in increasing numbers. They are coming in later, are
often sicker, and their length of stay is shorter.
On average, they enter at about 82 years and
die at about 86 (Hyatt, 1979). The chance
of institutionalization for older persons at
any time in the United States is 5 in 100;
and the risk of ever being institutionalized
for sustained periods after age 65 is about
25 in a 100 (Maddox, 1979). The 4 or 5
percent of older people in nursing homes
who do not have families may be widowed,
immigrants, or have no children or kin (Hall,
1980). The majority in nursing homes are
women, simply because they live longer. Many
have not always been poor, but inflation has
eroded their funds over the years.

The number of persons in nursing homes

rises sharply with age. About 5 percent of
those age 65 and older are in nursing homes;
and these include 1 percent of those ages 65
to 74, 7 percent of those ages 75 to 84, and
22 percent of those age 85 and older. Overall
the health status of about one-seventh of all
those over age 65 requires their being institutionalized or confined to bed (Fowles, 1983).
Eighty-five percent of them die in the nursing home after an average stay of just 1.1
years. A third die within the first year, and
another third live up to 3 years.

While most people refer to all residential
community facilities for the elderly as "nursing homes," commercial nursing homes differ from homes for the aging. Commercial
homes operate for profit, while homes for
the aging, sponsored by various fraternal,
religious, or trust organizations, are nonprofit and voluntary, and are sometimes operated by federal, state, or municipal governments. The commercial homes receive
more federal monies than the nonprofit ones,
and they house about 80 percent of the institutionalized elderly. The care in most institutions of both types is very expensive, although Medicaid has helped considerably.

Deficiencies. It has been widely publicized that many nursing homes are severely
deficient. They often have few or no nurses,
and hardly qualify as homes. Robert Butler
(1975c) visited many, frequently disguising
himself as a family member. Sometimes he
saw "patients lying in their own urine and
feces. Food is frequently left untouched on
plates" (p. 263). In many cases drug pre-
scriptions were wrongly administered, fundamental hygiene standards were neglected,
and in order to keep down food costs, many
homes often served meals that could have
caused malnutrition.

In contrast to the noninstitutionalized elderly, those in nursing homes spend almost
all their time within the same general setting
(Brent, Brent & Mauksch, 1984). The non-

institutionalized, especially in smaller towns, may use porches, street corners, and shopping malls, to socialize—perhaps talking with friends or playing games. Nursing home residents, on the other hand, must satisfy all their needs, both private and social, within a relatively confined environment; yet little effort has been made systematically to relate the planning of such homes to an analysis of the residents' varied needs.

Few of the homes have social or therapeutic progams, and few are reimbursed by Medicare or Medicaid for putting such programs into effect (Gottesman, Quarterman & Cohn, 1973). The employees are often grossly overworked, and just as grossly inefficient and untrained. The patients themselves are often treated in a highly authoritarian manner. Such care is no bargain at any price, and certainly not at the current high costs.

The worst abuses are at the commercial homes. Sometimes patients may be arbitrarily shifted from one facility to another, with little regard for the consequences. Those individuals who experience involuntary relocation, and who are financially dependent, indicate considerable life dissatisfaction (Smith & Brand, 1975). Often they are cut off from their only close friends and experience feelings of isolation. Any move, including going to a nursing home in the first place, is less traumatic when the older person makes a voluntary decision to do so.

Most old people fare better if they can somehow manage to remain in the community. In a study of three groups of the elderly—one group a year after institutionalization, another 1 to 3 years after institutionalization, and a third a community sampling—the community sampling proved superior in mental health and cognitive functions and had experienced fewer difficulties with illness, economics, and social interaction. After just 3 weeks of institutionalization, residents indicated some decline in capacity for self-care, and an increase in body

preoccupation. After a year, 49 percent of the institutionalized subjects showed extreme deterioration, including death, compared to 18 percent of the community sampling. Nevertheless, it is uncertain to what extent the community and nursing home groups were completely comparable (Tobin & Lieberman, 1976).

Individual Reports. Answers to the following questions by several elderly persons—almost all of them women—who currently live in nursing homes afford a glimpse of what it is like to reside in such places.

Why did you come to the nursing home?
FEMALE, AGE 77:   I had a partial paralyzing stroke, and was unable to take care of myself.
FEMALE, AGE 68:   I work daily, Monday to Friday, in arts and crafts, mostly on hook rugs. I also go to all the activities here, like Bingo, movies, sing-a-long, and to group activities. Also to holiday parties, picnics, boat rides, and field trips, and I watch TV. Last but not least, I have bull sessions with two of the residents.
FEMALE, AGE 86:   Because I walk very little (with a walker), I am very slow getting around. I wash my one room daily and take entire care of my finances. I even order drugs from the Retired Person's Pharmacy. I spend some time each morning waiting for help—to bring my dress (I keep underwear where I can reach it, to save time). I cannot wear elastic hose, so apply my own elastic bandage to my "good" leg. I have a severe foot and back ailment, so am unable to help out or play Bingo. There's too little time to read or write much—I love both.
What do you like most about living in a nursing home?
FEMALE, AGE 86:   I was sent by the doctor. I lived alone and had a broken thigh bone. The same hip was broken 13 years before.

I had no family left, no near relatives in town. Also I knew of this home's good reputation. I was unable to care for myself.

What did you give up of special importance by coming to the home?

FEMALE, AGE 74: Home life, going on trips, going to church and stores, and visiting with relatives and friends.

MALE, AGE 75: Getting out. To church, friends' homes. Eating out with friends. I had to give up driving several months before, and was too lame to walk alone. I had enjoyed using my car and took many trips with friends who had no car. I always had a friend who could help drive. I advise callers to keep going. I say, you'll enjoy memories of trips and travels.

How do you spend your time, other than eating or sleeping?

FEMALE, AGE 68: Making friends and keeping busy in doing crafts.

FEMALE, AGE 68: Feeling I'm cared for, not being responsible for the care of a large house. I'm in a two-bedroom suite, and have made some fine new friends. I found I could write "jingles" and have written one each year. I also wrote a "Night before Christmas" for the home's *Gazette*. Institution food is not "like home."

What do you like least about living in a nursing home?

FEMALE, AGE 74: Missing my own home, and not being able to go out for rides, church, and lunches.

FEMALE, AGE 68: Having to give up my own home—and my own pace of living.

FEMALE, AGE 86: Constant (though unavoidable) change of employees—three shifts per day—and losing one or more who have come to seem like friends. In my case, it means a lot that an aide can help dress my feet with various pads and bandages. The ones who do it most comfortably and quickly have had lots of experience.

What things worry you the most? What are your chief anxieties? Also, what do you rely on most to keep your morale up?

FEMALE, AGE 74: Worrying about a small house I still own. And wishing I was still there. My prayers and faith in God.

FEMALE, AGE 68: Not hearing from seven of my nine children. I rely on the activities program here to keep up my morale!

Retirement Parks, Communities, and Communes

At least until they become incapacitated, growing numbers of old persons are choosing to live in communities, apartment houses, or other places either restricted to, or catering especially to older persons. Also communes for older persons are being developed—for example, one in Winter Park, Florida, consists of twelve older people, all over 70. Other older persons enjoy living in mobile home parks that involve a life style and culture all of their own (Deck, 1972).

One technique is networking—for example, in a housing development each resident may become responsible for making contact each week with at least two others (Freeman, 1984).

To what extent should older people in group-care facilities be helped, and at what point does such care produce a hospital atmosphere and result in overdependence? In one study, elderly people in a retirement hotel and an apartment tower were provided little in the way of special services, but did not appear to miss them. At two other sites, a life-care home and a retirement village, the residents were provided with many services that nevertheless did not seem to create dependency. Such services permitted the residents to be more independent by helping them maintain themselves at "optimal levels" (Sherman, 1975).

Elderly migration is a long-standing phenomenon—many retirees move to other areas (Biggar, Cowper & Yeatts, 1984). For some decades retired persons, especially the more well-to-do, have moved to the Sunbelt to live. Some moves are "quasi-migrations"—that is, only for the winter months; others are permanent. Contributing to the increase in out-of-state moves have been earlier retirement and pension payments, including Social Security.

Selecting Appropriate Facilities

As at any age, the choice of a place to live in later years is a highly individual matter, depending upon life styles and personalities. The old saying, one person's meat is another's poison, is certainly applicable in such situations. The important thing is that such facilities be expanded, upgraded, and constantly evaluated by government agencies, to prevent profiteering off the age group that can least afford it. Advisory services should also exist to disseminate information and effect a favorable match between persons and facilities.

The following young-old discuss where they would prefer to live in their later years.

MALE, AGE 64:   In order of preference: my own home, with a family member, in a nursing home.

FEMALE, AGE 65:   I want to remain in my own home as long as possible. I'd rather take chances on broken bones and stay there until I am helpless. Then I will go to a nursing home. I do not want to live with, and be a burden on, my children.

MALE, AGE 53:   I want to stay in my own home; and I expect to leave enough money to employ a housekeeper, or nurse, or someone to take care of me there.

FEMALE, AGE 63:   Several of my friends (whom I have known for years) and I plan to form a small retirement commune and hire a nurse to live there to take care of any immediate medical needs.

Some elderly people live in retirement communities, especially in California, Flor-

ida, and Arizona. In one development—Sunset City, Arizona, 12 miles north of Phoenix, the largest all-retirement community in the country—there is a large hospital, a shopping center, recreation centers, and golf courses as well as seven swimming pools, both indoor and outdoor, air-conditioned shuffle-board courts, ceramic and art facilities, and machine and wood shops.

Some of these communities are restricted to people over 50, although the rules vary considerably from place to place. Residents of these areas have more friends than the elderly in a general community, although they have fewer contacts with members of their families. While they may lack the stimulation of regular association with children and younger people, they apparently feel greater satisfaction in places that cater to older people. Many older people find it difficult to adapt to younger people's life styles and children's noisy behavior.

One housing innovation is the elder cottage, the American version of the Australian granny flat (Guion, 1984). This relocatable garden cottage is designed for use by older persons who want to live close to their relatives. Certainly such housing, especially designed for older persons, could fill a real need. It is estimated that at least 1 in 5 older persons live in inappropriate housing, which may be too large or expensive to maintain. The cottages would relieve the problem of attempting to shelter aging parents in their children's homes, and they would allow many individuals, who must have some assistance, to avoid being institutionalized. It is estimated that as many as a third of residents in nursing homes do not belong there. Unfortunately, lack of space in residential areas and zoning regulations often preclude taking advantage of this housing alternative.

Contrary to what one might expect, older persons who live in planned housing rely mostly on supportive networks outside these facilities. While proximity does foster some relationships it counts less than family bonds and other long-term relationships. Residents with sensory impairments and chronic health problems are more likely to be isolated than others from other housing residents; however, when they experience some condition requiring hospitalization they receive more support from other residents than those impaired but not hospitalized (Stephens & Bernstein, 1984).

THE OLDER WORKER

Arguments for Early Retirement

Various arguments have been advanced in favor of early retirement: (1) Industry may be spared older, less productive employees who would be difficult to retrain in newer techniques. (2) Early retirement is especially beneficial for those in unusually boring, arduous or hazardous occupations. (3) Early retirement allows individuals to indulge in various forms of leisure that they lacked time for before. (4) Retirement of older workers affords opportunities for younger ones to enter the work force or to advance more easily through the ranks (Litras, 1979).

Arguments for later retirement may be equally cogent. (1) Inflation has cut into retirement persons' real income to the point that they cannot feel secure economically. (2) Since increasing numbers of people are living to an advanced old age, their early retirement places an unusual burden on the Social Security system. (3) Many older persons are returning to work because they find retirement boring or they need extra money. They are also encouraged by recent laws that make it easier for them to obtain jobs. Nevertheless, many of them have great difficulty finding work.

Whether early retirement is wise depends on the individual. A study of persons over age 55, by the American Association of Retired Persons, indicated that half of those who had retired had done so by choice. Most of them were glad they had retired, but 36 percent would rather be working. Among those still working, 62 percent were glad they were and only 21 percent said they would retire if they could afford it (Stevens, 1979).

Many older people continue their high level work performance into advanced years. In 1984, Nobel scientist Barbara McClintock, 82, still worked in a Long Island laboratory; Johnny Kelley, 76, had run in 53 Boston marathons; and dancer-choreographer Martha Graham, 90, was still teaching dance and took her dance company to perform in Europe. Graham's formula for living is: "I am excited about life, and I don't look back" (Dynamic Elderly, 1984, p. 48).

Social Security itself was initiated partly to move people out of the workforce and make room for younger workers but failed to take into account certain factors (Butler, 1983). Older workers have a special value, and work might contribute to older persons' continued mental and physical health. In developing such policies both psychosocial and biomedical factors should be taken into consideration.

Older People at Work

Since older workers have a harder time than younger ones obtaining work, they are sometimes exploited. Often people who pass the usual retirement age, including professors, will work for less pay than they did before. Fiske (1980) asks whether we may need laws against exploiting older people such as now exist against child labor.

Many people oppose employment of older persons, because they presumably take jobs away from younger ones. The fact is that some older persons need the work as much as younger people do. Also, they do not always compete for the same jobs, the service and retail sectors being exceptions. Overall, older like younger, workers vary greatly, and should be treated as individuals.

Although older, like younger, workers vary greatly, the research suggests few reasons for employers' reservations about hiring older workers (Coverly & Newquist, 1984). True,

Margaret Hester

Typically, older workers perform as well as, or even better than, young ones.

the costs of some employee benefits increase with age; however, such costs relate more to length of employment than to age. As for productivity, ratings do not decline with age. Indeed, in most job situations older employees perform as well or better than younger ones. Nor do older workers lose more time from work—an average of 4.2 days compared with 4.1 for workers ages 17 to 24 and 5.7 for those ages 45 through 64. Persons over age 45 have 52 percent fewer cases of acute illness a year than do younger persons; and, though they have more chronic conditions, these do not always impair functioning. Older workers are even safer than younger ones, accounting for 10 percent of all accidents, although they constitute 14 percent of the work force.

In terms of psychological factors older workers also rate as well as younger ones. They, like all workers, have their special work preferences. Many are quite interested in remaining at work, but often confront barriers. However, they may be offered only low-paying jobs with few, if any, fringe benefits. Few part-time jobs provide high pay or status.

RETIREMENT

The Pluses and Minuses

The issue of retiring from work has come to affect increasing numbers of people. Years ago, a far higher percentage of the population were self-employed, and continued to work almost all their lives. The average life span was shorter, so fewer people reached retirement age. Today increasing numbers are retiring at an earlier age than in the past.

Causes of Stress. Retirement can produce stress for various reasons. Retirees' loss of a dominant social role, that of worker, means loss of status in a work-oriented society (Hochschild, 1973). Retirees must also cope with other aspects of retirement: the end of a work career, decreased income, increased awareness of the aging process, greater potential for declining health, much more free time, changed interpersonal relations, and society's image of the retiree (Thurnher, 1974).

All of these factors can cause distress. Men's sexual interest may decline if they have difficulty adjusting to their new role—or non-role. They are especially anxious if their wives are still working, for they are not psychologically prepared for the role reversal in such cases (Troll, 1971). Those who cannot create a satisfactory postretirement life style, suffer from the so-called "retirement syndrome," which includes gastrointestinal problems, irritability, and nervousness.

Yet the responses to and the problems of retirement are highly variable. In Atchley's study (1975), fewer than a third of retired persons had difficulty adjusting. Forty percent reported problems in adapting to a reduced income, which was by far the most common problem. About a quarter of the adjustment difficulties concerned missing work, and 38 percent such factors as the death of a spouse or declining health, both of which relate to retirement adjustment in that they affect the overall situation.

Two major conflicting theories are employed to assess the consequences of retirement—crisis theory suggests that retirement has negative effects because of the centrality of occupational identity, at least in men (Palmore, Fillenbaum & George, 1984). In contrast, continuity theory proposes that such an identity is not the more central one for most people, and that retirement allows the continuity of other roles. Retirement also permits the development of new leisure roles, which encourage status and self-esteem.

Longitudinal data help determine to what degree retirement does, or does not, impact on important areas of life. About a half to three-fourths of the difference between incomes of retired and working men can be charged to retirement. Some persons' health deteriorates after retirement; others' improves. There are few effects on activities except a small incresae in solitary entertainment, time with friends, and nonemployment work. Nor is there evidence that retirement makes people depressed or dissatisfied. Early retirement, however, does have greater effects than at the usual ages.

Early-retired men report less income, a reduced living standard, and less happiness. Overall, the effects of retirement are not great, in terms of basic attitudes or life satisfaction.

Compensations. Retirement can, and often does, yield a variety of satisfactions. It provides freedom from restricting routines, and time for pursuing special interests. The mental and physical health of persons whose occupations were unusually strenuous, boring, or time consuming, often improves. For retired persons in general, health improvement is more common than decline (Eisdorfer, 1972).

In the following retired people discuss their feelings:

MALE, AGE 72:   I have neither been happier nor the reverse [since retirement]. I miss my students but they continue to contact me, and sometimes my colleagues invite me to lecture on favorite subjects. I don't run out of things to do.

MALE, AGE 65:   If I could change my life style I would hope to find a totally satisfying employment that I could follow my whole life.

MALE, AGE 69:   My feelings are mixed. I have felt the loss of prestige and feelings of worth. I feel relief from responsibility and criticism. I have many warm friends, old and new.

FEMALE, AGE 68:   Since retiring I am very happy because I continue to do part-time work for a wonderful family during the summer. I'm active and have some time for travel.

FEMALE, AGE 74:   I've been happier because I can do things I want to do and do not feel pushed.

MALE, AGE 65:   So far retirement has been the least rewarding period of my life. I have no competition and very limited satisfaction.

The Situation. Especially important is the total overview of retirees' lives. The elderly who live in retirement communities have a higher morale than those who live in age-integrated communities (Seguin, 1973). Other factors that promise good adjustment include a rich, fulfilling family life, good health, and satisfying avocations. In sum, retirement adjustment relates to how particular types of individuals operate in complex environments.

Advance Planning. Also of significance are certain preretirement factors, including advance adjustment and planning. Those who feel good about themselves and the world continue to cope well throughout their lives. Those who disintegrate at critical times such as retirement or death of a spouse, are those who have been falling apart all along (Troll, 1975).

Bromberg (1981), former senior center director and consultant, offers the following suggestions to persons anticipating retirement: (1) Decide what kind of life you want after retirement, keeping in mind that you must plan for 20 or more years. (2) Carefully budget for retirement, including an inflation factor of at least 12 percent. Expenses are lower in rural areas or the south. (3) Check out the place where you plan to retire, including the weather and quality of medical care. Subscribe in advance to a paper; and become familiar with the local property, tax, and inheritance laws. If you anticipate living in a retirement village investigate the sponsor's "track record," and talk to people who live there. Do not sell your home or cut home ties until you feel secure in your new surroundings. (4) Check your federal taxes and benefits, including Social Security regulations. About 300,000 Americans have retired abroad, mostly in Europe; and Social Security checks will be sent to most countries except those in the Communist bloc. Medicare payments, however, are limited to the United States and its dependencies. (5) Also check your company's retirement benefits—many persons have found their pensions invalidated by unnoticed provisions. (6) Become acquainted with helpful sources of information. Larger libraries, as well as government agencies, have mounds of material. The Small Business Administration and Government Printing Office can supply information about second careers and hobbies. (7) Become involved in community affairs, perhaps helping to promote legislation for older persons, or serving as a volunteer in community agencies or schools. (8) Explore your pre-retirement options. Does your company allow gradual, partial, or perhaps trial retirement or leaves of absence? (9) Do not simply assume that you know the answers. A national survey indicated that only 10 percent of retirees had properly prepared for the years ahead.

Retirement Activities

Typical Patterns. The retired individual has many possibilities for recreation including reading, gardening, watching television, attending sports events, visiting friends and relatives, taking walks, pursuing creative interests, or taking special courses. It is not easy to evaluate the way elderly people spend their leisure time. Some may consider lonely an old man who spends much time sitting in a park; however, he may have been a satisfied loner all along.

Life style derives from all such activities and is determined by the way they are patterned. In general, such preferences are stable and become more sedentary with the years. In one study, the elderly were found to spend less time in certain leisure activities as they grew older, and about the same time in others. In general, they spent less time listening, drinking, dancing, attending movies, traveling, hunting, reading, and in physical exercise. However, from their middle to older years they showed stable patterns in entertaining friends, watching television, cultural consumption (for example, listening to music) and cultural production (such as painting and playing music). Participation in clubs and organizations peaks during the years 40 to 54, discussions of important issues by age 65, and observing spectator sports, either in public places or on television, by age 40 (Rosenzweig, 1972).

While the elderly engage in about the same range of activities as younger people, rarely do these two age groups participate in them together. Ordinarily there is a rather firm segregation in leisure activity—either because of generational preferences or fear of embarrassment, which causes older people to avoid situations where they might perform poorly (Miller, 1965).

In later years, most people have more unstructured time on their hands than their past experiences or interests have prepared them to use properly. Suzanne Haynes of the National Heart, Lung, and Blood Institute observes that most retired people go through a "honeymoon phase" when they do many things that they had long wanted to do, but then they run out of resources and begin to feel dissatisfied. Retirees begin to feel a sense of loss—"loss of job, loss of identity, which they attach to their work, loss

of peers who died, and loss of their own good health" (Stevens, 1979, p. 1). As a result, some individuals may participate only minimally, which is hardly experiencing true leisure, for leisure is not merely time free from job demands. Some individuals may react by participating in work-related activities, some in pure relaxation, and others prefer merely to rest.

A study of older persons' religious practices disclosed a decline in formal participation, and increasing homogeneity over the years in matters of religious involvement (Ainlay & Smith, 1984). Because of declining health and mobility, older people attend church less with advancing years, but read the Bible and watch televised religious programs more. Meantime, they grow more alike in their religious interest and participation, perhaps because of their common and increasing awareness of physical decline and ultimate demise.

Hendricks and Hendricks (1977) raise the question whether leisure assumes a different meaning when it is not related to the work cycle. For about 40 years, work, whether rewarding or not, structures the average per-

Retired individuals have many possibilities for recreation.

Margaret Hester

son's life style. During that period, leisure activities may become a sort of "anticipatory socialization"—a preparation for the future use of leisure time (p. 249).

Even in later years, a work orientation may persist, but increasing numbers of older people are finding equally significant values in other areas of life (Hendricks & Hendricks, 1976). In future years older people will have had many years of exposure to mass media and commercial entertainment, and their leisure activities will undoubtedly reflect this earlier experience. Moreover, improvements in health care will enable them to participate more actively and satisfyingly in recreational activities, although passive leisure pursuits may be just as satisfying.

Although most research shows a positive relationship between activity and sense of well-being, much depends on such factors as health, presence of a spouse, or the nature of the activity (Fengler, 1984). When resources hitherto provided diminish, remaining activities assume added significance. In a meal site program in New England, persons experiencing the greatest deficits in resources derived most benefit from becoming volunteers, employees, or participants. The most consistent source of satisfaction for the more disadvantaged elderly was participation in the Retired Senior Volunteer Program, which involves assisting with a broad variety of activities.

Some older persons lead exciting, ever-changing lives, but the majority retrench a bit. The number of solitary, passive activities increases despite more opportunities for physical activities and time to pursue them (Gordon & Gaitz, 1977). To some extent this slowing down may represent almost an unconscious adaptation to diminishing internal resources. Some retirees find that simply getting up in the morning, getting dressed, eating, shopping, resting a bit, playing cards or visiting, and going to bed, exhausts their physical resources. Even unusually healthy people may choose to slow down simply because it is a good way to live. For years they

may have lived at a breakneck pace governed by inflexible routines. Now they can pause in their walks to enjoy the birds and flowers, or simply sit in a rocking chair on the porch, reflecting deeply on ideas they only considered superficially before.

Older people also become more honest with themselves. After retirement, in a less competitive environment, they have little need to hide the unfavorable aspects of their personalities. They can glorify the victories of their past and be treated quite indulgently. They share confidences with each other, including complaints about their infirmities and confessions of deviancy. They form pseudo-friendships and intimacies without serious commitments that might have been damaging in earlier years. Later on, the very old and infirm have difficulty being intimate because other people do not choose to be intimate with them (Bensman, 1979).

Also characteristic of later years, especially the late-late ones, is modification in activity required by physical impairment. Disabled individuals are less able to participate in household activities such as money handling and shopping; and most have left the work force. At any one point in time, half of Americans age 65 and over have some major health incapacity, although fewer than 5 percent are institutionalized (Bengtson & Treas, 1980).

The small minority who live with their children may have more cause for unhappiness than satisfaction. When the burden of tending an aging parent falls on a family with teen- or college-aged children, it imposes some difficult choices. "Will money be used for grandma or for the children's college? Will a couple take a postretirement trip abroad or remain at home to look after the aging parent? The result is a no-win situation . . . either way, you feel guilty" (Bennett, 1979, p. 40). Guilt also arises if an older person is placed in a nursing home.

The result is personality conflict, great changes in life style, and loss of privacy. In one case a grandmother who watches TV in the living room prevents the 16-year-old daughter from playing the piano. The parents are never alone except after they go to bed. The teen-agers find that there is "an extra listener to their private conversations" (p. 40). The greatest problem often lies in personality differences. Younger members may also be called on for a great many small tasks: to bring the older person pills or to turn up the TV sound volume. Or grandparents may have to share the family bathroom.

The family life style must be planned around the aging parent. Even when government-paid attendants provide some assistance, there is the problem of being unable to leave overnight or for weekends. Often these very persons who sacrifice years looking after an aging parent themselves can anticipate having no one to look after them in their later years (Bishop, 1979). Older people have a certain security living among people they love, but they often feel that they are an unwanted burden—and this is often the case. In addition, most of their resources—money, space, and life routines—are largely controlled by their children. For older people with no blood kin, neighbors and friends may constitute pseudo-families (Shanas, 1980).

Kinship Support Patterns. Neugarten speaks of the extended kinship pattern, not a horizontal one but a vertical one, as in four-generation families. Up and down this "generational tree there is a service exchange including giving advice, child care, help during times of illness, housekeeping, and money; and more aid flows down than up." In such families the middle aged have two older generations with whom to be concerned. They may have to worry about both parents and aging grandparents (Hall, 1980).

In some cases kinsfolk are missing or live too far away to provide assistance. Although some support can be provided from a distance, such services as transportation, meal preparation, and home maintenance can be performed only by those close at hand—a for a significant minority such assistance is lacking. Data obtained from the obituary section of a paper indicated that 24.7 percent of the deceased, ages 65 and older, had no surviving children or siblings living near enough to have provided regular direct assistance (Hays, 1984).

Individual Differences. All individuals face the crises of old age from their own perceptions; the retirement experience that rejuvenates one ages another (Marris, 1978–79). Indeed, personality is a more important determinant of physical activity than age. Among 184 retired men with a median age of 65 years, involvement in physical activity was associated with such characteristics as greater orientation toward helping professions, altruistic interests, and greater extroversion, but not with age. Involvement in cultural events related to a theoretical orientation and extroversion.

Personality factors are also important in retirement. Far-sighted and flexible persons often enjoy the challenge posed by their new role, and are practically certain to make a good adjustment (Bynum, 1972). The internally controlled, who believe that personal rewards depend on their own behaviors and attitudes differ sharply from the externally oriented, who feel that rewards are controlled by forces outside themselves (Cox, Bhak & Kline, 1978).

People also differ in the way they organize their time, and how much organization means to them. Some of the elderly find it hard to structure their time. By contrast, younger and middle-aged persons' time is usually structured for them. Some older people become disturbed at finding the days slipping away aimlessly. Others enjoy unstructured time and spend it in casual activities.

Among women over age 60 in Los Angeles, reports psychologist Beckman, the quality and amount of time and activity spent with neighbors, friends, and relatives other than children, added more to their feelings

. did contacts with their
ᴨ, 1982).

ds, which becomes increas-
ᴨ later years, hinges on var-
ᴣr early adulthood men tend
ᴜ their associates while women
gain tᴜᴜ ᴣcher & Oliker, 1983). For one
thing, men's friends die earlier; and women,
being more often widowed, may seek friends
to compensate for the missing husband. On
the other, such women begin making more
friendships, perhaps because of the dispo-
sitional factor, even before their difference
in longevity becomes a factor. Note that unmarried women and men have networks equal
in size despite the advantages that men have
for making friends in terms of career status,
greater income and fewer home duties.

Hour-long interviews with a sampling of
noninstitutionalized persons, ages 60 and
older, were employed to determine the most
salient parameters of friendship (Usui, 1984).
Friendship networks of blacks proved less
homogeneous than those of whites in terms
of race, sex, and marital status—that is, blacks
were more likely than whites to include persons of different race, sex, and marital status. For both races, homogeneity was low
except on race and sex—friends were almost
always of the same race and sex. Fewer than
half the friends were of the same marital
status or within 10 years of the respondent's
age; and only a minority of friends named
had attained the same educational level.
Closeness of the relationship did relate positively to the age level and sex homogeneity
of the network.

Life Styles

Social Class Differences. Adaptation to
retirement varies considerably by social class.
Many upper-middle-class men (Vaillant,
1977; Sears, 1977) come to value interpersonal relationships as much as their work.
They wish to balance their lives better and
to nurture as well as be nurtured. Many lower-
middle-class men become bored and re-

signed a decade or two before they retire,
after realizing they have risen as far in their
jobs as they ever will. The question arises:
"Does too little stress in itself become, so to
say, stressful?" Such individuals' primary
stimulation in late middle and old age comes
from the mass media, and vicarious mastery
becomes their substitute for real living (Fisk,
1980). Meantime, they enjoy being pam-
pered by their wives; and the women often
feel good about "becoming the strong shoul-
der on which their mellowing spouses could
now allow themselves to lean" (Fiske, 1980,
p. 351). Freed from their burdens of childrearing and jobs, some of these women seek
to expand their horizons, reflecting the
changing norms for women (p. 353).

Sex Differences

It has been commonly presumed that performance of household tasks is far more acceptable to older retired men than to young
men. Young men are thought to perceive
such work as a threat to their masculinity
and a frustration to concentration on their
careers. Besides, given his superior status as
a male, he may feel entitled to be served. In
contrast, older people are more often viewed
as somewhat unisexual, or androgynous,
which makes older men more adaptable and
willing to do housework.

Interviews with older, married men employed full-term, part-time, or retired,
showed the retired men to be more involved
in such activities, and with generally enhanced feelings of well-being (Keith, Powers
& Goudy, 1981). Retired men, whose wives
still worked, performed more masculine and
feminine tasks, without negative effects, although participation in masculine household tasks produced greater satisfaction. Nor
did men in two-job older households feel
upset by helping with housework. By this
time couples have presumably worked out
their respective role responsibilities.

The retired husband's role in housework
is becoming increasingly important as greater

numbers of wives work, and as husbands are usually older than they are. Besides, growing numbers of remarriages in later life, usually involving an older husband, will create even more families with working wives and retired husbands.

To the extent that men become more androgynous in later years, and fewer sex-typed behaviors are expected of them, the change to performing more feminine tasks in the home becomes easier (Keith & Brubaker, 1979). Strongly sex-typed individuals will have more difficulty making the adjustment than more flexible individuals.

Typical Life Styles. In a study of men and women in California (Maas & Kuypers, 1974), forty-seven retired middle-class fathers' life styles were seen as falling into four groups: family-centered (19), hobbyist (11), remotely sociable (9), and physically unwell-disengaged (8). The family-centered fathers' life styles focused on marriage, parenting, and grand-parenting; the hobbyist fathers' on leisure activities and special interests. The remotely sociable fathers were concerned with interpersonal associations and large social issues; the unwell-disengaged fathers were in poor health and perceived themselves as withdrawn from the world. Collectively, most of the fathers seemed pleased with their work or retirement situation, the critical factor being that they had the freedom to choose whether to work full-time, part time, or not at all.

Among the middle-class women interviewed in this study, six life-style groups were found: husband-centered (23), uncentered (21), visiting mothers (16), work-centered (12), disabled-disengaged (12), and group-centered (11). The largest group, the husband-centered wives, did most things together with their spouses; the uncentered mothers had few recreational interests and no involvement with work. The visiting mothers enjoyed frequent social interaction and close, meaningful relationships. The work-centered mothers worked either part time or

full time. The disabled-disengaged mothers were dissatisfied with everything, especially their health. The group-centered mothers spent much time at clubs or other formal, structured groups such as their church.

This study provides significant insight into aging, at least for the type of population involved. According to popular stereotypes, aging brings progressive decrements in psychological functioning and a more closed mode of life. Most of these parents were still healthy, both physically and psychologically. The few who had unfortunate personality dispositions, had had them as young adults. The diversity of life styles involved seemed limited only by the number of people studied. A more broad-based study would have suggested a still wider range of life alternatives. Even within these life-style patterns, individuals demonstrated unique methods of interaction, satisfaction, and involvement and expressed highly varied preferences for where they wanted to live.

The most remarkable finding of the study was the similarity in life style and personality in young adulthood and old age. Nor did old age necessarily bring new psychological problems. Instead, problems that had existed already were at worst exacerbated. For old age to be understood, it must be viewed as an integral part of the total life cycle, rather than as a period set apart from the rest of life. Societal planning must be done within the context of adulthood as a whole.

SUMMARY

Older people have diverse, more or less satisfactory life styles. While some undesirable features of their way of living may derive from physiological changes, others reflect society's failure to adapt properly to older people's needs. Still, some life styles are highly rewarding and largely the creations of individuals themselves.

Common types of household arrangements in later years include living with one's spouse, living alone, or living with others, either unrelated or kin. Among those living alone, the never-marrieds adapt better than the widowed. Others live in nursing homes, in retirement parks, or in communities and communes; each of these places has its own characteristic life style, advantages, and disadvantages.

Retirement is especially critical in its effect on morale—for better or worse. Problems relating to this event include deciding when to retire, how to modify one's life style after retirement, where to live and with whom—whether alone or with relatives, in one's own home, or in a commune. Kinship and friendship support systems are especially important, as well as the older individual's attitudes and coping skills. Life styles in retirement vary according to social class, financial status, age, and personality. There is tremendous overall diversity, reflecting a tendency to continue lifestyles initiated in earlier years.

A persistent theme in the literature on aging is that activities developed early in life can be maintained throughout life, but only within supportive and unthreatening environments. Ideally, every individual should develop and maintain resources, interests, and activities that give satisfaction in later years. After the age of 70, health problems may increasingly interfere with all but sedentary leisure activities, but even these may be creative and personally satisfying.

SUGGESTED READINGS

A retirement planning guide. (1984). The National Association of Mature People. Oklahoma City, OK.

BIGGAR, J. C., COWPER, D. C. & YEATTS, D. E. (1984). National elderly migration patterns and selectivity. *Research on Aging, 6*(2), 163–188.

BRENT, R. S., BRENT, E. E., & MAUKSCH, R. K. (1984). Common behavior patterns of residents in public areas of nursing homes. *Gerontologist, 24*(2), 186–192.

DICKINSON, P. A. (1981, March-April, May-June). Practical answers to personal questions about retirement planning. *Aging,* 4–11.

FORMAN, B. L. (1984). Reconsidering retirement. Understanding emerging trends. *The Futurist, 18*(3), 43–47.

HARDY, M. A. (1984). Effects of education on retirement among white male wage-and-salary workers. *Sociology of Education, 57,* 84–98.

JOHNSON, C. L. (1983). A cultural analysis of the grandmother. *Research on aging, 5*(4), 547–567.

KEITH, P. M., POWERS, E. A., & GOUDY, W. J. (1981). Older men in employed and retired families wellbeing and involvement in household activities. *Alternative Lifestyles, 4*(2), 228–241.

KOURI, M. K. (1984). From retirement to re-engagement. *The Futurist, 18*(3), 35–42.

KRAUSE, D. R. (1982). *Home bittersweet home: Old age institutions in America.* Springfield, IL: Charles C. Thomas.

LAWTON, M. P., MOSS, M., & MOLES, E. (1984). The suprapersonal neighborhood context of older people: Age heterogeneity and well-being. *Environment and Behavior, 16*(1), 89–109.

LEE, G. R. & ELLITHORPE, E. (1982). Intergenerational exchange and subjective well-being among the elderly. *Journal of Marriage and the Family, 44*(1), 217–224.

PALMORE, E. B., FILLENBAUM, G. G., & GEORGE, L. K. (1984). Consequences of retirement. *Journal of Gerontology, 39*(1), 109–116.

PAMPEL, F. C., LEVIN, I. P., LOUVIERE, J. J., MEYER, R. J., & RUSHTON, G. (1984). Retirement migration decision-making. The integration of geographic, social, and economic preferences. *Research on Aging, 6*(2), 139–162.

QUINN, W. H. (1983). Personal and family adjustment in later life. *Journal of Marriage and the Family, 45*(1), 57–73.

SIMONS, R. L. (1983–84). Specificity and substitution in the social networks of the elderly. *International Journal of Aging and Human Development, 18*(2), 121–139.

STREIB, G. F., FOLTS, W. E., & LaGRECA, A. J. (1984). Entry into retirement communities. Process and related problems. *Research on Aging, 6*(2), 257–270.

USUI, W. M. (1984). Homogeneity of friendship networks of elderly blacks and whites. *Journal of Gerontology, 39*(3), 350–356.

WARD, R. A., SHERMAN, S. R., & LCGORY, M. (1984). Subjective network assessments and subjective well-being. *Journal of Gerontology, 39*(1), 93–101.

CHAPTER THIRTEEN

Problems of Later Years

OLD AGE IN AN AGE-GRADED SOCIETY

Later Years in the United States

In terms of developmental stage theory, old age is distinctive in several ways. Unlike other age stages, it has a clear-cut and identifiable beginning, age 65, at least as far as working life is concerned; at this age many people retire and begin to collect Social Security (Hareven, 1976). From this time on, older people's social value declines sharply. Butler comments upon the popularity of the phrase, "the graying of America." Unfortunately, he says, "when we speak of graying we create an image of a doddering, unproductive, stagnant society. That's very unfair and inaccurate. We may simply have a maturer population with a very different age distribution" (p. 27). This older society may be superior in many ways—for example, it deemphasizes youth culture and possesses a greater sense of growth and maturity. He suggests that "we'll see more novels with an older protagonist, different kinds of music; and perhaps . . . new sports, and . . . changes in consumer interests" (p. 27).

Butler feels that society should be challenged to deal with this change, and he laments the popularity of products designed to disguise aging skin, gray hair, and wrinkles in efforts to pretend that aging does not exist (Hyatt, 1979). As Butler (1975c) aptly states it: "In America childhood is romanticized, youth is idolized, middle age does the work, wields the power and pays the bills, and old age, its days empty of purpose, gets little or nothing for what it has already done" (p. xii). Nor can people at this stage look forward to things to come; for this stage is the only one from which there is no exit except death.

Ageism

The problems associated with later years are not so much inherent in aging itself as the result of *ageism,* the process of systematically stereotyping and discriminating against people simply because they are old. Older people are often viewed as inflexible in thought and manner, senile, and old-fashioned in their skills and morality. Of course, ageism is not confined to the elderly. Some young people may not trust anyone over 30, and some over 30 may not trust those younger than they (Butler, 1977b). Nevertheless, the term is most often used to describe negative attitudes toward the elderly.

Expressions of ageism in this sense cover a broad range of phenomena, including myths and stereotypes, "outright disdain and dislike, or simply subtle avoidance of contact; discriminatory practices in housing, employment, and services of all kinds; epithets, cartoons, and jokes" (Butler, 1975a, p. 12). Another instance of ageism is the unfortunate attitude of many health practitioners. In general such persons give lower priority to the elderly than to younger groups.

Another form of ageism is the we-versus-they syndrome. (Butler, 1983). Although all of us will grow old—if we live long enough—we tend to think of the elderly as "they," when from the long-term perspective, the elderly are all of us.

Stereotypes of the elderly take root when we are very young. In one study (Hickey, Hickey & Kalish, 1968, p. 224), over 200 third-graders were asked to write about an old person. The most common characteristic ascribed such a person was "kind," but oddly enough, the second most common rating was "mean." Here are some more of their observations:

My sister and I like to walk down to the corner with old Mr. Smith, but we have to walk slower when we are with him.

They always ask you to talk louder.
Old people usually die, or lose a leg or an arm.
Old people are mean, and they don't let you walk on their lawn.
Old people are funny.

In general, the elderly are stereotyped as being different, a minority group—not just in numbers but disadvantages—but this image may be changing (Lawton, 1983). In 1967 the income status of the elderly began to turn around, and given the same trend, should approach 73 to 90 percent of younger adults' incomes. The education differential is changing, too; by 1994 about 80 percent of older men and 83 percent of older women will be as well-educated as the middle-aged. In addition, the health gap is narrowing, and declines in mobility and activity are less conspicuous. Meanwhile, the elderly are organizing and gaining greater political clout. In short, concludes Lawton, "we are moving in the direction of an age-irrelevant society where socioeconomic status is concerned, and the elderly are losing some of their minority group status" (p. 8).

Unfortunate Effects. The effects of ageism are often subtle, but always damaging. Like all prejudice, it affects persons' views of themselves. They tend to adopt the very stereotypes that serve them so poorly; in so doing they reinforce them. Meantime younger people often avoid old people, who remind them that their day, too, will come. Ageism becomes a defense mechanism that makes it easier to ignore the plight of older people. By ignoring them we can, at least for a time, avoid reminders of the reality of our own future aging and death.

PROBLEMS WITH INTERPERSONAL RELATIONSHIPS

Conflict Between Generations

Certain of the elderly's interpersonal problems reflect generational friction. This conflict derives from several factors, one of which is in the increasing burden older people impose on younger ones. This dramatically growing minority will place still heavier burdens on societal and support systems in the future. Meantime, medical advances will increase the number of the chronically ill by decreasing the incidence of mortality from acute illnesses (Eisenberg, 1977).

The middle aged will find this burden hard to bear. It is their own parents who are the aged, and for whom they feel a deeply personal responsibility. They must also care for the young, both individually and collectively. Often such responsibilities "trap them in their careers or life styles until the children grow up or their parents die" (Butler, 1975c, p. 15). Hence, the middle aged may become somewhat ambivalent toward both the young and old, because both groups serve as reminders of their own fading youth. Moreover, the responsibilities of the middle aged will increase in the future as their parents and grandparents live longer. Nevertheless, a middle-aged offspring's reluctance to take on the major responsibility for a failing parent may not indicate "hardheartedness" as much as a "strong reality orientation." The situation may simply be too difficult for the son or daughter to cope with. At the same time, the older person who becomes dependent on the generosity of "a former subordinate" cannot easily adapt to "a self-image constructed out of active mastery over a lifetime, which could explain why older men are often more reluctant than women to seek help from children" (Hess & Waring, 1978, p. 251).

In such a situation conflicts often arise for all sorts of trivial and not-so-trivial reasons. Sometimes disharmony arises between middle-aged children and elderly parents, as when the parents insist on living alone after it has become physically hazardous for them to do so: or when parents use up property that otherwise might be left to their children. Hostility may be subtle or overt, and sometimes even take the form of physical abuse (Cohen, 1980). To the degree that government takes over the special needs of the elderly, tension between the middle-aged and older generations may decrease (Kreps, 1977). The middle-aged are thus freed from difficult choices between their children and their parents' needs, while the elderly are relieved from being put in the role of "petitioners" for assistance from those whom they once controlled (Hess & Waring, 1976).

The baby boomers, those now in their 40s, face a dual problem, one in middle age, another in later years (Butler, 1983). In later middle age they will be supporting more older parents, perhaps grandparents; and after they retire, they must be supported by a smaller generation. This situation will exacerbate, as numbers of the old-old increase. Now the old-old constitute a third of *all* the old, but they will number 40 percent in just one more decade. The answer, advises Butler, must be through insuring maintenance of incomes and improving support systems.

To bridge the generations various techniques are being employed so that young people may tap "the vast reservoir of life and wisdom found in older people" (Tice, 1982, p. 80). The Foster Grandparent Program currently pairs about 18,000 foster grandparents with about 54,300 children throughout the country. In a Teaching-Learning Communities program, older volunteers help in school programs, sharing their own special skills and knowledge. They help children in creative writing, filmmaking, cooking, gardening, or whatever. Meanwhile, workshops are being held on ways to link the generations.

Marriage Problems

One of the most difficult problems of the widowed in later years is finding another mate. Some older people do marry, occasionally for the first time, and undoubtedly more would, given the opportunity. The older that singles of either sex become, the less their chances of marriage or remarriage; and the chances grow progressively slimmer each year. A woman between 65 and 69 is twice as likely to marry as one between the ages of 70 and 74. A woman's chances to have a relationship with an older man diminish because of differential mortality rates. At age 65 there are 4 women for every 3 men; at at age 85 women outnumber men 2 to 1.

Also, as individuals get older they have less control over their social relationships, including the ability to maintain contact with friends. Their adult children may indiscriminately move them from here to there for practical reasons. They may be relocated in new neighborhoods because of urban renewal; or they may be uprooted from their own homes because they are no longer able to take care of themselves. It is difficult to make friends in their new environment, partly because they have less mobility. In addition, new neighbors and friends rarely provide the same feelings of security as old ones (Kalish, 1975).

The sexual double standard is especially apparent, for older men are six times more likely to marry than older women. Society portrays women as sexually unattractive at an earlier age than men, and accepts the marriage of younger women to older men. In addition, there are three single women for every single man over 65. In the case of the widowed of either sex, heirs, children, and even the memory of the departed spouse may interfere with remarriage.

Old people in the South and West remarry twice as often as those in the Northeastern and North Central states. In those parts of the country, retirement communities facilitate finding a mate, especially for those who are relatively healthy and well-to-do. Those who do marry are quite romantic; they favor religious ceremonies and June weddings.

Candidates for remarriage also include older divorced persons. In 1980 a mere 3 percent of individuals in their 30s had been divorced, although that figure is rising, but a much larger number will have had more than one divorce by old age (Glick, 1984). The chances of eventual redivorce of today's young adults are about one in five. When it occurs, grief and anxiety stem not simply from the loss of a particular person, but from what that individual meant in one's own life style. In case of divorce one may have a great sense of failure or even guilt, as well as loss; and it is more difficult for elderly persons, especially women, to find a new mate at this age. Still, more people over age 65 are becoming divorced each year, which can bring concomitant loss of possessions and familiar surroundings (Streever & Wodarski, 1984).

Sexual Relationships Married couples, as well as those who live together without being married, may be confused or misled by recent counseling. They have been urged to try for "a second honeymoon" marriage and to continue to have a sex life. However, the new norms may be as unhealthy as the old ones, if they encourage older couples to believe that they can maintain youthful sexual patterns throughout life—a physiological impossibility (Cleveland, 1976, p. 236). The most realistic and healthy goal is "to gain intimacy, joy, and fulfillment through a broad spectrum of sensual sexual interactions" (p. 236). This ideal is constructed on the basis of the physiological fact that people continue to be capable of sexual response, but it also acknowledges that physiological changes do occur.

Certainly people retain sex intimacy needs throughout their lives; however, older people have greater problems achieving it. Either sex may lose a spouse, and women, especially, have trouble finding a remarriage partner. For every 150 women over age 65 there are just 100 men, and for those over 80, for every 250 there are just 100 men. One answer, suggests Butler (Today's senior citizens, 1984) is to expand the concept of human intimacy beyond the physical act of sex. Needs for closeness and tenderness, including caressing and touching, can be met through close friends.

Social Relationships

With support from adult children weakening, friends in later years assume correspondingly greater importance. Interviews with working-class grandparents in the Madison, Wisconsin area, whose average age was about 65, indicated that interaction with friends contributes more positively to older persons' morale than interaction with kin (Wood & Robertson, 1978). Parents may perceive their children's relationships with them as somewhat obligatory; the generations have different interests; and the younger adults have no special need for their older parents.

Especially after widowhood and retirement, older people seek out relationships with their contemporaries. Only their contemporaries can share their interests and experiences and hence sustain their own feelings of self-esteem and usefulness. At older ages, when peers are unavailable, sibling relationships may become important because again they are of similar age. Indeed, sibling relationships take on friendship aspects in later life. Older people naturally feel more comfortable with those their own age; they correctly feel somewhat unwanted in groups of younger people. They also get along better with persons who have shared the same

period of early socialization and who have lived through the same historical times. They "share recollections of the same ball players, movie actors, automobiles, and politicians; they remember dancing the same dances, using the same slang, fighting in the same wars, wearing the same clothing styles" (Kalish, 1975, p. 87).

Isolation. Loneliness may be another problem for the elderly. It is estimated that within a several-week period, over a quarter of all American adults feel very lonely (Rubin, 1979). While loneliness is a psychological state, it helps produce physical ailments and may even lead to suicide. People who are often lonely report feelings of being "self-enclosed, hopeless, and abandoned . . . (Rubin, 1979, p. 86). Robert Weiss believes that everyone has a need for attachment or intimate relationship, as with a spouse or lover—and a sense of community, most adequately fulfilled by a network of friends who have similar concerns. Either of these needs, if not met, may result in loneliness; and the only cure is to replace what is miss-

Contacts with friends help dispel loneliness.

Elaine Buhl

ing. Aging people may feel cut off from their social and material environment because their senses are failing. They also sense that they have been put up on a shelf just because they are old. Becoming unable to drive is especially damaging, since almost any satisfying life style involves much going and coming. Cohen (1980) concludes that for the elderly isolation without some social support is an important problem.

Although research is consistent in disclosing the therapeutic value of congenial companionship, all except the 5 percent of older persons in institutions live in the community, increasing numbers of them alone. Just over the past two decades, two and a half times as large a fraction of them were living alone, having increased from 17 percent in 1960 to 26 percent in 1982. The largest increases among those living alone were among women and the very old (Fowles, 1983).

An especially acute misfortune for the elderly, and one that occurs with some frequency, is loss of intimate friends (Matthews, 1983). Some older people are very independent, going out mainly with groups; others have only one, or a few, intimate friends. The consequences when they lose such friends may be devastating, especially for those who lack close family ties. Yet this loss is hardly recognized—consider how the old are sometimes uprooted from one environment to another, in the process perhaps leaving friends who are the closest persons to them in the world.

A special form of isolation is that resultant from being removed from familiar objects and surroundings which, in a sense, are part of the extended self. When older persons, unable to take total care of themselves are relocated, they experience losses of familiar surroundings and possessions, such as furniture or momentos, as well as independent income. Sometimes they must sell treasured possessions just to survive (Freeman, 1984).

The timing of such relocation is also important. Often it occurs immediately after the death of some significant other, perhaps a spouse, or loss of some physical function. Yet significant others, at this time, often focus on the move itself, ignoring all the ways such a move impacts on the individual involved. When older persons are relocated others often make all the decisions without any real input from the older person involved. At least they should be allowed to choose from among viable alternatives.

Some individuals find pet ownership to be a satisfying antidote to loneliness; others may react indifferently, even negatively, to pets. Certainly, when people become unwilling participants in a pet program, as when grandparents become reluctantly involved in their grandchildren's pet care, outcomes will hardly be positive. The critical factor appears to be individual reaction to pets—for some poeple, by no means all, "a pet can be an extremely salient aspect of life" (Lawton, Moss & Moles, 1984).

One reason it is important to understand the significance of pets in some older persons' lives, is to be aware of the traumatic effect of a pet's loss (Curtis, 1982). At such times, support systems should be available. Grief over a pet's loss can be as traumatic as that of any member of the family. Giving up, psychotic depression, or even suicide may follow. Certainly laws should protect the rights of older people to keep pets, in publicly supported housing if they are compelled to move there, especially those they already have. The writer would add that it is also the only humane way to treat the pets.

In certain ways the loss and grief sustained by the elderly are distinctive. More often than younger persons they experience multiple losses within relatively brief periods, at times when their own coping resources and capacities are diminished. On the one hand, the effective resolution of earlier problems and adaptations to losses may facilitate acceptance of one's current life and ultimate death (Freeman, 1984). Many older people remain remarkably resilient in the face of all too frequent challenges to their stamina and resourcefulness. On the other hand, the same personality traits that serve as coping mechanisms in the young may become coping inhibitors in later years. Independence and direct-action strategies that were successful and self-enhancing in earlier years may prove ineffective and frustrating later on. Besides, such persons have greater difficulty adapting to the passive role sometimes required of them or accepting help even when it is needed (West & Simons, 1983).

The Homeless. It is easy to overlook the homeless, who are mostly men and city dwellers (Koenig, 1984). It is estimated that in Philadelphia alone, from several hundred to 8,000 fit this category. They sleep in such varied places as moving vans, abandoned buildings, subway stations, on park benches, or even in a future rail tunnel. In winter they sit over vents or grates in the sidewalk to keep warm. One such individual opened a shelter for the homeless himself, which has 40 beds but sometimes shelters as many as 70.

A few of these people are homeless by choice; others are highly varied. Their numbers are swollen by economic dislocation, welfare cuts, and unemployment. Some are mentally ill, discharged from institutions without being able to care for themselves. They become the "bag ladies" and the "vent men," called such names as "Spiderman, Duck Lady, and Rising Sun." (Koenig, 1984).

PERSONAL PROBLEMS OF COPING, HEALTH, AND ADJUSTMENT

Coping Problems

Age-Related Limitations. Another reason for older persons' growing isolation is their failing sensory, motor, and sometimes mental capacities. Over ten times as many older persons as younger ones are unable to read ordinary newsprint; and of the 500,000 legally blind persons in this country, about half are over 65 (White House Conference on Aging, 1972). Hearing impairments are even more common than visual problems; they involve 13 percent of those 65 to 74, and 26 percent over the age of 75 (Riley, Foner, et al., 1968). Visual deficiencies arise either from disease or naturally occurring "deteriorative processes," and to some extent from accidents, while hearing losses more often involve such environmental variables as noise pollution (Kalish, 1975).

Problems of Space and Movement. Other coping problems are broad, including those of time, movement, and space. Readaption to problems of space grows harder as people's movements become increasingly hampered by such difficulties as arthritis, general weakness, and failing senses. The elderly may have trouble driving because of failing sight or other physical problems (Kalish, 1975). While only a small number of all automobile accidents involve elderly drivers, their accident rate is high indeed if it is based on the number of miles they drive. Accident rates of persons aged 70 to 79 are about equal to those of teen-agers; for drivers 80 and older it is even higher (Riley, Foner, et al., 1968). Older drivers' errors most typically include failing to yield the right of way, turning improperly, and running red lights. Rarely do their accidents result from speeding.

In mass transportation they must cope with "cumbersome entrances, stairways, difficult traffic islands, and the high step-up features of buses" (Pepper, 1980, p. 16).

Older persons' decreased capacities have far-reaching ramifications. An older person may simply be unable to engage in activities that were absorbing in earlier years. Those who are handicapped are less likely either to engage in physical activities that they formerly enjoyed or to increase their associations with others. Individuals suffering from arthritic conditions may find walking, or even dressing, difficult. Although older people may adapt pretty well, these problems may prove ego threatening, partly because this society attaches great importance to continuing per-

l physical integrity. Besides,
ation that one can no longer
ve in certain ways can be
:.

Utilization of Potential. Despite their
handicaps, older people possess important
potentials both for personal growth and for
making contributions to society, which have
been too long ignored. As early as 1874, psychologist George Beard was researching the
limitations of age and reported that 70 percent of the world's creative works are completed by age 45, and 80 percent by age 50.
Within this time period, he named ages 30
to 45 as life's most creative and productive
years (Hareven, 1976).

However, older people need not be unproductive. We can give some dramatic examples of highly productive older people:
Among them are creative octogenarians
Georgia O'Keefe, who continues to paint,
and Pope John XXIII, who revitalized his
church. Examples of creative septuagenari-
ans were Duke Ellington, who continued to
compose and had a full concert schedule until his death, and Golda Meir, who served as
Israel's prime minister. Some older people
express their creativity for the first time in
their late years, when they finally have enough
leisure time to develop their talents. When
productive incapacity does exist, it ordinarily derives from various losses, diseases, or
circumstances rather than any "aging process" (Butler, 1975c).

Society, as traditionally constituted, has
done little to foster the creativity and continued growth of older persons. Instead, the
roles and environments accorded the elderly
have tended to frustrate more complex individuals, and have seemed best suited to the
psychologically simplistic type.

Type and Incidence of Physical Disorders.

In order of importance, the chief causes of
limited physical activity in later years are heart
condition, arthritis and rheumatism, or-
thopedic impairment, and mental and nervous conditions. Every year approximately

15 percent of 45-to-65 year-olds are hospitalized, compared with 25 percent of those
over 65 (U.S. Dept. of HEW, 1978). The
mortality rate for heart disease, pneumonia,
influenza, and accidents has diminished significantly; however the cancer death rate
shows no signs of slowing; and over three-
fourths of all cancer victims are over age 65
(Pepper, 1980).

About 6 percent of people over 65 and
20 percent of those over age 80 have Alzheimer's disease, which derives from changes
in the brain, the death of cells, and impairment of mental function. The second major
form of brain disease is caused by circulation
difficulties in the small blood vessels, which
also cause the death of brain tissue. Although treatment can help, there are, to date,
no cures for either. There are hopeful signs
in drug research, and ultimate breakthroughs cannot be ruled out (Today's senior citizens, 1984).

Certain observations may help to place
these figures in perspective. For one thing,
as we have stated before, some systems and
organs of the body begin to fail earlier than
others (Kalish, 1975), so that we cannot measure decline by age alone. For another, older
people, as opposed to younger ones, suffer
more from chronic diseases than from acute
illnesses. Often such disabilities cannot be
expected to improve, so older people must
somehow adjust to them.

The almost universal symptom of aging
is fatigue—"which may be an internalized
harbinger of almost any systemic disease"
(Leventhal, 1984). If this "internal cue is associated with aging and separated from the
more tangible symptoms associated with familiar diseases (for example, joint pain)" one
may unnecessarily delay having it checked,
and a "potentially treatable" condition may
be overlooked (p. 134).

Cataracts are another common problem
in later years. Three in five people, ages 65
to 74, manifest initial signs of them, and by
age 80 almost everyone's vision is clouded
by them to some extent (Langone, 1984).

Surgery is still the only effective treatment; however, laser beams are being used increasingly as a diagnostic and surgical tool. Looking ahead, surgeons anticipate finding alternatives to surgery, including ways to prevent cataracts from forming and highly specific enzymes which would dissolve them chemically.

One hazard experienced increasingly with aging is surgery, and much of it is unnecessary. A poor risk 60 year-old woman loses 14 days of life after elective gall bladder surgery, yet she is never told this. There is no evidence that those who undergo radical mastectomy live any longer than those who undergo simple mastectomy, yet the extra cost in psychic stress and dollars is great (Surgery, 1978).

Another hazard relates to use of instructions and warnings on medicine labels, that can be read only with difficulty, if at all, by many of the elderly (Ralph, 1982). Many are not able to read small print, and some not anything printed on colored paper. Cataracts, in particular, which are common in later years, reduce contrast and color recognition. Yet warnings on drug bottles are often written in such small type on such low-contrast papers as to be made, in effect, invisible. This writer would add that the child-proof caps placed on various medications are often aged-proofed as well, making it difficult or impossible for the very old and infirm to open. Perhaps the best solution is to stop using such caps and place warning labels, in large print, on such bottles, to alert parents to the need to keep them out of children's way.

Many problems of the elderly receive little publicity. For example, from fifty to eighty-eight hearing aid batteries are swallowed annually, being mistaken for pills, and require immediate care. Over 10,000 of the elderly are killed each year by hypothermia, produced by an abnormally low internal body temperature, which can occur in rooms where the temperature is below 65 degrees or in outside cold. Some older persons living on meager incomes keep their quarters cold in order to save heating costs (Briefs on Aging, 1984).

A major need for any physical problem is for early and correct diagnosis. For example, in cases of senility—the popular designation for mental deterioration, disorientation, confusion, and memory loss—15 percent are caused by depression and 85 percent by some physical problem which may have been caused by brain disease as well as nutritional deficiencies and drug reactions (Today's senior citizens, 1984). The medications that act on the central nervous system—tranquilizers, antidepressants, and antihypertensive drugs—can produce mental confusion and symptoms resembling brain disease. One problem is dosage—a person over age 65 will have twice the reaction to a drug as will a young person (Today's senior citizens, 1984). Senility caused by depression or drugs is reversible to some degree, much depending on how long it has progressed before diagnosis.

The elderly are more confident than younger persons that they can cope with a new illness, but like adults of all ages, they are fearful of cancers (Leventhal, 1984). Also, if they have thus far escaped major illness, they feel more secure about the future. They may resist special diets and dietary control as treatment for disease, as in diabetes and ulcers—perhaps because eating is one of their few remaining pleasures.

How older people perceive their physical limitations depends both upon the degree to which such limitations actually curtail activities and how they are perceived by significant others. Individuals who are treated as ill are more likely to define themselves as ill (Myles, 1978). In general, the chronically ill feel that they have time on their hands and that their lives are over.

Improving Physical Health. Attempts to improve the health of older persons must take place on both the individual and professional level. Older people should be educated about good health care, including whatever modifications are required by aging. Changes in the body over the life span necessitate psychological adaptations, or maladjustments will result. An older man who has always perceived himself as the epitome of strength and health may tax himself unduly and precipitate a heart attack. The wife often becomes concerned about her husband's health and his apparent indifference to seeking medical advice (Fiske, 1980).

A common error, especially in hospitals, is to overprescribe medication for the elderly. Older patients are likely to be sensitive to drug effects, and medication should be held to a minimum. Physicians should "assume that the patient may have an impaired capacity to metabolize and/or excrete any drug . . ." (Hicks, Funkenstein, Dysken & Davis, 1980). More information is needed about the long-term effects of psychotropic medication (Cohen, 1980, p. 977).

Professionals must keep abreast of the latest developments, particularly in the area of adult disease. A panel of the National Cancer Institute has warned that too many women under 50 are undergoing X-ray examinations for breast cancer in spite of the possibility that the risks of the procedure may outweigh the benefits. It has been recommended that routine X-raying of the breasts (mammography) be discontinued in women under 50 who are not in high-risk categories, because X-rays may cause cancer (Women under 50, 1977).

A Perspective on Physical Health. Both professionals and laymen should modify their concepts of physical aging, for much of what we view as aging nowadays is caused by illness and disease rather than by the aging process. Eventually the chief diseases of later life will become preventable, or at least treatable. Already acute brain syndromes and the mental depression experienced by old people, are "treatable and reversible." We have learned that physical appearance will deteriorate much less if people stop smoking cig-

arettes and avoid excessive exposure to the sun, because both cause the skin to wrinkle. Eventually even such physical changes as the graying of hair and baldness may become controllable. The physical health of many older persons is already much better than is generally known.

Physical Self-Image. One problem of aging is adapting to a revised physical self-image. Sometimes older people make such statements as, "When I look into the mirror, I see the face of an old person. It isn't me—I have the spirit of a younger person" or, "I am a prisoner of my body. It's not really me with arthritis, with sagging breasts and loose skin—it's someone else" (Kalish, 1975, p. 58). On the other hand, such attitudes are not universal. An individual's physical self-concept does not relate to age per se, but reflects particular life circumstances (Plutchik, Weiner & Conte, 1971).

Individual Testimony Many old people describe their health as good and then go on to name various ailments. They are generally quite aware of the importance of health and take various precautions to stay well.

FEMALE, AGE 68: I'm healthy. I visit the doctor, get rest and exercise, and eat properly.

FEMALE, AGE 73: I am not able to do what I want to do. The mind and heart are willing but the flesh is weak. I'm not complaining—just thankful I can do as much as I can.

MALE, AGE 72: Physically I can't do some of the things I could when I was 50. I have a problem with glaucoma that requires regular treatment and for this reason it is a nuisance, but I don't worry about it.

Nutrition. Despite their growing concern about health, older people often eat poorly and unwisely. An aging body needs all the support it can get. Symptoms that suggest a serious organic change in the brain sometimes result from nutritional deficiency, and pathological symptoms disappear as a proper diet is introduced. Yet the diets of the aging poor are often not adequate for maintaining mental and physical health; and even those who are more affluent may experience nutritional deficiencies because of faulty eating habits.

Many factors contribute to poor nutrition in the elderly. In spite of the growing popularity of meals at senior citizens' centers and home-delivered meals, 83 percent of deaths due to malnutrition involve people over age 65 (Pepper, 1980). A high percentage of people over age 75 have no teeth and consequently have trouble eating a balanced diet. Since most younger people today are covered by dental insurance, more future oldsters may retain their teeth. For another thing, their decreased mobility can make it difficult for them to prepare a meal. They may have to shop by telephone and are thus unable to be selective. They may eat little—or too much—because they are lonely or depressed.

Alcohol, the fourth leading killer in the United States (after liver diseases, highway and other accidents, and crime), poses significant problems for older people. Some people also become alcoholics for the first time in old age because they frequently experience grief and loneliness. Sometimes alcohol is too casually prescribed for older people to help them sleep or to improve their appetite. Alcohol, in turn, "blocks reaction time, impairs coordination, and fuzzes mental abilities, especially memory. Serious falls and misjudgments can result" (Butler, 1975c, p. 363). In addition, alcoholism and its accompanying malnutrition often account for memory impairments in old age that may be wrongly attributed to hardening of the arteries. On the other hand, older people who have long been moderate drinkers may benefit from cocktails, especially when they share them with friends.

Mental Health Problems

Definition and Incidence of Major Problems.
All these problems contribute to the disproportionate number of older persons with major mental health problems. A consistent finding of mental health pathology in the elderly is the prevalence of chronic brain syndrome in people aged 65 and over. Of these, 3 to 4 percent are moderately impaired and 1 to 2 percent severely impaired, the proportion increasing with age. At any point in time, most of them are at home being cared for by relatives and neighbors instead of being in institutions. A large majority of cases suffer from senile or arteriosclerotic dementia (Kay & Bergmann, 1980). Many who are institutionalized as mentally ill are actually suffering from some physical ailment, perhaps extreme malnutrition, that makes them appear to be mentally ill. For another thing, many of the quite disturbed elderly are in nursing homes instead of mental institutions. More older women than men are institutionalized, partly because older women ordinarily do not have a spouse to take care of them. Older men more often have younger wives to care for them (Kay & Bergmann, 1980).

The mental disorders of later years fall into two main categories: those that are organic, and those that are related to individual personality and experience (Kalish, 1975). Many older people grow senile and incompetent for social reasons and not because of any factors inherent in aging. Some may be labeled senile and may be treated that way until they do, in fact, deteriorate. Often, the same sort of behaviors labeled expressions of individualism in the middle-aged may be termed senility in the elderly (Cawthon, 1981).

Nevertheless, some do have a brain disease, with its accompanying personality change, memory loss, and depression. The organic disorders, also termed *organic brain syndromes,* may be either chronic or reversible. Reversible brain syndromes can frequently be treated. By contrast, chronic brain syndromes, which derive from permanent damage to the brain, as in senile brain disease or cerebral arteriosclerosis, may be treated symptomatically but not reversed. Functional disorders include various kinds of neuroses, psychotic disorders, personality disorders, and psychophysiological disorders.

Acute reversible brain syndromes represent "major psychiatric medical emergencies," and afflict over half the geriatric patients admitted for mental illness. If properly treated, a significant proportion of such persons improve sufficiently to return to society. Nevertheless, many mentally confused older people are returned home untreated, even when they are suffering from "reversible confusional states" that are often caused by anemia, alcoholism, malnutrition, or undiagnosed physical ailments such as infections, congestive heart failure, and even fecal impaction. In other cases, such conditions may be induced by drugs, sometimes by tranquilizers prescribed by physicians.

Neuroses. A very large number of older people suffer from neuroses, particularly depressive neuroses, the number-one mental disorder among the elderly. A large majority receive no formal psychiatric help (Bronson, 1979). Causes of neuroses of the elderly are not completely understood but probably include "acute and chronic physical illness, adverse social conditions, isolation and widowhood, personality difficulties, problems in family relationships, and previous psychiatric illness . . ." (Kay & Bergmann, 1980, p. 52).

We should also pay more attention to the trauma involved in apparently ordinary situations. For example, older people who lose their teeth and must eat without dentures may experience real trauma, to the point that it brings on senility almost "overnight." "Instant senility" may also be brought on when an older person is advised to wear a hearing aid. Such "harbingers of old age" can pro-duce severe breakdown in some persons, especially those who have always prided themselves on being healthy and intact. In short, the ideal is that senility be treated as a curable mental disorder until it is proven otherwise, and that positive attitudes and therapeutic programs be developed.

Immediate diagnosis and treatment of emotional and mental disorders is critical, especially with regard to reversible brain disorders. Otherwise, these conditions may become chronic and irreversible, though they may be subject to some improvement.

Financial Problems

Now let us have a look at older workers' financial status, as of the early 1980s. Over 80 percent of men ages 55 through 59, 60 percent of those 60 through 64, and 1 in 8 of those ages 70 or older were still working (Donovan, 1984). Older women have greatly increased their presence in the work force—of those ages 55 to 65, 42 percent were working in 1982 compared to just 27 percent in 1950. Of retirees, 1 in 5 returns to work part-time.

A major reason for continuing to work is the increasing cost of living. Just about half the total work force is covered by pension plans. Of Americans over age 65, Social Security accounts for 37 percent of their income, pensions 13 percent, and earnings 25 percent, mostly from part-time work. These earnings are among the few sources of "unfixed" income that help cope with rising costs.

An individual's economic status in retirement is limited by family roles, occupation, and education over the years and since the sexes' pathways through life differ, so does their ultimate financial well-being. In consequence, the financial status of the two main categories of elderly households—those headed by married males and those by unmarried females—differs sharply. For a woman, each of her children and each year missed from full-time labor participation di-

Margaret Hester

One of the elderly person's problems is the rising cost of living.

minishes her occupational status and later retirement income. True, many women share their husbands' benefits, but the numbers of elderly unmarried women are increasing due to growing numbers of the never-married, widowed, and divorced (O'Rand & Landerman, 1984).

Financial problems can be a major cause of stress at any age. It is not clear whether, or to what extent, the financial plight of older people is worse than that of younger adults; however, older people are hit harder by high inflation and soaring living costs than younger groups. Besides, many older people with low incomes have just enough money to disqualify them from receiving Medicaid. Besides, many differences exist among the states in the forms and levels of health benefits that Medicaid provides.

Women's economic situation in later years is worse than men's, for at least two reasons. About half of all employed women and 80 percent of retired women have no pension; women's average retirement income in 1981 was $6,600 for women compared to $11,000 for men (Briefs on Aging, 1984). Besides, because of women's greater longevity, they

have to provide for more post-employment years, in times when the dollar buys less each succeeding year.

When asked what their greatest needs are, older people most often mention money for goods and services. Financial resources decrease along with other resources. Younger people might walk in order to save the cost of transportation, but older ones may have trouble walking. Younger persons can borrow money against future prospects, but older ones can rarely look forward to an increase in their future income. Younger individuals can often increase their income by moonlighting; older ones have difficulty obtaining any work at all. They may be arbitrarily retired and experience age bias when they attempt to get new jobs. They may not be physically able to work, or they may be compelled to work (if they find any) at a marginal job with very low pay. If they earn too much money, they must sacrifice much of their Social Security benefits, even though an equivalent income from private pensions or other assets involves no such penalty.

Worry over financial problems in later years is a functon of both income and, to some extent, the personality of the individual involved. Often such worries are realistic and are produced by continuing inflation rather than the failure to lay up a nest egg.

MALE, AGE 72:   After I made the decision that I could get along without the million-dollar yacht that attracted me at age 18, I have had no overwhelming financial problems. We have coped by matching plans with incomes.

MALE, AGE 71:   I do have serious financial problems and cope by careful budgeting.

The elderly of the future may be better off than the current aged. The education of persons over age 65 has steadily increased in recent years (Fowles, 1983). The median number of years completed, from 1940 to 1960, was just over 8 years. From 1960 to 1980, the median rose from 8.3 to 11.1; and by 1990 will reach 12. Since better education means higher earnings, succeeding age groups should be correspondingly better off financially.

Clothing. A rarely noticed but important problem for older people is obtaining clothing that is both attractive and practical. A study of thirty-eight women, aged 65 to 85 (mean age 74.17) provided insight into their clothing preferences and problems. In general, their clothing did not allow for their decreased height nor for increased weight around the trunk. The type and placement of garment fasteners did not take into account the limited muscular movements and physical weakness of older women. Although the zipper was the preferred fastener, the types used were not the best to be had. Clothing research is also needed for individuals with particular physical limitations who must use prosthetic devices and braces or need to carry a hearing aid (Smathers & Horridge, 1979).

ENVIRONMENTAL AND SOCIAL PROBLEMS

The Environment

A commonly overlooked problem of older people is that imposed by an environment that is largely planned by and for younger persons. They can easily become disheartened by an endless succession of frustrations and obstacles that would be no problem to younger persons: high bus steps, the need to cross wide, busy streets to catch a bus, fast-changing traffic lights, high curbs, and inadequate building labels (Birren, 1977).

Satisfaction with the neighborhood is especially important in determining satisfaction with residence. Older people are especially concerned about access to facilities and services, while younger adults are more concerned with neighbors' social characteristics and maintenance habits (Kasl & Rosenfield, 1980, p. 480). Often they live in neighborhoods where even "good" children treat them with little respect, make too much noise, and race their bikes about in such a way as to unnerve them. Yet older people cannot simply move out of a neighborhood as readily as younger ones can (Pepper, 1980).

John Logan (News notes, 1984), expert on the sociology of neighborhoods, points out that many of the suburbs, to which the city elderly have been increasingly migrating, share many of the worst features of inner cities but few of their benefits. Many suburbs are crowded with the elderly, the poor, and minorities, and they have a high crime rate and poor police protection. Such suburbs are less residential and more segregated than most, a development Logan describes as the "ghetto-ization of suburbia." Central cities would accord older people better transportation, senior activity centers, and nursing homes.

Elderly people may not be in housing or neighborhoods congenial to their age preferences (Lawton, Moss & Moles, 1984). Some of them prefer considerable age-homogeneity. They are made to feel old by constantly being treated as such by persons around them. Or they may find children too noisy and thoughtless. Others prefer a wider age mix. They say young people help keep them young and count on them to lend a hand when necessary. Just 15 percent of those who preferred mixed-age groupings included such "ageistic" reasons as not wanting to hear them talk about sickness or dying, or not liking old people's mental outlook.

Building Designs. Common building designs can present problems to the elderly (Jordan, 1983). For example, consider the 73-year-old who enters a public office building to check on a claim. He cannot read the claim office's listing in the lobby directory because it is near the top, out of range of his bifocals. In the elevator he cannot read the numbers etched into the stainless steel plate beside the call buttons because of the lack of color contrast. At home an aging individual may have trouble opening an outer door against a strong winter wind. Thus, characteristics of surroundings become in varying degree critical, depending on the nature and extent of a person's impairment. More subtle needs should be considered, too—for example, the need for adequate privacy without sacrificing opportunities to socialize. Analysis of such needs should become a significant part of designing environments used mostly by the elderly, while, at the same time, taking into account that they differ greatly among themselves (Jordan, 1983).

Crime

Violent Crime. Another environmental hazard is violent crime, which more often victimizes older than younger persons. Even the middle aged are quite vulnerable to violent crime, especially robbery. As a result

many of the elderly bec[...] they practically become p[...] homes. Many older pec[...] cover after being crimin[...] woman, age 75, was be[...] when she entered the b[...] sister lived, and she died[...]. For some time she had been making a 2 hour trip several times a week to care for her sister who had also been mugged. Residents in the building were mostly older couples who refused to be quoted by name about the incident because of fear of being mugged themselves (Woman, 75, 1981).

Crimes of violence against the elderly are committed by all sorts of people, including those in need of drugs, armed robbers, gangs, and muggers, most of them young. Much of this crime is never reported because the elderly fear retaliation, or they may fear the expense of hiring a lawyer and taking the case to court. Even among crimes reported by persons of all ages, only 12 percent culminate in arrest, 6 percent in convictions, and 1 percent in imprisonment—figures that hardly constitute a deterrent to crime. When older people resist assault, their chances of death and injury increase. Ten percent of all robbery victims are killed, and another 10 percent are seriously injured.

The elderly are easy marks because of their increasing confusion, forgetfulness, and diminished sight and hearing. They are generally weaker and more vulnerable; and often there is no one else to help (Montgomery, 1979). In one year in the area north of 59th Street in Manhattan, there were 480 robberies and 256 con games against the elderly. In San Diego 20 percent of all street crime is against the elderly, who comprise just 8.5 percent of the population (Montgomery, 1979).

Measures Against Violent Crime. The victims of crime ought to be compensated for losses they have incurred, including medical and legal costs, and property damage. They uld be protected against reprisal by alert neighbors and friends, and by increased police surveillance. Their apartment buildings should be provided with intercom systems to announce the arrival of visitors, locked mailboxes, sturdy door locks, doormen, and TV monitors. Lighting should be improved in the streets, parks, and any other places especially conducive to assault. Special protective measures should be required in elevators, laundry rooms, and subway stations. Especially in high-crime communities, or in any areas where there are rowdy young adolescents, escort services should be provided. Older people could organize in order to monitor their buildings, report the presence of strangers, and check the functioning of such security devices as locks and alarms. Police protection would improve if officers were educated about the sociology of crime and how to take care of vulnerable persons. The elderly should be told to carry little or no money, walk close to the curb, and go in groups, especially at night. Special police protection is needed wherever older people are concentrated. Older people should also attend survival and defense classes especially designed for them.

Another tactic for discouraging crime against the elderly is to make examples of offenders. Sometimes a group of elderly people will sit in the courtroom during trials of those who have hurt one of them, in order to exert silent pressure for sterner sentences to be meted out to offenders.

Various factors—including loss of hearing, poor vision, slower motor and mental responses, and poorer physical coordination—enhance older persons' vulnerability to crime. Problems of isolation due to widowhood, the death of friends, poverty, mandatory retirement, transportation problems, and physical impairments are already hard for older people to cope with. When the fear of crime is added to these problems, it causes many older people to remain locked in their homes day and night.

Organized efforts to protect older people from crime are essential. Among the few such efforts available the National Council of Senior Citizens is sponsoring a project which employs senior volunteers to help persons who are robbed or criminally attacked (News Notes, 1981). However, resources to aid senior victims—and such persons are many—are all too rare. Two elderly women were duped into investing part of their meager savings in real estate, which proved to be mostly under water. Another woman's home was vandalized and the windows smashed with rocks. The youthful offenders were identified, but no one helped the widow pursue the matter. One of the rare organized efforts to help such victims derives from a grant by the Justice Department, under which senior volunteers conduct field studies in a victim assistance program; materials for guiding such volunteers are provided (News Notes, 1981).

Fraudulent Schemes. Often older people are victimized in other ways, too. Door-to-door salesmen offer them "bargains" that prove to be worthless. Persons with poor vision may be cheated when change is made. Also, "by telephone, by peddlers at the door, and in advertising, the old folks at home—mostly widows—are deluged with misleading sales pitches for worthless and overpriced insurance policies, home repairs, quack remedies, dance lessons, earning-money-at-home deals, vacation certificates, discount clubs, investment plans, unordered merchandise, and cemetery plots" (Montgomery, 1979, p. 1).

In other cases quack doctors prey upon the elderly, peddling all sorts of cures and anti-aging schemes, capitalizing on their intense desire to improve their physical condition. One of the most widespread areas of fraud is that of medical misrepresentation. A related fraud is the sale of so-called medigap health insurance policies by high-pressure salesmen, presumably to pay the expenses not covered by Medicare. One insurance commissioner calls these "medi-scare" insurance. People are coaxed into buying many policies when only one will pay on duplicate claims. Other medical frauds peddle pills for phony ailments such as "delta cells in the lower torso."

Older people may also fall prey to the "loneliness industry," which offers all sorts of lures, ranging from lifetime dancing lessons to dating services. Other fly-by-night operators offer such get-rich-quick schemes as selling franchise rights to vending machines. These operators take their money and vanish forever. Because many older people wish to find an ideal retirement home, they prove easy prey for high-pressure land salesmen. Lots may be described as ready for building, yet lack a source of water or other vital facilities. Buying condominiums carries particular risks, for while they do offer certain tax advantages and services, buyers may be assessed later to pay for a garden, a pool, or other amenities. Often older people have not counted on such expenses, and with their fixed incomes, cannot afford them.

Rapid Change

Another, and often overlooked, problem of older people is change; and while everyone is affected by it, for better or worse, the most negative impact has probably been on the elderly. Rapidly changing times have caused the values of older people to become more quickly outdated, and they themselves are therefore less adequate guides for the young.

Fast change also helps to account for the cult of youth, because the older generations' ways of living and thinking so quickly go out of style. As youthful ways of life are considered more appropriate for a fast-changing society, so do their physical and behavioral traits become the norm. Hence, the physical features and characteristics associated with the "over-the-hill" generation are negatively viewed, while those associated with youth emerge as the ideal.

A PERSPECTIVE ON LATER LIFE PROBLEMS

An Encouraging Note

For better perspective on the problems of the elderly, the following points are pertinent. The elderly often have to cope continuously with a series of problems, with no breathing spells between them, at that state in life when it is hardest to cope. They must adjust to growing physical handicaps, the dying off of their own generation, and retirement, all of which require a critical reorganization of life purposes (Marris, 1978–79). Often these critical events occur in bunches.

In any case, the anticipation of the decrements of old age is often more foreboding than the reality proves to be. Declines occur quite gradually, so that aging individuals are continually adapting without realizing it. Older people often continue to enjoy life and adjust to chronic problems that appear overwhelming at first. These areas of decline are only one aspect of an individual's life; and if other parts of it prove satisfying, the importance of particular deficits shrinks.

In the following, several older people relate what has helped them most in making life adjustments. People most often mention remaining active, being religious, and having certain attitudes toward life. Even in later years they are used to coping somehow; and they are rarely defeatist.

FEMALE, AGE 68:   I get along by keeping active in church work, home, and the community.
FEMALE, AGE 74:   I've got common sense and a faith in God. It is fundamental that you

make the best of the situation in which you find yourself if you cannot better it.

MALE, AGE 69:   My religious faith and helping to build a better world keep me going.

FEMALE, AGE 65:   I have the belief in my own ability to cope, which I developed as a child. My own self-confidence, plus an exceptionally wide range of abilities developed over the years, has always carried me over the bumps without undue stress.

SUMMARY

It is generally agreed that in varying degree, older people in the United States experience many problems. One of these is ageism, or stereotyping and discriminating against people on the basis of age. Problems of interpersonal relationships occur in the areas of conflict between generations, family and marriage, sex, friendships, and isolation. Personal problems arise over such matters as age-related limitations, effective utilization of individual potential, and physical and mental health, including the physical self-image, nutrition, and disorders characteristic of later years. Other personal problems include those relating to finances and clothing.

Certain environmental and social problems, such as crime, have been recognized, but not coped with successfully; others, such as the older person's difficulty in dealing with environments designed mostly for younger people, or environments in constant process of change, have been ignored. Older people do a remarkably good job of coping with things as they exist. How much better they could do, given optimum assistance, can only be conjectured.

SUGGESTED READINGS

ACHENBAUM, W. A. (1983). *Shades of gray—old age, American values and Federal policies since 1920.* Boston-Toronto: Little, Brown and Company

BANKOFF, E. A. (1983). Social support and adaptation to widowhood. *Journal of Marriage and the Family 45*(4), 827–839.

BROWN, B. S. (1983).The impact of political and economic changes upon mental health. *American Journal of Orthopsychiatry, 53*(4), 583–592.

FREEMAN, E. M. (1984). Multiple losses in the elderly: An ecological approach. *Social Casework: The Journal of Contemporary Social Work, 65*(5), 287–296.

JOHNSON, D. F. & PITTENGER, J. B. (1984). Attribution, the attractiveness stereotype, and the elderly. *Developmental Psychology, 20*(6), 1168–1172.

LAZARUS, R. S. & DELONGIS, A. (1983). Psychological stress and coping in aging. *American Psychologist, 38*(3), 245–254.

LEVENTHAL, E. A. (1984). Aging and the perception of illness. *Research on Aging, 6*(1), 119–135.

MATTHEWS, S. H. & SPREY, J. (1984). The impact of divorce on grandparenthood: An exploratory study. *Gerontologist 24*(1), 41–47.

McCONNEL, C. E. (1984). A note on the lifetime risk of nursing home residency. *Gerontologist 24*(2), 193–198.

NISSENSON, M. Aging Americans. Therapy after Sixty. *Psychology Today 18*(1), 22–26.

O'RAND, A. M. & LANDERMAN, R. (1984). Women's and men's retirement income status. *Research On Aging, 6*(1), 25–44.

THOMPSON, L. W. BRECKENRIDGE, J. N., GALLAGHER, D. & PETERSON, J. (1984). Effects of bereavement on self-perceptions of physical health in elderly widows and widowers. *Journal of Gerontology, 39*(3), 309–314.

WAN, T. T. H. & ODELL, B.G. (1983). Major role losses and social participation of older males. *Research on Aging 5*(2), 173–196.

WEST, G. E. & SIMONS, R.L. (1983). Sex differences in stress, coping resources, and illness among the elderly. *Research on Aging, 5*(2), 235–268.

WESTBROOK, M. T. & VINEY, L. L. (1983). Age and sex differences in patients' reactions to illness. *Journal of Health and Social Behavior, 24* 313–324.

CHAPTER FOURTEEN

Policies and Programs

There are two main categories of programs in which older persons are involved. One includes adults of all ages, the other specific categories of older people. Those for adults in general are wide ranging and include such activities as study or discussion groups, continuing education, group therapy, and training for leisure pursuits. Other programs are designed for subgroups of the elderly, according to their special interests and needs. Thus Social Security and Medicare programs involve all the elderly, where part-time job programs concern those who desire or need to continue working.

ELDERLY ACTIVISM

Volunteer Work

All across the country, older people are becoming increasingly involved in a variety of volunteer organizations. The combination of considerable free time with better financial conditions, improved health, and more education will attract growing numbers of older people to volunteer community service (Cohen, 1980). Not only does such activity enrich the lives of the volunteers, it also taps a rich reservoir of vital resources for society. Certain of these programs are countrywide; others are less well known. Everyone is familiar with volunteers in hospitals and schools; less well known is the Retired Senior Volunteer Program. Volunteers work in such places as libraries, museums, schools, daycare centers, and hospitals. Members of the Service Corps of Retired Executives (SCORE) possess skills that they share with others. For instance, they provide free counsel to small businesses already in existence or to individuals who are planning new ventures. Project Find, developed by the

National Council on Aging, involves learning about the lives of the elderly poor, attempting to identify their greatest needs, and then locating resources to help them. The Senior AIDE Program (Alert, Industrious, Dedicated, Energetic), officially called the Senior Community Program, is designed to improve the low-employment, low-income status of many of the elderly poor, often by finding part-time employment for them. The Dial-a-Listener Program permits elderly persons to talk with others of their own age by dialing a particular number; ten elderly professional people answer their calls. This service helps to dispel the anxiety that many old people feel about suffering an injury or falling without having anyone to contact for help.

Political Activism

Future Prospects. Formerly the elderly were not prone to becoming involved in politics. However, they are as likely as adults in general, and more likely than young adults, to be politically active and to vote (Maddox 1979).

Knox (1980) predicts that society's attitudes toward the elderly will change as older people become more numerous and visible as well as politically powerful. However, it is still uncertain how much political clout older people will develop. While most minority groups are strongly held together by certain significant characteristics such as religion or race, older people cut across all the subgroups and strata of society.

Contrary to the stereotype that there is an elderly voting bloc they vote much more on such bases as social class, religion, ethnic group, and occupation, sources of identity which an individual has had much longer than the one factor of old age (Fowles, 1983). While older people may vote as a group on specific issues, such as Social Security payments, in general they vote more by income level than age. There is no politics of the elderly in this country (Hall, 1980). That is,

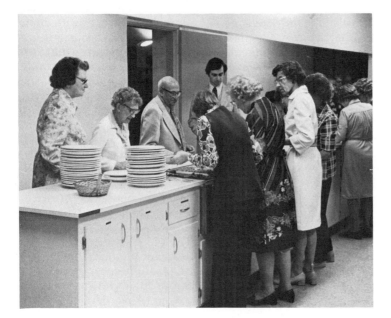

Some older persons serve as volunteers in senior centers.

they possess little sense of "weness" as a group. Only recently has this situation been changing.

Organizations That Represent the Elderly. Certain organizations have been formed to represent the interests of the elderly. The best known is the Association of Retired Persons (AARP). The AARP has developed a broad variety of services and programs. Some are concerned with keeping older people mentally active, including bringing library books to those who cannot get out, and arranging two-week vacations on college campuses. They also make available through themselves or related agencies, drugs, travel, and insurance at reduced cost. And they produce a newsletter at a minimal subscription rate through which AARP members can keep abreast of news and activities about their age group.

The Grey Panther movement is not a service organization, but "a grass-roots movement of social activists trying to take control of their lives" (Offir, 1975, p. 40). The Grey Panthers ascribe many problems of aging to deficiencies in the American society, which defines people in terms of economic production instead of the types of human beings that they are; and they call "this production-line ideology the Detroit syndrome" (p. 40). They claim that the obsolescence of both things and human beings is built into our society.

HELPING OLDER PEOPLE HELP THEMSELVES

Vocational Assistance

The Economic Hazard of Retirement. Most people prefer to retire by age 65, especially those employed in heavy manual labor, assembly-line jobs, or other tedious work. Adequate provision for persons who have worked for a specific period of time should be made. Both Social Security and company retirement plans are important steps in that

direction, but they remain inadequate. A big problem is inflation, which makes paychecks smaller and smaller. Another hazard is the uncertainty of company pensions, especially in less-stable industries. Unionized workers fare better than others, but they are still a minority. The main thing driving older people back to work is inflation, although other factors may be involved. As a result, Cohen (1980) predicts that retirement will become, increasingly, a "relative state, as older people undertake a variety of second or third careers—full and part time" (p. 973).

Discriminatory Policies. Some older persons would rather work than retire—either in a full- or part-time capacity. But they have problems finding jobs. Many older persons simply settle for menial jobs or part-time employment. One woman who sold her diner turned to work in a laundry. Another who had been a water department employee resorted to long hours in a supermarket. Because of such problems the median income of male workers over age 65 is less than half that of those aged 55 to 64 (Ragan & Wales, 1980).

Special Employment Programs. Several concrete suggestions are being made for helping older people cope with their employment problems. One adaptation is flexitime, in which employees can set their own hours. Social workers may help employers arrange a gradual reduction in responsibilities of employees approaching retirement. They may work fewer hours or days and have long weekends. Or employers may arrange information sessions for employees and their spouses regarding financial resources and new opportunities for the future (Freeman, 1984).

Some companies have retraining programs, and others allow a gradual retirement process. Leaves of absence may be extended over several years in order to acclimate prospective retirees to greater leisure time. A common recommendation is that older persons be trained to update obsolescent skills. Special assistance should be given to less efficient and handicapped persons, for their personal and financial needs are often greater than average.

A television station in Baltimore is trying to match older employees with suitable new jobs; an insurance company is retraining older employees; and the National Council on Aging has launched its "Retirement Planning for the 80s" (National Council, 1983). Alternatives to total retirement include part-time work, temporary assignments, tapered withdrawal preceding full retirement, shared job arrangements, and even voluntary demotion. Some people oppose mandatory retirement altogether. The pension systems, too, will inevitably require overhauling. However, political considerations and special interest groups often succeed in derailing reforms, and short-term gains typically prevail over long-term needs.

Forman (1984) takes a critical view of current retirement policies and warns of their consequences. Such policies have developed haphazardly, in piecemeal fashion. To make room for younger workers and to reduce widespread unemployment, early retirement inducements have mushroomed, and older people in growing numbers are taking advantage of them. In the longer-term, falling birth rates may produce an acute labor shortage and a tremendous strain on the pension system, as shrinking younger generations attempt to support vastly increased numbers of unproductive elders. Both short- and long-term, in view of advancing technologies, it is wasteful to create an "unproductive leisure class of parasitic elders" when their superior experience and expertise are badly needed (Forman, 1984, p. 47). For their part, many persons would not retire if attractive, flexible work policies prevailed.

If retirement policies are to be realistic they must take into account the diversity of the elderly population. For instance, individuals engaged in hard factory work have a health expectancy much poorer than that of white collar workers. Butler (1983) believes that retirement policies should distinguish between people who are no longer able to work at all and those who could carry on some gainful activity. The age of compulsory retirement should also take into consideration persons who have been able to work only a few years, or have worked at very low pay—hence receive poor benefits.

Developing Positive Attitudes Toward Retirement. This writer believes that the most important, though difficult, objective is to educate people throughout their lives so that they eagerly anticipate job retirement, not so much to rest and relax but to enrich their lives in ways they could not while still employed. To date, our institutions, including the government and the schools, have failed to recognize the need for a massive effort to educate people in the creative use of free time. Society itself is making some adaptations (such as classes in leisure-time activities, bowling clubs, and so on), but a large social lag remains.

The potential for early retirement, coupled with long-term creative training in the use of leisure, could make the later years the richest period of life. Flexibility of choice should be the ideal, and ultimately the reality. Even given optimum alternatives, some persons will choose not to retire because they are talented or ego-involved in a particular vocational skill.

Educational Programs

The senior adult education movement arose in the 1950s and gained rapid momentum in the 1960s and 1970s. A vast, somewhat amorphous network of programs was developed and sponsored by public school systems and by colleges and universities. (Hartford, 1980).

History and Aims. Educational programs for older persons should serve at least two basic purposes: to compensate for earlier educational deficiencies, and to enrich life. Many older people would enjoy and profit from courses that update earlier learning or open new vistas. A minority have not acquired even basic learning skills and are, in effect, functional illiterates. However, the interpersonal and group experience is considered as vital for the participants as the course content (Hartford, 1980).

Design of Programs. Times are changing so rapidly that intermittent lifelong education is viewed as increasingly essential. It would help to reduce the gap between generations, both in personal effectiveness and interpersonal compatibility. In the current older generation, the majority have had far fewer educational opportunities than younger people. Besides, continued learning helps to retard any intellectual deterioration that otherwise might occur.

Educational offerings should be designed to meet the special interests and needs of older persons. They should involve developing leisure activities, general intellectual enrichment, and practical matters such as consumer education, protection from crime, and mental and physical hygiene. Meantime, conditions must be such that people can avail themselves of such opportunities. Prerequisites for particular courses should be flexible; classes should be held in convenient places, including nursing homes; and motivation by the teacher should be positive and ego-building. Many of these people have been away from formal education for years; and apparent deficiencies may be a result, not of intellectual impairment, but of unfamiliarity with newer teaching methods, "rusty" learning skills, and a lack of self-confidence.

One effect of the changing student population will be a shift in emphasis in order to meet the needs of these older students. Some institutions, it is forecast, will become "three-tiered," serving traditional students, middle-aged students, and retirees. The overall trend in adult education is toward career-oriented credit courses, and not the "no-credit 'enrichment' and do-it-yourself courses (such as yoga and home rep... that some colleges have offered for year... (Graying of the campus, 1977, p. 1).

Group Therapy

Various forms of group therapy are appropriate for the aged. In group therapy the aged are helped by observing therapists at work with individual participants as well as by participating in the therapy themselves. Activity group therapy may include "drama, dance and movement, exercise, sports and games, art, music, poetry reading and writing, creative writing, autobiography and reminiscence or oral history, recreational programs and square and folk dancing." The difference between activity group therapy and recreational therapy is the "therapeutic focus" (Hartford, 1980, p. 818). Art therapy, also conducted in groups, may involve various forms of art appreciation; and the group provides feedback and support for each individual's work. Dramatic group therapy, widely used, may include play writing and play readings by older people as an avenue for expressing feelings, identifying with the characters, or assuming the role of another. In movement and dance therapy, the use of bodily movement helps in nonverbal expression, whereas interpretive dance steps help older people with emotional expression. Growing emphasis is being placed on creative writing as a means of helping older people establish links between past and present. It serves as a catharsis, a way of freeing themselves from burdens of the past and of expressing their reactions to the present. Family group therapy involves family sessions with a therapist and focuses on a particular problem as it relates to all family members. For example, the therapist may help family members work out alternative solutions to the problems of some dependent, needy or ill relative. Inappropriate therapies may bring unfortunate results; whereas well-conducted activities and programs have proved socially and mentally

(Hartford, 1980, p.

therapy proves to have weaknesses (Nissenson, e quite reassuring and re- provides a social network ...therwise lonely, and a healthy ... of helping others while being help... ...ers may dislike this invasion into their ow... ...r others' privacy or feel even further depressed than before after hearing others' outpourings of unhappiness.

GOVERNMENT POLICIES AND PROGRAMS

Some Basic Considerations

Realistic Appraisal of Need. For several reasons it is essential that the government make a large-scale commitment to helping older people. The government must make up for what former support systems no longer provide. In the past, the most common social support systems have been family, church, and immediate neighborhood (Klerman, 1979). The church, which formerly provided consolation in periods of despair, especially at times of death, has been displaced by secularized help from social service agencies such as family services, and the like. Meantime, neighborhoods are less important in this era of personal mobility and urban change, because they are no longer intact.

To meet the elderly's need, advises Butler (1975c), the national policy on aging should be broad-ranging and include the following points: (1) All high-risk groups, including children, the disabled, the sick, and the elderly, should be given priority in government programs. (2) Poverty should be defined in realistic terms, taking into account the current cost of living. (3) Property taxes should be drastically reduced for the aged in order to permit them to keep their homes. (4) Older persons should be allowed to work as long as their health permits. Those who wish to do so could be incorporated into a national senior service corps, Foster Grandparent, or other service programs. (5) Programs for continuing lifetime education should help the elderly to build new skills and thus allow them more flexible choices. (6) Aspects of elderly persons' environment, including parks, transportation facilities, crime protection, health clinics, and the like should be adapted to meet their needs. For example, sick elderly people should not have to wait their turn for hours in doctors' office or in clinics. (7) Other priorities should include the construction of nonprofit nursing homes, the right to mental health care, and adequate basic and applied research.

The National Council on Aging has already produced how-to manuals on replicating certain innovative senior citizen programs (National Council, 1983). Some central resource organizations, such as a university hospital, may provide the expertise and impetus for volunteer assistance programs in general. Specific programs might be developed to provide financial aid to the elderly for energy costs; to help companies develop part-time or temporary employment for their retirees; to establish a home-sharing service that matches elderly people who have space in their homes with others who seek housing; to develop self-help food delivery systems including gardens, food cooperatives, and buying clubs; and to suggest ways to raise revenue for supporting senior service programs—for example, those that provide congregate or home-delivered meals.

Funding Research. Another policy should be the funding of significant studies. Research proposals should be very carefully screened to insure that maximum benefits will be derived from the all-too-inadequate funds currently available. Most programs at present are based on the only data available, which are derived largely from studies of "middle-class, native-born white Americans . . . and they are therefore hardly representative of the pluralistic society of our contemporary United States" (Kessler, 1976 p. 56). Typically, findings about adults are skewed because of the large captive audiences of potential research subjects in schools (Hall, 1980).

Social Security

By far the most important and comprehensive form of assistance for older persons is the Social Security program. When the Social Security Act was first passed in 1935, various categories of persons, including the self-employed, were excluded; but by the 1970s, over 90 percent of those over 65 were eligible for Social Security benefits, although some of them chose to continue working and to postpone or reduce those benefits (Fitzpatrick, 1975).

Social Security currently covers most workers; and it is ordinarily paid for by both workers and their employers. Employed workers and their employers share the tax equally. (Self-employed individuals make their own Social Security contributions each year when they pay their income tax.) These contributions provide four major kinds of protection: retirement benefits, survivors benefits, disability benefits, and Medicare health-insurance benefits (*World Almanac*, 1980).

Recent law requires that job-based health insurance displace Medicare as the main health coverage for older workers. Naturally, business executives oppose this development because insurance for older workers costs more than that for younger ones (Butler, 1983).

Retirement Benefits. Workers become eligible for full retirement benefits at age 65, or they may retire at 62 with 80 percent of full benefits. The nearer they are to 65 when they begin to collect benefits, the larger the fraction of full benefits received. The amount of the retirement benefit that recipients are entitled to at 65 is the key to benefits under

other programs (Golenpaul, 1976). Workers who delay taking their benefits until after they reach 65, receive 3 percent over what they would have received for each year that they do not claim those benefits. A minimum benefit is provided for all persons under the Social Security system. If the wife was also 65, she would obtain half the husband's payment (*World Almanac*, 1980). On the other hand, if the wife is between 62 and 65, she may obtain a reduced benefit, depending on how long before age 65 she begins receiving checks. She will obtain this amount for the rest of her life unless her husband dies first, in which case she would get a widow's benefit. If the wife is eligible to receive retirement benefits based on her own earnings, she can get whichever is larger, her husband's or her own. When a woman worker receives a retirement benefit and has a dependent husband aged 62 or over, he may draw a benefit similar to that of his wife, beginning at age 62.

Survivors' Benefits. With survivors' benefits, the family is provided with life-insurance protection, the amount depending upon what the worker would have been entitled to at age 65. These benefits include a cash payment to help cover burial expenses, and a lump-sum death payment. A survivor benefit is paid to children until they reach 18, or until they are 22 if they are in school; or at any age if they are disabled before the age of 22. An eligible child receives 75 percent of the basic benefit.

Disability Benefits. Disability benefits are paid to three groups. The first is insured workers under 65 who have severe disabilities. These individuals collect the same amount as they would if they were 65. In the meantime, eligible dependents of such workers receive the usual benefits. Permanently disabled children of workers who receive retirement or disability benefits, or who have died, can collect benefits after age 18; and in such cases the mother can also obtain benefits if the children are under her care.

...ows, dependent widowers, or in ...tions, the surviving divorced wives ...ers who worked long enough under ...l Security, may receive benefits as early age 50 if they become disabled. The majority of people over age 65, and many under that age, who have been entitled to disability checks for at least 2 years under Medicare protection, also receive disability benefits. Medicare helps pay the costs of inpatient hospital care, as well as certain types of follow-up care. In addition, Medicare helps to defray the cost of physcian services, outpatient services, and certain other medical items.

Medicare has certain significant deficiencies. Over 5 million older Americans wear eyeglasses that need changing; 3.5 million people over 65 need their dentures refitted or replaced; and 1.5 million need hearing aids. Medicare pays nothing for such needs. In addition, older people are most susceptible to chronic illness, whereas Medicare is designed mostly for short-term acute care, the kind that the old need the least (Pepper, 1980).

Medicare also puts undue restrictions on health maintenance organizations (HMOs) and home health care. Most Medicare money (78 percent) goes to nursing homes, and only 0.4 percent to home health alternatives. Besides, prior hospitalization is required before an individual may qualify for home care under Medicare. Up to 40 percent of all nursing-home residents could be cared for better, more pleasantly, and less expensively on a part-time basis in their homes if such alternatives were available.

In the state of Washington, 90 percent of the hospitals keep patients longer than they need to because beds in nursing homes are lacking; yet care in the hospital costs four times as much. Pepper concludes that "the nursing-home situation could charitably be described as a mess" (p. 15).

Unfortunately, Social Security programs, as presently designed, are not geared to the aged's most pressing needs. Of the 26 million Americans over age 65, almost 40 percent have some chronic mental or physical handicap (Moore, 1983). Yet traditional support systems, including federal programs, are less well prepared than ever to provide the care required. Medicaid pays for nursing-home care, eyeglasses, hearing aids, dentures, and drugs, none of which Medicare provides, but proper care for chronic disorders is lacking. Nor does Medicare, even now—before projected further reductions occur—cover most long-term care outside the home, home care, and nearly all preventive medicine. Medicare is especially biased toward treating acute illness (those of shorter duration), although more people die of chronic diseases. More federal funds are contributed to hospitals, which remain 25 percent empty, than to nursing homes, which have waiting lists. Contributing to the problem is a critical shortage of geriatric physicians. Currently, there is no board certified specialty in this area, and just 720 of the almost 400,000 members of the American Medical Association have a major commitment to geriatrics. The field of geriatrics in America, including research, is still in its infancy. And just a miniscule fraction of the nation's 137 medical schools have professors of geriatrics or required courses in this area (Butler, 1983).

Medicare provisions, adopted in 1965, reflect what younger, not older, persons require. Its nursing home benefit is brief, designed for convalescence, after hospitalization. Coverage for custodial services, essential for those unlikely to recover completely, was omitted, causing some of the aged to become expensive institutional patients (Butler, 1983).

The current Social Security system is threatened because of slow economic growth, high inflation, and high unemployment. Early in the next century, Social Security taxes or their equivalent are anticipated to increase by as much as 300 percent (Sheppard & Rix, 1977). The economic viability of the system would be increased by raising the age at which people may claim benefits. The average life expectancy beyond age 65 is steadily increasing, and many older workers have amply demonstrated their continued vocational competence—hence, such a step seems feasible. Nevertheless, there seems to be strong public resistance toward taking it. Nor can the elderly rely on their savings. During most of their working years, wages were much less than they are today, and the buying power of what they have managed to save has been progressively reduced by inflation.

It is currently popular to consider reducing benefits to the elderly because of increased longevity, but to date illness and disability by age brackets have held constant. Hence, as the older population grows, so will the numbers of the sick and disabled (Butler, 1983). The fact remains that older people vary greatly in quality of health. Best projections indicate that the proportion of persons, ages 65 to 74, whose activities must be limited because of some chronic disability, will remain about 35 percent; and because of the baby boom, the numbers of such persons will double by 2020.

The elderly come to depend on Social Security and are fearful of projected cuts. Even the better-off elderly, and those anticipating retirement in the near future, are confused. They may not be critically in need of full benefits, but they have, for a long time, counted on this federal aid. They are used to a certain standard of life, and would feel poor—even if they were not—if they could not maintain it. Consider, for example, the recently enacted legislation that now requires the better-off elderly to pay taxes on half their Social Security payments—in effect, a major cut. Persons under the Medicare program are increasingly fearful of what may lie ahead (Lancaster, 1982).

Butler (1983) provides a penetrating look into the future. The baby-boomers, the outsized cohort born between 1945 and 1952, who are now adults, and will dominate America for the next several decades and retire between 2010 and 2020, face a changed

scenario and special challenge. The gloom-and-doom school of thought predicts chaos ahead as the smaller generation following after them attempts to care for its elders. True, the ratio of older individuals will rise from 3 to 1 to 2 to 1; but the total number of dependents—those under 18 plus those over 65—will actually be fewer per 100 working-age persons, given current fertility rates. In 2050, as now, half the population will be supporting the other half, the difference being a shift in numbers of dependents from the younger to the older generation.

HELP WITH MAJOR PROBLEMS

Mental Health

Although community mental health centers are now specifically required, many health clinics assume a passive attitude toward the public (Cohen, 1980). That is, such services are available, but the clinics do little to inform the public about them. As a result, many elderly persons are not aware that these services exist or how to avail themselves of them. Typically they "either receive no psychiatric attention at all, or are committed for long periods of time, often for life, to institutions which offer little more than custodial care" (Lowy, 1980, p. 828).

Among categories of help that older persons need is transitional counseling, for persons at risk for losses in the near future. Among them may be persons who expect soon to retire, have a recently diagnosed physical condition, face removal to a nursing home or other changed circumstances, or are facing losses in relationships through divorce, separation, death, or change in residence of significant persons (Freeman, 1984). Psychiatrists look on older people as "unattractive patients." Besides, Medicare pays only a fraction of psychiatrists' fees, and few older people can afford extensive private psychotherapy (Lowy, 1980). In short, many mental health professionals assume an attitude of "therapeutic nihilism toward both the young and old who become mentally disturbed and mainly employ sedation to soothe them. Nevertheless, many of their symptoms are reversible and modifiable by proper treatment" (Fiske, 1980, p. 365).

Patients with more serious disorders are usually placed in inadequate mental health centers or foster homes. Even the community mental centers of the National Institute of Mental Health fail to meet the needs of the poor, the old, and the chronically mentally ill (Chu & Trotter, 1974). Aged and infirm mental patients are in even worse condition in most so-called foster homes, where a mere pittance is paid for their care, and the homeowner makes a profit even from that.

The elderly are underrepresented among the total who receive psychological care, for several reasons (Nissenson, 1984). Just 3 percent of therapists' clients are over age 65; and only about 30 percent of clinical psychologists are treating even one older person. For one thing, many clinicians are reluctant to treat aging patients, believing their efforts are better spent on younger persons. Freud himself believed it inappropriate to try to treat older patients, whom he called all those over age 50. Also, therapists may feel threatened by such persons, who remind them of their own aging. This writer would add that few have had the special training needed for dealing with older persons, hence, feel inadequate. They may also have embraced the common notion that the elderly are too old to unlearn maladaptive behaviors, hence are poor prospects for successful therapy.

Therapists must take into account older persons' distinctive needs (Nissenson, 1984). They must schedule appointments differently, perhaps for briefer periods than usual. And they must be fully cognizant of older persons' greater sensitivity to various medications. They must be aware of the gender gap as patients age—for example, of the larger proportion of the female widowed. One psychoanalyst noted that many of his widowed patients found release in masturbation and need reassurance to resolve guilt feelings about it.

It is especially important to foster the attitude that something can and should be done for senile patients, for many people feel negatively toward them. Folsom (1972) has achieved quite dramatic reversals of senility among VA hospital patients. He describes the case of a 77-year-old man who had had two heart attacks and several strokes. "When we got him," recalled Folsom,

his family was convinced he would die. In three months, they had taken away all of his bodily functions (by enemas and the injection of a catheter) except breathing and eating. He had no purpose in living and was in a desperate state.

First we threw away the pages of instructions from the family. Then we started to bombard him with facts; his name, the date, time, his room number. We showed him the bathroom and started him on exercises. Two months later he was able to go home. But the family had ruled out his return psychologically. So he had furloughs at home until they got used to him again.

He subsequently got back to his vegetable gardening and keeps the freezers of two families well-stocked.

Physical Problems

Prevention. Physical, like mental, problems involve prevention as well as therapy. Preventive medicine is concerned with such matters as nutrition, smoking, physical activity, excessive drinking, and drug-taking, and styles of life that are endangering. For example, the effect of personality and life styles on heart attacks is now under scrutiny (Butler, 1975b). Prevention also involves the research required to head off or minimize the effects of illness and disease. Illness among older people produces a feeling of "spatial limits due to bodily restriction" (Levy, 1978). Mood becomes colored in this state of affairs and motivation to create plans and projects

Physical problems increase with age and may, among women especially, include broken bones.

decreases. . . . "[Without adequate support] the individual slips into living only one day at a time . . . with a consequent loss of a future extension." Especially deserving of attention are the chronic degenerative diseases such as strokes and heart attacks, which strike men with greater frequency than women.

All too rarely the focus is on older persons' potential rather than their presumed passivity, parasitism, and dependency. Furukawa and Shoemaker (1982) emphasize health promotion and maintenance and the wellness concept even among the terminally ill. The view that people need not wait until an illness is over to focus on wellness suggests a different and constructive approach to dealing with other adults.

There is at least some evidence that elderly subjects show significant gains in health after training (Sidney & Shephard, 1977).

In one study, a group of men and women over 60 had led relatively inactive lives. The women spent more time than the men in light physical effort, but neither sex spent much time in heavy physical work. However, after a year of programmed exercise, favorable changes were observed in body composition as well as in life style, including an increase in physical activity and a diminished use of cars.

Another important aspect of preventive medicine is diet. In practice, older people need a "meal guide" based on their own living habits and preferences. Nutrition for the elderly should also take into account conditions that are especially common at that age. Missing teeth, sore gums, and poorly fitting dentures may hinder eating, while a new set of teeth or a visit to the dentist may contribute to a better diet. When poor oral conditions exist, softer foods might be the answer. For older persons with chronic diseases, a modified diet should be a part of their routine medical care. Such diets are based on their regular eating habits, which are modified only to meet their current medical needs (Marble & Patterson, 1975).

Physicians who have specialized in preventive medicine should be available for the elderly. Typically, general practitioners and internists treat the elderly as they would any younger patient with the same condition, regardless of differences caused by age.

Research Geriatrics research focuses on special problems of the elderly and how to reduce or prevent them (Butler, 1983). Efforts are made to distinguish between older and younger persons' reactions to pain, heart attacks, infection, and drugs. For instance, mental confusion, rather than chest pain, may be a symptom of heart attack in older individuals. Senile dementia may be reversible if it is traced to a treatable origin, such as malnutrition, drug abuse, or infection.

Some significant research is already being pursued by government agencies and universities. The National Institute on Aging, a division of the National Institute of Health, has a major biomedical program that is attempting to learn, for example, why aging produces decreasing resistance to disease, why cells age and die, and so on. Institute researchers also intend to make extensive studies of the life experiences of people from their early years until old age, in order to find out how and why they age the way they do. At the University of Southern California's Gerontology Center, psychologists Diana Woodruff and David Walsh are trying to exploit ways of learning in which the elderly may do better than the young (New tricks, 1975).

One important problem that needs both research and appropriate implementation is how to provide adequate help for the elderly without its doing more harm than good. Krauskopf and Burnett (1983) note the conflict between older persons' desire for au-

tonomy and society's perception that they need protection. Certain legislation, designed to be protective, may have the effect of abuse. Courts may appoint guardians and conservators of estates of the elderly without their approval, or consign them to involuntary institutionalization. Although such legislation is designed to protect those who are no longer able to take care of themselves, it can victimize them instead. Such steps may be taken by family members for their own welfare, or by authorities who do not fully appreciate the situation of older persons in general, or of a particular person's needs. As a result, the imposition of an unlimited guardianship or conservatorship can produce a complete withdrawal of individual rights and civil liberties. It reduces an individual to the status of a child, deprives one of control over personal needs and private property, and decimates pride. Involuntary commitment also involves loss of freedom, as well as mandatory submission to whatever medical and other treatment may be provided. Such guardians are especially threatening since they are empowered to commit one to an institution by declaring it to be in the patient's interest. Especially essential in such cases is the presence of attorneys specially trained to deal with such matters, as well as having a genuine empathy for the elderly.

Needs. Only about 15 percent of people over 65 need special social and health services (Hall, 1980); however, medical expenses for this age category averages three times as much as for younger persons, less than half (44 percent) of which is paid by Medicare. Older persons, panicky in case they lack adequate funds in time of illness, gain feelings of false security by obtaining several health insurance policies. This situation encourages unscrupulous persons to prey on their fears and persuade them to buy overlapping policies ignoring the fact that in most cases only one policy will pay (Pepper, 1980).

Because of their special needs, the appropriation of disproportionate funds to the elderly goes unquestioned; however, congressional testimony recently challenged this concept (Ragan & Wales, 1980). When insufficient funds are available for all, is it more desirable to maintain the lives of "very sick, very aged persons" or to divert more of the money for preventive programs for younger adults?

Whatever programs are provided should meet particular criteria. Professionals who deal with older people should be equipped for the task by temperament and training. All too many people simply exploit the aged and give them minimal time for maximum fees. In addition, many psychiatrists cope with older persons' mental and emotional problems by "chemical straightjacketing"—that is, by giving them tranquilizers and antidepressants.

Certain facts should also be kept in mind regarding medical care of the elderly. Despite their poorer health, all but a few use health facilities no more than younger groups. A small number of them do make heavy use of such facilities, suggesting that greater attention should be paid their special needs. Looking ahead, the rapidly growing number of physicians, coupled with their tremendous influence on which and how many health care resources the elderly use, may lead to unnecessary physician visits, treatments, and hospitalization (Roos, Shapiro & Roos, 1984).

Long-Term Care

Home Care. Whenever possible, people who cannot take care of themselves should be maintained at home (Shore, 1972). Hence there should be home care hospitals, daycare centers, and care programs tailored to individual needs in order to prevent unnecessary institutionalization. To date, however, the vast majority of the incapacitated elderly are placed in nursing homes.

One problem is the ever-increasing cost of funding the bills for home care. In just 9 years, from 1973 to 1982, such costs increased by a multiple of about thirteen times, while the numbers of those served slightly over tripled. During the same period expenses for Medicare tripled (Briefs on Aging, 1984).

Miscellaneous Services. Other services for older people are highly varied. Under the nutrition program for the elderly, Title VII of the amended Older Americans Act, communal eating places have been established that serve 5 days a week (Lowy, 1980). All individuals in the vicinity, aged 60 and over, are eligible, and no means test is required (Lowy, 1980, p. 837). Most senior citizen centers offer recreational activities, counseling, medical diagnosis, home health care, financial and legal management, and advice, transportation and escort services, cash for emergencies, delivered meals, and volunteer services. The senior citizens center "works with older persons, not for them, enabling and facilitating their decisions and their actions . . ." (p. 838). Its philosophy is that aging is a normal process, that older people need peers with whom they can interact and that they should have a voice in decision making regarding their interests.

For a variety of reasons the use of the nation's estimated 5,000 senior centers is relatively low, with about 18 percent participation in any one year (Krout, 1983). Those who do participate, in comparison with nonusers, have lower incomes and education, and see their friends more often. Their main reasons for participation are having something to do and opportunities for making friends. Nonusers attribute their lack of participation to being too busy and simply having no interest.

Other types of services are available. Lifeline is a "formalized telephone emergency alarm system that connects older persons with a central station operator in case of emergency. The operator has lists of family, friends, or back-up agencies to turn to for assistance. If older persons do not use their telephone in a fourteen-hour time period or reset the alarm, an emergency signal is automatically triggered to alert a central station operator" (Lowy, 1980, p. 845).

The Friendly Visitng Organization involves having volunteers visit isolated homebound older persons regularly once or more a week. They do such things as "play chess and cards, write letters, provide an arm to lean on during a shopping trip, and just sit and chat" (Lowy, 1980, p. 845).

In 1984 the country had about 800 adult daycare centers, with 200 more anticipated annually. In 1984 these daycare centers, rapidly growing in number, provided 6 to 8 hours of care, including social and health services and one meal, for about twenty dollars a day. Many states provide subsidies to low-income families to help pay for such care (Briefs on Aging, 1984).

More informal assistance comes from peers; elderly neighbors check on one another, the better able on the less mobile. It may or may not be set up in a structured fashion. In general, services delivered to older people are fragmented and not universally available.

A large proportion of the vulnerable elderly have access to resilient informal support networks (Morris & Sherwood, 1983–1984). However, only about 35 percent have a particular helper who can be counted upon to care for them indefinitely. Many informal helpers would be willing to provide additional or different types of help, if needed, as the aged person's needs change; however, they may find themselves involved in forms of assistance and to a degree that they had not anticipated.

When asked what they would do if more formal services became available, about 31 percent of the informal helpers did not wish to be replaced; 23 percent would give up such services; 40 percent would cease help but continue contact; and just 6 percent would give up both help and contacts. The question arises: How can formal services best be integrated with these informal support systems? Too much formal help will be expensive in terms of dollars and diminishing the older person's quality of life. Possibly formal agencies had best assume an ancillary role, determining the extent of informal services available, behaving as a last resort mechanism, and giving informal helpers first opportunity to meet their needs. Besides, formal agencies can hardly remain aware of all the needs of the individual elderly. Well and good, this text writer adds, but the needs of the helpers should also be considered, many of whom are under considerable stress themselves. While the above scenario has real merit, an integral part of the program should be a continuous monitoring of the helper's morale and situation.

Care by Offspring. When children assume care of an aging parent, which still occurs quite often, the effects can be traumatic (Moore, 1985). Since females are still labeled the nurturers by society, it is the daughter or daughter-in-law who usually shoulders most of the burden. They may become angry with parents, whose behaviors are often exaggerations of those they had when younger; and siblings are forced to come together to make decisions, which test and sometimes harm such relationships and usually the burden falls mainly on one individual. When the parent finally dies, the offspring often feel a combination of sorrow and relief.

One divisive issue regarding care of the elderly is the filial responsibility concept recently incorporated into the Medicaid program, which allows the states, when possible, to recover nursing-home expenses from patients' children. Butler (1983) disapproves this measure, calling it an "administrative nightmare," which also creates family conflict because monies which otherwise would go to a couple's children are used for the elderly.

Elderly persons without adult children are far more likely to become institutionalized. In one survey just 55 percent of nursing home residents had a living child. Other studies show about three times as high a proportion of never-marrieds in such homes as are found in the general population (Briefs on aging, 1984).

Nursing-Home Care. McConnell (1984) notes that, at any one time, about 5 percent of the nation's elderly reside in nursing homes, a figure that deludes people into believing that they themselves will have small likelihood of such ultimate residence. It also makes them less concerned about the generally low quality of such care. This same "5 percent fallacy" has led politicians to believe it is safe to ignore the needs of such a small constituency. The fact is that such residencies are generally brief; but altogether a large percentage of the old spend some time in nursing homes, perhaps a half of all of us. About a third of such residents remain fewer than 30 days and 74 percent are discharged, 17 percent because of death, within the first year; and another 19 percent die shortly after discharge. Too brief a time to cause real concern, one might think—but should not one's last days on earth be as satisfying as society can make them?

Various authorities have outlined their conceptions of what nursing homes should ideally be. Kübler-Ross (1974) insists that they be made as much like homes as possible; "and that means that you include children, not only for visiting, but for residing there at least during the day in daycare centers so that the old people can help with the little ones. The elderly can perhaps plant a little garden and do some woodwork and all the other things that used to make life meaningful at home" (p. 148).

In the following, several female nursing-home residents reply to the question: "*If you were asked to design an ideal nursing home, what are some of the things that you would stress?*"

AGE 68: Separate the troublemakers from the people who are easy-going.

AGE 86: I would recommend pleasant, comfortably furnished rooms as in this one; and as far as possible, residents should be regarded as persons.

AGE 87: I'd stress cleanliness, good food, and courtesy, on the part of both patients and the help.

AGE 74: All residents should have their own rooms, big enough to have a chair or table from their own home and a big enough place to bring some of the things they hate to part with.

AGE 77: I'd like a better variety of food.

Despite some planned activities, nursing-home residents often feel alone. Staff members are too busy to listen to them talk; and in many cases older residents do not have family members who are able or willing to give this sort of companionship (Cohen, 1980).

The policy should be, to whatever extent possible, to preserve an individual's feelings of independence. All too many older persons, as a result of mental and physical losses, become unnecessarily dependent upon others in major areas of their lives—for example, bathing. As a result they experience a diminished sense of pride, self-esteem, and control. Hence, it is essential that they develop new sources of self-esteem, such as greater control over routine decisions about their lives. They should also not allow losses, such as a hip injury, to interfere unduly with future efforts at mobility (Freeman, 1984).

Custodial care, when inevitable, would "signify the highest quality of personal, social, and health care" (Butler & Lewis, 1973, p. 298). Ideally such facilities should become places for rehabilitation, "nurturing the sense of hope and self-esteem which can make the last, and often most difficult, years of life worthwhile, up to the moment of death" (p. 299). For example, institutionalized persons should be provided relationships with persons outside the institution.

The costs of entering and living in a nursing home can be devastating. Many patients quickly exhaust all their resources for such care, and may then, only then, convert to

Medicaid. Moreover, such care is often very poor, especialy for residents who have no family to keep tabs on conditions there. Often they are transferred from health-related to skilled care facilities because the proprietor receives more federal monies there. The patient may then "slip into senility because the only stimulation is the moaning and senseless palaver that goes on in such a ward" (Moore 1985 p. 26). One critic stated candidly: "Most people leave nursing homes horizontally" (p. 26).

In short, today's nursing homes suggest houses of death, and "psychologically, many older people consider themselves buried alive when they enter such a place" (Butler, 1975c, p. 229). Many commercialized facilities for the old in America have been described as "human junk yards" by Congressman David A. Prior and "warehouses" by Senator Frank Moss. The old-old often receive poorer quality help than do the young-old. They are less attractive, often poorer, frequently chronically ill, and very often too confused, too upset, or too proud to seek effective medical help. They are often treated as if they were in the way or as nuisances by relatives and friends, physicians, and nursing staff.

Gfeller (1978) tells of a case in point. A 70-year-old widower refused to use the bathroom in the presence of a woman attendant and often sneaked there in the middle of the night, which was contrary to the rules. When he was caught, the physician prescribed tranquilizers and physical restraint. The man, who would prefer to soil his bed than to use the bathroom in front of women observers, became incontinent. Restraints became used routinely and medication was increased. The man became confused, depressed, and soon died.

This case history illustrates several significant points: (1) So-called disturbed behavior may in fact not be so at all. This patient's problem was that he preferred not to use the bathroom with females present. (2) Disturbed behavior need not require restraints

or tranquilizers; merely providing a male attendant or changing the rules of the nursing home would have been as effective or more so in this case. (3) Individual differences should be taken into account. This old man was extremely stubborn and finally died because he refused to give in to toileting in front of a woman.

Nursing homes discourage and usually manage to prevent, the satisfaction of a basic human need, sexual intimacy. Nancy Fox (1980), former supervisor of a hospital's geriatric wing, deplores nursing homes' opposition to sex relations among their elderly patients. Certainly it is natural that people retain such needs, including their components of "trust, empathy, affectional and sexual expression" (p. 96). Fox insists that nursing homes should provide not only the necessities for survival, but environments where the aging can experience all the varied satisfactions of personal relationships.

Since older people prefer being in their own homes, it would seem wise to reduce the nursing home stay to the minimum essential. Jeffrey Zack and Judith Rubin found that only a minority of older nursing-home patients need more than a relatively brief period of convalescent care after leaving a hospital (Aging, 1979). The others are soon well enough to go home, though sometimes they need visits from nurses and meals-on-wheels services. Nevertheless, regulations encourage nursing homes to be constructed on the model of hospitals where the patient role requires an individual not to engage in any activities without the physician's permission. Doctors and nurses even control daily activities; and in such a passive status older people begin to lose the skills required to manage their own lives and ultimately come to resist leaving the home. Yet older people desire to remain active. In one study, residents given certain responsibilities in a nursing home became more active, happier, and more alert during a 2-year period than did a comparable group treated the usual way.

Zack and Rubin recommend eliminating the requirements to reduce financial resources or else making grants available for people to return to live in the community.

A special problem is that by the time nursing-home residents are well enough to go home, they often lack sufficient financial resources. In order to qualify for Medicaid, they must reduce their financial resources to a low level, leaving only enough for burial.

The one program which provides long-term benefits for the elderly is Medicaid, which was designed for the elderly poor and pays about half the costs of nursing home care (Butler, 1983). Expenses for other patients are paid by themselves and their families. Private health insurance normally excludes nursing home and homemaker services, making it unsuited for geriatric patients.

Residential Concerns. More should also be done about the residential problems of the majority of the elderly who live outside nursing homes. The older person's neighborhood should be safe, attractive, and close to shopping areas. Legal service organizations should make provision for the upkeep of older persons who cannot afford it. The same organizations, or perhaps interested friends or relatives, might help safeproof houses by installing fire alarms and locks, constructing railings for cellar stairs, and placing lights in dark corners where people might trip. Air conditioning is important because the elderly are especially vulnerable to severe heat. Housing might be planned to accommodate life's successive stages, including the childrearing, empty-nest, and retirement periods. In some cases, campuslike arrangements might be devised to offer a variety of services and activities especially adapted to older persons' needs. Communities may help older residents by reducing property taxes, or even providing subsidies and free membership in food cooperatives. Transportation programs could include provisions

for senior citizens, including reduced rates on transit systems during off hours.

Finally, it is important that older persons' housing situations permit opportunities for primary group relationships. In one study, people whose mean age was in the early 70s, and who lived in a hotel remodeled into apartments, were highly satisfied with their housing, partly because it provided an interactional network. Those who visited most with their adult children, least often expressed those feelings; whereas those who did much less visiting were bothered little by such sentiments (Hampe & Blevins, 1975). Apparently relationships with other elderly persons whose circumstances are the same, are more supportive of morale than those with adult children.

The less able and the very old may need assistance in maintaining their own residence. Home-care needs of the elderly include focused intensive short-term services with a treatment regime by skilled nursing and medical staff, besides homemaker services for personal grooming and housekeeping. Intermediate services may be needed during periods of convalescence, and the stage of recovery should be regularly monitored. However, the most needed services, not mainly medical, relate to homemaking and personal hygiene and can be performed by specially trained aides (Birenbaum, 1978). enbaum, 1978).

Some older persons choose to leave their own homes and move to senior housing, even if they have been provided some direct services. For one thing, the social and physical condition of their homes may be poor; or they may simply prefer a form of housing that provides a protected environment but with personal autonomy. Variables predictive of choice of senior housing include good memory capacity, friendship with same-age persons, and short traveling time to homes of relatives. Those relating to admission to institutions, include "advanced age, limited living space, long traveling time to home of nearest relative, health that is subjectively viewed as poor, and use of a number of non-prescription drugs" (Beland, 1984, p. 184).

The Age-Segregation Issue. Authorities' opinions differ about whether older persons do best in age-integrated residential settings. Dr. Kübler-Ross (1974) dislikes the segregation of older people, for that is not "what life is all about." Robert Butler (1976) agrees, favoring a "life cycle" kind of community that involves all age groups. He recalls that, "My kids saw an older couple across the street go from their 70s to their 80s and finally die. It shows children the realities of what aging is. And it is just as important for older people to keep in contact with the young, to share in their mentality. But some people can't stand kids. They never could. If they prefer to live in a retirement community with their peers, they should have that right" (p. 32).

In contrast, Rosow (1974) suggests putting older people together in residential settings where they can form strong friendship groups and be protected from the negative attitudes of society at large. Under these conditions they develop their own norms and images, which differ from those of the larger social order. Under these conditions certain individuals become role models for others. In summary, "the crucial conditions are the anchorage of older people in a group of similar peers and the insulation from conflicting external norms and definitions" (p. 167).

The Environment

Only recently has the importance of ecological factors in relation to older persons been recognized. *Ecology* is "the study of natural systems, emphasizing the interdependence of one element in a system upon every other element" (Lawton & Nahemow, 1973, p. 619). The elderly undoubtedly experience the environment somewhat differently from the way younger persons do, a factor of importance to gerontologists, architects,

planners, and engineers. In particular, the environment should take into account normal age-related decrements in perceptual and cognitive function as in vision, memory, and learning (Fozard & Popkin, 1978). For example, almost all old people's falls on stairs occur when taking the first step down, which calls for adapting to a changing level of light. The simple matter of placing a light above the top stair would greatly reduce such falls. Again, older people with adequate depth and acuity perception under ordinary visual conditions, are seriously handicapped in driving tests when they have to read road signs in bright daylight. The challenge is to develop signs that take into account older persons' difficulties with light adaptation. Fozard and Popkin recommend that contrast in visual information displays be maximized, as on switch and control panels of household appliances; and that local lighting of ramps be provided to offset age-related difficulties in dark-light adaptation and sensitivity to glare.

Certain principles are especially relevant here. First, the effect of environments depends upon their significance for the individuals who live in or react to them. The aesthetic qualities that architects often stress are rarely important to the elderly.

Among the elderly, many individual differences exist. Some older people prefer rural, and others urban, environments. Some prefer quite traditional, others very modern, surroundings; and the same is true of younger persons. For some, flowers, pets, and possessions are especially important; others need contacts with friends and neighbors. Some appreciate environments in which they feel free and unrestrained. For example, they especially value a neighborhood where they feel secure and can move about freely.

Research indicates that environmental engineering for the elderly pays off. A group of older persons exposed to an environment with increased opportunities for activity, as compared with a similar group in unenriched environments, considerably expanded their own activities (Carp, 1978–79). Their greater participation in activities persisted across the next eight years and related positively to other indexes of well-being. It proved important, however, to match environmental resources with individual needs and the varieties of persons involved.

TECHNOLOGICAL ADVANCES

Technology has produced, or is in process of achieving, many advances with significance for older persons (Faris, 1983). Communications technologies are making possible a proliferation of new entertainment, security, and communications devices. Some operate through telephones, or television screen displays. Many allow the tailoring of entertainment and information to particular audiences; mass markets would make possible tailoring such services to the elderly's needs at little cost. Communications technologies also make possible a degree of personal and home security hitherto impossible. Since many older people live alone, security systems can alleviate much anxiety and alert appropriate sources to the need for help. These include various alerts which can be obtained singly or in combination: "a fire alert, based on heat and smoke sensors, an intrusion alert, a medical alert, usually a push button, and a panic alert for miscellaneous emergencies. Impulses, activated by home sensors, are transmitted by cable to police and fire departments and a central security station" (Faris, 1983).

Exciting health technologies have emerged from the space program. Persons with heart problems will be protected by implantable defibrillators which continuously monitor EKGs and emit electric shock to restore normal function in cases of fibrillation. New types of pacemakers with a 30-year life and 99 percent reliability will replace those requiring surgical replacement of batteries every 18 months or so. Already created has been a mitt-like unit for rehabilitating or relieving discomfort of patients suffering from burns, stroke, injury, or arthritis. An implantable urinary sphincter is being developed to return voluntary control to patients suffering from permanent incontinence, with its risk of serious bacterial infection. Already on the market is a lightweight bathrobe-type coat, for persons with circulatory and respiratory diseases, which retains 80 percent of one's body heat.

Predicted for the future are "aging-retardation treatments, computer-based mental therapies, vitamin-based preventive medicine, and the possibility of cloning parts for replacement" (Faris, 1983, p. 16). Tissue samples would be taken from individuals in childhood, frozen, and if needed, used to grow eyes, hearts, or other vital replacement parts in later years.

Rapidly developing food technologies also involve great benefits for older people. Food costs are a major problem for many older people, but advances under way will make available lower-cost but nutritious substitutes and extenders. Such analogs save up to 25 percent of cost, and there is no waste, no preparation or cooking shrinkage. Already available are meat, cheese, and fish analogs. For preparing foods microwave ovens, convection units, and induction cooktop units prepare food rapidly, and are not hot to the touch, thus reducing the risk of burns. In addition, advances in home communications will allow grocery shopping directly from one's own home.

As technological breakthroughs continue, the elderly will suffer correspondingly less from various disabilities. For example, recently developed special lenses eliminate the glare that older people who suffer from light-sensitive conditions such as cataracts, glaucoma, diabetic retinopathy, and macular degeneration have had to avoid. In the past such people have had to live highly restricted lives, avoiding such activities as reading, shopping, or visiting friends, not because they could not see well enough to do those things, but because even a normal amount of brightness was uncomfortable for them (Logan, 1984).

CONCLUDING OBSERVATIONS

Certain points are generally relevant to all programs for older people. Programs should be continuously modified to meet the rapidly changing characteristics of the older population. As a group they are becoming more numerous, better educated, and action oriented. They have more time, energy, resources, and know-how than their counterparts of past years (Cohen, 1980). Increasingly, they will, and should, assume an active role in shaping programs designed to help them. They should also be educated concerning their own rights and how to procure them.

It would be a good idea to survey adults in general in order to determine what kind of programs they believe are needed. Here a number of adults suggest how programs for older Americans should be improved.

FEMALE, AGE 73: Stop entertaining older Americans! Encourage them to give as long as they can, physically, mentally, and emotionally.

MALE, AGE 72: Programs could be improved by a change in thought patterns. To think of the elderly as assets rather than as liabilities would make them into assets.

FEMALE, AGE 43: Locally ways should be devised to bring recreation into these people's lives. A careful plan of field trips should take place.

FEMALE, AGE 58: When they reach 75 years old, provide half price on telephone and lights.

Older people should be treated as fully human, and not as some other order of being.

Old age is often treated as though it were distinct from the rest of life. Most hobbies and busy work recommended to the elderly are hollow and meaningless. But old age is a matter of circumstance. Older people have the same personalities they had when young. They must make readaptations that will enable them to find new ways of being themselves and of being true to themselves (Marris, 1978–79).

The formula for a mentally and physically healthy old age includes developing a network of social relationships and friends and having special interests and goals. The latter "may mean going to every Yankee baseball game, doing community work or starting a new career" (Today's senior citizens, 1984, p. 51).

Meantime, efforts to assist the elderly should take future trends into account. For example, medical advances will make better health possible, which in turn will dictate new kinds of programs for more active older generations. The future older generation—the young people of today—should receive "a life-course orientation in all of our social, educational, and economic institutions, so that when they approach the 20- to 30-year postparental stage, they will not be forced to project as empty a future as do many people who now make up the postparental and retirement cohorts" (Lowenthal, Thurnher & Chiriboga, 1975, p. 244). Besides, this education would teach young people how their present habits and life styles will affect their adjustment in later years.

Increasingly, younger adults should be encouraged to support such programs. They should relate to older people and the programs designed to help them in a personal, ego-involved fashion. Considering the growing emphasis on life-span development in college curricula and the stream of publications on life style and lifelong adjustment, adults of all ages—and even youth—may come to have a feeling of common cause and of mutual identity.

Youth, large, lusty, loving—
youth, full of grace, force, fascination,
Do you know that Old Age may come after you,
with equal grace, force, fascination?

WALT WHITMAN, *Leaves of Grass*

SUMMARY

Various programs have been designed for promoting the welfare of older people, including vocational and educational programs, group therapy, political activism, and government assistance, especially Social Security. Older people may themselves become involved in such work, either as employees or volunteers.

Help with mental and physical problems involves prevention and treatment, both short- and long-term, either at home or in institutions. Growing attention is being paid to such environmental concerns as residential and community adjustment, and to programs for assisting the elderly who live at home.

There is some disagreement over the degree to which the elderly should be integrated with other age groups in environmental settings. It is generally acknowledged that a great deal remains to be done, that older people should become involved in structuring these programs, and that greater attention should be placed on continuously modifying programs to meet the needs of changing times.

SUGGESTED READINGS

ADAMCHAK, D. J. & FRIEDMANN, E. A. (1983). Societal aging and generational dependency relationships. Problems of measurement and conceptualization. *Research on Aging, 5*(3), 319–338.

ARLING, G., HARKINS, E. B., & ROMANIUK, M. (1984). Adult day care and the nursing home. The appropriateness of care in alternative settings. *Research on Aging, 6*(2), 225–242.

BÉLAND, F. (1984). The decision of elderly persons to leave their homes. *Gerontologist, 24*(2), 179–185.

CHELLIS, R. D., SEAGLE, J. F., & SEAGLE, B. M. (1982). *Congregate housing for older people: A solution for the 1980s.* Lexington, MA: Lexington Books.

COHEN, C. I. & ADLER, A. (1984). Network interventions: Do they work? *The Gerontologist, 24*(1), 16–22.

DIAMOND, M. (1984). A love affair with the brain. *Psychology Today, 18*(11), 62–73.

FARIS, J. B. (1983, May–June). Technology promises increased convenience and challenges to the nation's elderly. *Aging,* 12–17.

HARE, P. H. & HASKE, M. (1983–84, December–January). Innovative living arrangements: A source of long-term care. *Aging,* pp. 3–8.

JORDAN, J. J. (1983–84, December–January). The challenge: Designing buildings for older Americans. *Aging,* pp. 18–25.

KROUT, J. A. (1983). Correlates of senior center utilization. *Research on Aging, 5*(3), 339–352.

MORRIS, J. N. & SHERWOOD, S. (1983–84). Informal support resources for vulnerable elderly persons: Can they be counted on, why do they work? *International Journal of Aging and Human Development, 18*(2), 81–98.

PETERSON, D. A. (1983). *Facilitating education for older learners.* San Francisco: Jossey-Bass.

ROOS, N. P., SHAPIRO, E., & ROOS, L. L. JR. (1984). Aging and the demand for health services: Which aged and whose demand? *Gerontologist, 24*(1), 31–36.

STEPHENS, M. A. & BERNSTEIN, M. D. (1984). Social support and well-being among residents of planned housing. *Gerontologist, 24*(2), 144–148.

VANDENBOS, G. R. & BUCHANAN, J. (1983). Aging, research on aging, and national policy. *American Psychologist, 38*(3), 300–307.

CHAPTER FIFTEEN

Death

CONCEPTS OF DEATH

Until recently the subject of death was avoided as much as possible in the United States. Only of late have philosophers, psychologists, sociologists, and others begun seriously to consider its impact on personal development, social adjustment, and society (Acceptance, 1975). New ways of thinking about the issues of life and death have been precipitated by "the lessening sense of permanence in modern society, exacerbated by the spectre of mass annihilation and the pressing problems of the nuclear family . . ." (Bryer, 1979, p. 255).

Depending upon their frame of reference, these authorities view death in a variety of ways; biological (the death of organic tissue throughout the life span and then ceasing to exist entirely), psychological (the impact on the person and others who witness it), sociological (its meaning to society at all levels), theological (religious concepts of an afterlife), philosophical (causes of death and its meaning), commercial (the cost and ritual of burial), and legal (the death certificate and the prolonged probating of willed property). Thus, dying is not simply the process of removal from life; rather it embraces a complex variety of situations and circumstances (Bischof, 1976, p. 357).

Definitions of Death

Traditionally, death has been interpreted as the "permanent cessation of functioning of the organism as a whole. . . ." (Bernat, Culver & Gert, 1982, p. 103). Some authorities insist upon "the total and irreversible loss of functioning of the whole brain as the sole criterion of death" (p. 103). However, in practice this definition may pose problems, in deciding whether it means the irreversible cessation of all neuronal activity, or the anatomical destruction of brain tissue (p. 112).

Current criteria of death vary not only among laymen but also among physicians and hospitals. Death is sometimes defined as the absence of certain clinically detectable vital signs. A person is dead "if his heart stops beating and he quits breathing. For an extended period of time, his blood pressure drops as low as to be unreadable, his pupils dilate, his body temperature begins to go down, and so forth" (Moody, 1975, p. 101). However, in a small but growing number of cases, technological intervention has rendered inadequate the definition of respiration and heart beat as signs of continuing life; the heart beat can be stimulated electrically, and before long the heart itself may be replaceable by a mechanical pump, while respiration can be maintained with a mechanical respirator (Hausman & Kappler, 1979).

More recently, death has sometimes been defined as the lack of brain-wave activity. This concept has resulted from the development of increasingly sensitive techniques for detecting biological processes, including those which cannot be observed overtly. A recent trend has been to interpret true death as the lack of electrical activity in the brain, as demonstrated by flat EEG (electroencephalograph) tracings. However, even experienced technicians may have to work with an EEG machine for some time to obtain correct readings. Moreover, it does not infallibly rule out resuscitation in particular cases, because overdoses of drugs may depress the central nervous system.

However, Hausman and Kappler (1979) question such definitions of death. Already some of the more vegetative brain functions are being corrected, duplicated, or artificially induced. It seems reasonable to believe that ultimately medical science will have made sufficient progress that technological substitutes, at least for vegetative brain functions, will become common. Currently physicians are as powerless to prevent death when brain failure occurs as they once were when a person's kidneys or heart failed. Ultimately we must give up definitions of death in terms of certain organic aspects of life and think of death as whatever currently produces the irreversible death of a person. Besides, it seems that it is impossible at present to determine exactly what the point of no return is. It may very well vary with the individual, and it is likely not a fixed point but rather a shifting range on a continuum" (Moody, 1975, p. 103).

According to the concept of *terminal drop*, death can be predicted from certain dramatic changes in cognitive function in the period preceding demise. That is, significant changes both in personal adjustment and performance may indicate impending death (Riegel & Riegel, 1972). Apparently terminal drop may occur anywhere between 1 and 5 years prior to death.

There are several reasons that it is difficult to determine when death has occurred. Death is defined as the absence of certain functions but there are no positive characteristics by which it may be immediately recognized. Second, the whole body does not die at once—heart beat and respiration may cease while cells for a time live on, a factor which is the basis of biological transplants. This practice also makes the exact determination of time of death especially important (Kelly, 1982, Part 1).

Because of conflicting views on when death has occurred legal definitions vary by state. Some states still follow the old common law definition, that death has occurred when all circulatory and respiratory functions have ceased; others follow the Harvard criteria. A report from the President's Commission for the Study of Ethical Problems in Medicine and Biomedical and Behavioral Research, endorsed by various legal groups, calls that individual dead who "has sustained either irreversible cessation of circulatory and respiratory functions, or irreversible cessation of all functions of the entire brain, including the brain stem . . ." (Gregory, 1982, p. 115).

Persons or Agencies that Define Death. Traditionally, societies and their religious leaders have defined time of death; more recently medical science, religious tradition, and popular consensus have all influenced concepts of death. Because of the matter of individual rights, says Kelly (1982, Part 2), there should be some flexibility in the definition of death. Patients' and their families' views should be respected by hospitals. The dying person, in effect, should have the right to make the decision.

Some Caveats. Robert M. Veach of the Hasting Institute of Society, Ethics, and the Life Sciences suggests several caveats in pinpointing time of death. The physician should be free of any important conflict of interest whether it relates to the patient, research, continued treatment fees, or transplantation. A judge, Michael T. Sullivan, believes individuals should be able to choose their course to death and to prescribe their death style. Nor should organ transplants be allowed unless agreed to in advance by the patient, or later by the kin or legal guardian (Kelly, 1982, Part 3).

THE EXPERIENCE OF DEATH

Humans have often wondered, usually with foreboding, what it was like to die—and reports from persons who have journeyed to the threshold of death offer some reassurance. They generally say that there is much less terror and discomfort than is commonly believed; and some of them have even felt happiness or ecstasy. One individual's last violent reaction was to fight against the sense of dying, even though she was no longer afraid. "She then gave in, knowing that she wanted it—death. Next she witnessed in rapid succession a great many scenes from her life. They began around the age of five and were marked by vivid impressions of color. She had the sense of a beloved doll and was impressed by how bright a blue the glass eyes were. She also had a picture of herself on a bright red bicycle on an equally bright green lawn. Other scenes followed, not of her whole life, but of her early childhood, and she emphasized that the death scenes all made her ecstatically happy . . ."(Holcomb, 1975, p. 256).

Among the experiences most commonly reported in near-death episodes are the "out-of-the-body experience, a sense of displacement of the conscious self from the physical body, possibly watching resuscitation attempts; a sense of rapid travel through space, a tunnel, a passage; awareness of a comforting presence, being, or light; a feeling of peace, calm, and acceptance, perhaps with sympathy for others; a sense of rapid review of scenes from one's life; awareness of approaching but not crossing some sort of barrier or frontier; and perhaps some mild reluctance to return" (Simpson, 1979, p. 122). In addition, terminally ill individuals sometimes hallucinate the presence of dead persons they once knew, who help them with their transition into their existence to come.

Interviews with forty-one persons, aged 18 to 67 years, who had been near death or declared clinically dead as a result of accident, illness, or attempted suicide, revealed four core components of death experiences: an affective cluster involving feelings of calm, peace, and painlessness; an out-of-body feeling; "the tunnel," or finding themselves in a dimensionless dark space; and observing, then entering, a light. Other related phenomena included hearing familiar voices, religious experiences, and seeing past events (Green & Friedman, 1983).

Mormon leaders interpret such experiences as glimpses into a second world inhabited by dead spirits. At death the spirit leaves the body but retains its individuality. While out of the body one meets others, usually close kin, who have come either to escort the spirit to the other world or to tell him or her to return to the body (Lundahl & Widdison, 1983).

Explanations proposed for these phenomena in purely physical terms are not convincing—psychological factors are involved, too. The circumstances under which these experiences occur, such as severe illness or accident, may enhance the brain's tendency "to perceive images and emotions determined by psychological mechanisms," including wish fulfillment and defense mechanisms (Simpson, 1979, p. 122). Collections of unscientifically gathered anecdotes have been misrepresented as evidence of survival of the human spirit after death. However, there is no scientific proof of life after death for "death is beyond the point from which any normal subject can return and tell us anything" (p. 123).

Although it is accepted that "elementary particles of physical matter survive corporate annihilation to become reabsorbed into the environment, . . . the degree to which such matter can be imprinted with consciousness, personality patterns, individual memories, or other 'essences' of the body is less certain" (Siegel, 1980, p. 927). Near-death recollections closely resemble dissociative hallucination experiences; hence, such data should not be taken as evidence of survival. Proof of the existence of an afterlife, if such is forthcoming, must await future breakthroughs in science and technology.

The belief in life after death influences attitudes, behaviors, and decisions during life, however (Siegal, 1980). Some people want their bodies to be frozen rather than be buried or donated to medical schools. Some even want to be prepared immediately for the life that follows—for example, the now-deceased woman who asked that her body be clad in a negligee and put in a slightly reclining position before burial. Or consider some Berkeley students' ridiculous new cause, CADAVER (Citizens Activated to Defend the Aspersed Value of the Eternally Reposed),

which demands "better living conditions for the dead, jobs for the dead, an end to media stereotyping of the dead, creation of a Dead Studies Department, and inclusion of the dead in affirmative action" (Lasagna, 1979, p. 17).

DEATH IN CULTURES PAST AND PRESENT

Philosophical and Historical Views

In all ages and all societies, death has been a matter of keen interest and speculation. The Bible contains little about events after death or the exact nature of the life that follows. Only two passages in the entire Old Testament (Isaiah, 29:16 and Daniel, 12:2) refer specifically to life after death. Isaiah declares that "They should live; together with my dead body shall they arise. Awake and sing, ye that dwell in dust . . . the earth shall cast out the dead." Plato, who lived in Athens from 428 to 348 B.C., and was one of the greatest philosophers of all time, portrayed death as the separation of the soul from the body. He discusses physical death in several of his dialogues—especially in *Phaedo, Gorgias,* and the *Republic.* Presumably, after separation from the body, the soul meets and talks with the departed spirits of others and is guided to the next life by guardian spirits. Some souls are met after they die by a vessel that transports them across water to another shore. Nevertheless, Plato confessed that his own representations of life after death were at best probabilities (Moody, 1975).

The Hindu and Buddhist concepts of death differ sharply from the Western one of complete dissociation from life. They perceive death as "anything but the endless time of never coming back or the absence of presence" (Kübler-Ross, 1975, p. 53). The "conquest of death" involves "the cultivation of a disciplined mind and body . . ." (p. 71). Once an individual has come to accept the reality of death, that person begins to "transcend both life and death and to [come] into unity with the Changeless Absolute" (p. 71).

In the history of Western philosophy, death sometimes has been glorified as that which gives meaning to life and is the precondition for the "true" life. Another view is that death is grim and terrifying. In this sense "it lies in ambush and strikes unexpectedly from the side as it claims the young, the innocent, the high-minded, and the frivolous . . ." (Holcomb, 1975). Death's "ultimate victory is in persuading us that the good God of all beginnings . . . is turned by the power of death into what James Joyce called . . . the hangman God and what C. S. Lewis called the cosmic vivisectionist" (pp. 275–276). Those who fear it most are accustomed to being in charge of their own existence. They feel terror that they cannot manipulate the forces of death (Kübler-Ross, 1975).

In contrast to the death ideal of speed and painlessness in much of Western culture, the Hutterites prefer a more prolonged period of dying, which lets the dying individual socialize other Hutterites into a happy acceptance of the promise of a better life to come (Stephenson, 1983–84).

Among the Amish, dying individuals live out their final days at home, surrounded by their loved ones who help them plan their death. Their strong religious beliefs afford them a calm acceptance of death. Death is perceived as a natural part of life's rhythm; it provides a sense of continuity across generations and is facilitated by living among their own people. Also, the dying know that their families will be supported by the community (Bryer, 1979).

Most people simply evade the reality of death, except when the loss of family members or friends rudely forces it into their consciousness. Ordinarily we are too wrapped up in the business of living to waste time on what we cannot ultimately prevent. We simply take living for granted, and do not sit around congratulating ourselves that we are

alive. It is only when death is imminent for ourselves or those we love, that we feel a certain life hunger (Imara, 1975). Middle age brings an increasing awareness of aging. Peterson (1980) calls the midlife crisis "the confrontation of the inevitability of total impotence . . . total loss of self" (p. 926). A common reaction is denial, or avoiding confrontation with death's inevitability. Thus, people engage in a "ritual of pretense, saying to the dying patient 'You are looking better today' or 'The nurse said you had a good night'" (Peterson, 1980, p. 928). Peterson defends denial as necessary; its very universality indicates its functional value for individual and society. It may "not square with modern mental health practices in which one must confront reality at all costs [but] at times [it] is essential to hope, to serenity, and to a good death. Individuals vary in their ability to confront the going from which is no return" (p. 929).

Family members and therapists should be careful to determine whether or not confrontation with the truth is wise. Sometimes "mutual pretense" is best for all. For many individuals the last hours are spent in "doubt and ambiguity," and these doubts may not be resolved. For individuals for whom denial has been a way of life there is simply hope. In an "ironic sense [denial] is fulfillment—[the] completion of lives of emptiness" (Peterson, 1980, p. 931).

Decreasing Emphasis on Maintaining Life Regardless of Circumstances. This negative view of death is paralleled by a corresponding deemphasis on maintaining life for life's sake, resulting in part from the growing world population and our shrinking natural resources. Hall and Cameron (1976) observe Americans' growing support for capital punishment. Even suicide no longer repels us, and its rate is climbing. Psychologist Robert Kastenbaum believes that suicide may win society's approval and will become an ethical alternative and "strengthen the social fabric"

(p. 108). Theologian Richard Rubenstein defends some suicides as examples of applying reason to human problems; and he argues that it is "irrational to prolong suffering, to keep alive the malformed or the unconscious, to support murderers at public expense, or to allow unwanted babies to be born" (Hall & Cameron, 1976, p. 108).

Euthanasia. Nationally, over the past 30 years, the idea of euthanasia has become increasingly accepted among all major population subgroups, with the largest increase in approval among Catholics and the young (Ostheimer, 1982). The issue of employing euthanasia has become especially important because of modern technology's potential for delaying the moment of death, and because most people these days die in hospitals or nursing homes.

Euthanasia may be voluntary, involving the wishes of patients or those acting on their behalf, or involuntary, in the absence of such wishes. In order that an incompetent individual's rights not be violated, a legal representative might be appointed or the immediate family might be allowed to act on the patient's behalf. The latter procedure should be made legal since it is the one commonly employed for the protection of the physician or the family involved. If freedom from potential criminal immunity is desired, an elective of some private ethics committee should be available (Ward, 1982).

Mercy killing may be advocated for various reasons. Most often stressed is the poor quality of life, especially when there is much pain or no hope of recovery. Also the individual might be regarded as expensive to keep alive and of no further value to the community.

A major issue, since life support systems can now maintain respiration and heartbeat, is whether, and under what conditions, to prolong life. Although the pulling of the plug on life support machines has become a highly controversial question, among nurses it is not a matter of whether to pull it but when. A large majority favor freeing dying patients from prolonged pain, although 6 in 10 would keep the person alive to allow a "chance to harvest his kidneys, heart, or corneas for transplant use," provided that the patient had previously agreed, the family approves, and a recipient is available (Is it right, 1982, p. 39).

Unfortunately, we have no way of knowing before people become unconscious whether or not they would choose to have life-sustaining machines turned off. In one case a technician who had hooked up 600 patients to such machines indicated that 400 of them had been able to communicate their desires and that not one of them had asked to be permitted to die (Hall & Cameron, 1976).

In a questionnaire study, to which 20 percent of 1,300 physicians responded, over a third (37.4 percent) said that within the past 2 years not one of their patients had requested withdrawal of life support. Of these, 43.37 percent had complied after consultation with the patient's family. Those who withheld such support had consulted with their colleagues. Almost half (48.7 percent) favored legislation allowing medical procedures which might hasten death in order to alleviate pain, and 1 in 3 felt circumstances might make it advisable to hasten the death of a dying patient through some positive act. Two in three believed the physician possesses the sole ultimate responsibility for such decisions, and about two-fifths thought that further legal clarification was needed. Half approved legislation allowing the terminally ill the right to have support suspended (Wershaw, Ritchey & Alphin, 1982).

Hall speculates that manipulating the time of death may one day become acceptable under certain circumstances. In 1975 over half of a sample of Americans under age 30 said that "incurable disease or continual pain confer upon a person the moral right to end his life" (p. 108).

If this trend continues, we may one day institute the euthanasia parlors like those portrayed in the movie *Soylent Green*. In this picture of the future, people who wish to end their lives report to a government building, where beautiful girls welcome them and administer a lethal drug. As they lie dying, the volunteers watch movies of idyllic pastoral settings and listen to Beethoven's Ninth Symphony; and while *Soylent Green* is mere fiction, we must not forget that science fiction has been on target with many of its conjectures. Of course there are great dangers here. Ultimately, bureaucrats might decide that only certain people would be permitted access to medical technology; or mercy death might be the reward that people would receive on retirement, and the date of retirement would be arbitrary (Hall & Cameron, 1976).

These new problems are brought on by advances in medical technology. If there were enough machines in our hospitals, large numbers of people who would otherwise die would continue to survive and "the prospect of hospitals made up of bed after bed filled with terminal patients is chilling but possible" (p. 106). Moreover, the cost of such care is rising astronomically: as the financial costs grow, "our eroded reverence for life may wear away entirely" (p. 108).

The happiness of the patient is not always the deciding factor. In one case, the night before surgery was planned on a woman, her son-in-law called the doctor and reminded him that he had already performed almost the same operation on her and asked him not to perform it again. If the physician operated, the family's savings would be fully depleted, and they would be denied "a color TV, a second car, and a larger home" (Hall & Cameron, 1976, p. 106). Therefore, the physician called off the operation, believing that the few extra years the patient would gain would not make up for the family's material deprivation. (The author, incidentally, takes sharp issue with this decision.)

Death as Positive. Most current authorities on the subject perceive death as both natural and positive, especially in its impact on life. Corr (1979) points out that "there can be no life without death. . . . Our problem is a tendency to withdraw from nature and construct an artificial living space populated by plastic flowers, gala figurines and pet rocks—none of which will ever die" (p. 67). Alienation from nature diminishes humanity; and "by holding death at a distance and not permitting it into our lives, we have failed to realize the guidance it could provide as a steering force in helping to determine the ways we might live" (p. 67). Imara (1975) believes that it is necessary to learn to die in order to learn to live; and new growth requires the death, or throwing off of, restricting shackles.

Recent films, books, and television dramatizations are representing death more realistically than formerly, suggesting that it need not be portrayed in offensive or shocking ways. In their writings, many exceptional individuals have shared their struggles with grief and terminal illness; and this sharing has proved therapeutic and helpful in coming to understand death and dying (Corr, 1979).

The Function of Fear of Death. On the other hand, coming to view death as a friend could have unexpected consequences. Perhaps a "healthy fear" of death keeps us from taking undue chances and motivates us to live as healthy a life as possible in order to prolong it. A total lack of fear of death would produce a mass suicide partly because much of humankind's life is a burden and only the terror of death keeps human beings going. Absence of fear of death might also lead to the crumbling away of all law and order. Society is made possible because people in authority can dominate the masses by utilizing the threat of death, as by war or legal verdict (Simpson, 1979). In addition, Kastenbaum (1974) suggests that too little fear of death might result in a dangerously low level of procreation, which would threaten the continuation of the species. In a study that included both tenth-graders and college undergraduates, young people perceived various alternatives for continuing themselves beyond death. This yearning for self-continuation is especially high among those who feel strong anxiety about death. Such individuals prefer to postpone their death and "to keep the torch burning to the option of passing it on to the next generation" (p. 76). Others perceive procreation as a satisfying way of reducing their concern over their personal mortality.

A Changing Concept. In general, evaluations of death vary according to place, time, circumstance, and individual philosophies. Studies of attitudes toward death and death ceremonials over the years and around the world indicate its significance to be highly fluid. We can only guess what its status would become if, as has been predicted, the life span should be extended by several decades, or if some eons from now, its length should become optional. A number of times the

writer has posed the question to college undergraduates: If you could choose to live forever, and have good health and a good body characteristic of whatever age you designate, throughout eternity, would you do so, or would you choose to have a normal life span? In addition, those questioned are told that once they have made the decision, they cannot change it. A large majority always settle for a normal life span.

Individual Feelings about Death

Typical Views. Certain attitudes toward death are typical. Even when approaching death, people ask, "Why me?" and seek a meaning for their suffering. The act of dying itself may involve a certain amount of anticipatory grief over the loss of one's own life. In addition, fear of dying is often associated with unfounded beliefs that dying itself is painful, that death involves an ultimate

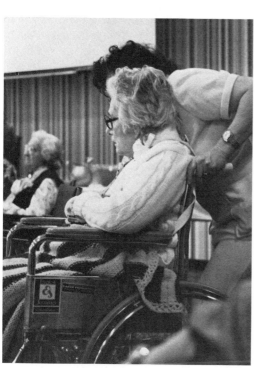

The very old may come to welcome death.

T.G. Bell

aloneness, and "that there may be final medical procedures that will further dehumanize [one] by being turned into a sort of plumbing shop . . ." (Holcomb, 1975). The fear of pain can be relieved by a knowledge of modern pain-relieving processes. It can help to know that though dying is rarely pleasant, it is neither as painful nor as unpleasant as often feared.

Attitudes Toward Death. In a sampling of adults of varying sex, race, age, the factor relating most significantly to fear of death was age. (Big leveler, 1978). The middle aged worried about and feared death the most, while the elderly appeared to have faced up to it. The middle aged have increasing experiences with illness and death, as it occurs among their former teachers and mentors or even among their contemporaries. Their own gradual decline and growing physical limitations heighten the reality of their own mortality. Yet men and women differ in responding to such issues. Men react angrily when they realize that death and illness are realities; women who have been brought up to assume the caretaking role, feel less conflict about accepting their own ultimate dependency (Mann, 1980).

The very old may even come to welcome death. Deprived of people they love and limited in their activities because of pain and disabilities, many of them "are ready to welcome the Reaper who no longer seems too grim" (Lidz, 1980, p. 36). Some who fear death the most have never been able to live fully because of their own personality problems. Yet even these people come to accept the inevitable (Lidz, 1980).

Individual Views of Death. Here several successively older adults tell how they feel about death:

MALE, AGE 33, RESEARCH PSYCHOLOGIST: Thoughts of my own death scare me so badly I don't even like to talk about it.

FEMALE, AGE 34, HAIR STYLIST: I don't fear death. I believe in life everlasting and that heaven is better than life on earth. Maybe when the time actually comes, if I know it is near, I won't have quite as positive an attitude. But I still won't fear it.

MALE, AGE 59, JOURNALIST: One of the most shameful aspects of the human condition is that man's final moment is likely to be one of pain, and his final days, even years, ones of discomfort and helplessness, a soul abiding in a decaying carcass. One's greatest reward would be to go quickly and peacefully. Even so, the vista of a universe continuing for an eternity without being a part of it is intellectually appalling, incomprehensible, unacceptable.

MALE, AGE 69, RETIRED COLLEGE PRESIDENT: If I should go to hell (which isn't likely) and find it didn't exist, I'd be relieved. If I go to heaven (as I expect to) and find there is no such place, I'd be disappointed but I would not regret trying to live an upright Christian life.

Factors That Modify Attitudes Toward Death. Feelings about death involve many factors, one of which is individual conviction about the worth of past accomplishments. Those who have not fully lived, who still have unsettled matters and unrealized dreams of accomplishment, who have not availed themselves of the significant things in life, such as loving, being loved, and contributing effectively to others' welfare, are the most unwilling to die (Ross, Braga & Braga, 1975).

Religious persons typically view death differently from nonbelievers. To the religious person, death is simply the last stage in earthly life; but it is not a complete death because only the body dies (Ross, Braga, & Braga, 1975). Those who have truly integrated religion into their lives have the most positive feelings toward death. The better educated are also better adjusted, perhaps because they are generally more financially secure and hence can leave their affairs in better order.

Even among the old fear of death varies considerably. In a study of 293 elderly persons (mean age 75.4 years), those who lived in institutions or who perceived time as slow were more anxious about life after death (Baum, 1983).

Sex also relates to attitudes toward death. Females are more concerned than males about loss of identity and self-annihilation, and males more about effects on family and friends and punishment in the life hereafter (Florian & Kravetz, 1983).

The Best Place to Die. Dr. Melvin J. Krant (1972) observes that "helping someone to die well is one aspect of health care." But the meaning of dying well depends on the person involved. Unless patients are mentally incompetent, they should be part of whatever decisions are made about their welfare (Carey, 1975). Members of the family can help most by maintaining an environment that is compatible with the individual's preferred life style, as much as circumstances permit. All too often at this stage, people are simply handled like inert pieces of baggage, to be stashed wherever the caretakers decide.

Over two-thirds of the people in the United States die outside the home, in contrast with about half, three decades ago (Acceptance, 1975). Yet patients often prefer to spend their last days in a familiar environment; and their will should prevail when circumstances permit. Instead of being in a "sterile hospital" they want "companionship and relief from pain; hypnosis, drugs, wine and music . . . (Huyck, 1974, p. 163).

In a study of a hundred elderly patients, all expressed a desire to remain in their homes until death, but only fifty-five did so. The others died either in hospitals or nursing homes. Nineteen were taken from their homes because of physical and emotional exhaustion either on the part of the patients or their families (Groth-Juncker & Mc-Cusker, 1983).

For those who must spend their last months or days away from home, the *hospice* provides special care. The hospice is a place designed for providing support, comfort, and dignity for individuals who are dying; but it need not be a specific place. Rather it is an attitude that can be utilized by all hospitals and nursing homes (Butler, 1978–79).

The hospice is a concept of care for the terminally ill, providing more pleasant, homelike surroundings than most hospitals provide—or indeed, providing care in the home (AMA Council on Medical Service, 1982). It complements rather than competes with other forms of care; and it also involves those who care for the patient. The hospice team deals with patients and their families as a unit and helps provide for the terminally ills' social, physical, emotional, and economic needs (Martin, 1982).

Gibson (1984) questions the hospice concept on several grounds. While such care is advocated as being less costly, it also cuts patients off from help they might otherwise receive in a hospital. Besides, although the hospice concept was intended to apply to patients in their last weeks or days, it has been stretched to a half year or more, the apparent reason being to save money. Thus the value of life becomes secondary to cost efficiency. In effect, treatment is suspended and the patients are given up to die.

Care of the Dying. The terminally ill need much tender, loving care, "for [while] they may be as helpless as a child . . . they seldom arouse tenderness" (Weissman, 1972, p. 144). They should be helped to feel, even in their final days, that they are of value; and they should have people readily at hand with whom they can share their fears, feelings, and anxieties (Kübler-Ross, 1974). Everything possible should be done to relieve their feelings of isolation from others.

The dying have their own special concerns. Among situations that influenced the sense of dignity of twenty-four terminally ill persons, 90 percent named a sense of help-lessness, feelings of unrelatedness, lack of control, and an overpowering sense of loss (Nash, 1977). Another concern is death itself. Most of the elderly do not fear it, but often want to discuss it, even if their listeners are supportive and caring. They also enjoy reviewing their lives; and this reminiscing helps them to perceive their lives as a whole and to reflect upon what they have done. Some of them even write their life stories, often at length, perhaps with a double motive: to leave a legacy for their descendants and to review their own past (Kalish & Reynolds, 1975). Meantime, they should be protected from excessive pain, for the greater discomfort individuals suffer on approaching death, the less able they are to retain a high level of positive emotion. On the other hand, they should not be drugged simply so that they will not be troublesome.

Many of the dying simply want to talk with any sympathetic person. In the San Francisco Bay area, Charles Garfield, a clinical psychiatrist, has established a hot line to provide emotional counseling for the dying and those close to them (Goleman, 1978). Medical advances have lengthened the time required to die, thus allowing the dying and those they love to "renew their intimacy, be together, share their sorrow, anger, fears, and the joy that comes from the experience of their loving. . . . However, because our culture has taught us to deny and camouflage dying and death, few of us—patients, families, friends, and medical personnel—know how to use this gift in a positive way" (p. 34).

An important issue that arises is whether patients should be told of an unfavorable prognosis. Most patients, including those with diagnosed cancer, would rather be told the truth about their medical condition—but there are exceptions. Physicians themselves indicate a preference for telling patients as little as possible because of fear of producing feelings of depression and helplessness (Weir, 1977). If patients ask, they may be informed that they are seriously ill, but also be told of all treatment possibilities. They should not be told that they are going to die at a particular time because no one can predict such a thing accurately, and many persons have lived far beyond medical expectations. Patients also need to know that their physicians will not simply give up but will make every effort to prolong their lives.

Since it is not always appropriate, or possible, to make one's wishes known in case of severe illness or deterioration, it is a good idea for intimates to share with each other their feelings about whether to be told about survival prospects, whether they favor the use of life-sustaining machines, and whether to have a funeral. Some individuals do not want to be told their condition is probably terminal; and one cannot know, without asking, who these few are.

People are often given up for dead long before death has occurred. As Butler (1975c) points out, "we are so preoccupied with defending ourselves from the reality of death that we ignore the fact that human beings are alive until they are actually dead. At best, the living old are treated as if they were already half dead" (p. xi). Relatives and friends of the terminally ill often write them off.

The Right to Die. The issue of the right to die is of growing importance, because of the increasingly sophisticated life-sustaining equipment available. *Passive euthanasia* means letting patients die naturally instead of exercising artificial means to keep them alive, when living would involve a vegetative existence or continuous suffering. *Active euthanasia* means the deliberate killing of persons who are presumed to be helplessly and hopelessly disabled or ill. Doctors themselves often support the biological preservation of the individual, even at the price of the patient's loss of dignity. However, passive euthanasia is receiving some consideration as a medical practice under carefully safe-guarded circumstances, including the individual's own wish to die. Already, most authorities oppose artificially keeping a patient alive after extensive and irreversible brain damage has been done.

The majority of laymen, too, oppose indefinitely maintaining a person who has no future prospect but pain and who has expressed a willingness to die. Mark and Dan Jury (1976) tell the poignant story of their grandfather, an old miner, who, after his retirement, was afflicted with various infirmities associated with old age. His habits gradually changed; he stopped hanging around the local garage, which had become a ritual ever since his retirement; and he lived in his own mind, indulging in all sorts of fantasies. At night he would get up, tear his room apart, and strew the bedclothes around, sometimes totally losing control of his bowels. One day he simply decided to stop eating, and he adamantly refused food despite his family's coaxing. His family rejected the only alternative, which was to resort to hospitalization and intravenous feeding. They felt that to strap this man to a hospital bed, "with tubes protruding from his arms was completely alien to the sort of person he had always been" (p. 61). They decided that it was Gramp's right to determine his own destiny and to die through his own will if he so desired.

Increasingly, people are coming to believe that the individual concerned should make the final decision on whether or not and how long their lives should be sustained by machine. And to insure that their wishes will be known, they make out a so-called living will in the presence of at least two witnesses, testifying to that person's soundness of mind, which indicates whether or not life support should ever be used in his or her case (Kutner, 1982). A committee of physicians or a hospital board might then decide whether or when it should be honored; however, such wills are not as yet legally binding. An individual might carry the will, besides giving copies to a doctor or some intimate. Such wills might be specifically tailored to take into account religious principles, special wishes,

and feelings about specific support measures.

The living will poses two main challenges to medicine. Does the patient, by rejecting prolonged treatment, have the right to die; and should physicians who honor such requests, by withholding or continuing such treatment, be held legally liable? The will, whatever the patient's choice, respects the autonomy and dignity of the individual. About three-fourths of Alabama physicians, when questioned, approved them, and just 12 percent disapproved. Just 3 percent felt that withdrawal of life support should never be an acceptable option (Wershaw, Ritchey, & Alpin, 1982). Still missing, but needed, is legal support for such wills, in order to clarify matters of the physician's liability and the patient's rights (Baker, 1982).

Organ Donation. A major issue relating to death is that of organ donation, and interest in it is growing (Organ donor recruitment, 1982). One reason is the rate of cadaver graft survival of transplanted hearts and kidneys of 50 to 70 percent, and of kidney host survival up to 90 percent, for 2 years. Corneas, bone, and skin may also be transplanted, and the list of transplantable parts will surely grow. Certainly, the quality of life, or life itself, of large numbers of potential recipients is at stake.

The problem lies in obtaining sufficient and appropriate donors. A large majority of people claim that they would be willing to make such donations, but few sign the cards that make the act legal. The Uniform Anatomical Gift Act, adopted by all states, makes donors' wishes binding after they die. However, in Maryland, where the donor card is on the driver's license, only 1.3 percent have signed it. Various suggestions have been made for increasing positive responses, including broader education about this matter. As methods of transplantation improve and rejection phenomena come under increasing control, the demand for organs will become correspondingly greater.

The Rights and Tasks of The Dying. Even fatally ill persons have certain rights and tasks (Noyes & Clancy, 1977). One chore is to accept reality, which includes cutting back their former freedom; and they must also stick to necessary rules and routines imposed by their caretakers. Yet the fatally ill should also remain independent to whatever extent possible—for example, they should be willing, if able, to feed themselves.

One anticipatory act to one's inevitable demise is estate planning, to insure the welfare of dependents and distribution of property according to one's wishes (Laikin, 1982). Such planning involves finding ways to reduce estate shrinkage, caused by taxes and estate expenses, payment of death costs, and arranging for distribution of property among the heirs.

Another task, in anticipating death, is somehow to establish the significance of one's life and selfhood. The dying include two categories (Marshall, 1980): those who are aware that the end is not too far off and those with a condition that makes death probable within a short time. The awareness of impending death is enhanced by witnessing the death of others and recognition of the stages of one's own life. In either case, the result is an intensive self-reflection, a life review, and a solidifying of one's identity—perhaps through memoirs, letters, and reflections left behind.

People also preserve their identities over time through collecting various objects and endowing them with meaning, a sort of "identity kit" (Unruh, 1983). Family photographs, scrapbooks, souvenirs, jewelry—all represent their owners' identities; and these items symbolically represent to the elderly who they are or once were. These possessions, in turn, symbolize identities which remain with the survivors.

Especially revealing is when unorthodox distribution of particular artifacts are made. Thus the deceased's own prior identities may be revealed. The animal lover bequeaths money for maintaining pets; or the liberal may leave money for some special political cause. Sometimes money is left to a friend, perhaps whom one came to know well in a nursing home. As a result of new identities and friendships established in later life, artifacts are often left to persons outside the family. Disinheritance, too, can help maintain one's identity. Such exclusion may be one's way of asserting one's own independence or punishing someone, perhaps for neglect or some disapproved action.

Survivors, in turn, sift through their memories for events, large and small, that endow the deceased with special identities, or even create them. Or they may choose to preserve particular identities of the deceased to the exclusion of others. In general they tend to idealize the deceased—for example, a man may be perceived as having failed in business because he was too honest.

Survivors may persist in bonding activities after the loved one dies. They may continue to go to places the two had enjoyed together. Or special funds may be named after the deceased. Streets may be named for them; or money may be given in their name to some charity (Unruh, 1983).

Dying persons also have certain rights. They have the right to be cared for by society or their intimates; and they are entitled to respect, status, and care. If at all feasible, people should be allowed to die where they wish. About 25 percent find their greatest help from the family, and over 90 percent of one sampling questioned desired to die at home, naturally and with dignity (Peterson, 1980). Over 85 percent would refuse heroic attempts to keep them alive. Yet over 70 percent are taken out of their homes and die in hospitals or nursing homes, "surrounded by strangers and often maintained by pipes and tubes" (Peterson, 1980, p. 932).

Putting Death in Perspective

Death as The Natural Culmination of Life. Ideally, we should view death as both natural and positive. Typically an individual's normal state is presumed to involve the best of health, while death is viewed as the ultimate "calamity" (Katchadourian, 1976, p. 52). Perhaps if "medicine could convey the notion that illness and death are part of life rather than aberrations imposed upon it, conceptual and practical gains in understanding the life cycle would be considerable" (p. 52). If we realize that ultimately everyone will share the same fate, we will also be able to comprehend that in life we should become "as one, aware and appreciative of our differences, and yet accepting that in our humanness, we are all alike" (p. 3). Such attitudes, by contrast with dread and fear, would not only improve the quality of life but also the quality of dying (Acceptance, 1975).

Developing Healthy Attitudes Toward Dying. Authorities advise that everyone seek to develop healthy attitudes toward dying. Robert J. Lifton speaks of achieving healthy attitudes toward death through attaining some variation of symbolic immortality. One man attains a certain biological or biosocial immortality through his children and descendents. He comes to understand that his life is a link between former and future generations and has its own place in history. This idea is expressed by Paul in a letter from his final imprisonment in Rome to his young apprentice Timothy: "As for me, already my life is being poured out on the altar, and the hour for my departure is upon me. I have run the great race; I have finished the course; I have kept the faith" (2 Tim 4:7). Creative immortality is gained through one's works—such as teaching, writing, or some creative art or craft. Natural immortality is through an individual's continuity with nature, "dust to dust," or recycling one's substance by rejoining the substance from which one came. Spiritual immortality refers to some afterlife in relation to the divinity (Simpson 1979; Lifton & Olson, 1974).

Kübler-Ross (1975) advises that people relate to death in various contexts, including viewing people in the dying process, attend-

ing their burials, or perhaps interacting with the body. She believes that we err in sheltering children from death and the dying, and that we are depriving them of an experience with which they should become familiar.

One reaction to death is acting as if the deceased has not lived at all. Such tie-breaking reflects the fact that in long-term relationships mutual patterns of living are a significant part of the survivor's life. These habits may require drastic alteration when the relationship is broken by death. This tie-breaking has received too little recognition as a part of the bereavement process. It means relinquishing the old roles that involved the departed, without acting as if the past had not existed, and then acquiring a new role congruent with the fact that the old relationship is dead (Rosenblatt, Walsh & Johnson, 1976).

Healthy attitudes toward death should be developed in the early years, sometimes through death education courses. Apparently such courses do not decrease death anxiety significantly during the course itself but result in less death anxiety later on. Changes in attitude are unlikely to be complete, if achieved at all, until some time has passed (Simpson, 1979).

Coping with the Death of Loved Ones. Death not only affects the dying but the loved ones who are left behind. Often their hardest task is the process of letting the dying go. A mother whose only son, a young adult, died of cancer, felt first a shock and then a certain numbness; and as she progressed through later stages of grief, she experienced certain psychosomatic symptoms. Finally she concluded that "grief cannot be hurried, but eventually an emotional balance returns. . . . You cannot bring back the one you love but you have to face reality. A change has occurred in my life, and my life must now have more meaning. I watched our son fight to live and stood by as he accepted death. He knew there was not much hope for him and became very brave. I could not disappoint him and I had to be strong for him" (Mize, 1975, p. 101).

Coping with a parent's death may be especially difficult. Usually a life-time of love is involved—besides, after parents die an individual feels exposed, recognizing that one's own generation comes next. A theme of anticipatory orphanhood throughout life helps middle-aged individuals—those most likely to sustain parents' loss—prepare for their death (Moss & Moss, 1983–84).

The reaction to another's death depends on several factors, one of which is an individual's feelings about the death of that specific person. One may feel differently depending on whether it is a young person, an older individual, or a terminally ill person. Another element is the degree of devotion felt toward the dying person. Watching a stranger die is not the same as seeing a loved one die. Also involved are matters of dependence and distance—whether one has been constantly caring for the dying person or has been physically removed from the place of death (Bischof, 1976).

Authorities on the subject of death generally stress the need to express sorrow, anger, and pain openly, and to deal with feelings honestly instead of holding them back. However, Klein (1978) suggests that some people do better working through their grief internally; individuals and subcultures have different ways of dealing with this experience.

Usually the most intense period of bereavement is immediately after the significant person has died. However, other intense periods involve preparation for, and participation in, the funeral service or memorial ceremony, and coming home afterward. The funeral or memorial service itself may provide a catharsis for deep feelings and help the individual achieve a reintegration and restabilization of the self. Even after the service is over, there is much to do in working through grief. There is the matter of coping with the meaninglessness of simple

daily routines because they are no longer shared with the deceased. Sometimes grief work is neurotic; it either persists too long, or is delayed and appears long after the death. When the pain of grief work is great it may not result in healing, but instead in sadistic actions toward others, or masochistic self-punishment.

Grief also takes its toll on health, at least temporarily. Older widows and widowers, 2 months after the loss of a spouse, reported a significant increase in new illnesses, and worsening of conditions already there, as well as greater use of medication, and poorer health in general. Women reported slightly more illnesses than men, perhaps because men have been conditioned to deny symptoms of weakness (Thompson, Breckinridge, Gallagher & Peterson, 1984).

Grief is sometimes portrayed as involving stages. The first, observes Miller, (1982), is the *impact stage*, characterized by numbness. In the next, or *recoil stage*, the truth of the loss begins to take hold, and one feels depressed and angry. It is during this stage that suicide by widows or widowers is most likely. In the final, or *readjustment stage*, a large majority of the bereaved sever their links with the past and face the future.

Grief, adds Miller, varies considerably according to the circumstances of the death. People have had time to adjust to losses sustained after a loved one's prolonged illness. In contrast, reactions to a loved one's suicide are especially painful, as the bereaved often have feelings of guilt. Also the community is less likely to be supportive in such cases, which adds to one's burden.

Another authority, Lee (1982), defines four stages in grief, the first being *shock*, especially in cases of sudden loss or natural disasters. A second stage is *cognitive resolution*, or coming, intellectually at least, to realize what has happened after a brief period of near-disbelief. After such realization, the bereaved may express *hostility*, or despair, or "overwhelming sadness" (p. 185). The final stage is *conative* (behavioral) *resolution*, or reorganization, which often occurs about 3 or 4 months after the loss; this stage may involve disposing of possessions the deceased left behind or becoming involved again in outside interests. If the loss was anticipated long in advance, much of the grief process may already have occurred.

Lee surmises that about 2 in 3 cases of grieving are normal. The third may involve abnormal reactions—for example, such behaviors as frigidity or impotence—and the sooner professional help is obtained the better. However, persons involved in helping the bereaved rarely possess in-depth knowledge of counseling or psychopathology. In any case it is assumed that the usual grief rituals—funerals, church services, and so forth, are of great help, to most people at least. Also essential are intimates who will listen to the bereaved and counsel them patiently.

Last Rites. Another task is taking care of the details of the final rite of passage—including those relating to family preferences, individual desire, and religious affiliation. Cremation and donating bodies to medical research, and contributing to worthy causes instead of sending lavish floral displays are increasingly common. Funeral directors, although unprepared to deal with extreme

cases, can provide considerable help through sympathetic listening, reassurance, patience, and helpful suggestions (Miller, 1982). Family physicians may also be of help, through their understanding of grief and of circumstances surrounding the death (Secundy, 1982.

Of considerable importance to the families involved, especially those of limited means, is the cost of funerals. Funeral expenses can mount rapidly, especially since costs are rarely itemized in advance. Embalming is unnecessary if the body is to be buried immediately, but many funeral directors simply assume it is to be done. State laws vary—some do not require it; in others it depends on how long the body is held before burial. A cheap pine box is the cheapest casket, but most people settle for a medium-priced one. Extras add up, too, including the costs of casket display, grave plot, and the funeral itself.

Some money can be saved by electing cremation, which is growing in popularity. Most Protestant denominations permit it, and Roman Catholics can request permission for it. Jewish and Greek Orthodox faiths oppose it, as do some Lutheran and fundamentalist Protestant churches.

Some individuals make all the final arrangements for themselves, including pre-

There is a growing concern over the cost of burial.

payment of expenses and making their wishes known. They may join a funeral or memorial society—a nonprofit society for helping people arrange "simple, dignified services at low cost" (Planning a funeral, 1982, p. 146). Such societies may advise regarding donating one's body to science, and they often recommend memorial services as alternatives to funerals. They do not carry out funeral arrangements themselves, but provide information about options. They also urge their members to discuss plans with their families, thus anticipating the reality of death (Funerals: The memorial service alternative, 1982).

Individuals should also be aware of any special funeral customs or rituals employed in their own faith. Overwhelmingly, the clergy in general favor some rite of passage and that it be public, in recognition of the dignity of the individual and to provide survivors support in their grief. Otherwise, there are religious differences regarding such matters as viewing and visiting, and whether a funeral should be traditional or not (Minton, 1982).

A CLOSING COMMENT

Significant changes are taking place in society's attitudes and practices regarding death. The subject itself is no longer taboo; and a host of psychologists, philosophers, and other professionals are debating the significant issues. A look at history and a glance around the world readily disclose that views and practices relating to death derive, often in obscure ways, from the total context of a culture; and they inevitably evolve at varying speeds, according ot the rapidity of change within society itself.

In the main, attitudes and practices relating to death in this society are becoming healthier, mostly because we are looking at them squarely and beginning to do something about them. Consider the decision by many persons to dispense with such costly traditions as purchasing fine caskets or having elaborate funerals. Nevertheless, we must realize that death cannot be turned into a wholly rational matter, because it may represent the loss of a self that one deeply values, even for those who believe that the self may assume another form in eternity.

SUMMARY

The topic of death has been accorded increased interest in recent years, sparked by issues concerning the definition of death, the experience of death, as reported by individuals who have had near death experience, and interventions to delay death, especially by life-sustaining machines. A degree of perspective is gained on such issues by examining attitudes and practices relating to death both historically and cross-culturally. Individuals, too, vary in their feelings about death, according to age, physical condition, and personality.

Practical issues on the matter relate to treatment of the dying, the right to die, coping with the death of loved ones and with the prospect of one's own ultimate demise, and developing appropriate attitudes toward death. Authorities recommend facing up to the topic with a view to establishing healthier attitudes toward it.

SUGGESTED READINGS

BAUM, S. K. (1983). Older people's anxiety about after life. *Psychological Reports, 52*(3), 895–898.

COOLIDGE, F. I. & FISH, C. E. (1983–1984). Dreams of the dying. *Omega: Journal of Death and Dying, 14*(1), 1–8.

GEYMAN, J. P. (1983). Dying and death of a family member. *Journal of Family Practice, 17*(1), 125–134.

GRAYSON, B. (1982). Near-death studies, 1981–1982: A review. *Anabiosis, 2*(2), 150–158.

GREEN, J. T. & FRIEDMAN, P. (1981). Near-death experiences in a southern California population. *Anabiosis, 3*(1), 77–95.

GREENE, F. G. (1983). Multiple mind/body perspectives and the out-of-body experience. *Anabiosis, 3*(1), 39–62.

GROTH-JUNCKER, A. & MCCUSKER, J. (1983). Where do elderly patients prefer to die? Place of death and patient characteristics of 100 elderly patients under the care of a home health care team. *Journal of the American Geriatrics Society, 31*(8), 457–461.

JETER, K. (1983). Analytic essay: Family stress and bereavement. *Marriage and the Family Review, 6*(1–2), 219–225.

LOVELL, A. (1983). Some questions of identity: Late miscarriage, still birth and prenatal loss. *Social Science and Medicine, 17*(11), 755–761.

MOSS, M. S. & MOSS, S. Z. (1983–84). The impact of parental death on middle-aged children. *Omega: Journal of Death and Dying. 14*(1), 65–75.

MOUNT, E. (1983). Individualism and our fears of death. *Death Education, 7*(1), 25–31.

RYAN, J. (1983–84). Silent barter. *Omega: Journal of Death and Dying, 14*(2), 145–154.

SOLOMON, J. K. & ALMQUIST, E. (1983). Psychogenic mortality syndrome: Choosing to die by the institutionalized elderly. *Death Education, 6*(4), 353–364.

STEPHENSON, P. H. (1983–84). "He died too quick!" The process of dying in a Hutterian colony. *Omega: Journal of Death and Dying. 14*(2), 127–134.

UNRUH, D. R. (1983). Death and personal history: Strategies of identity perservation. *Social Problems, 39*(3), 340–351.

WALTON, D. N. (1983). *Ethics of withdrawal of life-support systems: Case studies on decision-making in intensive care.* Westport, CN: Greenwood Press.

CHAPTER SIXTEEN

Perspectives on Adulthood

SOME GENERALIZATIONS

The foregoing survey of the adult life stages yields a few general conclusions. First of all, our humanness dictates a certain commonality within our lives, while the unique blending of individual heredity and patterns of experience creates infinite variations within them. To a certain extent we all remain, in varying degrees, out of synchrony with each other. While the fundamental principles that govern development bind us all, we may be grappling with different tasks at somewhat different stages in our development.

The Unevenness of Progress Through Life

In a way, progression across the life span is uneven, like broken-field running. It is inaccurate to think of everyone as experiencing a gradual and equal decline in each

decade between the ages of 20 and 70. Decline may be focused in one or two decades, while plateaus or even improvements may occur during others. In other words, changes in behavior do not follow a straight-line course across the years. Nor do changes in the body proceed at a homogeneous pace. Individuals differ greatly in pace of aging and rates at which their various sensory and motor mechanisms age. An individual can be old in one respect and somewhat young in another—hence, any unitary index of aging has little use or meaning. Each individual should learn to employ that "mixture of strategies that will be for him or her optimum" (Welford, 1980, p. 210).

Neither do individual personalities and life trajectories follow a straight course. In the Longitudinal Study of Transitions, which involved lower-middle-class men and women, goals, commitments, values, and self-concepts proved less continuous than had been expected. One reason may have been the increasing velocity of sociohistorical change (Fiske, 1980).

Growth processes themselves are unique for every individual and do not follow a set sequence. Of course, there are normal transitions in life such as finishing school, graduation, leaving home, getting married, or having a first child. However, not everyone finds these events major turning points. For many people, less anticipated events— even inner experiences—sometimes abrupt, sometimes stretched over a period—have far greater impact on feelings and actions. These may include such events as falling in love or reaching some peak of achievement (Fiske, 1980, p. 344).

The Predictability of Personality

Despite this unevenness, development does not proceed in a random fashion. Within broad limits, individuals grow along paths that are predictable from earlier points in their lives and from knowing something about their personality structure, ways of coping, success in adapting to earlier life events, and expectations of life (Neugarten, 1971). In order to understand people, it is important to be familiar with their previous life experiences (Lowenthal & Chiriboga, 1973).

Individual variations in certain characteristics, especially, appear to persist over the years—for example, activity level. Individuals may slow down somewhat over the years, but they will tend to remain in the same position relative to their age peers, throughout life. The incentive to engage in activities also persists through the life span, although approaches to them may change and barriers to participation may exist (Wigdor, 1980). Another characteristic that persists over the years is degree of conventionality. Unconventional thought is one of the most stable characteristics from early adolescence to late adulthood, as are the related traits of rebel-

liousness and sex-typed behaviors (Haan & Day, 1974). Although in adolescence, females are a bit more conventional than males, they become less conventional by young adulthood; and by middle age, they are even less so than males.

Certain other life-style characteristics, such as humanitarianism, intellectualism, aestheticism, and practicality, tend to become more important from late adolescence to early adulthood and to remain stable or even increase a bit over the adult years (Haan & Day, 1974). By their late 20s most people have established core interest and value patterns, which in general resemble those of their parents.

Participants in the Berkeley longitudinal studies rated at age 30, and by different raters at age 70, demonstrated consistency in 10 of 16 personality variables over the 40-year period. The most stable personality variable was talkativeness; other stable ones were self-esteem, excitability, cheerfulness, and energy output. It is possible that these characteristics have at least in part a genetic base because they were stable not only among a sample of mothers over a 10-year period, but also among their children from adolescence to middle age (Mussen, Eichorn & Honzik, 1980).

Although a degree of consistency is the rule, earlier characteristics do sometimes appear to change. In the Grant study, at least half the men who as adolescents had appeared colorless had become interesting and full of life by their mid-40s (Vaillant, 1977). One such individual took up deep-sea diving; another had an exciting love affair; and still another, a frightened, mother-dominated boy in adolescence became a well-known and unusually independent scientist.

Besides, individual variation in the age at which successive stages appear is large, and composite patterns (statistical patterns) round out whatever stages, if any, exist. In other words, the lumping together of test scores obscures widespread individual variations (Botwinik, 1977).

Viable Alternatives

Over and over, life histories demonstrate the legitimacy of highly varied life styles. In Ross Firestone's book, *The Success Trip* (1976), thirty-four people who have been successful in a variety of fields, including such diverse persons as Albert Ellis, Howard Cosell, and Mike Wallace, describe in what manner they achieved success. The predictably common denominators were driving ambition, intelligence, and hard work. Otherwise there was no pattern, because some were rich and some poor; some were pushed to achieve when they were children, and others did not find their niche until they were well into their adult years. Many of them indicated that sheer luck had much to do with reaching the top, but the majority added that one must have the potential for taking advantage of this luck.

CAUTIONS REGARDING STAGE THEORY

As discussed earlier in this volume, the value of stage theory is that it establishes a certain order in viewing the life experience. However, it often suggests a precision that may not exist. For example, the woman's life cycle is commonly viewed as a sequence of inflexible stages: "home-centered activities in childhood, work before and after marriage, bearing and rearing children, caring for the retired husband, widowhood, and death" (Movius, 1976, p. 57). These hypothetical stages do not take into account such life discontinuities as returning to school or developing new interests (Lopata, 1971).

Stage theory erroneously suggests that development is a unitary process. For example, formal thinking normally emerges in adolescence, but the ability to use such thinking is not global. A particular adolescent may be capable of employing formal reasoning in science but not with semantic content (Berzonsky, 1978).

Objections may also be raised to the characterization of particular age stages. Erikson (1982) rejects viewing the last years in terms of finality, when life is over. Every life stage has its developmental tasks and capacity for growth. "Old people," to use his terminology, have at least one great advantage—they can see the totality of life and how it all "hangs together."

Chance Encounters. Sheer chance interrupts the progression of individuals through predictable invariant stages (Bandura, 1982). Developmental models of behavior presume a certain determinism in which early experiences define the course of subsequent development. Socialization theorists, in general, portray life patterns as the outcome of childhood socialization. Stages theorists define development in terms of unvarying life stages, preordained.

However, paths are strongly influenced by chance encounters or unplanned meetings between people who do not know each other. For example, Nancy Davis, later Nancy Reagan, while an actress began receiving announcements through the mail of Communist meetings intended for someone who had her same name. Concerned that her career might be harmed by this mistaken identity, she arranged a meeting through her film director with Ronald Reagan, then president of the Screen Actors' Guild. In this case the mere likeness of names, and a mix-up of the postal service, altered her life. In his Nobel Lecture Herbert Brown tells how receipt of a gift from his girl friend launched his career. If she had not given him this particular chemistry book, because it was the least expensive one available in the university bookstore, his career might have taken another direction.

The impact of chance encounters depends somewhat on one's readiness to be influenced in particular ways. Lives cannot be shaped independently of an individual's own preparedness for the impact. These chance meetings have their greatest effect when one finds the persons they meet satisfying so that their encounter often leads to lasting relationships. The effect of such encounters is less predictable when an individual does not have strongly developed standards for assessing impact. People can better resist the entrapment of such encounters if there are societal safeguards in the form of previous education. Affiliation with individuals and groups is greater when the rewards are high.

According to society's own conception of stages, people are assigned age roles. As a result most people submit to the age stereotypes foisted upon them. According to Montagu & Coleman (1977), however, people should remain forever young in spirit. They should preserve "the spirit of a child, of youthfulness, of inquisitiveness—an open-mindedness that is free to consider everything, a sense of humor, playfulness—all of these qualities we are designed to develop rather than outgrow" (p. 46).

The Divergence of Physiological and Psychological Development

It is important to remember that "there is not necessarily a correlation between chronological and biologic age. . . . The aging process varies from individual to individual . . ." (Hicks, Funkenstein, Dysken & Davis, 1980, p. 769). For most people, life is not all downhill after they have passed their physical peak. Instead, people move "toward greater comfort, candor, and an objective sense of self as displayed by now 40- and 50-year old people who have been followed over a period of time" (Haan, 1976, p. 64). Even in the young-old, and often in the old-old years, large numbers of people continue to grow, arriving at successively higher stages of self-actualization.

A FEW RECOMMENDATIONS

Research Needs

If people are to make the most of adulthood, they need to have the results of certain kinds of research. It is especially important that the life styles of people who age successfully be studied. In a longitudinal study of aging begun in 1958 by Dr. Nathan W. Shock, director of the Gerontology Research Center in Baltimore, a panel of over 1,000 men, aged 20 to 103, have been seen at least once, and over 100 of them at least four times. While they are not representative of the entire population, they do portray aging under favorable conditions (Tobin, 1977).

Certain categories of adults have been almost ignored or underrepresented. Psychological studies of the elderly have been based largely on institutionalized subjects, partly because it is hard to obtain the cooperation of the aged in a community for psychological testing. Studies on community samples are often biased because they overrepresent the middle class (Thomae, 1980).

On certain topics men have been neglected. In studies of sex equality and love, women have held the limelight. Gardiner (1978) suggests a need to go beyond romantic heterosexual love and to create a new literature not solely based on women's love for men. She sees as the core an undeniable female relationship between mother and daughter.

In most areas of adult research, women have been misrepresented or neglected. Empirical research especially is scattered and theoretical work only beginning (Barnett & Baruch, 1978). This point of view is often reflected in researchers' choice of subjects for study. In one major study of menopause, working women were excluded from the sampling, apparently because they were too atypical (VanKeep & Kellerhals, 1975).

Nor are adequate differentiations among

subcategories of women often made; sales clerks and physicians, homemakers and career committed are all lumped together (Barnett & Baruch, 1978). Nevertheless, various aspects of work status—such as degree of commitment and status level of occupation—are highly significant for women's experience, especially at middle age.

Two matters relevant to human development have been largely overlooked, the first concerning the sheer uniqueness of the individual (Howe, 1982). The individual should be used more as a study unit. The second topic deals with time dimension, for when events occur is as important as what events occur. The so-called developmental research is somewhat static as individuals may be observed briefly on only a few occasions and average scores for groups are compiled.

Finally, research regarding adulthood must greatly increase in quantity and improve in quality if significant theories are to emerge. A common theme among researchers "is the apparent absence of convincing findings on the nature of developmental processes in adulthood and the observation that directionality of age changes is in considerable doubt" (Schaie, 1973a, p. 151). As the pieces fall into place and gaps are closed, a more meaningful psychology of adulthood will emerge.

Many authorities are urging that developmental psychologists become more concerned with naturalistic ecology. Certainly "the description of relationships in naturalistic environments, while not sufficient to establish that factor X does cause factor Y, is necessary for such a conclusion. Yet historically, description is not one of the psychologist's delights—it is a second-class method of study . . . because it does not permit one to infer causality" (p. 336).

Improving Relations Between Age Groups

Much has been made of the need to improve relationships between youth and their parents. Communication between them is poor and relatively infrequent. Adolescents talk with their age peers far more than with adults; and the need to improve the relations between middle-aged and older persons is just as great.

Tice (1982) believes it more important than formerly to insure a sense of continuity between the generations. In times past the generations engaged in many activities together—for example, when they preserved food for the winter through picking, drying, and canning. Family traditions and family recipes were passed down through the generations, as grandparents or aging relatives shared their knowledge and told stories of their past. In contrast, these days occupations are fragmented, family structures changed, and age groupings more distinct. Increasingly, the retired are living in special housing and communities of their own.

One way of improving relations between the middle-aged and the elderly is to provide those older people assistance to live in their own homes who otherwise must be cared for by institutions or individuals. There are many individuals in long-term care facilities that need not be there (Hare & Haske, 1983–84). Many older people are given a higher level of care than is necessary anyhow. Most of them would prefer not living in a nursing home if it were not necessary, for going into one means severing ties in the community, dependence, separation from society, and isolation.

Many long-term care patients are taken care of in their own homes or in homes of relatives, which normally presents great difficulty. The caretaker is usually a spouse or sibling about the same age who may be having problems, too, or a daughter-in-law who has her own marital and family priorities and often is in the workforce.

Another problem is the sacrifice of privacy. One survey showed that 4 in 5 home owners over age 55 with large homes would prefer maintaining separate apartments in their homes to sharing their homes with an-

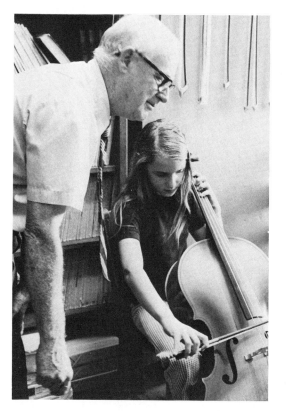

A sense of continuity between generations is important.

other. The older person, like the host, could also benefit from the privacy thus achieved.

Such problems are complicated because families' own life cycles do not always match those of their individual members. When parents require assistance with certain problems of aging, their adult children may be facing problems of climacteric, menopause, and retirement; grandchildren are experiencing the problems of adolescence, new marriages, or first children; great-grandchildren are being born and demanding the attentions of parents and grandparents (Kirschner, 1979).

The institutionalization of support for the elderly has weakened intergenerational cooperation, but it has also reduced a powerful source of tension. For one thing, neither generation can coerce the other on the basis of money. On the other hand, the elderly no longer have an image of "abject dependency" (Bengtson & Traes, 1980, p. 414). Public services and Social Security have mostly eliminated the necessity of older people being supported by their children. Also the childcare function of grandparents has diminished because of demographic forces that have made small grandchildren a phenomenon of midlife and not later years.

Communication between the generations is still quite frequent, partly as a result of such factors as "universal literacy, the development of a reliable and inexpensive postal service, the ubiquitous telephone, the family automobile, the expansion of the highway, the discount air fare. . . . Kinspeople are more accessible today than ever before" (Bengtson & Traes, 1980, p. 414).

Tensions may also arise between young and middle-aged adults, or between the young-old and old-old. Often middle-aged workers are bypassed for promotion in favor of younger ones. Or young adults may resent middle-aged ones for clinging too long to society's reins. The young-old may avoid the old-old, who represent what they realize with dread they will shortly become, and with whom they are unwillingly lumped into the same general category.

The writer believes that intermingling should be encouraged, not forced, and probably for brief rather than long periods, unless cultural factors make such extended association natural and satisfying.

Life-Span Education

Compton and Parish (1978) stress the importance of adult educators expanding adult learners' perspectives to achieve a broader world view and increase their awareness of their personal relationships to that larger world. Nations that hold power will use it intelligently if their citizens are world-minded. Adults must realize the interdependence of all nations and the need for a global society. A humanistic society rather than a thing-centered materialistic one must arise.

During the past years, the goals of technology and science have overshadowed humanistic ideals and produced an overwhelming materialistic emphasis. Education itself has catered to society, which is perceived as "a producing and consuming unit" (p. 31). Little attention has been paid the quality of civilization and more to a "concept of progress measured in terms of the gross national product . . ." (p. 31).

Education should help adults to conceptualize and structure an emerging society of the future. Adults should be educated to a "heightened awareness of the profound changes that are taking place in the world. They must be sensitive to the implications of such changes for all human institutions" (p. 32). Only thus can people begin to make

order out of "the chaos" of their lives and achieve new directions and hope for humankind (Compton & Parish, 1978, p. 73).

Environmental Control and Social Engineering

It is increasingly recognized that exploitation of the environment can work for or against us. Therefore, the varying impact of particular environments on different age groups and kinds of people should be determined. For example, the tempo and conditions of adult life should become properly related to adult physiological processes. One reason for the increase in psychosomatic ailments and life stresses is that the socially defined pace of life in industrial societies is "out of phase with its basic metabolic rhythms" (Katchadourian, 1976, p. 51).

Social engineering, employed to change our environment, might take many forms. Butler (1975a) recommends diverting the money now spent on spectator sports to facilities that encourage physical recreation for the entire population. The large chunks of public park space now "gobbled up by golfers could be more equitably divided among hikers, swimmers, and other sports enthusiasts" (p. 367).

Much emphasis is being placed today on environmental hazards to health. One health hazard is the profusion of new synthetic chemical products, including cancer-causing food additives, the discharge of asbestoslike fibers into the air and water, and birth-control pills. Although the birth-control pill has "freed millions of users from sexual constraint, it has proved, in more than a decade on the market, to have serious, even fatal side effects for some users. And the returns on its long-term consequences are not yet in" (Nation of guinea pigs, 1979, p. 10).

Some cities provide better environments than do others. One study of the quality of life in metropolitan areas considered several categories: economic development; political and government activities; environmental safety; climate; health and education; and social, recreational, and cultural activities. The best large city to live in proved to be Portland, Oregon. The best medium-sized city was Eugene, Oregon, and the best small one Lacrosse, Wisconsin (Kent, 1980).

LOOKING AHEAD

Planning and imaginative forecasting should become an integral aspect of government, social and educational programs, and research. Even now, although the dim outlines of the future are just emerging, contingency programs subject to continuing modification should be devised. Here are some possible developments.

Changes in the Family

Conger (1981) points out that in the 1980s the future of the family has displaced the tremendous concern of the 1960s and 1970s with youth. Pickett (1977) agrees, predicting that the family will remain a basic element.

The following are a summary of some predictions concerning the future of the family:

1. Harry and Joan Constantine (1973) believe that ultimately, lifetime partners who have sex only with each other will constitute a substantial minority. Most families will center around pairs who "share a primary but not exclusive commitment." The family will be permeable, allowing new members of other families to join it.
2. James Ramey (1976) foresees an increase in multiadult households, a situation that will afford an enriched environment for both children and adults, all of whom will relate easily to each other, regardless of kinship.
3. Jessie Bernard (1975) believes that marriage in the future can only succeed on an egalitarian basis. Many women have come to realize that traditional marriage favors their husbands. They reject the present inequities of most marriages, such as when the woman holds

a job outside the home and still does most of the housework. Some women will marry but refuse to have children; those who have children will insist that parenting and childrearing should be shared.
4. Other authorities foresee a two-step marriage; the first phase will be legal cohabitation; and in the second, permission to have children will be granted. Among the young, the de facto two-step marriage often exists already.

Rubenstein (1982) describes the current dual-career family and predicts little change ahead, at least short-term. Dual-career marriages, in which the wife makes more money, involve more problems than do those where the husband is chief provider. Social epidemiologist, Carlton Horung, found that 4 in 5 men in this situation received psychological abuse from their wives and were more likely to die prematurely. For underachieving men married to overachieving wives, the death rate from ischemic heart disease is eleven times greater than the norm. Moreover, the higher the woman's status relative to her husband's, the higher was the men's mortality rate.

This financial inequality hurts the husbands in other ways. Traditionally, money has meant power in marriage—besides, many men evaluate their masculinity in terms of the size of their pay checks. Hence, a large majority feel threatened when the wife earns more.

Nor does there seem to be much chance of change in the years just ahead. Researchers Regula Jerzog and Jerald Bachman found that just 13 percent of males in a population of 3,000 high school seniors wanted their wives not to work, and 92 percent of the girls expected to have a career; both sexes said couples should share housework equally. However, when asked to imagine having their own children, they discarded their progressive views. The woman should stay at home with preschool age children, and the men should be the chief providers. Both sexes opposed any arrangement by which the husband should spend less time on the job than the wife.

Conger (1981) portrays the women's movement as the single most significant event of the 1970s. He believes that women's need to be perceived as individuals is an evolutionary process that will persist, despite resistance from a good many men and some women. Whatever solutions emerge in this area will be highly significant for all areas of family and all human relationships.

In short, the family of the future will involve varied "family profiles. The traditional family, as we have known it, will survive in a smaller, more flexible form, but it will be joined by other forms which were once considered deviant" (Pickett, 1977, p. 332). The boundaries of marriage will shift and change, with continued variations. Future marriages will contain forms as contrasting as traditional unions and homosexual marriages. For "those who like kaleidoscopes, the future is beautiful indeed. Those who prefer a still life may find it less to their liking" (p. 332). Pickett concludes by observing that most social scientists' future projections are based on current findings, and forecasting almost never takes into consideration the inevitable "dramatic scientific achievements or the sudden events that change the course of history" (p. 332).

Predictions about the family's future continue to appear in a steady stream. Herb Seal, in his book *Alternative Life Styles,* predicts that tribal families will appear even in the middle class, as a reaction to the somewhat isolated life styles that have emerged from a complex, computerized, automated society. Seal predicts increasing equality in the family for both women and children. Children may have their own houses to allow some alternative to being with their parents, and teenagers might live in them at times while they work out identity problems or simply to escape the constant meddling and nagging of parents who want to impose (Revival of tribalism? 1979).

Slesin (1979) notes that since only 7 percent of American households fit the traditional mold of working husband, wife at home, and two children, contemporary housing needs have changed. Cooked food and facilities for child care might be available in housing complexes; or work and residence might be united in the same place. Large housing complexes might have daycare centers; or there might be several bedrooms in an apartment complex for single persons with perhaps three living rooms. Housing in general would contain more storage space, no more interior kitchens, low window sills, and other improvements in the allocation of space. In general, the house would be "reinvented." No longer would houses be built with master bedrooms when there are no masters, or dining rooms when most people no longer dine in a formal sense.

Potential for Increasing the Life Span

Even more dramatic changes may be in store for us. In the future we may know enough about aging to modify the process directly—perhaps by altering the body chemistry—or indirectly, through health care and improved nutrition. Also, genetic factors that cause such changes as baldness or graying may be modifiable. While humans may never be able to live forever, as a result of future breakthroughs "they can live much longer and more comfortably, mostly free from the violent ravages of disease, with perhaps a gradual and fairly predictable decline toward eventual death" (Butler, 1975c, p. 17).

Conjectures on Longevity. More dramatic changes in longevity may occur. Since 1900 life expectancy has increased from 47 to 74. From 3000 B.C., the Bronze Age, to

1900 the gain was 29 years, which means as much gain occurred in just 84 years as in the past 3,000 (Today's senior citizens, 1984).

Already the normal life span has been extended in certain species. In a study of rats fed 60 percent of the normal intake, their mean length of life was extended. Two-thirds of these rats lived longer than the longest-lived rat fed full rations (Yu, Masoro, Murata, Bertrand & Lynd, 1982). Aging is apparently affected by three different but interrelated systems: the brain, the endocrine system which secretes hormones, and the immune system which makes numerous antibodies that combat disease (Batten, 1984). The brain does not seem to deteriorate with age and its neurons might continue 150 to 200 years if other systems did not fail. However, "just as muscle cells are designed to contract, so the brain's cells are designed to receive stimuli, and just as regular exercise makes muscles strong, so regular stimulation keeps the brain healthy," says Marian Diamond, of the University of California at Berkeley.

One cause of aging is genetic—some people simply live longer; but life style makes a difference, too, including stress, diet, and environment. Seventh Day Adventists who are vegetarians live 7 years longer on average than do other Americans.

Various approaches have proved successful in prolonging the lives of certain animals. Rats, carefully tended and provided with "toys" producing a stimulating environment, lived an average of 900 days instead of the normal average of 700 days. Mice fed low-calorie diets, supplemented with vitamins and minerals, lived from 25 to 100 percent longer (Batten, 1984).

If no special research effort is made, the date for controlling aging will be delayed until the beginning of the next century, which is too late to help most of us living today. Some opponents of such research believe that the world would become populated with "decrepit, patched up, wizened, senile people, perhaps fed through tubes and moving with the aid of electronic prostheses" (Strehler, 1977, p. 54). Such a picture is simply not true, because the life span can hardly be increased if the body's overall condition is not improved. Persons who lived 150 years would be correspondingly healthy for most of their life span, and even those of a less advanced

The number of older people is increasing relative to the general population.

age would have bodies like those of much younger persons.

Many scientists have concluded that aging and cancer are "opposite sides of the same coin. Normal cell division contains all the body's natural repair systems, but, as people age, cells divide less efficiently. There is cellular damage and errors accumulate in the cell nucleus. When repair mechanisms fail altogether and abnormal cells begin to liberate, the result is cancer" (Cranston, 1980, p. 17). Untangling the secrets of molecular and cellular changes basic to the aging process will possibly lead to cures for many medical problems, from "cancer to senile dementia, kidney failure, and hardening of the arteries, among others" (pp. 17–18).

Cranston notes the mushrooming number of older people and the tremendous need to win battles against crippling disabilities and killer diseases in later years. He raises the question: Why do we want old people around? Will they supply solutions possibly only from persons with long and vast experience? As George Bernard Shaw once wrote: "Men do not live long enough. They are, for all purposes of high civilization, mere children when they die" (Cranston, 1980, p. 18).

The potential impact of a greatly expanded life span would produce a revolution in human societies. Because of the vastly better health and the greater time available to assimilate the world's wonders and wisdom, the mentality of the future will be more advanced than that of today. And since the healthy middle years of life would at least double, people would have more time to contribute to society. Professionals today require many years for their training; if their posttraining years doubled, they could make a far greater contribution than at present.

Besides, if machines take over more of the burdensome, repetitive tasks, human beings, with their vastly increased physical resources, will be able to experience more creatively the varied worlds of music, art, poetry, and entertainment. However, such a utopia will be made possible for the readers of this book only if society provides far greater support for aging research than it does at present.

Questions are even being raised about how long it is desirable to live (Batten, 1984). Philosopher Thomas Hobbes believed that a stringent life and early death were best for most species, because only the fittest would survive and reproduce. Many people predict that for humans—if they lived much longer—conflicts would occur between generations, as older people held on to jobs. In informal surveys on this topic, which the author has taken in her college classes across the years, an overwhelming majority would settle for the normal life span and would oppose vast government expenditures to underwrite research designed to increase it.

Population Control

The quality of life in the future will relate in no small measure to the number of persons on this planet, and to what kind of people they are. Dr. Kingsley Dunham, a geologist, notes that the world's resources are "nonrenewable and finite" and that unless population growth can be curbed, famine and pollution could lead to mass death within a few decades (p. 6). In consequence, people must be called upon increasingly to control their personal parenting desires for the good of society (Population proliferation, 1973, p. 6).

"Short of nuclear annihilation, the greatest threat to humanity," writes Szulc (1984), "is, ironically, its own sheer mass. . . . What could happen by the mid-21st century (when babies born in this decade approach old age) defies imagination, unless acceptable ways are found of curtailing population growth" (p. 16). The world's population has doubled over the past two decades; already "over half the world's people live in cities that cannot house, feed, or support them" (p. 17). In some places, notably Africa, "mass starvation may become inevitable."

Donald Mann, president of Negative Population Growth paints a scenario of doom (Simon, 1983). He points out that in 1900 the world population was 1.6 billion, a figure it took millions of years to reach; but increases that great now occur every 15 to 20 years. The Global Report to the President, a committee of experts, projected that in just 17 more years, hundreds of thousands of animals and plant species may have disappeared; half the forests will be gone; and severe water and energy shortages will have arrived, all being the effect of sheer numbers. The only solution is population control, best achieved through tax incentives to have smaller families. Overpopulation has the effect of reducing the carrying capacity of the environment.

In contrast, Julian Simon, economics professor, notes that the resource base does not remain fixed—people continue to create more. Even metals, the natural supplies of which are diminishing, may be recycled. As for energy, the sun affords an infinite future potential.

As one option, Sol Tax, an anthropologist, visualizes model colonies isolated from the rest of the world, though perhaps not from each other, dotted around the globe. The model colony system might even develop into a sort of international university, serving as a kind of international technical core (Next 30 years, 1977).

The idea of placing large artificial structures in space for permanent human habitation has aroused increasing interest. The idea is to implement the "concept of self-contained, spinning worldlets assembled at the stable earth-moon, LaGrangian points (mathematically defined regions of space leading and trailing the moon in its orbit around the earth)" (Setting up model space colonies, 1979, p. 14). Lunar minerals and solar energy would allow colonies of 10,000 or more to support themselves in orbit through their own industry and agriculture. The human interaction aspects of such settlements might be worked out in simulated colonies where intended space dwellers might devise their own living patterns, in the same way that societies have evolved over the centuries.

Genetics. In another area, genetics, giant strides are being made; much debate arises concerning how far man should go in attempting to control his own genetic destiny. Cal Tech biologist, James Bonnes, points out that countless millions of organisms evolved on earth have vanished; he suggests that humans should create a new and better species, through selective breeding (Foote, 1982). The idea would be to select for such characteristics as longevity, energy, intelligence, and freedom from genetic disease. However, molecular geneticist, Robert Sinsheimer, doubts that such powers would be used solely for positive purposes and questions tampering with the human gene pool.

Issues Relating to Adoption. Genetic advances, in terms of increasing fertility options, and more sophisticated genetic counseling for both parent and offspring, are raising issues about the rights of adoptees and offspring of surrogate mothers (Rosenfeld, 1981). A 33-year-old leukemia victim requiring a bone marrow transplant, had been adopted as an infant and was trying desperately to locate some family member as a possible donor through gaining access to sealed records. However, in almost every state records are sealed by law when babies are adopted; an amended birth certificate lists the adoptive parents as the child's legal ones. Part of the reason for such laws was the stigma previously attached to illegitimacy.

Nevertheless, groups have formed through the country to help adoptees find their natural or birth parents, perhaps partly because there are seven times as many adopted children as others among psychiatric patients. In one case an adoptee married a birth parent. Another time a birth mother found out that her son's fiancee was her own daughter.

Adoptees do not have enough information to receive adequate genetic counseling.

At the University of Washington geneticists discovered five cases where birth mothers found that the children they had given up for adoption would have a 50-50 chance of being afflicted with a genetic disease. Attempts to find the birth parents in such cases often involve difficult protracted searches and negotiations.

Individuals who were conceived by artificial insemination, perhaps over 100,000 Americans, do not know who their fathers are nor do their legal parents. In such cases records are poor, if any; the legal status of such insemination is cloudy. In one case an obstetrical resident noted an unusual blue birthmark, exactly like one he himself had, on the thigh of a newborn he was in the process of delivering. As a medical student he had been a sperm donor and concluded that he must be the child's genetic father.

Still another problem is that of surrogate mothers, women who bear babies, often conceived through use of the father's sperm, that they have agreed to deliver to a couple. The status of such infants is doubtful, particularly if the surrogate mother decides to keep the baby.

Relationships Between Generations

By the year 2000 a sharp increase will occur in numbers of persons aged 85 and over, an estimated 6.7 million. The over-age-65 population will double between 2010 and 2019 and almost double again in the years 2020 to 2029, assuming a further reduction in mortality rates (Butler, 1983).

This progressive graying of America, or the increasing average age of our population, may have several effects. In time increasingly larger numbers of older people must be maintained by smaller numbers of younger ones. Moreover, because of their larger numbers, the elderly's demands for special benefits will have greater force. Consequently, warn some sociologists, there may develop "a war between the ages that [will]

make the generation gap of the 1960s seem tame" (End of youth culture, 1977).

Besides, as the proportion of younger to older people declines, the nation's preoccupation with matters of youth may decrease. There may be fewer pop music fans, and less juvenile programming on television. After decades of stress on very active sports, recreation may focus on less energetic pursuits. There has already been a revival of more sedate, leisurely pastimes such as ballroom dancing and ocean liner cruises.

Older people can also be expected to acquire more sophistication and power. They are becoming increasingly better educated and are gaining more income and acquiring greater experience in promoting their concerns.

Where parents and children are concerned, the line is increasingly difficult to distinguish between legitimate parental authority and their children's rights (Cory, 1982). In a survey of 1,002 residents of Los Angeles, aged 17 to 94 (42 percent of them parents), the majority lent strong support to parental guidance in teenagers' sex lives when asked whether they would side with the parents or their teenage child. They would allow teenagers more freedom in matters of educational choice, personal grooming, and religion. With regard to sex, 60 percent would support the father who asks the pharmacist not to sell his 14-year-old son condoms after learning that the son had bought some. Respondents were split about 50-50 on whether the father may insist on going to a doctor with his 14-year-old-son who thinks he might have VD. Yet 70 percent would support the 14-year-old girl whose parents ask the family doctor not to see her when they find out that she has asked the doctor for birth control advice. Just 42 percent supported parents who would insist that their 12-year-old son cut his hair to a length that they liked.

The respondents were sympathetic with some of the parents' concerns about their children's religion but not others. About 4 in 5 (78 percent) supported parents who wouldn't let their 14-year-old girl accept a scholarship to attend a school run by advocates of an oriental religion, and 71 percent would back parents who made their 10-year-old son go to church with them even though he had decided that there was no God. The greatest support for the adolescents came on such less significant issues as length of hair.

A certain amount of generational friction may be inevitable. A study of fathers indicated that they perceived emerging values and behaviors as the inevitable concomitant of change, others as matters of personal conviction (Nydegger, Mitteness & O'Neil, 1983). They perceived past generations as strongly familistic and changes in this area as major. Almost three-fourths (72 percent) disapproved younger generations' diminished interest in marriage and children, and blamed them for the "imminent collapse of the family" (p. 542). They also strongly disapproved the young's rejection of the Protestant Ethic, which endorses fiscal responsibility and the value of work.

Significantly, the fathers saw their generation as amidst certain long-term, consistent trends, including rejection of social morality. At least half the changes they attributed to historical processes outside personal control; the others, with which they disagreed, to younger people's "wrong-headed" decisions. The continuation of these disapproved trends is interpreted as a sort of "generational ethnocentrism." In any case, change makes such differences inevitable and the matter of distinct generations a fact of life.

On the other hand, as the generations share more common experiences the generation gap may not grow as predicted, but rather, it may narrow (When family, 1983). Besides, older generations are much better educated than formerly; hence, they keep up with the current trends and are better able to relate to their middle-age children—and even grandchildren. The current emphasis on continuous renewal throughout adulthood should reduce the gap and enable all generations to grow and help each other.

The Impact of Futurism

The growing emphasis on futurism should afford a better perspective on these matters. Futurism focuses on anticipating technological and scientific advances and making the most of their effects (Spekke, 1976).

Paul Dickson calls futurism the "fastest growing educational phenomenon in history, the most important new concept of government in a hundred years, invaluable, too, for industry and a major breakthrough in human thinking" (Worst forecasts, 1978, p. 127).

Another factor is the rapid pace of change in all life areas. The structure of organizations, patterns of work life, scientific ideas, even vocabularies, are changing so fast that people are experiencing a certain "future shock." Meanwhile, people should realize that there is no escape from the future—they cannot turn back the clock (Mortimer & Simmons, 1978). Nor can a science of adulthood simply be extrapolated from psychologies of earlier stages. While much can be learned from them, their assumptions about adults must be tested throughout the life span. Until recently most longitudinal studies originated in child research suggested that the consequences of what happened in the early years would be with a person forever. However, as subjects in such studies grow older, it became apparent that changes can occur (Lowenthal, 1977).

The study of adulthood raises complex questions extending into all areas of human life. Hence, Lerner and Spanier (1978) endorse moving from "unidisciplinary, noninteractive, static views of individuals, social units, and contexts to an interdisciplinary, dynamic, interactional conception of individual and social changes across the life span, social context, and history" (p. 328).

Already increasing attention is being paid the complex interactional features of family life structures. For example, at one time researchers focused on how the mother affects the child; later they began to consider how each affects the other. More recently—and perhaps partly because computers make such involved research more feasible—interactions within whole networks are being studied (Pruchno, Blow & Smyer, 1984). Networks may be viewed as people around whom a web is spun as multiple life events interweave several lives. The networks themselves are seen as changing over time, as roles of participants and participants themselves change. One aspect of such study may involve considering how a single life-event experienced by one participant may impinge on all the others. Such an approach departs from the traditional analysis of individuals, toward one accounting for the networking effect of multiple lives. This writer perceives validity in both, each approach helping to validate and give meaning to the other.

Considering the brief history of adult psychology, tremendous gains have been made. Undoubtedly, the growing focus on this area will give us insights impossible to imagine at present. The challenge is to find ways to convert this information into more rewarding life styles at all stages of aging. Meanwhile, considering the constantly changing environments in which humans interact, replications of earlier research are desirable and maintaining a permanently tentative attitude becomes necessary.

SUMMARY

The survey of adult life stages, as provided in this book, yields certain generalizations: (1) Progress in life is relatively uneven. (2) Consistency of personality development is the rule, despite some change. (3) Physical and psychological health interrelate but are not locked in tandem. Stage theory allows a certain orderliness in viewing adult life, but

its shortcomings should be taken into account.

Recommendations for improving the quality of adult life include fostering more adequate research, improving relationships between age groups, making adequate provision for lifelong education, and encouraging environmental control and social engineering. Especially important is imaginative forecasting and planning for the future, subject to continuous modification.

SUGGESTED READINGS

ABELES, R. P., TIETELBAUM, M. S., & RILEY, M. W. (Eds.). (1982). *Aging from birth to death: Sociotemporal perspectives*. Boulder, CO: Westview Press.

BOULDING, K. E. (1984). The meaning of the twenty-first century: Reexamining the great transition. *World Future Society Bulletin*.

BRAUN, P., & SWEET, R. (1983–84). Passages: Fact or fiction? *International Journal of Aging and Human Development, 18*(3), 1–15.

CHERLIN, A., & FURSTENBERG, F. F. Jr. (1983). The American family in the year 2000. *The Futurist, 17*(3), 7–14.

FREEMAN, M. (1984). History, narrative, and life-span developmental knowledge. *Human Development, 27*(1), 1–19.

HANCOCK, T. (1982, August). Beyond health care. Creating a healthy future. *The Futurist*, pp. 4–13.

HOARE, C. H. (1982). Future issues in adult education: A review of the literature of the seventies. *Adult Education, 33*(1), 55–69.

LUSZCZ, M. A. (1983). An attitudinal assessment of perceived intergenerational affinities linking adolescence and old age. *International Journal of Behavioral Development, 6*(2), 221–231.

MORF, M. (1983). Eight scenarios for work in the future. *The Futurist, 17*(3), 24–30.

MUMFORD, M. D. & OWENS, W. A. (1984). Individuality in a developmental context: Some empirical and theoretical considerations. *Human Development, 27,* 84–108.

PECCEI, A. (1984). The alternatives of the human future. *World Futures, 19,* 199–208.

PRUCHNO, R. A., BLOW, F. C., & SMYER, M. A. (1984). Life events and interdependent lives: Implications for research and intervention. *Human Development, 27*(1), 31–41.

SIMON, J. L. (1983). Life on earth is getting better, not worse. *The Futurist, 17*(4), 7–15.

SIMON, J. L. (1983). The population debate. Growth means progress. *Science Digest, 91*(4), 76–81.

Slaughter, R. A. (1984, July-August). Towards a critical futurism. *World Future Society Bulletin,* 19–25.

Yinon, Y., Sharon, I., & Malkiman, B. A. (1983). Age similarity and helping intentions. *International Journal of Behavioral Development, 6*(2), 233–240.

Zimberg, S. (1974). The elderly alcoholic. *Gerontologist, 14,* 221–224.

Zimbardo, P. G., & Ruch, F. (1979). *Psychology and Life* (10th ed.). Glenview, IL: Scott, Foresman.

Zube, M. (1982). Changing behavior and outlook of aging men and women: Implications for marriage in the middle and later years. *Family Relations, 31*(1), 147–156.

Zubin, J. (1973). Foundations of gerontology: History, training, and methodology. In C. Eisdorfer & M. P. Lawton (Eds.), *The psychology of adult development and aging.* Washington, D.C.: American Psychological Association.

Glossary

Acute brain syndrome: A mental disorder characterized by relatively severe, diffuse, but reversible impairment of brain tissue function.

Affiliative: Characterized by a close relationship to others.

Ageism: The process of systematically stereotyping and discriminating against people on the basis of age.

Aging: The process by which an organism progresses through the stages of immaturity, maturity, and deterioration from conception until death.

Alienation: The condition of feeling distinct from, isolated from, and to some degree opposed to the dominant social group.

Alzheimer's disease: A to-date incurable disorder, usually beginning in middle age, characterized by progressive hardening of tissue and nerve degeneration.

Amniocentesis: Perforation or tapping, as with a needle, of the innermost membrane of the sac enclosing the embryo.

Amphetamine: A white, odorless powder that acts as a stimulant to the nervous system.

Analog: That which is similar or comparable in certain respects.

Adrogyny: Integration of both masculine and feminine characteristics within one individual.

Anomie: A state of normlessness characterized by personal and social demoralization and disorganization; a psychological state characterized by feelings of rootlessness and lack of a firm identity; often experienced by persons in cultures undergoing rapid change.

Anorexia: Absence of appetite for food.

Anthropologist: One who makes comparative studies of the chief human characteristics, including somatic characteristics, social habits and customs, and languages.

Antibodies: Proteins produced in the body having the capacity of neutralizing or reacting with an antigen, a substance which causes the production of antibodies.

Anticipatory socialization: The process of engaging in activities that prepare one for later roles in society.

Arteriosclerosis: A condition distinguished by thickening, hardening, and diminished elasticity of the arteries.

Atrophy: Wasting away, especially of body tissue or an organ.

Autonomic: Pertaining to that division of the nervous system concerned with the largely automatic regulation of smooth muscles and glands.

Baby boomers: The generation born in the late 1940s and early 1950s, characterized by a larger-than-normal birthrate.

Biofeedback: The employment of instrumentation to increase the self-control and awareness of the bodily processes.

Biological determinism: The doctrine that an individual's growth, development, and behaviors are the inevitable consequences of influences stemming from the nature of the body itself.

Bonding: In child psychology, the process of establishing a close, enduring relationship between caretaker and infant.

Born again: A phenomenon characterized by dedicating oneself to fundamentalist spiritual values and transforming one's life style to that end.

Butch: A lesbian who behaves in a masculine manner.

Caesarian section: An operation in which a fetus is removed by cutting through the walls of the abdomen and uterus.

Calcify: To harden; to change into a very hard substance.

Carcinogenic: Tending to produce cancer.

Cardiovascular: Pertaining to the heart and blood vessels.

Catharsis: A cleansing or purgation; in Freudian terms, the patient purges the mind of repressed material (catharsis) by telling whatever occurs to her or him (free association).

Cerebrovascular disease: Mental impairment due to the malfunction of the cerebral blood vessels.

Cholesterol: A physiological signficant substance found in animal fat and tissues. The gall bladder is composed almost wholly of cholesterol.

Chronic: Of lengthy, persistent duration.

Chronic brain syndrome: Psychiatric syndrome caused by impairment of brain tissue function characterized by continued decline and without expectation of reversal or recovery.

Climacteric: The syndrome, or pattern of symptoms (somatic, hormonal, and psychic), that signals the termination of the reproductive period in the female or the normal diminution of sexual activity in the male.

Cognitive: Pertaining to the process of knowing and thinking.

Cohabitation: The state of living together, most commonly applied to unmarried couples.

Cohort: Category of persons who share some characteristic, such as age or period in history.

Commune: A close-knit community of people who share common interests and activities, such as childrearing.

Confucianism: Ethical teachings introduced in China by Confucius; Confucius stressed devotion to family and friends, ancestor worship, and justice and peace.

Congenital: An anomaly marked by physical deviation present at, or usually before, birth.

Conservatorship: An arrangement by which some person or persons are appointed as custodian of funds, as for an elderly or mentally disabled person.

Conventional stage (Kohlberg): The second stage of moral development, occurring during later childhood, when good and evil are first identified with the concepts of "good girl" and "good boy" and the concepts themselves are allied with social standards of law and order.

Critical period: Time during which particular experiences may have especially profound and enduring effects.

Cross-sectional research: The description of a number of persons in terms of one or more variables as they appear at a given time.

Cruising: In popular terminology, the practice of deliberately setting out to find sexual companions, especially in bars.

Culture: The way of life—material and behavioral—of a society, including its customs, knowledges, beliefs, and morals.

Decrement: Reduction.

Defense mechanism: In Freudian theory, any behavior employed to achieve mental stability and ward off anxiety.

Delusion: A false belief maintained in the face of contrary evidence.

Dementia: A general term for mental deterioration.

Demographic: Pertaining to the study of human populations, with reference to population trends, distribution, and differential birth rates in subcultures.

Depressive neurosis: A relatively persistent state of depression precipitated by situational factors such as sustaining some loss and often associated with feelings of guilt for past failures or actions.

Determinism: The doctrine that all events and choices are subject to, and decided by, natural laws.

Development: A process involving all the many changes, both qualitative and quantitative, that occur during progress toward maturity. It embraces both changes inherent in the maturing process and those resulting from interaction between the individual and the environment.

Developmental approach: The frame of reference for studying the life span in which each phase of life is viewed in terms of both antecedent and anticipated phases.

Developmental psychology: · The branch of psychology concerned with characteristic behaviors at successive stages of development and the processes involved in moving from one stage to another.

Developmental task: A skill or accomplishment that should be satisfactorily mastered at a particular age stage if an individual is to be ready for the next stage.

Diabetes mellitus: A metabolic disorder characterized by the loss, or the almost complete loss, of the ability to oxidize carbohydrates because of faulty pancreatic activity and consequent disturbance of the normal insulin mechanism.

Discrete: Consisting of distinct, individual parts.

Disengagement: The mutual withdrawal by aging persons and those in their social environment from each other.

Dissociation: The segregation of certain mental processes from others, resulting in the loss of normal interrelationships between them.

Dissociative hallucination: A mental process characterized by dissociation and hallucinations. *See also* hallucination.

Double sex standard: A code of morality that involves different standards for judging the behavior of each sex.

Down's syndrome. *See* Mongolism.

Downward mobility: Progression toward a lower status in the social hierarchy.

Dyad, dyadic: Pertaining to a relationship in which two persons or objects are involved.

Ecological: Pertaining to that branch of biology that concerns the relationship between living organisms and their environment.

Ego: Self, as distinguished from other; the aspect of the psyche (general psychological function) that is conscious and most in touch with reality.

Egoism: The tendency to be self-centered and to consider only one's own interests.

Electrocardiograph: An instrument for making electrocardiograms, or tracings of electric currents produced by the contraction of the heart muscles.

Emasculated: Deprived of virility or manhood.

Emphysema: A swelling caused by the presence of air in the interstices of connective tissues of the lungs.

Empirical: Based on experience, careful experiment, and/or observation.

Empty nest: The period in parents' lives immediately after grown children leave home.

Encounter group: A group characterized by frank, intimate, often emotional interaction.

Endemic: Peculiar to a particular geographic location or category of persons.

Environmental engineering: Conscious planning and manipulation of the environment to achieve certain desired effects.

Enzyme: An organic compound, often a protein, capable of producing or accelerating some change in its substrate, for which it is often specific.

Epiphenomenon: An occurrence or phenomenon that occurs with and appears to result from another.

Erogenous: Pertaining to zones or parts of the body which, when stimulated, arouse sexual desire and erotic feelings.

Estrogen: Female hormone.

Ethnicity: Cultural, racial, or linguistic affiliation.

Ethnocentrism: Belief in the inherent superiority of one's own culture.

Euthanasia, active: The deliberate killing of persons presumed to be hopelessly disabled or ill.

Euthanasia, passive: The practice of simply permitting a patient to die naturally instead of exerting special efforts to maintain life, when such life would, in all likelihood, consist in a vegetative existence or involve much suffering.

Experimental method: The procedure in which specific conditions are arranged under which a phenomenon is to be observed to determine the influences of these conditions. The observed phenomenon is called the *dependent variable;* the arranged conditions are called *independent,* or *experimental, variables.*

Expressive: Relating to behaviors that convey feelings, as distinct from those designed to get something done or achieve some goal.

Extended family: A family unit that includes the parents, children, and assorted kin, usually grandparents.

Familism: A social pattern in which the family and family solidarity take precedence over individual rights and interests.

Family cluster: An arrangement in which persons of different marital and age statuses and their children meet regularly together. They share activities, leisure, and mutual support without living together, swapping mates, or pooling income.

Family network: A living arrangement in which three or four nuclear families live together in the same neighborhood and regularly share companionship and leisure pursuits and exchange services.

Fem: The individual who assumes a feminine role in a lesbian relationship.

Filial: Pertaining to son or daughter.

Flexitime: The practice of allowing employees considerable flexibility and autonomy in determining their work schedules.

Formal operations (Piaget): The period (between ages 11 and 15) when truly logical thinking begins and the final step is taken toward abstract thinking and conceptualization.

Free radical: An atom or compound in which there is an unpaired electron.

Functional age: An age status based on what an individual is capable of doing, as distinct from number of years lived.

Functional psychosis: A serious mental disorder for which there is no known or detectable organic base. It apparently derives from the abnormal operation of an organ or organ system but not from known changes in structure.

Futurism: The science of anticipating and planning for years to come.

Gender: Mode of transaction of sex role in terms of behaviors considered to be masculine or feminine.

Generation gap: Discrepancy in understanding or values between one age cohort and another. *See also* cohort.

Generation unit: A group within the same generation that organizes its common experience in distinctive ways.

Generations effect: The differential impact of life events on successive age cohorts, not merely because of age difference, but because they have experienced different historical events.

Generativity: The impulse toward procreation; interest in establishing and guiding the next generation.

Geriatrics: The branch of medicine that deals with the health and diseases of the aged.

Gerontology: Study of the elderly.

Global: Relating to the whole.

Gonadal: Pertaining to the primary sex glands—the ovaries in the female and the testes in the male.

Group marriage: An arrangement in which two or three couples live together or share sex partners.

Gynecological: Relating to the study and treatment of women's diseases, especially of the rectal and genito-urinary tract.

Hallucination: The perception of objects, sounds, and visions that are not actually present.

Heterogeneous: Of various types.

Heterosexual: A person who is sexually attracted to the opposite sex.

Homosexual: A person who is sexually attracted towards others of the same sex.

Hospice: A nursing home especially designed for the care of the terminally ill.

Humanist: One who is philosophically concerned with the ideas and ideals of human beings.

Hypochondriac: A person unusually preoccupied with his or her own health.

Hypertensive: Causing increased tension and pressure.

Hysterectomy: Surgical removal of all, or part, of the uterus.

Identical twins: Monozygotic twins; developed from a single fertilized ovum.

Identity: A sense of uniqueness as a person, equivalent to answering the question, "Who am I?"

Identity crisis: A major turning point in life related to defining what and who one is.

Immune system: Parts and processes of the body which, collectively, provide protection against disease and decrement.

Instrumental: Associated with doing, or accomplishing objectives.

Intelligence quotient (IQ): A score derived from an intelligence test indicating how the individual's demonstrated mental ability compares with that of others at the same developmental stage.

In vitro: In a test tube, as in fertilization.

Kibbutz (pl., kibbutzim): A collective farm settlement in Israel cooperatively owned and managed by the members.

Lesbian: A female whose sexual preference is for another of her own sex.

Lesion: Injury, damage.

Libido: The life force underlying all activity; sexual craving or erotic desire.

Life cycle: The complete set of phenomena and events that comprise the total life span.

Life style: The overall pattern of motives, coping techniques, and behaviors that generally characterize an individual's behavior.

Living will: An individual's expressed desires regarding whether or not his or her life will be maintained by extraordinary efforts or life sustaining machines when that individual's condition may no longer allow making such a decision.

Locus of control: The perception of being controlled either internally by oneself, or externally by others.

Longitudinal research: Study involving repeated observations or measurement of the same individual or group over time.

Macho: Behaving in the highly assertive, dominant fashion, traditionally approved for males.

Mastectomy: Surgical removal of the breast.

Meditation: A twice daily procedure for inducing complete relaxation, ordinarily lasting about twenty minutes each time, in which one sits with eyes closed, focuses on the rhythm of his or her breathing, and says some word or number in rhythm with the breathing.

Menarche: First menstruation.

Mentor: A loyal friend or advisor, usually older or having higher status.

Metabolic: Characterized by, or resulting from, *metabolism*—the physical and chemical processes that proceed continuously in living organisms and cells, by which assimilated food is built into protoplasm (*anabolism*) and broken down into waste and simpler substances (*catabolism*), as energy is released for vital processes.

Midlife crisis: A critical period during middle age when an individual is induced by personal, physical, and social factors to examine his or her life; it may result in important modifications of life style and philosophy.

Molecular geneticist: A specialist in dealing with basic cellular properties and hereditary phenomena of the organism.

Mongolism: A congenital mental condition characterized by slanting eyes, large tongue, flat skull, stubby fingers, and other physical abnormalities.

Morbidity: The state or quality of being unhealthy and diseased.

Narcissistic: Self-loving.

Necrotizing: Tending to produce decay or death.

Neuron: A nerve cell, or structural unit of the nervous system.

Neurosis: A somewhat poorly defined mental disorder, less serious than psychosis, and leaving the personality relatively intact.

Neurotic: (Also **psychoneurotic**): Tending to behave in predominantly emotional rather than rational ways.

Normative: Relating to the norm or standard.

Nuclear family: A family composed only of father, mother, and children, as opposed to an *extended family*, which also includes the descendants of a common grandparent and all their relatives.

Nurturant: Characterized by warmth, involvement, personal love, and compassion.

Nurturer: One involved in the caretaking of others.

Octogenarian: An individual between 80 and 90 years of age.

Oedipus complex: In psychoanalytic theory, excessive emotional attachment, involving conscious or unconscious incestuous desires of the son for his mother. The oedipus complex specifically refers to the boy's sexual desire for his mother, but in theoretical discussions it includes the analogous love of the girl for her father, more specifically called the electra complex.

Ontogeny: Biological development of the individual as distinguished from *phylogeny*, or racial (evolutionary), development of any plant or animal species.

Open marriage: The practice in which two or three couples live together and share sex partners.

Organic brain syndrome: A pattern of symptoms characteristic of acute and chronic brain disorders, any one of which may predominate in individual cases.

Ovulation: The physiological process by which a mature ovum (female germ cell) escapes from a ruptured follicle (sac or cavity).

Ovum transfer: The placement of the fertilized egg cell in the womb of a host mother, where it is brought to term.

Pacemaker: An instrument placed beneath the skin for providing a normal heartbeat by electrical stimulation of the heart muscle.

Palimony: The equivalent of alimony for persons who have lived together as husband and wife without getting married.

Paranoia: A functional psychosis characterized by delusions of persecution or grandeur.

Parkinsonian: Relating to *paralysis agitans*, a progressive disease of later life and characterized by weakening muscles, tremors, and slowing of voluntary movements.

Pathogenic: Tending to cause disease.

Pathological: Pertaining to a diseased or abnormal condition of the organism or its parts.

Patriarchal family: A family headed by the father or eldest male.

Phallic: A psychoanalytic term concerning the penis, usually in reference to the stage of infantile sexuality.

Phenomenologic: Relating to how others subjectively experience reality.

Phylogenetic: Pertaining to *phylogeny,* or the evolutionary development of a species.

Pluralism: The stessing of multiple components instead of unity, as in social or cultural pluralism, which focuses on the variety of groups and subcultures composing a society.

Polyfidelitous: Being faithful to all persons concerned.

Precocity: In the case of a child, the quality or condition of being unusually advanced, in some respect, for one's age.

Preconventional stage: The lowest stage in Kohlberg's theory of moral development; involves relatively self-centered concepts of right and wrong—that is, of what one can do without getting caught or what leads to greatest personal gratification.

Premenstrual syndrome (PMS): A pattern of general stress and instability associated with the menstrual cycle.

Primal therapy: Under the guidance of a therapist, the psychic pain of certain childhood events is experienced again in order to free the individual from the adverse effects of such events.

Proceptive: Designed to, or having the effect of, improving the chances of fertilization.

Progenesis: The capacity for producing offspring.

Progesterone: A female hormonal compound, sometimes produced commercially for treating various menstrual disorders.

Projective techniques: Tests consisting of relatively unstructured or ambiguous situations designed to elicit reactions that indicate the subject's characteristic attitudes, motives, and traits.

Psychiatric: Pertaining to the branch of medicine concerned with mental disorders.

Psychiatrist: A physician who specializes in the diagnosis and treatment of mental disease.

Psychic: Pertaining to the mind; beyond known physical processes.

Psychoanalytic: Relating to a body of doctrine associated with Freud and modified by his followers; a special technique for discovering hidden motivation.

Psychogenic: Of mental or emotional origin.

Psychoneuroses: A somewhat poorly defined class of mental disorders, less serious than psychoses, that leave the personality relatively intact.

Psychopathology: The science that deals with mental diseases or disorders.

Psychoses: The scientific name for severe mental disturbances; commonly called insanity.

Psychosomatic: Pertaining to the mind-body relationship; having bodily symptoms of mental or emotional origin.

Psychotherapy: The use of any psychological technique in treating emotional maladjustment or mental disorders.

Psychotic: Having, or relating to, severe mental disturbance.

Pubertal rites: A program of precepts and rituals by which an individual, on reaching sexual maturity, is initiated into the adult life of the community.

Reconstituted family: The family produced by marriage of formerly married persons, at least one of whom has one or more children.

Reference group: The group of persons with which an individual identifies; a reference group determines standards of behavior, values, and status aspirations of that individual.

Reify: To treat an abstraction as substantially existent.

Reinforcement: Increase in strength of a response when the response produces a reduction in drive.

Replication: Repetition.

Rite of passage: A ritual of induction into adult society.

Role: A pattern of behavior associated with functions in various groups.

Schism: A split or division.

Schizophrenia: A serious mental disorder characterized by withdrawal, delusions, and hallucinations, often with impaired intelligence.

Self-actualization: The process of moving through sequentially higher stages of motivation and organization to adequate achievement of one's potential.

Semantic: Relating to meaning in language.

Semen storage: The storing, for purposes of subsequent artificial insemination, of fluid containing the male reproductive cells or spermatozoa.

Senescence: The process of growing old.

Senile dementia: A condition associated with later years, characterized by memory gaps, imaginary memories, frequent disorientation, preoccupation with personal needs, and at times, feelings of persecution and suspicion.

Senility: Old age, ordinarily with the connotation of mental and physical degeneration.

Septuagenarian: An individual aged somewhere between 70 and 79.

Sex role: The characteristic behavior patterns of males or females in a particular society.

Significant other: Someone of unusual importance to an individual's life or welfare.

Socialization: The process by which an individual learns to behave in ways approved by the society.

Sociodemographic: Relating to matters of population and society.

Somatic: Pertaining to body structure or framework of the body, as distinct from mental processes.

Stage theory: The conceptualization of human development as involving several relatively discrete stages that can be identified physiologically, psychologically, and sociologically.

Stereotype: A preconceived, prejudiced picture of the members of some particular group.

Straight: A slang term for heterosexual.

Stress: A condition created by abnormal tension, especially when no ready solution is available for a crucial problem.

Surrogate: Substitute.

Swinging: The consensual and occasional exchange of sex partners by married couples.

Synapses: Points of contact between adjacent neurons that transmit nerve impulses from one neuron to another.

Syndrome: Pattern.

Systemic disease: A disorder relating to, or affecting, the body as a whole.

Tactile: Pertaining to touch.

Terminal drop: Accelerated decline in cognitive development within the years just preceding death.

Testosterone: Male sex hormone.

Thematic Apperception Test: A projective test in which the subject responds to a series of pictures of people involved in various situations in order to assess the subject's characteristic traits, attitudes, and motives.

Transsexual: An individual who feels like a member of the opposite sex.

Trauma: An experience that inflicts serious physical or psychological shock on an organism.

Triad: A group of three.

Type As: Individuals who are unusually competitive, hard-driving, and presumably subject to stress.

Ubiquitous: Everywhere; quite widespread; omnipresent.

Ulcer: An open sore, other than a wound, on the skin or some mucous membrane, characterized by disintegration of the tissue and often by the discharge of pus.

Upward mobility: Progression toward higher status in the social hierarchy.

Vascular: Having vessels or ducts for conveying blood or lymph.

Vas deferens: The duct that conveys sperm from the testicle to the ejaculatory duct of the penis.

Vasectomy: Surgical removal of the vas deferens.

Zeitgeist: Spirit of the age or times.

References

Challenges of "midlife" affecting 44 million. (1984 July). *AARP Bulletin*, p. 2.

AMA Council on Medical Service. (1982). Hospice programs. In J. A. Franklin (Ed.), *Source book on death and dying*, (1st ed.) (pp. 193–197). Chicago: Marquis Professional Publications.

ABRAMS, B. (1982, January 21). "Middle generation" growing more concerned with selves. *The Wall Street Journal*, p. 29.

Acceptance of the idea of mortality. (1975). *Intellect, 103*(2362), 215–216.

ACOCK, A. C. (1984). Parents and their children: The study of intergenerational influence. *Sociology and Social Research, 68*(2), 151–171.

ADAMS, R. D. (1980). The morphological aspects of aging in the human nervous system. In J. E. Birren & R. B. Sloane (Eds.), *Handbook of mental health and aging* (pp. 149–160). Englewood Cliffs, NJ: Prentice-Hall, Inc.

ADLER, N. E. (1975). Emotional responses of women following therapeutic abortion. *American Journal of Orthopsychiatry, 45*(3), 446.

Advantages and disadvantages of having children. (1979). *USA Today, 108*(2411), 6–7.

Age of miracles in science and technology. (1983, May 9). *U.S. News & World Report*, A20–A21.

Aging: The nursing home gulag. (1979). *Psychology Today, 13*(2), 22.

AHLSTROM, S. E. (1978). National trauma and changing religious values. *Daedalus, 107*(1), 13–30.

AINLAY, S. C., & SMITH, D. R. (1984). Aging and religious participation. *Journal of Gerontology, 39*(3), 357–361.

ALEKSANDROWICZ, M. K. (1974). The effect of pain-relieving drugs administered during labor and delivery on the behavior of the newborn: A review. *Merrill-Palmer Quarterly, 20*, 123–141.

ALBIN, R. S. (1980). Demythologizing cancer blues. *Psychology Today, 13*(8), 25–26.

ALLEN, L. R., & BEATTIE, R. J. (1984). The role of leisure as an indicator of overall satisfaction with community life. *Journal of Leisure Research, 16*(2), 99–109.

American Family, The. (1980, June 16). *U.S. News & World Report*, 48–50.

AMMONS, P., & STINNETT, N. (1980). The vital marriage: A closer look. *Family Relations, 29*(1), 37–42.

ANDERSON, D., & BRAITO, R. (1981). A mental health of the never-married. *Alternative Lifestyles, 4*(1), 108–124.

ANDERSON, S. B. (1979). Educational measurement in a new decade. *College Board Review, 112*, 2–23.

ANGIER, N. (1982). Dr. Jekyll and Mrs. Hyde. *Discover, 3*(11), 28–34.

ANTONUCCI, T. (1976). Attachment: A life-span concept. *Human Development, 19,* 135–142.

ARBEIT, S. A. (1976). A study of women during their first pregnancy. Unpublished doctoral dissertation, Yale University.

ARIÉS, P. (1975). The family prison of love, *Psychology Today, 9*(3), 53–58.

ATCHLEY, R. C. (1972). *The social forces in later life: An introduction to social gerontology.* Belmont, CA: Wadsworth Publishing Co.

———. (1975). *The sociology of retirement.* Cambridge, MA: Schenkman.

AXELSON, L. J., & GLICK, P. C. (1979, April). Family specialists look ahead: Their attitudes, beliefs, consensus, and perceptions of future issues. *Family Coordinator,* 149–155.

BA or MRS? Finding fulfillment at college or home. (1978). *Human Behavior.* 7(4), 51.

BABCHUK, N. (1981). Primary friends and kin: A study of the associations of middle-class couples. In L.D. Steinberg (Ed.), *The life cycle: Readings in human development* (pp. 311–322). New York: Columbia University Press.

BAGNÉ, P. (1983). High-tech breeding. *Mother Jones, 8*(7), 23–29.

BAILEY, S. K. (1976). The several ages of learning. *Change, 8*(4), 36–39.

BAILYN, L. (1973). Family constraints on women's work. *Annals of the New York Academy of Science, 19*(208), 82–90.

———. (1976, April). Will the real middle-aged woman please stand up? Toward an understanding of adult development in women. Symposium presented at the meeting of the Eastern Psychological Association, New York.

BAKEMAN, R., & CAIRNS, R. B. (1985). Describing and analyzing interactional data: Some first steps. In R. B. Cairns (Ed.), *Social interaction: Methods, analysis, and illustrations.* Hillsdale, NJ: Erlbaum.

BAKER, C. (1982). The living will: The final expression. In J. A. Fruehling (Ed.), *Source book on death and dying* (1st ed.) (pp. 88–97). Chicago: Marquis Professional Publications.

BALTES, P. B. & SCHAIE, K. W. (1974). On the plasticity of intelligence in adulthood and old age: Where Horn and Donaldson fail. *American Psychologist, 31*(10), 720–725.

BALTES, P. B., & WILLIS, S. L. (1982). Plasticity and enhancement of intellectual functioning in old age. Penn State's adult development and enrichment. In F. I. M. Craik & S. E. Trehub (Eds.), *Aging and Cognitive Processes.* New York: Plenum.

BANDURA, A. (1982). Psychology of chance encounters and life paths. *American Psychologist, 37*(7), 747–755.

BANKOFF, E. A. (1983). Social support and adaptation to widowhood. *Journal of Marriage and the Family, 45*(4), 827–839.

BARAN, A., SOROSKY, A., & PANNOR, R. (1975). The dilemma of our adoptees. *Psychology Today, 9*(7), 38.

BARDWICK, J. M. (1974). Evolution and parenting. *Journal of Social Issues, 30*(4), 39–62.

BARNETT, R. C., & BARUCH, G. K. (1978). Women in the middle years: A critique of research and theory, *Psychology of Women Quarterly, 3*(2), 187–197.

BARRETT, K. (1984, December). Two-career couples. How they do it. *Ms.,* 111, 114.

BASSETT, J. (1981). But that would be wrong—*Psychology Today* survey report on cheating, lying, and bending the rules on everyday life. *Psychology Today, 15*(11), 34–51.

BATTEN, M. (1984). Life spans. *Science Digest, 92*(2), 46–51; 98.

BAUM, S. K. (1983). Older people's anxiety about afterlife. *Psychology Reports, 52*(3), 895–898.

BAUM, S. K. (1983–84). Age identification in the elderly: Some theoretical considerations. *International Journal of Aging and Human Development, 18*(1), 25–30.

BAUMRIND, D. (1974). Coleman II: Utopian fantasy and sound social innovation. *School Review, 83*(1), 69–84.

BAXTER, L. A. (1984). Trajectories of relationships disengagement. *Journal of Social and Personal Relationships, 1,* 29–48.

BAYER, L. M., WHISSELL-BUECHY, D., & HONZIK, M. P. (1981). Health in the middle years. In D. H. Eichorn, J. A. Clausen, N. Haan, M. P. Honzik, & P. H. Mussen (Eds.), *Present and past in middle life.* New York: Academic Press.

BECKMAN, L. (1983). Do the elderly need their children? Help cross-talk. *Psychology Today, 17*(2), 81.

BELAND, F. (1984). The decision of elderly persons to leave their homes. *Gerontologist, 24*(2), 179–185.

BELFER, M. L., MULLIKEN, J. B., & COCHRAN, T. C. (1979). Cosmetic surgery as an antecedent of life change, *American Journal of Psychiatry, 136*(2), 199–201.

BELL, D. H. (1981). Up from patriarchy: The male role in historical perspective. In R. A. Lewis (Ed.) *Men in difficult times* (pp. 306–323). Englewood Cliffs, NJ: Prentice-Hall.

BELL, D. H. (1982). *Being a man: The paradox of masculinity.* Lexington, MA: Lewis Publishing Company.

BELL, D. H., & TREAS, J. (1980). The changing family context of mental health and aging. In J. E. Birren & R. B. Sloane (Eds.), *Handbook of mental health and aging* (pp. 400–428). Englewood Cliffs, NJ: Prentice-Hall, Inc.

BENNETT, A. (1979, November 16). Aging Americans: Caring for the elderly greatly changes lives of many U.S. families. *Wall Street Journal,* (pp. 1, 40).

BENSMAN, J., & LILIENFELD, R. (1979). Friendship and alienation. *Psychology Today, 13*(4), 56–66.

BERGER, M. (1979). Men's new family roles—some implications for therapists. *The Family Coordinator, 28*(4), 638–646.

BERGIN, A. E. (1975). Psychotherapy can be dangerous. *Psychology Today, 9*(6), 96–100, 104.

BERMAN, H. J. (1975). Prologue to aging: Societal structure and the aged. In M. G. Spencer & C. J. Dorr (Eds.), *Understanding aging: A multidisciplinary approach.* New York: Appleton-Century-Crofts.

BERNARD, J. (1972). *The future of marriage.* New York: Bantam Books, Inc.

————. *The Future of Motherhood.* (1975). New York: Bantam Books, Inc.

BERNARD, J. (1981). The good-provider role. *American Psychologist, 36*(1), 1–12.

BERNARDO, S. & ROSE, K. J. (1984, March). Research on aging. *Science Digest,* 95.

BERNAT, J. L., CULVER, C. M., & GERT, B. (1982). On the definition and criterion of death. In J. A. Fruehling (Ed.), *Source book on death and dying* (1st ed.) Chicago: Marquis Professional Publications.

BERZONSKY, M. D. (1978). Formal reasoning in adolescence: An alternate view. *Adolescence, 13*(50), 279–290.

BEST, F. (1984). Technology and the changing world of work. *Futurist, 18*(2), 61–66.

BIELBY, D. D. V. & BIELBY, W. T. (1984). Work commitment, sex-role attitudes and women's employment. *American Sociological Review, 49,* 234–247.

BIELBY, D., & PAPALIA, D. E. (1975). Moral development and perceptual role taking egocentrism: Their development and interrelationship across the life span. *International Journal of Aging and Human Development, 6*(4), 293–308.

Big Leveler, The. (1978). *Human Behavior, 7*(2), 60.

BIGGAR, J. C., COWPER, D. C., & YEATTS, D. E. (1984). National elderly migration patterns and selectivity. *Research on Aging, 6*(2), 163–188.

BIRD, C. (1983, April/May). Profile of tomorrow. *Modern Maturity,* April/May, 36–39.

BIRD, D. (1972). The case against marriage. In L. K. Howe (ed.), *The future of the family.* New York: Simon & Schuster.

BIRENBAUM, A. (1978). Home care: An alternative to the high cost of hospitalization, *USA Today, 107*(2398), 52–54.

BIRREN, J. E. Synopsis of senescence. *Quest/78, 2*(2), 126.

————. (1977). The abuse of the urban aged. In S. H. Zarit (Ed.), *Readings in aging and death: Contemporary perspectives,* (pp. 128–131). New York: Harper & Row.

————. & RENNER, V. J. (1980). Concepts and issues of mental health and aging. In J. E. Birren & R. B. Sloane (Eds.), *Handbook of mental health and aging.* (pp. 3–33). Englewood Cliffs, NJ: Prentice-Hall, Inc.

BISCHOF, L. J. (1976). *Adult psychology,* (2nd ed). New York: Harper & Row.

BISHOP, J. E. (1979, November 16). Jogging a lot won't ensure immunity from heart attacks. *Wall Street Journal,* 18.

————. (1979, April 5). Age of anxiety. Research in indicating that stress is linked to physical illness. *Wall Street Journal,* 28.

BISHOP, J. M., & KRAUSS, D. R. (1984). Depictions of aging and old age on Saturday morning television. *Gerontologist, 24*(1), 91–94.

BLACK, S. M. & HILL, C. E. (1984). The psychological well-being of women in their middle years. *Psychology of Women Quarterly, 8*(3), 282–292.

BLAKE, J. (1982). Demographic revolution and family evolution: Some implications for American women. In P. W. Berman & E. R. Ramey (Eds.), *Women: A developmental perspective* (pp. 299–312). Washington: U.S. Dept. of Health and Human Services, NIH Publication No. 82-2298.

BLOCK, J. H. & BLOCK, J. (1983). The role of ego-control and ego-resiliency in the organization of behavior. In W. Damon (Ed.), *Social and personality development: Essays on the growth of the child* (pp. 282–320). New York: Norton.

BLUMBERG, P. M. & PAUL, P. W. (1975). Continuities and discontinuities in upper-class marriages. *Journal of Marriage and the Family, 37*(1), 63–76.

BORKAN, G. A., & NORRIS, A. H. (1980). Assessment of biological age using a profile of physical parameters. *Journal of Gerontology, 35*(2), 174–184.

BOTWINICK, J. (1973). *Aging and behavior.* New York: Springer Publishing Co.

————. (1977). Intellectual abilities. In J. E. Birren & K. W. Schaie (Eds.), *Handbook of the psychology of aging.* (pp. 580–605). New York: Van Nostrand Reinhold.

BOUWSMA, W. J. (1976). Christian adulthood. *Daedalus, 105*(2), 77–92.

BOWEN, G. L. & ORTHNER, D. K. (1983). Sex-role congruency and marital quality. *Journal of Marriage and the Family, 45*(1), 223–242.

BOWER, T. (1974). Repetition in human development. *Merrill-Palmer Quarterly, 20*(4), 303–318.

BOWLING, A. & CARTWRIGHT, A. (1982). *Life after death.* London: Tavistock.

BOZETT, F. (1981). Gay fathers. Identity conflict resolution through integrative sanctioning. *Alternative Lifestyles, 4*(1), 90–107.

BRAM, S. (1974). To have or not: A comparison of parents, parents-to-be, and childless couples. Unpublished doctoral dissertation, University of Michigan.

BRANCO, K. J. & WILLIAMSON, J. B. (1982). Stereotyping and the life cycle: Views of aging and the aged. In *In the eye of the beholder* (pp. 364–410). New York: Praeger.

BRANDWEIN, R. A., BROWN, C. A., & FOX, E. M. (1974). Women and children last: The social situation of divorced mothers and their families. *Journal of Marriage and the Family, 36*(3), 498–514.

BRAUN, P. & SWEET, R. (1983–84). Passages: Fact or fiction? *International Journal of Aging and Human Development, 18*(3), 1–15.

BRENT, R. S., BRENT, E. E., & MAUKSCH, R. K. (1984). Common behavior patterns of residents in public areas of nursing homes. *Gerontologist, 24*(2), 186–192.

BRIDGWATER, C. A. (1984). The phases of mentorship. Work, crosstalk. *Psychology Today, 18*(6), 74.

Briefs on aging. (1984, February/March). *Aging.* p. 3.

BRINKERHOFF, D. B., & WHITE, L. K. (1978). Marital satisfaction in an economically marginal population. *Journal of Marriage and the Family, 40,* 259–267.

BRITTON, J. H. & BRITTON, J. O. (1972). *Personality changes in aging.* New York: Springer Publishing Co.

BROMBERG, J. (1981, May/June). Retirement—Boredom or bliss. *Aging,* pp. 317–318, 17–21.

BROWER, K. (1979). In warm blood: Earth. *Omni, 2*(1), 20–22.

BRUCK, C. (1979). Menopause. *Human Behavior, 8*(4), 38–46.

BRYER, K. B. (1979). The Amish way of death: A study of family support systems. *American Psychologist, 34*(3), 255–261.

Buddyships. (1979). *Human Behavior, 8*(4), 35.

BURRIS, B. H. (1983). The human effects of unemployment. *Social Problems, 31*(1), 96–110.

BUTLER, R. N. (1975a). Man does not die, he kills himself. *International Journal of Aging and Human Development, 6*(4), 367–370.

———. (1975b). Psychiatry and psychology of the middle aged. In A. M. Freedman, H. J. Kaplan, & B. J. Sadock (Eds.), *Comprehensive textbook of psychiatry,* (2nd ed.), (pp. 2390–2404). Baltimore: Williams & Wilkins.

———. (1975c). *Why Survive? Being Old in America.* New York: Harper & Row, Publishers.

———. (1976). We should end commercialization in the care of older people in the United States: Some thoughts. *International Journal of Aging and Human Development, 7*(1), 87–88.

———. (1978–79). Public interest report No. 26: Compassion and relief from pain. *International Journal of Aging and Human Development. 9*(2), 193–195.

———. (1983). Current data inconclusive about aged's health and work. *Aging and Work, 6*(3), 187–196.

———, & LEWIS, M. I. (1973). *Aging and mental health: Positive psychosocial approaches.* St. Louis, Mo.: C. V. Mosby Company.

BRYER, K. B. (1979). The Amish way of death: A study of family support systems. *American Psychologist, 34*(3), 255–261.

BYNUM, J. E. JR. (1972). An exploration of successful retirement adjustment: The formulation of hypotheses. Ph.D. dissertation, Washington State University.

CAMERON, P. (1976). Masculinity/femininity of the generations: As self-reported and as stereotypically appraised. *International Journal of Aging and Human Development, 7*(2), 143–151.

———, & CROMER, A. (1974). Generational homophyly. *Journal of Gerontology, 29,* 232–236.

CAMPBELL, A. (1975). The American way of mating: Marriage si, children only maybe. *Psychology Today, 8*(12), 37–42.

CAMPBELL, C. (1975). Economic reality—intruder on the American dream. *Psychology Today, 9*(1), 36–37.

CARLSON, C. M. (1984). Reminiscing: Toward achieving ego integrity in old age. *Social Casework: The Journal of Contemporary Social Work, 65*(2), 81–89.

CAPEL, W. C., GOLDSMITH, V. M., WADDELL, K. J., & STEWART, G. T. (1972). The aging narcotic addict: An increasing problem for the next decades. *Journal of Gerontology, 27,* 102–106.

CAREY, R. G. (1975). Living until death: A program of service and research for the terminally ill. In E. Kübler-Ross (Ed.), *Death: The Final Stage of Growth* (pp. 75–86). Englewood Cliffs, NJ: Prentice-Hall, Inc.

CARP, F. M. (1978–79). Effects of the living environment on activity and use of time. *International Journal of Aging and Human Development, 9*(1), 75–85.

CATH, S. H. (1980). Suicide in the middle years: Some reflections on the annihilation of self. In W. H. Norman & T. J. Scaramella (Eds.), *Midlife: Developmental and Clinical Issues,* (pp. 53–72.) New York: Brunner/Mazel Publishers.

———. (1975). The orchestration of disengagement. *Journal of Aging and Human Development, 6*(3), 199–213.

Causes of emotional distress. (1979). *USA Today, 107*(2407), 16.

Changing attitudes towards marriage and parenthood, (1979). *USA Today, 108*(2411), 7–8.

CHEDD, G. (1981a). A simple blood test raises an awesome question: Who shall be born? *Science, 2*(1), 32–40.

———. (1981b). Wrongful life. *Science, 2*(1), 40.

CHERLIN, A. (1980). Postponing marriage: The influence of young women's work expectations. *Journal of Marriage and the Family, 42*(2), 355–365.

CHERRY, L. (1978). On the real benefits of eustress. *Psychology Today, 11*(10), 60–63, 69–70.

CHILMAN, C. S. (1974). Some psychosocial aspects of female sexuality. *Family Coordinator, 23*(2), 123–131.

CHRISTENSON, J. A., HOUGLAND, J. G. JR., GAGE, B. A., & HOE, L. V. (1984). Value orientations of organized religious groups. *Sociology and Social Research, 68*(2), 194–207.

CHRISTOFFERSEN, T. (1974). Gerontology: Towards a general theory and a research strategy. *Acta Sociologica, 17*(4), 393–407.

CHU, F. D., & TROTTER, S. (1974). *The madness establishment.* New York: Grossman Publishers.

CLARK, R. W. (1980). *Freud: The man and the cause.* London: Cale/Weidenfeld.

CLEARY, P. D. & MECHANIC, D. (1983). Sex differences in psychological distress among married people. *Journal of Health and Social Behavior, 24,* 111–121.

CLEVELAND, M. (1979). Divorce in the middle years: The sexual dimension. *Journal of Divorce, 2*(3), 255–262.

———. (1976). Sex in marriage: At 40 and beyond. *Family Coordinator, 25*(3), 233–240.

COBERLY, S. & NEWQUIST, D. (1984, February-March). Hiring older workers employer concerns. *Aging,* pp. 23–25.

COHEN, G. D. (1980). Prospects for mental health and aging. In J. E. Birren & R. B. Sloane (Eds.), *Handbook of Mental Health and Aging,* (pp. 971–993). Englewood Cliffs, NJ: Prentice-Hall, Inc.

COLE, S. G., & BYRON, D. (1973). A review of information relevant to vasectomy counselors, *Family Coordinator, 22*(2), 213–221.

COLEMAN, J. S. (1976). *Abnormal Psychology and Modern Life* (5th ed.), Chicago: Scott, Foresman and Company.

COMPTON, J. L., & PARISH, A. H. (1978). E pluribus unum: Adult education for a global society. *Lifelong Learning: The Adult Years, 1*(10), 30–33.

CONGER, J. J. (1981). Freedom and commitment: Families, youth and social change. *American Psychologist, 36*(12), 1475–1484.

Connubial depression. (1977). *Human Behavior, 6*(7), 52.

CONSTANTINE, L. L. (1983). Dysfunction and function in open family systems. I: Application of a unified theory. *Journal of Marriage and the Family, 45*(4), 725–738.

CONSTANTINE, L. L., & CONSTANTINE, J. M. (1973). *Group Marriage.* New York: Collier Books.

Coping with stress. (1976). *Human Behavior, 5*(5), 38.

CORBY, N., & SOLNICK, R. L. (1980). Psychosocial and physiological influences on sexuality in the older adult. In J. E. Birren & R. B. Sloane (Eds.), *Handbook of Mental Health and Aging* (pp. 893–921). Englewood Cliffs, NJ: Prentice-Hall, Inc.

CORNISH, E. (1979). The future of the family: Intimacy in an age of loneliness. *The Futurist, 13*(1), 45–59.

CORR, C. A. (1979). Living with the changing face of death. In Hannelore Wass (Ed.), *Dying: Facing the Facts.* (pp. 44–72). Washington: Hemisphere Pub. Corp.

CORY, C. T. (1982). Parent-teacher space wars. *Psychology Today, 16*(10), 18–22.

COVEY, H. C. (1983). Some theoretical considerations. Part II. *Educational Gerontology, 9,* 95–109.

COWING, D. E. (1975). Sexual behavior in college students. *American Journal of Orthopsychiatry, 45*(2), 284–285.

COX, H., BHAK, A., & KLINE, A. (1978, Winter). The motivation and marital adjustment patterns of older Americans. *Family Perspective,* 41–50.

CRANSTON, A. (1980). Progress in controlling the aging process. *USA Today, 108*(2420), 17–18.

CRITES, J. O., & FITZGERALD, L. F. (1978). The competent male. *Counseling Psychologist, 7*(4), 10–14.

CROCKER, J., & McGRAW, K. M. (1984). What's good for the goose is not good for the gander. *American Behavioral Scientist, 27*(3), 357–369.

CROSBY, J. F., GAGE, B. A., & RAYMOND, M. C. (1983). The grief resolution process in divorce. *Journal of Divorce, 7*(1), 3–18.

CROWLEY J. E., & SHAPIRO, D. (1982). Aspirations and expectations of youth in the United States. Part I. Education and fertility. *Youth and Society, 13*(4), 391–422.

CUNNINGHAM, J. D., BRAIKER, H., & KELLEY, H. H. (1982). Marital-status and sex differences in problems reported by married and cohabiting couples. *Psychology of Women Quarterly, 6*(4), 415–427.

CUNNINGHAM, W. R., & CLAYTON, V. (1973). "Fluid" and "crystallized" intelligence in the elderly, *Proc. 81st Ann. Conv., APA.*

CURTIS, P. (1982). Our pets, ourselves. *Psychology Today, 16*(8), 66–67.

Dad decision, The (1978). *Human Behavior, 7*(8), 34–35.

DALOZ, L. (1981). Shared parenting: The male perspective. In R. A. Lewis (Ed.), *Men in difficult times* (pp. 284–288). Englewood Cliffs, NJ: Prentice-Hall.

DAMON, W. (1983). *Social and personality development.* New York: Norton.

DATAN, N. (1980). Midas and other midlife crises. In William H. Norman & T. J. Scaramella (Eds.), *Midlife: Developmental and clinical issues* (pp. 3–19). New York: Brunner/Mazel Publishers.

DE BOER, C. (1978). The polls: Attitudes toward work. *Public Opinion Quarterly, 42,* 415–423.

Decades of decision: Alternating currents. (1979). *Omni, 2*(1), 96; 144.

Decades of decision: The human family. (1979). *Omni, 2*(1), 102.

Decades of decision: Micro/macro. (1979). *Omni, 2*(1), 100; 144.

DECARLO, T. J. (Ed.), (1974). Recreation participation patterns and successful aging. *Journal of Gerontology, 29,* 416–422.

DECK, J. (1972). *Rancho paradise.* New York: Harcourt Brace Jovanovich.

Depression epidemic, The. (1979). *USA Today, 107*(2407), 15–16.

DIBNER, A. S. (1975). The psychology of normal aging. In M. G. Spencer & C. J. Dorr (Eds.), *Understanding aging: A multidisciplinary approach.* New York: Appleton-Century-Crofts.

DONNELLY, C. (1976). A free-spending, job-squeezed, house-proud future. *Money, 5*(5), 96.

DONOVAN, R. J. (1984, February/March). Planning for an aging work force. *Aging,* 4–7.

DOUGLAS, S. P., & WIND, Y. (1978). Examining family roles and authority patterns. *Journal of Marriage and the Family, 40*(1), 35–47.

DOUVAN, E. (1975). Sex differences in the opportunities, demands, and development of youth. *Youth: 74th Yearbook of National Society for the Study of Education, Part I* (pp. 27–45). Chicago: University of Chicago Press.

DOWD, J. J. (1979–80). The problems of generations and generational analysis. *International Journal of Aging and Human Development, 10*(3) 213–229.

DOYLE, J. A. (1983). *The male experience.* Dubuque, IA: William C. Brown.

DRACHMAN, D. A. (1980). An approach to the neurology of aging. In J. E. Birren & R. B. Sloane (Eds.), *Handbook of mental healh and aging* (pp. 501–519) Englewood Cliffs, NJ: Prentice-Hall, Inc.

DREYER, P. H. (1975). Sex, sex roles, and marriage among youth in the 1970s. *Youth: 74th Yearbook of National Society for the Study of Education, Part I.* (pp. 194–223). Chicago: University of Chicago Press.

DUBOS, R. (1976). The despairing optimist. *American Scholar, 45*(2), 168–172.

DULLEA, G. (1980, February 3). Is joint custody good for children? *New York Times Magazine,* 32–53.

DUVALL, E. M. (1971). *Family development* (4th ed.). Philadelphia: Lippincott.

Dynamic elderly: Busier, healthier, happier. (1984). *U.S. News & World Report, 97*(1), 48–52.

EATON, W. W. & MCLEOD, J. (1984). Consumption of coffee or tea and symptoms of anxiety. *American Journal of Public Health, 74*(1), 66–68.

EBAUGH, H. R. F., RICHMAN, K., & CHAFETZ, J. S. (1984). Life crises among the religiously committed: Do sectarian differences matter? *Journal for the Scientific Study of Religion, 23*(1), 19–31.

Economics of being single, The. (1976). *Money, 5*(7), 32–38.

EISDORFER, C. (1972). Adaptation to loss of work. In F. Carp (Ed.), *Retirement* (pp. 245–265). New York: Behavioral Publications.

———, & LAWTON, M. P. (Eds.). (1973). *The Psychology of adult development and aging.* Washington, D.C.: American Psychological Association.

EISENBERG, L. (1977). On the humanizing of human nature. *Impact, 23*(3), 213–224.

ELDER, G. H. JR. (1975). Adolescence in the life cycle. In S. E. Dragastin & G. H. Elder, Jr. (Eds.), *Adolescence in the life cycle* (pp. 1–22). Washington, D.C.: Hemisphere Publishing Corp.

ELKIND, D. (1979). Growing up faster. *Psychology Today, 12*(9), 38; 41–42; 45.

ELL, K. (1984). Social networks, social support, and health status: A review. *Social Service Review, 58*(1), 133–149.

ELMAN, M. R., & GILBERT, L. A. (1984). Coping strategies for role conflict in married professional women with children. *Family Relations, 33,* 317–327.

End of youth culture. (1977, October 3). *U.S. News & World Report,* 54–56.

Equality between the sexes. (1979). *USA Today, 108*(2415), 5–6.

ERIKSON, E. (1959). Identity and the life cycle. *Psychological Issues,* Monograph, 1.

ERICKSON, V. L. (1982). Counseling psychologists in business and industry: Some questions from a developmental lens. *Counseling Psychologist, 10,* 33–35.

ERICKSON, V. L. & MARTIN, J. (1984). The changing adult: An integrated approach. *Social Casework, 65*(3), 162–171.

ETZIONI, A. (1978–79). Protecting the rights of research subjects. *Nutshell,* 125–126.

EWER, P. A., CRIMMINS, E., & OLIVER, R. (1979). An analysis of the relationship between husband's income, family size, and wife's employment in the early stages of marriage, *Journal of Marriage and the Family, 41*(4), 727–738.

Exercise peril. (1984). In the news. *Discover, 5*(4), 10.

Family health in an era of stress. (1979). *USA Today, 108*(2411), 1–2.

FARIS, J. B. (1983, May–June). Technology promises increased convenience and challenges to the nation's elderly. *Aging,* 12–17.

FARRELL, W. (1978). The liberated man and woman. *Public Welfare, 36*(1), 22–27.

FELSON, M., & KNOKE, D. (1974). Social status and the married woman. *Journal of Marriage and the Family, 36*(3), 516–521.

FENGLER, A. P. (1984). Life satisfaction of subpopulations of elderly. *Research on Aging, 6*(2), 189–212.

FERBER, M. A. (1982). Labor market participation of young married women: Causes and effects. *Journal of Marriage and the Family, 44*(2), 457–468.

FERRAR, K. (1982). Experiences of parents in contemporary communal households. *Alternative Lifestyles, 5*(1), 7–23.

FERRIS, P. (1977). *Dylan Thomas.* London: Hodder & Stoughton.

FILLENBAUM, G. G. & WALLMAN, L. M. (1984). Change in household composition of the elderly: A preliminary investigation. *Journal of Gerontology, 39*(3), 342–349.

FIRESTONE, S. (1976). *The success trip.* Chicago: Playboy Press.

———. *The dialectic of sex: The case for feminist revolution.* New York: Bantam Books, Inc.

FISCHER, J. & CARDEA, J. M. (1981). Mothers living apart from their children. A study in stress and coping. *Alternative Lifestyles, 4*(2), 218–227.

FISCHER, C. S. & OLIKER, S. J. (1983). A research note on friendship, gender, and the life cycle. *Social Forces, 62*(1), 124–131.

FISHER, E. O. (1973). A guide to divorce counseling. *Family Coordinator, 22,* 55–61.

FISKE, M. (1980). Tasks and crises of the second half of life: The interrelationship of commitment, coping, and adaptation. In J. E. Birren & R. B. Sloane (Eds.), *Handbook of mental health and aging* (pp. 327–373) Englewood Cliffs, NJ: Prentice-Hall, Inc.

FITZGERALD, J. M., NESSELROADE, J. R., & BALTES, P. B. (1973). Emergence of adult intellectual structure: Prior to or during adolescence? *Developmental Psychology, 9,* 114–119.

FITZPATRICK, B. (1975). Economics of aging. In M. G. Spencer & C. J. Dorr (Eds.), *Understanding aging: A multidisciplinary approach* (pp. 105–133). New York: Appleton-Century-Crofts.

FLAVELL, J. H. (1970). Cognitive changes in adulthood. In L. R. Goulet & D. B. Baltes (Eds.), *Life span developmental psychology.* (pp. 248–257). New York: Academic Press.

FLEMING, C. B. (1981). Mothers' milk—you can bank on it. *Science, 2*(1), 78–79.

FLERZ, V. C., FIDLER, D. S., & ROGERS, R. W. (1976). Sex-role stereotypes: Developmental aspects and early intervention. *Child Development, 47*(4), 998–1007.

FLORIAN, V. & KRAVETZ, S. (1983). Fear of personal death: Attribution, structure and relation to religious belief. *Journal of Personality and Social Psychology, 44*(3), 600–607.

FOLKINS, C. H. & SIME, W. E. (1981). Physical fitness training and mental health. *American Psychologist, 36*(4), 373–389.

FOLSOM, J. C. (1972). Simple physical activities for the elderly and disabled. *Gerontologist, 12,* 139.

FOOTE, C. A. (1982). Human nature. Designing better humans. *Science Digest, 90*(10), 44.

FOOTE, F. H. & SLAPION-FOOTE, M. J. (1984). Do men and women love differently? *Journal of Social and Personal Relationships, 1,* 177–195.

FORMAN, B. L. (1984). Reconsidering retirement. Understanding emerging trends. *The Futurist, 18*(3), 43–47.

FOWLER, J. (1983). PT Conversation. Stages of faith. *Psychology Today, 17*(11), 56–62.

FOWLER, J. (1983). PT Conversation. Stages of faith. *Psychology Today, 17*(11), 56–62.

FOWLES, D. (1983, May–June). The changing older population. *Aging,* 6–11.
95–97). Guilford, CN.: Dushkin.

FOX, G. L. (1980). The mother-adolescent daughter relationship as a sexual socialization structure: A research review. *Family Relations, 29*(1), 21–28.

FOZARD, J. L., & POPKINS, S. J. (1978). Optimizing adult development: Ends and means of an applied psychology of aging. *American Psychologist, 33*(11), 975–989.

FRANCKE, L. B. (1978). *The ambivalence of abortion.* New York: Random House.

FREEDMAN, J. L. (1978). Love-marriage-happiness (still). *Public Opinion, 1*(5), 49–53.

FREEDMAN, M. (1975). Homosexuals may be healthier than straights. *Psychology Today, 8*(10), 28–32.

Freeing up after forty. (1976). *Human Behavior. 5*(5) 50–51.

FREEMAN, E. M. (1984). Multiple losses in the elderly: An ecological approach. *Social Casework: The Journal of Contemporary Social Work, 65*(5), 287–296.

FREEMAN, M. (1984). History, narrative, and life-span developmental knowledge. *Human Development, 27*(1), 1–19.

FREUDIGER, P. (1983). Life satisfaction among three categories of married women. *Journal of Marriage and the Family, 45*(1), 213–219.

FRIED, B. (1967). *The middle-age crisis.* New York: Harper & Row.

Funerals: the memorial service alternative. (1982). In J. A. Fruehling (Ed.) *Source book on Death and Dying* (1st ed.) (pp. 147–148). Chicago: Marquis Professional Publications.

FURRY, C. A., & BALTES, P. B. (1973). The effect of age differences in ability-extraneous performance variables on the assessment of intelligence in children, adults, and the elderly. *Journal of Gerontology, 28,* 73–80.

FURUKAWA, C. & SHOMAKER, D. (1982). *Community health services for the aged.* Rockville, MD: Aspen Systems Corporation.

Future work (1977). *Human behavior, 6*(7), 47.

GAEDDERT, W. P., KAHN, A., FREVERT, R. L., & SHIRLEY, R. (1981, April). Role model choice: Who do women say their models are? Paper presented at the meeting of the Midwestern Psychological Association.

GAITZ, C. (1971). Aging and the brain. A symposium at the University of Texas Medical Center, Houston, Texas. New York: Plenum Publishing Corporation.

GALLUP, G. JR. (1977). U.S. in early stage of religious revival? *Journal of Current Social Issues, 14*(2), 50–52.

GARDINER, J. K. (1978). The new motherhood. *North American Review, 263*(3), 72–76.

GARDINER, B. B. (1974). The awakening of the blue collar woman. *Intellectual Digest, 4*(7), 17–19.

GEARING, J. (1978). Facilitating the birth process and father child bonding. *Counseling Psychologist, 7*(4), 53–56.

GEE, E. M. & VEEVERS, J. E. (1983). Accelerating sex differentials in mortality: An analysis of contributing factors. *Social Biology, 30*(1), 75–85.

GELLES, R. J. (1976). Abused wives: Why do they stay? *Journal of Marriage and the Family,* 659–668.

Generation in the middle. (1970). *Blue Cross Report, 23*(1), 11.

GERBER, T. (1980). Life in a single room. *Psychology Today, 14*(2), 34.

GERSON, M., ALPERT, J. L. & RICHARDSON, M. S. (1984). Mothering: The view from psychological research. *Journal of Women in Culture and Society, 9* 434–453.

GFELLER, E. (1978). Pinpointing the cause of disturbed behavior in the elderly. *Geriatrics, 33*(12), 26–30.

GIBBS, J. C. (1979). The meaning of ecologically oriented inquiry in contemporary psychology. *Geriatrics, 34*(2), 127–140.

GIBSON, D. E. (1984). Hospice: Morality and economics. *The Gerontologist, 24*(1), 4–8.

GILES-SIMS, J. (1984). The stepparent role. *Journal of Family Issues, 5*(1), 116–130.

GILFORD, R. & BENGTSON, V. (1979). Measuring marital satisfaction in three generations: Positive and negative dimensions. *Journal of Marriage and the Family, 41*(2), 387–398.

GILL, S. J., COPPARD, L. C., & LOWTHER, M. A. (1983). Mid-life career development theory and research: Implications for education and work. *Aging and Work, 6*(1), 15–30.

GILMARTIN, B. G. (1975). That swinging couple down the block. *Psychology Today, 8*(9), 54–58.

GLANTZ, L. H. (1984). Limiting state regulation of reproductive decisions. *American Journal of Public Health, 74*(2), 168–169.

GLASS, L. L. (1984). Man's man/Ladies' man. Motifs of hypermasculinity. *Psychiatry, 47,* 260–278.

GLENN, N. D. (1982). Interreligious marriage in the United States: Patterns and recent trends. *Journal of Marriage and the Family, 44*(3), 555–566.

GLENN, N. D. & McLANAHAN, S. (1982). Children and marital happiness: A further specification of the relationship. *Journal of Marriage and the Family, 44*(1), 63–72.

GLICK, P. C. (1984). Marriage, divorce, and living arrangements. *Journal of Family Issues, 5*(1), 7–26.

GLICK, P. C. (1975). Some recent changes in American families. *Current Population Reports,* P–23(52).

GOETHALS, G. W. (1975). Adolescence: Variations on a theme. *Youth: 74th Yearbook of National Society of the Study of Education, Part I* (pp. 46–60). Chicago: University of Chicago Press.

GOLEMAN, D. (1980a). Leaving home: Is there a right time to go? *Psychology Today, 14*(3), 52–61.

———. (1980b). Still learning from Terman's children. *Psychology Today, 13*(9), 44–53.

———. (1978). Who's mentally ill? *Psychology Today, 11*(8), 34–41.

GOLENPAUL, A. (Ed.). (1976). *Information please almanac: atlas and yearbook, 1976.* New York: Simon & Schuster.

GONGLA, P. (1982). In H. Gross & M. B. Sussman (Eds.). *Alternatives to traditional family living.* New York: Haworth Press. 3–20.

GOODMAN, N., & FELDMAN, K. A. (1975). Expectations, ideals, and reality: Youth enters college. In S. E. Dragastin & G. H. Elder (Eds.) *Adolescence in the life cycle* (pp. 147–150). Washington, D.C.: Hemisphere Publishing Corporation.

GORDON, C., & GAITZ, C. M. (1977). Leisure and lives: Personal expressivity across the life span. In R. H. Binstock & E. Shanas (Eds.), *Handbook of aging and the social sciences.* New York: Van Nostrand Reinhold.

GORE, S., & MANGIONE, T. W. (1983). Social roles, sex roles and psychological distress: Additive and interactive models of sex differences. *Journal of Health and Social Behavior, 24,* 300–312.

GOTTESMAN, L. E., QUARTERMAN, C. E., & KOHN, G. M. (1973). Psychosocial treatment of the aged. In C. Eisendorfer & M. P. Lawton (Eds.), *The psychology of adult development and aging.* Washington D.C.: American Psychological Association.

GOTTFREDSON, G. D. (1972). Career stability and redirection in adulthood. *Journal of Applied Psychology, 62,* 436–446.

GOULD, R. (1975). Adult life stages: Growth toward self-tolerance. *Psychology Today 8*(9), 74–78.

GOVE, W. R., & HUGHES, M. (1979). Possible cause of the apparent sex differences in physical health: An empirical investigation. *American Sociological Review, 44,* 126–146.

GOVE, W. R., HUGHES, M., & STYLE, C. B. (1983). Does marriage have positive effects on the psychological well-being of the individual? *Journal of Health and Social Behavior, 24,* 122–131.

GRAUBARD, S. R. (1976). Preface to the issue "Adulthood." *Daedalus, 105*(2), v–viii.

Graying of the campus. (1977, January 24). *Wall Street Journal,* 1; 20.

GREEN, J. T., & FRIEDMAN, P. (1981). Near-death experiences in a southern California population. *Anabiosis, 3*(1), 77–95.

GREENBERG, J. (1980, July 20). Some experts say genetics helps women live longer. *Atlanta Journal-Atlanta Constitution.*

GREENBLAT, C. S. (1983). The salience of sexuality in the early years of marriage. *Journal of Marriage and the Family, 45*(2), 289–300.

GREGORY, D. R. (1982). A new definition of death. In J. A. Fruehling (Ed.) *Source book on death and dying* (1st ed.) (pp. 115–118). Chicago: Marquis Professional Publications.

GRINDER, R. E. (1969). The concept of adolescence in the genetic psychology of G. Stanley Hall. *Child Development, 40,* 355–369.

GROSS, H., & SUSSMAN, M. B. (Eds.) (1982). *Alternatives to traditional family living.* New York: Hayworth Press.

GROTEVANT, H. D., SCARR, S., & WEINBERG, R. A. (1978). Are career interests inheritable? *Psychology Today 11*(10), 88–96.

GROTH-JUNCKER, A., & McCUSKER, J. (1983). Where do elderly patients prefer to die? Place of death and patient characteristics of 100 elderly patients under the care of a home health care team. *Journal of the American Geriatrics Society, 31*(8), 457–461.

GRUBER, H. E. (1973). Courage and cognitive growth in children and scientists. In M. Schwebel & J. Raph (Eds.), *Piaget in the Classroom.* New York: Basic Books, Inc.

GUBRIUM, J. F. (1975). Being single in old age. *Aging and Human Development, 6*(1), 29–41.

GUION, E. W. (1983–84, December-January). A new feature on the housing horizon. *Aging,* pp. 9–11.

GUNTER, B. G. & MOORE, H. A. (1975). Youth, leisure, and postindustrial society: Implications for the family. *Family Coordinator, 24*(2), 199–207.

HAAN, N. (1976). ". . . Change and sameness . . ." reconsidered. *International Journal of Aging and Human Development, 7*(1), 59–65.

———. (1981). Common dimensions of personality development: Early adolescence to middle life. In D. H. Eichorn, J. A. Clausen, N. Haan, M. P. Honzik, & P. H. Mussen (Eds.), *Present and past in middle life.* New York: Academic Press.

———, & DAY, D. (1974). A longitudinal study of change and sameness in personality development: Adolescence to later adulthood. *International Journal of Aging and Human Development, 5*(1), 11–39.

HALL, E. (1980). Acting one's age: New rules for old. *Psychology Today, 13*(11), 66–80.

——— (1974). People plan their lives in terms of imaginary systems: Nobody lives in the real world. *Psychology Today, 8*(2), 61–70.

———, & CAMERON P. (1976). Our failing reverence for life. *Psychology Today, 9*(11), 104–108; 113.

HAMMITT, W. E. & BROWN, G. E. (1984). Functions of privacy in wilderness environments. *Leisure Sciences, 6*(2), 151–166.

HAMPES, G. D., & BLEVINS, A. L. (1975). Primary group interaction. *International Journal of Aging and Human Development, 6*(4), 309–320.

HANNA, S. L. & KNAUB, P. K. (1981). Cohabitation before remarriage. Its relationship to family strengths. *Alternative Lifestyles, 4*(4), 507–522.

Happy daddies. (1978). *Human Behavior, 7*(11), 37.

HARE, P. H. & HASKE, M. (1983–1984, December–January). Innovative living arrangements: A source of long-term care. *Aging, 3–8.*

HAREVEN, T. K. (1976). The last stage: Historical adulthood and old age. *Daedalus, 105*(4), 13–27.

HARRIS, D. (1981). The middle-aged rush. *Psychology Today, 15*(11), 31.

HARRY, J. (1976). Evolving sources of happiness for men over the life cycle: A structural analysis. *Journal of Marriage and the Family, 38,* 289–296.

———. (1979). The "marital" liaisons of gay men. *Family Coordinator, 28*(4), 622–629.

HARTFORD, M. E. (1980). The use of group methods for work with the aged. In J. E. Birren & R. B. Sloane (Eds.), *Handbook of mental health and aging,* (pp. 806–826). Englewood Cliffs, NJ: Prentice-Hall, Inc.

HATFIELD, E., GREENBERGER, D., TRAUPMANN, J., & LAMBERT, P. (1982). Equity and sexual satisfaction in recently married couples. *Journal of Sex Research, 18*(1), 18–32.

HAUSER, P. M. (1976). Aging and world-wide population change. In R. H. Binstock & E. Shanas (Eds.), *Handbook of aging and the social sciences,* (pp. 59–86). New York: Van Nostrand Reinhold Company.

HAUSMAN, D. B., & KAPPLER, A. S. (1979). Death as irreversible coma: An appraisal. *Journal of Inquiry, 12*(1), 49–52.

HAVENS, E. M. (1973). Women, work, and wedlock: A note on female marital patterns in the United States. *American Journal of Sociology, 78,* 975–981.

HAVIGHURST, R. J. (1972). *Developmental tasks and education* (3rd ed.). New York: McKay.

———. (1974). Youth in crisis. *School Review, 83*(1), 5–10.

———., NEUGARTEN, B. L., & TOBIN, S. S. (1968). Disengagement and patterns of aging. In B. L. Neugarten (Ed.), *Middle age and aging.* Chicago: University of Chicago Press.

HAYFLICK, L. (1984). When does aging begin? *Research on Aging, 6*(1), 99–103.

HAYIM, G. J. (1984). Review of Barry Schwarts, Vertical classification: A study of structuralism and the sociology of knowledge. Chicago: University of Chicago Press, 1981. In *Social Forces, 62*(3), 842–844.

HAYS, J. A. (1984). Aging and family resources: Availability and proximity of kin. *Gerontologist, 24*(2), 149–152.

HAYS, R. B. (1984). The development and maintenance of friendship. *Journal of Social and Personal Relationships, 1,* 75–98.

HEILBRUN, A. B. JR. (1981). *Human sex-role behavior.* Elmsford, NY: Pergamon Press.

HENDRICKS, J., & HENDRICKS, C. D. (1977). *Aging in mass society: Myths and realities.* Cambridge: MA: Winthrop.

HENLEY, J. R., & ADAMS, L. D. (1973). Marijuana use in post-college cohorts: Correlates of use, prevalence patterns, and factors associated with cessation. *Social Problems, 20*(4), 514–520.

HERTEL, B., & NELSEN, H. M. (1974). Are we entering a post-Christian era? Religious belief and attendance in America, 1957–1968. *Journal for the Scientific Study of Religion, 13*(4), 409–419.

HESS, B. B., & WARING, J. M. (1978). Parent and child in later life: Rethinking the relationship. In R. M. Lerner & G. B. Spanier (Eds.), *Child influences on marital and family interaction: A life-span perspective* (pp. 241–273). New York: Academic Press.

HESSON, J. E. (1978). The hidden psychological costs of unemployment. *Intellect, 106*(2395), 389–390.

HICKS, R., FUNKENSTEIN, H. H., DAVIS, J. M., & DYSKEN, M. W. (1980). Geriatric psychopharmacology. In J. E. Birren & R. B. Sloane (Eds.), *Handbook of mental health and aging* (pp. 745–774). Englewood Cliffs, NJ: Prentice-Hall, Inc.

HIEMSTRA, R., GOODMAN, M., MIDDLEMISS, M. A., & VOXCO, R. (1983). How older persons are portrayed in television advertising: Implications for educators. *Educational Gerontology, 9,* 111–122.

HILL, C. T., RUBIN, Z., & PEPLAU, L. A. (1981). Breakups before marriage: The end of 103 affairs. In L. D. Steinberg (Ed.), *The Life Cycle: Readings in Human Development* (pp. 224–239). New York: Columbia University Press.

HILTZ, S. R. (1975). Helping widows: Group discussions as a therapeutic technique. *Family Coordinator, 24*(3), 331–336.

HIRSCH, G. T. (1974). Nonsexist childrearing: Demythifying normative data. *Family Coordinators, 23*(2), 165–170.

HOCHSCHILD, A. R. (1973). *The unexpected commmunity.* Englewood Cliffs, NJ: Prentice-Hall, Inc.

HOFFMAN, E. (1979–1980). Young adults' relations with their grandparents: An exploratory study. *International Journal of Aging and Human Development, 10*(4), 299–310.

HOFFMAN, L. W., & MANIS, J. D. (1978). Influences of children on marital interaction and parental satisfactions and dissatisfactions. In R. M. Lerner & G. B. Spanier (Eds.), Child influences on marital and family interaction: A life-span perspective (pp. 165–213). New York: Academic Press.

HOLAHAN, C. K. (1984). Marital attitudes over 40 years: A longitudinal and cohort analysis: *Journal of Gerontology, 39*(1), 49–57.

HOLCOMB, W. L. (1975). Spiritual cases among the aging. In M. G. Spencer & C. J. Dorr (Eds.), *Understanding aging: A multidisciplinary approach* (pp. 234–278). New York: Appleton-Century-Crofts.

HONZIK, M. P. (1984). Life-span development. *Annual Review of Psychology, 35,* 309–331.

HOOPER, J. O. & TRAUPMANN, J. A. (1983). Older women, the student role and mental health. *Educational Gerontology, 9,* 233–242.

HORN, J. C. (1975). Retirement—a dirty word, a depressing time. *Psychology Today 9*(1), 95–96.

———. (1979). The anxiety parade. *Psychology Today 13*(7), 32–34.

———. (1978). The youngest workers care the least. *Psychology Today 12*(5), 34–38.

HORN, P. (1975). A new teen-age course: Learning to be parents. *Psychology Today 8*(10), 79–80.

HOUSEKNECHT, S. K. (1977, May). Reference group support for voluntary childlessness: Evidence for conformity. *Journal of Marriage and the Family,* 285–292.

———. (1982). Voluntary childlessness in the 1980s: A significant increase? *Marriage and Family Review, 5,* 51–69.

———., & PANKHURST, J. G. (1983). The fate of alternative lifestyles in an era of "pro-family" politics. *Alternative Lifestyles, 5*(4), 190–205.

———., VAUGHN, S., & MACKE, A. S. (1984). Marital disruption among professional women: The timing of career and family events. *Social Problems, 31*(3), 273–284.

HOUSER, B. B. & GARVEY, C. (1983). The impact of family, peers, and educational personnel upon career decision-making. *Journal of Vocational Behavior, 23,* 35–44.

HOWE, M. J. A. (1982). Biographical evidence and the development of outstanding individuals. *American Psychologist, 37*(10), 1071–1081.

HOWE, M. J. A. (1980). *The psychology of human learning.* New York: Harper & Row.

How's your sex life? *Redbook's* survey on female sexuality. (1975, September 1). Reported in *Newsweek,* 57, 86.

HOYT, D. R. & BABCHUK, N. (1983). Adult kinship networks: The selective formation of intimate ties with kin. *Social Forces, 62*(1), 84–101.

HÜBNER, F. S. (1983). Transition into occupational life: Environmental and sex differences regarding the status passage from school to work. *Adolescence, 18*(71), 709–723.

HUETHER, C. A., HOWE, S., & KELAGHAN, J. (1980). Knowledge, attitudes and practice regarding vasectomy among residents of Hamilton County, Ohio, 1980. *American Journal Of Public Health, 74*(1), 79–82.

HUNT, M. (1983). Sexual behavior in the 1970s. *Playboy, 20*(10), 84–88.

———. (1974). Sexual Behavior in the 1970s. Chicago: Playboy Press.

HURLBURT, R. T. (1979). Random samplings of cognitions and behavior. *Journal of Research in Personality.* Cited in J. C. Gibbs, The meaning of ecologically oriented inquiry in contemporary psychology. *American Psychologist, 34*(2), 127–140.

HUYCK, M. H. (1974). *Growing older.* Englewood Cliffs, NJ: Prentice-Hall, Inc.

HYATT, J. C. (1979, October 25). Aging Americans: As lives are extended, some people wonder if it's really a blessing. *Wall Street Journal,* 1; 27.

If you live to be a hundred—it won't be unusual. (1983, May 9). *U.S. News & World Report,* A-10.

IMARA, M. (1975). Dying as the last stage of growth. In E. Kübler Ross (Ed.), *Death: The final stage of growth,* (pp. 147–163). Englewood Cliffs, NJ: Prentice-Hall, Inc.

Interview: Philip Morrison. (1979). *Omni, 2*(1), 93–94; 146–147.

Is it right? . . . To turn off life support? . . . To keep a body alive for its organs? . . . To give illegal narcotics to the dying? (1982). In J. A. Fruehling (Ed.), *Source book on death and dying* (1st ed.), (pp. 38–41). Chicago: Marquis Professional Publications.

JACKSON, E. L. (1983). Activity-specific barriers to recreation participation. *Leisure Services, 6*(1), 47–60.

JACOBY, S. (1974, February 17). 49 million singles can't all be right. *New York Times Magazine.*

JARVIK, L. F., EISDORFER, C., & BLUM, J. E., (Eds.). (1973). *Intellectual Functioning in Adults.* New York: Springer Publishing Co.

JENCKS, C. (1979). Making it: Can the odds be evened? *Psychology Today, 13*(2), 35–39.

Job and family. (1980, June 16). *U.S. News & World Report,* pp. 57–58.

JOHNSON, C. L. (1983). A cultural analysis of the grandmother. *Research on Aging, 5*(4), 547–567.

JORDAN, J. J. (1983–1984, December-January). The challenge: Designing buildings for older Americans. *Aging,* 18–25.

JORDAN, W. D. (1976). Searching for adulthood in America. *Daedalus, 105*(4), 1–11.

JORGENSEN, S. R. (1979). Socioeconomic rewards and perceived marital quality: A reexamination. *Journal of Marriage and the Family, 41*(4), 825–835.

JUHASZ, A. M. (1980). Adolescent attitudes toward childbearing and family size. *Family Relations, 29*(1), 29–36.

JURICH, A. P., & JURICH, J. A. (1975). The lost adolescent syndrome. *Family Coordinator, 24*(3), 357–361.

JURY, M., & JURY, D. (1976). Gramp. *Psychology Today, 9*(9), 57–65.

KAGAN, J., KEARSLEY, R. B., & ZELAZO, P. R. (1978). *Infancy: Its place in human development.* Cambridge, MA: Harvard University Press.

KAHN, A. (1984). The power war: Male response to power loss under equality. *Psychology of Women Quarterly, 8*(3), 234–247.

KALISH, R. (1975). *Late adulthood: Perspectives on human development. Monterey, CA: Brooks/Cole Publishing Company.*

———., & REYNOLDS, D. K. (1975). Death and bereavement in a cross-ethnic context. Unpublished manuscript.

KANGAS, P. E. (1978, February). The single professional woman: A phenomenological study. *Dissertation Abstracts International, 38*(8–B), 3888.

KANTER, M. K. (1978, March). Psychological implications of never married women who live alone. *Dissertation Abstracts International, 38*(9–B), 4464.

KASLOW, F. W., & SCHWARTZ, L. L. (1978). Self-perceptions of the attractive, successful female professional. *Intellect, 106*(2393), 313–315.

KASTENBAUM, R. (1974). Fertility and death. *Journal of Social Issues, 30*(4), 63–78.

KAUFMAN, D. R. & RICHARDSON, B. L. (1982). *Achievement and women: challenging the assumptions.* New York: The Free Press.

KAY, D. W. K., & BERGMANN, K. (1980). Epidemiology of mental disorders among the aged in the community. In J. E. Birren & R. B. Sloane (Eds.), *Handbook of mental health and aging* (pp. 34–56). Englewood Cliffs, NJ: Prentice-Hall, Inc.

KAY, E. (1974). *The crisis in middle management.* New York: American Management.

KEEN, S. (1978). Eating our way to enlightenment. *Psychology Today, 12*(5), 62–66; 79; 82; 87.

KEITH, P. M., & BRUBAKER, T. H. (1979). Male household roles in later life: A look at masculinity and marital relationships. *Family Coordinator, 28*(4), 497–502.

KEITH, P. M., POWERS, E. A., & GOUDY, W. J. (1981). Older men in employed and retired families. Well-being and involvement in household activities. *Alternative Lifestyles, 4*(2), 228–241.

KEITH, P. M. & SCHAFER, R. B. (1984). Role behavior and psychological well-being: A comparison of men in one-job and two-job families. *American Journal of Orthopsychiatry, 54*(1), 137–145.

KELLY, J. R. (1983). Leisure styles: A hidden care. *Leisure Sciences, 5*(4), 321–328.

KELLY, J. R. (1975). Life styles and leisure choices. *Family Coordinator, 24*(2), 185–190.

KELLY, T. E. (1982). What is death? Parts I & II. In J. A. Fruehling (Ed.), *Source Book on death and dying* (1st ed.) (pp. 123–128). Chicago: Marquis Professional Publications.

KEMPLER, H. L. (1976). Extended kinship ties and some modern alternatives. *The Family Coordinator, 25*(2), 143–149.

KENT, S. (1980). *The life-extension revolution.* New York: William Morrow & Co., Inc.

KERCKHOFF, R. K. (1976). Marriage and middle age. *Family Coordinator, 25*(1), 5–11.

KESSLER, J. B. (1976). Aging in different ways. *Human Behavior, 5*(6), 56–60.

KIMMEL, D. (1974).*Adulthood and aging.* New York: John Wiley & Sons, Inc.

KINKADE, K. (1973). Commune: A Walden Two experiment. *Psychology Today 6*(9), 71–82.

KINSEY, A. E., POMEROY, W. B., MARTIN, C. E., & GEBHARD, P. H. (1948). *Sexual behavior in the human male.* Philadelphia: Saunders.

KIRSCHNER, C. (1979). The aging family in crisis: A problem in living. *Social Casework: The Journal of Contemporary Social Work, 60*(4), 209–216.

KITAHARA, M. (1982). Male puberty rites: A path analytic model. *Adolescence, 17*(66), 293–304.

KIVETT, V. R. (1976). *The aged in North Carolina: Physical, social and environmental characteristics and sources of assistance,* Technical Bulletin No., 237, Raleigh, N.C.: Agricultural Experiment Station.

KLEIN, N. (1978). Is there a right way to die? *Psychology Today, 12*(5), 122.

KLERMAN, G. L. (1979). The age of melancholy. *Psychology Today, 12*(11), 37–42; 88.

KNOX, A. B. (1979). Programming for midlife. In A. B. Knox (Ed.), *Programming for adults facing midlife change,* (pp. 37–43). San Francisco: Jossey-Bass, Inc.

KNOX, D. (1980). Trends in marriage and the family—the 1980s. *Family Relations, 29*(2), 145–150.

KOCH, J. & KOCH, L. (1976). Sex therapy: Caveat emptor. *Psychology Today, 9*(10), 37.

KOCH, S. (1981). The nature and limits of psychological lessons of a century qua "science." *American Psychologist, 36,* 257–269.

KOENIG, R. (1984, February 28). Philadelphia shelter for the street people knows the score. *Wall Street Journal,* 1.

KOHLBERG, L. (1975). The cognitive developmental approach to moral development. *Phi Delta Kappan, 51*(10), 670–673.

KOLBENSCHLAG, M. (1976). Dr. Estelle Ramey: Reclaiming the feminine legacy. *Human Behavior, 5*(7), 25–27.

KOMPARA, D. R. (1980). Difficulties in the socialization process of stepparenting. *Family Relations, 29*(1), 69–73.

KRANT, M. J. (1972). The organized care of the dying patient. *Hospital Practice,* (7), 101–108.

KRAUSKOPF, J. M. & BURNETT, M. E. (1983, December). The elderly person: When protection becomes abuse. *Trial,* 61–71.

KREPS, J. M. (1977). Intergenerational transfers and the bureaucracy. In E. Shanas & M. B. Sussman (Eds.) *Family, bureaucracy, and the elderly.* Durham, NC: Duke University Press.

KRESSEL, K. (1980). Patterns of coping in divorce and some implications for clinical practice. *Family Relations, 29*(2), 234–240.

KROUT, J. A. (1983). Correlates of senior center utilization. *Research on Aging, 5*(3), 339–352.

KÜBLER-ROSS, E. (1974). *Questions and answers on death and dying.* New York: Macmillan, Inc.

KUTNER, L. (1982). Euthanasia: Due process for death with dignity: The living will. In J. A. Fruehling (Ed.), *Source book on death and dying,* (1st ed.) (p. 64). Chicago: Marquis Professional Publications.

LACY, W. B., & HENDRICKS, J. (1980). Developmental models of adult life: Myth or reality? *International Journal of Aging and Human Development, 11*(2), 89–110.

LAIKIN, G. J. (1982). Planning your estate—death and taxes. In J. A. Fruehling (Ed.), *Source book on death and dying,* (1st ed.) (pp. 219–226). Chicago: Marquis Professional Publications.

LAMB, M. E. (1978). Influence of the child on marital quality and family interaction during the prenatal, perinatal, and infancy periods. In R. M. Lerner & Graham B. Spanier (Eds.), *Child influences on marital and family interactions: A life-span perspective* (pp. 137–163). New York: Academic Press.

LAMB, M. E. (1982). Second thoughts on first touch. *Psychology Today 16*(4), 9–11.

LAMOTT, K. (1978). The money revolution. *Human Behavior, 7*(4), 18–23.

LANCASTER, H. (1982, January 8). The anxious aged. *Wall Street Journal,* p. 1.

LANGONE, J. (1983). B. F. Skinner: Beyond reward and punishment. *Discover, 4*(9), 38–46.

LASAGNA, L. (1979, December). Deathwatch. *Sciences,* 17.

LASSWELL, M. E., (1974). Is there a best age to marry? An interpretation. *Family Coordinator, 23*(3), 237–242.

LAUDICINA, E. V. (1973). Toward new forms of liberation: A mildly utopian proposal. *Social Theory and Practice, 2*(3), 275–288.

LAWRENCE, L. (1983). Stages of faith: PT conversation with James Fowler. *Psychology Today, 17*(11), 56–62.

LAWTON, M. P. (1983). Environment and other determinants of well-being in the aged. *Gerontologist, 23,* 349–357.

LAWTON, M. P., MOSS, M., & MOLES, E. (1984). The suprapersonal neighborhood context of older people: Age heterogeneity and well-being. *Environment and behavior, 16*(1), 89–109.

LAWTON, M. P., & NAHEMOW, L. (1973). Ecology and the aging process. In C. Eisdorfer & M. P. Lawton (Eds.). *The psychology of adult development and aging.* Washington, DC: American Psychological Association.

LEAHEY, M. (1984). Findings from research on divorce: Implications for professionals' skill development. *American Journal of Orthopsychiatry, 54*(2), 298–317.

LEE, G. R. (1978). Marriage and morale in later life. *Journal of Marriage and the Family, 40*(1), 131–139.

LEE, R. R. (1982). Object loss and counseling the bereaved. In J. A. Fruehling (Ed.), *Source book on death and dying,* (1st ed.) (pp. 183–188). Chicago: Marquis Professional Publications.

LEMASTERS, E. E. (1973). *Parents in modern America.* Homewood, IL: Dorsey Press.

LEMKAU, J. P. (1984): Men in female-dominated professions: Distinguishing personality and background features. *Journal of Vocational Behavior, 24,* 110–122.

LERNER, R. M. & SPANIER, G. B. (Eds.). (1978). *Child influences on marital and family interaction: A life-span perspective.* New York: Academic Press.

Lesbian life styles. (1977). *Human Behavior, 6*(11), 51–52.

LESHAN, E. J. (1973). *The wonderful crisis of middle age.* New York: David McKay.

LEVENTHAL, E. A. (1984). Aging and the perception of illness. *Research on Aging, 6*(1), 119–135.

LEVINE, S. B. (1984). Single living. *Ms., 13*(5), 47.

LEVINE, E. M. (1984). The middle-class family and middle-class adolescents in a state of disarray: A social-psychiatric analysis. *Psychiatry, 47,* 152–161.

LEVINGER, G., & SNOEK, J. D. (1972). *Attraction to relationship: A new look at interpersonal attraction.* Morristown, NJ: General Learning Press.

LEVINSON, D. J. (1977). The midlife transition: A period in adult psychosocial development. *Psychiatry, 40,* 99–112.

LEVY, S. M. (1978). Some determinants of temporal experience in the retired and its correlates. *Genetic Psychology Monographs, 98,* 181–202.

LEWIN, B. (1982). Unmarried cohabitation: A marriage form in a changing society. *Journal of Marriage and the Family, 44*(3), 763–773.

LEWIS, R. A., FRENEAU, P. J., & ROBERTS, C. L. (1979). Fathers and the postparental transition. *Family Coordinator, 28*(4), 514–520.

LEWIS, R., KOZAC, E. B., MILARDO, R. M., & GROSNICK, W. A. (1981). Commitment in same-sex love relationships. *Alternative Lifestyles, 4*(1), 22–42.

LIBBY, R. W. (1983). Sex, "the" family, and the religious new right. *Alternative Lifestyles, 5*(4), 206–235.

LIDZ, T. (1980). Phases of adult life: An overview. In W. H. Norman & T. J. Scaramella (Eds.), *Midlife: developmental and clinical issues.* (pp. 20–37). New York: Brunner/Mazel Publishers.

LIFTON, R. J. (1975). On death and the continuity of life: A psychohistorical perspective. *Omega: Journal of Death and Dying, 6*(2), 143–159.

———., & OLSON, E. (1974). *Living and dying.* New York: Praeger.

LITRAS, T. S. (1979). The battle over retirement policies and practices. *Personnel Journal, 58*(2), 102–110.

LIONELLS, M., & MANN, C. H. (1974). *Patterns of midlife in transition.* New York: William Alanson White Institute.

LOFLAND, L. (1982). Relational loss and social bond: An exploration into human relations. In W. Ickes & E. S. Knowles (Eds.), *Personality, roles, and social behavior.* New York: Springer-Verlag.

LOGAN, R. D. (1983). A re-conceptualization of Erikson's identity stage. *Adolescence, 18*(72), 943–946.

LONDON, P. (1974). The psychotherapy boom: From the long couch for the sick to the push button for the bored. *Psychology Today, 8*(1), 63–68.

Lonely die, The. (1978). *Human Behavior, 7*(2), 61.

LONG, I. (1976). Human sexuality and aging. *Social Casework, 57*(4), 237–244.

LOPATA, H. Z. (1971). *Occupation: Housewife.* London: Oxford University Press.

LOWENTHAL, M. F. (1975). Psychosocial variations across the adult life course: Frontiers for research and policy. *Gerontologist, 15*(1), 6–12.

———. (1977). Toward a sociopsychological theory of change in adulthood and old age. In J. E. Birren & K. W. Schaie (Eds.), *Handbook of the psychology of aging,* (pp. 116–127). New York: Van Nostrand Reinhold Co.

———., & CHIRIBOGA, D. (1973). Social stress and adaptation: Toward a life-course perspective. In C. Eisdorfer & M. P. Lawton (Eds.), *The psychology of adult development and aging.* Wahington, D.C.: American Psychological Association.

———., THURNHER, M., CHIRIBOGA, D., & ASSOCIATES. (1975) *Four stages of life: A comparative study of women and men facing transitions.* San Francisco: Jossey-Bass.

LOWY, L. (1980). Mental health services in the community. In J. E. Birren & R. B. Sloane (Eds.), *Handbook of mental health and aging,* (pp. 827–853). Englewood Cliffs, NJ: Prentice-Hall, Inc.

———. (1975). Social welfare and the aging. In M. G. Spencer & C. J. Dorr (Eds.), *Understanding aging: A multidisciplinary approach* (pp. 134–178). New York: Appleton-Century-Crofts.

LUCKEY, E. B. (1974). What I have learned about family life. *Family Coordinator, 23*(3), 307–313.

LUNDAHL, C. R. & WIDDISON, H. A. (1983). The Mormon explanation of near-death experiences. *Anabiosis, 3*(1), 97–106.

LYNESS, L. L., LIPETZ, M. E., & DAVIS, K. E. (1972). Living together: An alternative to marriage. *Journal of Marriage and the Family, 34*(2), 305–311.

MAAS, H. S. & KUYPERS, J. A. (1974). *From thirty to seventy.* San Francisco: Jossey-Baas, Inc.

MACCOBY, E. E. & JACKLIN, C. N. (1974). What we know and don't know about sex differences. *Psychology Today, 8*(7), 108–112.

MACE, D. R. & MACE, V. C. (1975). Marriage enrichment—Wave of the future? *Family Coordinator, 24*(2), 131–135.

MACHLIS, G. E. & WENDEROTH, E. L. (1984). Cultural variation in the use of leisure time: Foreign tourists at the Grand Canyon. *Leisure Sciences, 6*(2), 187–204.

MACK, P. (1984). A response to Shirley Glubka's "out of the stream: An essay on unconventional motherhood." *Feminist Studies, 10*(1), 145–150.

MACKE, A. S., BOHRNSTEDT, G. W., & BERNSTEIN, I. N. (1979). Housewives' self-esteem and their husbands' success: The myth of vicarious involvement. *Journal of Marriage and the Family, 41*(1), 51–57.

MACKLIN, E. D. (1972). Heterosexual cohabitation among unmarried college students. *Family Coordinator, 21*(4), 463–472.

MADDOX, B. (1982). Homosexual parents. *Psychology Today, 16*(2), 62–69.

MADDOX, G. L. (1979). Sociology of later life. *Annual review of Sociology, 5,* 113–135.

MALATESTA, C. Z. & KALNOK, M. (1984). Emotional experience in younger and older adults. *Journal of Gerontology, 39*(3), 301–308.

MALIA, M. E. (1976). Adulthood refracted Russia and Leo Tolstoy. *Daedalus, 105*(2), 169–183.

MANN, C. H. (1980). Midlife and the family: Strains, challenges, and options of the middle years. In W. H. Norman & T. J. Scaramella (Eds.), *Midlife: developmental and clinical issues.* New York: Brunner-Mazel.

MARBLE, B. B., & PATTERSON, I. M. (1975). Nutrition and aging. In M. G. Spencer & C. J. Dorr (Eds.), *Understanding aging: A Multidisciplinary approach* (pp. 195–208). New York: Appleton-Century-Crofts.

MARCIANO, T. D. (1979). Male influences on fertility: Needs for research. *Family Coordinator, 28*(4), 561–568.

MARGULES, D. L. (1979). Obesity and the hibernation response. *Psychology Today, 13*(4), 136.

MARIN, P. (1983). A revolution's broken promises. *Psychology Today, 17*(7), 50–57.

MARINI, M. M. (1978). The transition to adulthood: Sex differences in educational attainment and age at marriage. *American Sociological Review, 43,* 483–507.

Marriage—still a popular institution? (1978). *USA Today, 107*(2399), 7.

MARRIS, P. (1978–79). Conservatism, innovation, and old age. *International Journal of Aging and Human Development, 9*(2), 127–135.

MARSH, G. R., & THOMPSON, L. W. (1973) Effects of age on the contingent negative variation in a pitch discrimination task. *Journal of Genontology 28,* 56–62.

MARSHALL, V. W. (1980). *Last chapters: A sociology of aging and dying.* Monterey, CA: Brooks-Cole.

MARSHALL, V. W. (1978–79). No exit: A symbolic interactionist perspective on aging. *International Journal of Aging and Human Development, 9*(4), 345–359.

MARTIN, M. C. (1982). Hospice care update: Many questions still to be answered. In J. A. Fruehling (Ed.), *Source book on death and dying,* (1st ed.) (pp. 208–210). Chicago: Marquis Professional Publications.

MASH, D. J. (1978, Winter). The development of lifestyle preferences of college women. *Journal of National Association of Women Deans and Counselors,* 72–76.

MASNICK, G. (1983, March 10). Some continuities and discontinuities in historical trends in household structure in the United States. Unpublished discussion paper prepared for the Seminar on Family History and Historical Demography, Harvard Center for Population Studies.

MATTHEWS, S. H. (1983). Analyzing topical oral biographies of old people. *Research on Aging, 5*(3), 569–589.

MATTHEWS, S. H. & SPREY, J. (1984). The impact of divorce on grandparenthood: An exploratory study. *Gerontologist, 24*(1), 41–47.

MAYNARD, C. E., & ZAWACKI, R. A. (1979). Mobility and the dual-career couple. *Personnel Journal, 58*(7), 468–472.

MAZOR, M. D. (1979). Barren couples. *Psychology Today, 12*(12), 101–8; 112.

MCCONNELL, C. E. (1984). A note on the lifetime risk of nursing home residency. *Gerontologist, 24*(2), 193–198.

MCCREA, F. B. (1983). The politics of menopause: the "discovery" of a deficiency disease. *Social Problems, 31*(1), 111–123.

MCFALLS, J. A. (1980). *Psychology and subfecundity.* New York: Academic Press.

MCGEE, J. & WELLS, K. (1982). Gender typing and androgyny in later life: New directions for theory and research. *Human Development, 25,* 116–139.

MCLAUGHLIN, S. D. & MICKLIN, M. (1983). The timing of the first birth and changes in personal efficacy. *Journal of Marriage and the Family, 45*(1), 47–55.

MCMORROW, F. (1974). *Midolescence: the dangerous years.* New York: Strawberry Hill Publishing Company.

MCQUADE, W. (1972). What stress can do to you. *Fortune, 85,* 102–107.

MEAD, M. (1950). *Male and female.* New York: Morrow.

MEDAWAR, P. B., & MEDAWAR, J. S. (1977). Revising the facts of life. *Harpers, 254*(1521), 41–61.

MEDLEY, M. L. (1977). Marital adjustment in the post-retirement years. *Family Coordinator, 26*(1), 5–11.

MEDVED, M., & WALLECHINSKY, D. (1976). *What really happened to the class of '65?* New York: Random House, Inc.

MENDES, H. A. (1976). Single fathers. *Family Coordinator, 1976, 25*(4), 439–444.

MENGE, C. P. (1982). Dream and reality: Constructive change partners. *Adolescence, 17*(66), 419–442.

Menstrual myths. (1977). *Human Behavior, 6*(2), 62.

MERRIAM, S. (1979). Middle age: A review of the research. In A. B. Knox (Ed.), *Programming for adults facing midlife change* (pp. 7–15). San Francisco: Jossey-Bass, Inc.

MICHAEL, J. M. (1982). The second revolution in health. *American Psychologist, 37*(8), 936–941.

Middle-age grief process. (1978). *Intellect, 108*(2394), 355.

Midlife may be the start of better things for men. (1981, July 26). *Atlanta Constitution,* 5E.

MILLER, B. (1979). Gay fathers and their children. *Family Coordinator, 28*(4), 544–552.

MILLER, F. W. & LESESNE, B. B. (1982). Should the funeral director be considered a counselor? In J. A. Fruehling (Ed.), *Source book on death and dying* (1st ed.) (pp. 178–179). Chicago: Marquis Professional Publications.

MILLER, M. (1982). Surviving the loss of a loved one: An inside look at grief counseling. In J. A. Fruehling (Ed.), *Source book on death and dying* (pp. 189–192). Chicago: Marquis Professional Publications.

MILLER, M., & MILLER, J. (1980, January). The plague of domestic violence in the U.S. *USA Today, 108* 26–28.

MILLER, M. J. (1983). The role of happenstance in career choice. *Vocational Guidance Quarterly, 32*(1), 16–20.

MILLER, S. J. (1965). The social dilemma of the aging participant. In A. M. Rose & W. A. Peterson (Eds.), *Older people and their social world* (pp. 77–92). Philadelphia: F. A. Davis Company.

MILLER, P. Y., & SIMON, W. (1979). Do youth really want to work: A comparison of the work values and job perceptions of younger and older men. *Youth and Society, 10*(4), 379–404.

MINTON, F. (1982). Clergy views of funeral practices: Part One. In J. A. Fruehling (Ed.), *Source book on death and dying* (1st ed.) (pp. 159–162). Chicago: Marquis Professional Publications.

MIZE, E. (1975). A mother mourns and grows. In E. Kübler-Ross (Ed.), *Death: The final stage of growth* (pp. 97–104). Englewood Cliffs, NJ: Prentice-Hall, Inc.

MONEY, J. (1977). Destereotyping sex roles. *Society, 14*(5), 25–28.

Monogamous laws. (1978). *Human Behavior, 7*(4), 26.

MONTAGU, A. (1982). *Growing young. Anthropology and Aging.* New York: McGraw-Hill.

MONTAGU, A., & COLEMAN, D. (1977). Don't be adultish. *Psychology Today, 11*(3), 46–55.

MONTGOMERY, J. E. (1979, November 9). Aging Americans: Predators find elderly are often easy prey for array of rip-offs. *Wall Street Journal,* 1; 28.

MONTGOMERY, J. E. (1982). The economics of supportive services for families with disabled and aging members. *Family Relations, 31*(1), 19–27.

MOODY, R. A. JR. (1975). *Life after life.* Atlanta: Mockingbird Books.

MOORE, D. (1983, January 30). America's neglected elderly. *New York Times Magazine,* 30–32; 34; 37.

MOORE, P. (1975). What we expect and what it's like. *Psychology Today, 9*(3), 29–30.

MORRIS, J. N. & SHERWOOD, S. (1983–84). Informal support resources for vulnerable elderly persons: Can they be counted on, why do they work? *International Journal of Aging and Human Development, 18*(2), 81–98.

MORRISON, R. F. (1977). Career adaptivity: The effective adaptation of managers to changing role demands. *Journal of Applied Psychology, 62,* 549–558.

MORTIMER, J. T., & LORENCE, J. (1978). Work experience and occupational value socialization: A longitudinal study. Presented at the 73rd annual meeting of the American Sociological Association, San Francisco.

———, & SIMMONS, R. G. (1978). Adult socialization. *Annual Review of Sociology, 4,* 421–454.

MOSS, M. S. & MOSS, S. Z. (1983–84). The impact of parental death on middle-aged children. *Omega: Journal of Death and Dying, 14*(1), 65–75.

MOTT, F. L. (1978). *Women, work, and family*. Lexington. MA: Lexington Books.

MOUSSEAU, J. (1975). The family, prison of love. *Psychology Today, 9*(3), 52–54; 56–58.

MOVIUS, M. (1976). Voluntary childlessness: The ultimate liberation. *Family Coordinator, 25*(1), 57–63.

MUELLER, C. W., PARCEL, T. L., & PAMPEL, F. C. (1979). The effect of marital-dyad status inconsistency on women's support for equal rights. *Journal of Marriage and the Family, 41*(4), 779–791.

MUSON, H. (1979). Moral thinking: Can it be taught? *Psychology Today, 12*(9), 48–58; 67–68; 92.

———. (1977). The lessons of the Grant study. *Psychology Today, 11*(4), 42; 48–49.

MUSSEN, P. H., EICHORN, D. H., HONZIK, M. P., BIEBER, S. L., & MEREDITH, W. M. (1980). Continuity and change in women's characteristics over four decades. *International Journal of Behavior and Development, 3* 333–347.

MUSSEN, P. H., HONZIK, M. P. & EICHORN, D. H. (1982). Early antecedents of life satisfaction at age 70. *Journal of Gerontology, 37*, 316–322.

MYLES, J. F. (1978). Institutionalization and sick role identification among the elderly. *American Sociological Review, 43*, 508–521.

MYRICKS, N. (1980). "Palimony": The impact of *Marvin* vs. *Marvin. Family Relations, 29*(2), 210–215.

NAFFZIGER, C. C., & NAFFZIGER, K. (1974). Development of sex-role stereotypes. *Family Coordinator, 23*(3), 251–258.

NASH, M. L. (1977). Dignity of person in the final phase of life: An exploratory study. *Omega, 8*, 71–80.

National Council on Aging. (1983). Program innovations in aging. Washington D.C.: National Council on Aging.

Nation of guinea pigs, A. (1979). *USA Today, 108*(2415), 10.

NEUGARTEN, B. L. (1974). Age groups in American society and the rise of the young-old. *Annals of the American Academy*, 187–198.

———. (Ed.) (1968). *Middle age and aging*. Chicago: University of Chicago Press.

———. (1972). Personality and the aging process. *Gerontologist, 12*, 9–15.

———., & WEINSTEIN, K. K. (1964). The changing American grandchildren. *Journal of Marriage and the Family. 22*, 199–204.

NEUGARTEN, B. L. & DATAN, N. (1981). The subjective experience of middle age. In L. D. Steinberg (Ed.), *The life cycle: Readings in human development* (pp. 273–283). New York: Columbia University Press.

NEULINGER, J. (1974, April 29). On leisure. *Behavior Today*, 120.

NEWMAN, B. M. (1979). Coping and adaptation in adolescence. *Human Development, 22*, 255–262.

NEWMAN, B. M., & NEWMAN, P. R. (1975). *Development through life: A psychosocial approach*. Homewood, IL: Dorsey Press.

NEWMAN, S. (1976). *Housing adjustments of older people: A report from the second phase*. Ann Arbor: Institute for Social Research, University of Michigan.

News Notes. (1981, July–August). *Aging*. 48–49.

News Notes. (1983–84, December–January). *Aging*. p. 34.

New tricks to teach the old (1975). *Intellect, 104*(2369), 147.

NILSON, L. B. (1978). The social standing of a housewife. *Journal of Marriage and the Family, 40*(3), 541–548.

NISSENSON, M. (1984). Aging Americans. Therapy after sixty. *Psychology Today, 18*(1), 22–26.

NOELKER, L., & HARVEL, Z. (1978). Predictors of well-being and survival among institutionalized aged. *Gerontologist, 8*(6), 562–567.

NORMAN, M. (1978). Substitutes for mother. *Human Behavior, 7*(2), 18–22.

NORTON, A. (1974). The family life cycle updated. In R. F. Winch & G. B. Spanier (Eds.), *Selected studies in marriage and the family*, (9th ed.). New York: Holt, Rinehart & Winston.

NOTMAN, M. T. (1980). Changing roles for women at midlife. In W. H. Norman & T. J. Scaramella (Eds.), *Midlife: Developmental and clinical issues* (pp. 85–109). New York: Brunner/Mazel Publishers.

NOYES, R. JR., & CLANCY, J. (1977). The dying role: Its relevance to improved patient care. *Psychiatry, 40*, 41–47.

NYDEGGER, D. N. (1976). Middle age: Some early returns—a commentary. *International Journal of Aging and Human Development, 7*(2), 137–141.

NYDEGGER, C. N., MITTENESS, L. S., & O'NEIL, J. (1983). Experiencing social generations. *Research on Aging, 5*(4), 527–546.

O'CONNOR, P. & BROWN, G. W. (1984). Supportive relationships: Fact or fancy? *Journal of Social and Personal Relationships, 1*, 159–175.

O'LEARY, V. E., & DEPNER, C. E. (1976). Alternative gender roles among women: Masculine, feminine, and androgynous. *Intellect, 104*(2371), 313–315.

Only married men need apply. (1976). *Human Behavior, 5*(5), 63.

O'RAND, A. M. & LANDERMAN, R. (1984). Women's and men's retirement income status. *Research on Aging, 6*(1), 25–44.

Organ donor recruitment. In J. A. Fruehling (Ed.), *Source book on death and dying* (1st ed.). (pp. 242–244). Chicago: Marquis Professional Publications.

ORTHNER, D. K. (1975). *Familia Ludens:* Reinforcing the leisure component in family life. *Family Coordinator, 24*(2), 175–183.

ORY, M. G. & GOLDBERG, E. L. (1983). Pet possession and well-being in elderly women. *Research on Aging, 5*(3), 389–409.

OSHERSON, S. & DILL, D. (1983). Varying work and family choices: Their impact on men's work satisfaction. *Journal of Marriage and the Family, 45*(2), 339–357.

OSMOND, M. W., & MARTIN, P. Y. (1975). Sex and sexism: A comparison of male and female sex-role attitudes. *Journal of Marriage and the Family, 37*(4), 744–758.

OSTHEIMER, J. M. (1982). The polls: Changing attitudes toward euthanasia. In J. A. Fruehling (Ed.), *Source book on death and dying* (1st ed). (pp. 42–47). Chicago: Marquis Professional Publications.

PALISI, B. J. (1984). Symptoms of readiness for divorce. *Journal of Family Issues, 5*(1), 70–89.

PALMORE, E. (Ed.). (1974). *Normal aging II.* Durham, NC: Duke University Press.

PALMORE, E. B., FILLENBAUM, G. G. & GEORGE, L. K. (1984). Consequences of retirement. *Journal of Gerontology, 39*(1), 109–116.

PAPALIA, D. E. (1972) The status of some conservation abilities across the life span. *Dissertation Abstracts International, 32,* 4901.

———., & BIELBY, D. Cognitive functioning in middle and old age adults. *Human development, 17,* 424–443.

PARDINI, A. (1984, April-May). Exercise, vitality and aging. *Aging,* 19–29.

PARKE, R. D. & SAWIN, D. B. (1977). Fathering: It's a major role. *Psychology Today, 11*(6), 108–112.

PARKER, F. (1978). Women at work and in school: The new revolution. *Intellect, 106*(2393), 310–312.

PARKES, C. M. (1972). *Bereavement: Studies of grief in adult life.* New York: International Universities Press.

PARLEE, M. B., & The Editors of *Psychology Today.* (1979). The friendship bond. *Psychology Today, 13*(4), 42–54; 113.

PATRUSKY, B. (1982). What causes aging? *Science, 3*(1), 112.

PEABODY, S. A. (1982). Alternative life styles to monogamous marriage: Variants of normal behavior in psychotherapy clients. *Family Relations, 31*(3), 425–434.

PEPPER, C. (1980) Will there be a brighter tomorrow for the nation's elderly? *USA Today, 108*(2420), 14–16.

PEROSA, S. L. & PEROSA, L. M. (1983). The midcareer crisis: A description of the psychological dynamics of transition and adaptation. *Vocational Guidance Quarterly, 32*(2), 69–79.

PERRIN, E. B., WOODS, J. S., NAMEKATA, T., YAGI, J., BRUCE, R. A., & HOFER, V. (1984). Long-term effect of vasectomy on coronary heart disease. *American Journal of Public Health, 74*(2), 128–132.

PETER, L. J. (1978). The satisfaction of opting for simplicity. *Human Behavior, 7*(8), 70–71.

PETERSON, J. A. (1980). Social-psychological aspects of death and dying and mental health. In J. E. Birren & R. B. Sloane (Eds.), *Handbook of mental health and aging* (pp. 922–942). Englewood Cliffs, NJ: Prentice-Hall, Inc.

PICKETT, R. S. (1977). Tomorrow's family. *Intellect, 105*(2383), 330–332.

PINES, M. (1982). Restoring law and order in the family: Haley, J. interviewed by Maya Pines. *Psychology Today, 16*(11), 60–69.

PINES, A. & ARONSON, E. (1981). Polyfidelity: An alternative lifestyle without jealousy? *Alternative Lifestyles, 4*(3), 373–392.

Planning a funeral at a fair price. (1982). In J. A. Fruehling (Ed.), *Source book on death and dying* (1st ed.) (pp. 145–146). Chicago: Marquis Professional Publications.

PLECK, J. H. & SAWYER, J. (Eds.). (1974). *Men and masculinity.* Englewood Cliffs, NJ: Prentice-Hall, Inc.

Population proliferation and pollution. (1973). *Intellect, 102*(2351), 6.

PORTER-GEHRIE, C. (1979). Models of adulthood: An ethnographic study of an adolescent peer group. *Journal of Youth and Adolescence, 8*(3), 253–269.

POSTMAN D. (1981). The emergence of the adult child. *Psychology Today, 15*(10), 98.

POWELL, T. J. (1978). Self-help movement. *Intellect, 106*(2392), 269.

PRATT, M. W., GOLDING, G., & HUNTER, W. J. (1983). Aging as ripening: Character and consistency of moral judgment in young, mature, and older adults. *Human Development, 26,* 277–288.

Preretirement home . . . Rates get fixed . . . Industrial sales. (1981, December 23). *Wall Street Journal,* p. 13.

PRINGLE, B. M. (1974). Family clusters as a means of reducing isolation among urbanites. *Family Coordinator, 23*(2), 175–179.

PROEFROCK, D. W. (1981). Adolescence: Social fact and psychological concept. *Adolescence, 16*(64), 851–858.

PRUCHNO, R. A., BLOW, F. C. & SMYER, M. A. (1984). Life events and interdependent lives: Implications for research and intervention. *Human Development, 27*(1), 31–41.

RADIN, N. (1982). Primary caregiving and role-sharing fathers. In M. E. Lamb (Ed.), *Nontraditional families: Parenting and child development.* Hillsdale, NJ: Erlbaum.

RAGAN, P. K., & WALES, J. B. (1980). Age stratification and the life course. In J. E. Birren & R. B. Sloane (Eds.), *Handbook of health and aging* (pp. 377–399). Englewood Cliffs, NJ: Prentice-Hall, Inc.

RALPH, J. B. (1985). Visual booby traps for our aging population. In H. Cox (Ed.), *Aging* (4th ed.) (pp. 100–103). Guilford, CN: Dushkin.

RAMEY, J. (1976). Multiadult households: Living groups of the future. *Futurist, 10,* 79–83.

RAMOS, S. (1979, November 15). Deterring parents who steal their own children. *New York Times,* 1; 14.

RAO, S. N. (1974). Academic achievement and anxiety. *Psychological Studies, 19*(1), 38–42.

RAPOPORT, R., & RAPOPORT, R. N. (1975). *Leisure and the family life cycle.* London: Routledge and Kegan Paul.

———., & BUMSTEAD, J. (Eds.). (1978). *Working couples.* New York: Harper & Row.

RANK, M. R. (1981). The transition to marriage. A comparison of cohabiting and dating relationships ending in marriage or divorce. *Alternative Lifestyles, 4*(4), 487–506.

RASCHKE, H. J., & RASCHKE, V. J. (1979). Family conflict and children's self-concepts: A comparison of intact and single-parent families. *Journal of Marriage and the Family, 41* (2), 367–374.

Recreation for all is latest goal in cities. (1977, May 23). *U.S. News & World Report,* 72–73.

Revival of tribalism, A? (1979, February). *The Futurist,* 63.

RHODES, J. P. & RHODES, E. L. (1984). Commuter marriage. The toughest alternative. *Ms., 12*(12), 44–48.

RHODEWALT, F. & AGUSTSDOTTIR, S. (1984). On the relationship of hardiness to the type A behavior pattern: Perception of life events versus coping with life events. *Journal of Research in Personality, 18,* 212–223.

RIEGEL, K. F., & RIEGEL, R. M. (1972). Development, drugs and death. *Developmental Psychology, 6*(2), 306–319.

RILEY, M. W., FONER A., & ASSOCIATES. (1968). *Aging and society, Vol. 1: An inventory of research findings.* New York: Russell Sage Foundation.

RIPLEY, T., & O'BRIEN, S. (1976). Career planning for leisure. *Journal of College Placement, 36*(3), 54–58.

RIVERA, W. M. (1978). Life-cycle change: How does it affect the "target population"? *Lifelong Learning: The Adult Years, 1*(10), 15; 35.

ROBERTS, W. L. (1979–80). Significant elements in the relationship of long-married couples. *International Journal of Aging and Human Development, 10*(3), 265–270.

ROBBINS, J. M. (1984). Out-of-wedlock abortion and delivery: The importance of the male partner. *Social Problems, 31*(3), 334–350.

ROGERS, D. (1977). *Psychology of adolescence,* (3rd ed.). Englewood Cliffs, NJ: Prentice-Hall, Inc.

———. (1981a). *Adolescents and youth* (4th ed.). Englewood Cliffs, NJ: Prentice-Hall, Inc.

———. (1981b). *Life-span developmental psychology.* Monterey, CA: Brooks-Cole.

———. (1985). *Adolescence and youth* (5th ed.). Englewood Cliffs, NJ: Prentice-Hall, Inc.

ROLL, S., & MILLEN, L. (1978). Adolescent males' feeling of being understood by their fathers as revealed through clinical interviews. *Adolescence, 13*(49), 83–94.

ROLLINS, B. C., & CANNON, K. L. (1974). Marital satisfaction over the family life cycle: A reevaluation. *Journal of Marriage and the Family, 36,* 271–283.

ROLLINS, B. C. & FELDMAN, H. (1981). Marital satisfaction over the family life cycle. In L. D. Steinberg (Ed.), *The life cycle: Readings in human development* (pp. 301–310). New York: Columbia University Press.

ROOS, N. P., SHAPIRO, E., & ROOS, L. L. JR. (1984). Aging and the demand for health services: Which aged and whose demand? *Gerontologist, 24*(1), 31–36.

ROSENBERG, S. D., & FARRELL, M. P. (1976). Identity and crisis in middle-aged men. *International Journal of Aging and Human Development, 7* (2), 153–170.

ROSENBLATT, P. C., WALSH, R. P., & JACKSON, D. A. (1976). *Grief and Mourning in cross-cultural perspective.* New Haven, CN: HRAF Press.

ROSENFELD, A. (1981). The adoptees union. *Science, 2*(8), 20–23.

ROSENMAYR, L. (1980). Achievements, doubts, and prospects of the sociology of aging. *Human Development, 23,* 46–62.

ROSENZWEIG, M. R. (1972, May 7). Keep that brain busy. *Parade Magazine.*

ROSOW, I. (1974). *Socialization to old age.* Berkeley: University of California Press.

ROSS, K., BRAGA, J., & BRAGA, L. D. (1975). Omega. In E. Kübler-Ross (Ed.), *Death: The final stage of growth* (pp. 164–166). Englewood Cliffs, NJ: Prentice-Hall, Inc.

ROSSI, A. (1977). A biosocial perspective on parenting. *Daedalus, 106*(2), 1–32.

———. (1981). Transition to parenthood. In L. D. Steinberg (Ed.), *The life cycle: Readings in human development* (pp. 243–254). New York: Columbia University Press.

ROSSI, A. S. (1984). Gender and parenthood. *American Sociological Review, 49,* 1–19.

RUBENSTEIN, C. (1979). Sex repel. *Psychology Today, 13*(7), 102.

———. (1980). Survey report: How Americans view vacations. *Psychology Today, 13*(12), 62–66; 71–76.

———. (1981). Money and self-esteem, relationships, secrecy, envy, satisfaction. *Psychology Today, 15*(5), 29–44.

———. (1982). Wellness is all. A report on *Psychology Today's,* survey of beliefs about health. *Psychology Today, 16*(10), 28–37.

RUBENSTEIN, C. (1983). The modern art of courtly love. *Psychology Today, 17*(7), 40–49.

RUBIN, L. B. (1981). Work and its meaning. In L. D. Steinberg (Ed.), *The life cycle: Readings in human development* pp. 255–270. New York: Columbia University Press.

RUBIN, Z. (1979). Seeking a cure for loneliness. *Psychology Today, 13*(4), 82–90.

RUBLE, T. L., COHEN, R., & RUBLE, D. N. (1984). Sex stereotypes. *American Behavioral Scientist, 27,*(3), 339–356.

RUDINGER, C. (1972). Determinants of intellectual performance: Results from the Bonn Gerontological Longitudinal Study. *Archives of Psychology, 125,* 23–38.

RUDOLPH, S. H., & LLOYD, J. R. (1976). Rajput adulthood: Reflections on the Amar Singh diary. *Daedalus, 105*(2), 145–167.

RYFF, C. D. & MIGDAL, S. (1984). Intimacy and generativity: Self-perceived transitions. *Journal of Women in Culture and Society, 9*(3), 470–481.

SAWHILL, J. C. (1978–79). Lifelong learning: Scandal of the next decade? *Change, 10*(11), 7; 80.

SCANLON, J. (1979). *Young adulthood.* New York: Academy for Educational Development.

SCARF, M. (1979a). Roots of depression: The power of the dominant other. *Psychology Today, 12*(11), 54–58; 92–93.

———. (1979b). The more sorrowful sex. *Psychology Today, 12*(11), 45–52; 89–90.

SCHACTER, S. (1982). Don't sell habit breakers short. *Psychology Today, 16*(8), 27–34.

SCHAIE, K. W. (1973). Developmental policies and aging. In L. R. Goulet & M. P. Lawton (Eds.), *The psychology of adult development and aging.* Washington, D.C.: American Psychological Association.

———., & GRIBBIN, K. (1975). Adult development and aging. In M. R. Rosenzweig & L. W. Porter (Eds.), *Annual review of psychology, vol. 26* (pp. 65–95). Palo Alto, CA: Annual Reviews, Inc.

———., LABOUVIE, G. V., & BUECH, B. V. (1973). Generational and cohort-specific differences in cognitive functioning: A fourteen-year study of independent samples. *Developmental Psychology, 9,* 151–166.

———., & MARQUETTE, B. (1972). Personality in maturity and old age. In R. B. Dreger (Ed.), *Multivariate personality research: Contributions to the understanding of personality in honor of Raymond B. Cattell* (pp. 612–632). Baton Rouge: Claitor's Publishing.

SCHOENFELD, C. G. (1982). Mercy killing and the law—A psychoanalytically oriented analysis. In J. A. Fruehling (Ed.), *Source book on death and dying,* (1st ed.). (pp. 48–57). Chicago: Marquis Professional Publications.

SCHONFIELD, A. E. D. (1980). Learning, memory, and aging. In J. E. Birren & R. B. Sloane (Eds.), *Handbook of mental health and aging* (pp. 214–244). Englewood Cliffs, NJ: Prentice-Hall, Inc. 1980.

SCHWARTZ, H. (1979, November 15). A look at the cancer figures. *Wall Street Journal,* p. 26.

SEARS, R. R. (1977). Sources of life satisfaction of the Terman gifted men. *American Psychologist, 32,* 119–128.

SECUNDY, M. G. (1982). Bereavement: The role of the family physician. In J. A. Fruehling (Ed.), *Source book on death and dying* (1st ed.). (pp. 180–182). Chicago: Marquis Professional Publications.

SEEMAN, M. & SEEMAN, T. E. (1983). Health behavior and personal autonomy: A longitudinal study of the sense of control in illness. *Journal of Health and Social Behavior, 24,* 144–160.

SEGRE, S. (1975). Family stability, social classes, and values in traditional and industrial societies. *Journal of Marriage and the Family, 37*(2), 431–436.

SEGUIN, M. M. (1973). Opportunity for peer socialization in a retirement community. *Gerontologist, 13,* 208–214.

Self-help movement. (1978). *Intellect, 106*(2392), 269–270.

SELTZER, M. M., & ATCHLEY, R. C. (1971). The concept of old: Changing attitudes and stereotypes. *Gerontologist, 11*(3:1), 226–230.

SELYE, H., (1974). Stress. *Intellectual Digest, 4*(10), 43–46.

Setting up model space colonies. (1979). *USA Today, 107*(2405), 14–15.

Sexist surveys. (1979, March). *Human Behavior,* pp. 26–27.

SHANAN, J. & SAGIV, R. (1982). Sex differences in intellectual performance during middle age. *Human Development, 25,* 24–33.

SHANAS, E. (1980). Older people and their families: The new pioneers. *Journal of Marriage and the Family, 42*(1), 9–15.

SHANE, H. G. (1981). Significant writings that have influenced the curriculum: 1906–1981. *Phi Delta Kappan, 62*(5), 311–314.

———. (1977). Curriculum change toward the 21st century. Washington, D.C.: National Education Association.

SHEEHY, G., (1976). *Passages: The predictable crises of adult life.* New York: E. P. Dutton.

SHEFF, D. (1980, Summer). Gay life in Frisco. *Forum,* 106–111.

SHEPPARD, H. L., & RIX, S. E. (1977). *The graying of working America: The coming of retirement.* New York: Free Press.

SHERMAN, J., KOUFACOS, C., & KENWORTHY J. A., (1978). Therapists: Their attitudes and information about women. *Psychology of Women Quarterly, 2*(4), 299–313.

SHERMAN, N. C., & GOLD, J. A. (1979–80). Perceptions of ideal and typical middle and old age. *International Journal of Aging and Human Development, 9*(4), 67–73.

SHERMAN, S. R. (1975). On-site services in retirement housing. *Aging and Human Development, 6*(3), 239–247.

SHORE, H. (1972). Institutional care for the aged: Letter to HEW secretary Elliott Richardson. *Gerontologist,* (2), 114.

SHULMAN, N. (1975). Life-cycle variations in patterns of close relationships. *Journal of Marriage and the Family, 37*(4), 813–821.

SIDNEY, K. H., & SHEPHARD, R. J. (1977). Activity patterns of elderly men and women. *Journal of Gerontology, 32*(1), 25–32.

SIEGEL, R. K. (1980). The psychology of life after death. *American Psychologist, 35*(10), 911–931.

SILVERMAN, P. R. (1972). Widowhood and preventive intervention. *Family Coordinator, 21,* 95–102.

SIMON, A. (1980). The neuroses, personality disorders, alcoholism, drug use and misuse, and crime in the aged. In J. E. Birren & R. B. Sloane (Eds.) *Handbook of mental health and aging,* (pp. 653–670). Englewood Cliffs, NJ: Prentice-Hall, Inc.

SIMON, J. L. (1983a). Life on earth is getting better, not worse. *The Futurist, 17*(4), 7–15.

SIMON, J. L. (1983b). The population debate. Growth means progress. *Science Digest, 91*(4), 76–81.

SIMON, W., GAGNON, J. H., & BUFF, S. A. (1972). Son of Joe: Continuity and change among white working-class adolescents. *Journal of Youth and Adolescence, 1*(1), 13–34.

SIMONS, R. L. (1983–84). Specificity and substitution in the social networks of the elderly. *International Journal of Aging and Human Development, 18*(2), 121–139.

SIMPSON, M. A. (1979). Social and psychological aspects of dying. In H. Wass (Ed.), *Dying: Facing the facts* (pp. 108–136). Washington, D.C.: Hemisphere Publishing Corp.

SINEX, F. M. (1975). The biochemistry of aging. In M. G. Spencer & C. J. Dorr (Eds.), *Understanding aging: A multidisciplinary approach* (pp. 21–39). New York: Appleton-Century-Crofts.

Single mothers keeping a baby by default. Newsline. (1980). *Psychology Today, 14*(7), 100.

SKOLNICK, A. (1981). Married lives: Longitudinal perspective on marriage. In D. H. Eichorn, J. A. Clausen, N. Haan, M. P. Honzik, & P. S. Mussen (Eds.), *Present and past in middle age.* New York: Academic.

SKOVHOLT, T. M. (1978). Feminism and men's lives. *The Counseling Psychologist, 7*(4), 3–10.

SLESIN, S. (1979, November 22). Changing housing as families change. *New York Times,* 1; 5.

SLESINGER, D. P. (1980). Rapid changes in household composition among low-income mothers. *Family Relations, 29*(2), 221–228.

SMATHERS, D. G., & HORRIDGE, P. E. (1979). The effects of physical changes on clothing preferences of elderly women. *International Journal of Aging and Human Development, 9*(3), 273–278.

SMITH, C., & LLOYD, B. (1978). Maternal behavior and perceived sex of infant: Revisited. *Child Development, 49*(4), 1263–1265.

SMITH, M. J. (1980). The social consequences of single parenthood: A longitudinal perspective. *Family Relations 29*(1), 75–81.

SMITH, P. K. (1979). How many people can a young child feel secure with? *New Society, 48*(869), 504–506.

SMITH, R. T., & BRAND, F. N. (1975). Effects of enforced relocation on life adjustment in a nursing home. *Journal of Aging and Human Development, 6*(3), 245–259.

SPAKE, A. (1984). The choices that brought me here. *Ms., 13*(5), 48–52; 138.

SPANIER, G. B. (1983). Married and unmarried cohabitation in the United States: 1980. *Journal of Marriage and the Family, 45*(2), 277–288.

SPEKKE, A. A. (1976). America: The next 200 years. *Intellect, 105*(2376), 49–50.

SPENCE, D. L., & LONNER, T. D. (1978). Career set: A resource through transitions and crises. *International Journal of Aging and Human Development, 9*(1), 51–65.

SPENCE, J. T., & HELMREICH, R. L. (1978). *Masculinity and femininity: Their psychological dimensions, correlates, and antecedents.* Austin: University of Texas Press.

SROLE, L., LANGNER, S., Michael, S. T., OPLER, M. K., & RENNIE, T. A. C. (1962). *Mental health in the metropolis: The midtown Manhattan study.* New York: McGraw-Hill.

STEFFENSMEIER, R. H. (1982). A role model of the transition to parenthood. *Journal of Marriage and the Family, 44*(2), 319–334.

STEGNER, W. (1976). The writer and the concept of adulthood. *Daedalus, 105*(4), 39–48.

STEIN, P. J. (1976). *Single.* Englewood Cliffs, NJ: Prentice-Hall, Inc.

STERN, P. H. (1976). The Jung triangle. *Human Behavior, 5*(5), 17–23.

STEVENS, C. W. (1979, November 15). Aging Americans: Many delay retiring or resume jobs to beat inflation and the blues. *Wall Street Journal,* 1; 22.

STEVENS, J. H. JR. (1984). Child development knowledge and parenting skills. *Family Relations, 33,* 237–244.

STEPHENS, M. A. & BERNSTEIN, M. D. (1984). Social support and well-being among residents of planned housing. *Gerontologist, 24*(2), 144–148.

STEPHENSON, P. H. (1983–84). "He dies too quick?" The process of dying in a Hutterian colony. *Omega: Journal of Death and Dying, 14*(2), 127–134.

STOKOLS, D. (1978). Environmental psychology in *Annual Review of Psychology.* Palo Alto: Annual Reviews, (pp. 253–296).

STOLLER, F. H. (1970). The intimate network of families as a new structure. In H. A. Otto (Ed.), *The family in search of a future.* New York: Appleton-Century-Crofts.

STONE, K., & KALISH, R. (1973). Of poker, roles and aging: Description, discussion, and data. *Aging and Human Development, 4,* 1–13.

STORCH, P. A., LOOFT, W. R., & HOOPER, F. H. (1972). Interrelationships among Piagetian tasks and traditional measures of cognitive abilities in mature and aged adults. *Journal of Gerontology, 27,* 461–465.

STORY, M. L. (1974). Vocational education as contemporary slavery. *Intellect, 102*(2356), 370–372.

STRAUS, M. (1977, March). Normative and behavioral aspects of violence between spouses: Preliminary data on a nationally representative USA sample. Paper presented at the Conference on Violence in Canadian Society, Ottawa.

STREEVER, K. L. & WODARSKI, J. S. (1984). Life-span developmental approach: Implications for practice. *Social Casework: The Journal of Contemporary Social Work, 65*(5), 267–278.

STREHLER, B. L. (1977). A new age for aging. In S. H. Zarit (Ed.), *Readings in aging and death: Contemporary perspectives* (pp. 49–55). New York: Harper & Row, Publishers.

STREIB, G. F. (1976). Social stratification and aging. In R. H. Binstock & E. Shanas (Eds.), *Handbook of aging and the social sciences* (pp. 160–185). New York: Van Nostrand Reinhold.

STRIBLING, F. T. (1842). Annual report of the court of directors of the Western Lunatic Asylum to the legislature of Virginia, with the report of the physician, 1841 (pp. 15–16). Richmond, VA: Shepard and Conlin.

STRYKER, S., & MACKE, A. S. (1978). Status inconsistency and role conflict. In R. H. Turner, J. Coleman, & R. C. Fox (Eds.), *Annual review of sociology, vol. 4* (pp. 57–89). Palo Alto: Annual Reviews, Inc.

SUPER, D. E. & HALL, D. T. (1978). Career development: Exploration and planning. In M. R. Rosenzweig & L. R. Porter (Eds.) *Annual Review of Psychology, 29,* 333–372.

Surgery: Costs, risks, and benefits. (1978). *Intellect, 106*(2396), 442–443.

SZULC, T. (1984, April 29). One person too many? *Parade Magazine,* 16.

TARG, D. B. (1979). Toward a reassessment of women's experience at middle age. *The Family Coordinator 28*(3), 377–382.

TAVRIS, C. (1976). Women: Work isn't always the answer. *Psychology Today, 10*(4), 78.

TAYLOR, A. R. (1976). Habits, fears and desires of the genius graduate student. *Change, 8*(4), 31–34.

Television image of women, The. (1975). *Intellect, 103*(2365), 424–425.

Ten forces reshaping America. (1984). *U.S. News & World Report, 96*(11), 40–41.

TESCH, S. A. (1983). Review of friendship development across the life span. *Human Development, 26*(5), 266–276.

The latest line on birth control risks. (1981). *Science, 2*(4), 6.

The Revolution is over. (1984, June). *Time* 74–80.

The worst forecasts. (1978, April). *The Futurist,* 127–128.

THOMAE, H. (1980). Personality and adjustment in aging. In J. E. Birren & R. B. Sloane (Eds.), *Handbook of Mental health and aging* (pp. 285–309). Englewood Cliffs, NJ: Prentice-Hall. Inc.

THOMPSON, A. P. (1984). Emotional and sexual components of extramarital relations. *Journal of Marriage and the Family, 46*(1), 35–42.

THOMPSON, L. W., BRECKENRIDGE, J. N., GALLAGHER, D., & PETERSON, J. (1984). Effects of bereavement on self-perceptions of physical health in elderly widows and widowers. *Journal of Gerontology, 39*(3), 309–314.

THOMPSON, L., & MARSH, G. (1973). Psychological studies of aging. In C. Eisdorfer & M. P. Lawton (Eds.), *The psychology of adult development and aging.* Washington, D.C.: American Psychological Association.

THOMPSON, L. & SPANIER, G. B. (1983). The end of marriage and acceptance of marital termination. *Journal of Marriage and the Family, 45*(1), 103–113.

THURNHER, M. (1974). Goals, values, and life evaluations of the preretirement stage. *Journal of Gerontology, 29,* 85–96.

THURSTON, C. (1983). The liberation of pulp romances. *Psychology Today, 17*(4), 14–15.

TICE, C. H. (1982, September-October). Continuity: A gift from the older generation. *Children Today,* 2–6.

TIDBALL, M. (1975, February). Study of American women achievers. *Executive Woman.* 45–50.

TIERNEY, J. (1982, May). The aging body. *Esquire,* 543.

TIGER, L. (1984) *Men in Groups* UK: M. Boyars.

TIMIRAS, P. S. (1972). *Developmental physiology and aging.* New York: Macmillan.

TOBIN, S. S., & LIEBERMAN, M. A. (1976). *Last home for the aged.* San Francisco: Jossey-Bass.

Today's senior citizens: "Pioneers of new golden era." (1984). *U.S. News & World Report, 97*(1), 51–52.

TROLL, L. E. (1975). *Early and Middle Adulthood.* Monterey, Calif.: (1975). Brooks-Cole Publishing Co.

———. (1971). The family of later life: A decade review. *Journal of Marriage and the Family, 33,* 274.

TSOI-HOSHMAND, L. (1976). Marital therapy and changing values. *Family Coordinator, 25*(1), 57–63.

TUCKMAN, J., & LORGE, I. (1954). Classification of the self as young, middle aged, or old. *Geriatrics,* (9), 534–536.

TURNER, J. D. (1975). Patterns of intergenerational exchange: A development approach. *Aging and Human Development, 6*(22), 111–115.

TU WEI-MING. (1976). The Confucian perception of adulthood. *Daedalus, 105*(2), 109–124.

UNKEL, M. B. (1981). Physical recreation participation of females and males during the adult life cycles. *Leisure Sciences, 4*(1), 1–27.

UNRUH, D. R. (1983). Death and personal history: Strategies of identity preservation. *Social Problems, 39*(3), 340–351.

U.S. Bureau of the Census. (1976). Number, timing, and duration of marriages and divorces in the U.S.; June 1975. Current Population Reports (P-20, No. 297). Washington, D.C.: U.S. Govt. Printing Office.

U.S. Department of HEW. (1978). Statistical reports on older Americans: Some prospects for the future elderly population. DHEW Publication No. (OHDS) 78–20288.

U.S. Senate hearings, Special Committee on Aging, 91st Congress, 2nd Session, Part 10A. (1970). *Pension aspects of the economics of aging* (p. 1426). Washington, D.C.

USUI, W. M. (1984). Homogeneity of friendship networks of elderly blacks and whites. *Journal of Gerontology, 39*(3), 350–356.

VAILLANT, G. E. (1977). How the best of the brightest came of age. *Psychology Today, 11*(4), 34–41; 107–108; 110.

VANKEEP, P. A., & KELLERHALS, J. M. (1975). The aging woman. *Acta Obstetrica et Gynecologica,* Scandinavica Supplement, *51,* 17–27.

VEEVERS, J. E. (1975). The life style of voluntarily childless couples. In L. Larson (Ed.) *The Canadian Family in Comparative Perspective.* Toronto: Prentice-Hall of Canada.

———. (1974). Voluntary childlessness and social policy: An alternative view. *Family Coordinator, 1974, 23*(4), 397–406.

VERBRUGGE, L. M. (1983). Multiple roles and physical health of women and men. *Journal of Health and Social Behavior, 24,* 16–30.

———. (1975). Sex differentials in morbidity and mortality in the United States. Paper presented at the Annual Meeting of the Population Association of America.

VERZARO-LAWRENCE, M. (1981). Shared childrearing. A challenging alternative lifestyle. *Alternative Lifestyles, 4*(2), 205–217.

VITTITOW, D. (1981). Changing men and their movement toward intimacy. In R. A. Lews (Ed.) *Men in difficult times* (pp. 290–296). Englewood Cliffs, NJ: Prentice-Hall, Inc.

WACHOWIAK, D., & BRAGA, H. (1980). Open marriage and marital adjustment. *Journal of Marriage and the Family, 42*(1), 57–62.

WALTERS, J., & WALTERS, L. H. (1980). Trends affecting adolescent views of sexuality, employment, marriage and childrearing. *Family Relations, 29*(2), 191–198.

WARD, H. N. (1982). Euthanasia: A medical and legal overview. In J. A. Fruehling (Ed.), *Source book on death and dying* (1st ed.), (pp. 3–14). Chicago: Marquis Professional Publications.

WARD, R. A., SHERMAN, S. R., & LaGORY, M. (1984). Subjective network assessments and subjective well-being. *Journal of Gerontology, 39*(1), 93–101.

Warning—Living alone is dangerous to your health. (1980). *U.S. News, 88*(25), 47–48.

WATTS, W. (1981). The future can fend for itself. *Psychology Today, 15*(9), 36–48.

WEAVER, M. J. (1979, October 12). Single blessedness? *Commonwealth,* pp. 588–591.

WECHTER, S. L. (1983). Separation difficulties between parents and young adults. *Journal of Contemporary Social Work, 64*(2), 97–104.

WEIR, R. F. (1977). *Ethical issues in death and dying.* New York: Columbia University Press.

WEISSMAN, A. (1972). *On dying and denying.* New York: Behavioral Publications, Inc.

WEITZMAN, L. J. (1975). To love, honor, and obey? Traditional legal marriage and alternative family forms. *Family Coordinator, 24*(4), 531–548.

WELFORD, A. T. (1980). Sensory, perceptual, and motor processes in older adults. In J. E. Birren & R. B. Sloane (Eds.), *Handbook of mental health and aging* (pp. 192–213). Englewood Cliffs, NJ: Prentice-Hall, Inc.

WENTE, A. S., & CROCKENBERG, S. B. (1976). Transition to fatherhood: Lamaze preparation, adjustment difficulty, and the husband-wife relationship. *Family Coordinator, 25,* 351–357.

WERSHOW, H. J., RITCHEY, F. J. & ALPHIN, T. H. (1982). Physicians' opinions toward legislation defining death and withholding life support. In J. A. Fruehling (Ed.), *Source book on death and dying* (1st ed.) (pp. 33–37). Chicago: Marquis Professional Publications.

WESSEL, D. (1984, September 7). Working fathers feel new pressure arising from childrearing duties. *Wall Street Journal,* 31; 37.

WEST, G. E. & SIMONS, R. L. (1983). Sex differences in stress, coping resources, and illness among the elderly. *Research on Aging, 5*(2), 235–268.

WEST, S. (1982). Fertility fizzle. *Science, 3*(4), 12.

Western world's "silent revolution." (1978). *Intellect, 106*(2396), 435–437.

What future for the American family? (1976). *Changing Times, 30*(12), 7–10.

When "family" will have a new definition. (1983, May 9). *U.S. News & World Report,* A1–A4.

When middle-aged women start looking for jobs. (1979). *U.S. News & World Report, 87*(19), 58–61.

Where are the role models? (1977). *Psychology Today, 6*(2), 60–61.

White House Conference on Aging. (1972). *Aging and blindness.* Special Concerns Session report, Washington, D.C.: U.S. Government Printing Office.

WHITE, L. K. (1983). Determinants of spousal interaction: Marital structure or marital happiness. *Journal of Marriage and the Family, 45*(3), 511–519.

WHITE, L. K. (1979). Sex differentials in the effect of remarriage on global happiness. *Journal of Marriage and the Family, 41*(4), 869–876.

Why millions hate their jobs. (1976, September 27) *U.S. News & World Report,* pp. 87–90.

WIGDOR, B. T. (1980). Drives and motivations with aging. In J. E. Birren & R. B. Sloane (Eds.), *Handbook of mental health and aging* (pp. 245–261). Englewood Cliffs, NJ: Prentice-Hall, Inc.

WILLIAMS, R. (1969). *Biochemical individuality: The basis for the genetrophic concept.* Austin: University of Texas.

WISWELL, R. A. (1980). Relaxation, exercise, and aging. In J. E. Birren & R. B. Sloane (Eds.), *Handbook of mental health and aging* (pp. 943–958). Englewood Cliffs, NJ: Prentice-Hall, Inc.

WOHLWILL, J. F. (1980). The confluence of environmental and developmental psychology: Signpost to an ecology of development? *Human Development, 23,* 354–358.

WOLFARTH, G. A. (1973). An examination of family need fulfillment in an experimental extended family setting. Unpublished professional paper, Texas Woman's University.

Woman survives crash landing. (1982, January 11). Oswego, New York *Palladium-Times,* 11.

Woman, 75, slain after aiding sister. (1981, December 3). *Syracuse Post-Standard,* B-1.

Women under 50 are warned on the risks of breast X-rays. (1977, March 3). *New York Times,* 16.

WOOD, V., & ROBERTSON, J. F. (1978). Friendship and kinship interaction: Differential effect on the morals of the elderly. *Journal of Marriage and the Family, 40*(2), 367–375.

WOODEN, W. S., KAWASAKI, K. & MAYEDA, R. A. (1983, Summer). Alternative lifestyles. 236–243.

WOODY, R. H. (1978). Fathers with child custody. *Counseling Psychologist, 7*(4), 60–63.

World Almanac, 1980. (1980). New York: Newspaper Enterprise Association, Inc.

Worst forecasts, The. (1978, April). *Futurist,* pp. 127–128.

YANKELOVICH, D. (1972). *The changing values on campus.* New York: Simon & Schuster.

——. (1974). Turbulence in the working world: Angry workers, happy grads. *Psychology Today, 8*(7), 81–87.

———. (1979). Who gets ahead in America? *Psychology Today, 13*(2), 28–34; 40–43; 90–91.

———. (1984, December-January). Talking with Daniel Yankelovitch. American values. *Public Opinion,* 2–8.

YORBURG, B. (1973). The future of the American family. *Intellect, 101*(2346), 253–260.

YOUNG, R. A. (1983). Toward an understanding of wilderness participation. *Leisure Sciences, 5*(4), 339–357.

YOUNG, R. A. & CRANDALL, R. (1984). Wilderness use and self-actualization. *Journal of Leisure Research, 16*(2), 149–160.

Youth on the move. (1980). *U.S. News & World Report,* 1980, *89*(26), 72–73.

YU, B. P., MASORO, E. J., MURATA, I., BERTRAND, H. A., & LYND, F. T. (1982). Life-span study of SPF Fischer 344 male rats fed ad libitum on restricted diets: Longevity, growth, lean body mass and disease. *Journal of Gerontology, 37,* 130–141.

ZABLOCKI, B. (1975). Urban communes project. Unpublished data, Columbia University.

ZARIT, S. H. (1977). Gerontology: Getting better all the time. In S. H. Zarit (Ed.), *Readings in aging and death: Contemporary perspectives.* New York: Harper & Row.

ZILBERGELD, B. (1983). *The shrinking of America.* New York: Little Brown.

Index